Here is some of my best
work. Enjoy!

Personal Finance

SIXTH EDITION

E. THOMAS GARMAN
Virginia Polytechnic Institute and State University

RAYMOND E. FORGUE
University of Kentucky

HOUGHTON MIFFLIN COMPANY
Boston   New York

Editor-in-Chief: Bonnie Binkert
Assistant Editor: Bernadette Walsh
Senior Project Editor: Kathryn Dinovo
Senior Manufacturing Coordinator: Marie Barnes
Marketing Manager: Melissa Russell

Cover design: Harold Burch, Harold Burch Design, New York City
Cover images: Picture Book/Photonica; Wayne Calabrese/Photonica; © John
   Still/Photonica

This book is written to provide accurate and authoritative information concerning the covered topics. It is not meant to take the place of professional advice for any specific situation.

Printed in the U.S.A.

Library of Congress Catalog Card Number: 99-72010

ISBN: 0-395-95048-1

123456789-VH-03 02 01 00 99

Contents

iii

3 | Managing Taxes   55

5 | Managing Your Cash 125

What Is Cash Management? 126

Today's Providers of Financial Services 127

Banks and Depository Institutions • Mutual Funds • Stock Brokerage Firms • Financial Services Companies

Electronic Funds Transfer 129

Debit Cards • ATMs • Point-of-Sale Terminals • Smart Cards and Stored-Value Cards • Preauthorized Deposits and Payments • Electronic Benefits Transfer • EFT Regulations

Cash Management Tool 1: Interest-Earning Checking Accounts 134

Types of Checking Accounts • Checking Account Charges, Fees, and Penalties • Ownership Rights

Cash Management Tool 2: Savings Accounts 140

How to Save • Savings Account Interest

Cash Management Tool 3: Money Market Accounts 144

Super NOW Accounts • Money Market Deposit Accounts • Money Market Mutual Funds • Asset Management Accounts

Cash Management Tool 4: Low-Risk, Long-Term Savings Instruments 146

Certificates of Deposit • U.S. Government Savings Bonds

6 | Credit Use and Credit Cards 156

Distinguishing between Installment and Noninstallment Credit 157

Reasons for and against Using Credit 158

Why People Use Credit • Reasons against Using Credit

Types of Open-Ended Credit Accounts 163

Revolving Credit Card Accounts at Retail Stores • Revolving Credit Card Accounts at Financial Institutions • Travel and Entertainment Accounts • Other Forms of Open-Ended Credit

The Process for Opening an Open-Ended Charge Account 166

The Credit Application • The Credit Investigation • Credit Ratings and Risk Scoring

9 | The Housing Expenditure   231

12 | Life Insurance Planning   332

Why Buy Life Insurance?   333

How to Determine Your Life Insurance Needs   333

Life Insurance Needs over the Life Cycle • Financial Factors Affecting Life Insurance Needs • Calculating the Dollar Amount of Loss

Types of Life Insurance   339

Term Life Insurance • Cash-Value Life Insurance • Interest-Sensitive Life Insurance

Understanding Your Life Insurance Policy   349

Organization of an Insurance Policy • Terms and Provisions Unique to Life Insurance • Settlement Options • Special Features of Cash-Value Life Insurance Policies

Strategies for Buying Life Insurance   356

Should Your Life Be Insured at All? • Choosing the Right Type of Life Insurance • Choosing a Company • Choosing an Agent • Making Cost Comparisons in Life Insurance

PART 4

Investment Planning   367

13 | Investment Fundamentals and Portfolio Management   368

Preparations for Investing   369

Why People Invest • Prerequisites to Investing • Investment Returns

Discovering Your Own Personal Investment Philosophy   371

How Do You Handle Risk? • Ultraconservative "Investment" Strategies • Your Investment Philosophy: Conservative, Moderate, or Aggressive

15 | Investing Through Mutual Funds   431

Reasons for Investing Through Mutual Funds   432

Mutual Funds Dispense Profits to Investors • Investors Expect Dividend Income • Investors Expect Price Appreciation

The Different Objectives of Mutual Funds   434

Funds with a Current Income Objective • Funds with a Long-Term Growth Objective • Funds with a Growth and Income Objective • Funds with a Balanced Objective

Classification of Mutual Funds According to Their Portfolios   436

Common Stock Funds • Balanced Funds • Bond Funds • Specialty Funds • Money Market Funds

Unique Benefits of Mutual Funds   440

Automatic Reinvestment • IRS-Qualified Tax-Sheltered Retirement Accounts • Easy Purchase and Sale • Recordkeeping and Reporting • Collateral for Loans • Withdrawal Plans

The Costs of Investing Through Mutual Funds   443

Management Fees • Load Funds • No-Load Funds • Hidden Fees • Disclosure of Fees • Which Is Better, a Load or No-Load Fund?

Strategies for Selecting a Mutual Fund   448

Match Your Goals • Locate Sources of Comparative Performance Data • Interpret Comparative Performance Information over Time • Read Prospectuses and Annual Reports

When to Sell a Mutual Fund   451

16 | Buying and Selling Securities   457

Securities Markets   458

Primary Markets • Secondary Markets • Organized Stock Exchanges • Regulation of Securities Markets

Appendixes   A-1

Preface

The twentieth century has brought individuals the benefits of many new savings, credit, insurance, and investment options. Now more than ever, making sound financial decisions is exceedingly complex, even when compared with just 15 or 20 years ago. A solid understanding of the concepts and principles of personal finance is vital. *Personal Finance,* Sixth Edition, provides a comprehensive examination of these principles and offers solid strategies for successful management and planning. This edition has been thoroughly revised to reflect the most recent changes in our economic environment and describes the most up-to-date options available for readers as we transition into the next century. The new Garman/Forgue *Personal Finance* Web site, for example, offers exercises and experiences that parallel the text and offer the industry's best opportunities for learning on the Internet.

For a person to achieve financial success, he or she must plan, analyze, and control financial resources. This involves developing the knowledge and skills necessary to take advantage of favorable financial opportunities, resolve personal financial problems, achieve self-satisfaction, and strive toward financial security. This book is not about "headlines" and "highlights."

Competence and confidence are the two broad goals that underlay our efforts in writing *Personal Finance.* To develop competence in personal finance, the reader needs a text wide in scope. We have worked to make *Personal Finance* the most comprehensive and thorough textbook available. To help the reader become a lifelong skillful manager of personal finances, we take a how-to approach, explaining, for example, how to manage cash, determine personal credit limits, reduce income taxes, buy a car, calculate an affordable home mortgage loan, select an insurance agent, project life insurance needs, choose a life insurance policy, select a stockbroker, compare mutual fund investments, and project the anticipated return on an investment. We outline step-by-step procedures for the more complex financial activities, such as developing a total personal financial plan, planning and reconciling a 12-month budget, calculating personal income taxes, determining how much life insurance is needed, and figuring how much money will be needed for retirement.

To develop confidence in the area of personal finance, the reader needs to be led through, not simply to, the material. We aim to acquaint the reader with the subject matter logically and to offer no surprises. For students in personal finance with little background in finance, economics, or mathematics, our text offers clear explanations and instructions. Numerical examples are always explained parenthetically, and the benefits and costs of different personal finance decisions are examined closely. Key words and concepts—which are printed in boldface type—are clearly and completely defined when they first occur and often *again* in later chapters. Instructors who assign chapters out of sequence will find this feature particularly convenient.

More than 130 tables, charts, and illustrations support the text, including facsimiles of forms that are used in personal finance, such as checks and up-to-date income tax tables. Beginning- and end-of-chapter pedagogical materials are all designed to develop the reader's confidence in the area of personal finance.

As an aside, the Houghton Mifflin Company is pleased to report that *Personal Finance* is the required text for the first of a two-part examination process for the certification program, Accredited Financial Counselor, sponsored by the Association for Financial Counseling and Planning Education.*

Major Changes in the Sixth Edition

We have thoroughly enjoyed the challenge of updating and revising *Personal Finance*. It is popular with students because of the informal writing style and with instructors because it is so readable that students come to class prepared. We have again aimed to keep the narrative conversational and yet clear and concise. Responding to the comments and suggestions of both users and nonusers, we have added more topics, reorganized chapters for a better flow, highlighted important topics in special boxed features, updated and expanded use of Internet Web site exercises, and updated all tables and figures, as well as improved the overall pedagogy.

The new Personal Finance course links the Web site that accompanies this text and brings our package into full interface with the Internet. Developed in tandem with Courseworks Publishing, Inc., the Courselinks site provides both students and instructors with a wealth of supplemental materials to enhance learning and aid in course management. Included among the features of the Courselinks site are

- PowerPoint Chapter Outlines for instructor use as class notes.

- Regularly updated lists of supplemental Web sites for additional reading and enhancement of understanding the world of personal finance.

- Many of the applied mathematics problems from the text with links to the appropriate calculator or worksheet to be used to answer the problem.

- Each of the Exploring the World Wide Web exercises from the text with links to the appropriate external Web site for completing the exercise.

- Multiple-choice quizzes that are instantly graded to provide feedback to students on their mastery of personal finance concepts.

- Sites for students and instructors to share insights, questions, and information with fellow students and faculty.

- Many of the formulas and worksheets from the text plus present and future value calculators for doing all of the mathematical computations illustrated in the text.

---

* For more information, contact Accredited Financial Counselor Program, The Association for Financial Counseling and Planning Education, 6099 Riverside Drive, Suite 100, Dublin, OH 43017; telephone (614) 798-4107; fax (614) 798-6560; e-mail: *request@afcpe.org;* Internet: *www.afcpe.org.*

Topical Treatment

To keep pace with changes in the financial services industry and to provide a complete perspective on personal finance, we have added a number of current topics, such as

- The effect of work decisions on success in personal finance
- Flexible spending accounts that offer tax sheltering
- Hope scholarship and lifetime earning credits
- Maximization of the benefits from a tax-sheltered retirement account
- The relationship between financial planning and budgeting
- Smart card and stored-value cards
- How much to save
- Prioritization of wants
- New vehicle leasing regulations
- Evaluation of your decisions as a guide for future purchasing behavior
- Second mortgage loans
- Price-to-Sales ratio
- Inflation-indexed savings bonds
- The Roth IRA
- Cash-balance pension plans
- Strategies to legally avoid overpayment of income taxes
- Survivorship life insurance
- New alternative mortgage loans
- The proper forms of asset ownership (discussed in all appropriate chapters)
- Disability income insurance
- Bond premiums and discounts
- How a sideline business can reduce income taxes

We have also expanded coverage on more than 40 topics, including

- Financial tasks and challenges of divorced and remarried persons
- Advice on how to get out of debt
- Managing educational loan debts
- Resolving the dilemma of long-term health care
- Maintaining health care coverage when changing jobs
- Hidden hazards of decreasing premium life insurance
- The tax-planning principles of estate planning

Organization

We have retained the successful format of the fifth edition, with some improvements:

- Chapter 1, "The Importance of Personal Finance," has been strengthened by the addition of a new section on "How Work Decisions Affect Success in Personal Finance," based on material that was formerly in a separate chapter on careers.

- The "Managing Taxes" and "Estate Planning" chapters have been revised to emphasize all the tax-planning principles of estate planning.

Boxed Features

"Tax Considerations and Consequences," a boxed feature in every chapter, focuses on the key tax aspects of the subject at hand. Other boxed features provide basic personal financial advice or knowledge. "How to . . ." boxes offer concrete information on how to carry out a specific financial task, whereas "Did You Know?" and "What if . . ." boxes relay interesting anecdotes and information intended to increase the reader's overall knowledge.

There are more than 100 boxed inserts, including new ones on

- How to Search for Investments on the Internet
- Did You Know? Buying a Home Can Reduce Income Taxes Because Interest and Real Estate Taxes Are Tax-Deductible
- How to Calculate Taxable and Tax-Exempt Yields
- How to Keep Your Money Safe
- How to Discuss Personal Finances
- Did You Know? You Can Do Banking from Home
- How to Manage if You Become Overindebted
- Did You Know? About Direct-Investment Plans and DRIPs
- Did You Know? How Most Investors Select Stocks
- Did You Know? That Zero-Coupon Bonds Pay No Annual Interest
- How to Get at Your Qualified Retirement Funds Early
- How to Use Advance Directives
- How to Investigate a Brokerage Firm and Its Sales Representatives

Decision-Making Worksheets

New decision-making worksheets designed to help students solve personal finance problems by following a step-by-step procedure include

- Should You Buy or Rent (Based on Costs for the First Year)?
- Estimating Retirement Needs in Today's Dollars

Tables and Figures

We have updated all tables and figures and added several new ones, including

- Rule of 72
- Budgets and Financial Statements
- Classifying Annuities
- The Value of Tax-Sheltered Contributions

Internet Addresses

Every chapter offers Internet addresses for businesses, nonprofit organizations, and government agencies useful to the student of personal finance. Web sites are indexed for convenience.

End-of-Chapter Pedagogy

The end-of-chapter pedagogy has been revised to give more specific direction for a serious study of personal finance.

- Financial Math Questions are collectively designed to review *every* key math concept in personal finance.
- The new Exploring the World Wide Web of Personal Finance exercises let students and faculty apply chapter concepts using calculators and the vast resources of the Internet.
- Money Matters: Life-Cycle Cases can be used intermittently or in a logical series. We've included the popular Harry and Belinda Johnson case study of a young family from previous editions as well as a case study that follows the Hernandez family from midlife into retirement.

Overview of the Sixth Edition

The contents have been arranged so that as each new topic is introduced, it is fully explained and its fundamentals are thoroughly examined before commencing further study. For example, Chapter 13, "Investment Fundamentals and Portfolio Management," precedes chapters on specific types of investments. In addition, not only does each chapter follow an overall logical sequence but each is also a complete entity. Thus, the chapters can be rearranged to follow any instructor's developmental sequence without losing students' comprehension.

Part 1 provides an introduction to financial planning. Chapter 1 discusses what will be gained from the study of personal finance, describes the goals of financial planning, and helps the reader understand the economic environment so he or she can succeed financially by forecasting the state of the economy and understanding how work decisions affect success in personal finance. In Chapter 2, we explain how to plan financially over one's lifetime, and we review the types of financial records and statements that are pertinent to success in effective personal financial management, such as tax records and documents, balance sheets, and income and expense statements. In Chapter 3, we take the student through all phases of personal income taxation—especially how to legally avoid taxes—and we give advice on how to successfully win an audit with the IRS. "Managing Taxes" offers sufficient detail to enable a reader to adequately and accurately fill out an income tax form. Expanded coverage illustrates the 13 principles of effectively reducing tax liability.

Part 2, comprising six chapters, discusses the specifics of managing expenditures. Chapter 4 takes a cash-flow approach to the subject of budgeting. It provides basic information about money and then illustrates a complete financial plan before examining the specifics of budgeting and cash-flow management (goal setting, organizing, decision making, implementing, controlling, and evaluating). Chapter 5 examines the new concept of cash management, which involves making effective use of today's changing financial services industry to earn maximum interest on all one's money. Chapter 6 discusses credit use and credit cards, including new legal protections that are available, and Chapter 7 treats the subjects of the planned use of credit, non–credit-card borrowing, and what happens should one become overextended using credit. We cover automobiles and other major expenditures in Chapter 8, discussing several ways to save money when purchasing goods and services, detailing the several steps in the planned buying process, with emphasis on automobile purchases, and showing how to compare leasing with financing. Chapter 9 focuses on the housing expenditure, covering all aspects in the home-buying process, including new methods of financing, as well as renting (especially because renting is sometimes the wiser choice), and we provide information on both refinancing and selling a home.

Part 3 emphasizes income and asset protection. Chapter 10 thoroughly explains the concepts fundamental to understanding risk management, insurance, and how to purchase coverage. It emphasizes automobile and home-related property and liability coverage. Chapter 11 takes a new approach to health care planning that recognizes that most people's health insurance is really a health care plan; thus we have strengthened coverage on health maintenance organizations, preferred provider organizations, and managed care systems. Chapter 12 covers all the key concepts in term and cash-value life insurance, including single-premium life insurance and universal life insurance.

Part 4 contains five separate chapters on investment fundamentals and portfolio management, stocks and bonds, mutual funds, buying and selling securities, and real estate and advanced portfolio management. Because the topic of investments is too complex to treat superficially, this chapter-by-chapter breakdown offers instructors more flexibility in deciding which topics to teach. Importantly, Chapter 13 is a comprehensive study of investment fundamentals for those instructors who have time to teach only one chapter from Part 4. In each chapter, we provide enough detail for the reader to decide which investment alternatives are most suitable. We also offer specific guidelines on when each investment should be sold.

Part 5 concludes the text with two valuable chapters on financial planning for the future. Chapter 18 examines how to develop and implement a plan for a secure retirement, and Chapter 19 reviews the tax-planning principles of estate planning, with coverage on wills and trusts.

Students will find the four appendixes in *Personal Finance* useful beyond the course. Appendix A has more than two dozen key illustrations on how to use the present and future value tables. Appendix B permits students to accurately estimate Social Security benefits: retirement, survivor's, and disability. Appendix C explores careers in personal financial planning and counseling. Appendix D offers a concise explanation on using a financial calculator for personal finance decision making. The Glossary defines all key terms listed at the end of each chapter.

Supplements

These supplements are available with *Personal Finance,* Sixth Edition:

- *Instructor's Resource Manual with Test Bank*
- *Study Guide* (with three sets of sample test questions)
- A computerized *Test Bank*
- Over 70 *Color Transparencies*
- *PowerPoint Slides*
- Garman/Forgue *Personal Finance* Web site

The *Instructor's Resource Manual with Test Bank,* written by Professor Linda Gorham of Northeastern University and Berklee College of Music, has six components: suggested course outlines to emphasize a general, insurance, or investments approach to personal finance; detailed outlines for each chapter; outside research projects and class assignments; and answers and solutions to all end-of-chapter questions and problems. The manual also includes a test bank of more than 2200 questions, with the correct answers identified as well as textbook pages on which the responses can be found. Nearly 130 transparency masters are included that illustrate almost all text tables and figures as well as many boxed features and formulas.

A completely revised *Study Guide,* written by the authors, requires students to define 20 important terms from each chapter and provides three sets of sample examinations for each chapter. Each exam consists of true–false, matching, multiple-choice, and completion questions, plus some applied math problems. Correct answers are provided at the back of the *Study Guide* chapters.

A computerized version of the *Test Bank* in the *Instructor's Manual with Test Bank* is also available to instructors. The new program is very user-friendly and permits editing of test questions.

Color Transparencies are available to adopters of 50 copies or more of *Personal Finance.* These transparencies—which include selected tables, figures, formulas, and boxed features from the text—illustrate the most commonly taught concepts in personal finance.

PowerPoint Slides are a new supplement for this edition. Dr. Susan Jenkins and Janiel Nelson of Idaho State University have created over 450 slides that outline the text and include a selection of the text art. These slides are a valuable asset for use in the classroom, both as presentations and as PowerPoint Chapter Outlines for instructor use as class notes.

The new Courselinks *Personal Finance* Web site includes downloadable PowerPoint slides, links to the sites required to work through the World Wide Web exercises, links to additional web resources, self-testing quizzes that are instantly graded, and online access to formulas and worksheets. The new Garman/Forgue *Personal Finance* Web site enhances and extends the scope of the text.

Acknowledgments

We would particularly like to thank the members of our Advisory Board, who provided helpful suggestions and criticisms during the preparation of this edition:

Bala Arshanapalli, Indiana University Northwest; Anne Bailey, Miami University; Richard Bartlett, Muskingum Area Technical College; John J. Beasley, Georgia Southern University; Kim Belden, Daytona Beach Community College; Pamela J. Bennett, University of Central Arkansas; Daniel A. Bequette, Hartwell College; Peggy S. Berger, Colorado State University; David Bible, Louisiana State University in Shreveport; George Biggs, Southern Nazarene University; Susan Blizzard, San Antonio College; Anne Bunton, Cottey College; Anthony J. Campolo, Columbus State Community College; Chris Canellos, Stanford University; Diana D. Carroll, Carson-Newman College; Gerri Chaplin, Joliet Junior College; Steve Christian, Jackson Community College; Carol M. Cissel, Roanoke College; Thomas S. Coe, Xavier University of Louisiana; Edward R. Cook, University of Massachusetts—Boston; Kathy Crall, Des Moines Area Community College; Ellen Daniel, Ed.D., Harding University; Carl R. Denson, University of Delaware; A. Terrence Dickens, California State University; Charles E. Downing, Massasoit Community College; Gregory J. Eidleman, Alvernia College; Evan Enowitz, Grossmont College; Judy Farris, South Dakota State University; Fred Floss, Buffalo State College; Paula G. Freston, Colby Community College; H. Swint Friday, University of South Alabama; Wafica Ghoul, Detriot College of Business; Joseph D. Greene, Augusta State University; Jeri W. Griego, Laramie County Community College; Michael P. Griffin, University of Massachusetts—Dartmouth; Andrew Hawkins, Lake Area Technical Institute; Janice Heckroth, Indiana University of Pennsylvania; Diane Henke, University of Wisconsin—Sheboygan; Jeanne Hilton, University of Nevada; Laura Horvath, University of Detroit Mercy; David Houghton, Northwest Nazarene College; Roger Ignatius, University of Maine—Augusta; James R. Isherwood, Community College of Rhode Island; Marilyn S. Jones, Friends University; Andrew H. Lawrence, Delgado Community College; Charles J. Lipinski, Marywood University; Diane R. Morrison, University of Wisconsin—La Crosse; Oris L. Odom, II, University of Texas at Tyler; Angela J. Rabatin, Prince George's Community College; Gwen M. Reichbach, Eastern Michigan University; Edmund L. Robert, Front Range Community College; Clarence C. Rose, Radford University; David E. Rubin, Glendale Community College; Marilyn K. Skinner, Macon Technical Institute; Rosalyn Smith, Morningside College; Edward Stendard, St. John Fisher College; Eugene Swinnerton, University of Detroit Mercy; Lisa Tatlock, The Master's College; Stephen Trimby, Worcester State College; John W. Tway, Amber University; Jon D. Wentworth, Southern Adventist University; Gloria Worthy, State Technical Institute—Memphis; Alex R. Yguado, L.A. Mission College; Robert P. Yuyuenyongwatana, Cameron University; Martha Zenns, Jamestown Community College; Larry Zigler, Highland College; Virginia S. Zuiker, University of Minnesota.

We would also like to thank our reviewers, who offered helpful suggestions and criticisms to this and previous editions. We especially appreciate the assistance of:

Dori Anderson, Mendocino College; Robert E. Arnold, Jr., Henry Ford Community College; Hal Babson, Columbus State Community College; Rosella Bannister, Bannister Financial Education Services; Robert Blatchford, Tulsa Junior College; Paul L. Camp, Galecki Financial Management; Anthony J. Campolo, Columbus State Community College; Andrew Cao, American University; Gerri Chaplin, Joliet Junior College; Charlotte Churaman, University of Maryland; Patricia Cowley, Omni Travel; Joel J. Dauten, Arizona State University; Elizabeth Dolan, University of New Hampshire; Sidney W. Eckert, Appalachian State University; Jacolin P. Eichelberger, Hillsborough Community College; Don Etnier, University of Maryland, European Division; Vicki Fitzsimmons, University of Illinois; Elizabeth Goldsmith, Florida State University; Hilda Hall, Surry Community College; Janice Heckroth, Indiana University of Pennsylvania; Roger P. Hill, University of North Carolina—Wilmington; Naheel Jeries, Iowa State University; Peggy D. Keck, Western Kentucky University; Joan Koonce, University of Georgia; Eloise J. Law, State University of New York at Plattsburgh; Jean Lown, Utah State University; Janet K. Lukens, Mississippi State University Cooperative Extension Service; Ruth H. Lytton, Virginia Tech; Kenneth Marin, Aquinas College; Kenneth Mark, Kansas City, Kansas Community College; Julia Marlowe, University of Georgia; Jerald W. Mason, Texas Tech University; Billy Moore, Delta State University; John R. Moore, Navy Family Service Center, Norfolk; Steven J. Muck, El Camino College; Randolph J. Mullis, University of Wisconsin at Madison; Donald Neuhart, Central Missouri State University; William S. Phillips, Memphis State University; Carl H. Pollock, Jr., Portland State University; Mary Ellen Rider, University of Nebraska; Eloise Lorch Rippie, Iowa State University; Michael Rupured, University of Georgia; Barry B. Schweig, Creighton University; Elaine D. Scott, Bluefield State University; Wilmer E. Seago, Virginia Tech; Peggy Schomaker, University of Maine; Horacio Soberon-Ferrer, University of Florida; Mary Stephenson, University of Maryland at College Park; Francis C. Thomas, Personal Finance Specialist, Port Republic, NJ; Jerry A. Viscione, Boston College; Stephen E. Wagner, Attorney at Law, Blacksburg, Virginia; Rosemary Walker, Michigan State University; Robert O. Weagley, University of Missouri—Columbia; Grant J. Wells, Ball State University; and Dorothy West, Michigan State University.

In addition, we wish to thank the many students who had the opportunity to read, critique, and provide input for various components of the *Personal Finance* project.

Celia Hayhoe (University of Kentucky) reviewed all the financial math questions. Jing-jang Xiao (University of Rhode Island) prepared the financial calculator appendix.

Bonnie Binkert, editor-in-chief of Houghton Mifflin's College Division, has been a superlative editor who demanded nothing less than excellence in every aspect of this project; she led by example. This edition of *Personal Finance* was blessed with the tough questioning and careful editing of Kathryn Dinovo, Bernadette Walsh, and Jill E. Hobbs. The text and the ancillaries have been unquestionably strengthened by all these contributions. We would also like to thank Linda Gorham for her contributions to the IRM and Susan Jenkins and Janiel Nelson for their work on the PowerPoint slides. We are deeply appreciative of the generous assistance given by all.

A project of this dimension would never have been completed without the patience, support, understanding, and sacrifices of our friends and families during the book's development, revision, and production. Thanks are also offered to those who have supported our work on this project—for Tom: Lucy Garman; for Ray: Gary Forgue, Joe Forgue, and Irene Leech.

Finally, we wish to thank the hundreds of personal finance instructors around the country who have generously shared their views, in person and by letter, on what should be included in a high-quality textbook and ancillary materials. We've listened and have attempted to meet those needs in every way possible because we share the strong bias that students need to study personal finance concepts thoroughly and learn them well so that they may apply them effectively and successfully in their personal lives.

E. Thomas Garman
tgarman@vt.edu

Raymond E. Forgue
rforgue@pop.uky.edu

PART ONE

Financial Planning

The Importance of Personal Finance

1

OBJECTIVES

After reading this chapter, you should be able to:

1 Discuss what you will gain from the study of personal finance.

2 Describe five lifetime financial objectives of most people.

3 Understand the economic environment of personal finance so you can forecast the state of the economy, inflation, and interest rates.

4 Explain fundamental economic considerations that affect decision making in personal finance.

5 List objectives and steps to achieving your personal financial objectives.

6 Recognize how decisions at work affect success in personal finance.

Whether you are 20, 31, or 58 years old, you are fortunate to be reading this book because few people have the opportunity to study personal finance formally. Most Americans spend 12 to 16 years in school to become capable of earning an income, but they probably have never taken a course on how to manage that income. For some people, making money may seem easier than managing money.

Financial literacy refers to knowing the facts and vocabulary necessary to manage one's personal finances successfully. This ability is not widespread among Americans. Obstacles to financial literacy include a lack of knowledge about personal finance, the complexities of financial life today, being overburdened with too many choices in financial decision making, and a lack of time to learn about personal finance. To make matters worse, most workers today face the challenges of managing their own retirement funds. It is no wonder that many adults feel incompetent, confused, and a little frightened about financial matters. This concern may even be expressed by successful business people because it is one thing to know how to manage a company's finances, but quite another thing to manage one's own money.

The lack of financial literacy can result in one falling prey to investment scams, buying the wrong kind of life insurance, having excessive levels of consumer debt, spending money unconsciously or frivolously, and ultimately being unable to reach financial objectives.

The goal of this book is to educate you to be able to make the proper decisions to control your personal financial destiny. Like everyone else, you will make mistakes in financial matters. Studying this text will help you to make fewer personal finance errors and will help you to become an effective and successful manager of your personal finances for the rest of your life.

This chapter begins by examining what you will gain by studying personal finance and by reviewing five lifetime financial objectives. Finding success in financial matters requires an understanding of the economic environment so you can be aware of how the state of the economy, inflation, and interest rates will affect your financial goals. It is also useful to recognize the fundamental economic considerations in financial decision making, including opportunity costs, marginal analysis, income taxes, and the time value of money. Following an overview of the objectives and key steps to achieving your personal financial objectives, we examine how decisions at work can affect success in personal finance.

Why Study Personal Finance?

1 Discuss what you will gain from the study of personal finance.

You probably recognize that life sometimes can be difficult and that it will become even more involved as you grow older. You will make many complex decisions—some related to your education, your career, and your personal lifestyle, and many that affect your financial success. Although the decision-making process may be accompanied by some anxious and uncomfortable moments, you will become prepared to choose more wisely as you gain experience and education.

Many people do not learn about financial matters until they become mired in financial problems—they "learn from bad experience." Studying personal finance now will help you avoid such difficulties and show you how to take advantage of financial opportunities. **Personal finance** is the study of personal and family resources considered important in achieving financial success; thus, it involves how people spend, save, protect, and invest their financial resources.[*] Topics typically include tax management, budgeting, cash management, use of credit cards, borrowing, major expenditures, risk management, investments, retirement planning, and estate planning.

A solid understanding of personal finance topics will offer you a better chance of success in facing the financial challenges, responsibilities, and opportunities of life. Such successes might include paying minimal credit costs, not paying too much in income taxes, purchasing automobiles at low prices, financing housing on excellent terms, buying appropriate and fairly priced insurance,

---

[*] The reader is encouraged to use the Glossary, which includes hundreds of key terms, whenever needed.

selecting successful investments that match your personality, planning for a comfortable retirement, and passing on your estate with minimal transfer costs.

Closely associated with personal finance is the topic of **personal financial planning**—the development and implementation of coordinated and integrated long-range plans to achieve financial success. This book focuses on providing you with the "nuts and bolts"—knowledge, skills, tools, strategies, and tactics—necessary for you to plan effectively and achieve personal financial success.

Five Lifetime Financial Objectives

2   Describe five lifetime financial objectives of most people.

Financial success is the achievement of financial aspirations that are desired, planned, or attempted. It is defined by the individual or family that seeks it. For some people, such success may involve a financially secure retirement. Others may want vast wealth by the age of 50, while still others may desire enough money to educate their children. Many people simply want a comfortable life.

Financial objectives are rarely achieved without restraining **current consumption** (spending on present needs and wants). This restraint is accomplished by putting money into **savings** (income not spent on current consumption) and **investments** (spending intended to promote further income by adding to the stock of capital assets, such as investing money in stocks and mutual funds). By saving and investing, people are likely to have funds available for **future consumption** (goods and services expected to be consumed in the future). Saving for future consumption represents a good illustration of the human desire to achieve a certain **standard of living**. An individual or group earnestly seeks and strives to attain, to maintain if attained, to preserve if threatened, and to regain if lost this plane or content of living. At any particular time, individuals experience their actual **level of living** but save and invest to reach their desired standard of living.

The lifetime financial objectives that people pursue can be categorized into five groups: (1) to maximize earnings and wealth, (2) to practice efficient consumption, (3) to find life satisfaction, (4) to reach financial security, and (5) to accumulate wealth for retirement and a financial estate for heirs. These broad objectives are closely related, however; to achieve one, people typically need to achieve the others. The following sections describe these objectives.

Maximizing Earnings and Wealth

Wealth is an abundance of money, property, investments, and other resources. A fundamental truth of personal finance is that you cannot build wealth unless you spend less than you earn. To attain the objective of maximizing wealth, you must first seek to maximize earnings. Whether you choose to maximize earnings primarily through employment or through investments will depend on your tastes, interests, and abilities.

Practicing Efficient Consumption

We use money for two purposes: consumption and savings. Because consumption spending (buying goods and services) uses up the largest portion of income (often 90 percent or more), it is important to practice such spending efficiently. Evidence of efficiency is provided by a number of personal finance skills and techniques, such as keeping sound financial records, preparing a functional budget, using credit and checking accounts inexpensively, choosing economical insurance policies, and establishing appropriate criteria to select investments. Failure to practice efficient consumption is often characterized by the careless use of money on nonessentials, abuse of credit, and poor judgment on purchases. Obtaining a 10 percent saving through efficient consumption is equivalent to a 10 percent increase in income—or even more, because this income is not taxed. Careful study of currently unfamiliar areas of consumption (e.g., automobiles, television sets, VCRs, compact discs) can help you be a more efficient shopper and make more money available for purchase of other products and services or for saving or investment.

Finding Life Satisfaction (Some Aspects of Which Are Financial)

What gives you satisfaction in life? Perhaps it is having enough savings, owning a home, being free of debt, owning a late-model car, having a job that pays well, moving ahead in your career, traveling when you want, owning a vacation home, retiring early, living well in retirement, and being able to leave an inheritance. These examples suggest that money lies at the root of many intimate and critical decisions in life relating to career, lifestyle, family, and retirement. Moreover, you may feel that accumulating many costly material goods is one measure of quality of life. Alternatively, you may appreciate good health, strong friendships, a job that you like, a happy home life, giving your children a good education, having enough free time, and providing service to your community. To reach the life satisfaction you seek—whatever it is—you must make decisions related to your personal finances, such as which career to pursue, what to buy, how much to save and invest, and where to live. Financial success represents a means to a better quality of life, whether you intend to live well or donate most of your income to charity.

Reaching Financial Security

Financial security is the comfortable feeling that your financial resources will be adequate to fulfill any needs you have as well as most of your wants. It allows you to have confidence in your money matters, perhaps enjoy occasional indulgences, and remain largely free from doubt, anxiety, or fear about financial concerns. Indicators of financial security can include a steady income to provide a basic lifestyle, a career with potential for advancement (or retirement from such a career), an adequate emergency savings fund, a home with an affordable mortgage debt, adequate insurance coverage, investments in real estate other than a primary residence, a long-term investment program that might include mutual funds and corporate securities, a tax-sheltered retirement plan, an estate plan, and a will.

To reach financial security, first you need to set and prioritize your long- and short-term goals. These goals will give direction to your spending, saving, and investing. For example, if you spend most or all of your earnings on basic necessities plus recreation and entertainment, you will have little money left for the saving and investment needed to reach financial security.

Accumulating Wealth for Retirement and an Estate

Retirement is the primary reason why many people save money. A popular objective is to have a retirement income sufficient to live in a style that is considered "comfortable." Another reason to accumulate wealth is to build a financial estate that can be passed on to heirs after death.

Understanding the Economic Environment of Personal Finance

> **3** Understand the economic environment of personal finance so you can forecast the state of the economy, inflation, and interest rates.

Your success in personal finance partly depends on how well you understand and utilize information to cope with the economic environment. **Forecasting** is predicting, estimating, or calculating in advance. You should easily be able to forecast your income, income taxes, and living expenses. In addition, you need to be able to forecast the state of the economy, inflation, and interest rates so that you can have advance warning of the economic trends affecting your personal finances. While precise forecasts are impossible, it is important to make accurate estimates of the direction and strength of changes in economic trends. Armed with thoughtful insights, you can develop plans and take actions that reduce your risk of exposure to economic conditions beyond your control. Your planning should involve the development of a detailed scheme, program, or method for accomplishing a personal finance objective given certain assumptions.

The State of the Economy

An **economy** is a system of managing the productive and employment resources of a country, community, or business. The U.S. government, for example, attempts to regulate the economy to maintain stable prices (low inflation) and stable levels of low unemployment. In this way, the government seeks to achieve sustained **economic growth**, which is a condition of increasing production and consumption in the economy—and hence increasing national income.

Growth in the U.S. economy varies over time. A **business cycle** (also called an **economic cycle**) is a wavelike pattern of economic activity that includes temporary phases that undulate from boom to bust: expansion, recession (or depression), and recovery (see Figure 1.1).

The preferred stage of the economic cycle is the **expansion** phase, where production is at high capacity, unemployment is low, retail sales are high, and prices and interest rates are low or falling. Under these conditions, consumers find it easier to buy homes, cars, and expensive goods on credit, and businesses are encouraged to borrow to expand production to meet the increased demand. The stock market also grows because investors expect greater profits. As the demand for credit increases, short-term interest rates rise because more borrowers want

Figure 1.1

Phases of the Business
(Economic) Cycle

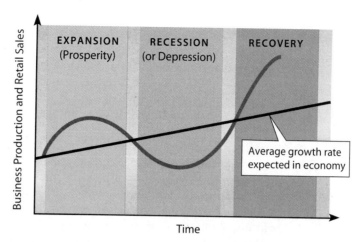

money. Consumers and businesses purchase more goods, exerting upward pressure on prices. Eventually, prices and interest rates climb high enough to stifle consumer and business borrowing, send stock prices down, and choke off the expansion. The result is negligible economic growth or even a decline.

In such situations, the economy often moves toward a **recession**, which is generally described as a decline in business activity or a downturn in the economy. More precisely, the federal government's Business Cycle Dating Committee officially defines a recession as "a recurring period of decline in total output, income, employment and trade, usually lasting from six months to a year and marked by widespread contractions in many sectors of the economy." During recessions consumers typically become pessimistic about their future buying plans. The typical U.S. recession is marked by an average economic decline of 2.1 percent that lasts for ten months with an average unemployment rate of 7.8 percent; the economic decline during 1990–1991, for example, was 1.5 percent, while unemployment reached 7.7 percent.

A **depression** is a severe downward phase of the economic cycle where unemployment is very high (perhaps 20 percent), prices are very low, the level of living decreases sharply, and economic activity virtually ceases. Depressions no longer occur in the U.S. economy because of the existence of so many social and economic safety-net programs, such as insured bank deposits, unemployment benefits, and Social Security. (The last depression occurred during the 1930s and into the early 1940s.) Instead, the U.S. economy now occasionally experiences prolonged periods of "low economic growth" (below 2.0 percent).

Eventually the economic slowdown ends, and consumers and businesses become more optimistic. The economy then moves into the **recovery** phase, where levels of production, employment, and retail sales begin to improve (usually rapidly), allowing the overall economy to experience some growth from its previously weakened state. To complete the business cycle, the economy moves from the recovery phase into an expansion phase. The entire business cycle normally takes four to five years.

Tracking at least two statistics may help you understand the direction of the economy: the nation's gross domestic product and the index of leading economic indicators. **Gross domestic product (GDP)** is the value of all goods and services produced by workers and capital located in the United States, regardless of ownership. It provides the broadest measure of the economic health of the nation because it reports how much economic activity has occurred within the U.S. borders. The government regularly announces the annual rate at which the GDP has grown during the previous three months. An annual rate of less than 2 percent is considered low growth; 4 percent or more is considered vigorous growth.

The **index of leading economic indicators (LEI)** is a composite index, reported monthly as a percentage by the federal government, that suggests the future direction of the U.S. economy. The LEI averages 11 components of growth from different segments of the economy, such as new orders for consumer goods and materials, new business formation, new private housing starts, average weekly claims for initial unemployment insurance, and growth of money supply. Taken together, these measures generally offer a relatively reliable prediction about future directions in the economy. A falling index for three or more consecutive months has been associated with slower economic growth in the months ahead; in contrast, three or more monthly increases suggest robust economic growth in the future.

To make sound financial decisions, you need to know the current state of the economy and where it is headed in the next few years. For example, when the economy begins to show clear signs of a slowdown, it may be a good time to invest in fixed-interest securities because interest rates are sure to fall as the government lowers its own interest rates to boost the economy. Furthermore, a point at which the economy is in the trough of a recession may be an excellent time to invest in stocks because the economy will soon expand into the recovery stage.

Information on the economic projections of government and private economists can be obtained in numerous periodicals on personal finance (such as *Kiplinger's Personal Finance Magazine, Worth, Smart Money,* and *Money*) and business (such as *Business Week* and *Forbes*), as well as in newsmagazines (such as *U.S. News & World Report, Time,* and *Newsweek*) and daily newspapers. After considering their views, you can make your own projections and then make financial decisions accordingly.

The Impact of Inflation

Inflation is a steady rise in the general level of prices; **deflation** involves falling prices. Inflation is measured by the changing cost over time of a "market basket" of goods and services that a typical household might purchase. Inflation occurs when the supply of money (or credit) rises faster than the supply of goods and services available for purchases. It also may be attributed to excessive demand or sharply increasing costs of production.

Inflation can be self-perpetuating. Workers may ask for higher wages, thereby adding to the cost of production. In response to the increases in the costs of labor and raw materials, manufacturers will charge more for their products. Lenders, in turn, will require higher interest rates to offset the lost purchasing power of the loaned funds. In addition, consumers will lessen their resistance to price increases because they fear even higher prices in the future. In times of moderate to high inflation, buying power declines rapidly, and people on fixed incomes suffer the most.

How Inflation Affects Income and Consumption   When prices are rising, an individual's income also must rise to maintain its **purchasing power**, which is a measure of the goods and services that one's income will buy. From an income point of view, inflation has a significant impact. Consider the case of Scott Marshall of Chicago, a single man who took a job in retail management three years ago at a salary of $32,000 per year. Since that time, Scott has had annual raises of $800, $900, and $1000, but he still cannot make ends meet because of inflation. Although Scott received raises, his current income of $34,700 ($32,000 + $800 + $900 + $1000) did not keep pace with an annual inflation rate of 4.0 percent ($32,000 × 1.04 = $33,280; $33,280 × 1.04 = $34,611; $34,611 × 1.04 = $35,996). If Scott's cost of living rose at the same rate as the general price level, in the third year he would be $1296 ($35,996 − $34,700) short of keeping up with inflation. He would need $1296 more in the third year to maintain the same purchasing power that he had in the first year. Personal incomes rarely keep up in times of high inflation.

Your **real income** (income measured in constant prices relative to some base time period) is the more important number. It reflects the actual buying power of your **nominal income** (also called **money income**) that you have to spend as measured in current dollars. Rising nominal income during times of inflation creates the illusion that you are making more money, when in reality you may not be. Figure 1.2 illustrates inflation rates of recent decades and the **half-life of a dollar** (the time required for a dollar to lose half its purchasing power). If inflation in the early years of the twenty-first century continues to be low, the dollar will maintain its purchasing power longer.

Figure 1.2

Inflation and the Half-Life of a Dollar

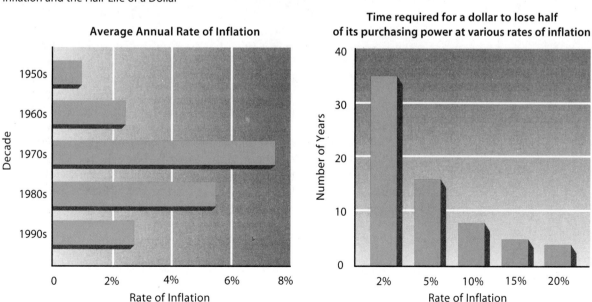

Source: Used by permission of The Conference Board, 845 Third Avenue, New York, NY 10022.

To compare your annual wage increase with the rate of inflation for the same time period, you must first convert your dollar raise into a percentage, as follows:

$$\text{Percentage change in personal income} = \left(\frac{\text{nominal income after raise}}{\text{nominal income last year}} - 1\right) \times 100 \quad (1.1)$$

For example, if Edward Mazone, a single parent and assistant manager of a convenience store in Columbia, Missouri, received a $1600 raise to push his $37,000 annual salary to $38,600 after a year during which inflation was 4.0 percent, he did better than the inflation rate because his raise amounted to 4.3 percent. First, convert the current dollar raise into a percentage:

$$\frac{\$38,600}{\$37,000} = 1.043$$

Then use Equation (1.1) to find the percentage change in personal income:

$$(1.043 - 1) \times 100 = 4.3\%$$

Measured in real terms, Edward's raise was 0.3 percent (4.3 − 4.0). In dollars, his real income after the raise can be calculated using Equation (1.2) by dividing his new nominal income by 1.0 plus the previous year's inflation rate (expressed as a decimal):

$$\text{Real income} = \frac{\text{nominal income after raise}}{1.0 + \text{previous inflation rate}} \quad (1.2)^*$$

$$= \frac{\$38,600}{1 + 0.040} = \$37,115$$

Clearly, a large part of the $1600 raise Edward received was eaten up by inflation. To Edward, only $115 ($37,115 − $37,000) represents real economic progress, while $1485 ($1600 − $115) goes for inflated prices on goods and services. Note that the $115 real raise is equivalent to 0.31 percent ($115 ÷ $37,000) of his previous income, reflecting the difference between Edward's percentage raise in nominal dollars and the inflation rate.

The U.S. government measures inflation using the **consumer price index (CPI)**, which is a broad measure of prices, or the cost of living for consumers. The CPI is published on a monthly basis by the U.S. Bureau of Labor Statistics (BLS). The prices of more than 400 goods and services (a "market basket") sold across the country are tracked, recorded, weighted for importance in a hypothetical budget, and totaled. The index has a base time period—or starting reference point—from which to make comparisons. If 1986–1988 prices represent the base period of 100 and the CPI is 167 on January 1, 2000, the cost of living has risen 67 percent since the base period [(167 − 100) ÷ 100]. Similarly, if the index rises from 167 to 172 on January 1, 2001, then the cost of living has increased by 3.0 percent over the previous year (172 − 167 = 5; 5 ÷ 167 = 3.0%). The formula for figuring the *percentage increase in the CPI* is the second index period minus the first index period, with the result divided by the first index period.

When prices rise, the purchasing power of the dollar declines, but not by the same percentage. Instead, it falls the *reciprocal amount* of the price increase (the counterpart ratio quantity to produce unity). In the preceding example, prices

*   This equation can be found on the *Garman/Forgue* Web site.

rose 67 percent over eight years while the purchasing power of the dollar declined 67 percent over the same period. [The base-year index of 100 divided by the 2000 index of 167 equals 0.6; the reciprocal is 0.4 (1 − 0.6), or 40 percent.] Similarly, in the preceding case in which prices rose 3.0 percent in one year, the purchasing power declined 2.9 percent [167 ÷ 172 = 0.971; the reciprocal is 0.029 (1 − 0.971)].

Inflation pushes up the costs of the products and services we consume. If automobile prices rose 20 percent over the past five years, for example, then it will take $24,000 now to buy a car that once sold for $20,000. Conversely, the purchasing power of the car-buying dollar has fallen to 83.3 percent of its original power ($20,000 ÷ $24,000) five years ago. Of course, if your market basket of goods and services differs from that used to calculate the CPI, you might have a very different **personal inflation rate** (the rate of increase in prices of items purchased by a person).

How Inflation Affects Borrowing, Savings, and Investments

Interest is the price of money. Interest rates on various forms of loans become higher during times of high inflation. Lenders want more for the money they lend because inflation reduces the value of the money to be repaid in the future. Thus, they will charge higher interest on loans. Savers can be hurt by inflation as well, because they, in effect, lend money to the bank when they save. Savers make no money if the inflation rate is 4 percent or higher when the interest rate on their savings accounts is 4 percent. In fact, they will be worse off as they must pay income taxes on interest earnings. Likewise, stock market investors will be negatively affected as inflation reduces the value of future corporate earnings. Basically, high inflation affects all financial decisions as people attempt to avoid its drag on buying power. In contrast, low inflation increases real investment returns (after inflation and income taxes) and makes long-term financial planning, such as for retirement, much easier.

How You Can Estimate Future Inflation

Projections about future inflation rates are made by the U.S. government's Office of Management and Budget (OMB), as well as by a number of economists and private organizations. Projections are reported in popular newspapers and magazines, including the *Wall Street Journal, Barron's, Business Week,* and *Kiplinger's Personal Finance Magazine.* To make sound financial decisions in the future, you need to make your own inflation estimates, both for the near term and for several years to come.

Your views on future inflation might be affected by how successfully you think that Congress, the president, and the Federal Reserve Board (commonly referred to as the *Fed*) will hold down inflation. The rate of inflation is directly related to policies of the federal government. In addition, unanticipated world events, such as war, peace, and supply cutbacks by the oil-producing countries, may affect inflation estimates. You should be able to project inflation relatively accurately over the near term, perhaps for the next one or two years. Although accurate long-term projections are more difficult to make, they still must be attempted because inflation will significantly affect many of your financial decisions. Be cautious in your estimates, however, perhaps erring slightly on the high side to be safe.

How You Can Estimate Future Interest Rates

Knowledge about interest rates gives you insight into the true cost of borrowing money. The degree of risk is higher for longer-term lending because a greater likelihood of error emerges when more time is involved. Thus, long-term interest rates are generally higher than short-term interest rates.

You also should know how changing interest rates affect investments. Rising interest rates depress stock prices for three reasons: (1) businesses must pay more when they borrow, thereby reducing profits; (2) future earnings will not be worth as much as today; and (3) stock investors are lured away to interest-paying investments that may pay higher rates, such as bonds.

You can forecast interest rates by focusing on changes in the **federal funds rate**, which is the rate banks charge one another on overnight loans. Because it is set by the Fed and regularly reported by the news media, the federal funds rate provides an early indication of Fed policy and trends for longer-term interest rates.

Because interest rates and the inflation rate typically move in the same direction, your estimates of near- and long-term interest rates should be consistent with your estimates of inflation. In general, short-term interest rates on conservative- and moderate-risk investments are 1 to 3 percent higher than the inflation rate, while long-term interest rates are 3 to 5 percent higher.

Economic Considerations That Affect Decision Making

4 Explain fundamental economic considerations that affect decision making in personal finance.

Your understanding of a number of basic economic considerations will certainly affect your financial success in life. Important among these factors are opportunity costs, marginal analysis, income taxes, and the time value of money.

Opportunity Costs in Decision Making

The **opportunity cost** of a decision is measured as the value of the next best alternative that must be foregone. For example, suppose that instead of reading this book you could have gone to a movie or watched television, but most of all you wanted to sleep. Therefore, the lost benefits of that sleep—the next best alternative—are the opportunity cost when you choose to read. Knowing the opportunity cost of alternatives aids decision making because it indicates whether the decision made is truly the best option.

In personal finance, opportunity cost reflects the best alternative of what one could have done instead of choosing to spend, save, or invest money. For example, by deciding to purchase 100 shares of General Motors stock rather than keeping the funds in a savings account, you are giving up the option of using the money for a down payment on a new automobile. Of course, if the money is not invested in the stock, future dividend payments will be foregone. In another example, you might travel across town to look at a possible real estate investment opportunity. In this case, the opportunity cost encompasses other things you could have done with the money you paid for the costs to drive there and back, plus the time spent traveling.

The Top Ten Money Mistakes That Waylay Young People

Just about everyone who has raised a family has made a number of errors in personal finance. Based on their sad experiences of not building wealth, here are ten doozies to avoid:

10 Failed to pay self first by saving on a regular basis.

9 Took out a five-year new car loan instead of buying a more affordable used automobile, and drove an automobile that was always worth less than the amount owed.

8 Bought life insurance years before the birth of the first child.

7 Did not comparison shop for the best insurance rates.

6 Used high-interest credit card debt instead of paying the bills in full each month with savings from the bank and later replenishing the savings account.

5 Did not start investing for retirement early enough and did so too conservatively.

4 Overlooked joining a credit union, which pays higher interest on savings and charges less for loans.

3 Purchased overpriced credit life and disability insurance as part of a credit package when taking out a loan.

2 Did not contribute to a tax-deductible retirement plan with money that otherwise would have gone to the Internal Revenue Service.

1 To avoid borrowing the money, did not finish college. As financial columnist Jane Bryant Quinn says, "Money couldn't be better spent because all the best jobs of the future will need smarts."

Opportunity costs usually involve money amounts, quantities of time, and certain psychic pluses or minuses. Although these factors should be considered carefully in decision making, in reality opportunity costs are difficult to quantify because most involve personal tastes and preferences. While the task is challenging, effective managers of personal finances need to carefully calculate some of the dollar costs and noneconomic costs (such as time) in their decision making.

A significant opportunity-cost decision that some people face involves the alternative of returning to college for a graduate degree. Another difficult decision might be the opportunity cost of renting an apartment versus buying a home. If these costs are underestimated, then decisions will be based upon faulty information, and judgments may prove wrong. Properly valuing the costs and benefits of alternatives represents a key step in rational decision making. The mathematics of these two opportunity cost decisions are illustrated later in this chapter and in Chapter 8.

Marginal Analysis in Decision Making

Utility is the ability of a good or service to satisfy a human want. A key task is to determine how much utility you will gain from a particular decision. For example, if you decide to spend $40 on a ticket to a concert, you might begin by thinking about what you might gain from the expenditure. Perhaps you'll enjoy a nice evening, good music, and so on. **Marginal utility** is the extra satisfaction derived from having one more incremental unit of a product or service. The concept of marginal analysis can help us when many variables must be considered in decision making because it reminds us to compare only important variables. It requires that we examine what we will gain if we also experience a certain extra cost. Marginal analysis suggests that people always attempt to maximize dollar satisfaction when choosing between products by using basic logic. In effect, people are inclined to do something until the marginal cost equals (or exceeds) the marginal utility.

Marginal cost is the additional (marginal) cost of one more incremental unit of some item. When known, this cost can be compared with marginal utility received. To illustrate, assume that you consider spending $60 instead of $40 (an additional $20) to obtain a front-row seat at the concert. What marginal utility will you gain from that decision? Perhaps an ability to see and hear more, the satisfaction of having one of the best seats in the theater, and the like. The concept of marginal utility helps to determine the extra benefits that you will receive from your decision.

In another example, two new automobiles were available on a dealership lot in Prescott Valley, Arizona, where retired engineer Dennis O'Barts and his wife, Paige, were trying to make a purchase decision. Both vehicles were similar models, although one was a Mercury and the other a Ford. The Mercury, with a sticker price of $25,100, had a moderate number of options, while the Ford, with a sticker price of $26,800, had numerous options. Marginal analysis suggests that Dennis and Paige do not need to consider all of the options when comparing the vehicles. Instead, the concept of marginal cost says to compare the benefits of the additional options with the additional costs—$1700 in this instance ($26,800 − $25,100). Dennis and Paige need decide only whether the additional options are worth $1700.

Income Taxes in Decision Making

Effective managers of their personal finances should regularly consider the economic effects of paying income taxes when making decisions. Of particular importance is the **marginal tax rate**, which is the tax rate at which your last dollar earned is taxed. As income rises, taxpayers pay progressively higher marginal income tax rates. Most financially successful people must pay U.S. federal income taxes at the 28 percent, or higher, marginal tax rate. For example, if Juanita Martinez, an unmarried office manager working in Atlanta, Georgia, has a taxable income of $32,000 and receives a $1000 bonus from her employer, she must pay an extra $280 in taxes on the bonus income ($1000 × 0.28 = $280). Juanita must also pay state income taxes of 6 percent, or $60 ($1000 × 0.06 = $60), and Social Security taxes of 7.65 percent, or $76.50 ($1000 × 0.0765 = $76.50). Thus, Juanita pays an *effective marginal tax rate* of almost 42 percent (28% + 6% + 7.65% = 41.65%), or $416.50, on the extra $1000 of earned income.

People who pay high marginal tax rates often can gain by making tax-exempt investments, such as bonds issued by various agencies of states and municipalities. For example, Stephanie Miller, a married chiropractor with two children from Cleveland, Ohio, currently has $5000 in utility stocks earning 5 percent, or $250, annually ($5000 × 0.05). She pays $70 in federal income tax on that income at her 28 percent marginal tax rate ($250 × 0.28), leaving her

Figure 1.3

Tax-Sheltered Returns Are Greater Than Taxable Returns

(Illustration: 8 Percent Annual Return and $2000 Annual Contribution)

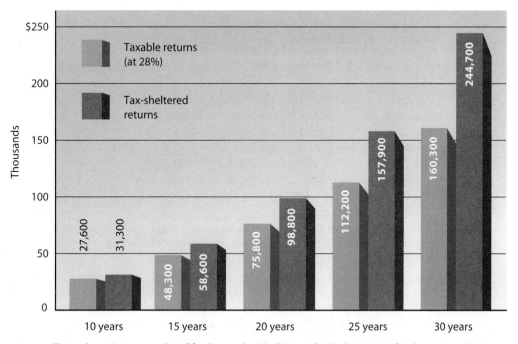

The mathematics assumes that all funds were deposited/invested at the beginning of each year. Note that income taxes must be paid on both the earnings and the previously tax-exempt investment contributions when the funds are eventually withdrawn. This topic is examined in more detail in Chapters 3 and 18.

$180 after taxes. Alternatively, a tax-exempt $5000 state bond paying 4 percent will provide Stephanie with a better after-tax return, $200 instead of $180. She would receive $200 tax-free from the state bond ($5000 × 0.04) compared with $180 ($250 − $70) after taxes on the income from the stocks.

As this discussion implies, the *very best kind of income* is tax-exempt income, which is totally free of taxes. For example, you are ahead of the game if you can legally receive $1000 and not pay taxes on that amount. If your situation mirrors that of Juanita Martinez, you save $416.50 in taxes on the $1000 in earned income ($1000 × 41.65%). The added impact of opportunity cost is even more dramatic. By legally avoiding paying an extra dollar in income taxes, you gain by not paying the dollar in taxes. In addition, you gain the alternative use for that dollar. Finally, you benefit by not having to earn another dollar to replace the one that might have been paid in taxes.

The second best kind of income for individuals is **tax-sheltered**—that is, income exempt from current income taxes. As demonstrated in Figure 1.3, tax-sheltered returns on savings and investments provide much greater returns than returns upon which income taxes must be paid because more money remains available to be invested. In addition, tax-sheltered funds grow more rapidly because compounding (the subject of the next section in this chapter) is enhanced when larger dollar amounts are invested as well as in the last years of growth. You should realize, however, that while current taxes are reduced, eventually one must pay income taxes on the income deferred.

The Time Value of Money in Decision Making

One of the most important concepts in personal finance is the **time value of money**, which is the idea that paying or receiving money over time is affected by the fact that money can earn a positive rate of return over time (as a result of earned interest). That fact must be considered to make mathematically correct decisions in personal finance. Calculating the time value of money allows the comparison of money to be received in different time periods or in different cash-flow patterns over time. For example, you might win the lottery and be offered the choice to receive a lump sum of $1,000,000 now or payments of $60,000 per year for 20 years for a total of $1,200,000. The more favorable answer for you depends upon the interest rate you could earn if you invested the $1,000,000 lump sum on your own. Time value of money calculations can provide the needed information.

Present value (or **discounted value**) is the current value of an asset that will be received in the future. **Future value** (**FV**) is the valuation of an asset projected to the end of a particular time period in the future. Given assumed rates of return for a number of years, both present and future values can be calculated. Time value calculations should be performed when setting financial goals, considering housing alternatives, determining life insurance needs, estimating the financial aspects of retirement, and analyzing investments.

For example, Alieu Demba, an unmarried automobile salesman from Knoxville, Tennessee, was considering two investments that paid certain sums of money in the future. First, a friend wanted to borrow $5000 for three years and pay Alieu back $6000 in a lump sum. Second, Alieu could invest the same $5000 for three years in a government bond paying 7 percent annual interest. Basically, Alieu needs to compare the future value of both alternatives. The future value of lending the money to the friend is $6000. There are multiple ways to determine the future value of the government bond, and each method gives the same answer. All of the calculations assume that the interest earned was not withdrawn but left to be reinvested. This **compound interest** is simply the calculation of interest on interest (because it is reinvested) as well as interest on the original investment.

Basic Calculation Method   Using Equation (1.3) results in the following answer, where i represents the interest rate:

$$FV = \text{(Present value of sum of money)}(i + 1.0)(i + 1.0)(i + 1.0) \dots \quad (1.3)$$
$$= (\$5000)(1.07)(1.07)(1.07)$$
$$= \$6125.22$$

Therefore, Alieu would earn more with the government bond because it would give him $125.22 more ($6125.22 − $6000).

Table Method   Table 1.1 provides a quick and easy way to determine the future dollar value of an investment. For the same example given above, use the table in the following manner: Go across the top row to the 7 percent column. Read down the 7 percent column to the row for three years to locate the factor 1.225.

Table 1.1

Future Value of $1 After a Given Number of Periods

Periods	1%	2%	3%	4%	5%	6%	7%	8%	9%	10%
1	1.0100	1.0200	1.0300	1.0400	1.0500	1.0600	1.0700	1.0800	1.0900	1.1000
2	1.0201	1.0404	1.0609	1.0816	1.1025	1.1236	1.1449	1.1664	1.1881	1.2100
3	1.0303	1.0612	1.0927	1.1249	1.1576	1.1910	1.2250	1.2597	1.2950	1.3310
4	1.0406	1.0824	1.1255	1.1699	1.2155	1.2625	1.3108	1.3605	1.4116	1.4641
5	1.0510	1.1041	1.1593	1.2167	1.2763	1.3382	1.4026	1.4693	1.5386	1.6105
6	1.0615	1.1262	1.1941	1.2653	1.3401	1.4185	1.5007	1.5869	1.6771	1.7716
7	1.0721	1.1487	1.2299	1.3159	1.4071	1.5036	1.6058	1.7138	1.8280	1.9487
8	1.0829	1.1717	1.2668	1.3686	1.4775	1.5938	1.7182	1.8509	1.9926	2.1436
9	1.0937	1.1951	1.3048	1.4233	1.5513	1.6895	1.8385	1.9990	2.1719	2.3579
10	1.1046	1.2190	1.3439	1.4802	1.6289	1.7908	1.9672	2.1589	2.3674	2.5937

Multiply that factor by the present value of the cash asset ($5000) to arrive at the future value ($6125). (Note that this figure varies by $0.22 from the precise calculation because of rounding.) Appendix A provides a more complete explanation of the time value of money and its applications.

You can appreciate the value of compounding by considering what happens when funds are left to grow over a long period of time. Figure 1.4 demonstrates the impact of various compounded returns on a $10,000 investment. The $10,000 will grow to $57,430 in 30 years at a 6 percent rate. Compounding $10,000 at 10 percent becomes $174,500 over the same time period; at 14 percent, it becomes a whopping $509,500!

Simple interest is the interest computed on principal only and without compunding. The interest earned each period is withdrawn and not invested to earn interest. This is illustrated in Equation (1.4).

Interest = principal × rate of interest × time (1.4)

or

$$I = P \times r \times T$$

In Alieu's situation, the simple interest amounts to $1050 ($5000 × 0.07 × 3), while compounding results in $1125.22 ($6125.22 − $5000). For the example in Figure 1.4, the simple interest calculates to $18,000 at a 6 percent rate for 30 years. When added to the $10,000 invested, this $18,000 in interest would total $28,000, which is $29,430 less than the $57,430 that compounding would yield. With compounding, the asset seems to grow slowly at first and then dramatically—a demonstration of the power of time and compound interest.

Figure 1.4

Future Value of $10,000 with Interest Compounded Annually

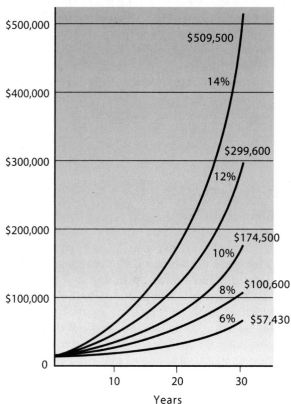

Algebraic or Financial Calculator Method   Time value of money calculations can be efficiently performed using algebra or a financial calculator. The following formulas can be used to solve for future value (*FV*), present value (*PF*), number of investment periods (*n*), and interest rate per investment period (*i*), where

FV = **Future** value	*n* = **Number** of investment periods
PV = **Present** value	*i* = **Interest** rate per investment period

$$FV = PV(1 + i)^n \tag{1.5}$$

$$PV = FV(1 + i)^{-n} \tag{1.6}$$

$$i = (FV/PV)^{1/n} - 1 \tag{1.7}$$

$$n = \frac{1n(FV/PV)}{1n(1 + i)} \tag{1.8}$$

If you are using a financial calculator for time value of money calculations, see Appendix D, "How to Use a Financial Calculator," or you can use the present and future value calculator found on the *Garman/Forgue* Web site.

Figure 1.5

The Rule of 72

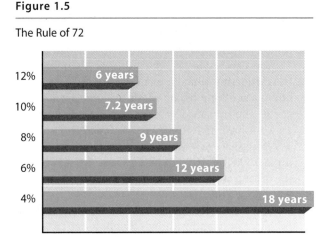

A handy formula for figuring the number of years it takes to double principal using compound interest is the **rule of 72.** You simply divide the interest rate the money will earn into the number 72. For example, if interest is compounded at a rate of 7 percent per year, your principal will double in 10.3 years (72 ÷ 7); if the rate is 6 percent, it will take 12 years (72 ÷ 6). The rule of 72 (see Figure 1.5) also works for determining how long it would take for the price of something to double given a rate of increase in the price. For example, if college tuition costs are rising 8 percent per year, the cost of a college education would double in just over nine years.

Objectives and Steps to Successful Management of Personal Finances

5 List objectives and steps to achieving your personal financial objectives.

Six steps must be completed to manage your personal finances successfully: (1) financial planning, (2) cash and credit management, (3) managing expenditures, (4) income and asset protection, (5) investment planning, and (6) retirement and estate planning. Taking well-informed actions in each area will be critical in helping you reach your lifetime financial objectives. Figure 1.6 implies that these key steps are generally related to one's lifetime financial objectives. Chapter 2 illustrates the details of putting together a comprehensive financial plan that includes all six key steps as you establish both long- and short-term goals. Figure 1.7 shows how the building blocks of a financially successful life fit together, and all of these factors are examined in the remainder of the text.

Figure 1.6

Objectives and Steps in Successful Management of One's Personal Finances

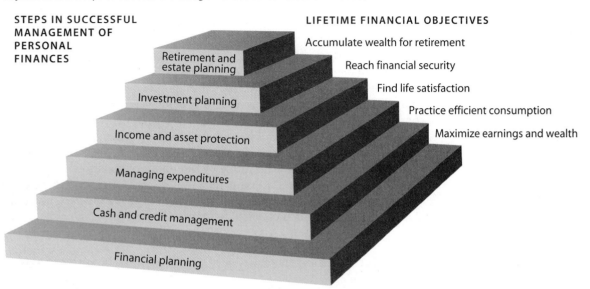

STEPS IN SUCCESSFUL MANAGEMENT OF PERSONAL FINANCES

- Retirement and estate planning
- Investment planning
- Income and asset protection
- Managing expenditures
- Cash and credit management
- Financial planning

LIFETIME FINANCIAL OBJECTIVES

- Accumulate wealth for retirement
- Reach financial security
- Find life satisfaction
- Practice efficient consumption
- Maximize earnings and wealth

Figure 1.7

The Building Blocks of Financial Success

ACHIEVE	Financially Successful Life				
INVEST	Mutual Funds	Stocks and Bonds	Real Estate	Pension Plans	
HANDLE	Credit Cards	Installment Loans	Savings Accounts	Education Costs	
MANAGE	Housing Expenses	Transportation Expenses	Insurance Expenses	Income Taxes	Contingencies
ESTABLISH	Long-Term Goals	Short-Term Goals	Organized Financial Records	Realistic Budget	Emergency Savings Fund
BASE	Checking Account	Savings Account	Money Market Account	Insurance Protection	Employee Fringe Benefits
FOUNDATION	Use of regular income to provide basic lifestyle and savings to meet emergencies				

How Work Decisions Affect Success in Personal Finance

6 Recognize how decisions at work affect success in personal finance.

Important financial aspects of one's working life will affect one's success in personal finance. It is vital to make effective use of the fringe benefits offered through an employer. A **fringe benefit** is compensation for employment that does not take the form of wage, salaries, commissions, or other cash payments. Examples include paid holidays, health insurance, and a retirement plan. Some fringe benefits are tax-sheltered, such as flexible spending accounts and retirement plans. Tax-sheltered means that the employee avoids paying current income taxes on the value of the benefits received from the employer. The taxes may be postponed, or deferred, until a later date (usually a good idea)—perhaps until retirement, when the individual's income tax rate might be lower. Smart decisions can increase your real income by thousands of dollars each year.

This section examines (1) comparisons of salary offers from employers located in cities that have different costs of living, (2) flexible spending accounts, and (3) employer-sponsored qualified retirement plans.

Comparing Salary Offers in Cities with Different Living Costs

Comparing salary offers from employers located in different cities can be difficult without sufficient information on the approximate cost of living in each community. Sometimes those costs vary drastically. Data from the American Chamber of Commerce Researchers Association reveal, for example, that life in a high-cost city such as Boston is, on average, 30 percent more expensive than life in a lower-cost city such as Portland, Oregon. The Chamber data are reported in index form, with the "average cost" community given a rating of 100.

The following example demonstrates how to compare salary offers in two different cities. In a recent year, the index was 130.6 for Boston (city 1) and 114.9 for Los Angeles (city 2). Let's assume you want to compare the buying power of a salary offer of $34,000 in Boston with a $31,000 offer in Los Angeles. The costs can be compared using Equations (1.9) and (1.10) below.

$$\text{Salary in city 1} \times \frac{\text{index city 2}}{\text{index city 1}} = \text{equivalent salary in city 2} \qquad (1.9)$$

$$\text{Boston's } \$34,000 \times \frac{114.9}{130.6} \text{ is equal to } \$29,913 \text{ in Los Angeles}$$

Thus, the $34,000 Boston salary offer would buy $29,913 of goods and services in Los Angeles—an amount less than the $31,000 Los Angeles salary offer. All things being equal (and they are both nice cities), the Los Angeles offer is better.

To compare the buying power of salaries in the other direction, reverse the formula:

$$\text{Salary in city 2} \times \frac{\text{index city 1}}{\text{index city 2}} = \text{equivalent salary in city 1} \qquad (1.10)$$

$$\text{Los Angeles's } \$31,000 \times \frac{130.6}{114.9} \text{ is equal to } \$35,236 \text{ in Boston}$$

Thus, the $31,000 Los Angeles salary offer can buy $35,236 of goods and services in Boston—an amount higher than the $34,000 Boston salary offer. All things being equal, the Los Angeles offer is still better.

You may compare salary figures and the cost of living in different communities in three ways:

1. By finding the index data in the American Chamber of Commerce Researchers Association's publication, *ACCRA Cost of Living Index* (found in your library or at *www.accra.org*).

2. By telephoning the local Chamber of Commerce in each city to obtain its researched-based index number.

3. By making a personal estimate of an index for each city based upon your impressions.

For the fairest comparisons, be sure to add or subtract from the salary offers the value of fringe benefits included or excluded, then do the calculations with the indexes.

Tax-Sheltered Flexible Spending Accounts

Examples of tax-sheltered fringe benefits are the **flexible spending account (FSA)**, **pretax set-aside account**, or **expense reimbursement account**. These fringe benefits are now offered by more than half of all large employers. These government-approved plans allow payment of selected employee-paid expenses for medical or dependent care to be reimbursed with pretax dollars. Under a typical FSA, the employee agrees to have a certain amount deducted from each paycheck that is then deposited in a separate account. As qualified expenses are incurred, the employee requests and receives reimbursements from the account. FSA accounts can be used to pay for three types of expenses: (1) care of a dependent under age 13; (2) care of another dependent who is physically or mentally incapable of caring for himself or herself, and who resides in the taxpayer's home; and (3) qualified unreimbursed medical expenses. Examples of the last kind of expenses include eye examinations, eyeglasses, routine physical exams, and orthodontia work.

The tax advantage of an FSA occurs because the deducted amounts of salary avoid federal income tax, Social Security taxes, and, in most states, state income taxes, thereby allowing selected personal expenses to be paid with pretax (rather than after-tax) income. Paying the expenses with **pretax dollars** (money income that has not been taxed by the government) *lowers* taxable income, *decreases* take-home pay, and *increases* effective take-home pay because of the reimbursements. For example, assume Jane Johnson, a married woman earning $30,000 annually, directs that her employer put aside $4920 of regular annual income ($410 per monthly paycheck) for child care expenses. During the year, Jane submits receipts for child care expenses to the employer and is reimbursed the $4920. Table 1.2 shows how Jane decreased her monthly take-home pay by $317 ($1651 − $1334), which, after plan reimbursements of $410 per month, increased her monthly effective take-home pay by $93 ($410 − $317). Jane's annual tax savings are $1116.

When Jane participates in the FSA, her federal income tax drops $62 per month and her Social Security tax drops another $31 monthly, which totals $93 per month or $1116 per year. In effect, the $4920 that Jane pays for child care consists of $3804 set aside by Jane and $1116 contributed by the federal government because, without the FSA, she would have had to pay the government the $1116 in the form of taxes on the $4920 of income.

Table 1.2

The Positive Effects of a Flexible Spending Account

	Without the Plan	With the Plan	Flexible Spending Account
Monthly salary	$2500	$2500	
To FSA account	—	(410)	$410
Taxable salary	2500	2090	
Income tax*	(248)	(186)	
Social Security tax	(191)	(160)	
Salary after taxes	2061	1744	
Medical and/or dependent care expenses	(410)	(410)	
Take-home pay	1651	1334	
FSA reimbursement	—	410	(410)
Effective take-home pay	1651	1744	
Net monthly savings increase with plan	—	$93	

* Based on annual salary of $30,000 with three W-4 exemptions and a "married filing jointly" filing status. Actual savings depend upon salary, number of exemptions, and filing status.

Before enrolling in an FSA, it is important to estimate expenses carefully so that the amount in the FSA does not exceed anticipated expenses. IRS regulations do not allow the plan to return unused amounts at the end of the plan year, nor can money be transferred from one account to another, or from one plan year to another. Thus, unused amounts are forfeited and are not returned to the employee—a condition called the "use it or lose it" rule. A nominal monthly fee is assessed to participate in these programs, and the maximum annual contribution is $5000. A negative aspect of FSAs for most workers is that eventual Social Security benefits may be slightly lower than anticipated (perhaps $10–$15 per month) because taxable income was reduced by the amount of the FSA withholding.

Employer-Sponsored Qualified Retirement Plans

More than half of all workers are covered by an **employer-sponsored qualified retirement plan**. These retirement plans have been approved by the Internal Revenue Service as vehicles in which to deposit tax-sheltered contributions; they offer tax advantages that can reduce a person's current income taxes and increase his or her retirement benefits. Thus, contributions to the retirement plans are exempt from current income taxes. Employer-sponsored qualified retirement plans provide two distinct advantages.

First Advantage: Tax-Deductible Contributions Create Larger Returns
Tax-sheltered retirement plans provide tremendous tax-deductibility benefits compared with ordinary savings and investment plans. Because pretax contributions to qualified plans reduce income, the current year's tax liability is low-

Table 1.3

The Value of Tax-Sheltered Contributions   (28 percent income tax rate, single)

Monthly salary	$3000		Monthly salary	$3000
Pretax retirement plan contribution	0		Pretax retirement plan contribution	500
Taxable income	3000		Taxable income	2500
Federal taxes	600		Federal taxes	460
Monthly take-home pay	2400		Monthly take-home pay	2040
You put away for retirement	0		Cost to put away $500 per month ($2400 − $2040)	360

ered. Thus, the money saved in taxes can be used to partially fund a larger contribution, which creates even greater returns.

As Table 1.3 illustrates, you can save substantial sums for retirement with minimal impact to monthly take-home pay. A single person with a monthly taxable income of $3000 who places $500 into a tax-sheltered retirement plan [for an annual contribution of $6000 ($500 × 12)] reduces monthly take-home pay from $2400 to $2040, not an enormous amount. The net effect is that it costs that person only $360 to put away $500 per month into a retirement plan. The immediate "return on investment" equals a fantastic 38.9 percent ($140 ÷ $360). In essence, the taxpayer puts $360 into his or her retirement plan and the government contributes $140. (Alternatively, the taxpayer could pay the $140 to the government.) A taxpayer paying a higher marginal tax rate realizes even greater gains. Because a substantial part of your contributions to a tax-sheltered retirement plan comes from money that you would have paid in income taxes, it costs you less to save more.

Second Advantage: Tax-Deferred Growth Enhances Earnings Because interest, dividends, and capital gains from qualified plans are taxed only after funds are withdrawn from the plan, investments in tax-sheltered retirement plans grow tax-free. The benefits of tax deferral can be substantial.

For example, if a person in the 28 percent tax bracket invests $2000 at the beginning of every year for 30 years and the investment earns an 8 percent taxable return compounded annually, the fund will grow to $160,300. If the same $2000 invested annually was instead compounded at 8 percent within a tax-sheltered program, it grows to $244,700! The higher amount solely results from compounding without paying income taxes. (Figure 1.3 on page 15 illustrates these differences in returns.) Indeed, when the funds are finally taxed upon withdrawal some years later, the taxpayer may be in a lower tax bracket.

Start Early and Become a Millionaire at Retirement

A tax-sheltered retirement plan is best begun at an early age. Consider two hypothetical cases of people who began making regular contributions to their IRA accounts at different stages in their lives. The early starter, age 30, invested $2000 annually but stopped the contributions at age 40. The late starter began investing the same amount at age 40 and continued until age 65. Thus, the early starter invested a total of $20,000 and the late starter invested $50,000. If both tax-sheltered investment accounts earned 9 percent per year, the early starter wins. The power of compounding earns a retirement nest egg of about $285,000 for the early starter, while the late starter will accumulate only about $185,000.

How to Maximize the Benefits from a Tax-Sheltered Retirement Plan

1. Start Early to Boost Your Retirement Because of the magic of compounding, the amount of money in your retirement plan can become quite large over time. For example, a worker who starts saving $25 per week in a qualified retirement plan at age 23 will have $450,367 by age 65, assuming an annual growth rate of 8 percent.

2. The Cost of Delaying Contributions Is High Waiting until age 33 to start saving, instead of beginning at age 23, results in a retirement fund of only $250,401. The cost of delay is nearly $200,000 ($450,367 − $250,401), even though ten years' worth of delayed deposits would have totaled only $13,000. This effect occurs because most of the power of compounding appears in the last years of growth.

3. Saving Just 1 Percent More of Your Pay Makes a Big Difference Employer restictions limit the maximum amount that workers may save in a qualified retirement plan. This limit might be 6 or 15 percent of income, for example. Most workers, however, do not save the maximum amount. A 23-year old worker earning $30,000 who saves just 1 percent more of his or her pay (only an extra $300 per year) will see a boost in the retirement fund of $91,273 (assuming an annual growth rate of 8 percent).

4. Avoid Making Withdrawals from a Tax-sheltered Retirement Plan The tax sheltering of funds in a qualified plan actually represents a deferment of taxes rather than a permanent avoidance of them. Income taxes must be paid when the funds are withdrawn. If money is withdrawn prior to a certain age—usually 59$^{1}/_{2}$—a 10 percent penalty may be assessed as well as the usual income tax.

In addition to paying a penalty and the income tax due on withdrawn funds from a retirement plan, the worker also loses the opportunity cost of keeping the funds invested. For example, assume that Ramsey Marshalla, a legal assistant from San Jose, California, withdraws $5000 from his employer-sponsored retirement plan for some reason (e.g., for an emergency, to pay bills, to buy a new vehicle when changing jobs, or to make a down payment on a home). As a result, Ramsey will not accumulate the $45,313 ($50,313 − $5000) that amount would have earned over the next 30 years. When faced with a financial problem, you should borrow from a credit union or bank (see Chapter 5) before withdrawing money from a retirement plan.

Summary

1. Effective management of your personal finances will enable you to face the financial challenges, responsibilities, and opportunities of life successfully.

2. Most people have five lifetime financial objectives: to maximize earnings and wealth; to practice efficient consumption; to find satisfaction in life; to reach financial security; and to accumulate wealth for retirement and an estate.

3. Your success in personal finance partly depends on how well you understand and utilize information to cope with the economic environment, including data about the state of the economy, inflation, and interest rates.

4. Four useful economic considerations that affect decision making in personal finance are opportunity costs, marginal analysis, income taxes, and the time value of money.

5. Successful management of personal finances involves six steps: financial planning; cash and credit management; managing expenditures; income and asset protection; investment planning; and retirement and estate planning. Success in these steps relates to the achievement of one's lifetime financial objectives.

6. Work-related decisions affect success in personal finance. These choices include selection of a salary offer, use of flexible spending accounts, and entry into employer-sponsored retirement plans.

Key Words & Concepts

business cycle   *6*
compound interest   *16*
consumer price index   *10*
employer-sponsored retirement plan   *22*
federal funds rate   *12*
financial success   *4*
flexible spending account   *21*
future value   *16*
gross domestic product (GDP)   *7*

index of leading economic indicators (LEI)   *8*
inflation   *8*
marginal cost   *14*
marginal tax rate   *14*
opportunity cost   *12*
personal finance   *3*
personal financial planning   *4*
personal inflation rate   *11*
present value   *16*
real income   *9*
tax-sheltered   *15*
time value of money   *16*

Questions for Thought & Discussion

1. Cite three examples of gains you are likely to make from the study of personal finance.

2. List the five lifetime financial objectives of most people.

3. Define "financial security" and give some examples of it.

4. Briefly summarize the phases in the economic cycle.

5. Explain how tracking the gross domestic product and the index of leading economic indicators can help you forecast the direction in which the economy is headed.

6. Provide a numerical example (using different numbers from the text) of how to measure the effect of inflation on a person's annual raise in salary.

7. Provide a numerical example (using different numbers from the text) of how to calculate the decline in the purchasing power of a dollar when prices rise.

8. Explain how inflation can dramatically affect your borrowing, savings, and investments.

9. Explain the difference between real income and money income.

10. Summarize why it is important to estimate future interest rates.

11. Define "opportunity cost" and give an example of how opportunity costs might affect your financial decision making.

12. Explain and give an example of how marginal analysis makes some financial decisions easier.

13. Describe and give an example of how income taxes can affect financial decision making.

14. Briefly explain the difference between simple interest and compound interest.

15. Using the Table Method, give an example (using different numbers from the text) that illustrates the importance of the time value of money.

16. Describe how the steps in successful management of personal finances are related to one's lifetime financial objectives.

17. Explain why the same dollar amount of salary offered by employers in two different cities may be important.

18. How do contributions to a flexible spending account work to benefit the finances of the worker?

19. How do contributions to an employer-sponsored qualified retirement plan benefit the finances of the worker?

DECISION-MAKING CASES

Case 1   Reasons to Study Personal Finance

Patricia Bailey of Gulfport, Mississippi, is a senior in college, majoring in sociology. She anticipates getting married a year or so after graduation. Patricia has only one elective course remaining and must choose between another advanced class in sociology and one in personal finance. As Patricia's friend, you want to persuade her to take personal finance. Give some examples of how Patricia might benefit from the study of personal finance.

Case 2   A Closer Look at Lifetime Financial Objectives

You have been asked to give a brief speech on the lifetime financial objectives of most people and their relationship to steps in successful management of personal finances. Make an outline of the points in your speech.

Financial Math Questions

1. As a graduating senior, Ann Coulson of Manhattan, Kansas, is anxious to enter the job market at an anticipated annual salary of $24,000. Assuming an average inflation rate of 5 percent and an equal cost-of-living raise, what will Ann's salary be in 10 years? In 20 years? (Hint: Use Appendix A.1 or calculations on the *Garman/Forgue* Web site.) To make real economic progress, how much of a raise (in dollars) must Ann receive annually?

2. Kathryn Berry, a freshman nutrition major at the University of Minnesota, has some financial questions for the next three years of school and beyond. Answers to these questions can be obtained by using Appendix A or the *Garman/Forgue* Web site.

   (a) If Kathryn's tuition, fees, and expenditures for books this year total $5000, what will they be during her senior year (three years from now), assuming costs rise 6 percent annually? (Hint: Use Appendix A.1 or the *Garman/Forgue* Web site.)

   (b) Kathryn is applying for a scholarship currently valued at $3000. If she is awarded it at the end of next year, how much is the scholarship worth in today's dollars, assuming inflation of 5 percent? (Hint: Use Appendix A.2 or the *Garman/Forgue* Web site.)

   (c) Kathryn is already looking ahead to graduation and a job, and she wants to buy a new car not long after graduation. If after graduation she begins a savings program of $2400 per year in an investment yielding 6 percent, what will be the value of the fund after three years? (Hint: Use Appendix A.3 or the *Garman/Forgue* Web site.)

   (d) Kathryn's Aunt Karroll told her that she would give Kathryn $1000 at the end of each year for the next three years to help with college expenses. Assuming an annual interest rate of 6 percent, what is the present value of that stream of payments? (Hint: Use Appendix A.4 or the *Garman/Forgue* Web site.)

3. Using the present and future value tables in Appendix A, the appropriate calculations on the *Garman/Forgue* Web site, or a financial calculator (see Appendix D), calculate the following:

    (a) The future value of $400 in two years that earns 5 percent.

    (b) The future value of $1200 saved each year for ten years earning 7 percent.

    (c) The amount a person would need to deposit today with a 5 percent interest rate to have $2000 in three years.

    (d) The amount a person planning for retirement would need to deposit today to be able to withdraw $6000 each year for ten years from an account earning 6 percent.

    (e) A person is offered a gift of $5000 now or $8000 five years from now. If such funds could be expected to earn 8 percent, which is the better choice?

    (f) A person wants to have $3000 available to spend on an overseas trip four years from now. If such funds could be expected to earn 7 percent, how much must be invested in a lump sum to realize the $3000 when needed?

    (g) A person who invests $1200 each year finds one choice expected to pay 9 percent per year and another choice that may pay 10 percent. What is the difference in return if the investment is made for 15 years?

    (h) A person invests $50,000 earning 6 percent. If $6000 is withdrawn each year, how many years will it take for the fund to run out?

4. You win a contest. The prize is cash, and you are offered several alternative payment plans. Which plan should you choose? Assume you can earn 5 percent on your money and ignore inflation.

    (a) $30,000 today.

    (b) $40,000 in five years.

    (c) $10,000 one year from today and $25,000 two years later.

    (d) $4000 per year starting today for the next ten years.

Exploring the World Wide Web of Personal Finance

To complete these exercises, go to the *Garman/Forgue* Web site at

www.hmco.com/college/business/

Select Personal Finance. Click on the exercise link for this chapter and answer the questions that appear on the Web page.

1. Visit the Bureau of Labor Statistics Consumer Price Index home page and link to information for various areas of the country and metropolitan areas of various sizes. Describe how prices have been changing for your area and city size during the past year.

2. Visit the Bureau of Labor Statistics Current Population Survey home page and link to a recent press releaase providing data on employment and unemployment for males and females. Compare the current unemployment rate for men and women older than age 20 and older than age 16.

3. Visit the Web site for the Federal Reserve Bank of Atlanta, where you will find a summary of economic information provided on the Web by agencies of the U.S. government. Select three Web sites that you feel would be especially useful for people seeking information on economic trends to help them with their personal financial planning.

4. Visit the Web site for WageWeb, where you will find the results of salary surveys in numerous career areas. Review the information for careers related to your college major. Does the information confirm what you had expected or does it open your eyes to a differing reality?

Financial Planning

2

OBJECTIVES

After reading this chapter, you should be able to:

1 Explain the concept of financial planning, its components, and its benefits.

3 Use financial ratios to evaluate your financial strength and progress.

5 Describe the use of computer software in personal financial planning.

2 Describe financial statements, particularly the balance sheet and the income and expense statement.

4 Identify the purposes and methods of financial recordkeeping.

6 Explain how to choose among the various types of professional financial planners.

Most people develop a pattern of financial behavior through trial and error. They want to succeed financially but typically lack clear goals for the future. Although they maintain financial records, often the records are poorly organized and difficult to locate. Thus, decision making is flawed because of a lack of understanding about the current economic conditions and their financial status. Instead of simply muddling through money matters, it is important to engage in explicit financial planning.

This chapter begins with an explanation of financial planning—what it is and how it can be important to you. We then examine two financial statements: the balance sheet and the income and expense statement. The section that follows explains how to use information from the financial statements to calculate financial ratios that evaluate your financial strength and progress. Next, we provide a detailed overview of recordkeeping to help you establish your own financial recordkeeping system. The chapter concludes with information on using a computer in personal financial planning and on the providers of financial planning assistance in today's marketplace.

The Components of Successful Financial Planning

1 Explain the concept of financial planning, its components, and its benefits.

Financial planning is the process of developing and implementing a coordinated series of financial plans to achieve financial success. Financial planning is unique to each individual or family, and should take into consideration all aspects of financial activity as an individual or family moves through life.

Table 2.1 on the following page provides an illustration of a financial plan. Most people do not make written financial plans in the broad areas indicated: spending, risk management, and capital accumulation. Many ignore certain areas (estate planning is a common example) and act with only partial knowledge in other areas (relying on generally inadequate employer-provided disability insurance, for example). Success in financial matters results from effective financial planning in all 15 specific areas. Each subsequent chapter will examine personal finance topics in enough detail so that you will feel comfortable and confident as you implement useful financial plans.

Financial planning begins by examining your values as they relate to financial activity. These values provide the underlying support and basis for financial goals. Successful financial planning includes the following components: (1) specified values that underlie the plans; (2) explicitly stated financial goals; (3) informed projections about the economy; and (4) logical and consistent financial strategies. Only after this development process is complete do you take actions to achieve the goals; planning comes before action.

Values Provide the Base for Financial Planning

Values are fundamental beliefs about what is important, desirable, and worthwhile. They serve as the basis for goals. Each of us differs in the ways we value education, spiritual life, health, employment, credit use, family life, and many other factors. Personal financial goals grow out of these values because we consider some things more important or desirable than others. We express our values, in part, by the ways we spend, save, and invest our money. Thus, our personal values dictate our financial plans.

Setting Financial Goals Follows from Values

Financial goals are the specific long- and short-term objectives to be attained through financial planning and management efforts. Goals should be consistent with values. They must be stated explicitly to serve as a rational basis for financial actions. Financial goals should be specific both in terms of dollar amount and the projected date they are to be achieved. Setting goals helps you visualize the gap between your current financial status and where you want to be in the future. Examples of general financial goals include finishing a college education, paying off debts (including education loans), taking a vacation, owning a home, accumulating funds to send children through college, owning your own business, and having financial independence at retirement. None of these goals, however, is specific enough to guide financial behavior. Specific goals should be measurable, attainable, relevant, and time-related. Figure 2.1 provides an overview of effective personal financial management.

Table 2.1

Financial Plans, Goals, and Objectives for Harry (Age 23) and Belinda (Age 22) Johnson   Prepared in January 1999

Financial Plan Areas	Long-Term Goals and Objectives	Short-Term Goals and Objectives
For Spending		
Evaluate and plan major purchases	Purchase a new car in two years.	Begin saving $200 per month for a down payment for a new car.
Manage debt	Keep installment debt under 10 percent of take-home pay.	Pay off charge cards at end of each month and do not finance any purchases of appliances or other similar products.
For Risk Management		
Medical costs	Avoid large medical costs.	Maintain employer-subsidized medical insurance policy by paying $85 monthly premium.
Property and casualty losses	Always have renter's or homeowner's insurance. Always have maximum automobile insurance coverage.	Make annual premium payment of $110 on renter's insurance policy. Make quarterly premium payments of $160 on automobile insurance policy.
Liability losses	Eventually buy $1 million liability insurance.	Rely on $100,000 policy purchased from same source as automobile insurance policy.
Premature death	Have adequate life insurance coverage for both as well as lots of financial investments so the survivor would not have any financial worries.	Maintain employer-subsidized life insurance of $34,200 on Belinda. Buy some life insurance for Harry. Start some investments.
Income loss from disability	Buy sufficient disability insurance.	Rely on sick days and seek disability insurance through private insurers.
For Capital Accumulation		
Tax fund	Have enough money for taxes (but not too much) withheld from monthly salaries by both employers to cover eventual tax liabilities.	Confirm that employer withholding of taxes is sufficient. Have extra money withheld to cover additional tax liability because of income on trust from Harry's deceased father.
Revolving savings fund	Always have sufficient cash in local accounts to meet monthly and annual anticipated budget expense needs.	Develop cash-flow calendar to ascertain needs. Put money into revolving savings fund to build it up quickly to the proper balance. Keep all funds in interest-earning accounts.
Emergency fund	Build up monetary assets equivalent to three months' take-home pay.	Put $200 per month into an emergency fund until it totals one month's take-home pay.
Education	Maintain educational skills and credentials to remain competitive. Have employer assist in paying for Belinda to earn a master's in business administration (MBA). Have Harry complete a master's of fine arts (MFA), possibly a PhD in interior design.	Both take one graduate class per term.
Savings	Always have a nice-size savings balance. Regularly save to achieve goals. Save a portion of any extra income or gifts. Save $15,000 for a down payment on a home to be bought within five years.	Save enough to pay cash for a good-quality video cassette recorder (VCR). Pay off Visa credit card balance of $390 soon.
Investments	Own substantial shares of a conservative mutual fund that will pay dividends equivalent to about 10 percent of family income at age 45. Own some real estate and common stocks.	Start investing in a mutual fund before next year.
Retirement	Retire at age 60 or earlier on an income that is the same as the take-home pay earned just before retirement.	Establish individual retirement accounts (IRAs) for Harry and Belinda before next year. Select the best retirement benefit plan offered by employer to meet long-term needs.
Estate planning	Provide for surviving spouse.	Each spouse makes a will.

Figure 2.1

Overview of Effective Personal Financial Management

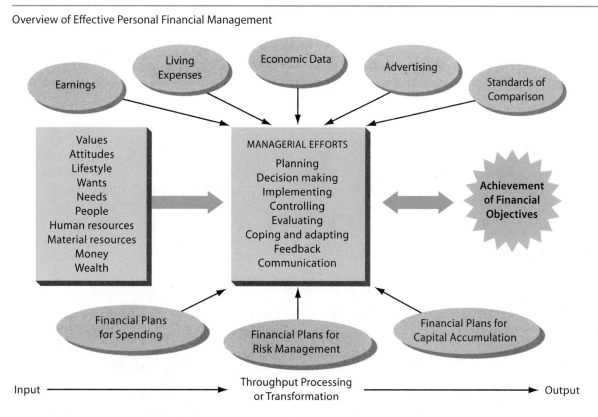

An example of a financial goal in risk management is provided by Judy Vogel of Cincinnati, Ohio. Judy is a single parent of two sons, aged 8 and 11. As a dance instructor, she was concerned about the risk of becoming disabled and being unable to work. After considering the matter thoroughly, Judy decided that a long-term goal was to protect herself from such losses until her sons finished college in approximately 15 years. Because her family has limited resources, Judy's short-term goal was to spend less than $40 per month on the necessary insurance coverage. After telephoning three insurance agents to compare premium costs, Judy bought a disability policy through her employer's group plan by paying $32 per month out of her $1450 per month after-tax income.

Informed Economic Projections Underlie Effective Planning

People who make informed projections about the economy are often rewarded with favorable financial opportunities. People should not assume that "inflation will be about the same for the next few years" or that "interest rates will probably remain steady for some time." For example, Laurie Wesswick of Laramie, Wyoming, is the owner of a fishing supply store. She correctly projected that savings account interest rates would decline during the last economic recession, so she put some of her funds into savings certificates of deposit (CDs) before rates declined from 5.5 percent to 3.75 percent. This decision enabled her to lock in the higher rates for three years. (Recall that strategies for assessing the economy were covered in Chapter 1.)

Financial Strategies Guide Financial Behavior

To be successful, financial plans must have logical and consistent strategies. **Financial strategies** are preestablished plans of action to be implemented in specific situations. For example, Carla Dall, an office manager for a textile company in Dobson, North Carolina, is a conservative investor. She decided that her strategy would be to sell most of her corporate stocks during times of economic prosperity when the stock market peaked and buy stock when prices were low during economic slumps. This approach permitted Carla to "buy low and sell high"—a strategy recommended by financial advisers. Financial strategies are identified throughout this book.

Financial Statements

2   Describe financial statements, particularly the balance sheet and the income and expense statement.

Financial statements are compilations of personal financial data designed to communicate information on money matters. They are used—often along with other financial data—to indicate the financial condition of an individual or family. The two most useful statements are the balance sheet and the income and expense statement.

A **balance sheet** (or **net worth statement**) describes an individual's or family's financial condition on a specified date (often January 1), showing assets, liabilities, and net worth. It gives a current status report as of a certain date and provides information on what you own, what you owe, and the net result if all debts were paid off. For example, if your balance sheet shows that you have a large cash balance, you can take action to achieve goals that require ready cash. An **income and expense** (or **cash-flow**) **statement** lists and summarizes income and expense transactions that have taken place over a specific period of time, such as a month or a year. It tells you where your money came from and where it went.

The Balance Sheet

If you are serious about your financial success, then you need to sit down today with pencil and paper to see exactly where you stand as indicated by your balance sheet—the value of what you own minus what you owe. Your balance sheet should be updated at least once each year. The information can then be compared with that on previous balance sheets to determine your financial progress and provide directions for future planning.

Components of the Balance Sheet   A balance sheet contains three parts: assets, liabilities, and net worth. Your **assets** include everything you own that has monetary value. Your **liabilities** are your debts—what you owe to others. Your **net worth** is the dollar amount left when what is owed is subtracted from the dollar value of what is owned—that is, when liabilities are subtracted from assets. Your net worth should grow at a rate at least equal to the rate of inflation.

What Is Owned—Assets The asset section of the balance sheet identifies things valued at their **fair market value**—what a willing buyer would pay a willing seller, not amounts originally paid. It is useful to classify assets as monetary, tangible, or investment assets.

Monetary assets (also known as **liquid assets**) include cash and near-cash items that can be readily converted to cash. They are primarily used for maintenance of living expenses, emergencies, savings, and payment of bills.

Tangible (or **use**) **assets** are physical items that have fairly long lifespans and could be sold to raise cash but whose primary purpose is to provide maintenance of one's lifestyle (e.g., a car). Tangible assets generally depreciate in value over time.

Investment assets (also known as **capital assets**) include tangible and intangible items acquired for the monetary benefits they provide, such as generating additional income and increasing in value. Successful financial planning generally requires **diversification** of investment assets by putting money in a variety of investments (such as real estate, stocks, bonds, and mutual funds). If one investment does not perform well, the others are available to maintain the overall value. Investment assets generally appreciate and are dedicated to the maintenance of one's future level of living.

Examples of each kind of asset are described next.

Monetary Assets

- Cash (including cash on hand, checking accounts, savings accounts, savings bonds, certificates of deposit, and money market accounts)
- Tax refunds due
- Money owed to you by others

Tangible Assets

- Automobiles, motorcycles, boats, bicycles
- House, mobile home, condominium
- Household furnishings and appliances
- Personal property (jewelry, furs, tools, clothing)
- Other "big ticket" items

Investment Assets

- Stocks, bonds, mutual funds, gold, partnerships, art, IRAs
- Life insurance and annuities (cash values only)
- Real estate investments
- Personal and employer-provided pension and retirement plans

What Is Owed—Liabilities The **liabilities** section of the balance sheet includes items that reflect debts owed, including both personal and business-related debts. The debt could be either a **short-term** (or **current**) **liability** (an obligation to be paid off within one year) or a **long-term liability** (an obligation to be paid off in a time period longer than one year). To ensure accuracy, be sure to include all debt obligations. Examples of items to include in the liabilities section of a balance sheet, with some suggested subheadings, are as follows:

Short-Term Liabilities

- Personal loans (owed to other persons)
- Credit card charge accounts, travel and entertainment credit cards

- Insurance premiums due
- Professional services unpaid (doctors, dentists, chiropractors, lawyers)
- Rent due but unpaid
- Taxes unpaid

Long-Term Liabilities

- Automobile or other installment loan balances
- Home mortgage balance
- Education loan balance
- Personal loan balance

Net Worth—What Is Left   Net worth is determined mathematically by subtracting liabilities from assets, as indicated in the **net worth formula** (2.1):

$$\text{Net worth } = \text{ assets } - \text{ liabilities} \tag{2.1}$$

or

$$\text{Net worth } = \text{ what is owned } - \text{ what is owed}$$

This formula assumes that if you converted all assets to cash and paid all liabilities, the remaining cash would be your net worth. The only way to increase net worth is to spend less than one's income. To get ahead in your personal finances, you must save and invest.

Sample Balance Sheets   The balance sheet serves as a statement of the assets and liabilities of a family, individual, or a business on a specified date. The total assets on a balance sheet must equal the total of the liabilities plus the net worth.

Table 2.2

Balance Sheet for a College Student		Bill Soshnik, January 1, 2000
	Dollars	**Percent**
ASSETS		
Cash on hand	$ 85	1.4
Checking account	335	5.5
Savings account	800	13.2
Personal property*	1240	20.5
Automobile	3600	59.4
Total assets	$6060	100.0
LIABILITIES		
Telephone bill past due	$ 70	1.0
Bank loan—automobile	3130	51.7
College loan	1000	16.5
Government educational loan	2500	41.3
Total liabilities	$6700	110.6
Net worth	($640)	(10.6)
Total liabilities and net worth	$6060	100.0

* At fair market value, schedule includes clothes, $800; dresser, $50; television, $150; chair, $30; table, $40; desk, $120; and dishes/tableware, $50.

Thus, both sides must balance, resulting in the name "balance sheet." The amount of detail shown on a balance sheet depends on the person or family for whom it is prepared. Accuracy and sufficiency are the keys. You must decide how much to include to show your financial condition accurately on a given date.

The balance sheets shown in Tables 2.2 and 2.3 reflect the degree of detail that might be included for a traditional college student and a couple with two children, respectively. Notice that Table 2.2 includes very few items. This pattern

Table 2.3

Balance Sheet for a Couple with Two Children	Victor and Maria Hernandez, January 1, 2000	
	Dollars	**Percent**
ASSETS		
Monetary assets		
Cash on hand	$ 260	0.12
Savings accounts	1,500	0.71
Victor's checking account	600	0.29
Maria's checking account	700	0.33
Tax refund due	700	0.33
Rent receivable	660	0.31
Total monetary assets	$ 4,420	2.1
Tangible assets		
Home	$76,000	36.2
Personal property	9,000	4.3
Automobile	11,500	5.5
Total tangible assets	$ 96,500	46.0
Investment assets		
Fidelity mutual fund	$ 4,500	2.1
Scudder mutual fund	5,000	2.4
General Motors stock	2,800	1.3
New York 2006 bonds	1,000	0.4
Life insurance cash value	5,400	2.6
IRA	6,300	3.0
Real estate investment	84,000	40.0
Total investment assets	$109,000	51.9
Total Assets	$209,920	100.0
LIABILITIES		
Short-term liabilities		
Dentist bill	$ 120	0.01
Credit card debt	1,545	0.01
Total short-term liabilities	$ 1,665	0.01
Long-term liabilities		
Sales finance company: automobile	7,700	3.7
Savings and loan: real estate	92,000	43.8
Total long-term liabilities	$ 99,700	47.5
Total Liabilities	$101,365	48.3
Net worth	$108,555	51.7
Total Liabilities and Net Worth	$209,920	100.0

is typical of single persons who have not acquired many objects of value. Observe also the excess of liabilities over assets. This situation is not unusual for college students, for whom debts often seem to grow much faster than assets. In such an example, the person is technically **insolvent** because he or she has a negative net worth. When students graduate and take on full-time jobs, typically their balance sheets change dramatically after a few years. The balance sheet in Table 2.3 shows greater detail and more items, reflecting the increasing financial complexity that occurs at later stages in a person's life.

Information Sources for the Balance Sheet To construct a balance sheet, you need to compile dollar values for your assets and liabilities. Your checkbook, savings account records, and receipts of various payments and investments will be good sources from which to begin. You may have to estimate approximate dollar values for household furnishings, jewelry, and personal belongings. Remember to value such items at their fair market value. The dollar values of homes, automobiles, investments, life insurance, and other cash items can be calculated more precisely. The degree of precision used to determine the values of assets depends on the purpose and use of a balance sheet. In most cases, your judgment will suffice, and detailed estimates are unnecessary. Many people find it useful to make a detailed list or *schedule of items* summarized on the balance sheet (as illustrated in the footnote to Table 2.2), because it helps them identify the fair market values.

The Income and Expense Statement

The income and expense (or cash-flow) statement is very different from a balance sheet. Whereas the balance sheet shows your financial condition at a single point in time, the income and expense statement summarizes the total amounts that have been received and spent over a time period, such as the previous year. The income and expense statement, therefore, shows whether you were able to live within your income during that time period.

An income and expense statement includes three sections: **income** (total income received), **expenses** (total expenditures made), and **net income** or **net gain** (total income minus total expenses where income exceeds expenses) or **net loss** (where expenses exceed income).

Income You may think of income as only what is earned from salaries or wages. Many other types of income exist that you should also include on an income and expense statement, however, such as the following:

- Bonuses and commissions
- Child support and alimony
- Public assistance
- Social Security benefits
- Pension and profit-sharing income
- Scholarships and grants
- Interest and dividends received (from saving accounts, investments, bonds, or loans to others)

- Income from the sale of assets
- Other income (gifts, tax refunds, rent, royalties)

Expenses All expenditures made during the period covered by the income and expense statement should be included in the expense section. The number and type of expenses shown will vary for each individual and family. Many people categorize expenses according to whether they are fixed or variable. **Fixed expenses** are usually paid in the same amount during each time period; they are often contractual. Examples of such expenses include rent payments and automobile installment loans. It is usually difficult—but not impossible—to reduce a fixed expense.

Variable expenses are expenditures over which an individual has considerable control. Food, entertainment, and clothing are variable expenses, for example. Note that some categories, such as savings, can be listed twice, as both fixed and variable expenses. Rather than use fixed and variable expenses categories, you might separate expenditures into savings/investments, debts, insurance, taxes, and household expenses. The following are examples of fixed and variable expenses that you might include in an income and expense statement:

Fixed Expenses

- Savings and investments (regular, fixed deposits)
- Pension contributions (employer's plan, IRA)
- Housing (rent, mortgage, loan payment)
- Automobile (installment payment, lease)
- Insurance (life, health, liability, disability, renter's, homeowner's, automobile)
- Installment loan payments (appliances, furniture)
- Taxes (federal income, state income, local income, real estate, Social Security, and personal property)

Variable Expenses

- Meals (at home and away)
- Utilities (electricity, water, gas, telephone)
- Transportation (gasoline and maintenance, licenses, registration, public transportation)
- Medical expenses
- Child care (nursery, baby-sitting)
- Clothing and accessories (jewelry, shoes, handbags, briefcases)
- Snacks (candy, soft drinks, other beverages)
- Education (tuition, fees, books, supplies)
- Household furnishings (furniture, appliances, curtains)
- Cable television (beyond basic services)
- Personal care (beauty shop, barbershop, cosmetics, dry cleaner)

- Entertainment and recreation (hobbies, socializing, health club, tapes/CDs, videotape rentals, movies)
- Contributions (gifts, church, school, charity)
- Vacations and long weekends
- Credit card payments
- Savings and investments
- Miscellaneous (postage, books, magazines, newspapers, personal allowances, domestic help, membership fees)

There is no rigid list of categories to be used in the expense section, but you do need to classify all expenditures in some way. The more specific your categories, the richer your understanding of your outlays.

Net Gain (Loss)   The **net gain (loss)** section shows the amount remaining after you have itemized income and subtracted expenditures from income, as illustrated by the following calculations of the net gain (loss) formula (2.2). (A business would term this amount as net profit or net loss.)

$$\text{Net gain (loss)} = \text{total income} - \text{total expenses} \qquad (2.2)$$
$$\$1100 \text{ net gain} = \$12,500 - \$11,400$$

or

$$(\$800 \text{ net loss}) = \$14,900 - \$15,700$$

It is important to strive to have a net gain rather than a net loss. A net gain demonstrates that you are managing your financial resources successfully and do not have to use savings or borrow to make financial ends meet. When the subtraction shows a net gain, that amount is then available (in your checking and savings accounts) to spend, save, or invest.

Sample Income and Expense Statements   Income and expense statements vary in detail depending on who prepares the statement. Tables 2.4 and 2.5 show income and expense statements for a college student and a couple with two children, respectively. Table 2.5 on page 40 vividly illustrates the additional income needed to rear children and shows the increased variety of expenditures that reflect a family's (rather than an individual's) lifestyle. As a person earns more income, the income and expense statement usually becomes more involved and detailed.

Information Sources for the Income and Expense Statement   Every check written, every receipt received, every payment made, and every earnings payment received represent sources of information to be included in the income and expense statement. Because the statement is a financial summary, the transaction data are taken from many sources. Some original sources of information include pay records, canceled checks, receipts, invoices, and bills marked paid.

Of course, if you keep poor records and save few documents, it will be difficult to prepare a sufficiently detailed income and expense statement. Several helpful examples of keeping detailed and accurate income and expense information appear later in this chapter, in the section entitled "Financial Record-keeping."

Table 2.4

Income and Expense Statement for a College Student   Bill Soshnik, January 1–December 31, 2000

	Dollars	Percent
INCOME		
Wages (after withholding)	$4,650	39.7
Scholarship	1,750	14.9
Government grant	2,500	21.3
Government loan	2,600	22.2
Tax refund	110	0.9
Loan from parents	100	0.9
Total Income	$11,710	100.0
EXPENSES		
Room rent (includes utilities)	$1,500	12.8
Laundry	216	1.8
Food	1,346	11.5
Automobile loan payments	1,292	11.0
Automobile insurance	422	3.6
Books and supplies	932	8.0
Tuition	3,160	27.0
Telephone	282	2.4
Clothing	475	4.1
Gifts	300	2.6
Automobile expenses	600	5.1
Health insurance	102	0.9
Recreation and entertainment	360	3.1
Taxes (Social Security)	356	3.0
Personal expenses	300	2.6
Total Expenses	$11,643	99.5
Net Gain (available to spend, save, and invest)	$67	0.5

Financial Ratios

3 Use financial ratios to evaluate your financial strength and progress.

Financial ratios are objective numerical calculations designed to simplify making judgmental assessments of financial strength over time. These ratios can serve as yardsticks to help manage financial resources more effectively and to develop spending and credit-use patterns consistent with your goals. The first ratio that we will discuss pertains to liquidity, the next three provide insight into the burden of debt, and the last ratio illustrates progress toward building wealth. Evaluate each ratio in light of the peculiarities of each individual and family circumstance, considering such factors as stage in the life cycle, marital status, and financial goals. Calculators for these ratios can be found on the *Garman/Forgue* Web site.

Table 2.5

Income and Expense Statement for a Couple with Two Children

Victor and Maria Hernandez, January 1–December 31, 2000

	Dollars		Percent
INCOME			
Victor's gross salary	$33,180		63.8
Maria's salary (part-time)	8,500		16.3
Interest and dividends	1,800		3.5
Bonus	600		1.2
Tax refunds	200		0.4
Rental income	7,720		14.8
Total Income		$52,000	100.0
EXPENSES			
Fixed expenses			
Mortgage loan and real estate taxes	$12,000		23.1
Homeowner's insurance	460		0.9
Automobile loan payments	4,400		8.5
Automobile insurance and registration	891		1.7
Life insurance	1,200		2.3
Medical insurance	1,580		0.3
Savings at credit union	360		0.7
Federal income taxes	4,500		8.7
State income taxes	1,400		2.7
City income taxes	220		0.4
Social Security taxes	3,234		6.2
Personal property taxes	950		1.8
Total fixed expenses		$31,195	60.0
Variable expenses			
Food	$ 5,900		11.3
Utilities	1,800		3.5
Gasoline, oil, and repairs	2,700		5.2
Medical expenses	1,425		2.7
Medicines	165		0.3
Clothing and upkeep	2,160		4.2
Church	1,200		2.3
Gifts	600		1.2
Personal allowances	1,160		2.2
Children's allowances	480		0.9
Miscellaneous	270		0.5
Total variable expenses		$17,860	34.3
Total Expenses		$49,055	94.3
Net Gain (available to spend, save, and invest)		$2,945	5.7

Basic Liquidity Ratio

Liquidity is the speed and ease with which an asset can be converted to cash. One useful financial yardstick is the **basic liquidity ratio**, which reveals the number of months a household could continue to meet its expenses from monetary assets after a total loss of income. For example, compare the monetary assets on the balance sheet for Victor and Maria Hernandez in Table 2.3 ($4420) with their monthly expenses in Table 2.5 ($49,055 ÷ 12 = $4088) using Equation (2.3):

$$\text{Basic liquidity ratio} = \frac{\text{monetary (liquid) assets}}{\text{monthly expenses}} \qquad (2.3)$$

$$= \frac{\$4420}{\$4088}$$

$$= 1.08$$

This financial ratio suggests that the Hernandezes have insufficient monetary assets, able to support them for only slightly more than one month (1.08) if they faced a loss of income. Researchers at the University of Texas found that experts recommend that people should have monetary assets equal to three months' expenses in emergency cash reserves. Of course, the exact amount of monetary assets necessary depends on your family situation and your job. A smaller amount may be sufficient for your needs if you have adequate income protection through an employee benefit program, are employed in a job that is definitely not subject to layoffs, or have a spouse who works outside the home. Households dependent on the income from a self-employed person with fluctuating income need a larger emergency cash reserve.

Debt-to-Asset Ratio

The **debt-to-asset ratio** compares total assets with total liabilities and is a broad measure of a household's financial liquidity. It measures solvency and ability to pay debts, as shown in Equation (2.4). Calculations based on the figures in the Hernandez's balance sheet (Table 2.3) show that the couple has ample assets compared with their debts because they owe only 48 percent of what they own. (Reversing the mathematics shows that they own 2 times what they owe.)

$$\text{Debt-to-asset ratio} = \frac{\text{total debt}}{\text{total assets}} \qquad (2.4)$$

$$= \frac{\$101,365}{\$209,920}$$

$$= 0.48$$

If you owe more than you own, then you are technically insolvent. While your current income may be sufficient to pay your current bills, you still do not have enough assets to cover all of your debts. Many people in such situations seek credit counseling, and some eventually declare bankruptcy. (These topics are discussed in Chapter 7, "Planned Borrowing.")

Debt Service-to-Income Ratio

The **debt service-to-income ratio** provides an incisive view of the total debt burden of an individual or family by comparing the dollars spent on gross annual debt repayments (including mortgages) with gross annual income. Using data in Table 2.5, Equation (2.5) shows that the Hernandez's $16,400 in annual loan repayments ($12,000 for the mortgage loan and $4400 for the automobile loan) amount to 31.5 percent of their $52,000 annual income. A ratio of 0.36 or less indicates that gross income is adequate to make debt repayments including housing costs and implies that one has some flexibility in budgeting for other expenses. This ratio should decrease as you grow older.

$$\text{Debt service-to-income ratio} = \frac{\text{annual debt repayments}}{\text{gross income}} \qquad (2.5)$$

$$= \frac{\$16,400}{\$52,000}$$

$$= 31.5\%$$

Investment Assets-to-Net Worth Ratio

The **investment assets-to-net worth ratio** compares the value of investment assets with net worth. This ratio reveals how well an individual or family is advancing toward their financial goals for capital accumulation. Inserting the data from their balance sheet in Table 2.3 into Equation (2.6) shows that the Hernandezes have a ratio of 1.0. Thus, 100 percent of their net worth is made up of investment assets, an excellent proportion for this stage in their lives. Researchers at the University of Texas found that experts recommend 50 percent or higher. Younger people often have an investment assets-to-net worth ratio of less than 20 percent, primarily because they have few investments.

$$\text{Investment assets-to-net worth ratio} = \frac{\text{investment assets}}{\text{net worth}} \qquad (2.6)$$

$$= \frac{\$109,000}{\$108,555}$$

$$= 1.0$$

Other Ways to Assess Financial Progress

In addition to calculating financial ratios, you can use data from your balance sheets and income and expense statements to analyze your finances. Consider the assets listed on the balance sheet for Victor and Maria Hernandez in Table 2.3. Do they have too few monetary assets compared with tangible and investment assets? Many experts recommend that 15 to 20 percent of your assets be in monetary form, and that this proportion increase as you near retirement. Do you have too much invested in one asset, or have you diversified, like the Hernandezes? Have your balance sheet figures changed in a favorable direction since last year? And, of course, are you making progress toward achieving your financial goals?

Examine your income figures to see what proportion comes from labor compared with the share that comes from investments. As demonstrated in Table 2.5 for the Hernandezes, most people desire to have a growing proportion of income from investments. Twenty percent is an achievable goal for many persons.

In the expense area, it is vital to ask, "Am I spending money where I really want to?" In which categories could you reduce expenses? In which categories could you increase income? The Hernandezes, for example, might consider increasing the amount they set aside for savings and investments.

Financial Recordkeeping

<table>
<tr><td>**4** Identify the purposes and methods of financial recordkeeping.</td></tr>
</table>

Records and documents of all types follow us throughout our lives. The Internal Revenue Service (IRS) expects people to maintain financial records for tax reporting, and banks encourage customers to keep a record of check writing. Your financial records will help determine where you are, where you have been, and something about where you are going in a financial sense. Good records can also help you avoid penalties for overlooking financial obligations and running up needless credit charges. In addition, organized records permit easier fact gathering when it is time to file income taxes. They enable you to review the results of financial transactions as well as permit other family members to find them in your absence. Having accessible, organized, and complete financial records is a prerequisite for effective financial management. It also takes less time to update and maintain good records than poor ones.

Original Source Records

Original source records are formal documents that provide a record of personal financial activities. Cash and credit receipts, canceled checks and receipts from bank deposits, individual retirement account (IRA) documents, insurance policies, and photocopies of filed income taxes are examples of original source records. You can use original source records to show the IRS, for example, that claims for a tax-deductible expenditure are justified, to document the price of a product purchased, or to demonstrate ownership of an automobile by displaying the title. The primary reason for keeping records of any kind is to have the information available for some future purpose. Table 2.6 shows categories of financial records and the contents that might be included in each.

Safeguarding Financial Records

It does little good to keep records and then run the risk that they will be misplaced, stolen, or lost through fire or other causes. Methods used to safeguard records need not be elaborate or expensive. A desk drawer, a ring binder, a box, a portable file, an expandable paper or cardboard file, or an inexpensive paperboard file box are examples of places to maintain records. More elaborate equipment to safeguard records, such as a fire-resistant file cabinet or a safe, can ensure an even higher degree of safety. Some records—such as investment documents,

Table 2.6

Financial Records: Categories and Contents

Category	Contents	
	In Home File	**In Safe-Deposit Box**
Financial plans	Copy of written financial plans and revisions Balance sheets and income statements List of safe-deposit box contents Names and addresses of all financial advisers and institutions where you have accounts	Names and addresses of your financial planner and all financial institutions Copy of financial plans
Financial services	Checkbook Unused checks Bank statements Savings passbooks Location information and number of safe-deposit box Deposit, withdrawal, and transfer slips Records of the purchase of securities not yet sold	List of checking and savings account numbers Savings certificates
Budgeting	Annual budget Deadlines and expiration dates for such things as certificates of deposit Annual cash-flow statement Current budget control sheet Old budget control sheets List of short- and medium-term budget goals	Copy of annual budget
Insurance	Original insurance policies List of insurance premium amounts and due dates Calculation of life insurance needs Automobile insurance policy Health insurance booklet explaining coverage Health insurance claim forms Historical medical information on family members Receipts for payment of premiums	List of insurance policy numbers Photographs or videotape of all personal property
Housing	Copies of legal documents (lease, mortgage, deed, title insurance, termite inspections, etc.)	Mortgage papers, deed, lease
Contributions	Receipts and canceled checks Correspondence Log of any volunteer expenses	Papers pertaining to expensive gifts
Taxes	Receipts for tax-deductible costs, such as medical expenses, real estate and personal property taxes, charitable contributions, and miscellaneous expenses	Copies of income tax forms and documentation for last six years Records of all retirement plan transactions

insurance policies, birth certificates, school records, marriage licenses, and items proving ownership—are clearly more valuable than others. Safe-deposit boxes are available to protect these records. **Safe-deposit boxes** are secured lockboxes available for rent in banks and are very safe from theft, fire, and other catastrophes. By design, two keys must be used to open the box. The customer keeps one key, and the bank holds the other. You can make arrangements for a safe-deposit box by requesting one from a bank official, completing the required signature cards, and paying a small annual fee ($15 to $300).

Another location in which to store papers or records is a secure spot at your place of employment. Many people keep duplicates of important records at their workplace, since the likelihood of records at home and in the office being stolen or destroyed simultaneously is very small.

Using Computer Software in Personal Financial Planning

> **5** Describe the use of computer software in personal financial planning.

Using computer software in personal finance offers many benefits. Laborious calculations are sharply reduced, banking transactions can be performed with automatic updating of financial records, the balance sheet and income and expense statements are automatically updated when transactions occur, and financial plans can be developed.

Many people use a computer to help manage their personal finances. A software program that costs less than $50 can be used to create a financial plan, calculate how much interest you will save by paying down debts, obtain a copy of your credit report, remind you when bills are due, figure your income taxes, and calculate your retirement needs. Some programs provide free or low-cost on-line services (including stock and mutual fund quotes), identify which stocks and mutual funds meet your criteria, monitor your investment portfolio, and calculate your investments' total returns. Quicken and Microsoft are the most popular vendors of personal finance software.

What to Know about Professional Financial Planning

> **6** Explain how to choose among the various types of professional financial planners.

Information and counseling about specific aspects of personal finance, such as income taxes, credit, insurance, investments, and estate planning, are available from financial publications, nonprofessional advisers, and professional financial planners. A professional, such as a family lawyer, accountant, insurance agent, credit counselor, or stockbroker, can help you within his or her special area of expertise. But, such people usually do not have the broad education required to develop a thorough financial plan. Many providers of financial services, such as banks and insurance companies, offer **computer-generated financial plans.** Typically these plans are based on information obtained from a questionnaire filled out by the customer. The fee for this service, if any, depends on the depth of the plan and the degree to which it is supplemented by a series of personal consultations between the customer and a financial adviser.

Individuals with an annual income of $50,000 or more should consider supplementing their own knowledge of personal finance with the expertise of a professional financial planner who possesses appropriate certifications. An estimated

500,000 people call themselves financial planners, although many are really nothing more than salespersons for insurance, stocks, tax shelters, income tax preparation services, and other investments. Such people may be biased or limited in the expertise they can provide, because they must sell a specific financial product to make a living.

Commission-only financial planners live solely on the commissions they receive on the financial products (such as investments or insurance) they sell to their clients. In this case, the plan will be "free," but the payment will come from the commission. For example, if you invest $10,000 in a mutual fund recommended and sold by a commission-only planner, only $9150 of that amount may be put to work because the remainder went to pay an 8.5 percent ($850) commission to the planner. Approximately 31 percent of financial planners are commission-only planners.

A **fee-only financial planner** earns no commissions and works solely on a fee-for-service basis—that is, he or she charges a specified fee for the services provided. Such planners typically charge $50 to $200 per hour or 1 percent of the client's assets annually, and they usually need five or more one-hour appointments to analyze a client's financial situation thoroughly and to present a plan. Fee-only planners do not sell financial products, such as stocks or insurance, and can, therefore, claim to be free of potential conflicts of interest in making recommendations. Because they are not trying to "sell" anything, however, the client bears more responsibility for making sure the plan is implemented. Finding a true fee-only financial planner is difficult because deceptive, but legal, advertising exists. The Certified Financial Planning Board of Standards allows planners to offer **fee-only services** to clients who desire them as well as to sell commission products to other customers. A **fee-only practitioner** should be a genuine fee-only planner. Thus, advertisements touting "fee only" have no meaning whatsoever.

The largest group of financial planners (43 percent) are those referred to as **fee-based financial planners.** These planners charge an up-front fee for provid-

What Questions to Ask a Financial Planner

When considering hiring a financial planner, you should ask the following questions:

1. What credentials do you have to practice financial planning?

2. How long have you been in financial planning and related fields?

3. How long have you resided in the community, and who can vouch for your professional reputation?

4. Will you provide references from three or more clients you have counseled for at least two years?

5. Will you or an associate be involved in evaluating and updating the plan you suggest?

6. May I see examples of plans and monitoring reports you have drawn up for other investors?

7. To what financial planning trade organizations do you belong?

8. If you earn commissions, from whom do you earn them?

ing services and charge a commission on any securities trades or insurance purchases that they conduct on your behalf. Thus, they may appear less costly than fee-only planners but supplement that fee with commissions earned.

Of course, it does not matter if you pay commissions for financial planning advice as long as you understand what you are paying for and what you are getting. A financial planner should be able to analyze a family's total needs in such areas as investments, taxes, insurance, education goals, and retirement and pull all of the information together into a cohesive plan. The planner may help a client select and prioritize goals and then rearrange assets and liabilities to fit the client's lifestyle, stage in the life cycle, and financial goals. In addition, financial planners should be problem solvers and coordinators. They often work with outside advisers, such as attorneys, accountants, trust officers, real estate brokers, stockbrokers, and insurance agents. You can locate a financial planner by searching the yellow pages, by contacting several of the organizations that accredit financial planners, or by asking family, friends, and colleagues for referrals.

Professional Designations and Credentials

The public believes that persons calling themselves professionals should meet a set of accredited educational standards, have significant professional experience, be licensed by a government regulatory agency, and exhibit a commitment to helping others. Many financial planners have voluntarily undergone training and satisfied various qualifications for particular professional certifications to respond to these desires. Most certification examinations require three years of work experience prior to sitting for the examination. An **MBA**, or master of business administration, is a university degree concentrating in marketing, economics, accounting, and finance. An **MFP**, or master of financial planning, is a university degree in financial services. An **MS**, or master of science, is a university degree specializing in one of many majors, including financial planning.

Perhaps the best-known certification recipient is the **certified financial planner (CFP)**, who has been approved by the International Board of Standards and Practices for Certified Financial Planners. More than 32,000 are certified as having completed a comprehensive program of study. To become a CFP, planners must pass a two-day examination, have three years of work experience in the field, agree to adhere to a code of ethics, and continuously update their financial planning knowledge. The professional association of CFPs is the Institute of Certified Financial Planners (ICFP).

The International Association for Financial Planning, a trade group, will provide a list of planners in your area [(800) 806-PLAN; *www.iafp.org*]. The National Association of Personal Financial Advisors [(888) FEE-ONLY; *www.feeonly.org*] will provide names of fee-only planners in your area who are paid only by the client, and who do not receive commissions from financial products they recommend. The American Institute of Certified Public Accountants [(800) 862-4272; *www.aicpa.org*] can recommend CPAs in your area who are personal financial specialists.

A **chartered financial consultant (ChFC)** has passed a financial services curriculum, with emphasis on life insurance. Approximately 15,000 people have met the ChFC standards. A **chartered life underwriter (CLU)** has received training in life insurance.

How to Check the Background of a Financial Planner

Government agencies and self-regulatory organizations are available to help check the background of a financial planner. The CFP Board of Standards [(888) 237-6275] keeps records on planners holding its credential. The National Association of State Insurance Commissioners [(816) 842-3600] directs inquiries to the appropriate state agency. The National Association of Securities Dealers Regulation [(800) 289-9999] oversees securities brokers. The North American Securities Administrators Association [(888) 846-2722] and the Securities and Exchange Commission [(800) 732-0330] regulate investment advisers.

An **accredited financial counselor (AFC)** has passed two examinations (one in personal finance and one in financial counseling) and subscribes to the AFC code of professional ethics. This accreditation program is offered through the Association for Financial Counseling and Planning Education.

A **mutual fund chartered counselor (MFCC)** has passed a nine-part education program and a final exam on topics ranging from what is a mutual fund to ethics and professional conduct. This designation is conferred by the National Endowment for Financial Education and the Investment Company Institute.

A **registered investment adviser (RIA)** is a person required by the federal Investment Adviser Act to register with your state officials or the Securities and Exchange Commission [(800) 732-0330] because he or she gives investment advice to more than five people each year. The RIA designation means simply that the person has paid the $150 application fee; it does not mean that the adviser has met any government professional standards or passed any tests. An **investment adviser** is anyone who is paid to offer financial advice. Many states require registration of investment advisers.

Summary

1. Most people need to undertake some form of financial planning to achieve their financial objectives. Financial planning should reflect an individual's or family's values and life-cycle circumstances and have appropriate objectives in three broad areas: plans for spending, plans against risk, and plans for capital accumulation. Success in financial planning requires an understanding of one's values, explicitly stated financial goals, certain assumptions about the economy, and logical and consistent financial strategies.

2. Financial statements are compilations of personal financial data designed to furnish information about how money has been used and about the financial condition of the individual or family. The balance sheet provides information on what you own, what you owe, and the net result if all debts were paid off. The income and expense statement lists income and expense transactions over a specific period of time, such as the previous year.

3. Financial ratios can be used to assess your financial condition and progress so that you can better manage financial resources and

develop spending and credit-use patterns consistent with your goals.

4. Having accessible, organized, and complete financial records is a prerequisite to effective financial management. Your financial records are useful in preparing financial statements that can help you to evaluate where you are, where you have been, and where you are going in a financial sense.

5. Computers are increasingly being used in personal financial planning as software programs become available.

6. When choosing a financial planner, you should recognize that many professional designations are meaningful, such as CFP and ChFC. Costs may be on a fee-only, commission-only, or fee-based basis.

Key Words & Concepts

balance sheet   *32*

certified financial planner (CFP)   *47*

debt service-to-income ratio   *42*

diversification   *33*

expenses   *36*

fair market value   *33*

fee-only financial planner   *46*

financial goals   *29*

financial ratios   *39*

financial statements   *32*

financial strategies   *32*

fixed expenses   *37*

income and expense (cash-flow) statement   *32*

insolvent   *36*

liabilities   *33*

liquidity   *41*

net gain (loss)   *38*

original source records   *43*

short-term liability   *33*

tangible assets   *33*

values   *29*

variable expenses   *37*

Questions for Thought & Discussion

1. Define and describe financial planning.

2. List the three broad areas in which financial planning occurs.

3. Give two examples of specific goals.

4. List the 15 specific areas of financial planning.

5. What are the two principal financial statements?

6. Why must assets be listed on a balance sheet at their fair market value?

7. What are the components of a balance sheet?

8. Differentiate between monetary, tangible, and investment assets.

9. Explain the difference between short- and long-term liabilities.

10. Explain how to derive net worth, and give an example.

11. What does an income and expense statement show the person who prepares it?

12. Differentiate between fixed and variable expenses.

13. Describe one change in an income and expense statement that would affect net worth.

14. Explain how you can use financial ratios to help to evaluate your financial progress. Give an example.

15. What does the basic liquidity ratio show?

16. What are the benefits of keeping good financial records?

17. List three categories in which financial records might be organized.

18. Give two examples of financial records that you should maintain in the home and two that you should put in a safe-deposit box.

19. Illustrate a benefit of, and an obstacle to, using personal computer software in personal financial planning.

20. What services do fee-only financial planners perform for their clients?

21. Explain the three methods that financial planners use to charge for their services.

22. Give two examples of important questions to ask financial planners.

DECISION-MAKING CASES

Case 1 Budgeting Advice for Two Young Men

Bill Bailey, a poultry scientist from Little Rock, Arkansas, thinks that his two sons, who live at home, need budgeting advice. Ralph, age 19, works as a sales representative for an electronics manufacturer, and regularly spends all of his $2400 monthly income. Wilfred, 24, is a midlevel manager in a psychological testing company. He has completed three evening classes toward a master's degree and usually saves about 10 percent of his monthly salary of $3400. Wilfred is also contemplating marriage. Bill would like you to offer suggestions to his sons in financial management.

(a) What advice would you offer Ralph regarding life's opportunities?

(b) Realizing that Wilfred is contemplating marriage, what advice would you offer him regarding life's opportunities? How might his goals differ from those of Ralph?

(c) Use the data in the balance sheets for Bill Soshnik and Victor and Maria Hernandez (Tables 2.2 and 2.3) to advise Wilfred on how his financial life will change as the length of his marriage grows.

Case 2 Manipulation of an Income and Expense Statement

Using the data from the income and expense statement developed by Bill Soshnik (see Table 2.4), enter the data from the *Garman/Forgue* Web site. The program will calculate the totals.

(a) Print the income and expense statement and compare the results with the text for accuracy.

(b) What original source records might Bill have used to develop the income and expense statement?

(c) Use the data in the income and expense statement for Bill (Table 2.4) and Victor and Maria Hernandez (Table 2.5) to advise Bill on how his financial life will change as he becomes older.

Financial Math Questions

1. Review the financial statements of Victor and Maria Hernandez (Tables 2.3 and 2.5), and respond to the following questions:

(a) Using the data in the Hernandezes' balance sheet, calculate an investment assets-to-net worth ratio. How would you interpret the ratio? The Hernandez family appears to have too few monetary assets compared with tangible and investment assets. How would you suggest that they remedy that situation over the next few years?

(b) Comment on the couple's diversification of investment assets.

(c) Calculate a debt-to-assets ratio for Victor and Maria. How does this information help you understand their financial situation? How do their total assets compare with their total liabilities?

(d) The Hernandezes seem to receive almost all of their income from labor rather than investments. What actions would you recommend for them to remedy that imbalance over the next few years?

(e) The Hernandezes want to take a two-week vacation next summer, and they have only eight months to save the necessary $1200. What reasonable changes in expenses and income should they consider to increase net income and make the needed $150 per month?

2. Bob Green has been a retail salesclerk for six years. At age 35, he is divorced with one child, Amanda, age 7. Bob's salary is $36,000 per year. He regularly receives $250 per month for child support from Amanda's mother. Bob invests $100 each month ($50 in his mutual fund and $50 in

EE savings bonds). Using the following information, construct a balance sheet and income and expense statement for Bob.

ASSETS	Amount
Vested pension benefits (no employee contribution)	$ 3000
Money market account (includes $150 of interest earned last year)	5000
Mutual fund (includes $200 of reinvested dividend income from last year)	4000
Checking account	1000
Personal property	5000
Automobile	3000
EE savings bonds	3000

LIABILITIES	Outstanding Balance
Dental bill (pays $25 per month included in uninsured medical/dental)	$450
Visa (pays $100 per month)	1500
Student loan (pays $100 per month)	7500

ANNUAL EXPENSES	Amount
Auto insurance	$ 780
Rent	9100
Utilities	1200
Phone	680
Cable	360
Food	3000
Uninsured medical/dental	1000
Dry cleaning	480
Personal care	420
Gas, maintenance, license	2120
Clothes	500
Entertainment	2700
Vacations/visitation travel	1300
Child care	3820
Gifts	400
Miscellaneous	300
Taxes	6400
Health insurance	1440

Exploring the World of Personal Finance

1. Develop your own balance sheet. Is your net worth at the level that you expected at this point in your life? Or is it higher or lower than your expectations? What are the prospects for change in your net worth over the next few years?

2. Develop your own income and expense statement for this month. Do you have a net gain or a net loss? What changes might you put into effect for next month to avert a net loss or enhance your net gain?

3. Conduct a telephone survey of two financial planners in your community. Ask them the questions provided in the boxed insert, "What Questions to Ask a Financial Planner," on page 46.

4. Visit two local computer software outlets. Make a list of the major features of financial management software programs available at the stores. Identify two software programs that you feel would meet your needs.

MONEY MATTERS: LIFE-CYCLE CASES

Victor and Maria Hernandez Analyze Their Financial Statements

Victor and Maria Hernandez spent some time making up their first balance sheet, which is shown in Table 2.3. Using the data in their balance sheet, complete the following calculations and interpret the results.

1. Victor and Maria are a bit confused about how various financial activities can affect their net worth. Assume that their home is now appraised at $82,000 and the value of their automobile dropped to $9500. Calculate and characterize the impact of these changes on their net worth.

2. If Victor and Maria take out a bank loan for $1545 and pay off their credit card debts totaling $1545, what impact would this have on their net worth?

3. If Victor and Maria take $300 from their earnings and put it into their savings account, what impact would this move have on their net worth?

The Johnsons' Financial Statements

Harry and Belinda both found jobs in the same city. Harry works at a small interior design firm and earns a gross salary of $1700 per month. He also receives $3000 in interest income per year from a trust fund set up by his deceased father's estate; the trust fund will continue to pay that amount until 2004. Belinda works as a salesperson for a regional stock brokerage firm. When she finishes her training program in another month, her gross salary will increase $200 per month to $2350. Belinda has many job-related benefits, including life insurance, health insurance, and a credit union.

The Johnsons live in an apartment located approximately halfway between their places of employment. Harry drives about ten minutes to his job, and Belinda travels about 15 minutes via public transportation to reach her downtown job. Harry and Belinda's apartment is very nice, but small, and it is

Balance Sheet for Harry and Belinda Johnson   January 31, 2000

	Dollars	Percent
ASSETS		
Monetary assets		
Cash on hand	$ 570	4.0
Savings (First Federal Bank)	190	1.3
Savings (Far West Savings and Loan)	70	0.5
Savings (Smith Brokerage Credit Union)	60	0.4
Checking account (First Interstate Bank)	310	2.2
Total monetary assets	$ 1,200	8.4
Tangible assets		
Automobile (1991 Toyota)	11,000	77.5
Personal property	1,200	8.5
Furniture	800	5.6
Total tangible assets	13,000	91.6
Total Assets	$14,200	100.0
LIABILITIES		
Short-term liabilities		
Electricity	$ 65	0.5
Visa credit card	390	2.7
Sears card	45	0.3
Rent due	400	2.8
Total short-term liabilities	$ 900	6.3
Long-term liabilities		
Education loan (Belinda)	3,800	26.8
Automobile loan (First Federal Bank)	8,200	57.1
Total long-term liabilities	$12,000	83.9
Total Liabilities	$12,900	90.2
Net worth	1,300	9.8
Total Liabilities and Net Worth	$14,200	100.0

Income and Expense Statement for Harry and Belinda Johnson
July 1, 1999–January 31, 2000 (First Six Months of Marriage)

	Dollars	Percent
INCOME		
Harry's gross income ($1700 × 6)	$10,200	39.1
Belinda's gross income ($2150 × 6)	12,900	49.4
Interest on savings accounts	15	0.006
Harry's trust fund	3,000	11.5
Total Income	$26,115	100.0
EXPENSES		
Fixed expenses		
Rent	$ 3,600	13.8
Renter's insurance	110	0.4
Automobile loan payments	1,710	6.5
Automobile insurance	320	1.2
Medical insurance (withheld from salary)	510	1.9
Student loan payments	870	3.3
Life insurance (withheld from salary)	54	0.2
Cable television	120	0.5
Health club	300	1.1
Savings (withheld from salary)	60	0.2
Federal income taxes (withheld from salary)	4,800	18.4
State income taxes (withheld from salary)	780	3.0
Social Security (withheld from salary)	1,620	6.2
Automobile registration	40	0.2
Total fixed expenses	$14,894	56.9
Variable expenses		
Food	$ 2,300	8.8
Electricity	450	1.7
Telephone	420	1.6
Gasoline, oil, and maintenance	400	1.5
Doctors' and dentists' bills	310	1.2
Medicines	40	0.2
Clothing and upkeep	1,300	5.0
Church and charity	800	3.1
Gifts	480	1.8
Christmas gifts	350	1.3
Public transportation	580	2.2
Personal allowances	1,040	4.0
Entertainment	780	3.0
Vacation (Christmas)	700	2.7
Vacation (summer)	600	2.3
Miscellaneous	440	1.7
Total variable expenses	$10,990	42.1
Total Expenses	$25,884	99.0
Net Gain (available to spend, save, and invest)	231	1.0

furnished mostly with old furniture given to them by their families.

Soon after starting their first jobs, Harry and Belinda decided to begin their financial planning. Each had taken a college course in personal finance, so after initial discussion, they worked together for two evenings to develop the two financial statements presented on pages 52 and 53.

1. Briefly describe how Harry and Belinda probably determined the fair market prices for each of the tangible and investment assets.

2. Using the data from the income and expense statement developed by Harry and Belinda, calculate a basic liquidity ratio, debt-to-assets ratio, debt service-to-income ratio, and investment assets-to-net worth ratio. What do these ratios tell you about the Johnsons' financial situation? Should Harry and Belinda incur more debt?

Exploring the World Wide Web of Personal Finance

To complete these exercises, go to the *Garman/Forgue* Web site at

www.hmco.com/college/business/

Select Personal Finance. Click on the exercise link for this chapter and answer the questions that appear on the Web page.

1. Visit the Web site of the International Association of Financial Planners. Identify its six steps in the financial planning process.

2. Visit the Web site for SRI Consulting, where you will find the VALS questionnaire. This short questionnaire will help you identify your values in the context of others in American society.

3. Visit the Web site of the International Association of Financial Planners. Read through the code of ethics for members of the organization. What does the code tell you about the members?

4. Visit the Web site set up to accompany this text, where you will find a balance sheet template that you can use to determine your net worth. Is your net worth at the level that you expected for this point in your life? What are the prospects for change in your net worth over the next three years?

5. Visit the Web site set up to accompany this text, where you will find an income and expense statement template that you can use to determine your net gain or loss over the past month. What changes might you put into effect for the next month to avert a net loss or enhance your net gain?

Managing Taxes

3

OBJECTIVES

After reading this chapter, you should be able to:

1 Explain how taxes are administered and classified.

2 Describe the concept of the marginal tax rate.

3 Determine whether you should file an income tax return.

4 Describe the two ways of paying taxes: payroll withholding and estimated taxes.

5 Identify the eight steps involved in calculating federal income taxes.

6 Understand planning strategies to legally avoid overpayment of income taxes.

7 Explain the basics of IRS audits.

Tax planning comprises the processes undertaken to reduce, defer, or eliminate some taxes. It includes the determination of one's current tax liability and how that liability affects, and is affected by, financial transactions. Not all income is subject to the federal income tax, however. You pay personal income taxes *only* on your **taxable income**. This amount is determined by subtracting your allowable exclusions, adjustments, exemptions, and deductions from your total income, with the result being the income upon which the tax is actually calculated. We will provide details on this calculation later, but for now remember that the key idea in successful tax planning is to legally reduce your taxable income as much as possible, which, in turn, reduces your tax liability.

This chapter examines the principles of income taxation in the United States and the impact of those taxes on your income. It then discusses who must pay taxes and how they are paid—through payroll withholding and estimated tax payments. Next, eight steps detail the process of paying federal income taxes, from the determination of gross income through the computation of taxes due. We also provide examples of how to calculate federal income taxes. Finally, we examine the appropriate and desirable methods of reducing tax liability, review how to survive an income tax audit successfully, and note the effects of a variety of other federal, state, and local taxes on personal finances.

Administration and Classification of Income Taxes

1 Explain how taxes are administered and classified.

Taxes are compulsory charges imposed by a government on its citizens and their property. To learn how to manage taxes effectively, you should know how taxes are administered and classified.

Federal Tax Laws

Taxes are administered at all levels of government. Because the largest amount of tax you pay is on your income, this chapter focuses primarily on the federal personal income tax. Three-fourths of all Americans pay federal income taxes. The U.S. Internal Revenue Service (IRS) is charged with the responsibility of collecting federal income taxes based on the legal provisions in the Internal Revenue Code. The code represents the major tax laws written by the U.S. Congress.

In addition, the IRS itself issues IRS regulations, which interpret and make specific the tax laws passed by Congress. These regulations have the force and effect of law; they are printed in thick volumes available in most public libraries. Finally, dozens of IRS rulings are issued each year; these Internal Revenue Service decisions are related to specific tax cases and are based on its interpretations of both the Internal Revenue Code and the IRS regulations. Tax rulings provide guidance on how the IRS may act in similar situations. The courts also issue decisions giving the judicial interpretation of the tax laws that Congress passes and the regulations and decisions of the Internal Revenue Service.

The Progressive Nature of the Federal Income Tax

Taxes can be classified as progressive or regressive. A **progressive tax** is one that takes a larger percentage of income from high-income taxpayers than from low-income taxpayers. In the United States, the federal personal income tax is progressive because the tax rate increases as a taxpayer's income (and thus implied ability to pay) increases. As Table 3.1 shows, the higher portions of a taxpayer's income are taxed at increasingly higher rates under the federal income tax.* A **regressive tax** operates in the opposite way. As income rises, the tax rate remains the same or decreases, so that the tax demands a decreasing proportion of a person's income as income increases. Such taxes are not based on ability to pay. Examples of regressive taxes include state sales taxes and Social Security taxes.

Table 3.1

The Progressive Nature of the Federal Income Tax

Segment of Taxable Income	Taxed Rate (percent)*
First $25,750	15.0%
Over $25,750 but not over $62,450	28.0
Over $62,450 but not over $130,250	31.0
Over $130,250 but not over $283,150	36.0
Over $283,150	39.6

* Rates are for a single taxpayer.

*   All tax rates cited in this chapter are for the most recent tax year available at the time of publication.

The Marginal Tax Rate Is Applied to the Last Dollar Earned

2   Describe the concept of the marginal tax rate.

Perhaps the single most important concept in personal finance is the **marginal tax rate.** Recall from Chapter 1 that this tax rate is applied to your last dollar of earnings. It tells you how much of any extra earnings—from a raise, investment income, or money from a second job—you can keep after paying income taxes; it also measures the tax savings benefits of a tax-deductible expense. This concept is illustrated in Figure 3.1.

A **marginal tax bracket (MTB)** is one of the five income-range couplets shown in the tax-rate schedules (as illustrated in Table 3.1 and Table 3.2). Depending upon their income, taxpayers fit into one of these tax brackets (as shown in Table 3.2 on page 58) and, accordingly, pay at one of those marginal tax rates: 15 percent, 28 percent, 31 percent, 36 percent, or 39.6 percent. Each year the taxable income levels for the tax brackets are adjusted to reduce the effects of inflation, a process called **indexing.** This process keeps taxpayers from being unfairly forced to pay more taxes only because inflation raises their incomes.

As an example, Susan Bassett (see Figure 3.1) is in the 28 percent marginal tax bracket because the *last* dollar Susan earned is taxed at that level. Part of her income ($2750 + $4300) is not taxed, the largest portion ($25,750) is taxed at 15 percent, and the remaining portion of Susan's income ($11,200) is taxed at 28 percent. Thus, Susan is in the 28 percent marginal tax bracket. The mathematics shown in Figure 3.1 is based upon the **tax-rate schedules** in Table 3.2. These income tax brackets must be used by persons with a taxable income of $100,000 or more. Another depiction of the income tax brackets is shown in the IRS's **tax tables.** These tables were designed to save computational time for taxpayers and must be used by people with taxable incomes of less than $100,000. The tax tables and tax-rate schedules yield nearly equal tax liabilities (differing by less than $10 because of rounding) if used for the same taxable income. Segments of the tax tables are provided in Table 3.3.

The marginal tax rate can greatly affect many financial decisions. For example, consider someone with a 28 percent marginal tax rate who wants to make a $100 tax-deductible contribution to a charity. The charity receives the $100, and

Figure 3.1

How Your Income Is Really Taxed (Example: Susan Bassett with a $44,000 Gross Income)

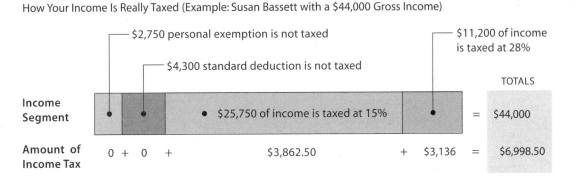

Susan's marginal tax rate is 28%.

Table 3.2

Tax-Rate Schedule

If 1999 Taxable Income Is		The Tax Is	Plus	This Percent	Of Amount Over
Over	But Not Over				
Single Return					
$ 0	$ 25,750	0	+	15 %	$ 0
25,750	62,450	$ 3,862.50	+	28	25,750
62,450	130,250	14,138.50	+	31	62,450
130,250	283,150	35,156.50	+	36	130,250
283,150		90,200.50	+	39.6	283,150
Married Filing Jointly					
$ 0	$ 43,050			15 %	$ 0
43,050	104,050	$ 6,457.50	+	28	43,050
104,050	158,550	23,537.50	+	31	104,050
158,550	283,150	40,432.50	+	36	158,550
283,150		85,288.50	+	39.6	283,150

Table 3.3

Illustration of Segments of the Tax Tables*

If Taxable Income Is		And You Are Filing		If Taxable Income Is		And You Are Filing	
At Least	But Less Than	Single	Joint	At Least	But Less Than	Single	Joint
$20,000	$20,050	$3,004	$3,004	37,000	37,050	7,020	5,554
20,050	20,100	3,011	3,011	37,050	37,100	7,034	5,561
20,100	20,150	3,019	3,019	37,100	37,150	7,048	5,569
20,150	20,200	3,026	3,026	37,150	37,200	7,062	5,576
25,900	25,950	3,912	3,889	37,350	37,400	7,118	5,606
25,950	26,000	3,926	3,896	37,400	37,450	7,132	5,614
26,000	26,050	3,940	3,904	37,450	37,500	7,146	5,621
26,050	26,100	3,954	3,911	37,500	37,550	7,160	5,629
28,900	28,950	4,752	4,339	48,000	48,050	10,100	7,851
28,950	29,000	4,766	4,346	48,050	48,100	10,114	7,865
29,000	29,050	4,780	4,354	48,100	48,150	10,128	7,879
29,050	29,100	4,794	4,361	48,150	48,200	10,142	7,893
29,800	29,850	5,004	4,474	57,000	57,050	12,620	10,371
29,850	29,900	5,018	4,481	57,050	57,100	12,634	10,385
29,900	29,950	5,032	4,489	57,100	57,150	12,648	10,399
29,950	30,000	5,046	4,496	57,150	57,200	12,662	10,413
30,800	30,850	5,284	4,624	60,000	60,050	13,460	11,211
30,850	30,900	5,298	4,631	60,050	60,100	13,474	11,225
30,900	30,950	5,312	4,639	60,100	60,150	13,488	11,239
30,950	31,000	5,326	4,646	60,150	60,200	13,502	11,253
31,200	31,250	5,396	4,684	80,000	80,050	19,587	16,811
31,250	31,300	5,410	4,691	80,050	80,100	19,602	16,825
31,300	31,350	5,424	4,699	80,100	80,150	19,618	16,839
31,350	31,400	5,438	4,706	80,150	80,200	19,633	16,853

* Derived from the tax schedules in Table 3.2.

the taxpayer may deduct $100 from taxable income. This deduction results in a $28 reduction in income tax ($100 × 0.28). In effect, the taxpayer gives $72 and the government "gives" $28 to the charity.

Your Effective Marginal Tax Rate Is Higher

In reality, most of us pay marginal tax rates higher than 15 or 28 percent. The **effective marginal tax rate** on income is even higher than that given in the preceding discussion because it includes all tax claims against a specific income. Workers usually must pay three other income-based taxes: (1) the combined Social Security and Medicare tax of 7.65 percent; (2) state income taxes of 6 percent or more; and (3) perhaps an additional 1 to 5 percent in local (city or county) income taxes.

To determine the effective marginal tax rate on income, you must add all of these other taxes to the federal marginal tax rate. For example, a taxpayer might have a federal marginal income tax rate of 28 percent, a combined Social Security and Medicare tax of 7.65 percent, a state income tax of 6 percent, and a city income tax of 4 percent. These taxes result in an effective marginal tax rate of 46 percent (28 + 7.65 + 6 + 4 = 45.65, rounded to 46). Thus, many employed taxpayers pay an effective marginal tax rate of 46 percent or more.

Your Average Tax Rate Is Also Revealing

Your **average tax rate** is a calculated figure showing your tax liability as a percentage of total income. Because your total income is not fully taxed by the federal government, your average tax rate is always less than your marginal tax rate. For example, as shown in Figure 3.1, Susan Bassett's average tax rate on total income is 15.9 percent ($6,998.50 ÷ $44,000). The average tax rate for all U.S. taxpayers is approximately 15 percent.

Determine Your Federal Marginal Tax Rate

You can calculate your federal marginal tax rate in the following way, assuming your taxable income can be found in the tax table income brackets illustrated in Table 3.3:

1. Assuming that you are single and have a taxable income of $37,014, find in the tables (segments of which are shown in Table 3.3) the amount of tax on that income ($7020).

2. Add $100 to that income for a total of $37,114, and find the tax on that amount ($7048).

3. Calculate the difference between the two tax amounts ($7048 − $7020 = $28) and divide by 100 (28 ÷ 100 = 0.28 = 28 percent). Thus, the extra $28 in taxes resulting from an increase in taxable income of $100 reflects a marginal tax rate of 28 percent.

Your federal marginal tax rate also can be determined by looking up your taxable income in the tax-rate schedules.

Who Should File a Tax Return?

3   Determine whether you should file an income tax return.

It is fairly easy to determine whether you should file a tax return. In fact, most people who earn an income should file a return. To **file** simply means to report formally to the IRS any income earned and your tax liability for the year.

Citizens and residents of the United States and Puerto Rico must file federal income tax returns if they have earned sufficient income. In general, the income thresholds that require filing a return are $7050 for single individuals and $12,700 for married people filing jointly. These figures represent the sum of the value of the personal exemption and the standard deduction for taxpayers of the appropriate filing status.

When Students Should File

Students often wonder whether they should file a tax return. Generally a return is necessary if the student had income from one or more of the following sources: (1) **earned income**—compensation for performing personal services, such as salaries, wages, tips, and net earnings from self-employment; (2) **unearned income**—rents, dividends, capital gains, interest, and royalties; and (3) **transfer payments**—payments by governments and individuals for which no goods or services are expected in return, such as welfare payments. The law also requires you to file a return (even if you owe no taxes) when someone (such as your parent) can claim you as a dependent and you have unearned income exceeding $700, or if you have earned income greater than $7050.

Other Times When You Should File a Tax Return

There are two other cases in which it is wise to file a tax return:

1. *To get a refund of any federal income taxes withheld.* People who have had federal income taxes withheld from paychecks but who did not receive enough income to be required to file should submit a return to obtain a refund. If you have neglected to file for refunds in the past, you can complete the appropriate tax form [1040EZ (which the IRS calls its "very short form"), 1040A (to be replaced by form 1040T), or 1040 (the long form)] for the year in question. **Form 1040-X**, Amended U.S. Individual Tax Return, can be used to amend returns filed in error during the past three years. If you moved and never received a filed-for deserved refund, send the IRS Form 8822, the official change-of-address notification, and the agency will forward you a check.

2. *To get a refund if you can qualify for a tax credit.* For example, if your earned income and adjusted gross income are less than $28,000, filing an income tax return might qualify you for a refund of as much as $1440. You also may qualify for other credits for children, adoption expenses, and education. (More information about credits is found on pages 73 and 74.)

Ways to Pay Income Taxes

4 Describe the two ways of paying taxes: payroll withholding and estimated taxes.

When taxpayers complete their tax returns for mailing to the Internal Revenue Service by the April 15 deadline,* they determine their **tax liability**—the amount of tax that must be paid based on income earned during the previous year. Note, however, that the federal income tax is a "pay as you go" tax. Accordingly, taxpayers are required to use one of two methods to discharge their tax liability gradually during the year prior to filing: payroll withholding or estimating taxes.

Method One: Payroll Withholding

Payroll tax withholding is money that an employer takes from an employee's paycheck that is used to pay part or all of the employee's income taxes. This money is deposited in government accounts. The amount withheld is based on the amount of income earned, the number of exemptions reported by the employee on Form W-4 (the Employee's Withholding Allowance Certificate), and other factors. An **exemption** is part of a person's or business's total income on which no tax is imposed. A **personal exemption** is a legally permitted deduction of a taxpayer's total income for each person supported by that income. A person can serve as an exemption on only one tax return—his or her own or another person's (usually a parent). Taxpayers can count themselves and their spouses (if filing jointly) as personal exemptions. **Dependent exemptions** also may be claimed for any of the taxpayer's qualifying dependents, such as children or parents. (A Social Security number is required for anyone aged 2 and older claimed as a dependent.) Each exemption claimed will reduce the amount of tax withheld through payroll withholding.

You may be exempt from payroll withholding (for example, if you are a student who works only summers) if you meet three tests: (1) you had no income tax liability last year and were entitled to a full refund of any tax withheld; (2) you expect to owe no tax in the current year on an income of $700 or less; and (3) you are not claimed as an exemption on another person's tax return. If you satisfy these criteria, request a Form W-4 from your employer and write in the word "exempt" in the appropriate place; if not, file a tax return after the end of the year to obtain a refund of money withheld. Withholding for Social Security and Medicare taxes occurs regardless of whether you are exempt from income tax withholding.

Overwithholding occurs when employees have employers withhold more in estimated taxes than the tax liability ultimately due the government. Approximately three-fourths of all taxpayers practice overwithholding, which actually represents a form of forced savings. These taxpayers receive a refund (which averaged about $1500 last year) approximately six weeks after filing their income tax returns. The IRS does not pay interest on such refunded monies. If you anticipate that your tax liability will be lower than the federal

---

* If you are unable to file your tax return on time, you may avoid a penalty for late filing by obtaining an automatic extension of four months by sending in Form 4868 (or a letter containing the same information) by the due date. A second extension for two months is also possible. Approximately 5 percent of all taxpayers ask for extensions. Despite a filing extension, interest is assessed on any tax liability that is not paid by April 15.

government's withholding schedule, you can refigure your withholding exemptions to decrease the amount withheld.

Method Two: Estimated Taxes

Many people are self-employed or receive substantial income from an employer that is not required to practice payroll withholding. Lawyers, accountants, consultants, movie actors, and owners of rental property are examples of such employees. Under the "pay as you go" requirements, tax laws require such taxpayers to estimate their tax liability and pay it in quarterly installments on April 15, June 15, September 15, and the following January 15. **Estimated taxes** represent the advance payments of one's current tax liability based on estimated tax liability. Form 1040-ES, Declaration of Estimated Tax for Individuals, must be filed if the estimated tax is $1000 or more and if any other withholdings will total less than 90 percent of the current year's tax.

Employed taxpayers who earn additional income by moonlighting can avoid paying estimated taxes by amending their Form W-4 to increase payroll withholding to cover the anticipated extra liability. In this way, the employer is directed to overwithhold taxes so that the taxpayer sufficiently prepays the taxes on the other income. In such a case, a Form 1040-ES will not have to be filed.

Eight Steps in Calculating Your Income Taxes

5 Identify the eight steps involved in calculating federal income taxes.

There are eight basic steps in calculating federal income taxes:

1. Determine your total income.

2. Determine and report gross income by subtracting exclusions.

3. Subtract adjustments to income.

4. Subtract the IRS's standard deduction amount for your tax status *or* list your itemized deductions.

5. Subtract the value of your personal exemptions.

6. Determine your tax liability.

7. Subtract appropriate tax credits.

8. Calculate the balance due the IRS or the amount of your refund.

The eight steps in the overall process of federal income tax calculation are illustrated in Figure 3.2. Our discussion of the eight steps will remain general so that you can grasp the "big picture" of federal income taxation. Although we provide a number of details, limitations, and qualifications throughout this chapter, we do not examine them in depth. The wise financial manager will call the IRS at (800) TAX-1040 to obtain Publication 17, *Your Federal Income Tax: For Individuals,* which is revised annually. All federal income tax forms can be obtained by telephoning the IRS at (800) TAX-3676. IRS information (such as forms, regulations, guides, and answers to common questions) may be accessed

Figure 3.2

The Process of Income Tax Calculation

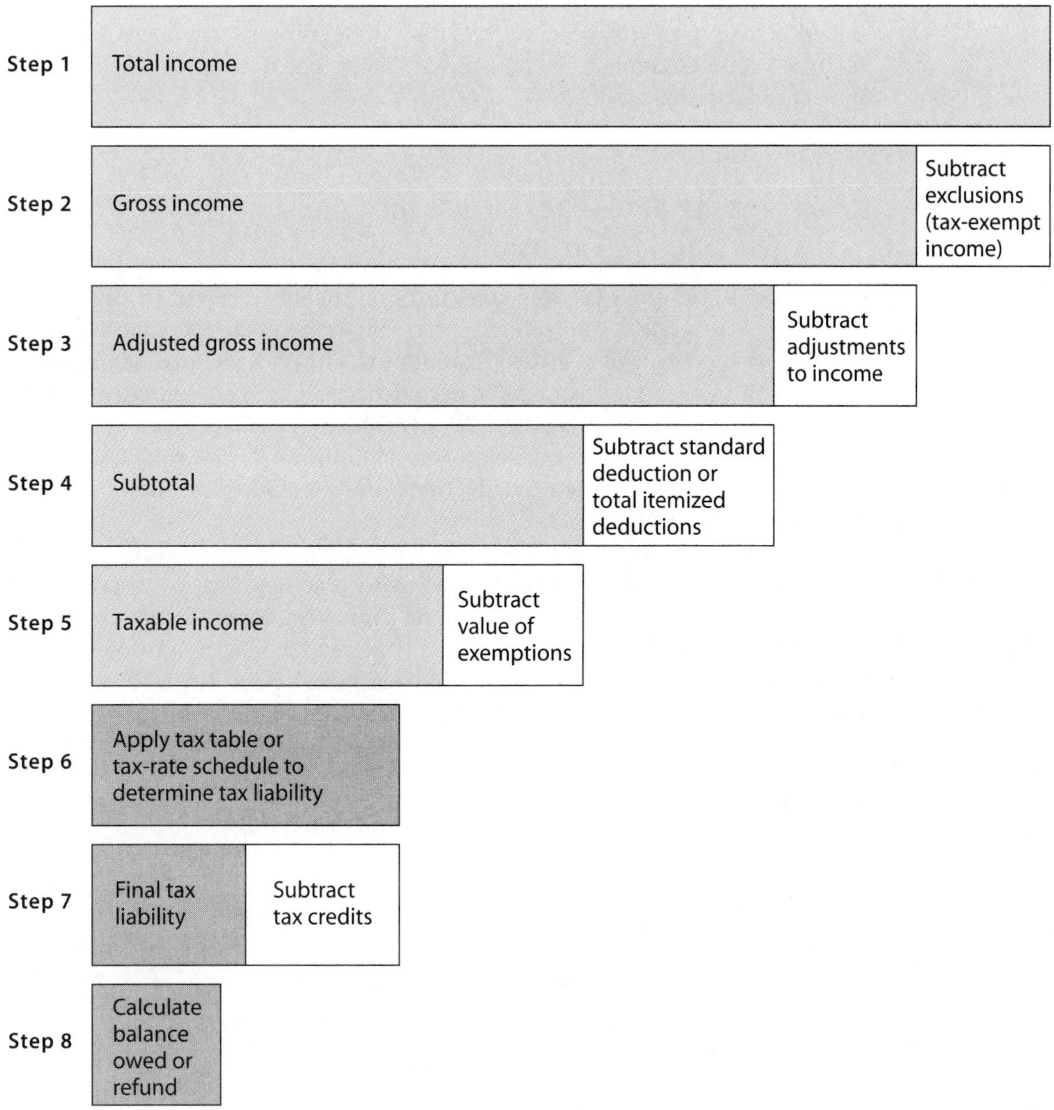

Step 1	Total income
Step 2	Gross income — Subtract exclusions (tax-exempt income)
Step 3	Adjusted gross income — Subtract adjustments to income
Step 4	Subtotal — Subtract standard deduction or total itemized deductions
Step 5	Taxable income — Subtract value of exemptions
Step 6	Apply tax table or tax-rate schedule to determine tax liability
Step 7	Final tax liability — Subtract tax credits
Step 8	Calculate balance owed or refund

from the World Wide Web at *www.irs.treasury.gov/prod/cover.html*. A visit to a bookstore will give you an opportunity to purchase privately produced tax guides that offer advice on how to reduce income taxes[*] and computer software to assist in filling out your return.[†]

[*] One of the best tax guides is the annual, authoritative, and readable J. K. Lasser's *Your Income Tax* (New York: Simon & Schuster).
[†] Popular computer software programs to help prepare income tax returns include Kiplinger Tax-Cut (Block Financial Software), Personal Tax Edge (Parsons), Simply Tax (4Home Productions), TaxCut (H&R Block), and Turbo Tax (Intuit).

1. Determine Your Total Income

Practically everything you receive in return for your work or services and any profit from the sale of assets are considered income, whether the compensation is paid in cash, property, or services. Listing these earnings will reveal your **total income**—compensation from all sources—most, but not all, of which will be subject to income taxes.

2. Determine and Report Gross Income by Subtracting Exclusions

On the tax form, **gross income** consists of all income received in the form of money, goods, services, and property that you are required to report. To determine gross income, you need to examine which kinds of income should be included and which kinds should be excluded, because many sources of income are not subject to federal taxation. You eventually calculate and pay personal income taxes only on your taxable income. (Subtractions from gross income will later be allowed in adjustments, deductions, and exemptions, as indicated in the unshaded boxes in Figure 3.2.)

Income to Include   Most people have their income reported to them annually on a Form W-2, Wage and Tax Statement. Employers must provide W-2 information by January 31 of the next year. If you earn income from interest or dividends or other sources, those sources may send you a Form 1099, Miscellaneous Income. That information is provided to the IRS.

Types of income included in gross income are as follows:

- Wages and salaries
- Commissions
- Bonuses
- Professional fees earned
- Interest income (including dividends from credit unions and any interest on federal income tax refunds)
- Dividends (including distributions from mutual funds even though they are reinvested)
- Tips earned
- Alimony received
- Scholarship and fellowship income spent on room, board, and other living expenses
- Graduate-level tuition reimbursements from employers
- Grants and the value of tuition reductions that pay for teaching or other services
- Annuity and pension income received (although portions are excluded)
- Military retirement income
- Social Security income (a portion is taxed above certain income thresholds)
- Disability payments received if you did not pay the premiums

- Punitive damage payments from personal injury lawsuits
- Value of personal use of employer-provided car
- Withdrawals and disbursements from qualified retirement accounts, such as an IRA, a 401(k) plan, or a Keogh account (discussed in Chapter 18, "Retirement Planning")
- State and local income tax refunds (only if the taxpayer itemized deductions the previous year)
- Fair value of anything received in a barter arrangement
- Withdrawals from a tuition prepayment plan
- Employee productivity awards
- Awards for artistic, scientific, and charitable achievements unless assigned to a charity
- Prizes, contest winnings, and rewards
- Gambling and lottery winnings
- Any kind of illegal income
- Fees for serving as a juror or election worker
- Unemployment benefits
- Partnership income or share of profits
- Net rental income
- Royalties
- Investment, business, and farm profits (or losses)

Capital Gains and Losses   A **capital asset** is property owned by a taxpayer for personal use or as an investment. Examples of capital assets include stocks, bonds, real estate, household furnishings, jewelry, automobiles, and coin collections. A **capital gain** is income received from the sale of a capital asset above the costs incurred to purchase and sell the asset. A **capital loss** results when the sale of a capital asset brings less income than the costs of purchasing and selling the asset.

Capital gains and losses on investment properties must be reported on the tax return. Capital gains from the sale or exchange of property held for personal use must be reported as income, but losses are not deductible.

A **long-term capital gain** (or **loss**) occurs when the asset was held for more than 12 months (except for art and collectibles). A **short-term capital gain** (or **loss**) occurs when the asset was held for one year or less. Long-term capital gains are taxed at 20 percent, although the rate is only 10 percent for those in the 15 percent marginal tax bracket; short-term capital gains are taxed at your marginal tax rate. Gains on assets aquired after the year 2000 and held by individual taxpayers for more than five years will be subject to reduced rates for taxable years beginning after December 31, 2000. The 20 percent and 10 percent rates will be reduced to 18 percent and 8 percent respectively.

It is important to realize that not all investments are profitable, so capital losses are deductible against capital gains (a tax break that encourages venturesome investments). If such losses exceed the comparable gains, the remaining losses can be matched against up to $3000 of other income. Any loss left over can be carried forward to successive years, up to an annual $3000 maximum.

Income to Exclude   Some sources of income are not considered legally as income for federal tax purposes; thus, such income is tax-exempt. These amounts are called **exclusions.** Some of the more common exclusions are as follows:

- Interest received on municipal bonds (issued by states, counties, cities, and districts)
- Income from a car pool
- Income from items sold at a garage sale for a sum less than what you paid
- Cash rebates on purchases of new cars and other products
- Scholarship and fellowship income spent on course-required tuition, fees, books, supplies, and equipment (degree candidates only)
- Prizes and awards made primarily to recognize artistic, civic, charitable, educational, and similar achievements
- Federal income tax refunds
- State income tax refunds (for a year when you did not itemize deductions on the federal return)
- Interest received on Series EE bonds used for college tuition and fees (discussed in Chapter 5, "Managing Your Cash")
- Child-support payments received
- Property settlement in a divorce
- Compensatory damages in physical injury cases
- Return of money loaned and money received from a loan
- Net proceeds from health and accident insurance policies
- Earnings accumulating within annuities, cash-value life insurance policies, Series EE bonds, and qualified retirement accounts
- Life insurance death benefits
- Gifts and inheritances
- Welfare, black lung, worker's compensation, and veterans' benefits
- Value of food stamps
- First $500,000 ($250,000 if single) gain on sale of principal residence
- Disability insurance benefits if you paid the insurance premiums
- Social Security benefits (subject to limits)
- Up to 14 days of rental income from vacation home
- Tuition reduction if not received as compensation for teaching or service
- The first $5000 of death benefits paid by an employer to a worker's beneficiary
- Travel and mileage expenses reimbursed by an employer (if not previously deducted by the taxpayer)
- Amounts paid by employers for premiums for medical insurance, worker's compensation, and Social Security taxes
- Moving expenses reimbursements received from an employer (if not previously deducted by the taxpayer)

- Employer-provided meals

- Employer-provided mass transit fares (up to $60 per month) for commuting purposes and subsidized parking (up to $170 per month)

- The first $50,000 worth of group-term life insurance provided by an employer

- Employer payments for dependent care assistance (for children and parents)

- Employee contributions to flexible spending accounts

- Employer-provided tuition assistance for undergraduate classes (up to $5250)

3. Subtract Adjustments to Income

Adjustments to income represent a selected group of legal subtractions from gross income that include contributions to personal retirement accounts, certain moving expenses, alimony paid, interest penalties for early withdrawal of savings certificates of deposit, interest (for five years only) on student loans for higher education ($1500 in 1999, $2000 in 2000, and $2500 in 2001), and certain expenses of self-employed persons. Adjustments are subtracted from gross income to determine **adjusted gross income (AGI)**. In addition to reducing your AGI directly, they help you qualify for other AGI-based write-offs, such as for some itemized deductions.

To illustrate the value of adjustments to income, consider a person with a gross income of $30,000 who contributes $1000 to a **qualified retirement account** (a tax-advantaged plan that the IRS has approved to encourage saving for retirement). The adjustment reduces gross income to $29,000 and, therefore, saves $280 in income taxes (calculated using Table 3.2). (Contributions to retirement plans are covered in Chapter 18.) Adjustments are called **above-the-line deductions** because they may be subtracted from gross income regardless of whether the taxpayer itemizes deductions or takes the standard deduction amount (these procedures are explained later in this section).

4. Subtract the Standard Deduction for Your Tax Status or Itemize Your Deductions

Over the years, Congress has approved a number of day-to-day living expenses that can be deducted from adjusted gross income. Taxpayers are permitted to reduce their adjusted gross income by the amount of the standard deduction or the total of their itemized deductions, whichever is larger. The **standard deduction** is the amount that all taxpayers (except some dependents) who do not choose to itemize deductions may subtract from their adjusted gross income. The amount varies according to filing status, age, and blindness. In effect, it consists of the government's legally permissible estimate of any likely tax-deductible expenses such taxpayers might have. For example, the standard deduction amounts are $4300 for single individuals and $7200 for married people filing jointly. Taxpayers whose total itemized deductions would not exceed the amount permitted for the standard deduction may instead use the appropriate standard deduction.

About one-fourth of all taxpayers have itemized deductions that total more than the standard deduction amount for their **filing status**—the description of family status that determines the taxpayer's tax bracket and rate at which income is taxed. A return can be filed with a status of a single person, a married person (filing separately or jointly), or a head of household.

Taxpayers whose tax-deductible expenses exceed the standard deduction amount may forego the standard deduction and list their **itemized deductions** instead. These items are part of a person's or business's total expenditures that can be deducted from adjusted gross income in determining taxable income. For example, a single person might list all of his or her possible tax deductions and find that they total $5000, which is more than the standard deduction amount of $4300 permitted for single taxpayers. In that case, the single person should deduct $5000 instead of taking the $4300 standard deduction amount. Some deductions are subject to limits based on one's adjusted gross income. The tax form lists the following classifications of itemized deductions:

- Medical and dental expenses
- Taxes
- Interest paid
- Gifts to charity
- Casualty and theft losses
- Miscellaneous expenses

Examples of legitimate deductions in each of these categories follow.

Medical and Dental Expenses (Not Paid by Insurance) in Excess of 7.5 Percent of Adjusted Gross Income

Medicine and drugs

Medical insurance premiums, including those for long-term insurance for the chronically ill (subject to limits) and for contact lenses

A Sideline Business Can Reduce Your Income Taxes

Some people moonlight from their regular jobs or do freelance work to increase income; others convert a hobby into a sideline business. In addition to the income it provides, a sideline business is associated with several tax advantages. These benefits include deductions for: home-office expenses (if the strict standards are met); expenses for vehicles, computers, and office equipment; hiring family members; a portion of related meals and entertainment costs (receipt or diary entry required for amounts above $75); gift expenses (limited to $25 per person); travel (including all expenses when staying over Saturday night to take advantage of reduced airfare); and a portion of the cost of health insurance premiums. A person with a sideline business also has additional opportunities to set aside

tax-deferred retirement funds, as well as move many previously nondeductible miscellaneous deductions to the business.

A simple hobby, however, will not qualify if you pursue it only to take tax losses every year. You may deduct expenses and even claim deductible losses when you can show that your business activity is profit-oriented. According to the IRS, the best way to prove that your sideline business is real is to earn a profit in at least three of five consecutive years, although court decisions frequently show that this criterion is *not* a firm requirement. If possible, you might want to consider a sideline business to reduce your income taxes to give you more money to spend, save, and invest.

Medical services (doctors, dentists, nurses, hospitals, long-term health care) and medical equipment (hearing aids, eyeglasses)

Home improvements made for the physically handicapped

Transportation costs to and from locations where medical services are obtained, using a standard flat mileage allowance

Taxes You Paid

Real property taxes (such as on a home or land)

Personal property taxes (such as on an automobile when any part of the tax is based on the value of the car)

State, local, and foreign income taxes

Interest Expenses

Interest paid on first and second home mortgage loans (up to $1 million debt)

Interest for some "points" and loan-origination fees paid for housing loans

Interest paid on home-equity loans for amounts up to $100,000 debt

Interest paid on loans used for investments (subject to limits)

Gifts to Charity

Cash contributions to qualified organizations, such as churches, schools, and other qualifying charities (receipt required for $250 or more)

Noncash contributions (such as personal property) at fair market value (a receipt is required for contributions of more than $500)

Travel expenses incurred while performing volunteer services for a charitable organization, using a standard flat mileage allowance

Casualty and Theft Losses (Not Paid by Insurance) in Excess of 10 Percent of Adjusted Gross Income

Casualty losses (such as from storms, vandalism, and fires) in excess of $100

Theft of money or property in excess of $100 (a copy of the police report provides good substantiation)

Mislaid or lost property if the loss results from an identifiable event that is sudden, unexpected, or unusual (such as catching a diamond ring in a car door and losing the stone)

Job Expenses and Most Other Miscellaneous Deductions in Excess of 2 Percent of Adjusted Gross Income (Partial Listing Only)

Union or professional association dues and membership fees

Fees for a safe-deposit box used to store papers related to income-producing stocks, bonds, or other investments

Custodial fees on a qualified pension plan (such as on an IRA)

Purchase and maintenance of specialized clothing that is not suitable for off-the-job use (such as protective shoes, hats, and gloves), including uniforms for members of the armed forces reserves

Unreimbursed employee business expenses (but only a portion of the cost of meals and entertainment), including long-distance telephone calls, cleaning and laundry, and car washes (of business vehicle)

Tax counsel and tax preparation fees

Investment advisory and management fees

Tools and supplies for use in a profession

Books and periodicals for use in a profession

Expenses for investment publications if you have investment income

Custodial fees for stock and mutual fund dividend reinvestment plans

Business use of a personal residence or home office (subject to limits if used regularly and exclusively for business and you have no other location where you conduct substantive activities of that business)

Fees paid to obtain employment through an agency

Travel costs between two jobs, using a flat mileage allowance

Job-related car expenses (but not commuting to work), using a flat mileage allowance or actual expenses

Commuting costs that qualify as a business or education expense

Medical examinations required (but not paid for) by an employer to obtain or keep a job

Appraisal fees on taxable types of items

Education expenses for an employee required by his or her employer to maintain and improve skills to advance his or her career, but generally not if the training readies the employee for a new career

Transportation, food, and entertainment costs for job hunting (which does not have to be successful) in your present career

Expenses for typing, printing, career counseling, want ads, telephone calls, employment agency fees, and mailing résumés for seeking a job in your present career field

Other Miscellaneous Deductions Allowed at 100 Percent

Gambling losses (but only to offset reported gambling income)

Business expenses for handicapped workers

Given the considerable list of deductions listed here and numerous others for which you might qualify, it makes sense to estimate your possible deductions very carefully. If the estimated total exceeds the standard deduction amount or is even close, go back and itemize deductions more carefully and then deduct the larger amount.

5. Subtract the Value of Your Personal Exemptions

As noted earlier, an exemption is a legally permitted deduction of a taxpayer's income for each person supported by that income (unless he or she is claimed as an exemption by another taxpayer, such as a parent). Each personal exemption reduces taxable income by $2750. You may claim an exemption for yourself, a spouse, and for other dependents. The value of a personal exemption is phased out for higher-income taxpayers.*

The number of exemptions you claim on your tax return may differ from the number claimed on the Form W-4 filed with your employer. For example, you may have chosen to claim fewer exemptions on your Form W-4 so that your employer would withhold a greater amount of taxes and ensure that you would receive a refund.

Claiming Another Person as an Exemption To claim someone else as a dependent for tax purposes and, therefore, that person's exemption value, the dependent must meet five criteria:

1. The dependent must be a relative or, if unrelated, must have resided in your home as a member of your household.

2. If the person was younger than age 19 or was a full-time student younger than age 24, his or her income does not matter. A person not meeting this age and student status requirement must have received less than $2750 in gross income for the year to be claimed as a dependent.

3. More than half of the dependent's total support must have been provided by you. (Exceptions include children of divorced parents, who generally can be claimed only by the custodial parent.)

4. The dependent must be a U.S. citizen or a legal resident of the United States, Canada, or Mexico.

5. The dependent must not have filed a joint return with his or her spouse. If the person and the person's spouse file a joint return only to obtain a refund, you may claim him or her if the other criteria apply.

What If You Are Claimed as an Exemption? If you are claimed as a dependent on someone else's return or are eligible to be claimed, you cannot claim a personal exemption for yourself, as only one person receives the exemption. For dependents who are claimed as an exemption by another person yet must still file a return, the amount permitted for that taxpayer's standard deduction is limited to $700 or the amount of income earned on a job, up to the amount of the standard deduction ($4300)—whichever is greater.

---

* The effective marginal rates for high-income taxpayers are 1 to 3 percent higher than the given marginal tax brackets because the value of their personal exemptions begins to be phased out when adjusted gross income exceeds these thresholds: $126,600 if filing as single and $189,950 if married filing jointly.

6. Determine Your Tax Liability

The steps detailed to this point are used to determine your taxable income. Taxable income is calculated by taking the taxpayer's gross income, subtracting adjustments to income, subtracting either the standard deduction or total itemized deductions, and subtracting the amount permitted for the number of exemptions allowed. The amount of taxable income is used to determine the taxpayer's tax liability via the tax tables or tax-rate schedules combined with the appropriate filing status (such as single or married filing jointly). Each filing status has a separate tax-rate table or schedule, which you then use to find your tax liability.* Table 3.3 shows segments from the tax tables.

The following examples show how to determine tax liability.

1. A married couple filing jointly has a gross income of $47,000, adjustments of $5350, itemized deductions of $4285, and two exemptions. They take the standard deduction of $7200 because their itemized deductions do not exceed that amount.

Gross income	$47,000
Less adjustments to income	−5,350
Adjusted gross income	41,650
Less standard deduction for married couple	−7,200
Subtotal	34,450
Less value of two exemptions	−5,500
Taxable income	28,950
Tax liability (from Table 3.3)	$ 4,346

2. A single person has a gross income of $47,300, adjustments of $5320, itemized deductions of $8400, and one exemption. He or she subtracts his or her total itemized deductions because the amount exceeds the $4300 permitted standard deduction value.

Gross income	$47,300
Less adjustments to income	−5,320
Adjusted gross income	41,980
Less itemized deductions	−8,400
Subtotal	33,580
Less value of one exemption	−2,750
Taxable income	30,830
Tax liability (from Table 3.3)	$ 5,284

3. A married couple with a gross income of $127,000 has adjustments of $3400, itemized deductions of $9800, and two exemptions. The itemized deductions are taken because they exceed the standard deduction value of $7200 for a married couple.

---

*   Taxpayers with several children, extremely high incomes, or substantial income from tax-exempt sources may have to pay an **alternative minimum tax (AMT)**, instead of the standard tax rates. The rate is 26 percent for the first $175,000 in taxable income; the rate then rises to 28 percent.

Gross income	$127,000
Less adjustments to income	−3,400
Adjusted gross income	123,600
Less itemized deductions	−9,800
Subtotal	113,800
Less value of two exemptions	−5,500
Taxable income	108,300
Tax liability*	$ 24,855

7. Subtract Appropriate Tax Credits

You also may be able to lower your tax liability through **tax credits**. A tax credit directly reduces tax liability, as opposed to a deduction that reduces income subject to tax. Tax credits are dollar-for-dollar subtractions from tax liability. Such subtractions reduce tax liability to *final tax liability*, which is the amount owed after subtracting tax credits. You may take tax credits regardless of whether you itemize deductions. Even if you have zero tax liability, you might be eligible for a refund of some tax credits. Most credits are subject to income limits, meaning that high-income taxpayers may not be eligible for the credit.

Hope Scholarship and Lifetime Learning Credits Two tax credits exist for qualifying higher education expenses. If you paid tuition and related expenses for yourself, a spouse, or a person you claim as a dependent for being enrolled in the first two years of post-secondary education, you may claim a **Hope Scholarship credit.** The amount is 100 percent of the first $1000 plus 50 percent of the next $1000 paid, for a maximum of $1500. The **lifetime learning credit** may be claimed for tuition and related expenses beyond the first two years of post-secondary school. This credit amounts to 20 percent of the first $5000 paid, for a maximum of $1000. You may not claim both the Hope credit and the Lifetime Learning Credit for the same tax year.

Adoption Credit A tax credit of up to $5000 is available for the qualifying costs of an adoption.

Child Tax Credit You may take a $500 **child tax credit** for each qualifying child younger than age 17 claimed as a dependent.

The Dependent/Child Care Credit The **dependent/child care credit** applies to workers who pay for dependent care of a child or disabled dependent that gives them the freedom to work, seek work, or attend school full time. Depending upon your income, the credit is 20 to 30 percent of child care expenses up to the $2400 (one dependent) or $4800 (two or more dependents) limit. The dependent/child care credit is phased out for incomes above $28,000. This credit is nonrefundable; it is limited to the taxpayer's tax liability.

---

* The tax liability here is calculated from the tax-rate schedules in Table 3.2 because the taxable income is higher than $100,000, which is the maximum for the tax tables. The tax liability is computed as follows: $23,537.50 + [0.31 \times (\$108,300 - \$104,050)] = \$24,855$.

The Earned Income Credit The **earned income credit (EIC)** is a refundable credit for low-income workers. It is a special subsidy that the government pays to low-income working people who are at least age 25 but younger than age 64. This credit is available for those whose earned income (wages, salaries, and so forth) and adjusted gross income are less than $28,000 (but at least $1). The credit can be as much as $1440 for a family or $720 with no qualifying children. Note that college students may qualify for the EIC. Anyone who was eligible for the credit may file to receive a credit retroactively for the previous three years.

8. Calculate the Balance Due or the Amount of Your Refund

The subtraction of your tax credits yields your final tax liability. Next, you should examine the Form W-2 for the year that summarizes the federal income tax withheld. If the amount withheld plus any estimated tax payments you made is greater than your final tax liability, then you should receive a tax refund. If the amount is less than your final tax liability, then you have a tax balance due. In such a case, you must send the government a check or money order made out to the IRS for the money owed.

Taxpayers generally hear from the IRS within three weeks if they have failed to sign the return, neglected to attach a copy of the Form W-2, made an error in arithmetic, or used the wrong tax tables or tax-rate schedules. Refunds are usually received within six weeks.

Avoid Taxes Through Proper Planning

6 Understand planning strategies to legally avoid overpayment of income taxes.

If you are knowledgeable about tax laws and regulations, keep reasonably good records, and are assertive in your planning, you can avoid overpayment of taxes. While the U.S. tax laws are strict and punitive about compliance, they remain neutral about whether the taxpayer should take advantage of every "break" and opportunity possible. As Judge Learned Hand said many years ago, "There is nothing sinister in so arranging one's affairs as to keep taxes as low as possible." Proper planning in personal finance requires that you apply the old saying, "Nothing ventured, nothing gained," to your income taxes. The strategies described here will enable you to accumulate more personal assets, to share those assets with family members in lower tax brackets, and eventually to pass the assets on to surviving relatives with a minimum of tax erosion.

Practice Tax Avoidance, Not Tax Evasion

Tax evasion involves deliberately and willfully hiding income, falsely claiming deductions, or otherwise cheating the government out of taxes owed. It is illegal. A waiter who does not report tips received and a baby-sitter who does not report income are both evading taxes, as is a person who deducts $150 in church contributions but who fails to actually make the donations. **Tax avoidance**, on the other hand, means reducing tax liability through legal techniques. It involves applying knowledge of the tax code and regulations to personal income tax planning.

Tax evasion results in penalties, fines, interest charges, and a possible jail sentence. In contrast, tax avoidance boosts your after-tax income because you pay less in taxes; as a result, you will have more money available for spending, saving, and investing.

A Dollar Saved from Taxes Is Really Two Dollars—or More

Sufficient reasons to avoid taxes can be summarized in three ways:

- **Opportunity cost** represents the most valuable alternative that must be sacrificed to satisfy a want. An opportunity cost is measured in terms of the value of this forgone opportunity, and it is reflected by the cost of what one must do without or what one could have bought instead. Giving the government money in the form of taxes has an opportunity cost. By paying $1 in taxes, you lose the alternative use of that dollar.

- If you pay a dollar too much in taxes, you may need to earn another dollar to replace it. Thus, a dollar saved in taxes may be viewed as two dollars in your pocket that become available for alternative uses; any second dollar earned is yours to keep if you did not pay that extra dollar to the government in the first place.

- If the two dollars saved are invested, the earnings from that investment expands the savings even further.

These three reasons should provide sufficient motivation for you to find legal ways to reduce your tax liability.

Strategy: Reduce Taxable Income When Possible

It may seem illogical to suggest that to lower tax liability you should reduce income. The key is to reduce *taxable* income, not all sources of income. Reducing your federal taxable income also usually reduces the personal income taxes imposed by states and municipalities.

A popular way to reduce taxable income is to pay some expenses with pretax dollars. Paying the expenses with **pretax dollars** (money income that has not been taxed by the government) lowers your taxable income, decreases your take-home pay, and increases your effective take-home pay because of the reimbursements. Two useful ways of reducing taxable income by paying with pretax dollars are premium conversion of health plan premiums and flexible spending accounts.

Premium Conversion of Health Plan Premiums An IRS-approved tax shelter that is frequently offered by large employers is **premium conversion** of health plan premiums. Under this plan, an employee has the amount he or she pays for health benefits premiums deducted from his or her salary before taxes are calculated. Premium conversion saves money for the employee because the health premiums are paid with pretax dollars. As a result, those amounts avoid Social Security, Medicare, and income taxes.

Flexible Spending Accounts   Many employers offer **flexible spending accounts** (also called **expense reimbursement accounts** or **pretax set asides**). Here an employee makes salary-reduction contributions to government-approved medical (up to $5000) and/or dependent care (up to $3000) reimbursement account(s). The pretax money may be used to reimburse selected employee-paid expenses. As with premium conversion, the taxpayer does not pay Social Security, Medicare, or income taxes on such salary reductions. The IRS is expected to approve a flexible spending account that allows workers to use pretax reimbursement account dollars to pay for transit fares and parking. (Flexible spending accounts were discussed in Chapter 1.)

An Example of How to Reduce Income Taxes

Ron and Marilyn West of Longmont, Colorado, have a complex income tax return because they have both made it a habit to learn about tax saving strategies and to take advantage of them whenever possible. The table at the right shows the Wests' total income and demonstrates how they arrive at a taxable income that is much lower. The Wests have two small children as well as Ron's mother living in their home. By thinking hard about how to reduce taxes, they have taken advantage of many applicable adjustments, deductions, exemptions, and credits. Part of their income also comes from tax-exempt sources. Their deductions and tax credits, typical for a couple with two children, result in a tax liability of only $3246. The marginal tax rate for the Wests is 15 percent. Their average tax rate for all income is 4.6 percent ($3246 ÷ $71,300). For a family with such a substantial income, they have been quite successful in lowering their tax liability.

TOTAL INCOME		
Ron's salary	$ 44,200	
Marilyn's salary	25,000	
Capital gains (sales of stock)	450	
Marilyn's year-end bonus	1,000	
State income tax refund (itemized last year)	180	
Interest on savings account	350	
Dividends on stocks	120	
Interest on tax-exempt state bonds	2,000*	
Gift from Marilyn's mother	2,500*	
Car-pool income (Ron's van pool)	250*	
Total all income		$71,300
MINUS EXCLUDABLE INCOME		
($2000 + $2500 + $250 from* above)		−4,750
GROSS INCOME		$66,550
ADJUSTMENTS TO INCOME		
Payment to Ron's retirement account	$1,000	
Payment to Marilyn's retirement account	1,000	
MINUS ADJUSTMENTS TO INCOME		−2,000
ADJUSTED GROSS INCOME (AGI)		$64,550
DEDUCTIONS		
Medical expenses	$5,500	
Exclusion (7.5% of AGI)	−4,841	
Total medical deductions	$ 659	
TAXES		
Real property	$1,800	
Personal property	210	
Total deductible taxes	$2,010	
INTEREST EXPENSES		
Home mortgage	$10,800	
Home-equity loan	160	
Total deductible interest expenses	$10,960	

Strategy: Seek Tax-Sheltered Returns on Investments

People often look for **tax-sheltered returns** on their investments because such income is exempt from current income taxes. A **tax shelter** is a tax planning tool that provides a reduction or postponement of income tax liability. Congress permits tax shelters in an effort to encourage certain types of investments or other taxpayer behaviors. Some tax shelters permit the money within the investment to grow and accumulate free of income taxes, thus postponing the tax liability. Other tax shelters allow money put into an investment to reduce income tax liability, either indirectly (with a deduction or an adjustment) or directly (with a credit). As a result, some of the money invested in tax-sheltered activities is partially "paid for" by the government—instead of sending a certain sum of money to the government in the form of taxes, the investor is permitted to keep those amounts.

Some tax shelters provide an immediate cash benefit (after the investor completes an income tax return), though most represent methods of deferring taxes until a later date when the tax rate might be lower. During the interim period, the taxpayer gains an alternative use for the money not yet given to the government as well as the time value of such funds. Strategies related to tax-sheltered returns include seeking long-term capital gains on investments, deferring income to later years, avoiding capital gains on your home, and considering investments that earn tax-exempt income.

Long-Term Capital Gains on Investments Because the tax rate on long-term net capital gains is 20 percent (10 percent for those in the 15 percent marginal tax bracket), taxpayers are motivated to seek investments that offer a return over a number of years rather than months. For example, a high-income taxpayer in the 39.6 percent tax bracket who earns a short-term net profit of $10,000 on stocks, bonds, or land is subject to ordinary income tax rates. Thus, he or she would owe $3960 in income taxes. In contrast, if that $10,000 income was earned over the *long term* (more than 12 months), the maximum income tax would be 20 percent, or $2000.

Deferred Income A number of methods are available to defer income to later years. Deferring income is important because IRS regulations permit such income to accumulate free of income taxes. When invested, deferred

CONTRIBUTIONS	
Church	$1,200
Other charities	240
Goodwill	300
Charitable travel	90
Total contributions	$1,830
CASUALTY OR THEFT	
Loss—diamond ring	$6,500
Insurance reimbursement	−0
Reduction	−100
Exclusion (10% of AGI)	−6,455
Total deductible losses	$45
MISCELLANEOUS	
Union dues (Ron)	$360
Safe-deposit box	30
Unreimbursed job expenses	460
Cost of Ron looking for a new job	900
Investment publications	60
Financial planning tax advice	50
Tax publications	20
Subtotal	1,880
Less 2% of AGI	−1,291
Total miscellaneous deductions	$589
TOTAL ITEMIZED DEDUCTIONS	−16,093
MINUS EXEMPTIONS (5 @ $2750)	−13,750
TAXABLE INCOME	$34,707
TAX LIABILITY (from Table 3.2)	5,206
TAX CREDITS	
Dependent care credit	−960
Child tax credit (2 children)	−1,000
Minus tax credits	−1,960
FINAL TAX LIABILITY	$3,246

The Principles of Reducing Taxes

There are a number of principles that people can use to reduce tax liability. Several are listed below along with some examples. The illustrations, of course, are subject to limits defined in this chapter. The several principles are as follows:

1. Earn tax-free income (such as from tax-exempt bonds, tax-exempt mutual funds, child support, and income earned while working overseas).

2. Have an employer pay for some of your living expenses (such as premiums for health care and group term life insurance, and education assistance).

3. Defer income to later years when you might be in a lower tax bracket by funding a qualified retirement account (such as a salary-reduction plan, an IRA, a Roth IRA, or a Keogh plan).

4. Save the maximum amount possible in a qualified retirement account when an employer offers some type of matching contributions (as sometimes occurs in a salary-reduction plan).

5. Within your qualified retirement account, buy income-producing investments (such as high-dividend stocks, mutual funds, and bonds) because such income avoids taxation until money is withdrawn.

6. Use other funds to invest in assets where the earnings will accumulate without being taxed (such as with annuities and municipal bonds as well as stocks and mutual funds in qualified retirement accounts).

7. If you have assets outside of your retirement fund, buy growth investments that will yield the largest capital gains outside of the retirement fund. This may reduce your income tax liability, as capital gains receive special treatment.

8. Be alert to special tax treatments for particular investments (such as tax swaps and like-kind free exchanges). (Note also that the tax law keeps changing to advantage or disadvantage certain investments.)

9. Itemize deductions on your income taxes.

10. Open a sideline business for the tax advantages it brings.

11. Buy a home for the tax advantages it brings.

12. Shift or split your income to someone in a lower tax bracket (avoiding the kiddie tax and using gifts and trusts).

13. Avoid or postpone estate taxes when possible [using wills and trusts (see Chapter 19)].

income will grow more substantially than when it is taxed every year. It will also provide income during later years, potentially when tax rates are lower. A number of investments qualify for tax-deferred status, including individual retirement accounts (IRAs); spousal IRAs; Roth IRAs; salary-reduction plans, such as 401(k), 403(b), 404(c), 457, SIMPLE, and Keogh plans; life insurance; and annuities. These tax-sheltered programs are detailed in Chapters 13 and 18.

Putting money into a qualified pension plan permits the taxpayer to use that amount immediately as an adjustment to income, thus lowering the tax liability for the current year. For example, a $2000 contribution to a qualified retirement plan immediately saves the taxpayer in the 28 percent tax bracket $560 ($2000 × 0.28) because that amount does not have to be sent to the IRS. Even minors may contribute up to $2000 of their wages (perhaps from a summer job) to an individual retirement account.

Contributions to a **Roth IRA**, while not tax-deductible, do accumulate without being taxed. The same is also true of nondeductible contributions ($500 limit) to an **education IRA**. The eventual withdrawals will be tax-free.

Buying a Home Can Reduce Income Taxes Because Interest and Real Estate Taxes Are Tax Deductible

Hanna Pallagrosi of Rome, New York, took a management position at a small retail chain store last year, where she earned a gross income of $39,240. Hanna wisely made a $1000 contribution to her qualified retirement plan. Her itemized expenses came to only $1800, so she took the standard deduction of $4300. As shown below, her tax liability was $5438, and Hanna became upset at such a large tax bill.

Gross income	$39,420
Less adjustments to income	−1,000
Adjusted gross income	38,420
Less standard deduction	−4,300
Subtotal	34,120
Less value of one exemption	−2,750
Taxable income	31,370
Tax liability (from Table 3.3)	$ 5,438

Because Hanna's employer experienced a difficult year financially, no employees received raises during the past year. Nonetheless, Hanna continued to contribute $1000 to the pension plan. To reduce her federal income taxes, Hanna became a homeowner after using some inheritance money to make the down payment on a condominium. During the year she paid out $6225 in interest expenses and $1595 in real estate taxes. After studying various tax publications, Hanna determined that she also had $1900 in other itemized deductions. As shown below, and using the current-year value of an exemption, these efforts reduced Hanna's tax liability dramatically.

Gross income	$39,420
Less adjustments to income	−1,000
Adjusted gross income	38,420
Less itemized deductions	−9,720
Subtotal	28,700
Less value of one exemption	−2,750
Taxable income	25,950
Tax liability (from Table 3.3)	$ 3,926

She correctly concluded that the IRS "paid" $1512 ($5438 − $3926) toward the purchase of her condominium and her living costs there, as she did not have to forward those dollars to the government. An additional benefit for Hanna is that she now owns a home whose value could appreciate in the future.

Avoidance of Capital Gains Taxes on the Sale of Your Home   In the past, capital gains on home sales were fully taxed. Effective May 7, 1997, however, homeowners with appreciated principal residences were allowed to avoid tax on gains of up to $500,000 if married and filing jointly and on gains up to $250,000 if single. The home must have been owned and used as the taxpayer's private residence for two out of the last five years prior to the date of the sale. You do not have to purchase replacement property. You can take advantage of this exclusion as often as you want, assuming that you meet the two-year ownership and residency rules.

Investments That Earn Tax-Exempt Income   Income from a **tax-exempt investment**, such as interest received from municipal bonds and types of money market mutual funds that invest solely in municipal bonds, is free from federal taxation. Taxpayers in higher income brackets (28 percent or more) often can gain by making these kinds of investments. (Bonds are discussed in Chapter 14, "Investing in Stocks and Bonds.")

For example, assume that Mary Ellen Rider, a retiree living in Lincoln, Nebraska, currently has $5000 in savings earning 4 percent, or $200 annually

($5000 $\times$ 0.04). She pays $56 in tax on this income at her 28 percent marginal tax rate ($200 $\times$ 0.28). A tax-exempt $5000 state bond paying 3.2 percent will provide her with a better after-tax return. She would receive $160 ($5000 $\times$ 0.032) tax-free from the state bond compared with $144 ($200 − $56) after taxes on the income from savings. The increase in after-tax income is $16 ($160 − $144).

Other examples of investments where the earnings are permitted to grow free of taxes are Series EE government bonds, state-sponsored college tuition prepayment plans, and education IRAs.

Strategy: If Possible, Split Income to Avoid the Marriage Penalty

Although most married taxpayers are subject to lower tax rates than single people or heads of households with the same income, some dual-earner couples must pay thousands of dollars in extra taxes. This inequity in the U.S. income tax system results from a **marriage penalty** that negatively affects people at both extremes of the income spectrum.

High-income, two-earner married couples pay more in income taxes than comparable single people because their pooled incomes boost them into a higher tax bracket than they would face individually as singles. This situation occurs because of the existence of so many tax brackets and because of the difference in **break points** (the points at which brackets change) for each filing status of taxpayer.

The following calculations, derived from Table 3.2, demonstrate the marriage penalty. When two $60,000-per-year earners marry, it costs them an extra $1562 in income taxes ($28,482 − $13,460 − $13,460) because their combined income is taxed at a marginal rate of 31 percent, rather than the 28 percent for single taxpayers. Note that the IRS has ruled that **quickie tax divorces** (such as divorcing in December and remarrying in January to save on income taxes) represent a form of tax evasion.

The marriage penalty is smaller for couples whose individual incomes are less equal. Note also that married couples receive a "tax bonus" when the sum of the individual tax liabilities that they have incurred by filing singly exceeds their liability under a joint return; this situation often arises when one person earns most of the couple's income.

Strategy: Shift or Split Your Income

Income shifting (or **splitting**) occurs when a person paying income taxes at a high marginal rate shifts or splits income to another person who is in a lower tax bracket. The result is that the income is taxed at a lower tax rate or not taxed at all. Splitting may also prove beneficial when one person has few deductions and the other has many. The key to successful income splitting and shifting is to move income from a higher to a lower marginal tax rate. Techniques to accomplish that end include avoiding the kiddie tax rate, giving gifts, establishing trusts, and buying Series EE savings bonds for children.

Avoid the Kiddie Tax Rate   Children younger than age 14 pay no tax on the first $700 of net investment income (such as interest, dividends, and capital gains)

Calculate Taxable and Tax-Exempt Yields*

Taxpayers in higher tax brackets have the opportunity to lower their income tax liabilities by investing in tax-exempt municipal bonds, money market funds that invest in municipal bonds, and other tax-exempt ventures. Because of their tax-exempt status, these investments offer lower returns than taxable alternatives. On the other hand, a net return from a tax-exempt investment may be better than one from a taxable investment when assessed on an after-tax basis.

Depending upon the information available, there are two ways to compare taxable and tax-exempt yields.

First, when you know the taxable yield, you can solve for the tax-exempt yield by using the **tax-exempt equivalent yield (TEEY) formula:**

$$TEEY = \text{taxable yield} \times (1.00 - \text{federal marginal tax rate}) \quad (3.1)$$

For example, assume that you are subject to the 31 percent federal marginal tax rate and you are considering investing in a taxable bond yielding 7.7 percent. Substituting these figures into Equation (3.1), we have

$$\begin{aligned} TEEY &= 7.7 \times (1.00 - 0.31) \\ &= 7.7 \times 0.69 \\ &= 5.3\% \end{aligned}$$

Thus, the tax-exempt equivalent yield of 5.3 percent provides the same return after the impact of income taxes as a taxable investment yielding 7.7 percent. When offered a 7.7 percent taxable investment, a person paying income taxes at the 31 percent rate would do better by taking a tax-exempt investment paying more than 5.3 percent.

Second, if you know the tax-exempt yield, you can change the mathematics to solve for the taxable yield by using the **taxable equivalent yield (TEY) formula:**

$$TEY = \frac{\text{tax-exempt yield}}{(1.00 - \text{federal marginal tax rate})}$$

$$(3.2)$$

Using the same assumptions and substituting figures, we have

$$\begin{aligned} TEY &= \frac{5.3}{1.00 - 0.31} \\ &= \frac{5.3}{0.69} \\ &= 7.7\% \end{aligned}$$

Thus, a 7.7 percent taxable return is equivalent to a 5.3 percent tax-exempt yield. You would need to receive a taxable yield of more than 7.7 percent to do better than a tax-exempt yield of 5.3 percent.

Your yield on an investment may be further reduced (or increased) by the impact of state and local tax regulations. For example, residents of New York City who buy municipal bonds also enjoy exemption from state and city income taxes on the earnings from these bonds. People living in places with high state and local taxes especially benefit from tax-exempt investments. The states with the highest combined tax burden are New York, Maryland, Rhode Island, Maine, Connecticut, Wisconsin, Massachusetts, and Ohio, plus the District of Columbia. Tax-exempt bonds are examined in Chapter 14.

* These equations can be found and used on the *Garman/Forgue* Web site.

and the next $700 is taxed at the child's rate. After $1400, the child's income is affected by the IRS's **kiddie tax rate**—the parent's marginal tax rate (probably 28, 31, 36, or 39.6 percent) is applied on the investment income of a dependent child under age 14 in excess of $1400. The kiddie tax rate disappears when the child reaches age 14, at which point federal income taxes again are figured at the child's rate, typically 15 percent. The stategy is for a parent to shift some investments into the child's name so that investment income is taxed at the child's lower rate. Such shifting can be accomplished by giving a gift that earns income.

Give Gifts   People are allowed to make tax-free gifts of cash or property of as much as $10,000 a year—$20,000 if the money is given jointly with a spouse—to anyone, including children. Gifts in excess of the limit may be subject to the federal gift and estate tax (Chapter 19 discusses this condition in detail), and any such taxes assessed would be due on the estate of the donor. Such gifts are not tax deductions for the donor. A recipient does not owe any federal taxes on the value of any gift, although an income tax liability may begin to occur on any income earned after the transfer occurs.

Suppose a parent wants to establish a college fund for a two-year-old child and currently has $5000 in savings earning 4 percent interest income ($200 annually). If the parent opens a custodial account in the minor's name and gives the $5000 to the child, the parent will escape taxes on the interest income. To a parent in the 31 percent tax bracket, shifting income creates an immediate gain of $62 ($200 × 0.31), as that amount will not go to the government. Assuming that the child has no other source of taxable income, no taxes on the child's interest earnings on the $5000 must be paid. After 16 years with compound interest at 4 percent, the child's college fund will have grown to $9365 (see Appendix A.1). Under the Uniform Transfers to Minors Act (or the Uniform Gifts to Minors Act), a custodian (such as the parent) controls the assets until the child reaches the designated age for the account to end, such as 18 or 21; the child then gains full control of the account's contents.

Income shifting can also occur when someone chooses to give appreciated stocks or property that earns an income to a minor child instead of selling it. If the child sells the asset at age 14 or older, the gains will be taxed at his or her rate rather than the parent's presumed higher rate.

In addition to the $10,000 gift exclusion, taxpayers may make separate gifts (of any amount) for the educational tuition and medical expenses of their children, grandchildren, or other persons. These tax-avoidance techniques are examined in Chapter 19.

Establish Trusts   A **trust** is a legal instrument that places the control of an asset with a trustee. Many people establish trusts for their children's education and to

Education Expenses

An **education IRA** (individual retirement account) is a trust or custodial account set up to pay for higher education expenses for the designated beneficiary who must be younger than age 18. The maximum contribution is $500 per year. Although contributions are not tax-deductible, amounts deposited accumulate tax-free until distributed. Also, education expenses are tax-deductible for employees who are required by their employers to maintain and improve skills to advance their careers; such expenses generally are not deductible if the training readies the worker for a new career.

manage particular assets. Establishing a trust for yourself, a spouse, a relative, a friend, or a charity sometimes reduces income taxes. An experienced attorney is required to set up a trust, and Chapter 19 offers suggestions on alternative types of trusts.

Buy Series EE Savings Bonds for Children   Another way to shift the tax liability from parents to children is to buy Series EE government savings bonds in the name of a child. Reporting the income annually for the child results in little or no taxes compared with waiting until the bonds are redeemed and reporting all of the accrued interest at once. This occurs because Series EE savings bonds (discussed in Chapter 5) provide the investor with the option of reporting the interest income each year it is earned instead of reporting it as a lump sum when the bond is finally cashed in.

Strategy: Actively Manage a Real Estate Investment

Tax losses are paper losses, in the sense that they may not represent out-of-pocket dollar losses. They are created when deductions generated from an investment (such as depreciation) exceed the income from the investment. In recent years, the IRS has tightened restrictions on tax losses, in part by limiting certain types of deductions, such as tax losses generated through passive activities. **Passive activities** include rental operations and all other businesses in which the taxpayer does not materially participate (such as limited partnerships), although certain exceptions exist. Investors generally may not use passive-activity tax losses to offset ordinary taxable income, such as salary, interest, dividends, annuity, self-employment income, and stock market profits. Passive tax losses can be used only to offset income from passive investments. Disallowed losses may be carried forward to the next taxable year, when they may be used to offset new passive income.

One key IRS exception does permit taxpayers to deduct passive losses against salary or self-employment earnings. Deductions are allowed for real estate investors who (1) have an adjusted gross income of $150,000 or less and (2) actively participate in the management of the property. In such a case, the investor may deduct up to $25,000 of net losses from passive investments against income from "active" sources, such as salary and dividends. For example, a residential real estate investment property might generate an annual cash income $1000 greater than the out-of-pocket operating costs. After depreciation expenses on the building are taken as a tax deduction, the resulting $1500 tax loss may then be used to offset other income. This tax break begins to phase out for those with an AGI of $100,000.

Strategy: Buy and Sell Investments in Ways That Enhance Tax Advantages

A **tax swap** occurs when an investor sells one depressed security to register a tax loss and then immediately purchases another security that is similar, but not identical, for approximately the same price. Tax swaps permit investors to sell securities for a capital gains tax loss while upgrading the quality of their investments and maintaining their same investment approach.

Likewise, the tax code permits **like-kind free exchanges** through which the investor avoids paying income taxes on capital gains created by selling real estate or another type of depreciable property. This situation occurs when property (often vacation housing) is exchanged for a "like kind" of real estate. The transaction need not be a direct exchange. The property may be listed and sold as an exchange property with the proceeds going into an escrow account, which are later used to buy replacement property.

You should understand that one should not make an investment decision based on tax considerations alone. Although a number of special tax breaks are available to investors, each investment opportunity should be analyzed based upon the merits of the situation. A tax-advantaged investment that loses money is still a lousy investment.

Strategy: Bunch Deductions and Postpone Income

Many people find that they do not have enough itemized deductions to exceed the standard deduction amount. By shifting the payment dates of some deductible items, however, you can increase your deductions. For example, if a single person has about $3500 of deductible expenses each year, he or she could prepay some items in December of one year to push the total over the $4300 threshold and receive the tax advantage of having excess deductions. The next year the person can simply take the standard deduction amount. This process is known as **bunching deductions**. Some items that may be prepaid are medical expenses, dental bills, real estate taxes, state and local income taxes, the January payment of estimated state income taxes, personal property taxes that have been billed, dues in professional associations, and charitable contributions. You may mail the payments or charge them on credit cards by December 31.

You also may be able to save taxes by **postponing income**. If you expect a year-end commission check of $2000, for example, the extra income might be enough to push you into a higher marginal tax rate. If your employer is willing to give the commission check a January date, the income need not be reported until the next year, when tax rates might be lower. You might expect to be in a lower tax bracket in the following year because you anticipate less sales commissions, know that you will not work full time (for example, if you return to school, have a child, or decide to travel), or another reason. Retired people may be able to postpone voluntary distributions of income from retirement plans, and entrepreneurs may delay billing customers for work.

Strategy: Take All of Your Legal Tax Deductions

Although you should not spend money just to create a tax deduction, you are encouraged to take all of the deductions to which you are entitled. An almost guaranteed way to increase itemized deductions, for example, is to purchase a home with a mortgage loan. The large amounts of money homeowners expend for interest and real estate taxes are deductible.

Here are some other approaches to increase your deductions and return more tax dollars to your pocket. Assume you are in the 28 percent marginal tax bracket and itemize deductions. Cash contributions made to people collecting door to door or at a shopping center during holidays are deductible, even though receipts are not given. (The IRS reasonably expects people to make such contributions.) Fifty dollars in contributions deducted can save you $14 in taxes. Instead of throwing out an old television set, donate it. An $80 charitable contribution for a TV (get a receipt) will save you $22 in taxes. The IRS requires receipts for contributions valued at $500 or more as well as for cash contributions of $250 or more.

Expenses for business-related trips can be a most fruitful area for tax deductions. If you take one business trip per year, perhaps incurring $400 in deductible expenses, you will save another $112 in taxes, assuming your miscellaneous deductions already exceed 2 percent of your AGI. The IRS also permits tax deductions for the costs expended on occasional job-hunting trips. In other words, the U.S. government foots the bill for 28 percent of such expenditures.

The IRS Audits Some Tax Returns

7 Explain the basics of IRS audits.

Filing an income tax return represents a taxpayer's "first offer" to the Internal Revenue Service, and sometimes the IRS conducts an audit to determine whether additional taxes are due. A **tax audit** is a formal examination of a taxpayer's tax forms by the IRS for accuracy and completeness. Audits are conducted to enforce the collection of the proper amounts due, and they are generally limited to a three-year period after you file. Audits also motivate other taxpayers to complete their tax returns properly; if audited, people usually tell friends about it.

The Taxpayer Bill of Rights

The "Taxpayer Bill of Rights" protects taxpayers during IRS audit examinations and tax collection procedures. It requires that you be informed of your rights, have your chosen representative handle your case, and be permitted to record the examination. In addition, it exempts certain property from seizure, offers taxpayers hardship relief from IRS actions (such as property seizures or other collection measures), prohibits penalties when you rely upon previous IRS advice that proves to be erroneous, limits penalties and interest, protects spouses who innocently sign a bad return, and permits recovery of attorney fees and $100,000 in civil penalties if you prevail in court when the IRS has been negligent. Contrary to what might be suggested by publicity surrounding the recent IRS reform, taxpayers in a *regular* audit must prove that they are right and the IRS is wrong. The reverse is true in court proceedings only *if* the taxpayer has good records, makes credible claims, and cooperates with the IRS.

Reasonableness Tests

Of the more than 120 million tax returns filed each year in the United States, 98 percent go unchallenged by the IRS. With computer assistance, however, the IRS subjects every return to a series of computer-based **reasonableness tests.** These tests are based on average amounts (that are revised each year) for each category of deductions. If medical deductions usually average x for a married couple with two exemptions and a certain income, returns that exceed this average are selected by the IRS computer and flagged for examination by IRS employees who decide whether a particular taxpayer will be audited. Although not required, many taxpayers try to eliminate audit questions in advance by attaching a written explanation to a return to document an unusually large deduction. This tactic sometimes convinces the IRS not to conduct an audit. Other returns are audited on a random basis. Five out of six people audited wind up paying more taxes.

The IRS Wants Money, Not Jail Sentences

Only about 2000 people are convicted of tax evasion each year. The IRS wants money, not jail sentences. If the IRS disagrees with your deductions and disallows something, you will owe the increased tax liability, interest on that liability from the date the tax "should have" been paid, and a 5 to 50 percent penalty applied to the portion of any underpayment.

More serious fines and penalties exist if you willfully failed to pay tax, did not file a return, or willfully made and subscribed to a false return. Having a deduction disallowed generally does not result in a penalty, so be confident and take the deduction to which you feel entitled.

 Other Types of Federal, State, and Local Taxes

Other types of taxes supplement the federal income tax. The most important is collected under the Federal Insurance Contributions Act (FICA), whose funds are primarily used to pay for Social Security and Medicare benefits. The Social Security tax is discussed in detail in Chapter 18 and in Appendix B.

The FICA tax represents a tax on earnings, with equal amounts being paid by employers and employees; self-employed workers pay both portions. The FICA tax that pays for Social Security benefits is 6.2 percent applied on the first $72,600 of wages (for a maximum tax of $4501.20). The 1.45 percent FICA tax that pays for Medicare hospital insurance benefits applies to all wages. Thus, the combined FICA rate (for both Social Security and Medicare) of 7.65 percent applies where wages are $72,600 or less. For example, an employee earning $72,600 pays $5553.90 in Social Security taxes and his or her employer pays an additional $5553.90, for a total of $11,107.80; a self-employed person pays both portions, for a total of $11,107.80. The only ways to reduce your Social Security taxes are to participate in an employee health benefits premium conversion plan and to establish a flexible spending account.

Taxpayers also pay a considerable amount in personal income taxes to state and local governments. Reduction of these tax liabilities generally can be accomplished by reducing your federal taxable income and by studying the state and local tax guidelines, because the latter often permit special deductions not allowed on the federal form. For example, renter's credits are allowed in California, Hawaii, and Massachusetts. Several states permit tax reductions for installing energy-saving equipment. Alternatively, you could move to a low-tax state, such as Alaska, Wyoming, Nevada, Tennessee, or South Dakota or to a state with no income tax, such as Florida, New Hampshire, or Texas.

In total, approximately 31 percent of the average household's income goes to pay the various types of taxes. By carefully analyzing the subject of income taxes and utilizing proper planning, you can have more money available every year to spend, save, and invest—activities that are the focus of the rest of this book.

Keep Your Tax Records a Long Time

You should keep your tax records for at least three years—the standard statute of limitations time period during which the IRS can audit you. The IRS does have up to six years to conduct an audit if you have understated your income by at least 25 percent, however. No time limit applies if the IRS suspects fraud. You should never discard records relating to home purchases, contributions to pension accounts, and investments held for a number of years. Because you have the burden of proving that the numbers you provided the IRS are accurate, when in doubt about keeping a tax record, do not throw it out. Recordkeeping is fundamental in tax matters, and being able to prove your deductions is crucial to surviving an audit and keeping more of your money.

Summary

1. Taxes are compulsory charges imposed by a government on its citizens and their property. The Internal Revenue Service (IRS) issues various regulations, which are its interpretations of the laws passed by Congress, that have the force and effect of law.

2. The most important concept in personal finance is the marginal tax rate—the tax rate applied to your last dollar of earnings. Your effective marginal tax rate is even higher.

3. People who definitely should file an income tax return are those who want to get a refund of federal income taxes withheld and those who qualify for a tax credit.

4. To ensure that it receives the tax liability due to it, the government requires payroll withholding for most people and tax estimation for others.

5. Eight steps are involved in paring total income down to final tax liability, including subtracting exclusions, adjustments, deductions, exemptions, and credits.

6. Avoiding taxes is both desirable and respectable. A number of ways exist to legally avoid income taxes, such as bunching deductions, shifting income, establishing a flexible spending account at your place of employment, and using tax shelters.

7. Income tax returns are subjected to reasonableness tests, and some are audited.

Key Words & Concepts

adjustments to income   *67*
average tax rate   *59*
capital gain   *65*
earned income credit (EIC)   *74*
exemption   *61*
Form 1040-X   *60*
gross income   *64*
kiddie tax rate   *81*
marginal tax rate   *57*
passive activities   *83*
progressive tax   *56*
reasonableness tests   *85*
standard deduction   *67*
tax audit   *85*
tax avoidance   *74*
tax credits   *73*
tax-exempt income   *125*
tax shelter   *77*
taxable income   *55*
unearned income   *60*

Questions for Thought & Discussion

1. Summarize the importance of IRS rulings and regulations.

2. Distinguish between a progressive and regressive tax.

3. Give an example showing how one's effective marginal tax rate is higher than one's marginal tax rate.

4. Summarize the components of Susan Bassett's tax liability (Figure 3.1).

5. Explain and illustrate how the marginal tax rate differs from the average tax rate.

6. Name two instances in which it would be wise to file a tax return even if not required by law.

7. What requirements must be met to be exempt from payroll withholding taxes?

8. List the five types of major subtractions from gross income when calculating one's income taxes.

9. List five examples of income that must be reported to the IRS (perhaps noting those with which you were not previously familiar).

10. What is a capital gain, and how do long- and short-term capital gains differ?

11. List five examples of exclusions to income (perhaps noting those with which you were not previously familiar).

12. What are adjustments to income? Give two examples.

13. Summarize how a sideline business can reduce your income taxes.

14. Explain the term "standard deduction" and describe who should use it.

15. List five examples of tax-deductible items, excluding the miscellaneous categories (perhaps noting those with which you were not previously familiar).

16. List five examples of miscellaneous deductions (perhaps noting those with which you were not previously familiar).

17. Explain why you might claim different exemptions on your tax return and on your Form W-4.

18. Explain whether the parent or the 21-year-old college student receives the personal exemption when the student earned $3800 last year.

19. Briefly describe the value of one type of tax credit.

20. Differentiate between tax evasion and tax avoidance.

21. Illustrate the concept of opportunity cost with income taxes using an example not given in the text.

22. List two principles of reducing income taxes (perhaps ones with which you were not previously familiar) and indicate why they could be important.

23. Describe how a tax shelter works.

24. Explain how deferring income might be of value to a taxpayer.

25. Summarize how buying a home can reduce your income taxes.

26. Give an example that demonstrates how to calculate the tax-exempt equivalent yield when you know the taxable yield.

27. Explain how the marriage penalty affects taxpayers.

28. Give two examples of how to shift some income.

29. Explain the tax advantage of actively managing a real estate investment.

30. Explain how bunching deductions works to reduce the tax liability of some taxpayers.

31. What kinds of penalties exist for a taxpayer who loses in an IRS audit?

32. Who must pay the FICA tax?

DECISION-MAKING CASES

Case 1 A New Family Calculates Income and Tax Liability

Holly Bender lives with her new husband and son in Summit, Mississippi. She is employed as a union organizer and her husband manages a fast-food restaurant. The couple needs your advice about their income taxes.

(a) Which of the following types of the Benders' family income must be included as total income for the IRS: $32,000 in Holly's salary, $30,000 in Joe's salary, $10,000 in life insurance proceeds of deceased aunt, $140 in interest savings, $4380 in alimony from Holly's ex-husband, $1200 in child support from her ex-husband, $500 cash as a Christmas gift from Joe's parents, $90 from a friend who rides to work in Holly's vehicle, $60 in lottery winnings gained from playing the lottery at $5 every week, a $420 state income tax refund (since the Benders itemized last year), a $570 federal income tax refund, $170 worth of dental services traded for a quilt Holly gave to the dentist, and a $1600 tuition scholarship Holly received to go to college part-time last year?

(b) What is the total of the Benders' reportable gross income?

(c) If Holly and Joe put $2800 into qualified pension plan accounts last year, what is their adjusted gross income?

(d) How many exemptions can the Benders claim, and how much is the total value allowed the household?

(e) How much is the allowable standard deduction for the Bender household?

(f) Holly and Joe have listed their itemized deductions, which total $6287. Should the Benders itemize or take the standard deduction?

(g) What is the Bender family's taxable income?

(h) What is their final federal income tax liability? [For your calculations, use Table 3.2 or the *Garman/Forgue* Web site.]

(i) If Holly's and Joe's employers withheld $12,000 for income taxes, do they owe money to the government or do the Benders get a refund? How much?

Case 2 Taxable versus Tax-Exempt Bonds

Art Williams, radio station manager in Franklin Township, New Jersey, is in the 28 percent federal marginal tax bracket and pays an additional 8 percent in taxes to the state of New Jersey. Art currently has more than $20,000 invested in various corporate bonds earning differing amounts of taxable interest: $10,000 in ABC earning 9.0 percent, $5000 in DEF earning 8.2 percent, $3000 in GHI earning 7.8 percent, and $2000 in JKL earning 7.1 percent. His stockbroker has suggested that Art consider investing these same sums into tax-exempt municipal bonds, which currently pay a tax-free yield of 5.2 percent. What is your advice?

Use the *Garman/Forgue* Web site to calculate your answers, or use the after-tax equivalent formulas on page 81.

Case 3 Taxable versus Nontaxable Income

Identify each of the following items as either (a) taxable income or (b) an exclusion from taxable income for Bob and Ellen Smithfield: Bob earns $45,000 per year; Bob receives a $1000 bonus from his employer; Ellen receives $40,000 in commissions from her work; Ellen receives $300 in monthly child support; Bob pays $200 each month in alimony; Bob contributed $2000 to his tax-sheltered retirement account; Ellen inherited a car from her aunt that has a fair market value of $3000; and the Smithfields received a $5000 gift from Bob's mother.

Financial Math Questions

1. What would be the marginal tax rate for a single person who has a taxable income of (a) $15,000, (b) $27,000, and (c) $100,000? (Use Table 3.2.)

2. What would be (a) the tax liability for a single taxpayer who has a gross income of $37,000, (b) that person's average tax rate based on gross income, and (c) that person's average tax rate based on taxable income? (Use Table 3.2 and don't forget to subtract the value of a standard deduction and one exemption.)

3. Ramona Peterson determined the following tax information: gross salary, $19,000; qualified pension plan contribution, $1000; interest earned, $90; dividend income, $40; personal exemption, $2550; and itemized

deductions, $3150. Calculate Ramona's taxable income and tax liability. (Use Table 3.2.)

4. Mary and Dennis Roddmann determined the following tax information: gross salaries, $34,000 and $22,500, respectively; qualified pension plan contribution, $2000; interest earned, $140; dividend income, $500; personal exemptions, $5100; itemized deductions, $8150. Calculate the Roddmanns' taxable income and tax liability. (Use Table 3.2.)

5. Rick and Susan Maxey determined the following tax information: gross salaries, $14,000 and $5000, respectively; qualified pension plan contribution, $500; interest earned, $140; dividend income, $500; personal exemptions, $5100; itemized deductions, $1750. Calculate the Maxeys' taxable income and tax liability. (Use Table 3.2.)

6. Add $135 in taxable income to each of the three tax examples on pages 72–73, and calculate the tax liabilities for each example. (Use Tables 3.2 and 3.3.)

7. Using Table 3.2, find the tax liabilities based on the taxable income of the following people:

    (a) a married couple earning a total of $21,230

    (b) a married couple earning a total of $55,580

    (c) a single person earning $34,240

    (d) a single person earning $55,615

MONEY MATTERS: LIFE-CYCLE CASES

Victor and Maria Reduce Their Income Tax Liability

The year before last, Victor earned $41,000 from his retail management position and Maria earned $35,000 as a dental hygienist. After they took the standard deduction and claimed four exemptions (themselves plus their two children), their federal income tax liability totaled more than $11,000. After learning from friends that they were paying too much in taxes, they vowed to never again pay

that much. Therefore, the Hernandezes embarked on a year-long effort to reduce their income tax liability. This year, they tracked all of their possible itemized deductions and they each made contributions to qualified pension plans at their places of employment.

1. Calculate the Hernandezes' income tax liability for this year as a joint return given the following information: gross salary income (Victor, $43,000; Maria $37,000); state income tax refund ($400); interest on checking and savings accounts ($250); stock dividends ($300); car pool income from Maria's coworkers ($240); contributions to qualified retirement accounts ($4000); itemized deductions (real estate taxes, $4000; mortgage interest, $1500; charitable contributions, $1700); and four exemptions.

The Johnsons Calculate Their Income Taxes

Harry and Belinda are both working hard and earning good salaries. They believe, however, that they are paying too much in federal income taxes.

The Johnsons' total income included Harry's salary of $20,400, Belinda's salary of $24,800, $355 interest on savings and checking, $3000 interest income from the trust, a $90 reimbursement from Belinda's health insurance claim, a $210 state income tax refund (they did not itemize last year), a $390 federal income tax refund, and a $400 cash gift from Harry's aunt. The interest income from the trust is taxed in the same way as the interest income from their checking and savings accounts.

1. What is the Johnson's reportable gross income?

2. If Harry put $500 into an individual retirement account last year, what is their adjusted gross income?

3. Assuming that the Johnsons file a joint federal income tax return, what is the total value of their exemptions?

4. How much is the allowable standard deduction permissible for the Johnsons?

5. The couple has $5400 in itemized deductions. Should they itemize or take the standard deduction?

6. What is the Johnsons' taxable income?

7. Because the Johnsons have no tax credits, what is their tax liability?

8. Because they each had $4800 in federal income taxes withheld, how much of a refund will the Johnsons receive?

9. What is their marginal tax rate?

10. Based on gross income, what is their average tax rate?

11. List four or five ways that the Johnsons could reduce their tax liability for next year. Even though they are renters, assume the Johnsons had a home with monthly payments of $800, or $9600 for the year. Of this amount, the sum of $8400 might go for interest and real estate property taxes, both of which are tax-deductible. The couple would then have $13,800 ($8400 + $5400) in itemized deductions. Calculate their taxable income and tax liability, assuming $13,800 in itemized deductions instead of taking the standard deduction.

12. What is your advice to the Johnsons about the tax wisdom of purchasing a home instead of renting?

Exploring the World Wide Web of Personal Finance

To complete these exercises, go to the *Garman/Forgue* Web site at

www.hmco.com/college/business/

Select Personal Finance. Click on the exercise link for this chapter and answer the questions that appear on the Web page.

1. Do you know the state income tax rates for your home state? Visit the Web site for the Federal Tax Administrators, where you will find a table with tax rates for all states with an income tax. Based on what you found, what is your combined federal and state marginal tax rate?

2. Would you like to get a head start on next year's taxes? Visit the Internal Revenue Service Web site to view draft copies of the forms for the next tax year and get their release dates for public use. What forms would you need to use to file your taxes for next year?

3. Visit the Ernst & Young Tax and Financial Planning Corner Web site, where you will find lists of the 25 most common income tax mistakes and 50 of the most often overlooked deductions. Select three from each list that might be applicable to your tax situation.

4. Visit the *Tax Prophet*'s Frequently Asked Questions Web page, where you will find a listing of tax-related articles from the *San Francisco Herald Examiner*. Select two articles to read that are most applicable to your tax situation.

Budgeting and Cash-Flow Management

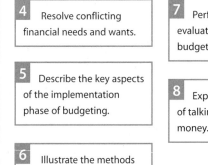

4

If you fail to plan, you plan to fail. Success in money matters requires that you implement your financial plans, which involves making choices and budgeting. Budgeting can help you make intelligent financial decisions that are consistent with your values and goals.

To start our discussion, we examine the relationship between personal financial planning and budgeting. This discussion prepares you for a fuller understanding of the process of budgeting: establishing specific financial goals, organizing, decision making, implementing, controlling, and evaluating. We end the chapter by describing how families can effectively talk about money, a topic difficult for many people to discuss.

The Relationship between Financial Planning and Budgeting

1 Describe the relationship between financial planning and budgeting.

The relationship between financial planning and budgeting is crucial to success in personal finance, because understanding this relationship serves as a positive motivation. In Chapter 2, we identified **financial planning** as the process of developing and implementing a coordinated series of financial plans and strategies to achieve financial success. This process includes the preparation of financial statements, such as the income and expense statement and the balance sheet. **Budgeting** is the process of projecting, organizing, monitoring, and controlling future income and expenditures (including cash and credit purchases as well as savings). Financial statements and budgets are some of the tools of financial planning.

Figure 4.1 illustrates an excellent way to think about budgets and financial statements. The income and expense statement focuses on where you have been financially, the balance sheet shows where you are are financially at the present time, and the budget indicates where you want to go in the future.

Your personal values are the starting point in financial planning and budgeting. **Values** are fundamental beliefs about what is important, desirable, and worthwhile. Your values serve as the basis for your financial goals. Once you identify your current financial position by examining information from your balance sheet and income and expense statement, plans can be developed for spending, risk management, and capital accumulation. Your financial goals evolve from plans, and both general and specific goals drive the creation of budgets.

A **budget** is a document or set of documents used to record both projected and actual income and expenditures over a period of time. The budgeting process represents the major mechanism through which financial plans are carried out and goals are achieved. Budgeting is narrower in scope than financial planning because it is primarily concerned with projecting future income and expenditures and reconciling the two with your financial goals.

Budgeting forces you to think about what is important in your life, what things you want to own, what it will take to obtain them, and, more generally, what you want to achieve in life. The process gives you control over your finances and empowers you to achieve your financial goals while simultaneously (and successfully) confronting any intervening events. The six-phase budgeting process illustrated in Figure 4.2 can be adapted to suit your needs while giving you the competence and confidence to manage your financial affairs successfully—forever.

Figure 4.1

Budgets and Financial Statements

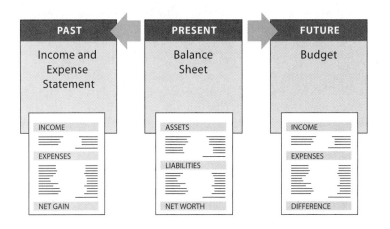

Figure 4.2

Phases in the Budgeting Process

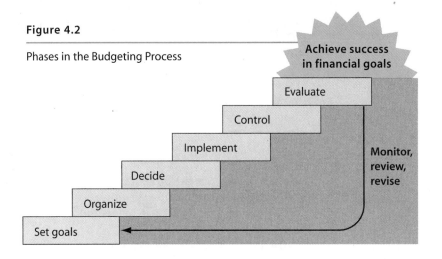

The Financial Goal-Setting Phase of Budgeting

Goal setting demands that you take a realistic look at future income and the amounts needed to reach established goals. It is *not* an exercise in wishful thinking, but requires careful and reasoned thinking. Financial goals were discussed in the context of financial planning in Chapter 2, although the goals discussed there were more general in nature and were tied directly to values. Here, in the **goal-setting phase of budgeting**, goals must be specific. They should contain dollar-amount targets (both in the long and short term) and target dates for achievement.

Setting Long-Term Goals

Long-term goals are financial targets or ends that an individual or family desires to achieve more than one year in the future—perhaps two, five, or even 30 years hence. Such goals provide direction for overall financial planning as well as shorter-term budgeting. For example, a long-term goal might be to save $22,500 within five years for a down payment on a home. Other goals might be more general, such as to have sufficient common stock investments by age 50 to receive dividends equivalent to 20 percent of your salary income.

If you have a small income or large debts, it may be unrealistic to think of long-term goals until any current financial difficulties are resolved. You may be unable to do much more than take care of immediate necessities, such as housing expenses, food, and utility bills. In such instances, you need to focus on short-term efforts to improve the financial situation.

Target dates may serve as checkpoints in your progress toward reaching long-term goals or as deadlines to indicate when a goal should be achieved. Nonetheless, long-term goals need to remain somewhat flexible given the length of time involved in achieving them. In addition, some goals may need to be changed if they prove unrealistic. As circumstances change, you should review and make adjustments or deletions. Likewise, as desired financial outcomes are achieved or changed, you can add new goals to your overall financial plans. An annual review of your progress in achieving long-term goals is a good idea.

Developing Short-Term Goals from Long-Term Goals

Short-term goals are financial targets or ends that can be achieved in a year or less. These goals should be consistent with the general direction of long-term goals and objectives. For example, if a long-term goal is to be debt-free in three years, a short-term objective might be to pay off a particular credit card balance within six months. Short-term goals provide the key input for the budget-making process. The task is to design a budget (perhaps covering one month at a time) that projects future expenditures and that, if followed, will permit you to reach your short-term goals.

You should explicitly express both long- and short-term goals when possible. The worksheet examples in Figure 4.3 provide rough estimates of how much must be saved to reach both types of goals. In particular, short-term goals must be stated clearly, or you will never know when you have achieved them. "To save enough for a down payment on an automobile," for example, is not as clear a

Figure 4.3

Goals Worksheet for Harry and Belinda Johnson

Date worksheet prepared	Jan. 20, 2000				
1	**2**	**3**	**4**	**5**	**6**
LONG-TERM GOALS	AMOUNT NEEDED	MONTH & YEAR NEEDED*	MONTHS TO SAVE	DATE START SAVING	MONTHLY AMOUNT TO SAVE (2 ÷ 4)
European vacation	$3,000	Aug. 2002	30	Feb. '00	$100
Down payment on new auto	5,000	Oct. 2003	45	Jan. '00	111
Down payment on home	22,500	Dec. 2004	60	Jan. '00	375

Date worksheet prepared	Jan. 20, 2000				
1	**2**	**3**	**4**	**5**	**6**
SHORT-TERM GOALS	AMOUNT NEEDED	MONTH & YEAR NEEDED*	MONTHS TO SAVE	DATE START SAVING	MONTHLY AMOUNT TO SAVE (2 ÷ 4)
Partial down payment on new auto	$1,332	Dec. '00	12	Jan. '00	$111
House fund	4,815	Dec. '00	12	Jan. '00	401
Christmas vacation	700	Dec. '00	12	Jan. '00	58
Summer vacation	600	Aug. '00	6	Feb. '00	100
Anniversary party	250	June '00	5	Jan. '00	50

* Goals requiring five years or more to achieve require consideration of investment return and after-tax yield, which will be presented in later chapters.

Achieve Your Financial Goals

The goal-setting process has six steps:

1. **Identify the goal** as specifically as possible.

2. **Set a deadline to reach it** and put intermediate target dates on long-term goals, thereby creating short-term goals.

3. **List obstacles** to the goal's achievement and devise strategies to overcome the obstacles.

4. **List your skills and knowledge and other people that will help you** reach the goal.

5. **List the benefits to yourself** that will occur when you reach the goal. You are most likely to achieve a goal when you are convinced that it really is "your goal," when you make an emotional commitment to the goal, when short-term goals lead to long-term goals, and when you can visualize yourself receiving its benefits.

6. **Establish an automatic savings account deposit plan** by using payroll withholding or electronic transfers from checking to savings accounts.

short-term goal as "to save $2400 by December of this year for a down payment on a new Ford Mustang."

Some short-term goals are ends in themselves because they can be fully achieved within one year. When placing dollar amounts on goals up to one or two years in the future, it is generally fair to assume that interest earned on savings will offset inflationary increases. Thus, you can simply divide the dollar amount of the long-term goal measured in today's price by the number of short-term time periods to determine the short-term goals.

For a time period exceeding one or two years, consider the example of Belinda Johnson, a salesperson for a stock brokerage firm, and her husband, Harry, an interior designer. Belinda and Harry are newlyweds who hope to buy their own home someday. They have decided to establish a five-year savings plan to purchase their first home. After studying the real estate market in their area, the couple figures that they will need 25 percent of the purchase price of the home for a down payment, moving expenses, and initial decorating costs. Condominiums that they would like and that seem to be affordable for first-time buyers are currently selling for around $90,000 in their area. Simple division would indicate that $22,250 would be necessary in five years. Belinda and Harry are sharp enough to realize, however, that housing costs have been rising about 3 percent per year in their community. Using Appendix A.1, they calculate that the type of housing they are considering will cost $104,310 ($90,000 × 1.159 from Appendix A.1) and require a nest egg of $26,078 ($104,310 × 0.25) in five years.* The Johnsons also know that their savings will earn interest that can be used to reach their goal. Using Appendix A.3, they calculate they would need to save $4815 per year ($26,078 divided by 5.416 from Appendix A.3) if they could earn 4 percent on their savings. Since the Johnsons budget monthly, they have

---

* You may wish to review the time value of money material from Chapter 1.

set a monthly goal of saving $401.25 ($4815 divided by 12) to achieve their first-year short-term goal (as indicated in Figure 4.3) on the way to buying their first home.*

Prioritizing Goals

Many people become discouraged in the goal-setting phase of budgeting because they quickly realize that they cannot achieve all of their goals immediately. Thus, it makes sense to attack the most important financial goals first. But what are the most important goals? One guideline is to pay off high-interest credit cards as soon as possible. Another is to contribute as much as possible to one's retirement plan. Don't be lured into following everyone else's approach. Many college graduates buy a new car soon after getting their first job because such a vehicle signifies having "made it." Give careful consideration to your priorities and recall that every action carries not only the dollar cost of the action taken, but also the opportunity cost of the alternatives foregone.

The Organization Phase of Budgeting

3 Establish the structural and mechanical aspects appropriate for your personal budget.

The **organization phase of budgeting** involves establishing the structural one's mechanical aspects appropriate for one's personalized budget. You should try to maintain a positive attitude toward budgeting by recognizing the value of recordkeeping, setting the recording format, selecting the cash or accrual basis of budgeting, determining which budgeting classifications are appropriate for you, and identifying the time period of your budget. Table 4.1 (p. 102) offers simple and complex budget classifications and Table 4.2 (p. 104) shows five sample budgets that you may consider using.

Select an Appropriate Recordkeeping Format

Recordkeeping, the process of recording the sources and amount of dollars earned and spent, is an integral part of the budgeting process. Its primary value lies in providing detailed information about what happened financially during any given period of time. Recording the estimated and actual amounts for both income and expenditures will help you monitor your money flow. Keeping track of income and expenses may seem an uninteresting task, but it is the only way to collect sufficient information to evaluate how close you are to achieving your financial objectives. You can create your own recordkeeping format to suit your needs or you can purchase forms that satisfy your needs. Figure 4.4 shows four samples of self-prepared budget records that vary in complexity. In the next section of this chapter, you will learn how budget data are recorded.

* Note that their savings each month would also earn interest resulting in monthly, rather than annual, compounding. Appendix A.3 cannot be used to make such fine distinctions. Using a financial calculator, we more accurately calculated a monthly savings amount of $398.34. While the difference is minor here, when long time horizons are involved, frequent compounding can mean additional thousands of dollars.

Figure 4.4   Recordkeeping Formats

(a) Simple form for each budget classification

Food Budget: $90			
DATE	ACTIVITY	AMOUNT	BALANCE
2-6	Groceries	$20	$70
2-9	Dinner out	8	62
2-14	Groceries	11	51

(b) More complex form for each classification

DATE	ACTIVITY	AMOUNT BUDGETED	EXPENDITURES	BALANCE
2-1	Budget estimate	$90		$90
2-6	Groceries		$20	70
2-9	Dinner out		8	62
2-14	Groceries		11	51
2-20	Groceries		25	26
2-26	Dinner out		10	16
2-28	Groceries		9	7
2-28	February Totals	$90	$83	$7

(c) Simple form for all expense classifications

DATE	ACTIVITY	Food Budget: $90	Clothing Budget: $30	EXPENDITURES Auto Budget: $60	Rent Budget: $275	Savings Budget: $60	Utilities Budget: $40	TOTAL Budget: $680	REMARKS
2-1	Gasoline			10				10	
2-6	Groceries	20						20	Had friends over
2-8	Gasoline			7				7	Good price
2-9	Dinner out	8						8	
2-14	Groceries	11						11	Pepsi on sale
2-15	Subtotals	/39		/17				/56	
2-16	Telephone						41	41	
2-17	Tire			64				64	Emergency

(d) More complex form for all income and expenditure classifications

			INCOME Salary	Other	TOTAL	EXPENDITURES Food	Clothing	Auto	Rent	Savings	Utilities	TOTAL	REMARKS
	Estimates		700	40	740	90	30	60	275	60	40	680	
	Balance forwarded from January		—	—	—	6	—	14	—	—	2	28	
	Sum		700	40	740	96	30	74	275	60	42	708	
DATE	ACTIVITY	CASH IN											
2-1	Paycheck	700	700										
2-1	Texaco-gasoline							10				10	
2-6	Safeway-groceries					20						20	Had friends over
2-8	7/11-gasoline							7				7	Good price
2-9	Dinner out-pizza					8						8	
2-14	Giant-groceries					11						11	Pepsi on sale
2-15	Subtotals	/700				/39		/17				/56	
2-16	AT+T-telephone										41	41	
2-17	Goodyear-tire							64				64	Emergency
2-28	Totals	700		40	740	83	28	87	275	60	41	660	Good month

Alternatively, you can purchase a computer software program designed specifically for budgeting or use a spreadsheet program such as Microsoft Excel. Quicken, a popular software program that accompanies this book, is excellent for budgeting. (The *Garman/Forgue* Web site provides a budget template as well as several financial calculators which might be useful for your budgeting needs.) Computerized recordkeeping has many advantages, especially the ability to make adjustments, corrections, and updates.

Use the Cash or Accrual Basis

You can use either of two systems of financial recording in your budgeting process. **Cash-basis budgeting** recognizes earnings and expenditures when money is actually received or paid out. **Accrual-basis budgeting** recognizes earnings and expenditures when the money is earned and expenditures are incurred, regardless of when money is actually received or paid. Most people follow the cash basis in the budgeting process because it is easier to use. Either method will work as long as you use it consistently.

Select Appropriate Budget Classifications

There are two broad budgeting classifications: *income* (money earned or received) and *expenditures* (money spent). Each can be subdivided into more detailed classifications.

Table 4.1 lists both simple and complex budget classifications for income and expenses. Even though the simple budgeting classifications illustrated in the table include only 12 expense items, they represent a suitable format for many people. (Some computer programs offer more than 100 budget classifications.) A danger exists when too many expenditures are classified under "miscellaneous," lowering the information value of the classification. You can divide any extraordinarily broad categories into more detailed classifications when more specificity is warranted. When the miscellaneous classification amounts to more than 5 percent of the total expenditures, for example, you could simply review the items included and create additional classifications.

It is important in setting up budget classifications to note the four different ways that savings can be categorized: (1) savings withheld from a paycheck and deposited directly to a savings account; (2) savings as a fixed expenditure; (3) savings as a variable expenditure; and (4) savings as the remainder after all other expenditures are paid. The first two methods embody the concept of "pay yourself first"—saving and investing before you pay other expenses—one of the major precepts of personal financial planning. The problem with relying solely on the last two methods is that you might not save at all.

Select Appropriate Time Periods

Many people who budget create a plan to cover income and expenses for a 12-month period. Most also develop monthly budgets because they receive their paychecks on a monthly or semimonthly basis. Using this shorter timeframe

Table 4.1

Sample Budget Classifications and Expense Guidelines

	Income	Fixed Expenses*	Variable Expenses*
Simple	Salary Nonsalary	Housing and utilities (25–45%) Insurance (2–10%) Savings and investments (6–20%) Taxes (8–20%)	Food (12–30%)[†] Transportation (3–10%) Clothing (1–10%) Health care (2–8%) Entertainment / vacations (2–10%) Personal / miscellaneous (2–5%) Credit payments (0–15%) Gifts and contributions (1–10%)
Complex	Salary Rent Interest Dividends Capital gains Tax refunds Loans Other	Pension contributions Individual retirement account Home mortgage loan Life insurance Health insurance Disability insurance Homeowner's insurance Automobile insurance Cable television Church Other contributions Christmas gifts Automobile loan or lease Loan 1 Loan 2 Dues and club memberships Savings (withheld from salary) Federal income taxes State income taxes Social Security taxes Real estate property taxes Personal property taxes Mutual fund investment Monthly investment plan Child support / alimony	Revolving budget savings fund Other savings Food at home Food away from home Electricity and gas Water Telephone Gasoline and oil Automobile maintenance / repairs Automobile licence renewal Automobile registration Public transportation Home maintenance / renovations Gifts Doctors and dentists Medicines and drugs Hospital bills Veterinary costs Legal advice Child care Domestic help Clothing and accessories Hobby supplies Sports equipment CDs, DATs, tapes, and records Books Newspaper / magazine subscriptions Tobacco products Alcoholic beverages Education and tuition School books and supplies Furnishings and appliances Personal care products Entertainment / recreation Vacations / long weekends Credit card 1 Credit card 2 Investments—other

* The percentages represent the range of expenses of various family units.

† The U.S. Department of Agriculture reports that more than half of all meals are eaten outside the home.

enables you to identify and control your financial activities and to maintain accurate records. These monthly budgets blend nicely with an annual budget and with financial statements (net worth and cash flow) that are also usually compiled on an annual basis.

The Decision-Making Phase of Budgeting

4 Resolve conflicting financial needs and wants.

The **decision-making phase of budgeting** focuses on the financial aspects of budgeting and the decisions about the sources of funds as well as their destination. As a financial manager, you should begin by examining the anticipated impact of inflation and economic conditions on your budget. You should next make realistic budget estimates for income and expenditures and then resolve conflicting needs and wants by revising estimates as necessary.

Inflation and Other Economic Factors

Inflation is perhaps the single most influential factor affecting budgets because it affects the prices you must pay for the expenditure items in your budget. If food prices are rising 5 percent per year, a food budget of $250 per month would need to increase to $262.50 after just 12 months. If you anticipate inflationary increases, you will be less likely to be caught unprepared for necessary changes in your budget.

An increase in interest rates can have a serious effect on budgeting because the amount allocated for credit purchases may need to be increased. Suppose it is January and you are planning to buy a $200,000 home with a $40,000 down payment; at that time you may obtain a 30-year mortgage loan at 7 percent for the balance. By July, the interest rates may have risen (or fallen). If you must wait until July to buy the home and interest rates have increased by just one percentage point, you may have a monthly mortgage payment of $1174 instead of $1064. Suggestions on how to predict inflation and other economic factors are offered in Chapter 1.

Realistic Budget Estimates

Budget estimates are the projected dollar amounts in a budget that one plans to receive or spend during the period covered by the budget. Most people begin by estimating either their total gross income from all sources or their disposable income. **Disposable income**—income received after taxes and all other employer withholdings—represents the money available for spending, saving, and investing.

Bear in mind that a budget is a working tool, and that it should remain flexible. Do not treat a budget as if it were engraved in stone. Instead, make and use a budget to fulfill your changing needs, wants, and goals. Another aspect of financial flexibility is planning your budget to produce substantial **discretionary income.** This income is the money left over once the necessities of living are funded.

Everyone's budgeted expenses are different because people's lives vary. Nonetheless, it is useful to review how other people allocate their money when

Table 4.2

Sample Monthly Budgeted Expenses for Various Family Units*

Classifications	College Student	Single Working Person	Young Married Couple	Married Couple with Two Young Children	Married Couple with Two College-Age Children
INCOME					
Salary	$ 300	$1700	$1600	$2000	$2200
Salary	—	—	1400	160	600
Interest and dividends	5	15	15	15	80
Loans / scholarships	200	—	—	—	—
Savings withdrawals	570	—	—	—	500
TOTAL INCOME	**$1075**	**$1715**	**$3015**	**$2175**	**$3380**
Fixed expenses					
Pension contributions	$ —	$ 20	$ 40	$ —	$ 100
Individual retirement account	—	20	160	—	105
Savings (withheld)	—	20	20	10	100
Housing	250	250	400	400	600
Health insurance	—	— †	60 †	70 †	70 †
Life and disability insurance	—	— †	10 †	15 †	15 †
Homeowner's or renter's insurance	—	—	10	10	15
Automobile insurance	—	40	60	40	60
Automobile loan payments	—	230	200	150	—
Loan 1 (TV and stereo)	—	80	80	40	—
Loan 2 (Other)	—	40	40	—	50
Federal and state taxes	30	290	520	320	480
Social Security taxes	23	130	230	165	210
Real estate taxes	—	—	—	—	40
Personal property taxes	—	5	10	10	10
Investments	—	—	60	5	50
Total fixed expenses	**$ 303**	**$1125**	**$1900**	**$1235**	**$1905**
Variable expenses					
Revolving budget savings fund	$ —	$ 40	$ 50	$ 50	$ 45
Other savings	—	—	150	—	—
Food	180	120	280	240	200
Utilities	40	50	60	70	90
Automobile gas, oil, maintenance	—	60	60	60	100
Medical	10	30	40	70	50
Child care	—	—	—	60	—
Clothing	20	50	60	50	40
Gifts and contributions	10	20	40	60	80
Vices	20	40	60	40	40
Education	400	—	—	—	500
Furnishings and appliances	10	10	30	20	20
Personal care	10	15	25	30	30
Entertainment	40	60	100	60	120
Vacations	17	30	40	30	60
Credit card 1	—	20	20	20	20
Credit card 2	—	—	20	20	—
Miscellaneous	15	45	80	60	80
Total variable expenses	**$ 772**	**$ 590**	**$1115**	**$ 940**	**$1475**
TOTAL EXPENSES	**$1075**	**$1715**	**$3015**	**$2175**	**$3380**

* Government surveys for a recent year reveal the following percentages of expenditures for various categories of spending: all food, 13.9; housing, 31.8; apparel and services, 5.2; transportation, 19.0; health care, 5.6; entertainment, 4.9; personal insurance and pensions, 9.3; and other, 10.3.

† Over and above the amount subsidized or provided by employer.

planning your own budget. Table 4.2 presents budget estimates for a college student, a single working person, a young married couple, a married couple with two young children, and a married couple with two college-age children.

Note that the college student's budget given in Table 4.2 requires monthly withdrawals of previously deposited savings to make ends meet. The single working person's budget allows for an automobile loan but not much else. The young married couple's budget permits one automobile loan, an investment program, contributions to individual retirement accounts, and significant spending on food and entertainment. The budget of the married couple with two young children allows for only an inexpensive automobile loan payment; note that one spouse has a part-time job to help with the finances. In contrast, the budget of the married couple with two college-age children permits a home mortgage payment, ownership of two paid-for automobiles, savings and investment programs, and a substantial contribution for college expenses.

To make realistic estimates of income and expenses, reliable financial information is critical. The more accurate the estimates, the more effective the budget. Most people begin by making budget estimates for one pay period and then multiply by the number of pay periods per year to obtain annual budget figures. Although accuracy is important, rounding figures to the nearest dollar (or sometimes even $5) is usually sufficient.

Information from the income and expense statement developed during the financial planning process (described in Chapter 2) is a good resource for making estimates. If such a statement is unavailable, other sources of information may be substituted. For income data, look at your copies of the previous year's income tax forms. Alternatively, you can review payroll stubs for gross income information as well as the amounts withheld for taxes, insurance, and the like.

For fixed expenses such as rent and automobile insurance premiums, use payment stubs and information from your checkbook. Variable expenses are more difficult to estimate, so review the sample budgets of others (as illustrated in Table 4.2) and the expense guidelines in Table 4.1. When you lack previous financial records, you might find it useful to keep a detailed log of expenditures for one or two months and then make your initial budget estimates.

It is essential to make reasonable estimates for things you already have planned. If you have seven Christmas gifts to buy and expect to spend $50 for each, it's easy to make an estimate of $350. If you want to go out to dinner once each week at $30 per meal, you might estimate an expense of $120 per month. Avoid using unrealistically low figures because these low estimates can prove very frustrating when higher expenditures occur in reality. Simply be fair and honest in your estimates. The next step is to add up your total budget estimates for monthly or annual income and expenses.

Reconciling Budget Estimates

Many people are shocked when their initial expense estimates far exceed their income estimates in their budget. Only three choices are available in such cases: (1) earn more income; (2) cut back expenses; or (3) try a combination of more income and less expenses.

Extra income, of course, is usually hard to find. Therefore, the immediate task is to decide what is really important in the budget. You must reconcile conflicting wants to revise your budget until total expenses do not exceed income.

This process is known as **reconciling budget estimates.** First, review the fixed expenditures to see if they are accurate and are all truly necessary. Next, look at each of the variable expenditures and change some "must haves" to "maybe next year." Perhaps you might keep some quality items but reduce their quantity. For example, instead of $120 for four meals at restaurants each month, consider dining out twice each month at $30 per meal. Table 4.3 on the following page illustrates the annual budget for Harry and Belinda Johnson and reflects their efforts to reconcile budget estimates until total planned expenses fall below total planned income. Note that Harry and Belinda are "paying themselves first," in the amount of $400 per month, to save to buy their own home.

While sometimes uncomfortable, the process of reconciling needs and wants is a healthy exercise. It helps identify your priorities by telling you what is important in your life at the present time. It also suggests sacrifices that you might make. The process of reconciling your financial wants and needs in making and revising budget estimates is vital to achieving your financial goals.

The Implementation Phase of Budgeting

> **5** Describe the key aspects of the implementation phase of budgeting.

In the **implementation phase of budgeting,** you put the budget into effect. Specifically, you record expenditures made and income received during the budget time period, manage cash-flow problems, determine totals for the time period, and prepare financial statements.

Recording Actual Income and Expenditures

An **expenditure** is an amount of money that has been spent. You may plan a budgetary expense but, when the money has been spent, it becomes an actual expenditure. It is important to keep an accurate and up-to-date record of expenditures. Having them handy may remind you to record expenditures frequently. If you have a good memory or keep a notepad in your pocket or purse for that purpose, expenditures can be formally recorded every few days.

When writing data in the "activity" column in your record, be descriptive (as shown in Figure 4.4), as you may need such information later. Many people also write comments in a "remarks" column in their records for the same reason, as shown in parts (c) and (d) of Figure 4.4. Use a pencil so that corrections or revisions are easier to make.

Managing with a Cash-Flow Calendar

For most people, income remains somewhat constant month after month, but planned expenses can rise and fall sharply. As a result, people occasionally complain that they are "broke, out of money, and sick of budgeting." As you will see, this problem can be *anticipated* by the creation of a cash-flow calendar and *eliminated* through the use of a revolving savings fund.

The budget estimates for monthly income and expenses in Table 4.3 have been placed in summary form in Table 4.4 on page 108, providing a **cash-flow calendar** for the Johnsons. Annual estimated income and expenses are recorded in this calendar for each budgeting time period in an effort to identify surplus or

Table 4.3

Annual Budget Estimates for 2000 for Harry and Belinda Johnson (Prepared December 15, 1999)

	Jan.	Feb.	Mar.	Apr.	May	June	July	Aug.	Sept.	Oct.	Nov.	Dec.	Yearly Total	Monthly Average
INCOME														
Harry's salary	$1,700	$1,700	$1,700	$1,700	$1,700	$1,700	$1,775	$1,775	$1,775	$1,775	$1,775	$1,775	$20,850	$1,737.50
Belinda's salary	2,150	2,150	2,350	2,350	2,350	2,350	2,350	2,350	2,350	2,350	2,350	2,350	27,800	2,316.67
Interest	15	20	20	30	30	35	35	35	35	40	40	20	355	29.58
Trust	—	—	—	—	—	—	—	—	3,000	—	—	—	3,000	250.00
TOTAL INCOME	$3,865	3,870	4,070	4,080	4,080	4,085	4,160	4,160	7,160	4,165	4,165	4,145	52,005	4,333.75
Fixed expenses														
Rent	600	600	600	600	600	600	625	625	625	625	625	625	7,350	612.50
Health insurance	85	85	85	85	85	85	85	85	85	85	85	85	1,020	85.00
Life insurance	9	9	9	9	9	9	9	9	9	9	9	9	108	9.00
Home purchase fund	400	400	400	400	400	400	400	400	400	400	400	400	4,800	400.00
Renter's insurance	—	—	—	—	—	110	—	—	—	—	—	—	110	9.17
Automobile insurance	—	—	—	—	—	320	—	—	—	—	—	320	640	53.33
Automobile loan payments	285	285	285	285	285	285	285	285	285	285	285	285	3,420	285.00
Student loan	145	145	145	145	145	145	145	145	145	145	145	145	1,740	145.00
Savings	60	60	60	60	60	60	60	60	60	60	60	60	720	60.00
Health club	50	50	50	50	50	50	50	50	50	50	50	50	600	50.00
Cable television	20	20	20	20	20	20	20	20	20	20	20	20	240	20.00
Federal income taxes	490	490	490	490	490	490	490	490	490	490	490	490	5,880	490.00
State income taxes	130	130	130	130	130	130	130	130	130	130	130	130	1,560	130.00
Social Security taxes	295	295	310	310	310	310	315	315	315	315	315	315	3,720	310.00
Total fixed expenses	$2,569	2,569	2,584	2,584	2,584	3,014	2,614	2,614	2,614	2,614	2,614	2,934	31,908	2,659.00
Variable expenses														
Savings/investments long-term	—	—	—	—	—	—	—	—	—	—	—	—	—	—
Revolving savings fund	220	220	220	220	220	(80)	70	(530)	70	70	—	(700)	0	—
Food	360	360	360	360	360	360	360	360	360	360	360	360	4,320	360.00
Utilities	100	100	100	100	50	50	50	50	50	75	75	100	900	75.00
Telephone	70	70	70	70	70	70	70	70	50	70	70	90	840	70.00
Automobile gas / maintenance	45	45	265	45	45	45	45	45	45	45	45	45	760	63.33
Medical	60	60	60	60	60	60	60	60	60	60	60	60	720	60.00
Clothing	160	160	160	160	160	160	160	160	160	160	160	160	1,920	160.00
Church and charity	100	100	100	100	175	100	100	100	100	100	100	100	1,275	106.25
Gifts	80	80	105	65	145	25	20	60	60	60	60	20	780	65.00
Christmas gifts	—	—	—	—	—	—	—	—	—	—	—	—	—	—
Public transportation	50	50	50	50	50	50	50	50	50	50	50	50	600	50.00
Personal allowances	155	155	155	155	155	155	155	155	155	155	155	155	1,860	155.00
Entertainment	130	130	130	130	130	130	130	130	130	130	130	130	1,560	130.00
Automobile license	—	—	—	—	—	40	—	—	—	—	—	—	40	3.33
Vacation–Christmas*	—	—	—	—	—	—	—	—	—	—	—	700	700	58.33
Vacation–summer*	—	—	—	—	—	—	—	600	—	—	—	—	600	50.00
Anniversary party*	—	—	—	—	—	250	—	—	—	—	—	—	250	20.83
Miscellaneous	75	75	75	75	75	75	75	75	75	75	75	75	900	75.00
Total variable expenses	$1,605	1,605	1,850	1,590	1,695	1,490	1,345	1,385	1,365	1,410	1,340	1,345	18,025	1,502.08
TOTAL EXPENSES	$4,174	4,174	4,434	4,174	4,279	4,504	3,959	3,999	3,979	4,024	3,954	4,279	49,933	4,161.08
Difference (available for spending, saving, and investing)	($309)	($304)	($364)	($ 94)	($199)	($419)	$201	$161	$3181	$141	$211	($134)	$2072	$172.67

* Provided for in revolving savings fund.

Table 4.4

Cash-Flow Calendar for Harry and Belinda Johnson

Month	1 Estimated Income	2 Estimated Expenses	3 Surplus / Deficit (1 – 2)	4 Cumulative Surplus / Deficit
January	$3,865	$4,174	− $309	− $309
February	3,870	4,174	− 304	− 613
March	4,070	4,434	− 364	− 977
April	4,080	4,174	− 94	− 1,071
May	4,080	4,279	− 199	− 1,270
June	4,085	4,504	− 419	− 1,689
July	4,160	3,959	+ 201	− 1,488
August	4,160	3,999	+ 161	− 1,327
September	7,160	3,979	+3,181	+ 1,854
October	4,165	4,024	+ 141	+ 1,995
November	4,165	3,954	+ 211	+ 2,206
December	4,145	4,279	− 134	+ 2,072
Totals	$52,005	$49,933	—	+$2,072

deficit situations. In the Johnsons' case, planned annual income exceeds expenses. However, they start out the year with many expenses, resulting in deficits for the next six months. Later in the year, income usually exceeds expenses, resulting in a planned surplus at year's end.

Effective management of cash flow can involve curtailing expenses during months with financial deficits, increasing income, using savings, or borrowing. If you borrow money and must pay finance charges, the credit costs further push up monthly expenses. It is better to borrow from yourself using a revolving savings fund.

Utilizing a Revolving Savings Fund

In its simplest form, a **revolving savings fund** is a variable expense classification in budgeting into which funds are allocated in an effort to create savings that can be used to balance the budget later so as to avoid running out of money. Establishing such a fund involves planning ahead—much like a college student does when saving money all summer (creating a revolving savings fund) to draw on during the school months. Most people need to establish a revolving savings fund for two purposes: (1) to accumulate funds for large irregular expenses, such as automobile insurance premiums, medical costs, Christmas gifts, and vacations; and (2) to meet occasional deficits due to income fluctuations.

The Johnsons' revolving savings fund is shown in worksheet format in Table 4.5 on page 109. It provides only enough savings to cover expenses for their planned vacations and anniversary party. Their revolving savings fund does not contain enough money to cover their frequent monthly deficits in cash flow,

Table 4.5

Worksheet for Revolving Savings Fund for Large Irregular or Revolving Expenses
(for Harry and Belinda Johnson)*

YEAR 2000 Month (describe expense items)	Amount Needed to Cover Large Expenses	Deposit in Reserve Savings Fund	Paid from Reserve Fund	Reserve Savings Fund Balance
Beginning balance				— †
January		$220		$ 220
February		220		440
March		220		660
April		220		880
May		220		1100
June —Anniversary party	$250	170	250	1020
July		70		1090
August —Vacation	600	70	600	560
September		70		630
October		70		700
November		—		700
December —Christmas	700	—	700	—†
Totals	$1550	$1550	$1550	

Total Large Irregular Expenses = __$1550__ divided by 12 = __$129.17__ , which is the
minimum amount to be deposited in reserve each month, depending when the funds are needed.

* Harry and Belinda, being newlyweds, started the year with a zero beginning balance. Next year they will
 begin the year with a balance of $2072 (see Tables 4.3 and 4.4).
† These amounts should be the same (zero for the Johnsons).

however. The revolving savings fund concept works wonderfully *only* if the fund contains enough money to cover the largest cumulative deficit. Thus, the Johnsons need $1689 (the June figure in Table 4.4). Lacking that much money, the couple has two alternatives: to borrow money to cover deficits during the first several months of the year or to cut back on expenses enough to create surpluses during these months. They could also use a combination of the two alternatives. Note also in Table 4.4 that the Johnsons have a planned surplus of $2072 at the end of December. This amount should be more than enough to create a revolving savings fund to begin the new year so that they will not face planned deficits again.

Calculating Time-Period Totals

After the budgeting period has ended—usually at the beginning of a new month—you need to add up the actual income received and expenditures made during that period. You can perform this calculation on a form for each budget classification, as shown in parts (a) and (b) of Figure 4.4, or on a form with all income and expenditure classifications, as in parts (c) and (d) of Figure 4.4. Such calculations indicate where you may have overspent within your budget categories. If you are new at budgeting, do not be too concerned about overspending; it occurs in some classifications almost always, only to be balanced by underspending in other categories. Use such information to refine your budget estimates in the future, and in three or four months you will be able to estimate your expenses much more accurately.

The Control Phase of Budgeting

6   Illustrate the methods and techniques to keep income and expenditures within planned budget totals.

In the **control phase of budgeting**, an individual or family uses various methods and techniques to keep income and expenditures within the planned budget totals. The control phase occurs *simultaneously* with the implementation phase, because the best time to control spending is during the budget time period.

Reasons for Budget Controls

Budget controls tell you whether you are on target and how well you are progressing on a financial level; they also alert you to such problems as errors, overexpenditures, emergencies, and exceptions or omissions. For example, when Postal Service employee Barbara DelRio of Dayton, Ohio, examined her budget figures for the month of May, she discovered that her "cash out" column equaled $1596 while all other expenditure columns totaled only $1532. The two figures should be the same if she had recorded all transactions and added all figures correctly. Thus, this cross-check serves as a built-in control. It is futile to try to account for every single dollar because some cash is bound to "slip away" every month. However, a difference of $64 ($1596 − $1532) indicates that something is wrong, and that Barbara likely omitted some expenditure item.

Comparing totals represents a valuable control built into the recording process. The controls used should not, of course, be treated as absolute mandates with penalties should there be errors. Instead, they simply inform you that you need to reexamine your budgeting practice and remedy any missteps.

Seven Budget Control Measures

Suggestions for controlling a budget include the following: (1) use a checking account; (2) employ a credit controlsheet; (3) check accuracy; (4) monitor unexpended balances; (5) justify exceptions; (6) use the envelope system; and (7) employ subordinate budgets.

Use a Checking Account   If you use cash frequently instead of checks, you may have trouble tracking the amount you spend. You must retain many receipts and write the purpose of each expense on the back of each receipt; you should also keep a daily log that includes expenditures for which you obtained no receipt. Checks, on the other hand, provide a record of the business or person with whom you did business, and each check contains a space to record the purpose, as shown in Figure 4.5. It is also good control to deposit all checks received to your checking account without receiving a portion in cash; if you need cash, write a check.

Figure 4.5

Check with Explanation Space

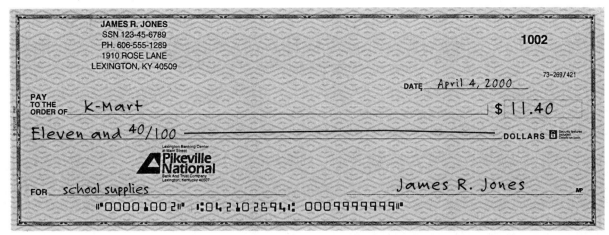

Source: Courtesy of Pikeville National Bank, Pikeville, KY.

Check Register

CHECK NO.	DATE	DESCRIPTION OF TRANSACTION	AMOUNT OF CHECK		FEE (–)	✔ T	AMOUNT OF DEPOSIT		BALANCE FORWARD	
									290	51
1001	4/2	Angelo's Pizza	9	80					9	80
		supper							280	71
—	4/3	Deposit					100	00	100	00
		Birthday from Aunt Lin							380	71
1002	4/4	K-Mart	11	40					11	40
		school supplies							369	31

It is easy to write a check in haste without recording its purpose on the front of the check. The check stub or register (also shown in Figure 4.5) provides a handy place to record explanations of expenditures. A special concern arises with people who use automatic teller machines (ATMs) frequently to withdraw cash or use debit cards for day-to-day expenditures. These withdrawals should be recorded in the check register *immediately*. Further, the budget expenditure category for which the funds were used must be recorded so that the budget balance can be appropriately adjusted. You should establish a habit of safeguarding ATM and debit card receipts by always putting them in the same place in your wallet or handbag and filing them safely when you return home.

Employ a Credit Controlsheet Figure 4.6 shows a sample **credit controlsheet** that can monitor credit use, amounts owed, and parties to whom debts are owed. This form can keep you abreast of outstanding credit obligations and allows you to cross-check easily the credit-flow checksheet with credit statements received in the mail.

Figure 4.6

Credit Controlsheet

Credit flow for		Jan.—Mar.								
DATE	PURPOSE FOR CREDIT	VISA		MASTERCARD		AMES Dept. Store		SUMMARY All Creditors		
		Chg (Pay)	Balance	Chg (Pay)	Balance	Chg (Pay)	Balance	Chgs	Paid	Balance
1-2	Gas for car	14.95	14.95					14.95		14.95
1-2	Clothing					32.00	32.00	32.00		46.95
1-15	Paid Visa	(14.95)	- 0 -						14.95	32.00
1-27	New desk			320.00	320.00			320.00		352.00
2-12	Gas for car	20.00	20.00					20.00		372.00
2-28	Paid Ames					(32.00)	- 0 -		32.00	340.00

People who keep budgets on a cash basis sometimes do not track credit transactions until they receive a statement noting the amount due. While this system works well for some people, others continue to buy on credit and fail to recognize the detail and amount of their indebtedness until they receive a statement. People who make credit purchases also need to keep the receipts for future reference so charges listed on a statement can be verified and any errors challenged. A credit controlsheet allows you to record each credit transaction when it occurs; if you misplace a receipt, you still have a record available for verification.

Check Accuracy Another way to control a budget is to double-check the accuracy of financial records. Many people increase the accuracy of their records by using a computer, a word processor, or a calculator. Accuracy in recordkeeping builds confidence in handling financial affairs.

Monitor Unexpended Balances The *best* method to control overspending is to **monitor unexpended balances** in each budget classification. You can accomplish this task by using a budget design that keeps a declining balance, as illustrated by parts (a) and (b) of Figure 4.4. Other budget designs, such as those shown in parts (c) and (d) of Figure 4.4, need to be monitored differently. As illustrated in parts (c) and (d), simply calculate subtotals every week or so, as needed, during a monthly budgeting period.

Justify Exceptions **Budget exceptions** occur when budget estimates in various classifications differ from actual expenditures, with discrepencies usually taking the form of overexpenditures. Exceptions may also occur in the over- or under-receipt of earnings. Allowing for exceptions keeps your budget flexible, although you still need to monitor them. Of course, to remain within your budget allocations, you must balance—or offset—overexpenditures with extra earnings received or with a reduction of spending elsewhere.

Use the Envelope System The **envelope system** of budgeting gets its name from the fact that exact amounts of money are placed into envelopes for purposes of strict budgetary control. If you wish to use the envelope system, place

Get Out of Credit Difficulties

The most carefully prepared budgets can be rendered virtually useless by careless use of credit. If overuse of credit is a problem, the following budget activities should be implemented:

1. **Make a credit controlsheet** similar to the one shown in Figure 4.6.

2. **Do not take out additional loans** or add to credit card balances.

3. **Budget a specific payoff amount monthly** for each debt. For installment loans, make the required monthly payment. For credit card debt, calculate the amount needed to pay the debt off within a specific time period (e.g., two years). (A method for calculating the necessary amount to be repaid each month will be covered in Chapter 7, "Planned Borrowing.") Make those payments as you would any other bill.

4. **If credit cards are to be used, record every usage** in colored ink in your check register and treat it like a cash expenditure. Pay off all new charges each month plus the amount needed to retire the debt as calculated in item 3.

money equal to the budget estimate for expenditure classifications in envelopes at the start of a budgeting period. Write the classification name and the budget amount on the outside of each envelope. As expenditures are made, record them on the appropriate envelope and remove the proper amounts of cash. When an envelope is empty, funds are exhausted for that classification. This technique works well in controlling expenditures for variable expenses such as entertainment, personal allowances, and food. It may also provide a good way for younger children to learn to budget allowances. Of course, the envelopes must be safeguarded to prevent theft.

Employ Subordinate Budgets A **subordinate budget** is a detailed listing of planned expenses within a single budgeting classification. For example, an estimate of $1200 for a week-long vacation could be supported by a subordinate budget as follows: motel, $700; restaurants, $300; and entertainment, $200. Without a subordinate budget to guide expenditures, the $1200 might last only four or five days becuase of overspending.

The Evaluation Phase of Budgeting

7 Perform the tasks of the evaluation phase of budgeting.

Evaluation has extreme importance in the budgeting process. Indeed, the **evaluation phase of budgeting** provides feedback for reexamining short-term goals and, if needed, for reclarifying long-term goals. Your basic financial planning values may then be reaffirmed or reorganized to fit your needs. More specifically, the purpose of evaluation is to determine whether the earlier steps in the budgeting process have worked.

Although evaluation is a continuous process, a formal evaluation phase should occur at the end of each budgeting time period. At that time, you should compare actual with budgeted amounts, decide whether the budget objectives have been achieved, and judge whether the overall process of budgeting has worked.

Compare Estimated and Actual Amounts

Making comparisons, sometimes called **variance analysis**, is important if you want to understand why expenditures were higher or lower than you estimated. This method is illustrated in Figure 4.7. In some budget expenditure classifications, the budget estimates rarely agree with the actual expenditures—particularly in variable expenses. The remarks column, as illustrated in parts (c) and (d) of Figure 4.4, can help clarify why discrepencies occur.

Decide How to Handle Balances

At the end of the budgeting time period, some budget classifications may still have a positive balance. For example, perhaps you estimated the electric bill at $50, and it was only $45. You may then ask, "What do I do with the balance?" You also may ask, "What happens to budget classifications that were overspent?"

People often deposit the **net surplus** (the amount remaining after all budget classification deficits are subtracted from those with surpluses) in a savings

Figure 4.7

Quarterly Budget Variance for Harry and Belinda Johnson

	JANUARY				FEBRUARY				MARCH			
	Budget	Actual	Variance	Cumulative Variance	Budget	Actual	Variance	Cumulative Variance	Budget	Actual	Variance	Cumulative Variance
INCOME												
Harry's salary	1,700	1,700	—	—	1,700	1,700	—	—	1,700	1,700	—	—
Belinda's salary	2,150	2,150	—	—	2,150	2,150	—	—	2,350	2,350	—	—
Interest	15	5	(10)	(10)	20	5	(15)	(25)	20	5	(15)	(40)
Trust	—	—	—	—	—	—	—	—	—	—	—	—
TOTAL INCOME												
EXPENSES												
Fixed expenses:												
Rent	600	600	—	—	600	600	—	—	600	600	—	—
Health insurance	85	85	—	—	85	85	—	—	85	85	—	—
Variable expenses:												
Food	360	390	(30)	(30)	360	400	(40)	(70)	360	390	(30)	(100)
Utilities	100	110	(10)	(10)	100	120	(20)	(30)	100	95	5	(25)
Telephone	70	60	10	(10)	70	55	15	25	70	45	25	50
Auto gas/maintenance	45	48	(3)	(3)	45	46	(1)	(4)	265	268	(3)	(7)

account, such as their revolving savings fund account, or put the money toward paying off credit card balances. Others treat it like "mad money" and spend it. Still others leave the funds in a checking account and carry the surpluses forward, thereby providing larger budget estimates for the following month. The budgeting form in part (d) of Figure 4.4 allows for carrying forward balances to the next period. Some people carry forward deficits, with the hope that having less available in a budgeted classification the following month will motivate them to keep expenditures low. Because variable expense estimates are usually averages, it is best not to change the estimate based on a variation that occurs over just one or two months. If estimates are too high or low for a longer period, however, you will want to make adjustments.

Be aware of any over- or underestimates of the amounts actually recorded for earnings or expenditures. Overages on a few expenditures may cause little concern. However, if excessive variances have prevented you from achieving objectives or making the budget balance, then take some action. New controls might have to be instituted or current controls tightened. Reflective thinking in this type of evaluation will ensure an improved budgeting process in the future.

Assess Progress toward Goals

Whatever your goals, it is exciting to know that some or all of them have been achieved or that progress has been made toward those ends. A successful budget reflects on the person behind it. Even though achieving such objectives as staying within the budget estimates, paying off a small debt, or saving a few hundred dollars within the budget period may seem unimpressive to some people, it allows you to say, "I achieved my goals because I made the plan and worked it successfully."

If you did not achieve some of your objectives, you can use the evaluation process to determine why and to adjust your budget and objectives accordingly.

What to Do with Extra Money

A common fear in budgeting is that spending will exceed income. But what if the opposite happens and income regularly exceeds budgeted expenditures? This can happen if you get a raise, if your projections for outgo were too high, or if you are simply frugal. If you find you have money left over at the end of the month, you might consider the following:

- *Pay off your credit card debt.* Paying on these high-interest loans will result in even lower expenditures as interest charges diminish.

- *Put the money in your employer-sponsored retirement plan.* Because these plans are tax-sheltered, you save on taxes at the same time that you add to your nest egg.

- *Invest in a mutual fund.* Investing is a habit that is hard to start but easier to continue. Starting when funds are readily available will help continue the pattern when money is tighter.

- *Pay down a mortgage or other loan.* Putting additional amounts toward monthly loan payments will get them paid off earlier and reduce overall interest expenses.

Suppose the Johnsons find that they are unable to set aside the planned $400 for their new home. By evaluating their budget, they might find that unexpected medical expenses and an out-of-state trip to visit a sick relative led them to dip into their savings. Under these circumstances, they can easily understand why the objective was not achieved and they can set their sights on reaching the goal during the next budgeting time period.

Evaluation of your progress toward reaching savings goals is especially important. As seen in Chapter 2, net worth can grow only when you spend less than your income. Success comes when savings goals are being met. If this is not the case, the budgeter must set up mechanisms to force savings to occur. Payroll deductions and automatic transfers from checking to savings accounts may aid this process by making saving automatic. Such mechanisms are especially helpful for first-attempt savers who are simply trying to build the three- to six-month emergency fund that is recommended for most people.

Discussions about Money

8 Explain the techniques of talking effectively about money.

A common cause of marital tension is conflict over money. Couples often disagree about what to spend their money on and how much to spend. Sometimes one person in a relationship will make a crucial financial decision without consulting the other person, thereby creating resentment and perhaps setting the stage for a series of retaliatory actions. Some couples seem unable to work together to perform the fundamental tasks of managing money, such as reconciling the checking account, creating a workable budget, and paying bills on time. It is quite common for at least one spouse to bring a great deal of debt to a marriage. Other couples get into financial trouble because they use credit too often. Mutual trust in money matters can be developed—and must be—in order to have happy interpersonal relationships and achieve financial success.

Money Management and Financial Decision Making for Couples

Managing money and making decisions about money matters are two different processes. Managing money includes such tasks as handling the checkbook, overseeing the budget, and doing the day-to-day shopping. While managing family money is an important responsibility, it is also vital to know which family members make the financial decisions, because disagreements typically arise in this area.

Decision making can be unilateral, shared, or divided. In some families, one person—usually the chief money earner—makes all financial decisions. Couples typically share decision making to some extent. They talk with one another and decide how much to spend on major purchases, such as appliances, jewelry, and recreation activities. They also share decision-making power on more expensive planned financial activities, such as buying automobiles and housing, as well as on key topics like estate planning and investments.

Many families divide financial decision making. Sometimes decision making is divided equally and at other times according to mutually approved specifications, such as respective knowledge, interest, experience, and temperament. Some cou-

Your Personal Spending Style

Personal spending styles are the different ways that people spend or deal with their money. Can you recognize these styles?

- **Givers** are generous to a fault. Regardless of whether they have the money, they always seem to be giving gifts or other financial support to others.

- **Me-spenders** love to spend money on themselves. They enjoy living the materialistic lifestyle.

- **Big spenders** simply like to spend money on themselves and others and enjoy it more if other people notice. They often reach for the bill when at a restaurant with a group.

- **Tightwads** save so compulsively that little is left even for essentials.

- **Normal people** usually do not have a pattern of excessive behavior, as do the previous four groups, but may occasionally exhibit spending faults.

If two people with sharply different spending styles commit to a relationship, they should be prepared for some problems that probably will arise.

ples also split recordkeeping chores. For example, one spouse might handle the checkbook and pay the bills, while the other might keep track of the budget, complete forms for health insurance claims, and fill out income tax returns.

Complications for Dual-Earner Households

The U.S. Census Bureau reports that 43 percent of all married households have two incomes. Although two earners can mean more income, expenses typically increase because of work-related costs such as clothing, eating out, income taxes, transportation, and sometimes child care. One or both earners may exhibit jealousy or possessiveness over their share of the income. A financial danger facing dual-earner households is that they would likely experience an unexpected decline in total income should one partner lose a job or take time off from work to make a career change, return to school, or raise children. Therefore, dual-earner households need to limit financial commitments that rely heavily on their "second" income in case their situation changes.

Questions facing dual-earner households include the following:

- Should we pool all our income and pay expenses out of one financial "pot" or keep accounts in two or more separate pots?

- Which partner should pay which household expenses and in what proportions?

- Should we pool our savings?

- Should homes and investments be put in joint names?

- How should we spend the joint income tax refund?

- Who should manage the checkbooks, recordkeeping, budgeting, health care claims, investments, and retirement and estate planning?

- How will we resolve money matters upon which we disagree?

Financial experts recommend that each person in a relationship keep some money of his or her own. This aim could be accomplished with three checking accounts for most dual-earner couples: a discretionary account for each individual (two accounts) and a third joint account. The budget categories related to each account should be clearly and jointly specified. Each partner can then feel that he or she has access to money that the other partner does not control. These feelings of autonomy encourage independence and self-control in a relationship rather than dependency on the other person.

Complications Brought by Remarriage

Remarriage merges financial histories, values, and habits as well as households. Some remarried couples will have substantial combined incomes bolstered by child-support payments from a former spouse. In many cases, at least one spouse may be paying (instead of receiving) alimony and child support. When "his," "her," and "our" children are included in the household, living expenses can be quite steep. Special concerns for blended families include determining who assumes financial responsibility for various progeny, meeting the needs of biological offspring without neglecting or offending spouses and stepchildren, resentment over alimony and child support payments, and management of unequal assets, incomes, responsibilities, and debts. Even gift giving can become a quandary. Many remarried people use "his" and "hers" funds and require the legally responsible parent owing financial support to a previous spouse or to children to make such payments out of his or her own money. Jean Lown, professor of home economics at Utah State University, suggests that, "What is best is what the couple can agree on."

Emotions and Money

Besides the economic goods and services that money can provide, people often ascribe a number of emotions to money, including freedom, trust, self-esteem, guilt, indifference, envy, security, comfort, power, and control. When talking

Did You KNOW?

The Difference between Prenuptial and Postnuptial Agreements

Many people contemplating remarriage are nervous about financial matters and may even exhibit a sense of distrust, guilt, or illusions about financial matters—especially when they are bringing substantial assets or debts to the new relationship. Therefore, some couples sign a **prenuptial agreement**, a contract specifying what (if any) share of each person's assets the other will be entitled to during marriage or in case of divorce. Another useful device is a **postnuptial agreement**, a contractual agreement signed after marriage to spell out each spouse's financial responsibilities. Such precautions may forestall grief later because courts generally uphold the validity of such agreements. The key is to make sure the agreement is congruent with laws protecting spouses and that both sides are equally represented by legal counsel.

about financial matters to others, particularly in family relationships, it is useful to recognize how money is valued emotionally by each person.

Many people consider their way of handling money to be a deeply private and personal matter. They may want to hold on to their fiscal autonomy as long as possible, and they may be embarrassed to inquire about how much others— even loved ones—spend, earn, or owe. For many people, money is a dark little area of self-suspected incompetence, and it is a difficult subject to discuss. Judith Viorst, author of *Necessary Losses*, suggests that becoming responsible and adept at managing one's financial matters represents a true passage into adulthood—a scary process for a lot of people. Nevertheless, learning to talk about money may be a precursor to reaching family financial security.

Talking about Financial Matters

Discussions about money matters are not always easy because they often reflect deeply held values that are difficult to change. Some people who are entirely rational about most things in life can prove unpredictable or even careless in money matters. While unrealistic values need to be identified and discussed, adults need to accept that honest differences may exist among people and that these values must be respected. The following techniques should help you discuss money with more confidence and candor.

 Discuss Personal Finances with Your Partner

Couples should discuss each person's values and attitudes in several areas that significantly affect a family's finances:

- **Childbearing** How many children do you want to have? How soon?

- **Employment** How do you feel about dual-career arrangements? Are you satisfied with your careers? Are you earning enough money? Are you willing to move for your spouse's advancement?

- **Clothing** How important is clothing to you? Are you satisfied with the amount, quality, and prestige value of clothing that you have?

- **Food** Is the food you are eating at home the quality you really want? Who should do the cooking and shopping for food? Do you want to eat out more often? Where?

- **Debt** How comfortable are you using credit to buy now, thereby committing future earnings?

- **Housing** How much do you want to spend on home furnishings? Do you really want to buy a home, or is renting acceptable? Where would you like to live?

- **Transportation** Could you cope by using mass transportation and by having just one automobile? Could one car be an inexpensive vehicle that gets high mileage? If so, who would drive it? Do you associate status with the car you drive?

- **Recreation** Would you be satisfied spending less (or more) money on recreational activities?

- **Vacations** What do you really want to do on vacations? Should you consider separate vacations? Do you prefer one long vacation each year or more frequent long-weekend breaks?

- **Future Security** How important are savings? Will your retirement plan actually provide you with a decent (or high) level of living? What would happen financially if you became disabled or died?

Get to Know Yourself and Your Partner   The first step in learning to talk with others about financial matters is to understand your own approach to money. Perhaps you could make a list of what money means to you. Consider the emotions described earlier to help get you started. Make a list of your financial fears, or "what would happen if . . . ." After your partner separately makes such lists, you will have much to discuss together. It will be constructive to discuss any differences in how you view yourself as compared with how your partner views you.

Learn to Manage Financial Disagreements   Give all family members time to express their views when discussing financial matters. Each family member also needs to listen to what others are saying and feeling. If talking proves too difficult, have each person separately write down his or her concerns. By swapping

Develop Money Sense in Children

Parents can help children develop money sense by providing them with opportunities to manage their own money while still young and guiding this behavior toward appropriate patterns. Five suggestions follow.

1. Give children access to money.
Even children as young as five years old should have some money of their own. An allowance and an opportunity to earn additional money ("pay") around the house should be the source of these funds in the preteen years. Later, work outside the home may be an option. The amounts of allowance and pay should fit the family income level. Some chores should be required and not be paid for; in contrast, special or extra jobs could result in some compensation, giving a young child a sense of the work ethic.

2. Give children the freedom to save as well as to spend their money.
Children should have autonomy over at least some of their own money. Consider requiring that the child deposit one-half of his or her allowance and "pay" in a savings account. The remainder could be available for discretionary spending in certain categories jointly determined by the parent and child.

3. Allow children the freedom to fail.
Parents should not stop children from "wasting their money." Advice is fine, but kids need to feel

the pain of a purchase gone bad. Similarly, kids should not be bailed out from every mistake. We sometimes learn best from experience, not from what somebody else tells us is best. Note that item 4 is designed to keep these mistakes from being too devastating.

4. Teach responsibility through increasingly complex activities.
The dollar amounts and the areas of discretionary spending should increase as the child becomes older. A seven-year-old might be allowed to spend his or her own money on toys, snacks, and gifts to charity at church or school. A 14-year-old might be allowed to buy meals and clothing as well. More responsibility and autonomy should be given only as the child exhibits the ability to handle previous tasks.

5. Talk about family finances with children.
In many families, money matters are a taboo subject. Children need to see that parents must work at managing the family finances. They should know what it costs to raise a family and how hard it can be to make ends meet sometimes. Otherwise, kids will grow up with unrealistic expectations and behaviors that will be passed on to their children as well.

notes, ideas and concerns can be shared. Schedule a time and place for financial talks, decide on agenda items, and leave other conflicts outside the door. When necessary, agree to disagree or postpone difficult decisions until a later time—but do so consciously and not simply out of procrastination.

Avoid "You" Statements "You" statements are blaming statements, such as "You always . . . ," "You never . . . ," "You are acting like . . . ," "You should forget that idea . . . ," and "If you don't, I will. . . ." These statements have a high probability of being condescending to other people, of making them feel guilty, and of making them feel that their needs and wants are not important.

Use "I" Statements Use such phrases as "I think" and "I feel" when discussing money. Messages focusing on "I" describe the behavior in question, the feelings you experienced because of the behavior, and any tangible effect on you. For example, a spouse might say, "I feel upset when you make credit purchases, because I do not know where we will find the money to pay the bills at the end of the month." "I" messages say three things: what (the behavior), I feel (feelings), because (reason). Using "I" messages helps build stronger relationships because they tell the other person that "I trust you to decide what change in behavior is necessary." Beware of "I" statements that end with "I need *you* to ...." These statements may be seen as attempts to exert power.

Focus on Commonalities Successful communication about money requires that the effort be aimed toward agreeing on common goals and reaching a consensus of opinion without substantially compromising the views of family members.

Be Honest Achieving consensus requires that each person be honest when talking about money matters; it further demands that family members regularly talk about finances, particularly when money decisions are not pressing. Be prepared to compromise. When you make decisions together, act on them.

People learning to discuss money matters often focus their attention on current financial activities and short-term issues to the exclusion of long-term financial planning. Recall, however, that values, financial plans, and long-term goals form the bases for short-term goals and issues. Therefore, you should try to use these discussions to forge overall long-term strategies for dealing with your family finances. Once the proper base has been established, short-term issues are more likely to fall into place.

Summary

1. Your personal values are the starting point in financial planning and budgeting. Budgeting is a process of projecting, organizing, monitoring, and controlling future income and expenditures (including cash and credit purchases as well as savings).

2. In the goal-setting phase of budgeting, goals must be specific. They should contain dollar amount target dates for achievement.

3. In the organization phase of budgeting—which focuses on the structural and mechanical aspects of budgeting—you choose a recording format, select either the cash or accrual basis of accounting, choose various budget classifications, and select the time period for the budget. It is important to maintain a positive attitude toward budgeting and to maintain flexibility.

4. The decision-making phase of budgeting requires you to make realistic budget estimates

for income and expenditures as well as resolve conflicting needs and wants by revising estimates as needed.

5. In the implementation phase of budgeting, you put the budget into effect primarily by recording actual income and expenditures. You then manage cash-flow and calculate time-period totals.

6. The control phase of budgeting includes the potential use of seven different means of control. Using a checking account, checking accuracy, and monitoring unexpended balances are popular controls. Formal budgeting controls include the credit controlsheet and the envelope system.

7. In the evaluation phase of budgeting, you compare actual with budgeted amounts, decide how to handle balances, and assess progress toward goals.

8. Many people find it difficult to talk with others about money and the tough financial decisions they must make. A number of useful strategies can be used to improve communications about money matters, including the use of "I" statements.

Key Words & Concepts

budget   *95*

budget controls   *110*

budget estimates   *103*

budgeting   *95*

cash-basis budgeting   *101*

cash-flow calendar   *106*

credit controlsheet   *111*

discretionary income   *103*

disposable income   *103*

expenditure   *106*

long-term goals   *96*

monitor unexpended balances   *112*

net surplus   *114*

personal spending styles   *117*

prenuptial agreement   *118*

reconciling budget estimates   *106*

recordkeeping   *99*

revolving savings fund   *108*

subordinate budget   *113*

values   *95*

Questions for Thought & Discussion

1. Concisely describe the relationships among the following terms: values, financial planning, goals, and budgeting.

2. List the six phases of budgeting.

3. Distinguish between long- and short-term goals.

4. What is the focus of the organization phase of budgeting?

5. Differentiate between cash- and accrual-basis budgeting.

6. Briefly explain how inflation affects budgeting.

7. What are the values of resolving conflicting needs and wants in budgeting?

8. Explain how a cash-flow calendar works.

9. Explain how a revolving savings fund works.

10. What purposes do budget controls serve?

11. How can you use a checking account as a budget control?

12. Explain how the envelope system of budget control works.

13. How can a subordinate budget be used on a vacation?

14. What is the purpose of the evaluation phase of budgeting?

15. What should be done during the evaluation phase of budgeting?

16. Briefly describe how decision making can be handled by families.

17. Give two suggestions for how parents can increase their children's money sense.

18. List three financial questions that dual-earner couples and remarried families face.

19. Describe two types of spending styles other than "normal."

20. Give three suggestions on how to help people talk about money matters.

DECISION-MAKING CASES

Case 1 A Couple Creates an Educational Savings Plan

Anne and Mike Washington of Gary, Indiana, have two young children and have been living on a tight budget. Their monthly budget is illustrated in Table 4.2 as the "married couple with two young children." Mike and Anne have been nervous about not having started an educational savings plan for their children. Anne has just started to work part-time at a local accounting firm and earns about $160 per month; this income is reflected in the Washingtons' budget. They have decided that they need to save $200 per month for the children's education, but Anne does not want to work more hours away from home.

(a) Review the family's budget and make suggestions about how to modify various budget estimates so that they could save $200 a month for the education fund.

(b) Briefly describe the impact of your recommended changes on the Washingtons' lifestyle.

(c) What factors should the couple remember as they attempt to discuss and resolve this important financial issue for their family?

Case 2 Budget Control for a Recent Graduate

Charles DiPinto, a political scientist from Tucson, Arizona, graduated from college eight months ago and is having a terrible time with his budget. Charles has a regular monthly income from his job and no really large bills, but he likes to spend. He exceeds his budget every month, and his credit card balances are increasing. Choose three budget control methods that you could recommend to Charles, and explain how each one could help him gain control of his finances.

Financial Math Questions

1. Sharon and Dick DeVaney of West Lafayette, Indiana, have decided to start a family next year, so they are looking over their budget (illustrated in Table 4.2 as the "young married couple"). Sharon thinks that she can go on half-salary ($800 instead of $1600 per month) on her job as a graduate assistant for about 18 months after the baby's birth and then return to full-time work.

(a) Looking at the DeVaneys' current monthly budget, identify categories and amounts in their $3015 budget where they realistically might cut back $800. (Hint: Federal and state taxes should drop about $250 as their income drops.)

(b) Assume that Sharon and Dick could be persuaded not to begin a family for another two to three years until Sharon finishes graduate school. What specific budgeting recommendations would you give them for handling (i) their fixed expenses and (ii) their variable expenses to prepare financially for an anticipated $800 loss of income for 18 months, as well as the expenses for the new baby?

(c) If the DeVaneys' gross income of $3015 rises 6 percent per year in the future, what will their income be after five years? [Hint: See Appendix A.1 or the *Garman/Forgue* Web site.]

MONEY MATTERS: LIFE-CYCLE CASES

Victor and Maria Hernandez Think about Their Budget

Victor and Maria Hernandez have begun the transition from being parents with children at home to being without children. As their children grow older and prepare to go away to college, Victor and Maria have been considering several issues related to their children's money matters. They could use some advice.

1. Explain five ways that the Hernandezes might create money sense in their children.

2. Use the sample budgets in Table 4.2 to explain to the couple how their budget might change when their children go to college.

The Johnsons Have Some Budget Problems

The Johnsons enjoy a high income because they both work at well-paying jobs. They cannot believe that less than a year ago they were both living the stressful financial lives of college students. Times have changed for the better.

The Johnsons have spent parts of three evenings over the past several days discussing their financial values and goals together. As shown in the upper portion of Figure 4.3, they have established three long-term goals: $3000 for a European vacation to be taken in 2¹/₂ years, $5000 needed in October 2003 for a down payment on a new automobile, and $22,500 for a down payment on a home to be purchased in December 2004. As shown in the lower portion of the figure, the Johnsons did some calculations to determine how much they had to save for each goal—over the short term—to stay on schedule to reach their long-term goals as well as pay for two vacations and an anniversary party.

After developing their balance sheet and income and expense statements (shown on pages 52–53), the Johnsons made a budget for the year (shown in Table 4.3). They then reconciled various conflicting needs and wants until they found that total annual income exceeded expenses. Next, they created a revolving savings fund (Table 4.5) in which they were careful to include enough money each month to meet all of their short-term goals. When developing their cash-flow calendar for the year (Table 4.4), however, they noticed a problem: a series of substantial cash deficits over the first several months of the year. In fact, despite their projected high income and anticipated substantial surplus at the end of the year, it is now January and the Johnsons are broke!

Harry and Belinda have very little money in savings to cover planned deficits. To meet this problem, they do not anticipate increasing their income, using savings, or borrowing. Instead, they are considering modifying their needs and wants to reduce their budget estimates to the point where they would have zero or positive balances during the first six months of the year.

1. Make specific recommendations to the Johnsons on how they could make reductions in their budget estimates. Do not offer suggestions that would alter their new lifestyle drastically, as the couple would reject these ideas.

Exploring the World Wide Web of Personal Finance

To complete these exercises, go to the *Garman/Forgue* Web site at

www.hmco.com/college/business/

Select Personal Finance. Click on the exercise link for this chapter and answer the questions that appear on the Web page.

1. Visit the Web site for Healthy Cash. There you find a series of short questionnaires designed to identify your spending style. What does that information tell you about potential problems you might have achieving your financial goals and what you might want to discuss with loved ones?

2. Visit the Web site for the U.S. Bureau of Labor Statistics, where you will find information on expenditure patterns for a typical family. Compare this information with both the absolute dollar amounts you spend and the percentages spent in each category.

3. Visit the Quicken Web site, where you will find an article on budgeting for a baby. How does the information compare with what you have done or seen other young families do as they prepare for a new arrival?

4. Visit the Web site for this book, where you will find a budget spreadsheet set up for your use. Create a budget for yourself for the next month. Track your income and spending for the month to see how well you are able to keep within the budgeted amounts.

5. Visit the Quicken Web site, where you will find an article addressing the question of whether two incomes are better than one for couples. What three issues are raised in the article that support the notion that the two incomes are not always better?

Managing Your Cash

5

OBJECTIVES

After reading this chapter, you should be able to:

1 Explain the importance of effective cash management and list the four tools of cash management.

2 Compare and contrast the primary providers of cash management opportunities in today's financial services industry.

3 Understand the uses of electronic funds transfer and the legal protections available for it.

4 Understand the criteria for choosing and using various types of checking accounts and the importance of having an interest-earning checking account.

5 Identify the potential benefits of opening a savings account as well as key factors to consider when comparing savings accounts.

6 Explain the importance of placing excess funds in a money market account.

7 List the potential benefits of putting money into low-risk, longer-term savings instruments.

The typical American household has one or more interest-earning checking and savings accounts and typically pays about $200 a year for these services. Accordingly, this chapter begins with a discussion of how you can manage these accounts so as to minimize their costs and maximize your interest earnings. Next, we provide an overview of the providers of today's financial services so you can better understand where to conduct your checking, saving, borrowing, insuring, investing, and other personal finance activities. Today's financial services industry increasingly relies upon electronic funds transfer, a process you can use to your advantage. The remainder of the chapter focuses on the four tools of cash management: (1) interest-earning checking accounts, (2) savings accounts, (3) money market accounts, and (4) various low-risk, longer-term savings instruments.

What Is Cash Management?

1 Explain the importance of effective cash management and list the four tools of cash management.

As your income increases, you will have ever more cash to manage. This fact requires that you develop a strategy about how much cash to keep on hand, in what forms, and in which financial institutions.

Cash management is the task of maximizing interest earnings and minimizing fees on all of your funds kept readily available for living expenses, recurring household expenses, emergencies, and saving and investment opportunities. Cash management involves the effective management of all your monetary assets, such as cash on hand, savings accounts, checking accounts, money market accounts, other short-term investment vehicles, and various longer-term savings instruments. The accounts into which such funds are placed are called **cash equivalents** because they maintain a constant or nearly constant value and because they have liquidity. Good cash management allows you to earn interest on your money while still providing reasonable liquidity and safety. **Liquidity** refers to the speed and ease with which an asset can be converted to cash; **safety** is freedom from financial risk. Wise financial managers place excess funds not needed for everyday living expenses into other types of accounts that pay higher rates of interest.

The four tools of cash management are illustrated in Figure 5.1. First, you need to have a low-cost interest-earning checking account from which to pay monthly living expenses. Second, you might want to maintain a small savings account in a local financial institution that earns interest and represents an easily accessible source of emergency cash. Third, when income begins to exceed expenses regularly, you can consider opening a **money market account**. Such an account allows you to earn the highest interest rates on excess funds while considering other savings and investment options. Fourth, your cash management plan is complete when you transfer some funds into low-risk, longer-term savings instruments (such as certificates of deposit and government savings bonds) because you want to earn even higher returns and still maintain safety. With this option, you commit the amounts for longer time periods (sacrificing some liquidity for higher interest). This procedure allows you to build up greater amounts to be used for later spending, saving, or investing.

Figure 5.1

Four Tools of Cash Management (with Illustrative Interest Rates Earned on Funds)

Interest-earning checking account (3.0%)	Savings account in a financial institution (3.4%)	Money market account (3.6%)	Other low-risk, longer-term savings instruments (5.2–5.6%)
• NOW checking account	• Statement savings account	• Super NOW account • Money market deposit account • Money market mutual fund • Asset management account	• Certificate of deposit • Government savings bond

Today's Providers of Financial Services

2 Compare and contrast the primary providers of cash management opportunities in today's financial services industry.

Today's **financial services industry** includes institutions and individuals offering one or more of the following services to individuals and families: checking, savings, traveler's checks, credit, insurance, stocks and bonds, real estate, credit and budget counseling, financial planning, and legal advice on financial matters. The financial services industry holds at least one promise for Americans—an increasingly complex financial marketplace. This complexity will occur because new players are entering the industry, an expanding redefinition of banking, wider use of computer networks, the availability of new products and services, greater competition, and deregulation.

Today's providers of financial services include depository institutions, money market mutual funds, stock brokerage firms, financial services companies, and others. Table 5.1 matches these providers with the financial products and services that they sell. We will discuss these providers in this and following chapters. At appropriate points, we offer suggestions about who might best use various providers of financial services.

Banks and Depository Institutions

Depository institutions are those recognized and regulated by the federal government to offer loans and banking services to businesses and individuals, such as commercial banks, savings and loan associations, mutual savings banks, and credit unions. Although each is a distinct type of institution, and their characteristics will be detailed in the following paragraphs, people often label them all as banks.

Commercial Banks **Commercial banks** are corporations chartered under federal and state regulations. They offer numerous consumer services, such as checking, savings, loans, safe-deposit boxes, investment services, financial counseling, and automatic payment of bills. Accounts in a federally chartered bank are insured against loss by the **Bank Insurance Fund (BIF)** of the **Federal Deposit Insurance Corporation (FDIC)**, which is an agency of the federal government. Accounts in state-chartered banks are usually insured by the FDIC's BIF program or a private insurance program.

Table 5.1

Today's Providers of Cash Management Services

Providers	What They Sell
Depository institutions (banks, savings and loan associations, mutual savings banks, and credit unions)	Checking, savings, lending, credit cards, investments, and trust advice
Mutual funds	Money market mutual funds, tax-exempt funds, bond funds, and stock funds
Stock brokerage firms	Stocks, bonds, mutual funds, real estate investment trusts, and tax shelters
Financial services companies	Checking, savings, lending, credit cards, real estate, investments, insurance, tax shelters, accounting and legal advice, and financial planning

Savings and Loan Associations   **Savings and loan associations (S&Ls)** focus primarily on accepting savings and providing mortgage and consumer loans. S&Ls provide checking services through interest-earning NOW accounts (discussed later in this chapter). S&Ls generally pay depositors an interest rate about 0.25 percent higher than commercial banks. The FDIC insures accounts in all federally chartered S&Ls and some state-chartered S&Ls; the insurance is provided through the FDIC's **Savings Association Insurance Fund (SAIF)**.

Mutual Savings Banks   A **mutual savings bank (MSB)** is similar to an S&L because MSBs accept deposits to make housing and consumer loans. These banks are legally permitted in only 17 states, primarily those in the eastern United States. They are called "mutual" because the depositors own the institution and share in the earnings. Generally, MSBs have FDIC's BIF coverage. Like S&Ls, they offer interest-earning NOW accounts to checking customers.

Credit Unions   A **credit union (CU)** is a not-for-profit cooperative venture that pools the deposits of member-owners which are then used to invest or lend to member-owners. Members have some common bond, such as the same employer, church, union, or fraternal association. Persons in the immediate family of a member are also eligible to join. Credit unions with federal charters have their accounts insured through the **National Credit Union Share Insurance Fund (NCUSIF)**, administered by the National Credit Union Administration (NCUA), which provides the same safety as deposits insured by the FDIC. State-chartered credit unions are often insured by NCUSIF, and most others participate in private insurance programs.

Credit unions accept deposits and make loans for consumer products; the larger institutions make home loans. They typically use payroll deductions for deposits and loan repayments, and they often offer free insurance to pay off a loan in the event of death or disability. In addition, many offer free financial counseling. Credit unions usually pay higher interest rates and charge lower fees than commercial banks, S&Ls, or MSBs.

Mutual Funds

A **mutual fund** is an investment company that raises money by selling shares to the public and then invests that money in a diversified portfolio of investments. Many mutual fund companies have created mutual fund accounts that can be used for cash management purposes. Money deposited in mutual funds is not insured by the federal government. Some mutual fund companies, however, purchase private insurance to cover potential losses. Cash management accounts in mutual funds provide a convenient and safe place to keep money while awaiting alternative investment opportunities.

Stock Brokerage Firms

A **stock brokerage firm** is a licensed financial institution that specializes in selling and buying stocks, bonds, and other investment alternatives. Such firms provide advice and assistance to investors and earn a commission based on the buy and sell orders executed by the company. Stock brokerage firms typically offer a

Keep Your Money Safe

Occasionally, a depository institution will fail, thereby putting at risk the deposits of its customers. As indicated in the text, two federal insurance funds protect depositors from losing their money in such circumstances. This protection has limits, however, so that you will have no more than $100,000 (combined deposits and interest) of protection for various classes of accounts at any one institution organized as follows:

1. $100,000 total on all of your single-ownership accounts (held in your name only). For example, if you had one checking account and two savings accounts with the same institution, your protection for the combined balances would be $100,000.

2. $100,000 total on all of your joint accounts held with other individuals. For example, a husband and wife might have joint accounts and other joint accounts with other combinations of individuals. The husband and wife would have a maximum of $100,000 each in protection across all of their joint accounts.

Thus the total protection that an individual might have with any one instutution (including all its branches) is $200,000, with protection of no more than $100,000 each on single-ownership and joint accounts. Additional protection is available for retirement accounts, however.

money market mutual fund account (operated by a mutual fund) into which clients may place money while waiting to make investments. Thus they provide cash management services as well.

Financial Services Companies

A **financial services company** is a national or regional corporation that offers a large number of financial services to consumers, including the traditional checking and savings accounts, lending and credit cards, accounts in money market mutual funds, and advice on investments, insurance, real estate, and general financial planning. These companies are also called **quasi-banks** or **nonbank banks** because they provide limited traditional banking services—either accepting deposits or making commercial loans, but not both. Large corporations operating in this area include Prudential Securities and Fidelity Investments. Money held in a money market mutual fund or another account at a financial services company is not insured against loss by the FDIC, although such companies generally purchase private insurance.

Electronic Funds Transfer

3 Understand the uses of electronic funds transfer and the legal protections available for it.

The most noteworthy feature of today's financial services industry is the blossoming of electronically assisted transactions available to consumers. These **electronic funds transfers (EFTs)** use a variety of systems and technologies to transfer funds electronically (rather than by check or cash) among various bank accounts. They move money between accounts in a fast, paperless way.

Many people use EFT systems to eliminate the inconvenience of writing checks and carrying large amounts of cash. The following discussions profile the most widely recognized forms of EFT: debit cards, automated teller machines (ATMs), point-of-sale transactions, smart cards, preauthorized payments and deposits, electronic benefits transfer, and on-line home banking services. Also discussed are the key government regulations that protect consumers who use electronic funds transfers.

Debit Cards

A **debit** (or **ATM** or **EFT**) **card** is a plastic card that provides access to the EFT system via the ATM or EFT point-of-sale system (see below). It is issued by the financial institution where the user maintains a checking account. A debit card differs from a credit card in that use of the debit card is not borrowing money but instead provides access to one's own money. A user initiates transactions by inserting the card into the ATM and entering his or her **personal identification number (PIN)**, which identifies that the user is, in fact, authorized to access the account. Debit cards and PIN numbers basically "unlock" your account. You should always memorize your PIN numbers rather than writing them down in your checkbook or wallet.

Debit cards come in two forms. An **on-line debit card** requires the use of a PIN number. A common example is a cash withdrawal from an account using an automatic teller machine. An **off-line debit card** does not require a PIN number; instead, the user signs a receipt for the transaction. For example, you could use an off-line debit card to purchase a meal at a restaurant. Funds to cover the purchase would be deducted from the account (usually checking) accessed by the card. Sometimes a bank credit card doubles as a debit card. Users need to be clear whether they are using their card as a credit card or a debit card and which type of debit card arrangement applies (on-line or off-line). This distinction is important because the protections for fraudulent usage differ for the various types of cards (discussed below). Off-line debit cards are particularly risky, because a crook needs only your account number to access your account.

ATMs

An **automated teller machine (ATM)** is an electronic computer terminal located on the premises of a financial institution or elsewhere through which customers may make deposits or withdrawals, or carry out other financial transactions just as they would through a human bank teller. Now often called **cash machines**, ATMs are activated by using a debit card and PIN. Some ATM security systems "read" your face, fingerprint, or the iris of your eye to confirm identity.

Fees are usually assessed for ATM use. Some financial institutions charge customers $4 per month for up to 10 ATM transactions. Other institutions assess a transaction fee, often $0.50 to $1.50, for each use of ATMs and point-of-sale terminals; higher fees (often $2) may apply to transactions carried out through terminals not in your bank's network. Fees may total as much as $8 in out-of-the-way locations. The average ATM wothdrawal is $60 with the most common withdrawal being just $20. A $2.00 fee is 10 percent of that amount and represents to three times the annual interest that would be earned on that amount.

Most ATM networks provide a toll-free telephone number to tell you where the closest network terminals are located. Responsibility for customer service rests with the institution that issued the card, not necessarily the one that provides the terminal.

Point-of-Sale Terminals

A **point-of-sale (POS) terminal** is an electronic computer terminal located at a store or other merchant location that allows the customer to use a debit card to make purchases. The transaction is transmitted over the **electronic funds transfer point-of-sale system (EFTPOS)**, and funds are taken from the user's account and deposited in the merchant's account. Some POS terminals are off-line, where the customer receives a receipt and the issuing bank withdraws funds from the customer's account within three or four days. Thus, this "delayed debit card system" operates much like a check system. In contrast, an on-line POS terminal instantly debits the customer's account—creating an "instant check." Examples of on-line ATM systems are Cirrus, Most, and Star.

Smart Cards and Stored-Value Cards

Approximately 80 percent of all consumer transactions in the United States are conducted with cash, with most involving amounts less than $20. In an attempt to appeal to that large market, many financial institutions and other organizations now issue smart cards and stored-value cards. These plastic payment devices use a built-in computer chip to store data and handle payment functions. The cards can be electronically "loaded" with a certain amount of money; this amount decreases every time the card is used to make a purchase. With a **smart card**, dollar amounts can be added to replenish the card. With a **stored-value card**, the user simply obtains a new card when funds run out. Such cards have uses ranging from buying gasoline to making long-distances telephone calls. Many of these cards can be used only with a PIN number, which confirms the user's identity. Some combination cards can also be used as credit and debit cards.

Students often become familiar with these cards at college, where they are employed for campus identification, dormitory security, bookstore and copying machines, library cards, student meal programs, and even sporting and special events admissions. Remember that these cards are basically "cash"—as a result, they may be used by anyone who finds or steals them.

Preauthorized Deposits and Payments

You (or anyone else you authorize) can make regular electronic "direct deposits" of paychecks, stock dividends, or Social Security benefits to your account. You also can authorize your financial institution to pay recurring bills in both regular amounts (such as mortgages or automobile loans) and irregular amounts (such as electric or telephone bills). Federal law permits you to stop a preauthorized payment by calling or writing the financial institution, provided that your new order is received at least three days before the payment date. Written confirmation of a telephone notice to stop payment may be required by the institution.

Electronic Benefits Transfer

Electronic benefits transfer (EBT) directs cash benefits to recipients using smart cards as the delivery mode. Recipients may include individuals lacking bank accounts and those who do not receive their benefits by direct deposit. An organization "puts" a certain amount of money or credit on the plastic card, which is then used by the recipient to make purchases at point-of-sale terminals or to obtain cash from ATMs. An example of an EBT includes the U.S. federal government's program to deliver benefits electronically through such programs as the Social Security Administration and Medicare. These efforts represent steps toward a **one-card system,** enabling an EBT recipient to access all of the benefits that he or she receives through a single card.

EFT Regulations

Both federal and state regulations have been adopted to provide protection for EFT users. The 1978 Electronic Funds Transfer Act is the governing statute, while the Federal Reserve Board's Regulation E provides specific guidelines on EFT-card liability. According to these regulations, a valid card can be sent only to a consumer who has requested it. Unsolicited cards can be issued only if the card can-

You Can Do Your Banking from Home

Home banking services allow an increasing number of people to conduct their banking by using a home computer or a touch-tone telephone.

Bank-Based Programs
Bank-based programs usually offer the greatest number of services. Typically, customers can summon an electronic checkbook to their computer monitor, double-check calculations and earlier payments, transfer cash between accounts, buy and sell stocks, transfer money into mutual funds, and communicate with a customer service representative.

Bill-Paying Programs
Using a telephone, you can access Payline [(800) 572-9546; requires only a touch-tone phone] or CheckFree [(800) 882-5280] to pay your bills, including fixed and variable expenses. These national electronic bill-paying services are available

to customers of any bank. From 5 to 8 percent of checkwriters use such services.

Computer-Based Programs
It may be less expensive to pay your bills electronically via computer. The four leading money management software programs—*Quicken, Managing Your Money, Microsoft Money,* and *Kiplinger's Simply Money*—all provide mechanisms for electronic bill paying. For increased security, on-line passwords for these services are longer than usual.

Financial Services Online (or Cyberbanking Online)
Internet banking offers above market interest rates on deposits, transfers among accounts, and access to automated teller machines for cash. Banks that offer pure Internet banking include Net.Bank Inc. of Atlanta (*www.netbank.com*), Telebank of Arlington (*www.telebank.com*), and Security First Network Bank of Atlanta (*www.sfnb.com*).

not be used until validated and the user is informed of his or her liability for unauthorized use as well as other terms and conditions. When you sign up for EFT services, your depository institution must inform you of your rights and responsibilities in a written **disclosure statement**.

Users must get written receipts when withdrawing money or making deposits with an ATM or using a point-of-sale terminal to pay for a purchase. These receipts show the amount of the transfer, the date it took place, and other information. General protection of a customer's account exists in the form of a **periodic statement** sent by the financial institution that shows all electronic

Send Cash in a Hurry

Consider this scenario: A friend is traveling in another state and has experienced an emergency. You must send cash to your friend quickly. What would you do? First, find out the amount needed, when it must be there, and a telephone number where you can reach the friend. This information may be necessary to call the person back so he or she will know where to pick the money up and what identification will be required. That person may need to present a photo ID to claim the funds, although some other option can usually be worked out when necessary. Sending money overseas is more complicated, but it can be done as well. There are six methods of sending cash.

Western Union Call Western Union at (800) 225-5227 to use its Money Transfer Service, which operates 24 hours per day using 16,000 agents in the United States and abroad. The company promises to deliver cash within 15 minutes of the request to the recipient, typically at a Western Union office, supermarket, convenience store, or drugstore. Amounts up to $2000 can be handled by telephone, using payment by cash advance from a Visa or a MasterCard; higher amounts require bringing cash or a cashier's check to a Western Union office.

MoneyGram Call MoneyGram at (800) 926-9400 to send money to more than 19,000 locations in 82 countries. MoneyGram, however, does not accept credit-card orders by telephone. Its prices are usually slightly below those of Western Union.

American Express American Express may be telephoned at (800) 926-9400 to send cash within ten minutes to 9000 locations, including American Express offices, airports, and bus stations. Cash advances on Visa, MasterCard, and American Express Optima cards are accepted, although such transactions are not permitted on the American Express green card.

U.S. Postal Service The U.S. Postal Service can send a postal money order by means of Express Mail, with overnight delivery by noon the next day guaranteed seven days a week. You must pay by cash.

Wire Transfers Any bank or savings and loan association in the United States can wire money to a designated bank anywhere in the world, although the transaction can be completed only during banking hours, with cash typically being received the day after the request is made. Cash advances on Visa and MasterCard are accepted. Wire transfers are almost always less expensive than the other methods described above.

ATM Network Funds can be instantly deposited into a checking or savings account that is part of an ATM network. A friend can immediately send funds via an ATM machine at any location on the network. You then can withdraw the funds up to the limit applied daily by your bank.

transfers to and from the account, fees charged, and opening and closing balances. A user of EFT services should regularly reconcile the information on this periodic statement with the written receipts.

If you find an error in your periodic statement, notify the issuing organization in writing as soon as possible. Use the notification procedures found in the disclosure statement accompanying your monthly statement. If the institution needs more than ten business days to investigate and correct a problem, generally it must return the amount in question to your account while it conducts the investigation (within a required 45 days). If an error occurred, the institution must correct it promptly by making the correction final. If no error occurred, the institution must explain its decision in writing and let you know that it has deducted any amount temporarily credited during the investigation. In such a case, the institution must honor withdrawals against the credited amount for five days. You may ask for copies of documents on which the institution relied in the investigation and again challenge the outcome if a mistake has been made.

The sooner you report the loss of a card, the more likely you will be to limit your liability if someone uses the card without your permission. Cardholders are liable for only the first $50 of unauthorized use if they notify the issuing company within two business days after the loss or theft of their card or PIN. After two days, cardholder liability for unauthorized use rises to $500. Some issuers have voluntarily lowered this maximum to $50. You risk *unlimited* loss for use if, within 60 days after the institution mails your financial statement to you, you do not report an unauthorized transfer or withdrawal. Thus, you could lose all of the money in your account plus any lines of credit attached to that account, such as an automatic overdraft loan agreement (discussed later in this chapter). These regulations apply to debit cards *and* to other cards used to make an electronic funds transfer (such as a bank credit card). All states have specific laws that provide additional protection for consumers in EFT transactions.

Most homeowner's and renter's insurance policies (discussed in Chapter 10, "Risk Management and Property/Liability Insurance") cover the liability for theft of both debit and credit cards. If you are not currently protected, such insurance coverage generally can be added. Many companies sell similar insurance as a separate policy for an annual premium of $30 to $60. In addition, some firms sell a **card registration service** that will notify all companies where you have debit and credit cards in the event of loss. For $15 to $50 per year, you need to make only one telephone call to report all card losses. Of course, you can also notify debit and credit card companies yourself at no cost.

Cash Management Tool 1: Interest-Earning Checking Accounts

4 Understand the criteria for choosing and using various types of checking accounts and the importance of having an interest-earning checking account.

Expenditures above and beyond your need for pocket money can be met by using an interest-earning checking account. A **checking account** at a depository institution allows checks to be written against amounts on deposit. Also known as a **transaction account**, it lets you transfer deposited funds to merchants and service providers as well as to accounts at other financial institutions. Three quarters of American adults pay bills and make purchases using a checking account. People access their checking accounts by writing checks, using an ATM, making electronic transfers (such as point-of-sale transactions and direct deposits), sending items by mail, giving instructions on the telephone, or talking with a teller inside a financial institution. This section examines the types of checking accounts available; checking account charges, fees, and penalties; other kinds of checking accounts; and types of accounts and ownership rights.

Types of Checking Accounts

A checking account has numerous benefits. It eliminates the need to carry a great deal of cash, and it is more convenient and less expensive to pay bills by mailing a check than by traveling all over town to make payments in person. Having a checking account also helps in budgeting because a written record of each check may be kept in an accompanying transaction register. In addition, the canceled check provides proof of payment and a tax record. Similarly, using an ATM or POS terminal provides a written receipt that should be kept with other checking documents.

We will use the traditional term **checking** from this point forward to include demand deposits, negotiable orders of withdrawal, and share drafts. The terms *banks, banking,* and *depository institutions* will be defined to include commercial banks, savings and loan associations, mutual savings banks, and credit unions. The person who opens the checking account and writes the check is known as the **drawer** or **payer.** The financial institution at which the account is held is the **drawee,** and the person or firm to whom the check is written is the **payee.** When a check is written, it becomes a **negotiable instrument,** which is an unconditional written promise to pay a specified sum of money as of a specific date to a specified payee or bearer.

Traditional checking accounts at commercial banks are technically known as **demand deposits.** A financial institution must withdraw funds and make payments whenever demanded by the checking account depositor. Current law permits only commercial banks to offer demand deposits. While these accounts permit unlimited checking, they also pay no interest. There are three types of non–interest-paying checking accounts.

A **special checking account** requires no minimum balance to open, does not earn interest, requires a monthly service charge (perhaps $3) or assesses fees for each check or transaction (perhaps $0.50), and carries restrictions on the maximum number of transactions allowed each month without additional fees. This type of account is meant for people who write few checks and keep low balances.

A **regular checking account** does not pay interest and generally does not assess a monthly fee as long as a minimum balance is maintained, such as $1200, although there may be charges for deposits and transactions made through an ATM.

A **lifeline banking account** (also called a **basic banking account**) offers access to certain

> **Did You KNOW?**
>
> ### Stop-Payment Orders Have Time Limits
>
> A **stop-payment order** specifies that the bank not honor a check when presented for payment. To accomplish this, you can telephone your bank and stop payment on the check. Many people are unaware that if the verbal stop-payment order is not followed up with a written instruction to the bank, the person or merchant to whom the check was written can cash the check after 14 days. Even with a written request, the check can be cashed after six months unless the order has been renewed.

minimal financial services that every consumer ought to have—regardless of income—to function in society. These services include cashing of government checks without charge and low-cost checking accounts for low- and moderate-income consumers in the bank's neighborhoods. An applicant's income and net worth determine acceptance into a lifeline program. College students generally do not qualify because their parents' assets and income are often considered part of the resources available to them. The cost of lifeline banking accounts is extremely low, often about $3 per month.

All depository institutions can offer some form of an **interest-earning checking account**, which is simply a checking account that pays interest to the depositor. Commercial banks, S&Ls, and mutual savings banks offer a **negotiable order of withdrawal (NOW)** account. This checking account earns interest or dividends as long as minimum-balance requirements are satisfied. A NOW account can be described as an "interest-earning checking account." When the financial institution receives the negotiable order of withdrawal (or "check"), the funds on deposit are used to make the payment.

A **share draft account** is the credit-union version of a NOW account. It is given its name because members of the credit union actually own the organization and their deposits are called shares. Technically, share draft accounts earn dividends instead of earning interest; for tax purposes, however, the earnings are "interest income." Costs for a share draft account are often lower than for checking at banks and savings and loan associations.

When you write share drafts, you simultaneously make a carbonless copy instead of having canceled checks returned to you. Some banks use this type of **check truncation** as well; others send customers **image statements** that show miniature computer pictures of canceled checks. For a fee, you can always obtain a legal double-sided photocopy of the original to prove payment, if necessary.

The Proper Way to Endorse Checks

Endorsement is the process of writing on the back of a check to legally transfer its ownership, usually in return for the cash amount indicated on the face of the check. When you sign, or **endorse**, the back of a check written to you, it can then be cashed, given to another person, or deposited.

A check with a **blank endorsement** contains only the payee's signature on the back. Such a check immediately becomes a **bearer instrument**, meaning that anyone who attempts to cash it very likely will be allowed to do so, even if the check has been lost or stolen. You would be wise to avoid making a blank endorsement prior to depositing or cashing a check.

A **special endorsement** can be used to limit who can cash a check by writing the phrase "Pay to the order of [name]" on the back along with your signature. A special endorsement can easily be put on a check that you want to sign over to another person. Such a "two-party check" is difficult to cash other than by depositing it in an account at a financial institution.

A **restrictive endorsement** uses the phrase "For deposit only" written on the back along with the signature. It authorizes the financial institution to accept the check only as a deposit to an account. Checks deposited by mail should always be endorsed this way.

Usually, NOW accounts pay about the same interest rate as savings accounts. Sometimes NOW accounts pay higher interest rates on larger balances (such as $1000), but the amount up to the minimum earns only the base interest rate. The combination of a base rate and a higher rate is called a **tiered interest rate.**

Checking Account Charges, Fees, and Penalties

Depository institutions often assess checking account customers a number of charges, fees, and penalties. For example, many institutions have monthly service fees, per-check charges, a transaction charge to use the bank's own ATMs, and a still higher fee to use other ATMs on its network.

In some cases, customers may have to pay **account exception fees.** These charges and penalties are assessed for what the financial institution considers unusual transactions, such as writing a check for insufficient funds; they may also include fees that kick in if a customer does not maintain a minimum balance in an account. Because of account exception fees, customers pay an average of $15 to $20 each month to maintain a checking account. People interested in getting their money's worth in banking would be wise to avoid as many as possible of the charges shown in Table 5.2 on the following page.

Check users must consider the amount of interest the account will earn and how much of it will be offset by any occasional imposition of fees. A NOW account with no balance requirement is preferable, but rare. Decision making becomes more difficult when the institution offers a NOW account in combination with either a minimum- or average-balance requirement. With a **minimum-balance account**, the customer must keep a certain amount (perhaps $400 or $500) in the account *throughout* the time period (usually a month or a quarter) to avoid a flat service charge or fee (usually $5 to $15). A charge is assessed whenever the triggering event occurs—that is, when the balance drops below the specified minimum. With an **average-balance account**, a service fee is assessed only if the *average* daily balance of funds in the account drops below a certain level (perhaps $400 or $500) during the time period (usually a month or a quarter). As an alternative, customers with only a small amount of funds to leave on deposit and who use fewer than ten checks a month might best be served with a non–interest-bearing special checking account that has no balance requirements and costs $0.15 to $0.50 per check or deposit.

Ownership Rights

The process of opening a checking (or savings) account requires that you fill out forms giving the financial institution certain personal information, complete some signature cards, and make your first deposit. A **signature card** is a form that can be used to verify the saver's signature against a signed withdrawal slip or check in the future.

You may need to decide whether to open an individual or joint account. An **individual account** has one owner who is solely responsible for the account and its activity. A **joint account** has two or more owners each of whom has legal rights to funds in the account. The forms of joint ownership discussed in this section apply to all types of property, including automobiles and homes, as well as to checking and savings accounts. There are three types of joint accounts:

1. **Joint tenancy with right of survivorship** (also called **joint tenancy**) is the most common form of joint ownership, especially for husbands and wives. In this case, each person owns the whole of the asset and can dispose of it without the approval of the other(s). When an owner dies, his or her share is divided equally among the other owners. With accounts at financial institutions, the financial institution will honor checks or withdrawal slips possess-

Table 5.2

Costs and Penalties on Checking and Savings Accounts

Account Exception	Reasons for Assessing Costs or Penalties	Assessed on Checking or Savings
Automated teller machine (ATM) transactions	A customer's account is assessed a fee (often $1.00) for each transaction on an ATM; an additional fee may be charged for using an ATM not owned by the financial institution.	Checking, savings
Telephone, computer, or teller information	Fees are assessed for access or requests for account information by telephone, by computer, or in person (often $0.50 per transaction) after a number of free requests (perhaps three) have been made.	Checking, savings
Maintenance fees on a minimum-balance account	An account balance falls below a set minimum amount, such as $300. A set fee of $5 to $15 per month is often charged.	Checking
Maintenance fees on an average-balance account	An average daily account balance for the month falls below a set amount, such as $300. The cost is usually based on a set fee, a scaled amount (the more the account falls below the average, the greater the cost), or a percentage of the amount the account falls below the average.	Checking
Tiered balances	Accounts earn varying interest rates depending on the amount on deposit, such as 2.5 percent on the first $500, 3.0 percent on amounts above $500 to $1000, and 3.5 percent above $1000.	Checking, savings
Stop-payment order	A customer asks the financial institution to not honor a particular check; the fee is $10 to $20 per check.	Checking
Bad check "bounced" for insufficient funds	Costs of $10 to $30 are assessed for each check written or deposited to your account marked "insufficient funds."	Checking
Early account closing	Charges are sometimes assessed if a customer closes an account within a month or quarter of opening it. Charges range from $5 to $10.	Checking, savings
Delayed use of funds	Amounts deposited by check cannot be withdrawn until rules specify.	Checking, savings
Inactive accounts	A monthly penalty may be assessed for inactive accounts (ones with no activity for six months to a year).	Checking, savings
Excessive withdrawals	Some savings institutions assess a penalty ($1 to $3) when withdrawals exceed a certain number per month.	Savings
Early withdrawal	Amounts withdrawn before the end of a quarter earn no interest for that quarter.	Savings
Deposit penalty	Deposits made during the present quarter earn no interest until the beginning of the next quarter.	Savings

ing *either* signature. An advantage of a joint account is that in case of death, and regardless of provisions in a will, the property automatically transfers by contract to the surviving account holder, who continues to have immediate access to the funds. A disadvantage is that one person can withdraw all of the money in the joint account without the other's knowledge.

2. **Tenancy in common** is a form of joint ownership in which two or more parties own the asset, but each owns a separate piece of the property rights. In most states, the ownership shares are presumed to be equal unless otherwise specified. When one owner dies, however, his or her share in the asset is distributed according to the terms of a will (or, if no will exists, according to state law) instead of automatically going to the other co-owners.

Checking Instruments for Special Needs

There are four other types of special checks: (1) traveler's checks, (2) money orders, (3) certified checks, and (4) cashier's checks. People who use these checking instruments must pay a fee for each use. If you have a checking account, you will need these checking instruments only occasionally.

Traveler's Checks   Cashing a personal check in a distant city is usually difficult. **Traveler's checks** are issued by large financial institutions (such as American Express, Visa, and Carte Blanche) and sold through various financial institutions. They are accepted almost everywhere. Purchasers typically pay a fee of 1 percent of the amount of the traveler's checks, or $1 per $100. Credit unions frequently waive the fee. Traveler's checks come in specific denominations ($10, $20, $50, and $100). After purchase, they should be immediately signed once by the purchaser. To use a traveler's check, the purchaser fills in the name of the payee, dates the check, and signs it for a second time. All traveler's check companies guarantee replacement of lost checks if their serial numbers are identified.

Money Orders   Many financial institutions and the U.S. Postal Service sell money orders. A **money order** is a checking instrument bought for a particular amount. Money orders are written for relatively small amounts, and the fee charged—

usually from $0.85 to $8.00—is based on the amount of the order. If you use three or more money orders per month, you would probably find it less expensive to open a checking account.

Certified Checks   Occasionally a merchant will accept your check only with a guarantee that the check is good. A **certified check** is a personal check drawn on your account on which your financial institution imprints the word "certified," signifying that the account has sufficient funds to cover its payment. The financial institution simultaneously freezes that amount in the account and then waits for the check to come back through the banking system before actually subtracting the funds. Checks certified by an officer of the financial institution generally cost $5 to $10.

Cashier's Checks   To be even more certain that a check is good, some payees insist on receiving payment in the form of a **cashier's check.** This check is made out to a specific party and drawn on the account of the financial institution itself; thus, it is backed by the drawee's finances. To obtain such a check, you would pay the financial institution the amount of the cashier's check and have an officer prepare and sign it. Generally, a fee of $5 to $10 is charged.

3. **Tenancy by the entirety**, which exists in about 30 states, is restricted to property held between a husband and a wife. Under this arrangement, no one co-owner can sell or dispose of his or her portion of an asset without the permission of the other. This type of account provides the tightest control over checking or savings because both signatures are required for checks or withdrawal slips. This restriction prevents withdrawals by one owner without the knowledge of the other. Upon the death of one owner, funds in this account pass automatically to the surviving joint account holder outside the terms of the deceased's will.

Generally, dual-earner couples should own some property together and some separately. If you own a business and default on a loan, your creditors usually cannot attach your home if it is in your spouse's name. On the other hand, a nonworking spouse should get his or her name on all deeds and investments; in the event of divorce, courts typically award property to the persons who legally own it. In **community property states**—where most of the money and property acquired during a marriage are legally considered the joint property of both spouses—the rights of both husbands and wives are equally protected. (These states include Arizona, California, Idaho, Louisiana, Nebraska, New Mexico, Texas, Washington, and Wisconsin.)

Two other types of ownership of checking accounts (as well as other assets) exist. A **minor's account** can be opened with the permission of a parent or guardian when a child is not old enough to sign his or her name. In this case, the minor owns the account and is the legal earner of the interest or dividends paid on the account. Another way to hold property is through a **trust**—a legal instrument that places control of one's assets with a **trustee**, a person or institution that manages the financial assets of another. An adult can set up a **trustee account** to hold the property for a child, who is, in turn, restricted from withdrawing money from the account without the adult's signature. The adult remains responsible for the account's activity, and any earnings generated from the account are considered taxable income for the adult.

Cash Management Tool 2: Savings Accounts

5 Identify the potential benefits of opening a savings account as well as key factors to consider when comparing savings accounts.

The second tool of cash management to consider is a savings account. **Savings** simply consists of current income that is not spent on consumption. A local savings account can provide you with an easily accessible source of emergency cash and a temporary holding place for funds in excess of those needed for daily living expenses. Interest rates on savings accounts are typically 0.10 to 0.25 percentage points higher than those paid on NOW checking accounts, although they are usually lower than the rates seen with money market funds or low-risk, longer-term savings instruments.

Funds on deposit in a **savings account** are considered time deposits rather than demand deposits. **Time deposits** are savings that are expected to remain on deposit in a financial institution for an extended period. Institutions usually have a rule requiring that savings account holders give 30 to 60 days' notice for withdrawals, although this restriction is seldom enforced. Some time deposits, however, are **fixed-time deposits**, which specify a period that the savings must be left on deposit, such as six months or three years; certificates of deposit (CDs), discussed later in this chapter, fit this description.

The most popular account offered by financial institutions is the **statement savings account** (also called a **passbook savings account**). Using a statement savings account permits frequent deposit or withdrawal of funds. No fees are assessed as long as a low minimum balance ($1 to $50) is maintained. Statement savings account holders are provided printed receipts to indicate the account transactions, and transactions usually can be accessed through ATMs. The process for opening a savings account is similar to that for a checking account.

All depository institutions offer time deposits. In the following subsections we examine how to save, savings account interest, grace periods, and the impact of the Truth in Savings Act.

How to Save

Most people find it difficult to save money because they look at savings as what is left over after they have met their needs and wants. Wise financial planners

A Checking Account Overdraft Protection Agreement Can Save You Money

Some people have difficulty keeping track of the amount of money in their checking accounts and occasionally write a **bad check**—that is, a check for which there are insufficient funds in the account. Several states allow merchants to sue bad-check writers for the amount of the original check plus a penalty of three times that sum, up to a maximum of $500. If you accidentally write a bad check (only 0.1 percent of all checks "bounce"), your financial institution can take one of four actions:

- If the check amount is not too large or if you are a good customer, your bank might honor the check by paying it and telephoning or writing to remind you to put the funds in the account as soon as possible. *Few* banks are this nice, however.

- Your bank may stamp the check "insufficient funds" and return it to the payee. In this case, the bank will charge you a fee of $10 to $30, and the payee will probably charge you a similar fee. Thus, your fees could total $60 for one bad check!

- If you have signed an **automatic funds transfer agreement** with your bank, the amount necessary to cover the check will be transmitted from your savings to your checking account, assuming you have money in the savings account.

- If you have signed an **automatic overdraft loan agreement** with your bank, needed funds are automatically loaned to you by your bank or from your Visa or MasterCard account. Note, however, that the loan may be advanced in fixed increments of perhaps $100. If you need only $10, you will consequently wind up paying interest on amounts not needed.

Overdraft protection agreements, as noted in items 3 and 4 above, can save you from having to pay overdraft charges if you write a check with insufficient funds in your account. Writing too many bad checks will reflect poorly in your credit rating too, and this topic is examined in Chapter 6.

take a different approach. They follow the adage **"pay yourself first,"** which means to treat savings as the first expenditure after (or even before) getting paid. In this way, they can effectively build a pool of funds to provide for large, irregular expenditures; meet short-term goals; save for retirement, a down payment on a home, or children's college; or simply build a cushion for the unforeseen

Reconcile Your Checking Account

The task in checking account reconciliation is to compare the financial institution's records with the check writer's own records. Most checking account holders receive monthly statements that itemize their checking and ATM transactions. Financial institutions usually return all canceled checks and provide a monthly statement of all transactions; people with truncated checking receive only a statement (not the checks themselves). It is important to reconcile the checking account soon after receiving a monthly statement to catch errors and to avoid the extra mathematics involved with numerous **outstanding checks** (checks written but presented for payment too late to appear on the statement). Research indicates that only about half of the U.S. population balances their checkbooks every month, and another one-fourth never balance their checkbooks.

Most errors in account reconciliation come from three sources: (1) failure of the check writer to add and subtract correctly; (2) failure of the check writer to subtract certain charges made by the financial institution (such as account activity fees, stop-payment charges, and costs for printing checks) or to add interest earned (on interest-earning accounts); and (3) failure of the check writer to record transactions made on ATMs, especially withdrawals.

Follow these steps in reconciling your checking account:

1. *Place the checks in order by check number or issue date.* Many financial institutions arrange the checks on the monthly statement in sequence as well.

2. *Compare the canceled checks with the information in your transaction register* to look for any

recording errors. Make any needed corrections in the transaction register, such as recording a forgotten ATM withdrawal. Place a check mark by each amount in the transaction register that correctly matches the amount shown on the monthly statement.

3. *Bring the transaction register up to date by subtracting any charges* that appear on the monthly statement and adding any interest earned.

4. *Compare your deposit slips* with the deposits listed on the statement and with deposit amounts noted in the transaction register. List **outstanding deposits** (amounts deposited too late to be included on the statement). Total all deposits.

5. *List all outstanding checks*—those written but not presented for payment in time to appear on the statement. Total all of these checks.

6. *See if the account balances.* Take the balance of the account as shown on the statement, add any outstanding deposits (from step 4), and subtract any outstanding checks (from step 5). The resulting amount should equal the amount in the transaction register. If not, you may have transposed digits, such as writing 786 for 876. This type of error often appears when the difference between your balance and that given by the bank is divisible by 9. In this case, locate and correct the transposition. If the error is not a transposition, recheck the arithmetic and carefully follow these six steps again. As a last resort, an officer at the financial institution can assist you—usually for a fee—in reconciling your account.

"rainy day." In Chapters 1, 3, and 4, we discussed ways to calculate the dollar amount to save for such goals. A first step is to accumulate enough savings to cover living expenses (perhaps 70 percent of gross income) for three to six months. This money will serve as an emergency fund in case of job layoff, long illness, or other serious financial calamity. For a person with a $30,000 gross annual income, three- to six-month savings might amount to $5250 to $10,500 ($30,000 ÷ 12 = $2500 × 0.70, or $1750 for each month). People who should consider keeping more funds available—perhaps income to cover six to 12 months of living expenses—include those who depend heavily on commissions or bonuses or who own their own businesses.

Most people rationalize not saving such a large amount for three reasons. First, most savings alternatives typically offer such a low interest rate that the return provides poor protection (if any) against inflation. Second, people usually have ready access to credit when needed for genuine emergencies. Third, many people feel that they have adequate job security as well as sufficient medical and disability insurance coverage to eliminate or greatly cushion the financial impact of such calamities. Nonetheless, you should remember that the purpose of a financial reserve is to provide *adequate* protection.

Savings Account Interest

The calculation of interest to be paid on deposits in financial institutions is primarily based on four variables: (1) how much money is on deposit; (2) the method of determining the balance; (3) the interest rate applied; and (4) the frequency of compounding (such as annually, semiannually, quarterly, monthly, or daily). The more frequent the compounding, the greater the effective return for the saver.

The Truth in Savings Act of 1991 requires depository institutions to disclose a uniform, standardized rate of interest so that depositors can easily compare various savings options. This rate, called the **annual percentage yield (APY)**, is a percentage based on the total interest that would be received on a $100 deposit for a 365-day period given the institution's annual rate of simple interest and frequency of compounding. The institution must use the APY as its interest rate in advertising and in other disclosures to savers.

An account with a grace period provides the depositor with a small financial benefit. A **grace period** is the time period (in days) during which deposits or withdrawals can be made and still earn the same interest as other savings from a given day of the interest period. For example, if deposits are made by the tenth day of the month, interest might be earned from the first of the month. For withdrawals, the grace period generally ranges from three to five days. Thus, if a saver withdrew money from an account within three to five days of the end of the interest period, the savings might still earn interest as if the money remained in the account for the entire period.

Wise money managers should select the savings option that pays the highest APY and avoid institutions that assess excessive costs and penalties. Given the same APY, savers should choose an institution that calculates interest daily. Comparison shopping could easily earn you an extra $10 to $20 each year on a $1500 savings account balance. Savers should also consider the fees and penalties outlined in Table 5.2 when deciding where to open a savings account.

Cash Management Tool 3: Money Market Accounts

6   Explain the importance of placing excess funds in a money market account.

Most people use checking and savings accounts at local financial institutions as the cornerstones of their cash management efforts. They may earn interest on both accounts. When income begins to exceed expenses on a regular basis, perhaps by $200 or $300 each month, a substantial amount of excess funds can quickly build up. Although this situation is a comfortable one, it is wise from a cash management point of view to move some of the excess funds to an account that pays even higher interest.

A **money market account** is any of a variety of interest-earning accounts that pay relatively high interest rates (compared with regular savings accounts) and offer some limited check-writing privileges. Such accounts are offered by banks, savings and loan associations, credit unions, stock brokerage firms, financial services companies, and mutual funds.

Interest rates on money market accounts are typically 0.5 to 1.5 percentage points higher than those paid on NOW checking accounts. Why earn only 3.0 percent on your money when 4.0 percent or more might be earned by opening a money market account? An investor who keeps $4000 in a NOW checking account might earn $120 interest annually, while the person with that amount in a money market mutual fund could well earn $160—a difference of $40. The four types of money market accounts are super NOW accounts, money market deposit accounts, money market mutual funds, and asset management accounts.

Super NOW Accounts

A **super NOW account** is a government-insured money market account offered through depository institutions; it takes the form of a high-interest NOW account with limited checking privileges (usually a maximum of six checks per month). The initial minimum deposit typically ranges from $1000 to $2500. If the average balance falls below a specified amount (such as $1000), the account reverts to earning interest at the lower rate offered on a regular NOW checking account. Depositors can withdraw their funds (using checks, ATMs, or electronic transfers) at any time without penalty.

Money Market Deposit Accounts

A **money market deposit account (MMDA)** is also a government-insured money market account offered through a depository institution. It has minimum-balance requirements and tiered interest rates that vary with the size of the account balance. Institutions are allowed to establish fees for transactions and maintenance, and account holders typically are limited to three to six transactions each month. Often the customer must deposit $1000 to open an account. If the average monthly balance falls below a certain amount, such as $2500, the entire account will earn interest at the lower rate of a regular NOW account. MMDAs generally pay higher interest rates than super NOW accounts.

Money Market Mutual Funds

A **money market mutual fund (MMMF)** is a money market account in a mutual fund investment company (rather than at a depository institution). It pools the cash of thousands of investors and earns a relatively safe and high return by buying debts with very short-term maturities (always less than one year). Interest is calculated daily, and an investor can withdraw funds at any time.

MMMFs, which require a minimum deposit ranging from $500 to $1000, can prove convenient in cases of special financial needs because checks can be drawn on the account. On the other hand, the minimum check limit is often $200, which serves to discourage use of a money market mutual fund as an everyday checking account; at least three dozen mutual funds offer unlimited check writing with no minimums on check amounts, however. Electronic transfers are permitted, but ATMs cannot be used because MMMFs are not depository institutions.

These mutual funds typically pay the highest rate of return that can be earned on a daily basis by small investors, which generally exceeds that offered on most NOW checking accounts by 1.5 to 2.5 percentage points. Although MMMFs are not insured by any federal agency, they are considered extremely safe. Some funds buy only debts of the U.S. government and therefore are virtually risk-free, paying a return only slightly lower than that of other MMMFs. Another group of MMMFs invests in only tax-free debts, which earn lower yields but pay tax-free returns to depositors. (This concept is examined in Chapter 3, "Managing Taxes.") To open an MMMF account, you can contact a mutual fund company; more details are provided in Chapter 15, "Investing through Mutual Funds."*

Investors in high income tax brackets may choose to invest money in tax-exempt securities because they may offer a higher after-tax return than taxable investments. For example, an investor who pays state and local income taxes at a combined 40 percent rate would earn an after-tax return of 6 percent on a taxable investment that returned 10 percent. Alternatively, that investor might choose to invest in a tax-exempt municipal bond with a 7 percent return. Because the latter investment is exempt from federal income taxes, it pays a higher after-tax return—7 percent versus 6 percent. To serve the needs of such investors, some MMMFs invest solely in tax-exempt securities, such as municipal bonds. Investments in these MMMFs are tax-exempt because they involve tax-free securities. (This subject is examined in detail in Chapters 3 and 14.)

Asset Management Accounts

An **asset management account (AMA)** (or **all-in-one account**) is a multiple-purpose coordinated package that gathers most of the customer's financial transactions into a unified account and reports them on a single monthly statement. Included can be transactions in a money market mutual fund, checking, credit card, debit card, automated teller machine, loan, and stock brokerage accounts. Also known as **central asset accounts**, AMAs are offered through stock brokerage firms, financial services companies, and mutual funds. Through an AMA, you may conduct all of your financial business with one institution. The required minimum to open an account is usually $5000 or more. Typically, $10,000 is required to open an AMA account spread across all subaccounts.

---

* Some of the largest money market mutual funds are managed by Dreyfus [(800) 782-6620], Fidelity [(800) 544-8888], Kemper [(800) 621-1048], T. Rowe Price [(800) 541-8832], and Twentieth Century [(800) 345-2021].

Institutions that offer AMAs use computer programs to manage the funds in the account. Daily or weekly, the program checks your various subaccounts and **sweeps** funds in and out of the MMMF to ensure that the highest interest rates apply to the funds. For example, imagine that you open an account with $2000 in cash deposited in the checking account, a $2000 certificate of deposit, a $2000 MMMF, and a $4000 stock brokerage account. Within days, all but perhaps $500 of the checking account funds will be swept into the mutual fund to earn a higher return. Should you write a check for $750, it will be covered by drawing upon the mutual fund. When your $3000 paycheck is deposited electronically into your checking account, much of it will soon be swept into the mutual fund, as will the certificate of deposit funds when the certificate expires. If you had a loan account within the AMA, the monthly payment would be made automatically when a sweep occurs, with the funds for the payment being drawn from the subaccount with the lowest interest rate. Again, the goal is to maintain the highest balances in the highest-paying accounts.

Some AMAs assess an annual fee, typically $100. Firms that handle AMAs usually offer several features to attract investors, such as free credit and debit cards, a rebate of 1 percent on card purchases, free traveler's checks, inexpensive term life insurance, and a free investment advisory newsletter.

Cash Management Tool 4: Low-Risk, Long-Term Savings Instruments

7 List the potential benefits of putting money into low-risk, longer-term savings instruments.

If you are an effective manager of your personal finances, you have established a NOW checking account, a savings account, and a money market account; you earn interest on all funds until they are expended. The fourth tool of cash management involves placing money into low-risk, longer-term savings instruments that allow you to earn even higher returns in exchange for giving up some liquidity. Funds for this part of cash management primarily come from amounts built up in your money market account when you commit some of this money for specific time periods—perhaps three to six months, or potentially even two years or more. Obligating amounts for longer time periods permits you to earn high returns while accumulating amounts to be used for later spending, saving, or investing. Interest rates on low-risk, longer-term savings instruments are typically 2.0 to 3.0 percentage points (or more) higher than those paid on NOW checking accounts.

Savings instruments of this type include certificates of deposit and U.S. government savings bonds. In addition, funds could be placed into higher-yielding, short-term Treasury issues (discussed in Chapter 14, "Investing in Stocks and Bonds"), although the minimum purchase requirements for these instruments range from $1000 to $10,000.

Certificates of Deposit

A **certificate of deposit (CD)** is an interest-earning savings instrument offered by a depository institution that accepts deposits for a fixed amount of time, commonly ranging from seven days to eight years. Certificates of deposit are insured through the FDIC or the NCUSIF. Deposits range from $100 to $100,000. The interest rate existing when the CD is purchased typically is locked in for the entire term of the deposit. Depositors collect their principal and interest at the end of the time period (although sometimes on a monthly basis). Be wary of CDs that are really "investment certificates." These instruments can be recalled and reissued at a lower interest rate prior to maturity at the discretion of the financial institution.

Interest rates on longer-term CDs are always higher than rates on shorter-term instruments to reward savers for accepting the risk that the longer they remain locked into a CD, the greater the chance that inflation will force interest rates to rise. If interest rates rise, savers will have missed out on earning even greater returns; if interest rates fall, they will benefit from the excellent return locked in. Longer-term CDs also pay higher interest rates than NOW accounts because financial institutions can count on having deposits for a specific length of time and can make investments accordingly.

Variable-rate certificates of deposit (sometimes called **adjustable-rate CDs**) are also available. These instruments pay an interest rate that is adjusted (up or down) periodically. Typically, savers are allowed to "lock in," or fix, the rate at any point before their CDs mature. Of course, this variability detracts from the main virtue of the fixed-rate CD—predictability. The best variable-rate CDs have a guaranteed minimum rate. **Bump-up CDs** allow savers to bump up the interest rate once to a higher market rate, if available, and to add up to 100 percent of the initial deposit whenever desired.

Money withdrawn from a CD before the end of the time limit is subject to interest penalties. On certificates held less than one year, the depositor may lose a minimum of one month's interest; on certificates held more than a year, the depositor may lose a minimum of three months' interest. If the penalty exceeds the interest amount, you will get back less than you deposited. Consequently, before putting money into a CD, be confident that it is appropriate to tie up your funds.

Did You KNOW? Interest Rates for Short-Term Cash Management Opportunities Vary

If you want to put your money in a safe "parking" place for a short period, consider the alternatives listed below. The interest rates show relationships during a time of low (3 to 4 percent) inflation. During times of higher inflation, these rates would be commensurately higher.

Type of Account	Interest Rate
NOW checking account	3.0%
Statement savings account	3.4
Super NOW account	3.5
Money market deposit account	3.5
Asset management account	3.5
Money market mutual fund	3.6
Three-month bank certificate of deposit	4.8
Six-month certificate of deposit	5.0
One-year certificate of deposit	5.2
Two and one-half year certificate of deposit	5.5
Five-year certificate of deposit	5.6

Because you do not make deposits and withdrawals after initially investing in a CD, you have no reason to restrict yourself to a nearby institution when searching for the highest yields. An extra 1 percent yield amounts to $100 on a $10,000 CD every year! Lists of institutions paying the highest yields on CDs are published monthly by *Kiplinger's Personal Finance Magazine* and *Money*. Most such financial institutions do 99 percent of their business by mail. You might also check with a stockbroker for high yields, as brokerage firms buy CDs in volume to resell to individuals; these instruments are called **brokered certificates of deposit**. All types of CDs are an excellent cash management tool, and as banking deposits, they enjoy the added protection of federal deposit insurance.

U.S. Government Savings Bonds

Series EE and Series HH savings bonds have been offered since 1980, and they replace the older Series E and H bonds. The bonds are backed with the full faith and credit of the U.S. government. Series EE savings bonds, which represent the most widely held security in the United States, are often purchased through employer payroll deduction plans. They also can be purchased (without any fees, charges, or commissions) from some other federally insured financial institutions. Six in ten U.S. households own government savings bonds. If U.S. savings bond certificates are ever lost, stolen, or destroyed, they can be replaced.

Series EE savings bonds are discount bonds of the U.S. government that are purchased for 50 percent of their face value. A **discount bond** is one sold at less than face value; the difference between its purchase price and its value at maturity represents the interest earned. As a result, Series EE savings bonds pay no periodic interest. For example, a Series EE $100 bond can be purchased for $50 and redeemed at maturity for $100. Series EE bonds can be purchased in denominations from $25 to $10,000, with a maximum purchase limit of $15,000 annually for individuals and $30,000 for couples.

The date at which your investment will double depends upon what happens to interest rates. (A bond earning an average of 5 percent interest would reach

Did You KNOW? *The Government Has an Education Bond Program*

An education bond program permits taxpayers with earnings that fall below certain income limits to exclude from their taxable income all or part of the interest earned on Series EE bonds. Series EE bonds purchased after 1989 by persons aged 24 or older qualify if the bond is redeemed and the principal and interest are used to pay tuition, fees, and other college expenses of a dependent or, in the case of adult education, the bond purchaser or spouse. Expenses for proprietary institutions, such

as beautician or secretarial schools, sometimes do not qualify.

The bonds must be in the taxpayer's name or the taxpayer and his or her spouse; a bond issued in a child's name does not qualify. The tax break goes into effect the year the bond is cashed. Couples earning less than $100,000 can utilize this tax savings idea; single people earning about $65,000 are also eligible. Higher-income people do not qualify for this program.

face value in about 14¹/₂ years; one earning 6 percent would reach face value in 12 years.) Bonds issued after May 1, 1995, that are held from six months to five years earn a rate equal to 85 percent of the yield on *six-month* **Treasury security issues** (debt instruments used by the federal government to finance the national debt). These six-month securities represent examples of **Treasury bills (T-bills)**. If the T-bill rate is 5.25 percent, the bond rate would be approximately 4.46 percent. The rate can change twice each year, on May 1 and November 1; to find out the rate, telephone (800) 487-2663. The rate increases, decreases, or remains the same for each half-year that the bond is held until it reaches maturity. A variation on the Series EE bond is the new **Series I bond**. With these savings bonds, the overall interest rate is tied to changes in the consumer price index (CPI) so as to give the holder some protection from inflation.

Because savings bonds earn market interest rates, it is impossible to predict when a bond will reach face value. The government promises that 17 years will be the maximum; therefore, Series EE bonds are expected to earn a rate of return of at least 4.2 percent. (If necessary, the government will add extra money to the

TAX Considerations & Consequences — *Cash Management*

Good cash management from the perspective of income taxes can be aided by keeping some funds in a tax-free money market mutual fund and using a college savings fund.

Tax-Free Money Market Mutual Funds These money market mutual funds invest in tax-free instruments such as municipal bonds (see Chapter 14). A person paying federal income taxes at the 39.6 percent rate often finds it advantageous to keep some excess funds in tax-free money market mutual funds rather than the standard money market mutual funds. Use the formulas on page 81 to compare taxable and nontaxable returns.

College Savings Funds Consider giving cash or other assets to children because they are likely to pay income taxes at a much lower income tax rate.

For children under age 14, all income earned by assets placed in a Uniform Gifts to Minors Act custodial account or a Uniform Transfers to Minors Act account (the law depends upon the state of residence) above an annually adjusted earnings level is taxable at the child's level. The first $650 of **unearned income** (the income from an invest-

ment) the child receives is tax-free; unearned income above $1200 is taxed at the parent's likely higher rate. As a result, the account will grow faster than if kept in a parent's name because the child's tax rate is 15 percent, which generally is much lower than the parent's tax rate. Starting at age 14, federal income taxes are figured at the child's rate (often 15 percent).

Consider the following example of a college savings fund. A $1200 annual investment, perhaps in a mutual fund, with an assumed 8 percent rate of return will grow to $44,940 in 18 years (Appendix A.3; index factor 37.45 × $1200). If taxed at a parent's rate during those years, the funds probably would not grow to more than $36,000.

College Savings Trust Funds The federal tax code permits families to contribute as much as $50,000 (without incurring a gift tax) to a **savings trust** for college expenses (or **529 plan**, named after the tax code section permitting them), where the investment grows free of taxes. The distributions, which must be used for college expenses beyond tuition, are taxed at the student's rate.

bond to bring it up to its face value.) Series EE bonds cashed in (**redeemed**) within the first six months earn no interest; after six months, no penalty is assessed.

Series EE bonds continue growing in value until the Treasury specifies that they stop accruing interest, 30 years after their issue date. Series EE bonds held for a long time—from five through 17 years—pay 85 percent of the average of *five-year* Treasury security yields (these rates are usually higher than the six-month rates), but that rate begins only in the sixth year that the bonds are held. All interest earnings are added to the bonds' value every month, figured from the month they were purchased.

The semi-annual interest earned on Series EE savings bonds, which is accumulated in the bond, is exempt from all state and local taxes. Federal income tax may be deferred until the bonds are redeemed and the money actually received. Alternatively, the owner may choose to report interest annually on his or her income tax return. This option is usually best when bonds are held in the name of a child who has little or no other reportable income, and this action could result in a zero tax liability on the child's interest income. In addition, interest on Series EE bonds can be deferred when a bondholder trades in the Series EE bonds for Series HH savings bonds.

Series HH savings bonds are U.S. government bonds that are purchased at face value only by exchanging Series EE bonds (or their predecessor E bonds); they may not be purchased with cash. Series HH savings bonds issued after May 1, 1995, pay interest semiannually until they reach maturity five years later. Series HH bonds held longer than five years pay 85 percent of the average yield of *five-year* Treasury security issues. For example, a $10,000 Series HH bond paying 6.0 percent interest annually will yield a semiannual interest payment of $300 [($10,000 × 0.06) ÷ 2 = $300]; the rate could vary in subsequent six-month time periods. Bonds redeemed early are cashed in at slightly less than face value, a penalty that effectively adjusts and reduces the interest rates paid earlier. For example, a $10,000 Series HH bond paying 6.0 percent at maturity will yield less than $10,000 if redeemed after $4^1/2$ years to reflect an overall interest rate of perhaps 5.2 percent.

The interest income earned from Series HH bonds is exempt from state and local income taxes but must be reported on federal income taxes unless deferred. In contrast, accrued interest amounts on a Series EE savings bond exchanged for a Series HH bond and included in its issue price are reportable for federal income tax purposes in the year of redemption, disposition, or final maturity, whichever is earlier. Old HH and EE bonds will continue to operate under earlier rules.

Summary

1. Cash management is the task of maximizing interest earnings and minimizing fees on all of your funds kept readily available for living expenses, recurring household expenses, emergencies, and savings and investment opportunities. The tools of cash management include an interest-earning checking account, a savings account at a local financial institution, a money market account, and various lower-risk, longer-term savings instruments.

2. The four primary providers of cash management services are banks and bank-like institutions, mutual funds, stock brokerage firms, and financial services companies.

3. The most widely recognized forms of electronic funds transfer (EFT) are debit cards, automatic teller machines (ATMs), point-of-sale (POS) terminals, "smart" cards, preauthorized payments and deposits, electronic benefits transfer (EBT), and computer money management. The Electronic Funds Transfer Act protects consumers who use EFT.

4. The first tool of cash management should be an interest-earning checking account for paying monthly living expenses. In choosing a financial institution at which to set up such an account, you should consider such criteria as charges, fees, and penalties.

5. The second tool of cash management is a local savings account. Given the same annual percentage rate, savers should choose an institution that calculates interest daily.

6. After establishing interest-earning checking and savings accounts as the cornerstone of cash management efforts, the third tool of cash management to consider is a money market account. When income begins to exceed expenses on a regular basis, it is wise to move excess funds into an account that pays a higher interest rate, perhaps while you consider later investment options. Money market accounts include super NOW accounts, money market deposit accounts, money market mutual funds, and asset management accounts.

7. The fourth tool of cash management consists of low-risk, longer-term savings instruments that allow you to earn even higher returns, but safely. Funds for this part of cash management primarily come from amounts building up in your money market account. The available choices are certificates of deposit and U.S. government savings bonds.

Key Words & Concepts

Questions for Thought & Discussion

1. What is cash management?
2. What are some of the benefits of effective cash management?
3. List the four tools of cash management. Which two generally pay the highest interest rates?

4. Describe briefly the four major providers of financial services and the products they sell.

5. Differentiate among the bank-like institutions: commercial banks, savings and loan associations, mutual savings banks, and credit unions.

6. How are stock brokerage firms and financial services companies related to cash management?

7. Give several examples of electronic funds transfers.

8. What is a PIN? Explain how PINs work.

9. Give some examples of what "smart" cards can do.

10. How might you quickly send cash to a relative vacationing in London, England? Why would you use that method rather than an alternative?

11. What provisions apply to lost or stolen EFT cards?

12. Why is it important to have an interest-earning checking account?

13. Distinguish between a NOW checking account and a non–interest-earning checking account.

14. Explain the difference between a certified check and a cashier's check.

15. Give some examples of unusual transactions that result in assessment of costs or penalties on checking and savings accounts.

16. Distinguish between a minimum-balance and an average-balance requirement for a checking account.

17. Compare and contrast an automatic funds transfer agreement with an automatic overdraft loan agreement.

18. Distinguish between joint tenancy with right of survivorship and tenancy by the entirety.

19. What does it mean to live in a community property state?

20. Describe the three types of endorsements: blank, special, and restrictive.

21. Identify the main reasons why people make errors when reconciling their checking accounts.

22. Give four important reasons why people save money.

23. Discuss how much money a person might save if he or she is employed at a good job and enjoys a number of fringe benefits.

24. Summarize the provisions of the Truth in Savings Act.

25. Who needs a money market account and why?

26. Differentiate between a money market mutual fund and a money market deposit account.

27. Summarize how an asset management account works.

28. What is a certificate of deposit? Who might want to purchase one?

29. Differentiate between the three types of government savings bonds.

DECISION-MAKING CASES

Case 1   A Lobbyist Considers Her Checking Account Options

Jane Wawrzyniak, a lobbyist for the textile industry living in Springfield, Virginia, has maintained a checking account at a commercial bank for three years. The bank requires a minimum balance of $100 to avoid an account charge, and Jane has always maintained this balance. Recently, she heard that a nearby savings and loan association is offering NOW accounts paying 3 percent interest on the average daily balance of the account. This institution requires a minimum balance of only $300, but a forfeiture of monthly interest occurs if the account falls below this minimum. Given her past habits at the commercial bank, Jane feels that the $300 minimum would not be too hard to maintain. She is seriously thinking about moving her money to the NOW account.

(a) What is the main reason Jane should move her checking account?

(b) What should Jane know about the differences among NOW accounts offered at various financial institutions?

(c) If Jane maintained an average balance of $350 in a NOW checking account earning 3 percent, how much interest would she have earned on her money after one year? (Hint: Use Appendix A.1 or visit the *Garman/Forgue* Web site. Do not forget to subtract Jane's initial lump sum from the derived answer.)

(d) How much more would Jane have earned in one year if she decided to invest in a money market mutual fund paying 4 percent interest instead of the NOW account? (Hint: Use Appendix A.1 or visit the *Garman/Forgue* Web site and make some subtractions.)

Case 2 Use of a Computer Banking Service

Trent Searle, a service station owner from Roy, Utah, pays a $25 monthly fee for a computerized home banking service. His friend Brad Simpson feels that Trent is wasting his money on the service. Trent has a net income of $3000 per month, plus other earnings from some investments. In addition, he is part-owner of an apartment complex, which gives him approximately $1000 per month in income. He always tries to put his excess earnings into solid investments so that they might bring future income and security.

(a) What specific services offered by computer banking would help a person such as Trent?

(b) Justify Trent's paying the $25 monthly fee for computer banking.

(c) Recommend to Trent a combination of the four cash management tools that will offer some alternative money management services. Defend your answer to Trent, making sure to consider factors such as convenience, cost, services, and safety.

Financial Math Questions

1. Twins Barbara and Mary are both age 22. Beginning at age 22, Barbara invests $2000 per year for eight years and then never sets aside another penny. Mary waits ten years and then invests $2000 per year for the next 33 years. Assuming they both earn 8 percent, how much will each twin have at

age 65? (Hint: Use Appendixes A.1 and A.3 or visit the *Garman/Forgue* Web site.)

2. You need to amass $20,000 in the next ten years to help with a relative's college expenses. You have $10,000 available to invest. What annual percentage rate must be earned to realize the $20,000? (Hint: Use Appendix A.1 or visit the *Garman/Forgue* Web site.)

3. You want to create a college fund for a child who is now three years old. The fund should grow to $30,000 in 15 years. If a current investment yields 7 percent, how much must you invest in a lump sum now to realize the $30,000 when needed? (Hint: Use Appendix A.2 or visit the *Garman/Forgue* Web site.)

4. How many years of investing $2000 annually at 8 percent will it take to reach a goal of $20,000? (Hint: Use Appendix A.3 or visit the *Garman/Forgue* Web site.)

5. You plan to retire in 22 years. To provide for your retirement, you initiate a savings program of $6000 per year yielding 7 percent. What will be the value of the retirement fund at the beginning of the twenty-third year? (Hint: Use Appendix A.3 or visit the *Garman/Forgue* Web site.)

MONEY MATTERS: LIFE-CYCLE CASES

Victor and Maria Hernandez Need to Save Money Fast

The Hernandez family is experiencing some financial pressures, even though the couple has a combined income of $70,000. Because she has a bad back, Maria may possibly quit work for money income ($32,000 per year) or work part-time, if she decides to return to college. Also, their eldest son, Joseph, will start college in only three years.

1. If Maria stops working full-time, how much federal income tax will the couple avoid paying to the government, assuming her income is being taxed at a 28 percent rate?

2. If Maria works only half-time, how much federal income tax will she be paying to the

government, assuming her income is being taxed at a 28 percent rate?

3.   Reducing income taxes is one thing, but experiencing an enormous drop in income is an entirely different situation. After calculating the bleak financial figures if Maria cut back her hours, the Hernandezes have decided to rough it out for another year with Maria's ailing back. They have also decided to rapidly increase savings for Joseph's education. How much should they save annually for the next three years if they want to build up Joseph's college fund to $6000, assuming a 7 percent rate of return? (Hint: Use Appendix A.1 or visit the *Garman/Forgue* Web site. Assume that the years until enrollment equal 2, number of years enrolled equal 1, and inflation is 0%.)

4.   How much should they save annually for the next three years if they want to build up Joseph's college fund to $10,000, assuming a 7 percent rate of return?

5.   How much should they save annually for the next five years if they want to build up Joseph's college fund an additional $10,000, assuming a 6 percent rate of return?

How Should the Johnsons Manage Their Cash?

In January, Harry and Belinda Johnson had $1200 in monetary assets (see page 90): $570 in cash on hand, $190 in a statement savings account at First Federal Bank earning 2.8 percent interest compounded daily, $70 in a statement savings account at the Far West Savings and Loan earning 2.9 percent interest compounded semiannually, $60 in a share account at the Smith Brokerage Credit Union earning a dividend of 3.1 percent compounded quarterly, and $310 in their non–interest-earning regular checking account at First Interstate.

1. What specific recommendations would you give the Johnsons for selecting a checking account and savings account that will enable them to effectively use the first and second tools of cash management?

2. Their cash-flow calendar (see Table 4.4 on page 108) indicates that by September the Johnsons will have an extra $1854 available. They also expect continued surpluses of more than $200 per month from that point on because of anticipated salary raises, which are not reflected in their current financial statements. You probably have some recommendations for the Johnsons on using the third and fourth tools of cash management.

   (a) What type of money market account would you recommend that they open? Why?

   (b) What low-risk, long-term savings instrument would you recommend for their savings, given their objective of saving enough to purchase a new car in five years? Support your answer.

3.   If the Johnsons could put all of their monetary assets ($1200) into a savings account earning 4 percent, how much would they have in the account after one year? (Hint: Use Appendix A.1 or visit the *Garman/Forgue* Web site.)

Exploring the World Wide Web of Personal Finance

To complete these exercises, go to the *Garman/Forgue* Web site at *www.hmco.com/college/business/*

Select Personal Finance. Click on the exercise link for this chapter and answer the questions that appear on the Web page.

1. Visit the Web site for *Economic Review,* published by the Federal Reserve Bank of Atlanta, where you will find an article on electronic payment mechanisms in retail trade. What is the major reasoning behind the contention in the article that such forms of payment are more evolutionary than revolutionary?

2. Visit the Web site for *Money* magazine, where you will find a wealth of information about rates of return on certificates of deposit. What is the best rate for a one-year and a five-year CD in a large city nearest your home (look in the state, then the city)? How do these rates compare to the average rates nationally and the highest rates nationally?

3. Visit the Web site for *Money* magazine, where you will find a wealth of information about automatic teller machine fees. What institution charges the lowest and highest fees in a large city near your home? Of the tips given on the site for how to save on fees, which is most practical and appropriate for you?

4. Visit the Web site for *Money* magazine to find a wealth of information about checking account interest rates, fees, and penalties. View the information for the banks in a large city nearest your home. How does the information compare with the information for your current checking account?

5. Visit the Web site for the Federal Reserve Board. There you will find an article titled "New Choices for Receiving Your Federal Government Payments" on the federal government's efforts to move many of the recipients of federal transfer payments to an electronic funds transfer payment plan. What members of your family might be affected by this effort?

Credit Use and Credit Cards

6

OBJECTIVES

After reading this chapter, you should be able to:

1 Compare and contrast installment and noninstallment credit and discuss the costs of credit.

2 Discuss reasons for and against using credit.

3 Describe the types of charge accounts.

4 Describe the process of opening a credit account and the procedures lenders use to evaluate credit applicants.

5 Manage your credit card and charge accounts properly.

M any people have conflicting feelings about the use of credit. On the one hand, they may be attracted to the ease of using a credit card to pay for vacation expenses or to purchase a new television through monthly payments. On the other hand, they may have vivid memories of a friend or relative who fell deeply into debt by overusing credit cards and ended up being pressured by creditors or even going bankrupt. A recent survey revealed that one out of three U.S. households truly fears becoming overextended on credit and more than one-half are concerned about making their credit card payments.

The purpose of this chapter is to show you how to use charge accounts and credit cards wisely. We will first distinguish between installment and noninstallment credit. Next, we will explore a number of positive reasons for using credit as well as some negative aspects of credit. The discussion will then turn toward the types of charge accounts available, explaining how to open such accounts and the procedures lenders use to evaluate credit applicants. The chapter concludes with information on how to manage a charge account properly.

Distinguishing between Installment and Noninstallment Credit

1 Compare and contrast installment and noninstallment credit and discuss the costs of credit.

Credit is a term used to describe any situation in which goods, services, or money are received in exchange for a promise to pay a definite sum of money at a future date. In essence, credit represents a form of trust established between a lender and a borrower. If the lender believes that a prospective borrower has both the ability and the willingness to repay money, then credit will be extended. The borrower is expected to live up to that trust by repaying the lender. For the privilege of borrowing, a lender typically requires that a borrower pay interest and some other charges, such as processing fees.

Consumer credit is nonbusiness debt used by consumers for expenditures other than home mortgages. (Borrowing for housing has investment aspects that result in a separate classification.) There are two types of consumer credit: installment credit and noninstallment credit. With **installment credit**, the consumer must repay the amount owed in a specific number of equal payments, usually monthly. For example, a $12,000 automobile loan might require monthly payments of $255 for 60 months. **Noninstallment credit** includes single-payment loans [such as a loan of $2000 at 12 percent interest with a single payment of $2240 ($2000 plus $2000 × 0.12) due at the end of one year] and open-ended

---

 The Five Criteria Used to Grant Credit

In evaluating a credit application, lenders consider the "five C's" of credit:

CHARACTER

Your honesty and reliability in meeting financial responsibilities make up your character. Your previous credit history indicates how highly you value paying bills on time.

CAPITAL

Capital is a measure of your financial net worth. Questions about assets (home ownership, mutual funds, savings accounts) and liabilities (credit limits and balances due on present credit accounts) reveal whether your net worth is sufficient to warrant the granting of credit.

CAPACITY

Capacity refers to the income available to make repayment. Having a substantial income, holding the same job for several years, and having few other debt payments suggest a strong financial capacity to repay.

COLLATERAL

Collateral is property offered and pledged to secure repayment of a loan and subject to seizure should the borrower fail to repay the loan. Lenders view credit backed by collateral as more secure.

CONDITIONS

General conditions of the economy affect credit. When rising interest rates result in a restriction in the supply of money, less money is available for lending. In such cases, many applicants who would have been approved for credit under better conditions will be rejected.

credit. With **open-ended credit**, credit is extended in advance of any transaction, so that the borrower does not need to reapply each time credit is desired; any amounts owed may be repaid in full in a single payment or via a series of equal or unequal payments, usually monthly. Open-ended credit includes revolving charge accounts (such as department store accounts and bank credit cards), travel and entertainment accounts (such as American Express), service credit, and other charge accounts.

With open-ended credit, the consumer makes any charges desired as long as the total does not exceed his or her **credit limit**, which is the preapproved maximum outstanding debt allowed on a credit account by the lender. Credit limits vary with the perceived credit worthiness of the borrower. Having too many accounts or high credit limits on your accounts may be viewed as a negative by potential lenders, however, even if the balance owed on the accounts is low. This viewpoint is especially true for mortgage lenders. This chapter is concerned mainly with open-ended credit; installment credit will be discussed in Chapter 7.

Reasons for and against Using Credit

2   Discuss reasons for and against using credit.

Consumer credit is widely used in the United States. At times, use of credit may be a good decision. On other occasions, credit may be inappropriate because of its costs and other disadvantages.

Why People Use Credit

Credit is not automatically bad. It can be used in very positive ways to enhance personal financial planning. Some of the reasons people use credit are summarized in the following list:

1. **For convenience.** Using credit—and credit cards in particular—simplifies the process of making many purchases. It provides a record of purchases, and it can be used as leverage in disputes over purchases. Convenience use of credit is growing. For example, the use of credit cards at grocery stores has increased greatly in recent years.

2. **For emergencies.** Consumers use credit to pay for such unexpected expenses as emergency medical services or automobile repairs.

3. **For identification.** For many activities, such as cashing a check or renting an automobile, consumers may need to show a bank credit card to verify their identities. Merchants are not allowed to charge bad checks against bank credit cards, and putting your card account number on your check increases the possibility of fraudulent use of your charge account.

4. **To make reservations.** Most motels, hotels, and car rental agencies require some form of deposit to hold a reservation. A credit card number usually will serve as such a deposit, allowing guaranteed reservations to be made over the telephone. Note, however, that the hotel might notify the credit card issuer to put a hold on your account for the anticipated total amount of the charge; this process is called **credit card blocking**.

5. **To consume expensive products earlier.** Buying "big ticket" items such as a computer or automobile on credit allows the consumer immediate use of the product. Many expensive items would not be purchased (or would be bought only after several years of saving) without the opportunity to pay for them over time. Note, however, that the product should last at least as long as the repayment period on the debt.

6. **To enjoy the good life.** Increasing numbers of people use credit as a way to raise their current level of living in anticipation of higher incomes in the future. In this way, they enjoy a rate of consumption today that is higher than their current income seemingly would permit. Unfortunately, this strategy for using credit gets many people into financial trouble.

7. **To take advantage of free credit.** Merchants sometimes offer "free" credit for a period of time as an inducement to buy. Referred to as "same as cash" plans, these programs allow the buyer to pay later without incurring finance charges. Usually the free credit lasts for a defined time period, such as 90 days or six months. Be careful using these plans, as interest may be owed for the entire time period if the buyer pays even one day after the alloted free credit period. One financial strategy is to use a cash advance or convenience check from a bank credit card (discussed later in this chapter) to "pay" the debt just before the deadline, thereby obtaining several months of free credit before finance charges begin.

8. **To consolidate debts.** Many consumers who have difficulty making credit repayments turn to a **debt-consolidation loan** through which the debtor exchanges several smaller debts with varying due dates and interest rates for a single large loan. Even when interest rates for such loans are higher, the new payment is usually smaller than the combined payments for the other debts because the term of the new loan is longer than the old ones.

9. **For protection against ripoffs and frauds.** Mail order and telephone purchases made on a credit card can be contested with the credit card issuer under the guidelines of the Fair Credit Billing Act (discussed later).

10. **To obtain an education.** The rising cost of higher education forces many to borrow. This may be the one of the better uses of credit, as one is investing in oneself to raise quality of life and/or income in the future.

Reasons against Using Credit

Reasons for not using credit include interest costs, fees for using (or misusing credit) in certain ways, privacy concerns, the potential for overspending, and its negative effect on financial flexibility.

Interest Is Costly **Interest** represents the price of credit. When stated in dollars, interest composes part of the **finance charge**, which is the total dollar amount paid to use credit, including interest and any other required charges such as a loan application fee. Since the 1968 passage of the Truth in Lending Act, lenders have been required to state the finance charge as an **annual percentage rate (APR)** that expresses the cost of credit on a yearly basis as a percentage rate. For example, a single-payment, one-year loan for $1000 with a finance charge of $140 has a 14 percent APR. The lower the APR, the lower the true cost of credit. The annual percentage rate can be used to compare credit contracts with different time periods, finance charges, repayment schedules, and amounts borrowed.

The Fair Credit and Charge Card Disclosure Act (FCCCDA) of 1988 has also made it easier to shop around for the best credit card. This act requires that key pieces of information be disclosed in direct-mail advertising and on applications for credit cards. Such information includes the APR, how it is calculated if it is a variable rate, all fees (including fees for late payments), the length of the grace period, and the method used to calculate the account balance (these topics are discussed below).* Many states have **usury laws** (sometimes called **small loan laws**) that establish the maximum loan amounts, interest rates, and credit-related fees for various types of loans from various sources. These maximum rates can vary from 18 percent to as much as 54 percent. Note that the laws of the state in which the lending institution is located apply, rather than the laws of the state in which the borrower lives. These regulations would apply to the annual fee, late payment fee, and other fees charged on a bank credit card.

Additional Fees Are Common A significant negative aspect of credit use is the large number of fees assessed by creditors. Some of these fees are associated with normal usage of the credit arrangement. Others are assessed when the borrower fails to comply with the stipulations of the contract in some way.

Bank credit card lenders typically assess annual fees ranging from $25 to $50 (or more). In addition, they may charge a **transaction fee** (a small charge levied each time a card is used). Some even charge a $3 fee for printing the monthly credit bill. These fees are not included in the APR calculation because they are not generally known in advance. Thus, an apparently low-cost card may turn into a high-cost card when all fees are considered.

Late payment fees of $10 and more are common when the borrower fails to make a payment by the due date. Many credit card issuers now charge a significant **over-the-limit fee** when the cardholder exceeds his or her credit limit. In addition, banks are increasingly likely to impose **punitive interest rates** on certain borrowers—that is, to raise the APR for the entire debt when a payment is late, the credit limit exceeded, or the creditor views some other aspect of the borrower to be a negative. The combination of these fees and higher rates can easily exceed the "normal" finance charge.

High-Priced Add-Ons May Be Difficult to Avoid Many lenders encourage borrowers to sign up for **credit life insurance** that pays the unpaid balance of a loan—to the lender—in the event of the borrower's death. People are often grossly overcharged for this insurance (the industry pays out an unusually low 43 percent of revenues for claims), and few people need it. Rates typically range from $0.50 to $0.70 per $100 of the outstanding balance—every month! Credit life insurance is one cost that can be avoided. *Term life insurance* (discussed in Chapter 12) is much less expensive, and proceeds go to the borrower's beneficiaries, not to a lender.

---

*   For $5 CardTrack [(800) 344-7714] offers monthly updates listing the lowest-cost bank credit cards.

Choose between a Low Annual Fee and a Low APR

When shopping for a credit card, you may encounter some cards with low or no annual fees and others with low APRs. Which is better? Generally speaking, you should choose a card with the lowest available APR if you are likely to carry a balance on the account. Similarly, you should choose a card without an annual fee if you are likely to pay your balance in full each month because the APR is irrelevant if no balance is carried.

One personal finance strategy is to use one credit card for convenience items that are paid for monthly and another for items where paying off the balance each month is not possible. Use a no annual fee card for the convenience purchases and a low APR card for purchases where you carry a balance.

Fortunately, the bank credit card business is highly competitive. Do not hesitate to contact your current card issuers and ask if you qualify for a lower annual fee or lower APR. Make sure they know that you are shopping for the lowest charges possible, and then switch cards if necessary.

Lenders may also offer **credit disability insurance**, which repays the outstanding loan balance if the borrower becomes disabled (with "disability" usually being very narrowly defined). In addition, **unemployment credit insurance** policies are sold. Rates charged for these protections may seem low, but on a percentage basis they are much higher than the actual cost of providing the protection.

Lenders that require credit life, credit disability, or credit unemployment insurance as a condition for granting a loan (because lenders find these add-ons highly profitable) should be avoided. The only exception might be credit life insurance for those people who cannot obtain life insurance through more traditional means.

Liability for Lost Credit Cards The Truth in Lending Act, as amended, limits a cardholder's liability for lost or stolen credit cards (including telephone calling cards) to $50 per card. This **credit card liability** applies only if you receive notification of your potential liability, you accepted the card when it was first mailed to you, the company provided you with a self-addressed form with which to notify it if the card was lost, and the card was used illegally before you notified the issuer of the loss. Although your financial liability is low, some companies specialize in selling **credit card insurance** (for an annual premium ranging from $15 to $49) that will pay creditors for the first $50 of unauthorized use of an insured person's lost or stolen credit cards. Such insurance is profitable for insurance companies and an unnecessary expense for you. In addition, most homeowner's and renter's insurance policies pay for such losses (see Chapter 10 for details). As a gesture of good will, most credit card companies will waive the $50 fee for unauthorized use when notified about a lost card promptly.

It Is Tempting to Overspend A major disadvantage of credit is that its use often leads to overspending. Buying $425 worth of new clothes on a charge account for $25 per month for 20 months (for a $75 finance charge) may appear easier than paying cash for a planned $200 worth of new clothes. It is even easier to buy more clothes on credit the next month, especially if you have nine credit cards—the number of cards held by the typical U.S. credit customer.

Overindebtedness can present a real problem for credit users. If a consumer has monthly nonmortgage debt repayments amounting to 20 percent of monthly take-home pay, he or she is seriously in debt. Instead of working at a job and spending the income, the consumer slaves at a job to pay the bills. It feels like "paying on Visa forever" instead of "paying off Visa." Misusing credit and not paying bills on time can give a consumer a poor credit reputation, damage employment prospects, and sometimes result in the loss of items purchased.

Privacy Is a Concern Protection of privacy is a vital concern to users of credit cards. Fraud can occur, as can "identity snatching." With very little personal information, a clever thief can borrow someone's credit identity and run up thousands of dollars in bills. To exercise caution with credit, follow these guidelines:

- Offer no personal information (such as your address, telephone number, or Social Security number) to merchants when using a credit card. If the merchant requires identification beyond the credit card (e.g., a driver's license) do not allow such information to be written down.

- Save all purchase and ATM receipts and check them against statements from creditors.

- Avoid giving out your credit card or checking account number on the telephone to anyone you do not know or did not telephone directly yourself.

Making Minimum Payments Can Keep You in Permanent Debt

Do you currently have a balance outstanding on your credit cards? How long have you carried the balance? If a person opens an account at age 20 and borrows $500 the first month and more the next month, he or she may find that the balance does not drop below that first $500 for years. If $500 is still owed on the account years later (perhaps at age 35), that person has **perma-debt**. In essence, the first month's borrowing was never paid off. At a typical 18% APR, the finance charges for $500 for 20 years would total $1800 (0.18 × $500 × 20).

Credit card issuers often require a minimum monthly repayment as low as $1/36$ or $1/48$ of the outstanding balance. Such a payment is mathematically guaranteed to keep the user in debt for a long time. In addition, paying only the minimum may lead a cardholder into severe financial difficulty. To

illustrate, a minimum payment of $25 ($1/48$) on an outstanding balance of $1200 with a 1.6 percent monthly periodic rate results in only $5.80 going to reduce the actual debt. The other $19.20 ($1200 × 0.016 = $19.20) is used to pay the monthly interest. At this rate of repayment, it would take more than seven years to repay the $1200.

Even worse, many card issuers today allow credit cardholders to skip a payment ($0 minimum payment) if a sufficiently large payment was made the month before. Note that interest will still be accrued for a month in which no payment is made. In essence, you increase your debt by allowing the interest to be charged as well. Low and $0 minimum payments illustrate the basic concept that lenders make their money from finance charges. The higher these charges, the more money the lender makes.

- Immediately change the status of a credit card account should you become married, separated, or divorced.

- Review your credit bureau report at least once each year.

- Report lost or stolen credit cards and suspicious billing information without delay. This is especially important when one uses cybercredit to make purchases over the Internet using a bank credit card.

Use of Credit Reduces Financial Flexibility   Perhaps the greatest disadvantage of credit use comes from the loss of financial flexibility in personal money management. If you have installment debts that claim 10 percent of your after-tax income, you have lost the opportunity to spend those dollars for some other purpose. Credit use also reduces your future buying power, as the money you pay out on a loan also includes a finance charge. Credit can be seen as a promise to work for the creditor in the future to pay off the debt.

Types of Open-Ended Credit Accounts

3 Describe the types of charge accounts.

Open-ended credit can be used to make purchases and, in some cases, to obtain cash advances. It is the most convenient type of credit and, therefore, the most abused. Many open-ended accounts (but not all) use a credit card. A **credit (or charge) card** is a plastic card identifying the holder as a participant in the charge account plan of a lender, such as a department store, oil company, or financial institution. Several types of consumer charge accounts are described in this section. All allow multiple uses without reapplication for credit, but some require that the entire balance be repaid each month. Credit cards and charge accounts are now the primary source of household debt other than home mortgages.

Revolving Credit Card Accounts at Retail Stores

A **revolving charge account** (also known as an **option account**) is any credit account for which the user has the option to pay the bill in full or to spread repayment over several months. If the latter payment scheme is selected, a fixed dollar minimum or percentage of the outstanding balance must be repaid each month. More than two-thirds of all cardholders maintain balances, and the average customer takes more than 15 months to pay for the charges even as other charges are being added to the account. The user may continue to make charges against the account as long as the total debt remains below the credit limit. Examples of revolving credit card accounts at retail stores include JCPenney, Best Buy, and Mobil Oil.

Revolving Credit Card Accounts at Financial Institutions

Revolving charge accounts are also offered through some 6000 commercial banks, savings and loan associations, and credit unions across the United States as well as by a number of consumer-products companies such as AT&T, Dean

When a Secured Credit Card Is Appropriate

Dozens of banks advertise that they will help people who want a credit card but are experiencing difficulty with obtaining one because they are new to use of credit or have insufficient income, some past delinquencies, or a previous bankruptcy. For such borrowers, lenders offer a **secured credit card** (also called a **collateralized credit card**). This credit card account is secured by a savings account opened at the financial institution that issues the card. If the credit card user fails to repay the debt, the bank can take legal action to seize the funds in the savings account.

Banks offering secured credit cards typically charge an application fee ($30 or more) and require the applicant to make a deposit of $300 to $600 into a savings account. The person then receives a credit limit in a like amount on a bank credit card,

such as Visa or MasterCard. The savings account balance cannot be withdrawn as long as the card is available for use. The deposit is refunded (with interest) when the balance is paid off and the account is closed.

Secured credit cards are sometimes marketed through "900" telephone numbers; the caller is charged a fee for the telephone call (often $30 or more) and a nonrefundable "application fee" (perhaps another $30 to $50). Shop locally for secured credit to avoid these extra costs.

Most people do not need a secured credit card, but those who have no alternative should consider obtaining one from a reputable institution. Proper usage can help improve the information in the cardholder's credit file so that the user can later qualify for a traditional unsecured credit card.

Witter Reynolds, General Motors, and GTE. Because these accounts can be accessed by a credit card (such as Visa, MasterCard, and Discover), they are usually called **bank credit card accounts**, or simply **bank cards**. Consumers use these accounts nationally and internationally in hundreds of thousands of retail outlets and thus may obtain the widest selection of goods and services through this type of credit card account. Note that the actual lender is the financial institution—not Visa, MasterCard, or their counterparts that provide the electronic network through which transactions are communicated. Participating merchants pay transaction fees of 2 to 8 percent for every dollar charged.

A **cash advance** is a cash loan from a bank credit card account. A transaction fee is usually assessed for each cash advance. Cash advances often are subject to a higher APR than are purchases, and interest is assessed as soon as the cash advance is granted. In most cases, the borrower receives the cash advance, such as from an automated teller machine (ATM). On other occasions, the funds are transferred automatically to cover a check written with insufficient funds in an account via an **automatic overdraft loan**.

Cash advances may be obtained at any financial institution that issues the type of card being used. Many bank credit card issuers periodically send three to five **convenience checks** to their cardholders that enable the customers to use the "checks" to access their credit card accounts and thereby make payments to others. Of course, these instruments are not genuine demand-deposit checks but simply a check-equivalent way to borrow money. If you receive such but do not want to use them, either put them in a safe place or destroy them immediately, as they could be used fraudulently if lost or stolen.

Some bank card issuers offer some form of **prestige card**, such as a "Gold" Visa, "Silver" MasterCard, or "Platinum" American Express card. These accounts require that the user possess higher credit qualifications and offer enhancements such as free traveler's checks and a higher credit limit. Most holders of regular bank credit cards do not realize that they could receive the higher credit limit on their standard card just by requesting one from the issuer. Prestige cards also may carry higher annual fees.

Some Visa and MasterCards are identified as **affinity cards**—that is, standard bank cards with the logo of a sponsoring organization imprinted on the face of the card. Typically, the issuing financial institution donates a portion of the annual fee and a small percentage of the amounts charged (perhaps 0.25, 0.5, or 1 percent) to the sponsoring organization. Sponsors may include charitable, political, sports, or other organized groups, such as the Sierra Club or Mothers Against Drunk Driving. Members of the sponsoring organizations may be motivated to use an affinity card because their organization receives money from each transaction. Creditors rightly calculate that fewer delinquencies will occur among the particular group of people, so they can afford to transfer some dollars to the named organization.

Travel and Entertainment Accounts

Travel and entertainment (T&E) accounts are similar to bank credit cards in that they allow holders to make purchases at numerous businesses; the entire balance charged must be repaid within 30 days, however. The best known of these cards are American Express, Diners' Club, and Carte Blanche. T&E cards are

---

Did You KNOW? *About Today's World of Bank Card Competition*

Increased competition in the credit card industry has provided both opportunities and problems for credit card users. Consumers who understand the innovations described below can take advantage of the opportunities and avoid the problems.

- Lenders now issue credit cards with **fixed** or **variable interest rates**. If the interest rate is variable—that is, it moves up or down monthly according to changes in some index of the lender's cost of funds—the borrower may see finance charges increase. Common indexes used include the prime rate and the federal funds rate (see Chapter 1). The rate used might be stated as "prime plus 8.8 percent." Thus, if the prime rate is currently 6.4 percent, the variable rate on the card will total 15.2 percent.

- An **introductory** or **teaser rate** is a temporarily low rate used to entice a borrower to sign up for

a new card. The rate typically reverts to a much higher fixed or variable rate after six or 12 months. Some borrowers sequentially open new accounts with introductory rates as introductory rates expire on their existing accounts to maintain low rates on a balance owed.

- A **co-branded card** is a normal bank credit card issued by a retail chain or manufacturer. As an example, Ford Motor Company offers a MasterCard account. Users of co-branded cards often pay reduced prices on the merchandise sold by the retailer or manufacturer (e.g., a new car), with discounts pegged to the amounts charged to their accounts.

- Some credit cards offer **rebates** that provide a partial refund of charges made on the cards. Occasionally these rebates take the form of frequent flyer miles on airlines cooperating with the plan.

Access a Personal Line of Credit

A **personal line of credit** is a lending arrangement that allows the borrower access to a prearranged revolving line of credit provided by the lender (usually a bank, savings and loan association, or brokerage firm). The essence of a line of credit is that borrowers can obtain a cash advance when needed and not reapply each time. Borrowers access the funds up to their credit limit in three ways:

• Contact the lender by telephone, wire, or in person.

• Use special checks, which may be used to make purchases or be deposited into one's checking account.

• Use a preapproved credit card.

Like all revolving accounts, a personal line of credit includes a credit limit and a flexible repayment schedule. For a home-equity line of credit, the equity in one's home is used as collateral for a secured revolving line of credit.

often used by businesspeople for food and lodging expenses while traveling. They are somewhat more difficult to obtain than bank cards because applicants must have higher-than-average incomes to qualify for an account; in addition, applicants must pay an annual membership of $35 or more. Furthermore, T&E cards are not accepted at nearly as many outlets as are bank credit cards. Travel and entertainment accounts are considered to be prestige cards, although, for example, American Express has more than 22 million "prestige" cards outstanding.

Other Forms of Open-Ended Credit

Service credit is the credit granted to consumers by public utilities, physicians, dentists, and other service providers that do not require full payment when services are rendered. For example, your electric company allows you to use electricity all month and then sends you a bill that may not be due for ten to 15 days. Service credit usually carries no interest, although penalty charges may apply if payments are made slowly, and future service may be cut off for continued slow payment or for nonpayment.

A **budget account** is a more limited charge account. Users must repay a specific portion of the charged amount (usually one-fourth to one-third) within 30 days and then pay the remainder over a few months. People with little or no credit experience may be able to open a budget account with some local department stores and small specialty shops.

The Process for Opening an Open-Ended Charge Account

4 Describe the process of opening a credit account and the procedures lenders use to evaluate credit applicants.

Obtaining credit requires that you complete a credit application. Based on the information in the application, the lender will have your credit history investigated. This information is then evaluated, and the lender decides whether to extend credit. If approved, you will receive a **credit card agreement** that outlines the rules and fees associated with the account. Of course, it is wiser to request and read such information before applying rather than after filling out the application form.

The Credit Application

A **credit application** is a form or interview that requests information that reflects your ability and willingness to repay debts. The information on credit applications helps lenders make informed decisions about whether they will be repaid by borrowers. Answering questions completely and honestly both on an application form and during an interview is important. If inconsistencies arise, the lender could refuse the request for credit.

A recent study revealed that about 12 percent of all people applying for credit are denied. Approximately half of the turndowns had no established **credit history** (a continuing record of a borrower's debt commitments and how well they have been honored) or their credit history contained adverse information. A bad credit history is like having high blood pressure—you may not know you have a problem until something bad happens, such as rejection of a loan application.

The Equal Credit Opportunity Act (ECOA) of 1975 prohibits certain types of **unfair discrimination** (making distinctions among individuals based on unfair criteria) when granting credit. Under this act, the lender must notify the applicant within 30 days as to the acceptance or rejection of a credit application. The

Establish a Good Credit History

After examining a credit-scoring chart (see page 169), most people who are new to the world of credit wonder whether they will ever get credit when they need it. The key is to establish a good credit history. The following steps can help you get started.

Establish both a checking and a savings account.
Lenders see persons who can handle these accounts as being more likely to manage credit usage.

Have a telephone installed and billed in your name.
Most risk-scoring systems view this condition as a positive factor, although the information must be offered voluntarily because the Equal Credit Opportunity Act prohibits inquiries about the topic.

Request, acquire, and use an oil-company credit card.
These cards are not difficult to obtain, but should one company refuse, simply apply to another company, as companies' scoring systems differ. Use the credit sparingly and repay the debt promptly.

Apply for a bank credit card.
Most bank card issuers have a program of test credit for people who lack an extensive credit history. The credit limit may be low (perhaps $300), but at least the opportunity exists to establish a credit rating. Later you can request an increase in the credit limit.

Ask a bank for a small short-term cash loan.
Putting these funds into a savings account at the bank will almost guarantee that you will make the required three or four monthly payments. In addition, the interest charges on the loan will be partially offset by the interest earned on the savings.

Pay off student loans.
Many people have their first exposure to credit through the student loans they use to attend college. Paying off these loans quickly through a series of regular monthly payments can show prospective lenders that you are a responsible borrower.

ECOA also requires creditors to provide the applicant with a written statement, if requested, of the reasons for refusing credit. Rejecting a credit application due to poor credit history is legal. In contrast, rejecting a person on the basis of gender, race, age, national origin, religion, or receipt of Social Security or public assistance is illegal. Credit applications cannot probe for information that could be used in a biased manner, such as marital status and childbearing plans. (Applicants may offer such information voluntarily, however.) If discrimination is proved in court, the lender may be liable for up to $10,000 in fines.

A creditor cannot require an applicant to disclose income from alimony, separate maintenance payments, or child support payments. If the borrower wants this income to be counted in evaluating the application, the creditor can consider whether that income stream is consistently received. Information about a spouse or former spouse may not be requested unless the spouse will use the account, it is a joint account, or repayment of debts will rely on the spouse's income or other financial support. The law requires that credit granted in both spouses' names must be used to build a credit history for both parties as well as for each individual.

The Credit Investigation

Upon receiving your completed credit application, the lender generally conducts a **credit investigation** and compares that information with the information on your application. Credit information is generally obtained from a **credit bureau** that keeps records of borrowers' credit histories for creditors to review. Credit bureaus compile information from various merchants, utility companies, banks, court records, and creditors. Most of the more than 2000 local credit bureaus belong to national groups that have access to the credit histories of more than 160 million people.

Members (lenders that also provide data to a credit bureau) pay both an annual charge and a specific fee for each **credit report** requested. Nonmember lenders must pay higher fees to receive these reports.

 ### *Find Out What Is in Your Credit Bureau File*

Credit bureaus are required by law to provide consumers with a credit report upon request. A report is free if it was used to deny credit within the past 60 days; otherwise a modest fee may be charged for a report. To obtain a report, you should provide the credit bureau with the following information:

- Your full name, including Jr., III, or other titles
- Your current and previous addresses for the last five years
- Your spouse's first name
- Your Social Security number and year of birth

For privacy reasons you should sign your request and provide a photocopy of your driver's license or other proof of your current address. Equifax [(800) 685-1111], TransUnion [(800) 916-8800], and Experian [(800) 682-7654] are the three largest national groups of credit bureaus. They provide consumers with copies of their credit report for a nominal fee. You may also ask to have your name withheld when they sell lists of consumers for credit card marketing purposes for two years by calling one number [(888) 576-8688].

Credit Ratings and Risk Scoring

A **credit rating** is an evaluation of a person's previous credit experience. Credit ratings may be determined in a subjective manner or by using a **credit scoring system** (also known as **risk scoring** or **behavior scoring**) in which a statistical measure is used to rate applicants on the basis of various factors relevant to creditworthiness. This process involves tracking the bill-paying patterns and other important characteristics of credit users to develop a statistical profile that seeks to predict future performance as a credit risk. Important characteristics typically

Your Score as a Credit Risk

Creditors are interested in extending credit to people who are likely to repay their debts and avoiding those who are most likely to default on their debts. The risk-scoring system shown here is hypothetical. Real systems are more precise and complex, and often involve 24 or more factors. The required number of points for approval might be as follows: local department store credit card (70), oil company credit card (74), major department store credit card (78), bank credit card (82), and travel and entertainment card (90). From the information provided, circle the points appropriate for yourself and total the number to obtain an impression of yourself as a credit risk.

Although these numbers are for purposes of illustration only, people with higher scores are likely to be better credit risks than those with lower scores, assuming, of course, that the person does not already have too much debt. The scores needed for approval vary among creditors, however, and depend upon economic conditions, a creditor's profit target, and its tolerance of risk. Some lenders have "red flags," such as bankruptcy, for which they will deny credit regardless of an applicant's overall score.

Factors	Points
Length of residence:	
Less than 1 year	1
1–3 years	5
4–5 years	10
6–9 years	14
10 or more years	20
Housing residence:	
Own	15
Rent	5
Other	1
Years at current job:	
Less than 1 year	1
1–2 years	5
3–5 years	10
6–9 years	15
10 or more years	20
Annual family income:	
Less than $10,000	2
$10,000–$19,999	6
$20,000–$29,999	8
$30,000–$49,999	18
$50,000 and over	20
Age in years:	
Under 21	0
21–24	4
25–34	9
35–44	11
45–54	12
55–62	13
63–65	14
Over 65	15

Factors	Points
Bank accounts:	
Checking and savings	20
Savings only	8
Checking only	6
Current bank loans:	
One or more	5
None	0
Small-loan company loans:	
Two or more	−10
One	−5
Telephone:	
Yes	8
No	0
Bank credit cards:	
Yes	8
No	0
Travel/entertainment cards:	
Two or more	0
One	5
Zero	10
Department store cards:	
Two or more	0
One	3
Zero	8
Credit bureau information:	
Excellent or satisfactory on 3+ accounts	20
Excellent or satisfactory on 1–2 accounts	6
No record	−5
Derogatory only	−20

include income, length of employment, home ownership status, and credit history.

In the credit rating procedure, creditors either determine credit scores themselves or rely upon a credit bureau to develop and provide scores. In all cases, the actual decision to grant credit is made by the lender. Consumers do not usually see their credit scores. When a credit bureau develops its own point system to help credit granters assess credit applications, the bureau needs to disclose these scores. Credit reports are often used for employment and insurance applications.

Risk scoring allows creditors or credit bureaus to categorize credit users according to the level of risk. Under the concept of **tiered pricing**, lenders offer lower interest rates to their customers having highest credit scores while charging steep rates to higher-risk borrowers. This difference represents another reason to make sure that your credit bureau file is accurate. Risk scoring also permits identification of borrowers who perhaps should have their credit limit increased or lowered, as well as those who could receive special marketing appeals.

Correct Your Credit History

The objective of the Fair Credit Reporting Act (FCRA) is to place certain restrictions on credit bureaus in an effort to reduce errors in credit reports. The law requires that reports contain accurate, relevant, and recent information, and that only bona fide users be permitted to review a file for approved purposes. One in five complaints to the Federal Trade Commission involves credit bureaus.

FCRA is partially enforced by credit-using consumers. For example, if you are denied credit, insurance, or employment because of information contained in a credit bureau report, the law requires that you be provided with the name and address of any credit bureau that supplied information about you. You then have 30 days to request a free summary of the contents of your file from the credit bureau; the bureau must provide the consumer with a copy of the same report it would send to a lender.

If you dispute an item, the law requires that it must be reinvestigated by the credit bureau. If the bureau cannot complete its investigation within 30 days, it must drop the information from your credit file. If the information was in error, it must be corrected. If the credit bureau refuses to make a correction (perhaps because the information was "technically correct"), you also may wish to provide your version of the disputed information (in 100 words or less) by adding a **consumer statement.** All new information (corrections or your side of the story) must be sent to anyone who received a credit report on you in the previous six months.

Negative information in your file is generally not reportable after a period of seven years (except for bankruptcy data, for which the time limit is ten years). If you have applied for life insurance or certain employment, your file may include comments from neighbors and friends about your morals, living habits, and personal information. For these kinds of investigations, you must be informed when a report is being compiled.

Some people are denied credit with the notation of "insufficient credit file" or "no credit file." In such cases, the credit file may not contain information on all of the accounts the applicant has had with creditors because not all creditors automatically report information to credit bureaus. To avoid this difficulty, provide your local credit bureau with all appropriate information that can verify the accounts you have now or had in the past.

Many companies interested in expanding their base of credit customers pay credit bureaus to **prescreen** their files and identify people who pass certain tests of creditworthiness. The company then sends the prescreened people an application for credit. Some have been **preapproved** and need only sign the notice to open the account. Note that being preapproved means only that you will be granted credit. The credit card debt limit will be determined after you apply.

Managing a Charge Account

5 Manage your credit card and charge accounts properly.

Credit can be a positive tool in personal financial management when used appropriately. The key is to manage credit use, which requires that you understand and monitor your credit statements and understand how finance charges are computed.

Credit Statements

Active charge account holders receive a monthly **credit statement** (also called a **periodic statement**) that summarizes the charges, payments, finance charges, and other activity on the account. The significant features of credit statements are the billing date, due date, grace period, payment schedule, and credit receipts obtained. You also need to know how to correct errors in your credit statements. Figure 6.1 on the following page shows a monthly statement for a credit card.

Billing Date The **billing date** (sometimes called the **statement date** or **closing date**) is the last day of the month for which any transactions are reported on the statement. In Figure 6.1, this date is 5/22/00. Any transactions or payments made after this date will be recorded on the following month's credit statement. The statement is mailed to the cardholder a day or so after the billing date. The billing date is generally the same day of each month, and the time period between billing dates is referred to as the **billing cycle**.

Due Date The **due date** is the specific day by which the credit card company should receive payment from you. In Figure 6.1, this date is 6/17/00. The period between the billing date and the due date—usually 20 to 25 days (with 20 days becoming more common)—represents the time allowed for statements and payments to be mailed and for the borrower to make arrangements to pay. Federal law states that bills must be mailed to cardholders at least 14 days before payments are due. If payment is received later than the due date, the customer is likely to be assessed a late fee ranging from $10 to $15. Even if a late fee is not assessed, a credit bureau may be notified of slow payment. If no payment is received by the due date, the cardholder may be declared in **default** (the borrower has failed to make a payment of principal or interest when due or has not met another key requirement of a legal credit agreement). The company will then begin collection efforts, often by mailing a "first notice" that a payment is overdue.

Transaction and Posting Dates The date that a credit cardholder makes a purchase (or receives a credit as described below) is known as the **transaction date**. In the past, several days would pass before the credit card company was

Figure 6.1

Sample Statement for a Revolving Charge Account

BANK CARD SERVICE CENTER **PO BOX 2947** **PIKEVILLE KY 41502-2947**			PLEASE INDICATE NAME OR ADDRESS CHANGE HERE			**0006**

VISA	MINIMUM PAYMENT DUE	PAST DUE AMOUNT	PAYMENT DUE DATE	NEW BALANCE	ACCOUNT NUMBER	PLEASE WRITE IN AMOUNT OF PAYMENT ENCLOSED
	15.00	0.00	06/17/00	$696.04	4444 1111 2222 3333	$.

USE ENCLOSED ENVELOPE AND MAKE PAYMENT TO

PLEASE COMPLETE AND ENCLOSE TOP PORTION WITH PAYMENT

PIKEVILLE NATIONAL BANK
PO BOX 2947
PIKEVILLE KY 41502-2947

Elizabeth Mountbatten
825 Kentucky Parkway
Lexington, KY 40509

FOR CUSTOMER SERVICE INQUIRIES CALL **800-426-9444**

ACCOUNT NUMBER	CREDIT LINE	AVAILABLE CREDIT	DAYS IN BILLING CYCLE	BILLING CYCLE CLOSING DATE	PAYMENT DUE DATE	MINIMUM PAYMENT DUE
4444 1111 2222 3333	2,000	1,304	31	05/22/00	06/17/00	15.00

DATE OF TRANS.	POST.	REFERENCE NUMBER	CHARGES, PAYMENTS, CREDITS AND ADJUSTMENTS SINCE LAST STATEMENT	AMOUNT
4 22	4 22	---------	PREVIOUS BALANCE	600.00
4 25	4 25	011223344	HARD ROCK CAFE	17.25
4 27	4 26	022333121	WAL-MART	104.50
5 02	5 02	---------	PAYMENT RECEIVED	15.00
5 13	5 12	142111321	WAL-MART	21.00-

PREVIOUS BALANCE	PAYMENTS	CREDITS	CASH ADVANCE	PURCHASES	ADJUSTMENTS	FINANCE CHARGE	NEW BALANCE
600.00	15.00	21.00	0.00	121.75	0.00	10.29	696.04

AN AMOUNT FOLLOWED BY A MINUS SIGN (–) IS A CREDIT OR A CREDIT BALANCE UNLESS OTHERWISE INDICATED.

Send Inquiries To: **BANK CARD SERVICE CENTER PO BOX 2947 PIKEVILLE KY 415022947**

VISA		AVERAGE DAILY BALANCE	MONTHLY PERIODIC RATE	ANNUAL PERCENTAGE RATES
	PURCHASES	686.31	1.5 %	18.0 %
	CASH ADVANCES	0.00	1.5 %	18.0 %

Source: Courtesy of Pikeville National Bank, Pikeville, KY.

informed of the transaction and the charge posted to the account (on the **posting date**). With the increased use of magnetic strip readers at retailers, these dates may be concurrent, with both matching the date the clerk "swipes" the card through the reader. Interest is charged from the posting date unless a grace period is offered; some lenders charge interest from the transaction date.

Grace Period A **grace period** is the time period between the posting date of a transaction and the due date, within which any *new* credit card purchases made during the billing cycle will avoid finance charges. Most cards provide a grace period only if the previous month's total balance was paid *in full and on time*. About 30 percent of all cardholders pay their bills in full by the due date and receive, in effect, an interest-free loan on their new purchases during the next billing cycle. An increasing number of cards do not offer a grace period even if the balance is paid in full each month. In Figure 6.1, the cardholder has a previous unpaid balance, $600, and was charged interest on the unpaid balance as well as on the new charges made within the billing cycle from the date they were posted to the account. Thus, this example contains no grace period.

Minimum Payments To meet his or her obligations, a borrower must make a **minimum payment** monthly that is no smaller than required by the creditor. In Figure 6.1, the cardholder has two options: pay the total amount due ($696.04), or make at least the minimum payment of $15. If the borrower pays the full amount due, finance charges on new purchases in the next billing cycle generally can be avoided. If a partial payment, such as the "total minimum payment due" of $15 is made, additional finance charges will be assessed and will be payable the following month.

Credit for Merchandise Returns and Errors If you return merchandise bought on credit, the merchant will issue you a **credit receipt**—written evidence of the items returned that notes the specific amount of the transaction. In essence, the amount of the merchandise credit is charged back to the credit card company and eventually to the merchant. A credit may also be granted by the credit card company when a billing error has been made (this topic is discussed later in this chapter) or an unauthorized transaction appears. Credits obtained in the current month should appear on the next monthly statement as a reduction of the total amount owed. The credit statement in Figure 6.1 shows a $21.00 credit.

Correcting an Error on Your Credit Card Statement The Fair Credit Billing Act (FCBA) went into effect in 1975 to help people who wish to dispute billing errors on revolving credit accounts. In effect, the FCBA permits a **chargeback**—that is, the amount of the transaction is charged back to the business where the transaction originated. Withholding payment to a credit card company is permitted when the cardholder alleges that a mathematical error has been made in a billing statement, when fraudulent use of the card appears to have occurred, or when (within certain reasonable limitations) a **goods and service dispute** asserts that the charges were for faulty, damaged, shoddy, defective, or poor-quality goods and services and you made a good faith effort to try to correct the problem with the merchant.*

* For goods and services disputes, the FCBA applies only to charges of more than $50 made in your home state or within 100 miles of your current mailing address. Most lenders apply the spirit of the Fair Credit Billing Act to any goods and services disputes, regardless of the geographic distances involved.

You must make a billing error complaint within 60 days after the date the first bill containing the error was mailed to you. The lender then has 30 days to acknowledge your notification and, within 90 days, must either correct the error permanently, return any overpayment (if requested), or provide evidence of why it believes the bill to be correct (such as a copy of a charge slip you supposedly signed). To secure their own evidence, some credit card issuers now use **signature capture** whereby you sign for the purchase on an electronic pad providing an instantaneous computerized record to verify the signature and record the purchase. In addition, some retailers that issue their own credit cards use **photo checkout** whereby the account holder's photograph is stored in the company's computer and appears on the terminal when a purchase is made with the card.

While the dispute is being investigated, creditors cannot assess interest on or apply penalties for nonpayment of the disputed amount, send **dunning letters** (notices that make insistent demands for repayment), or send negative information about your account to a credit bureau without stating that "some items are in dispute." A lender that does not follow the procedures correctly cannot collect the first $50 of the questioned amount, even if the bill was correct. Back interest and penalties may be owed if the disputed item is proved to be legitimately owed.

You should take several actions when disputing an item on a billing statement.

1. Send a written notice of the error to the credit card issuer. The notice must be in writing to qualify for the protections provided under the Fair Credit Billing Act. Instead of sending the notice to the same address where repayments are normally remitted, examine the billing statement thoroughly for an address under the heading "Send Inquiries to" or something similar.

2. Provide photocopies (not originals) of any necessary documentation. Keep the originals to challenge any finding by the company that no error occurred.

3. Withhold payment for disputed items. If possible, pay the remaining amount owed in full to isolate a disputed item. Under the provisions of the FCBA, the company must immediately credit your account for the amount in dispute.

4. After the dispute has been settled, review your credit bureau file to ensure that it does not include information regarding your refusal to repay the disputed amount.

Computation of Finance Charges

Companies that issue credit cards must tell consumers the annual percentage rate (APR) applied as well as what method they use to compute the finance charges. In addition, they must disclose the **periodic rate**, which is the APR for a charge account divided by the number of billing cycles per year (usually 12). For example, a periodic rate of 1.5 percent per month would result from an APR of approximately 18 percent (actually a bit higher because of compounding), and both figures must be disclosed. Typically, the finance charge is calculated by first computing the **average daily balance**—the sum of the outstanding balances owed each day during the billing period divided by the number of days in the period. The periodic rate is applied against that balance.

The method of computing the average daily balance is a critical feature of charge accounts and can be confusing. Several legally permitted computational approaches can push the effective interest rates higher than the stated APR. Especially problematic is the two-cycle average daily balance method.

To illustrate the calculation of the finance charge, consider an account with a 31-day billing cycle with an 18 percent APR. Assume that the beginning balance of $190 was owed for the first ten days. For the next 11 days the balance was $140, reflecting a $50 payment made on the eleventh day. The balance was $350 for the final ten days, reflecting a $210 purchase on the twenty-second day. The average daily balance is $223.87 [(10 × $190 = $1900) + (11 × $140 = $1540) + (10 × $350 = $3500) = $6940 ÷ 31 = $223.87]. Thus, a periodic rate of 1.5 percent (18 percent APR divided by 12) is multiplied by the average daily balance of $223.87, resulting in a finance charge of $3.36 ($223.87 × 0.015).

Calculating Average Daily Balances Affects Finance Charges

Four methods are commonly used to calculate the average daily balance on a credit card billing statement:

Average daily balance excluding new purchases.
In this case, the cardholder pays interest only on any balance left over from the previous month.

Average daily balance including new purchases with a grace period.
The balance calculation includes the balance from the previous month and any charges made during the billing cycle. The grace period allows for the exclusion of charges made during the billing cycle *only if* the balance from the previous billing cycle was zero.

Average daily balance including new purchases with no grace period.
The balance from the previous month and any charges made during the billing cycle are included in the balance calculation, even if the previous month's balance was paid in full.

Two-cycle average daily balance including new purchases.
This method is the least favorable for consumers. It eliminates the grace period on new purchases made during the current billing cycle and it *retroactively* eliminates the grace period for the previous month each time the account carries a balance. The

method effectively doubles the finance charges and is a device for advertising one interest rate and charging another. Unlike the one-cycle systems where each billing cycle stands alone, you must pay off your balance for at least two months to avoid finance charges.

The chart below illustrates how cardholders can sometimes be horribly (and legally) overcharged. The example demonstrates how finance charges vary for a hypothetical situation where a borrower charges $1000 per month and pays only the minimum payment, except for every third month when the balance is paid in full. Executing this scheme four times over the course of a year would result in the following finance charges under the three most common ways of computing the average daily balance and for low-, average-, and high-interest cards.

Annual Percentage Rate (APR)		
	12.0%	17.3%	19.8%
Average Daily Balance (excluding new purchases)	$ 40.00	$ 57.60	$ 66.00
Average Daily Balance (including new purchases)*	80.00	115.20	132.00
Two-Cycle Average Daily Balance (including new purchases)	120.00	172.80	198.00

* This is the most common method used by credit card issuers.

Summary

1. Borrowers use installment and noninstallment credit. Open-ended credit is an example of the latter form of credit.

2. People borrow for financial emergencies, to have goods immediately, and to obtain discounts in the future. Perhaps the greatest disadvantage of credit use is the ensuing loss of financial flexibility in personal money management. The annual percentage rate (APR) provides the best approximation of the true cost of credit.

3. Open-ended credit permits repeated access to credit without a new application each time money is borrowed. The consumer may choose to repay the debt in a single payment or to make a series of payments of varying amounts. Revolving charge accounts and travel and entertainment credit cards are the most commonly used open-ended credit accounts.

4. In the process of opening a credit account, the lender generally conducts an investigation into your credit history and assigns a credit score to the application.

5. Credit card statements provide a monthly summary of credit transactions and the calculation of any finance charges. Credit card issuers compute finance charges by multiplying the average daily balance by the periodic interest rate.

Key Words & Concepts

annual percentage rate (APR)   *159*
average daily balance   *174*
cash advance   *164*
chargeback   *173*
credit bureau   *168*
credit card liability   *161*
credit history   *167*
credit limit   *158*
default   *171*
dunning letters   *174*
finance charge   *159*

grace period   *173*
introductory rate   *165*
open-ended credit   *158*
periodic rate   *174*
revolving charge account   *163*
secured credit card   *164*
tiered pricing   *170*
two-cycle average daily balance including new purchases   *175*
unfair discrimination   *167*

Questions for Thought & Discussion

1. Describe the relationship between a lender and borrower that leads to successful credit use.

2. Identify the five C's of credit, and give an example of each.

3. Distinguish between installment credit and open-ended credit.

4. What two items of credit-cost information must lenders report according to the Truth in Lending Act?

5. Give six reasons to justify using consumer credit.

6. List three inappropriate uses of credit cards.

7. Describe four problems and disadvantages with credit use.

8. What are usury laws? Why can you not assume that your state's laws will apply to a particular credit agreement?

9. What two benefits or privileges might the cardholder receive from a bank credit card account that are typically not available from a revolving charge account at a retail store?

10. Identify the conditions necessary before a credit card holder can be liable for $50 for charges on a lost credit card.

11. Distinguish between a travel and entertainment credit card account and a bank credit card account.

12. Distinguish between a fixed and a variable rate credit card.

13. Why should borrowers be cautious about teaser rates?

14. Describe how a budget charge account works.

15. Explain what a secured credit card is and who might consider obtaining one.

16. Summarize what a credit investigation involves.

17. List some of the provisions of the Equal Credit Opportunity Act.

18. List the consumer rights outlined by the Fair Credit Reporting Act.

19. Describe the process of risk scoring.

20. Explain why some creditors offer tiered interest rates.

21. What are the most important factors that go into scoring a credit risk?

22. Name and describe briefly courses of action you can take to demonstrate that you can manage credit effectively.

23. What types of information are provided on a credit statement?

24. Summarize how you should go about correcting an error on a credit card bill.

25. Summarize the steps that creditors use when computing the monthly finance charges for a revolving credit card account.

26. Which method of computing average daily balances is least attractive to the consumer, and why?

DECISION-MAKING CASES

Case 1 Preparation of a Credit-Related Speech

Fred Marchese, of Auburn, Alabama, is the credit manager for a regional chain of department stores. He has been asked to join a panel of community members and make a ten-minute speech to graduating high-school seniors on the topic "Using Credit Wisely." Fill in the following outline Fred has prepared with things that he can say:

(a) What consumer credit is

(b) Reasons for using credit

(c) How graduates can use credit wisely

Case 2 A Delayed Report of a Stolen Credit Card

Joan Craycraft, of Athens, Georgia, had taken her sister-in-law Julia Johnson out for an expensive lunch. When it came time to pay the bill, Joan noticed that her Visa credit card was missing, so she paid the bill with her MasterCard. While driving home, Joan remembered last using the Visa card about a week earlier, and she started to become concerned that a sales clerk or someone else could have taken it and might be fraudulently charging purchases on her card.

(a) Summarize Joan's legal rights in this situation.

(b) Discuss the likelihood that Joan will be made to pay Visa for any illegal charges to the account.

Financial Math Questions

1. Jannelle Sampson, an antiques dealer from Sarasota, Florida, received her monthly billing statement for April for her Master-Card account. The statement indicated that she had a beginning balance of $600, on day 5 she charged $150, on day 12 she charged $300, and on day 15 she made a $200 payment. Out of curiosity Jannelle wanted to confirm that the finance charge for the billing cycle was correct.

   (a) What was Jannelle's average daily balance for April without new purchases?

   (b) What was her finance charge on the balance in (a) if her APR is 19.2%?

   (c) What was her average daily balance for April with new purchases?

   (d) What was her finance charge on the balance in (c) if her APR is 19.2%?

   (e) What was her finance charge using the two-cycle average daily balance if her average daily balance for March was $800? (Hint: Add the March average daily balance to the April average daily balance, and then divide by 2 to obtain the two-cycle average daily balance.)

2. Elizabeth Mountbatten is curious about the accuracy of her average daily balance as shown on her most recent credit card billing statement provided in Figure 6.1 on page 172. Use the posting dates for her account to calculate the average daily balance and compare it to that shown on the statement.

MONEY MATTERS: LIFE-CYCLE CASES

Victor and Maria Have a Billing Dispute

Maria Hernandez was reviewing her recent Visa account statement when she found two charges on her credit card statement that she and Victor could not have made. The charges involved rental of a hotel room and purchase of a meal on the same day in a distant city. These charges totaled $219.49 out of the $367.89 balance for the month.

1. What payment should Maria make on the account?

2. How should she notify her Visa issuer about this unauthorized use?

3. Once the matter is resolved, what should Maria do to ensure that her credit history is not negatively affected by this error?

The Johnsons Resolve Their Credit and Cash Flow Problems

Harry and Belinda have a substantial annual joint income—more than $52,000, in fact. They also have some cash-flow deficits planned for the first months of the year (see Tables 4.3 and 4.4).

To resolve this difficulty, the couple opened two Visa accounts and one MasterCard account at different banks and then obtained cash advances at interest rates above 19 percent. When they are supposed to pay on one account, the Johnsons obtain the needed money via a cash advance from another bank credit card. They now owe more than $1200, and it will be some months until Harry's trust income arrives in September.

1. What are the advantages and disadvantages of the Johnsons' opening more than one bank credit card account?

2. Comment on the costs involved in continually getting cash advances from one bank card to pay amounts due on the others.

3. Harry and Belinda have considered applying for additional installment credit to replace the old furniture given to them by their families. Regardless of the methods used for judging credit potential, the five C's of credit (on page 157) will continue to be factors

considered carefully in any credit approval. Using the five C's of credit, write a paragraph evaluating the Johnsons' application. Be sure to review their financial statements in Chapter 4 on pages 107–109.

Exploring the World Wide Web of Personal Finance

To complete these exercises, go to the *Garman/Forgue* Web site at

www.hmco.com/college/business/

Select Personal Finance. Click on the exercise link for this chapter and answer the questions that appear on the Web page.

1. Do you owe money on one or more credit cards? Visit the Financenter Web site, where you will find a calculator that will tell you how long it will take to pay off your balances.

2. Visit the Web site for one of the three major credit reporting firms. Order a copy of your credit report.

3. Visit the Web site for the Bank Rate Monitor Info Bank, where you will find information on bank credit card interest rates around the United States. View the information for the lenders in a large city nearest your home. How does the information compare with your current credit card account(s)? How do the rates in the city you selected compare with those found elsewhere in the United States?

4. Privacy is a big issue in credit reporting. Visit the Web site for Equifax and review its privacy policy.

5. Visit the Web site of the Consumer Information Center in Pueblo, Colorado, where you will find an on-line copy of the *Consumer Credit Handbook*. Download or print the *Handbook*. Identify one additional protection not discussed in this text provided by each of the following laws: the Fair Credit Billing Act, the Equal Credit Opportunity Act, and the Fair Credit Reporting Act.

Planned Borrowing

7

OBJECTIVES

After reading this chapter, you should be able to:

1 Discuss the elements of the planned use of credit.

2 Establish your own debt limit.

3 Understand the language of consumer loans.

4 Describe the sources of consumer loans.

5 Calculate the APR and finance charges on both single-payment and installment loans.

6 Recognize signs of overindebtedness, know what to do when it occurs, and explain your rights regarding credit collection and bankruptcy.

Most people use installment credit a dozen or more times during their life. Yet, only one out of every three borrowers shops for favorable credit terms. A wise financial manager investigates and compares costs so that he or she can avoid paying too much for credit. This goal is part of **planned borrowing**— a knowing decision to borrow to finance a purchase or simply to borrow cash. In this chapter we first discuss planned credit usage. We then examine the important terminology of consumer loans and describe where to obtain such loans. This discussion is followed by an explanation of how finance charges on consumer loans are computed. The chapter ends by considering the topics of credit overindebtedness and bankruptcy.

Planning Your Credit Usage

Using credit requires deliberate action and thinking, including considerations about when it is best to borrow. Planned borrowing typically is used for purchasing vehicles, personal loans, home improvements, furniture, computers, and major appliances. For many people, these items are too expensive to purchase without using credit.

Borrowing funds to pay for higher education or to make investments may prove advantageous because the returns may well exceed the cost of borrowing. In addition, buying on credit may offer benefits when inflation is high, the cost of credit is not prohibitive, and interest rates on savings are low; the after-tax cost of credit may be low as well. (This concept is detailed in Chapter 3, page 69.) Remember that credit is not income, however; rather, credit commits the use of future income. The financial management task is to determine when, how often, and how much to use installment credit. Your decisions will vary based on your needs and wants as well as your effectiveness in handling debt. Planned credit use requires establishing a debt limit, speaking the language of credit, knowing the best sources of credit available, calculating the costs of credit, and knowing what to do if credit usage gets out of hand.

Establishing a Debt Limit

Recall from Chapter 6 that credit card issuers set a credit limit for each of their cardholders. In a similar manner, you should also set your own **debt limit**, which is the overall maximum you believe you should owe based on your ability to meet the repayment obligations. Ironically, most peoples' debt limit is lower than what lenders might be willing to lend. When setting your debt limit, you do not need to include temporary use of revolving or service credit when the debt will be paid in full after the bill arrives. Three ways to determine debt limits follow:

- debt-payments-to-disposable-income method
- ratio of debt-to-equity method
- continuous-debt method.

Debt-Payments-to-Disposable-Income Method

To use the debt-payments-to-disposable-income method, you must decide the percentage of your disposable personal income (not gross income) that can be spent for regular debt repayments. Your **disposable personal income** is the amount of take-home pay remaining after all deductions are withheld for taxes, insurance, union dues, and other reasons.

Table 7.1 shows some monthly debt-payment limits expressed as a percentage of disposable personal income. As the table indicates, with monthly payments representing 16 to 20 percent of monthly disposable personal income, a borrower is fully extended and taking on additional debt probably would be unwise. (As mentioned, current debt excludes the first mortgage loan on a home.)

Table 7.1

Debt-Payment Limits as a Percentage of Disposable Personal Income

Percent	For Current Debt*	Take on Additional Debt?
10 or less	Safe limit; borrower feels little debt pressure	Could be undertaken cautiously
11 to 15	Possibly safe limit; borrower feels some pressure	Should not be undertaken
16 to 20	Fully extended; borrower hopes that no emergency arises	Only the fearless or foolhardy ask for more
21 to 25	Overextended; borrower worries about debts	No, borrower should see a financial counselor
26 or more	Disastrous; borrower may feel desperate	Impossible; borrower will probably declare bankruptcy

* Excluding home mortgage loans and convenience credit to be repaid in full when the bill arrives.

Table 7.2 on the following page demonstrates the impact of increasing debts on a budget. After deductions, disposable personal income is $1800 monthly. Current budgeted expenses (totaling the full $1800) are allocated in a sample distribution throughout the various categories.

As you can see, increasing debt payments from $180 to $450 per month (for example, to buy a new automobile, computer, or home entertainment system on credit) dramatically affects this budget. The financial manager must decide where to cut back to meet monthly credit repayments. As the debt increases, each 5 percent rise makes it much more difficult to "find the money" and make the cutbacks. In this case, the borrower reduced expenditures on savings and investments immediately and then finally eliminated all allocations in the category. Food was cut back, but only slightly. Utilities, automobile insurance, and rent are relatively fixed expenses; it is hard to reduce these amounts without moving or buying a less expensive car. Entertainment expenses were steadily reduced, and charitable contributions eliminated altogether. Further reductions in other areas would seriously affect this individual's quality of life.

Are you curious as to where you would have made reductions? Spending a few minutes changing the figures in Table 7.2 might give you an idea of your priorities and the size of the debt limit that you might establish. The debt-payments-to-income method focuses on the amount of the monthly debt repayments—not the total debt. As a result, it would be wise to consider the length of time that the severe financial situation due to high debt payments might endure.

Ratio of Debt-to-Equity Method

Another method of determining whether you have too much debt is to calculate the ratio of your consumer debt to your net worth. In this case, you would exclude the value of a primary residence and a first mortgage on that home. Most people have more assets than liabilities, resulting in a positive net worth. The net amount of assets greater than debts represents the equity one possesses. For example, a person with $14,000 in debts and $42,000 in assets has equity of $28,000 ($42,000 − $14,000), or a debt-to-equity ratio of 0.50 ($14,000 ÷ $28,000).

Table 7.2

Impact of Increasing Debt Payments on a Budget*
(One Person's Decisions on Where to Cut Back Expenses to Make Increasing Monthly Debt Payments)

Gross income	$ 26,000	
Deductions for taxes, retirement, insurance	$ 4,400	
Disposable personal income	$ 21,600	
Monthly	$ 1,800	

	No Debt	10% Debt	15% Debt	20% Debt	25% Debt
Rent	$ 550	$ 550	$ 550	$ 550	$ 550
Savings and investments	200	**100**	100	**60**	**0**
Food	180	**160**	160	**150**	150
Utilities (telephone, electricity, heat)	130	130	130	130	130
Insurance (automobile and life)	70	70	70	70	70
Transportation expenses	210	210	**180**	180	180
Charitable contributions	50	**30**	**20**	**0**	0
Entertainment	100	**80**	**60**	**50**	50
Clothing	50	**40**	**30**	30	**0**
Vacations and long weekends	25	25	**20**	**15**	15
Medical and dental expenses	20	20	20	20	20
Newspapers and magazines	10	10	10	10	10
Vices	40	40	**35**	35	35
Cable TV	15	15	15	15	15
Personal care	25	25	25	25	25
Gifts and holidays	25	25	25	**20**	20
Health club	30	30	30	30	30
Miscellaneous	70	**60**	**50**	50	50
Debt repayments	0	**180**	**270**	**360**	**450**
TOTAL	$1800	$1800	$1800	$1800	$1800

* Amounts in bold are the changes—cutbacks—made to make the increasingly larger debt payments.

This method provides a quick idea of your financial solvency. The larger the ratio, the riskier the likelihood of repayment. A ratio in excess of 0.33 is considered high, except for recent college graduates, who often accumulate large education loans. Such people would have a poor ratio of debt to equity, but their potential for substantial earning power offsets the ratio. If the situation has not changed three to five years later, however, then a problem likely exists.

Continuous-Debt Method

Another approach for determining when debts are too large is the continuous-debt method. If you are unable to get completely out of debt every four years (except for mortgage loans), you probably lean on debt too heavily. You could be developing a credit lifestyle, in which you never eliminate debt and continuously pay out substantial amounts of income for finance charges—possibly $2000 or more per year.

Setting Debt Limits for Dual-Earner Households

Aside from the companionship and other emotional benefits, entering into a relationship can be wonderful because it means joining incomes together. Two people each earning $26,000 per year will gross $52,000, with a disposable personal income from this total of around $39,000, or $3250 monthly. Such an amount seemingly means a couple can afford a much higher level of debt than before the incomes were combined. While the guidelines given in Table 7.1 are realistic, they would allow a doubling of debt payments if the addition of a second earner doubled household earnings.

If one of the earners reduces earnings to take care of growing family responsibilities (such as children), debts that had been manageable with two incomes may become burdensome and possibly overwhelming. Although some new debts are probably desirable and unavoidable, early in their relationship couples would be wise to build savings accounts and make investments that will ensure future financial security.

The Language of Consumer Loans

3 Understand the language of consumer loans.

Consumers typically obtain installment credit in the form of cash loans and purchase loans. A **cash loan** means that a person borrows cash and then uses it to make purchases, pay off other debts, or make investments. With a **purchase loan** (also called **sales credit**), a consumer makes a purchase on credit with no cash transferring from the lender to the borrower; instead, the funds go directly from the lender to the seller. For example, a buyer may obtain a purchase loan from General Motors Acceptance Corporation (GMAC) to buy a new Pontiac Grand Am.

Installment Loans

Consumer loans are usually classified as installment or noninstallment credit. Recall that **noninstallment credit** is debt that is repaid in a single payment or as **open-ended credit** (covered in Chapter 6), in which the borrower is permitted to repay either in full or over time. **Installment credit** (also called **closed-end credit**) requires that the consumer repay the amount owed in a specific number of equal payments, usually monthly. Installment loans typically come with a **fixed interest rate**, meaning that the rate will not change over the life of the loan.

To help you figure out the monthly payment for different loan amounts, Table 7.3 illustrates various monthly installment payments to repay a $1000 loan at commonly seen interest rates and time periods. For loans of other dollar amounts, divide the borrowed amount by 1000 and multiply the result by the

Table 7.3

Monthly Installment Payment (Principal and Interest) Required to Repay $1000*

Terms of Installments	Annual Percentage Rate								
	4%	6%	8%	10%	12%	14%	16%	18%	20%
1 year (12 months)	85.15	86.07	86.99	87.92	88.85	89.79	90.73	91.68	92.63
2 years (24 months)	43.42	44.32	45.23	46.14	47.07	48.01	48.96	49.92	50.90
3 years (36 months)	29.52	30.42	31.34	32.27	33.21	34.18	35.16	36.15	37.16
4 years (48 months)	22.58	23.49	24.41	25.36	26.33	27.33	28.34	29.37	30.43
5 years (60 months)	18.42	19.33	20.28	21.25	22.24	23.27	24.32	25.39	26.49

* To illustrate, assume you want to know how much the monthly payments would be to finance an automobile loan of $9000 at 10 percent for 3 years. To repay $1000, the figure is $32.27; therefore, multiply by 9 (for $9000) to determine that $290.43 is required for 36 months of payments. When using amounts greater or less than $1000, convert using decimals. For example, a loan of $950 at 10 percent for 3 years would be calculated as follows: $32.27 × 0.95 = $30.66. To perform these calculations for interest rates and time periods in addition to those listed, visit the *Garman/Forgue* Web site.

appropriate figure from the table. For example, an automobile loan for $12,000, financed at 10 percent interest, might be repaid in 36 equal monthly payments of $387.24 ($32.27 × 12).

Most installment loans involve a **loan book**—a coupon booklet with perforated pages that are torn out and sent to the lender along with each repayment. Each coupon gives details of each payment, such as the date and amount due. A recent survey revealed that four out of five people have never missed a scheduled debt payment.

Secured and Unsecured Loans

Loans can either be secured or unsecured. A **secured loan** requires a cosigner or collateral. A **cosigner** agrees to pay the debt should the original borrower fail to do so. Being a cosigner is a major responsibility, because a cosigner has the same legal obligations for repayment as the original borrower. In case of default, a lender will go after the party—either the borrower or the cosigner—from which it is most likely to collect.

A loan secured with collateral means that the lender has a **security interest** in that collateral. Typically, the lender records a lien in the county courthouse to make the security interest known to the public. A **lien** is a legal right to seize and dispose of (usually sell) property to obtain payment of a claim. When the loan is repaid, the lien will be removed. (The borrower should make sure this occurs.) In the event that the borrower fails to repay the loan, the creditor can exercise the lien and seize the collateral through **repossession**, sometimes without notice. Almost all credit contracts contain an **acceleration clause** stating that after a specific number of payments are unpaid (often just one), the loan is considered in default and all remaining installments are due and payable upon demand of the creditor. These clauses protect the lender's interest, but can prove very difficult for borrowers. Don't be fooled if you miss a payment and the lender does not exercise the acceleration clause immediately. It can do so at any time after default occurs. Do not ignore warning letters!

The Characteristics of a Variable-Rate Loan

It is becoming increasingly common for lenders to offer variable-rate loans as one alternative available to borrowers. Should you consider this type of loan? And just what is a variable-rate loan? A **variable-rate loan** (also called an **adjustable-rate loan**) includes a periodic rate that fluctuates according to some measure of interest rates in the economy. These loans can be structured such that the payment increases or decreases with changes in the simple-interest rate applied to the unpaid balance; or payment amount will stay the same, but the payments will last beyond the previously scheduled final payment; or the loan will feature a final **balloon payment** that is abnormally large in comparison with the other installment payments. The Truth in Lending Act requires that any payment more than twice the size of others be clearly identified as a balloon payment.

A variable-rate loan usually offers the advantage of a slightly lower initial annual rate (1 to 3 percent) than the fixed interest rate for an equivalent loan. The lender is willing to offer this rate because the risk of rising interest rates can be passed on to the borrower. Federal law requires lenders to set an upper limit, or an **interest-rate cap**, on an adjustable interest rate over the lifetime of second mortgage loans. In addition, some state laws demand similar caps on consumer loans. The disadvantage for the borrower is the obvious potential for a higher rate to be applied in the future. Interest rates also can decline. If you predict that interest rates in the economy will decrease in the years immediately ahead, a variable-rate loan could be a wise choice.

An **unsecured loan** has neither the assurance of collateral nor a cosigner. Instead, such a loan is given primarily on the good character of the borrower. Sometimes these forms of credit are referred to as **signature loans** because they are backed up only by the borrower's signature. Because unsecured loans carry higher risk than secured debts, the interest rate charged on them is usually quite a bit higher.

Purchase Loan Installment Contracts

Two kinds of contracts are used when purchasing goods with an installment loan: (1) **installment purchase agreements** (also called **collateral installment loans** or **chattel mortgage loans**), in which the title of the property passes to the buyer when the contract is signed; and (2) **conditional sales contracts** (also known as **financing leases**), in which the title does not pass to the buyer until the last installment payment has been paid. The installment purchase agreement provides a measure of protection for the borrower, as the creditor must follow all state-prescribed legal procedures when attempting to repossess the property. Some state laws permit the lender to take secured property back as soon as the buyer falls behind in payments, possibly by seizing a car right in a person's driveway.

Prepayment Penalties Many installment loan contracts include a **prepayment penalty**—a special charge to the borrower for paying off a loan earlier than the final due date. Prepayment penalties take into consideration the reality that

The Effect of Using Voluntary Repossession to Get Out of a Debt

When a lender takes back collateral or repossesses property because the borrower defaults on a loan, the borrower often still owes a deficiency balance on the debt. A **deficiency balance** is a sum of money owed after collateral or repossessed property is sold and the proceeds of the sale, less the expenses (collection, attorney, and court costs) involved in the repossession, are applied to the balance of the loan.

Deficiency balances are likely to occur whether repossession is voluntary or involuntary. Consider the example of Betty Peterson, an E4 in the U.S. Navy from San Diego, California, who came into serious financial stress three months ago when her husband became ill and lost his job. With such a

sharp reduction in family income, Betty voluntarily turned her Pontiac back to the finance company owing a balance of $6600. A month later, she found that the Pontiac had been sold at auction for only $4200, and the proceeds were reduced to $3900 due to collection and selling costs of $200 and attorney fees of $100. Thus, Betty was billed for a deficiency balance of $2700 ($6600 − $3900). Occasionally it may be necessary to sell an asset, but voluntary repossession is not usually the best way to do it. Betty would have been much better off had she sold the automobile herself, as repossessed property sold at auction often brings less than 50 percent of its value.

borrowers should pay more in interest early in the loan period when they have the use of more money and increasingly less interest as a debt is reduced over time. Recall, however, that the typical installment loan has equal payments. Thus, in early months the bulk of each payment is essentially devoted to interest. Most borrowers do not understand this concept, and it is irrelevant if the loan is paid over the agreed-upon time period. If the loan is paid off early, however, the lender will use some penalty method to reflect the high interest component in the early months.

The **rule of 78s method** (sometimes called the **sum of the digits method**) is a widely used method of calculating a prepayment penalty. Its name derives from the fact that on a one-year loan the numbers between 1 and 12 for each month add up to 78 (12 + 11 + 10 + 9 + 8 + 7 + 6 + 5 + 4 + 3 + 2 + 1). For a two-year loan, the numbers between 1 and 24 would be added, and so on for longer time period loans.

To illustrate the use of the rule of 78s method, consider the case of Devin Grigsby from Berea, Kentucky. He borrowed $500 for 12 months plus an additional $80 finance charge and is scheduled to pay equal monthly installments of $48.33 ($580 ÷ 12). Assume Devin wants to pay the loan off after only six months. He might assume (incorrectly) that he would owe only $250 more because after six months he had paid $250 (one-half) of the $500 borrowed and $40 (one-half) of the finance charge, for a total of $290 in payments ($48.33 × 6). Instead, Devin still owes $268.46, including a prepayment penalty of $18.46. To calculate this amount using the rule of 78s method, the lender adds together all of the numbers between 12 and 7 (12 for the first month, 11 for the second and so on for six months) where 12 + 11 + 10 + 9 + 8 + 7 = 57. The lender assumes that during the first six months $58.46 [(57 ÷ 78) × $80]—not $40—of

The Impact of Divorce on Your Credit

Besides the obvious emotional trauma of divorce, the breakup of a marriage impacts the credit of both partners. The Federal Trade Commission makes the following suggestions for individuals seeking a divorce.

Pay careful attention to credit accounts held jointly, including mortgages, second mortgage loans, and credit cards. The behavior of one divorcing spouse will affect the other as long as the accounts are held in both names. One party could make credit card charges, for example, and refuse to pay, leaving the burden on the other party. Accordingly, and where possible, ask creditors to close joint accounts and reopen them as individual accounts. Never accept a creditor's verbal assurance, either over the phone or in person, that an account

has been closed. Always insist on written confirmation, including the effective date of an account closure.

When debts were accumulated in both names, divorce decrees have no legal effect on who technically owes which debts. Creditors can legally collect from either of the divorcing parties. If the person absolved of responsibility for the debt under the divorce decree is forced by a creditor to pay off the account, that person must then go to court to seek enforcement of the divorce decree to collect from the former spouse.

Both before and after the divorce, get a copy of your credit report (see page 168). Check for accuracy and challenge any problem areas, such as accounts that continue to be shown in both names.

the finance charges was paid from the $290 in payments Devin had made on the loan.* Consequently, only $231.54 ($290 − $58.46) was paid on the $500 borrowed, leaving $268.46 ($500 − $231.54) still owed, for a prepayment penalty of $18.46 ($268.46 − $250.00).

Sources of Consumer Loans

4 Describe the sources of consumer loans.

Table 7.4 summarizes the features of the four major sources of typical consumer loans: depository institutions, second mortgage lenders, consumer finance companies and industrial banks, and sales finance companies. These institutions are discussed in the following sections, along with other sources and types of loans.

Depository Institutions

Depository institutions include commercial banks, mutual savings banks, savings and loan associations, and credit unions (see Chapter 5, page 127 for further descriptions). They tend to make loans to their own customers and to noncustomers with good credit histories. Because they prefer to make loans to good risks, such institutions typically require collateral or a cosigner for large or

---

* If the loan was paid off after one month, the amount of interest paid is assumed to be 12 ÷ 78 of the $80 finance charge, or $12.31. For a loan paid in full after two months, the amount of interest paid is assumed to be 23 ÷ 78 of the total (12 ÷ 78 for month 1 plus 11 ÷ 78 for month 2), or $23.59.

Table 7.4

Major Sources of Consumer Loans

Credit Source	Types of Loans					Lending Policies
	Single-payment loans	Installment loans	Passbook loans	Credit card loans	Automatic overdrafts	
Banks and S&Ls	✓	✓	✓	✓	✓	Loans to average and better credit-risk people Often require collateral Make secured and unsecured loans Rates vary according to type of loan and security Lower rates to their own customers
Credit Unions		✓		✓	✓	Lend to members only Average credit-risk people approved Require repayment by payroll deductions Make secured and unsecured loans Provide free credit life and disability insurance for the amount of the loan Often have lowest interest rates available
Consumer Finance Companies		✓				Most credit risks acceptable Collateral often required Rates are high and vary according to risk, type of loan, and security
Sales Finance Companies		✓				Loans to average and better credit-risk people Loans for collateral purchases only Loans tied to the seller (Sears, GMAC, etc.) that approves the application Rates are usually competitive with those of banks and S&Ls; special promotion rates are sometimes lower

higher-risk loans. For most loans, depository institutions offer highly competitive rates, partly because the funds loaned are obtained primarily from their depositors. The interest rate commonly ranges from 8 to 18 percent. Research indicates that many people who go elsewhere for loans actually meet the qualifications for depository institution lending and end up paying a higher interest rate than necessary.

Consumer Finance Companies

A **consumer finance company** specializes in relatively small loans and is, therefore, also known as a **small-loan company.** These lenders range from the well-recognized Household Finance Corporation (HFC) and Beneficial Finance Corporation (BFC) to many local neighborhood lenders. Such companies make secured and unsecured loans and require repayment on an installment basis. The interest rates they charge are higher than those of depository lenders because consumer finance companies make riskier loans that have greater default rates.

Approximately one-fifth of the loans granted by consumer finance companies are for the purpose of debt consolidation. Other common purposes of consumer finance company loans are for travel, vacations, education, automobiles, and home furnishings. Some small-loan companies specialize in making loans by mail. They advertise in newspapers and magazines to attract borrowers, who complete a credit application and receive approval via mail.

Sales Finance Companies

A **sales finance company** is a business-related lender (such as General Motors Acceptance Corporation, Ford Motor Credit, and JCPenney Credit Corporation) that is primarily engaged in financing the sales of the parent company. Such companies specialize in making purchase loans, with the item being purchased serving as collateral. Because the seller often works in close association with the sales finance company, credit can be approved almost immediately.

Because sales finance companies usually require collateral and deal only with customers that are considered medium to good risks, their interest rates can be competitive with those offered by depository institutions. Furthermore, the rate may be sharply lower than that offered by other sources if the seller subsidizes the rate to encourage sales, as exemplified by the special financing deals often offered on new cars. Most new car loans today are made by sales finance companies.

Loans from Investment Accounts

Many people build significant assets in investment accounts that may be earmarked for children's college, retirement, or other specific needs. Although many people prefer not to tap into these funds directly, it may be possible to borrow from or against these accounts. For example, it is possible to borrow from certain employer-sponsored, tax-sheltered retirement accounts (see Chapter 18, "Retirement Planning"), depending on the rules of the plan. Alternatively, if you have a margin account (see Chapter 17, "Real Estate and Advanced Portfolio Management"), you can borrow from your stockbrocker using your investments as collateral. In both of these cases, care must be taken to ensure that the loan plus interest is repaid lest the savings goal go unmet. Furthermore, tax consequences may arise if retirement account loans are not repaid.

Life Insurance Companies

Policyholders who have a **cash-value life insurance policy** can obtain loans from their life insurance companies based on the cash value built up in the policy. (This topic is examined in Chapter 12.) Such cash-value policies may take many years to build up to an amount sufficient to borrow.

An advantage to borrowing on a cash-value life insurance policy is that the interest rates are low, ranging from 4 to 6 percent. Of course, the policyholder is

About Alternative Lenders

A number of avenues are available to obtain credit that may not look like credit or credit may come from unusual sources. These sources include pawnshops, rent-to-own programs, check cashers, and rapid tax-refund services.

A **pawnshop** is a lender that offers single-payment loans, often for $100 to $500, for short time periods (typically one or two months), after an item of personal property is turned over to the pawnshop. The dollar amount loaned is usually based on the dollar value of the item pawned. In most states, a borrower need only turn over the item, present identification, and sign on the dotted line. The pawnshop owner can legally sell the item if the borrower fails to redeem the property by paying the amount due, plus interest, within the time period specified.

The interest charged by a pawnshop is usually about 5 percent per month plus a 2 percent monthly storage fee; thus, the annual combined "interest" amounts to 84 percent [(5 + 2) × 12]. Because the pawnshop typically loans only cash equal to one-third or less of the value of the property, the effective interest rate is often greater than 200 percent annually. Pawnshops represent the lender of last resort for borrowers.

A **rent-to-own program** provides a mechanism for buying an item with little or no down payment by renting it for a period of time after which it is owned. Furniture, appliances, and electronic entertainment items are commonly sold via rent-to-own, and this form of credit is often used by persons who feel they cannot qualify for credit purchases. These programs have two big drawbacks for con-

sumers. First, the renter does not own the item until the final payment is made. Paying late or stopping payments will cause the products to be seized with no allowance for the "rental" payments. Second, the actual cost for renting items is often exorbitantly high. A $300 TV might be rented for $15 per week for one year for a finance charge of $480 (52 × $15 − $300). Sadly, many people who use rent-to-own could qualify for more conventional—and less expensive—credit sources.

Check cashers (prohibited in some states) are businesses that cash checks for people who may not have bank accounts or access to traditional check-cashing outlets. Simply cashing someone's pay, government, or personal check is not technically considered credit. Check cashers do grant credit when they honor a personal check but agree not to deposit the check for a week or more. The fees for check cashing are sometimes 20 percent or more, pushing the APR (if the check is held for later deposit) to several hundred percent or more.

Rapid refund services include companies that agree to loan money based on the income tax refund to be received by a taxpayer. Some services complete the tax forms and loan the refund amount; others verify the refund amount from the taxpayer's completed forms before making the loan. In both cases, the borrower signs over the refund and pays a fee for the service to the lender. Like the rates charged by other alternative financial sector lenders, the effective annual APRs for these loans are extremely high (25 to 75 percent) relative to more traditional lenders.

borrowing his or her own money. Many people fail to pay back such loans because no fixed schedule of repayment is established and insurance companies do not pressure borrowers to repay the debt. In reality, the insurance company incurs no risk. Should the insured die before repaying the loan, the insurance company pays the beneficiaries the amount of the policy minus any outstanding debt and interest.

What It Costs to Borrow Money

Credit costs money. Just how much can be seen in the following table, which shows the cost of borrowing $1000 as an unsecured loan for two years and five years from various sources.

Lender	APR	Two-Year Loan		Five-Year Loan	
		Monthly Payment	Finance Charge	Monthly Payment	Finance Charge
Life insurance company	8	$45.23	$ 85.52	$20.28	$216.80
Credit union	12	47.07	129.68	22.24	334.40
Commercial bank	14	48.01	152.24	23.27	396.20
Mutual savings bank	14	48.01	152.24	23.27	396.20
Savings and loan association	14	48.01	152.24	23.27	396.20
Bank credit card	18	49.92	198.02	25.39	523.40
Consumer finance company	24	52.87	268.88	28.77	726.20
Pawnbroker	48+	n/a*	n/a	n/a	n/a

* Generally pawnbroker loans are granted for only a few months. A three-month loan for $1000 would have a finance charge of $120 {$1000 × [(0.48 ÷ 12) × 3]}.

Friends and Relatives

People usually borrow from friends and relatives when the purpose of the borrowed funds is too risky for conventional lenders or if the borrower has a poor or nonexistent credit history. Two considerations are important when borrowing from or lending to friends and relatives. First, make out a formal **promissory note** (a written loan contract). In case of default, the lender will need such a document to take an income tax loss, and the note simply makes things more businesslike. Second, establish a specific repayment schedule. Failure to follow these suggestions may result in the borrower deciding that the loan was actually a gift, and the lender may develop ill feelings. One advantage of these loans is the generally low—or nonexistent—interest rate.

Calculating Finance Charges and Annual Percentage Rates

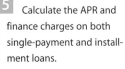

Calculate the APR and finance charges on both single-payment and installment loans.

The federal **Truth in Lending Act (TIL)** requires lenders to disclose to credit applicants both the interest rate expressed as an **annual percentage rate (APR)** and the finance charge expressed in dollars. The APR is the relative cost of credit on a yearly basis expressed as a percentage rate. Any interest rate quoted by a lender must be the APR. In some instances, lenders are ignorant of the law;

others may attempt to hide the federally mandated disclosure. Always inquire about the APR if it is not readily apparent and use it to compare rates from various sources to obtain the best deal.

The **finance charge** for a loan is the cost of credit measured in dollars. It must include all mandatory charges to be paid by the borrower. In addition to interest, lenders may charge fees for a credit investigation, a loan application, or credit life, credit disability, or credit unemployment insurance. When fees for such insurance are *required,* the lender must include them in the finance charge in dollars as part of the APR calculations. When the borrower elects these options voluntarily, the fees are not included in the finance charge and APR calculations, even though they raise the actual cost of borrowing.

Interest composes the greatest portion of finance charges. Three methods are used to calculate interest on installment and noninstallment credit: the simple-interest method, the add-on interest method, and the discount method. The following discussion illustrates the calculation of the annual percentage rate for single-payment and installment loans using each of these methods.

APR Calculations for Single-Payment Loans

Two methods are employed to calculate interest on single-payment loans: the simple-interest method and the discount method. The APR reveals the difference in the effective cost of credit for each.

The Simple-Interest Method With the **simple-interest method,** interest is calculated by applying an interest rate to the unpaid balance of the debt. The **simple-interest formula** given in Equation (7.1) is used as follows:

$$I = PRT \tag{7.1}$$

where

I = **interest** or finance charges
P = **principal** amount borrowed
R = **rate** of interest (simple, add-on, or discount rate)
T = **time** of loan in years

Suppose you took out a single-payment loan of $500 for two years at a simple interest rate of 12 percent. Your interest charges would be $120 ($500 × 12 percent × 2 years), which would be added to the debt, and you would make one payment of $620 at the end of two years.

To calculate the APR for a single-payment loan, divide the average outstanding loan balance ($500, as the full amount was owed during the entire loan period) into the average annual finance charge ($60, as $120 is the total for two years).

$$APR = \frac{\text{average annual finance charge}}{\text{average outstanding loan balance}} \tag{7.2}$$

$$= \frac{\$60}{\$500}$$

$$= 12\%$$

In this example, the APR is 12 percent. When the simple-interest method is used for any type of loan, the simple rate of interest and the APR are always equivalent.

The Discount Method The **discount method** is often used for single-payment loans. With this method, interest is paid up front and *subtracted* from the amount of the loan. The difference is the actual cash given to the borrower.

Using the same figures as in the last example, the denominator in Equation (7.2) changes. The average outstanding loan balance, or principal, is $380 [$500 − ($500 × 0.12 × 2)], because that is the amount actually received. Dividing $380 into the average annual finance charge of $60 gives an APR of 15.8 percent, as compared with the discount rate of 12 percent. This higher APR reflects the fact that the borrower does not have full use of the $500 borrowed.

APR Calculations for Installment Loans

The simple-interest, add-on, and discount methods are all used to determine the interest on installment loans. The simple-interest method is widely used by credit unions and sales finance companies to calculate interest. The add-on method predominates at banks, savings and loan associations, and consumer finance companies in installment loans for automobiles, furniture, and other credit requiring collateral.

The Simple-Interest Method With the **simple-interest method,** the interest assessed during each payment period (usually each month) is based on the outstanding balance of the installment loan. The lender initially designs a schedule (such as that given in Table 7.5) to have the balance repaid in full after a certain number of months. The borrower may vary the rate of repayment by making payments larger than those scheduled or repay the loan in full at any time.

It is easy to illustrate the simple-interest method applied to an installment loan. As shown in Table 7.5, at the end of the first month, a periodic interest rate (the stated rate applied to the outstanding balance of a loan) of 1.5 percent (18 percent annually, divided by 12 months) is applied to the beginning balance of

Table 7.5

Sample Repayment Schedule for $1000 Principal plus Simple Interest (1.5 Percent per Month)

Month	Outstanding Balance	Payment	Interest	Principal	Ending Balance
1	$1000.00	$91.68	$15.00	$76.68	$923.32
2	923.32	91.68	13.85	77.83	845.49
3	845.49	91.68	12.68	79.00	766.49
4	766.49	91.68	11.50	80.18	686.31
5	686.31	91.68	10.29	81.39	604.92
6	604.92	91.68	9.07	82.61	522.31
7	522.31	91.68	7.83	83.85	438.46
8	438.46	91.68	6.58	85.10	353.36
9	353.36	91.68	5.30	86.38	266.98
10	266.98	91.68	4.00	87.68	179.30
11	179.30	91.68	2.69	88.99	90.31
12	90.31	91.66	1.35	90.31	0

$1000, giving an interest charge of $15. Of the first monthly installment of $91.68, $76.68 goes toward payment of the principal and $15 goes toward the simple interest. For the second month, the interest portion of the payment drops to $13.85, as the outstanding balance after the first month is $923.32 ($1000 − $76.68). Because the simple-interest method of calculating interest on installment loans applies the periodic interest rate to the outstanding loan balance, the APR and the simple interest rate will differ only if there are fees, such as an application fee, that boost the finance charge. (This method of paying off a loan, called *amortization,* is discussed further in Chapter 9.) Note that simple-interest loans carry no prepayment penalties.

The Add-On Method   The **add-on method** is a traditional and widely used technique for computing interest on installment loans. Once again, Equation (7.1) is used to calculate the dollar amount of interest (the interest rate used in this equation for the add-on method is an add-on rate and should not be confused with the APR).

For example, assume that Mary Ellen Broman of New York, New York, borrows $2000 for two years at 9 percent add-on interest to be repaid in monthly installments. Using Equation (7.1), the finance charge in dollars is $360 ($2000 × 0.09 × 2). Adding the finance charge ($360) to the amount borrowed ($2000) gives a total amount of $2360 to be repaid. When this amount is divided by the total number of scheduled payments (24), we find that 24 monthly payments of $98.33 will be required. We know that the APR must be higher than the add-on rate of 9 percent, however, because monthly repayments mean that Mary Ellen does not have use of the total amount borrowed for the full two years. Equation (7.3), which shows the **n-ratio method** of estimating the annual percentage rate (APR) on an add-on loan, can be used to calculate the APR.

$$APR = \frac{Y(95P + 9)F}{12P(P + 1)(4D + F)} \tag{7.3}*$$

$$= \frac{(12)[(95 \times 24) + 9](360)}{12(24)(24 + 1)[(4 \times 2000) + 360]}$$

$$= \frac{(12)(2289)(360)}{(288)(25)(8360)}$$

$$= \frac{9,888,480}{60,192,000}$$

$$= 16.4\%$$

where

APR	=	**annual percentage rate**
Y	=	number of payment schedules in 1 **year**
F	=	**finance** charge in dollars (dollar cost of credit)
D	=	**debt** (amount borrowed or proceeds)
P	=	total number of scheduled **payments**

Using Equation (7.3), the APR is 16.4 percent. Note that the APR is approximately double the add-on rate because, on average, Mary Ellen has use of only half of the borrowed money during the entire loan period.

---

*   Equation 7.3 can be calculated on the *Garman/Forgue* Web site.

The Discount Method   Occasionally, the discount method may be used for an installment loan. When the discount method is applied to the preceding example, Mary Ellen would receive only $1640 ($2000 minus $360) at the beginning of the loan period. Using Equation (7.3), the APR would be 19.8 percent (the APR rises because only $1640 is borrowed while $2000 is repaid).

Dealing with Overindebtedness

6   Recognize signs of overindebtedness, know what to do when it occurs, and explain your rights regarding credit collection and bankruptcy.

People become **overindebted** when excessive personal debts make repayment difficult. Signs of overindebtedness are provided below. If these signs appear, debtors can take steps such as getting credit counseling to correct the situation. Lenders, of course, will attempt to collect the debts, but they are required to adhere to the stipulations of the Fair Debt Collections Practices Act (described in the next section). As a last resort, some debtors choose, or are forced by creditors into, bankruptcy.

Ten Signs of Overindebtedness

1. *Exceeding debt limits and credit limits.* Are you spending more than 20 percent of your take-home pay on credit repayments? Are you over the maximum approved credit limits on your credit cards?

2. *Running out of money.* Are you using credit cards on occasions when you previously used cash? Are you borrowing to pay insurance premiums, taxes, or other large, predictable bills? Are you borrowing to pay for regular expenses, like food or gasoline? Do you try to borrow from friends and relatives to carry you through the month?

3. *Paying only the minimum amount due.* Do you pay the minimum payment—or almost the minimum—on your credit cards instead of making a larger payment to reduce the balance owed?

4. *Requesting new credit cards and increases in credit limits.* Have you applied for additional credit cards to increase your borrowing capacity? Have you asked for increases in credit limits on your present credit cards?

5. *Paying late or skipping credit payments.* Are you late more than once a year in paying your mortgage, rent, car loan, or utility bills? Do you frequently pay late charges? Are you juggling bills to pay the utilities, rent, or mortgage? Are creditors sending overdue notices?

6. *Not knowing how much you owe.* Have you lost track of how much you owe? Do you avoid reality by not adding up the total? Are you afraid to add up how much debt you have?

7. *Taking add-on loans.* Taking **add-on loans**, or **flipping**, occurs when you refinance or rewrite a loan for an even larger amount before it has been completely repaid. Say that a loan of $1000 has been repaid down to $400. You decide to refinance the debt balance of $400 by borrowing $2000 and taking the additional $1600 ($2000 − $400) for other purposes.

8. *Using debt-consolidation loans.* Are you borrowing, perhaps from a new source, to pay off old debts? Such action may temporarily reduce pressure on your budget, but it also indicates that the borrower is using too much credit.

9. *Receiving notice of repossession or foreclosure.* **Foreclosure** is a legal proceeding by which the lender seizes a home for nonpayment of the mortgage. Has your home or other asset been seized to pay debts?

10. *Experiencing garnishment.* **Garnishment** is a court-sanctioned procedure by which a portion of the debtor's wages are set aside to pay debts. Wages and salary income, including that of military personnel, can be garnished. The Truth in Lending Act prohibits more than two garnishments of one person's paycheck. The total amount garnished cannot represent more than 25 percent of a person's disposable income for the pay period or more than the amount by which the weekly disposable income exceeds 30 times the federal minimum wage (whichever is less). In addition, the law prohibits garnishment from being used as grounds for employment discharge.

Federal Law Regulates Debt Collection Practices

The Fair Debt Collection Practices Act (FDCPA) of 1977 prohibits third-party debt-collection agencies from using abusive, deceptive, and unfair practices in the legitimate effort to collect past-due debts. Banks, dentists, lawyers, and others who make their own collections are exempt from the act. **Debt-collection agencies** are firms that specialize in making collections that could not be obtained by the original lender. In some cases, collection agencies assist the original lender (for a fee); in others, they take over (purchase) the debt and become the creditor. When a debtor offers to make payment for several debts, FDCPA requires that the amount paid must be applied to whichever debts the debtor desires.

Collection agencies are prohibited from telephoning the debtor at unusual hours, making numerous repeated telephone calls during the day, not applying payments to amounts under dispute, using deceptive practices (such as falsely claiming they are attorneys or government officials), making threats, or using abusive language. They also cannot telephone a debtor's employer. Even with these limitations, collection agencies can be irritatingly persistent when collecting past-due accounts. If the collection effort is not successful, as a last resort the creditor may take the debtor to court to seek a legal judgment against the debtor; this judgment may be collected by repossessing some of the debtor's property and/or garnishing wages.

Bankruptcy as a Last Resort

When debts are so overbearing that life seems really bleak—a situation that may be aggravated by recent unemployment, illness, disability, death in the family, or small business failure—many people consider seeking the advice of an attorney about filing a petition in federal court to declare bankruptcy. **Bankruptcy** is a constitutionally guaranteed right that permits people (and businesses) to ask a court to find them officially unable to meet their debts. When the bankruptcy court grants such a petition, the assets and liabilities of the person are then administered for the benefit of the creditors. This process provides for an orderly division of the borrower's property and repayment of each creditor as fully as

Manage if You Become Overindebted

Even the most well-meaning credit user can become overextended as a result of illness, unemployment, or serious inattention to credit usage. Reviewing the checklist of signals of credit overindebtedness can sound the alarm and motivate you to consider a "debt diet" before creditors begin collection procedures. What should you do if you begin to realize that you are overextended?

1. *Determine what you owe.* Find out exactly how much is owed, to whom, and the monthly payment amounts needed to pay off each debt. For credit card and other open-ended credit, you will need to set a target payoff date and determine the monthly payment required to meet that target. The *Garman/Forgue* Web site provides a calculator to help you do so. Remember, paying off debts provides a better "rate of return" than savings accounts and most investments. Invest your money in debt repayment first.

2. *Focus your budget on debt reduction.* Calculate the percentage of your budget necessary to make the payments listed in step 1, then add 5 percent. Use this extra money to help pay your creditors by applying the extra money to the debts with the highest APRs first and then, in turn, to others with lower APRs.

3. *Contact your creditors.* Try to work out a new payment plan with your creditors. Many lenders, including those that finance automobiles, may let you skip a few payments. They want to see you solve your financial problems so you can avoid bankruptcy. Creditors are more likely to work with borrowers who come to them first rather than after collection efforts begin.

4. *Take on no new credit.* Credit cards should be turned back to the issuer or locked up so they cannot be used. Disciplined action to reduce debt should show results in only a few months. If progress does not occur, seek professional help.

5. *Refinance.* Determine if some loans can be refinanced at a lower percentage rate. This is especially possible with mortgage loans. (See Chapter 9 for details.) Even if you refinance, keep making the same payment to pay the new loan off more quickly. Obtaining a debt-consolidation loan might be appropriate for someone who acquired too much debt; you should avoid the temptation to use this strategy simply to lower total monthly payments. It is smart to use debt consolidation to lower APRs.

6. *Find good help.* Many large employers offer budget counseling through their personnel offices. You also may be able to find free counseling at your credit union or labor union. Another place to seek help is with your creditors. Many creditors, such as banks and consumer finance companies, provide advice to help debtors. A **nonprofit consumer credit counseling organization** provides individual credit counseling, assistance with financial problems, educational materials on credit and budgeting, and a debt management plan as an alternative to bankruptcy. The organization negotiates with creditors to persuade them to accept reduced or partial payments and to pass those savings along to the debtor. A **debt management program** requires the consumer to provide one monthly payment (usually somewhat smaller than the total of previous credit payments) that is distributed to all creditors. Services are provided on a face-to-face basis or via the telephone for free or at a nominal cost. Nationwide nonprofit credit counseling organizations include Debt Counselors of America [(800) 680-3328], Genus Credit Management [(888) 436-8715], and National Foundation for Consumer Credit [(800) 388-2227].

7. *Avoid bad help.* Many people claim that they want to help people in debt. Some are not so reputable, however. A **credit repair company** (also known as a **credit clinic**) is a firm that offers to help improve or fix one's credit history for a fee; it typically requires an advance payment (often $250 to $2000). No company is able to remove or "fix" accurate but negative information in anyone's credit history. For-profit credit counseling organizations charge fees as high as 20 percent of the amount owed. These organizations should be avoided.

possible. Most of the bankrupt person's assets are given to the trustee and sold. State and federal laws govern what the debtor can keep; in general, bankrupt people are allowed to keep a small equity in their homes, an inexpensive automobile, and limited personal property. After division of assets not exempt from bankruptcy, the remaining debt is usually **discharged** (forgiven or canceled) by the court at the time a debtor emerges from bankruptcy.

Attorneys, although not absolutely necessary for bankruptcy filings, typically charge $500 to $1000, or more, depending on the complexity of the case. The advice of an attorney is a good idea when considering bankruptcy. Federal laws allow bankruptcy for consumers in two forms: Chapter 13 and Chapter 7.

Chapter 13—Regular Income Plan   **Chapter 13** of the Bankruptcy Act (also known as the **wage earner** or the **regular income plan**) is designed for individuals with regular incomes and secured debts up to $750,000 and unsecured debts up to $250,000 who might be able to pay off some or all of their debts given certain protections of the court. Under this plan, the debtor submits a debt repayment plan to the court that is designed to repay as much of the debt as possible, typically in 36 to 60 months. After the debtor files a petition for bankruptcy (accompanied by a $160 filing fee), the court issues an automatic **stay**—a court order that temporarily prevents all creditors from recovering claims arising before

Manage Student Loan Debt

1. *Choose the most advantageous repayment pattern allowed.* The standard repayment plan for student loan debt calls for equal monthly installments paid over ten years. If you owe more than $12,000, it may be possible to stretch payments over longer time periods. Alternatively, you can establish a graduated repayment plan whereby the payments are lower in the early years and increase in later years when income is anticipated to be higher. Finally, an income-contingent plan ties debt repayment requirements to the rise and fall of the graduate's income. The most advantageous approach is to pay the debt off as soon as possible, reducing total finance charges.

2. *Consolidate student loans.* It may be possible to consolidate more than one education loan made under various federal programs into a single plan administered by the federal government. This strategy may allow for a much more convenient repayment pattern. [For details on

consolidating a student loan, call the Federal Student Aid Information Center at (800) 433-3243.]

3. *Pay electronically.* In some programs, the graduate can make arrangements to have the monthly payment transferred electronically and automatically out of a checking account. As a reward for setting up such an arrangement, the graduate receives a one-quarter percentage point reduction in the interest rate.

4. *Be punctual with your repayments.* In some programs, if you make the first 48 payments on time, the interest rate will be reduced by two percentage points. This bonus is almost guaranteed when borrowers opt for electronic repayment.

5. *Refinance with a second mortgage loan.* This strategy may be useful since home equity interest is tax-deductible, whereas student loan interest is not.

the start of the bankruptcy proceeding. This action protects the debtor from collection efforts by creditors, including garnishments, and generally no assets may be sold by the borrower or repossessed by the lender after a stay is granted.

After the court notifies all creditors of the petition for bankruptcy, a hearing is scheduled. With the help of a **bankruptcy trustee** (or **U.S. trustee**)—who verifies the accuracy of a bankruptcy petition at a hearing and who distributes the assets according to a court-approved plan—the proposed repayment plan is reviewed (and modified, if necessary) and finally approved by the court. The debtor must then follow a strict budget while repaying the obligations. During this time, new credit is prohibited without permission of the trustee. If the debtor makes all scheduled payments, he or she is discharged of any remaining amounts due that could not be repaid within the period.

Chapter 7—Immediate Liquidation Plan Straight **bankruptcy**, known as **Chapter 7** of the Bankruptcy Act, is designed for an immediate liquidation of assets. This option is permitted when it would be highly unlikely that substantial repayment could ever be made. After receiving a Chapter 7 petition (the filing fee is $175), the bankruptcy judge can rule that the person can repay some debt and is referred to Chapter 13. Some debts are never excused or exempted from bankruptcy, including education loans that have come due within the previous seven years, fines, alimony, child support, income taxes for the most recent three years, debts not listed on a bankruptcy petition, and claims for punitive damages for malicious or wanton acts, such as causing injury while driving under the influence of alcohol or drugs.

Bankruptcy should be used as a last resort and not just as a quick fix or cure-all for overuse of credit. Because employers, landlords, and creditors check credit reports, people who have declared bankruptcy typically face years of trouble when renting housing, obtaining home loans, and getting credit cards. The fact that someone declared bankruptcy remains on his or her credit record for ten years.

Because a discharged debtor usually emerges with little, if any, debt and a much improved net worth, some creditors view former bankrupts who have a reliable source of income in a positive way. Because a Chapter 7 cannot be repeated for at least six years, the discharged debtors may represent improved credit risks. Although credit limits will be lower and will require hefty down payments, this renewed access to credit (at higher interest rates than usual) is tempting for some former bankrupts.

Summary

1. For many people, items such as automobiles, home improvements, and major appliances cannot be purchased without installment credit. The same may be true for payment of higher education and some investments. In such cases, people should consider planned borrowing, which is a knowing decision to borrow when the cost of borrowing is warranted by the benefits received.

2. It is important to establish your own debt limit. Three methods can be used: debt-payments-to-disposable-income method, ratio of debt-to-equity method, and continuous-debt method.

3. Consumer loans are classified as either installment or noninstallment credit. Borrowers must also distinguish between secured loans, which use collateral or a cosigner, and unsecured loans, which are riskier for the lender and, therefore, carry higher finance charges.

4. Three major sources of consumer loans are depository institutions, consumer finance companies, and sales finance companies. The last group specializes in secured loans, often at competitive interest rates, with the items sold serving as the collateral.

5. Both the simple-interest and add-on methods are used to calculate the cost of installment loans, although the annual percentage rate formula gives the correct rate in all cases.

6. Among the signals of credit overindebtedness are exceeding credit-limit guidelines and running out of money too often. People experiencing serious financial difficulties can obtain professional assistance through nonprofit consumer credit counseling service agencies or by submitting a petition under Chapter 7 or 13 of the Bankruptcy Act.

Key Words & Concepts

Questions for Thought & Discussion

1. When is it advantageous to borrow funds for planned purposes?

2. How does setting a debt limit help the borrower?

3. Explain how the "debt-payments-to-disposable-income" debt-limit method works.

4. Give an example of an individual's finances where the ratio of debt to equity is positive, and calculate the ratio. Create another example where the ratio is negative.

5. What suggestions about debt might you offer a recently married couple where both spouses work for money income?

6. Distinguish between noninstallment credit and installment credit.

7. For the borrower, what are the advantages and disadvantages of a variable-rate loan?

8. Distinguish between a secured loan and an unsecured loan.

9. What does it mean to cosign a loan?

10. What burden might an acceleration clause place on a borrower?

11. Would you recommend voluntary repossession as a method for getting out of debt?

12. Compare and contrast an installment purchase agreement with a conditional sales contract.

13. Summarize how the rule of 78s method works.

14. Describe how cash-value life insurance can be a source of funds for borrowing.

15. What process would a person interested in borrowing money from a pawnshop follow?

16. What fees must be included in the finance charge when calculating the APR on a loan?

17. For single-payment loans, summarize the differences between the simple-interest method and the discount method when calculating the APR.

18. For installment loans, summarize how the simple-interest method of APR calculation works.

19. Select three of the signals of credit overindebtedness and write a paragraph describing a hypothetical person who is exhibiting these characteristics.

20. Distinguish between "taking add-on loans" and "using debt-consolidation loans."

21. Compare and contrast the two forms of bankruptcy, Chapter 13 and Chapter 7.

DECISION-MAKING CASES

Case 1   Reducing Expenses to Buy a New Car

Ann Coulson recently graduated from college and accepted a position in Manhattan, Kansas, as an assistant librarian in the public library. Ann has no debts, and her budget is shown in the first column of Table 7.2. She now faces the question of whether to trade in her old car on a new one that will cost her a monthly payment of $330. Taking the role of a good friend of Ann, decide in what areas and how much in each area might Ann cut back on her expenses so that she can afford the vehicle.

(a) What areas might be cut back?

(b) How much in each area might be cut back?

(c) After finishing your analysis, what advice (and possibly alternatives) would you offer Ann about buying the new car?

Case 2   Clauses in a Car Purchase Contract

Virginia Rowland is a dentist in Hattiesburg, Mississippi, who recently entered into a contract to buy a new automobile. After signing to finance $12,000, she hurriedly left the office of the sales finance company with her copy of the contract. Later that evening Virginia read the contract and noticed several clauses—an acceleration clause, a repossession clause, a balloon payment for $900, and a rule of 78s clause. When she signed the contract, Virginia was told that "these standard clauses should not concern her."

(a) Should Virginia be concerned about these clauses? Why or why not?

(b) What are some fair warnings for Virginia regarding the balloon payment?

(c) Considering the rule of 78s clause, what will happen if Virginia pays off the loan before the regular due date?

(d) If Virginia had financed the $12,000 for four years at 12 percent APR, what would her monthly payment be, using the information in Table 7.3 or on the *Garman/Forgue* Web site?

Case 3   Debt Consolidation as a Debt Reduction Strategy

Isaac Granovsky, assistant manager at a small retail shop in Las Vegas, New Mexico, had an unusual amount of debt. He owed $1800 to one bank, $600 to a clothing store, $900 to his credit union, and several hundred dollars to other stores and persons. Isaac was paying more than $450 per month on the three major obligations and $425 per month for an apartment. He realized that his take-home pay of slightly more than $1200 per month did not leave him with much excess cash. Isaac discussed an alternative way of handling his major payments with his credit union officer. The officer suggested that he pool all of his debts and take out a debt-consolidation loan at a lower interest rate. As a result, he would pay only $230 per month for all his debts. Isaac seemed ecstatic over the idea.

(a) Is Isaac's enthusiasm over the idea of a debt-consolidation loan justified? Why or why not?

(b) Why can the credit union offer such a "good deal" to Isaac?

(c) What compromise would Isaac make to remit payments of only $230 as compared with $450?

(d) If you assume that the consolidation loan will cost more in total interest, what would be a justification for this added cost?

Financial Math Questions

1. Rosemary Jensen and Janice Parker of East Lansing, Michigan, are both single and share an apartment on the limited resources provided through Rosemary's disability check from Social Security and Janice's part-time job at a grocery store. The two grew tired of their old furniture and went shopping. A local store offers credit at an annual interest rate of 16 percent, with a maximum term of four years. The furniture they wish to purchase costs $2800, with no down payment required. Using Table 7.3 or the *Garman/Forgue* Web site, make the following calculations. Print your results.

    (a) What is the amount of their monthly payment if they borrow for four years?

    (b) What are the total finance charges over that four-year period?

    (c) How would the payment change if Rosemary and Janice reduced the loan term to three years?

    (d) What are the total finance charges over that three-year period?

    (e) How would the payment change if they could afford a down payment of $500 with four years of financing?

    (f) What are the total finance charges over that four-year period given the $500 down payment?

    (g) How would the payment change if they could afford a down payment of $500 with three years of financing?

    (h) What are the total finance charges over that three-year period given the $500 down payment?

2. Jack Sprater of Bozeman, Montana, has been shopping for a loan to buy a new car. He wants to borrow $12,000 for four or five years. His credit union offers a simple interest loan at 9.1 percent for 48 months, resulting in a monthly payment of $299.19. The credit union does not offer five-year auto loans under $15,000, however. If he borrowed $15,000, this payment would strain his budget. A local bank offered Jack a five-year loan at a 9.34 percent APR, with a monthly payment of $251.08. This credit would not be a simple-interest loan. Because Jack is not a depositor in the bank, he would also be charged a $25 credit check fee and a $45 application fee. Jack likes the lower payment but knows that the APR is the true cost of credit, so he decided to confirm the APRs for both loans before making his decision.

    (a) What is the APR for the credit union loan?

    (b) Use the n-ratio formula to confirm the APR on the bank loan.

    (c) What is the add-on interest rate for the bank loan?

    (d) By how much would Jack lower the APR on the bank loan if he opened an account to avoid the credit check and application fees?

3. Elliott Carson of Bishop, California, obtained a two-year installment loan for $1500 to buy some furniture eight months ago. The loan had a 12.6 percent APR and a finance charge of $204.72. His monthly payment is $71.03. Elliott has made eight monthly payments and now wants to pay off the remainder of the loan. The lender will use the rule of 78s method to calculate a prepayment penalty.

    (a) How much will Elliott need to give the lender to pay off the loan?

    (b) What is the dollar amount of the prepayment penalty on this loan?

MONEY MATTERS: LIFE-CYCLE CASES

Victor and Maria
Advise Their Niece

Victor and Maria have always enjoyed a close relationship with Maria's niece Teresa, who graduated from college with a pharmacy degree. Teresa recently asked Maria for some assistance with her finances now that her education debts are coming due. Teresa owes $19,000 in several student loans and earns $24,000 in disposable income. Teresa would like to take on additional debt to furnish her apartment and buy a better car.

1. What advice might Maria give Teresa about managing her student loan debt?

2. If on January 2, 2000, Teresa were to consolidate her loans into one loan at 8 percent interest, what advice could Maria give regarding Teresa's overall debt limit using both the debt-repayment-to-disposable-income and the continuous-debt methods outlined in the chapter? (Hint: Use Table 7.3 or visit the *Garman/Forgue* Web site to calculate monthly payments for various time periods.)

3. Evaluate monthly payments for loan terms of three, four, and five years. Compare the results.

The Johnsons' Credit Questions

Harry and Belinda need some questions resolved regarding credit. Their three-year-old car has been experiencing mechanical problems lately. Instead of buying a new set of tires, as planned for in March, they are considering trading the car in for a new vehicle so Harry can have dependable transportation for commuting to work. The couple still owes $3600 to the bank for their present car, or $285 per month for the remaining 18 months of the 48-month loan. The trade-in value of the car and $1000 that Harry earned from a freelance interior design job should pay off the auto loan and leave $1250 for a down payment on the new car. The Johnsons have agreed on a sales price for the new car of $14,250. The money planned for tires will be spent for other incidental fees associated with the purchase.

1. Make recommendations to Harry and Belinda regarding where to seek financing and what APR to expect.

2. Using the *Garman/Forgue* Web site or the information in Table 7.3, calculate the monthly payment for a loan period of three, four, and five years at 10 percent APR. Describe the relationship between the loan period and the payment amount.

3. Harry and Belinda have a cash-flow deficit projected for several months this year (see Tables 4.3 and 4.4). Suggest how, when, and where they might finance the shortages by borrowing.

 ### *Exploring the World Wide Web of Personal Finance*

To complete these exercises, go to the *Garman/Forgue* Web site at

www.hmco.com/college/business/

Select Personal Finance. Click on the exercise link for this chapter and answer the questions that appear on the Web page.

1. A key to getting out of debt quickly and at the least cost is to determine which debts should be paid off first. Visit the Web site for *Debt Analyzer.* Either enter your own data or enter hypothetical data to determine the most efficient way to pay off debts. What three insights did you learn about debt repayment priorities?

2. Visit the Web site for the Consumer Information Center in Pueblo, Colorado, where you will find an on-line copy of *Managing Your Debts: How to Regain Financial Health.* Download or print the handbook. What five tips would you give to someone who feels overindebted?

3. Visit the Web site for the Legg Mason Financial Calculator, where you will find a brief questionnaire asking for information about any simple-interest loan. Complete the questionnaire for a loan you have or for a hypothetical loan. The calculator will break down the monthly payments, indicating which portion of each payment goes to pay interest and which is used to pay down the principal of the loan.

4. Visit the Web site for Mortgage Market Information Service, where you will find a calculator that determines the monthly payment for any simple-interest loan given the time period, interest rate, and loan amount. Assume you wish to borrow $11,000 to buy a car. Vary the time period and interest rate of the loan to see how these variations affect your monthly payment.

Automobiles and Other Major Purchases

8

OBJECTIVES

After reading this chapter, you should be able to:

1 Describe several guidelines to save money on major purchases.

2 Employ the three steps in wise buying that occur prior to interacting with sellers.

3 Comparison shop when buying or leasing vehicles and other major purchases.

4 Negotiate effectively and make intelligent decisions when undertaking major expenditures.

5 Evaluate your purchase decision as a guide for future behavior.

This chapter focuses on the principles of wise purchasing as applied to vehicles and other major expenditures. We first provide some guidelines that can save you substantial amounts of money over your lifetime. These guidelines include life-cycle planning to give perspective on when people usually make major purchases. The steps in the buying process are then examined and illustrated. The first three steps occur prior to interacting with sellers: determining needs and wants, preshopping research, and fitting the budget. The important topic of comparison shopping follows as the fourth step in the buying process. The next two steps of negotiating and making the decision are then discussed with an emphasis on making the final decision at home. The seventh and final step—evaluation of the decision—is taken after making the purchase.

Guidelines for Wise Buying

1 Describe several guidelines to save money on major purchases.

Examples of ways that people waste money could fill the pages of dozens of books. Fortunately, the following simple guidelines can yield savings of 10 to 20 percent during a year, equivalent to a sharp tax-free increase in income.

Control Buying on Impulse

Simple restraint will help avoid **impulse buying**, which is simply buying without fully considering priorities and alternatives. For example, you may have shopped carefully by comparing various personal computers and then selected one at a discount store. While at the store, you impulsively pick up some games and entertainment software that you had not planned to buy. The extra $245 spent on an unplanned purchase ruins some of the benefits of the careful shopping for the computer itself.

Pay Cash

Paying cash whenever possible can save money in two ways. First, it helps control impulse buying, which becomes easier when credit cards are used for unnecessary purchases. Second, use of credit can make financial planning more difficult by taking away financial flexibility and by adding to the cost of items. As discussed in Chapters 6 and 7, you may pay 12, 18, or even 24 percent more for your credit purchases in the form of interest.

Buy at the Right Time

Paying attention to sales and looking for the right time to buy will save money. Many items, such as sporting goods and clothing, are marked down near certain holidays and at the end of each climate season. Another $5 or $10 weekly can be saved on food simply by stocking up on advertised specials. New vehicles are least expensive at the end of the month and the model year (because of sales) and near the close of a retailer's promotion. Make sure that what you buy on sale is something you will really use.

Don't Pay Extra for a "Name"

Some people have an "Excedrin headache" for $0.30 per dosage, while others have a plain aspirin headache for $0.02 per dosage. Scientific research (not the advertiser's research) consistently shows that the effectiveness of all over-the-counter pain relievers is roughly the same. Consequently, the ads for such products say "none better" rather than "we're the best." Gasoline, vitamins, laundry and other soaps, and many grocery items are all products with minor quality differences. Even some different makes of vehicles are essentially identical. For example, some automobiles made in the same U.S. plant are priced differently, such as the Chevrolet Blazer and the GMC Jimmy.

Buying generic products represents a good way to save money. **Generic products** are sold under a general commodity name such as "whole-kernel corn" rather than a brand name, such as Del Monte. Savings can be especially significant for generic prescription drugs. Many states allow consumers to request that the pharmacist dispense a generic equivalent even if the physician writes the prescription under a brand name. In other states, consumers can ask the physician to write the prescription for a generic drug. Realize, too, that many less-expensive, store-brand products (such as those sold by Sears or Kroger) are actually made by the brand-name manufacturers.

Many people feel more secure buying a "name." When taking vacations, they choose to stay at upscale hotels (Radisson, Hyatt, Sheraton) rather than save 50 percent or more by staying at budget inns like Motel 6, Super 8, or Days Inn—places that also offer satisfactory accommodations. Your informed financial decisions should be consistent with your personal values, and you can go first class if desired, but you should at least acknowledge the additional cost involved.

Recognize the High Price of Convenience Shopping

A bottle of ketchup or a jar of peanut butter bought at a supermarket probably costs 50 cents less than the same items purchased at a nearby convenience store, whereas bread and milk may be priced about the same. Buying a few items daily at a convenience store or neighborhood market rather than making a planned weekly visit to a supermarket can raise food bills by 30 percent or more through the combination of higher prices and the more frequent temptation of impulse purchases. In addition, although shopping for furniture and appliances in one's local community may be convenient, better prices on the same items may be found in larger, more competitive shopping areas.

Use Life-Cycle Planning for Major Purchases

"You can't have everything," the old saying goes, but many young Americans certainly try. This desire to have all of life's comforts early in life is one of the reasons why the average household headed by someone younger than age 25 spends 17 percent more than its disposable income. (How? By using credit, of course.) Because it is important to realize that one cannot have everything right now, life-cycle planning will help keep things in perspective. Comparing your possessions to those of your parents or more established relatives and friends is fine, but you should recognize that it takes many years to build up the same quantity and quality of possessions. Setting short- and long-term goals intelligently and recognizing budget limitations will enable you to reach goals for major purchases without jeopardizing your financial security.

It sometimes helps to think of the life cycle in terms of three periods: early singlehood, later singlehood/young couplehood, and mature singlehood/middle couplehood. Such a categorization has major benefits for individuals just starting their financial lives. First, it helps to plan purchases by setting up an appropriate timetable. Planning makes it easier to delay some purchases, knowing that the delay is not permanent. Second, defining these periods helps set up a budget category to save money for the purchase. Third, this approach makes clear that many major purchases are really replacements for older, obsolete items. The replacement process provides a good opportunity to upgrade the quality of a more basic model purchased early in life when funds were more limited.

Steps Taken Before Interacting with the Seller

2 Employ the three steps in wise buying that occur prior to interacting with sellers.

The planned buying process includes seven steps: (1) prioritizing wants, (2) preshopping research, (3) fitting the budget, (4) comparison shopping, (5) negotiating, (6) making the decision, and (7) complimenting or complaining appropriately. The first three steps should occur before you actually interact with sellers in any major way. They are, in a sense, the homework you do when preparing to buy.

Prioritize Your Wants

A **need** is something thought to be a necessity; a **want** is unnecessary but desired. In truth, very few needs exist, yet in everyday language people talk often of *needing* certain things. In the planned buying process, it is best to avoid such thinking and, instead, consider all options to be wants. Of course, some wants are very important. The most important can be determined by **prioritizing wants**, which results in a ranking of higher-priority and lower-priority wants. This approach provides two benefits. First, it allows careful consideration of benefits and costs of options. Second, it helps avoid short-circuiting the decision-making process by declaring something as a need and, therefore, as not open to careful consideration.

Prioritizing becomes more difficult when a decision has multiple facets. For example, consider the case of Sharon Danes, a respiratory therapist from St. Paul, Minnesota. Sharon has been late to work several times in the past few months because her 12-year-old car has malfunctioned more than once. She must first decide whether she should buy a new vehicle, buy a used vehicle, repair her current vehicle, or take the bus to work. After considering these options, Sharon decides to focus on buying a new vehicle. Next, she must determine which vehicle features are of higher or lower priority. To do so, Sharon developed the worksheet shown in Figure 8.1. Such a worksheet formalizes the prioritization process and aids decision making and shopping.

Do the Necessary Preshopping Research

Preshopping research means gathering information about products or services before actually beginning to shop for them. Manufacturers, sellers, and service providers represent important sources of information about products and services during preshopping research. Automobile manufacturers publish many brochures on their products and sponsor automobile shows that are used both to promote and to provide information on their vehicles. Two other sources of information are friends and consumer magazines. If you know someone who drives an automobile you are considering buying, ask the person about his or her experience with the vehicle. You also could read about the vehicle in a consumer magazine, such as *Consumer Reports*, which tests and reports on five to ten products monthly. In addition, *Consumer Reports Buying Guide,* which is published every December, lists facts and figures on numerous products. Monthly issues of *Consumer Reports* generally provide a two- to five-page narrative analyzing the products and summarizing the information in chart form. Figure 8.2 on page

Figure 8.1

Priority Worksheet
(for Sharon Danes)

AUTOMOBILE FEATURE	PRIORITY LEVEL		
	1	2	3
Adjustable steering column			✔
Airbag—driver	✔		
Airbag—passenger		✔	
Air conditioning		✔	
AM-FM radio	✔		
Antilock brakes		✔	
Automatic transmission	✔		
Central locking system			✔
CD player			✔
Cruise control		✔	
4-Wheel (all-wheel) drive			✔
Power windows			✔
Rear-window defroster	✔		
Sun roof / moon roof			✔
Theft-deterrent system			✔

209 provides an example of such a chart for a computer printer. Each year the April issue of *Consumer Reports* is devoted to the buying of vehicles.

When shopping for any product, it may help to review publications on a more specific topic, such as *Photography, PC World, Car and Driver,* and *Stereo Review.* Realize, however, that trade magazines accept advertising for the products they report on and thus are not likely to be as unbiased as *Consumer Reports,* which accepts no advertising. Another unbiased source of information on wise buying (and many other personal finance topics) is the federal government's Consumer Information Center, Pueblo, Colorado 81009 (*www.gsa.gov/staff/pa/cic/cic.htm*).

Price Advertising is a key source of information about prices. You can also obtain price information through catalogs, the telephone, and over the Internet. While the prices of "big ticket" items like furniture, appliances, and vehicles may be advertised, you may need to visit a showroom or dealership for prices on specific makes, models, and options. This first visit should not be a buying trip, but rather a mission to gather information only. A key piece of information is the **retail** or **manufacturer's suggested retail price (MSRP)**, which simply consists of the initial asking price. On new vehicles, the MSRP—called the **sticker price**—appears on a window sticker in the vehicle. The sticker price may bear little relationship to the price ultimately paid for a new vehicle. Many consumers have caught on to the fiction of new car sticker prices and now focus on the **invoice price** or **seller's cost**, which reflects the price the dealer paid for the vehicle. In fact, manufacturers sometimes offer **dealer holdback** programs that permit the dealer to retain (instead of paying) a portion of the invoice price, thereby providing the dealer with additional profit on the vehicle. Thus, even the invoice price may not represent the true dealer cost.

Figure 8.2

Consumer Reports Ratings on Computer Printers.

Ratings Computer printers
& Recommendations

Shopping strategy

An inkjet printer is the best choice for most households, thanks to its color-printing prowess. A laser printer is strictly for black and white.

Consider operating costs Check the Details on the Models to find the printers with the lowest printing costs, especially for graphics and photos.

Know where to shop You can find printers at office-supply and computer stores, wholesale clubs, in catalogs, or at online marts. Individual retailers as well as several computer makers package a printer with the rest of the hardware.

Overall Ratings *Within types, listed in order of overall score*

Key No.	Brand and model	Price	Overall score 0 P F G VG E 100	Text quality	Text speed B/W	Text speed COLOR	B/W GRAPHICS	B/W PHOTO	Color GRAPHICS	Color PHOTO
INKJET PRINTERS										
1	Hewlett-Packard DeskJet 895Cse	$410		◒	3.5 ppm	3.2 ppm	◔	◔	◔	◒
2	Hewlett-Packard DeskJet 712C	250		◒	3.1	2.5	◒	◔	◔	◒
3	Xerox DocuPrint XJ8C	240		◔	2.4	1.9	○	◔	◒	◔
4	Compaq IJ900	295		◔	2.4	1.9	◑	◔	◒	◒
5	Compaq IJ700	220		◒	2.3	2.0	◑	◔	○	◒
6	Epson Stylus Color 740	275		○	2.9	2.7	○	◔	◒	◔
7	Lexmark 3200	175		◔	1.8	1.5	◑	◔	◒	◒
8	Epson Stylus Photo 700	270		○	1.1	1.1	◒	◔	◔	◔
9	Epson Stylus Color 440	150		◒	1.6	0.8	○	◔	◒	◒
10	Lexmark 5700	245		○	2.4	2.0	◑	◔	○	◒
11	Canon BJC-5000	250		◒	2.0	1.5	○	◔	○	◒
12	Epson Stylus Color 640	200		○	1.7	1.7	○	○	○	◒
13	Canon BJC-7004 Photo	300		◒	2.0	2.0	◒	◒	○	◒
14	Hewlett-Packard DeskJet 697C	180		◒	1.7	0.6	○	◑	○	○
15	Canon BJC-4400	175		○	1.9	1.7	○	◔	◑	○
16	Okidata Okijet 2500	200		◑	1.0	0.9	○	◒	●	◑
17	Xerox DocuPrint XJ6C	150		◑	1.0	0.9	○	◒	●	◑
LASER PRINTERS										
18	NEC SuperScript 870	350		◔	4.6	—	◔	○	—	—
19	Hewlett-Packard LaserJet 1100 se	400		◔	4.5	—	◒	◑	—	—
20	Brother HL-1050	385		◔	4.6	—	○	○	—	—

The tests behind the Ratings

Overall score covers speed for text and print quality for text, graphics, and photos. We used default settings for text and graphics. **Text quality** indicates how crisply and clearly each printer reproduced text on copier paper. **Text speed** is for single-spaced pages per minute (ppm), based on the time needed from executing an "OK to print" command until the last page is finished. We printed a three-page document, then calculated an average speed. The **color** column gives the speed when the text included a small amount of a second color. **B/W** and **color** denote print quality for graphics and photos. **Price** is the estimated average, based on a national survey.

In the Details on the Models: All the printers run on Windows 95, 98, and NT; most also run on Windows 3.1, and a few run on Mac OS. Dimensions are HxWxD for the overall space needed to use the printer. • Printing costs include ink or toner as well as wear on print heads and drums. Text and graphics figures assume paper cost of 0.5¢ per sheet; photo figures, a paper cost of 67¢ per sheet. • "Banner" means the printer can print at least a 44-inch banner.

Most of these printers: • Are sold with and accommodate one set of color and black ink cartridges or one toner cartridge. • Have a 100-page paper feeder, an on/off switch, an on-screen ink monitor. • Offer technical support by telephone, fax, or Internet. • Use IEEE-1284 printer cable to connect to a Windows computer's parallel port, which should be set to the ECP mode for best results. • Have a 1-yr. warranty.

●	Excellent
◑	Very good
○	Good
◓	Fair
●	Poor

Trade-In   You may be able to trade in an old model when buying a new one, especially with automobiles. Buyers need to know the true value of any item they will trade in. You can determine the value of a car by telephoning someone at a bank or credit union who has access to the National Automobile Dealers Association (NADA) "red book" of used vehicle prices. Generally, people can receive a better price by selling a vehicle on their own rather than trading it in.

Cost of Financing   Major purchases, such as vehicles, are commonly purchased using credit. It is important to gather information on the current annual percentage rates (APRs) on vehicle and other purchase loans from various sources. An important source of loans for new vehicles is sales financing arranged through the dealer or manufacturer. In addition, buyers should always obtain quotes from local banks and credit unions.

Fit the Expenditure into Your Budget

Everyone asks "Can I afford it?" when making a buying decision. When the purchase is an expensive one, this question is crucial. An unaffordable cash purchase can wreck a budget for one or two months, but an ill-advised credit purchase may have negative effects for years.

One way to view the cost of a major expenditure is to consider the cost per use of the product. For example, Frank Lenz, an autoworker from Chicago, is considering buying a video camera. He has researched several models in the

Get Help When Buying a New Vehicle

The complexity and uncertainty involved in negotiating the price of a new vehicle has led to the development of a number of services that are offered to assist buyers. A **new vehicle buying service** provides people with aid ranging from retail and wholesale price lists to third-party negotiation of a purchase price from one or more dealers. One of the first such services to begin operation was the *Consumer Reports* New Car Price Service at (800) 933-5555. Others include AutoAdvantage at (800) 999-4227. All provide price reports for a fee ranging from $10 to $30 per report. Expanded services can be obtained from Nationwide Auto Brokers at (800) 521-7257, which will sell, finance, and deliver new vehicles; CarBargains at (800) 475-7283 and AutoAdvisor at (800) 326-1976 both offer bidding services. Although these services may cost from $30 to $300, the fee may be worth the expense to many car buyers, because of the lower prices they obtain and the freedom from hassles.

You can also search the Internet for new car buying assistance. Both Prodigy and America Online have multiple avenues for getting information by typing in just a few keywords such as "automobile" and "car." Edmund's Automobile Buyer's Guide can be found on the Web at *www.edmunds.com*. Car dealers in certain geographic areas have set up Web pages that can be accessed to determine availability of a make and model in the area. AutoSite *(www.autosite.com)* has links to automaker home pages. You can even use the Internet to make an offer to a dealership for a car, thus striking a deal electronically.

$700–$750 price range. Frank figures that he would use the camera about 20 times per year and knows that the average camcorder lasts about seven years, giving him 140 uses. Dividing this figure into the cost of a $700 model yields a cost per use of $5 ($700 ÷ 140), excluding the cost of videotapes and maintenance. It might be possible for Frank to save money by renting or borrowing a camera when he needs one.

Using a more expensive purchase, let's look at how Sharon Danes might fit a new car into her budget. She estimates that the base sticker price of the type of car she wants will be about $13,000. This price includes the four items she checked as highest priority because she would not consider buying a car that lacked them. The second-priority options will likely add a total of $2100 to the sticker price: passenger air bag, $500; air conditioning, $700; antilock brakes, $600; and cruise control, $300.

Buying a car with her first- and second-priority features might cost Sharon $16,000 ($13,000 + $2100 for the options + $900 for sales tax and title registration). She can use $2500 from her savings account as a down payment, receive $1000 for trading in her old car, and borrow the remaining $12,500. The prices for the car and its options are Sharon's estimates from her preshopping research. The actual price she will pay for the car will depend on her ability to negotiate the final price down from the sticker price. From her research, Sharon knows

Did You KNOW?

The Keys to Buying a Safe Car

The following pointers may help you purchase a safer new or used vehicle.

- *Check government safety test results.* The federal government crash-tests motor vehicles for safety. For results on various makes and models, call the National Highway Traffic Safety Administration (NHTSA) "auto hotline" at (800) 424-9393.

- *Check on recalls.* With more than ten million new vehicles sold in the United States each year, it is understandable that some will be recalled for repairs to safety features. When buying a used car, call the NHTSA auto hotline to see if the vehicle has been recalled. If so, confirm that the repairs have been made; if not, buy elsewhere. Dealers are required to fix vehicles recalled for safety reasons for free.

- *Look for a model with standard airbags.* All new cars now have driver's side airbags. For added protection, consider new and used models containing airbags for both the driver and the front-seat passenger. Seatbelts should be worn even if airbags are present.

- *Consider antilock brakes.* Antilock brakes are believed to reduce the possibility of skidding during sudden stops. They are especially helpful in rain and inclement winter conditions. (Antilock brakes should not be pumped during a skid; brake and hold.)

- *Consider side-impact protection.* All new passenger cars sold in the United States now meet federal side-impact regulations. Many vehicles met those requirements earlier and might be good candidates for the used car buyer.

- *Think about theft as well as accident safety.* Some makes and models of cars are much more attractive to thieves than others. These cars also require higher automobile insurance premiums. Call the NHTSA auto hotline for information on a new or used car's theft rating.

that the dealer cost of new vehicles averages about 12 percent less than the sticker price. By multiplying the sticker price by 12 percent, she can make a rough estimate of her bargaining room. For example, Sharon might bargain to reduce the price of the car with the wanted options and taxes by 10 percent to $14,400 [$16,000 − ($16,000 × 0.10)], leaving the dealer with a modest profit margin.

The monthly payment that Sharon must fit into her budget will depend on five factors: the price she actually pays for the car, the down payment she makes, the time period for payback of the loan, the amount she receives in trade for her old car, and the interest rate on the loan. For illustration, we will choose the down payment of $2500 and assume a 48-month time period (a common financing term). Sharon figures that she can get no more than $1000 for her old car. But what about the actual price and interest rate?

We will assume that Sharon has done a good job of estimating the price she might pay for the car. If she can reduce the price by 10 percent, she will need to borrow $10,900 ($14,400 − $2500 down − $1000 trade-in) instead of $12,500. This figure is only an estimate, however, and may vary by as much as $1000 depending on her negotiating skills. If the loan amount is $10,900, Sharon would then need to use the likely APR figure from her preshopping research to determine a monthly payment. If she obtains a loan with a 10 percent APR, Sharon estimates that her monthly payment would be $276.42 (10.9 × 25.36, from Table 7.3 on page 184).

Table 8.1 shows Sharon's monthly budget. Her monthly take-home pay of $1440 is totally committed. To buy the automobile with options, she will need $276.42 per month and will have to change her budget drastically. To commute

Table 8.1

Fitting an Automobile Payment into a Monthly Budget

	Budget Last Month	Possible Cutbacks	Budget with Automobile
Food	$ 230	$ −20	$ 210
Clothing	100	−25	75
Transportation	80	−80	0
Auto insurance	65		65
Gasoline	25		25
Housing	475		475
Utilities	85		85
Telephone	55		55
Entertainment	100	−50	50
Gifts	50	−25	25
Church and charity	30		30
Beautician	25		25
Savings	60	−10	50
Miscellaneous	60		60
Total	$1440	$ −210	$1230
Car payment			276
Total with car payment			$1506

to her former job, Sharon used public transportation at a cost of $80 per month; those dollars can now go toward a car payment. To find the rest of the money, she could cut food expenditures ($20 per month), spend less on clothing ($25), cut entertainment and gifts in half ($50 and $25, respectively), and put $10 less in savings. In all, these efforts would raise only $210 ($80 + $20 + $25 + $50

Did You KNOW ? *Rental Car Basics*

Getting a good deal when renting a car can be difficult.

- *Select the type of car needed.* Rental car rates are broken down by the size of the vehicle, such as subcompact, compact, and mid-size. Decide what type of car you want before shopping. You may receive a **free upgrade** if you reserve one size of vehicle and the company voluntarily rents you the next largest because your desired car size is unavailable. Be aware that the company will try to get you to agree to upgrade even if a free upgrade is forthcoming. Some people take a chance on a free upgrade and reserve a vehicle smaller than they need. If you really need a midsize car, however, reserve one.

- *Shop for price.* Rental car rates can vary by as much as 50 percent. Call or use the Internet to contact several companies asking for the absolute lowest rates (daily, weekend, or weekly) for the size of vehicle you desire. Check the travel section of your local newspaper for advertisements announcing special promotions. Discounts and other promotions are available only on a certain percentage of vehicles at a location. Calling early can ensure that you receive the best rate.

- *Ask about additional fees.* Quoted rates do not include taxes and additional fees assessed by airports and local communities. Fees may also be assessed for additional drivers, drivers younger than age 25, or not returning the car to the same location where it was rented.

- *Clarify mileage restrictions.* Free unlimited mileage may be available, although some companies restrict free mileage to 100 miles per day. Per-mile charges are then assessed. Some companies offer unlimited mileage but only to contiguous states, such as renting in California with unlimited mileage in Arizona, Nevada, and Oregon.

- *Avoid rental car insurance.* Rental car companies may pressure renters to buy various types of insurance at the time of rental. The most notorious is **collision damage waiver (CDW)** coverage, which waives the rental company's right to collect from a renter if the car is involved in an accident. Such insurance can add $10 or more to the daily rate, and it is generally unnecessary. A renter who has adequate insurance on his or her own automobile will likely be covered on rentals as well. Check with your insurance agent for confirmation.

  Rental companies will also offer a **loss-damage waiver (LDW) insurance coverage** (often $3 to $15 per day). This insurance pays a rental car company for each day a damaged vehicle is out of service for repairs. If you refuse CDW or LDW coverage, make sure your own insurance will pay these expenses.

- *Decide how to pay for gas.* When you rent a vehicle, its tank will be full. You then have two choices. First, you can agree to return the car with a full tank; but if it is not full, you will likely pay $2 to $3 per gallon to have the rental company fill it. Second, you can pay for the initial tankful at a price nearly equal to what local service stations charge per gallon; you then can return the car with its tank as near empty as you choose.

- *Inspect the vehicle.* Before driving off, check the car for dents, dings, scratches, and interior damage and stains. Make sure removable equipment such as the spare tire and jack are present. If such damage is present or items are missing, have them noted on the rental agreement before leaving the lot to ensure that you will not be charged upon return.

+ \$25 + \$10), still \$66 short of the amount she needs for the car. In addition, the gasoline, parking, and insurance costs on her new car would increase the needed amount even more. Sharon's alternatives are to make more cutbacks in her budget, to work overtime, or to get a part-time job. She could also reduce her payments to \$231.63 per month by taking out a longer 60-month loan (10.9 × \$21.25, from Table 7.3). She should be wary about having to operate on such a tight budget for five years, however. Sharon will pay much more in interest with a longer-term loan and might want to consider a less expensive new car or a used car.

Comparison Shopping

<table><tr><td>**3** Comparison shop when buying or leasing vehicles and other major purchases.</td></tr></table>

After completing the first three steps in wise buying, it is time to begin interacting with sellers by **comparison shopping**—the process of comparing products or services to find the best buy. A **best buy** is a product or service that, in the buyer's opinion, represents acceptable quality at a fair or low price for that level of quality. Purchasing the product with the lowest price does not necessarily assure a best buy, however; quality and features count, too. In comparison shopping, you visit different stores to gather specific information not obtained in your preshopping research. Some experts recommend use of the "rule of three," which says to compare at least three alternatives on any decision.

Comparison shopping takes time and effort, but the payoff in both satisfaction and savings can be considerable. During the early steps in the comparison shopping process, a shopper should narrow choices to specific makes and models and desired options. Then, he or she should visit the appropriate dealerships again. This time the shopper will be much closer to the decision to buy and will be ready to discuss details, although he or she should not buy at this point. When comparison shopping, tell the salesperson exactly what interests you and ask about price, availability, and any manufacturer's incentives, such as **rebates** (refunds from the manufacturer or dealer) that apply. You should inquire about warranties, service contracts, financing options, and leasing. Finally, test-drive the vehicle.* The goal is to narrow the choice even further prior to negotiating for the very best deal, which is the next step in the buying process.

Compare Warranties

Warranties are an important consideration in comparison shopping. Almost all products have **warranties**—assurances by sellers that goods are as promised and that certain steps will be taken to rectify problems—even if only in the form of implied warranties. Under an **implied warranty**, the product sold is warranted to be suitable for sale (a **warranty of merchantability**) and to work effectively (a **warranty of fitness** for a particular purpose) whether or not a written warranty exists. Implied warranties are required by state law. To avoid them, the seller can state in writing that the product is sold **"as is."** If you buy any prod-

---

*   Do not give your Social Security number or allow the dealer to photocopy your driver's license. The dealer might use the information to obtain your credit bureau report while you are on the test-drive.

uct "as is," you have little legal recourse should it fail to perform, even if the salesperson made verbal "promises" to take care of any problems.

Written and oral warranties accompany many products and are offered by manufacturers on a voluntary basis to induce customers to buy. These assurances are called **express warranties.** Companies that offer *written* express warranties must do so under the provisions of the federal Magnuson–Moss Warranty Act if the product is sold for more than $15. This 1975 law provides that any written warranty offered must be classified as either a full warranty or a limited warranty. A **full warranty** includes three stringent requirements: (1) a product must be fixed at no cost to the buyer within a reasonable time after the owner has complained; (2) the owner will not have to undertake an unreasonable task to return the product for repair (such as ship back a refrigerator); and (3) a defective product will be replaced with a new one or the buyer's money returned when that product cannot be fixed after a reasonable number of attempts. A **limited warranty** offers less than a full warranty. For example, it may offer only free parts, not labor. Note that one part of a product could be covered by a full warranty (perhaps the engine on a lawnmower) and the rest of the unit by a limited warranty. Read all warranties carefully, and note that both full and limited warranties are valid for only a specified time period.

Service Contracts Can Be Overpriced

A **service contract** is an agreement between the contract seller (a dealer, manufacturer, or independent company) and the buyer of a product to provide free (or nearly free) repair services to covered components of the product for some specified time period. This type of contract is purchased separately from the product itself (such as a vehicle, appliance, or electronics product). The cost is paid by the purchaser either in a lump sum or in monthly payments. Service contracts are very similar to insurance. For example, a 25-inch television priced at $600 could have a service contract that promises to fix anything free for the third and fourth years of ownership; the manufacturer's warranty covers the first two years. This contract might cost $60 for one year, or $5 per month, even if no servicing is done. Buying a service contract might provide peace of mind, but it is often unwise economically. More than 80 percent of all service contracts are never used, and total payouts to consumers to make repairs amount to less than 10 percent of money spent on the contracts.

Service contracts have become increasingly prevalent in the vehicle, appliance, and electronics markets because of the high profits involved and the persuasiveness of salespersons. All major automobile manufacturers and many dealers offer service contract plans; in addition, a number of independent companies offer service contracts for new vehicles. Service contracts are sometimes given names such as "extended warranty" and "buyer protection plan." The cost for such a contract can exceed $700, and, if offered by the manufacturer or dealer, it can be added to the purchase price of the vehicle and financed with the purchase loan. If $700 is charged for the plan, $400 or more may be dealer profit. A seller can afford to be more generous on a deal if he or she knows that most of the money will be made back on the service contract. Often, a deductible of about $100 must be paid with each use of the contract. Repairs are usually covered and may include preventive maintenance to covered components.

Get Things Fixed

Even the best-made products occasionally need repairs. Your first action should be to check your warranty. Before the repairs are begun, make sure you clearly understand what is covered and what is not. Some additional tips follow:

- *Get an estimate in advance.* Repairs are generally broken down into parts and labor. If you know what parts may be needed, ask the price that will be charged. In addition, ask about the labor charge, which is usually quoted as a flat fee or an hourly rate with some minimum. If an hourly rate is charged, ask for an estimate of the time required to make repairs. For in-home repairs, a charge for a house call may have to be paid even if repairs are minimal. Ask the repair shop to call first whenever repairs will exceed the estimate by 10 percent or more.

- *Ask how long repairs will take.* Waiting for an item while it is being repaired in the shop can be very frustrating. Ask if it is possible to keep the item at home while parts are ordered. Ask for the typical waiting period for parts to arrive.

- *Get a claim check.* When taking items into the shop, obtain a signed claim check that includes the date that the items were dropped off, along with the make, model, and serial number of the items, a brief description of the problem, any estimate of the cost, and instructions to call you if the estimate proves too low.

- *Ask to be given all replaced parts.* A check of the replaced parts will help ensure that the items for which you were charged were actually replaced.

- *Stay home when in-home repairs are made.* Your presence might prevent unnecessary repairs, and it allows the repairperson to ask questions to help diagnose the problem.

- *Get a written receipt.* A written repair receipt should include specifics of the repairs made and a breakdown of charges for each item rather than a lump-sum amount. Get the names of the persons to whom you talked and who did the repairs.

Consider Leasing instead of Buying

Leasing a new vehicle is an increasingly attractive option to many people in the market for a car. More than 30 percent of the new cars "sold" each year are actually leased, and for some makes (e.g., Mercedes) the percentage approaches 80 percent. It is even possible to lease used cars. Is leasing a better deal than financing? The answer cannot be known until some basics of leasing are understood.

When **leasing** a vehicle or any other product, you are, in effect, renting the product with the ownership title remaining with the lease grantor. Regulation M issued by the Federal Reserve Board governs lease contracts. A major requirement of this regulation is a mandatory disclosure of pertinent information about the lease that the consumer is considering. The disclosure form must summarize the offer of the lessee (leasing agency) to the lessor (consumer). The information in this form should be compared with the actual lease contract *prior to signing* to ensure that the lease signed is actually what was agreed upon verbally.

Five terms are important. First, the **gross capitalized cost** (gross cap cost) includes the price of the vehicle plus what the dealer paid to finance the purchase plus any other items you agree to pay for over the life of the lease, including insurance or a maintenance agreement. Second, **capitalized cost reductions** (cap cost reductions) are moneys paid on the lease at its inception, including any down payment, trade-in value, or rebate. Third, by subtracting the capitalized cost reductions from the gross capitalized cost, you can determine the **adjusted capitalized cost** (adjusted cap cost). Fourth, the **money factor** (or lease rate or lease factor) measures the rent charge portion of your payment. Although sometimes described by dealers as a figure for comparing among leases, lease forms must carry the following disclosure about the money factor: "This percentage may not measure the overall cost of financing this lease." Fifth, the **residual value** is the projected value of a leased asset at the end of the lease time period.

Leasing typically entails an initial outlay for the first month's lease payment and a security deposit. Payments are based on the capitalized cost of the asset (always negotiate a purchase price before discussing a lease) minus any capitalized cost reductions and the residual value. This difference represents the cost of using the asset during the lease period and, when divided by the number of months in the contract, serves to establish the base for the monthly lease payment. (Some new vehicles are offered with single-payment leases in which the entire difference between the capitalized cost and residual value is paid up front.) For monthly payment leases, the payments are lower than monthly loan payments for equivalent time periods because you are paying for only the reduction in the asset's value—not its entire cost. To compare the costs of leasing versus buying, use the Decision-Making Worksheet, "Comparing Automobile Financing and Leasing."

A lease may be either open-end or closed-end. In an **open-end lease**, you must pay any difference between the projected residual value of the vehicle and its actual market value at the end of the lease period. In recent years, some vehicle makes have depreciated more rapidly than expected, meaning that many holders of open-end leases have had to pay extra money when the lease expires. The Consumer Leasing Act of 1977 limits this end-of-lease payment to a maximum of three times the average monthly payment.

In a **closed-end lease** (also called a **walkaway lease**), the holder pays no charge if the end-of-lease market value of the vehicle is lower than the originally projected residual value. Closed-end leases may carry some end-of-lease charges if the vehicle has had greater than normal wear or mileage, however. For example, a four-year closed-end lease might require a $0.20 per mile charge for mileage in excess of 55,000 miles. If you actually drove the vehicle 60,000 miles during the four years, you would be charged an extra $1000 [0.20 × 5000 (60,000 − 55,000)]. With either open- or closed-end leases, you may purchase the vehicle at the end of the lease period. With an open-end lease you would pay the actual cash value. With a closed-end lease you would pay the residual value.

Other charges are possible with a lease. An **acquisition fee** is either paid in cash or included in the gross capitalization cost. It pays for a credit report, application fee, and other paperwork. A **disposition fee** is a charge assessed when you turn in the vehicle at the end of the lease and the lessor must prepare it for resale. An **early termination charge** may also be levied if you decide to end the lease prematurely. The **early termination payoff** is the total amount you would need to repay if you end the lease agreement early; it includes both the early termination charge and the unpaid lease balance. Be wary of a lease with a termination fee, even if you do not plan to end the lease early, because termination also occurs when a leased vehicle is totally wrecked or stolen. Make sure you obtain a written disclosure of these charges well before you actually make your decision. In its early years, your lease may be financially **"upside-down,"** which means that you owe more on the vehicle than it is worth. (This situation is also likely to occur when you buy on credit.)

Because it is still relatively new for most people, leasing has attracted its share of shady deals from some sellers. You should be wary of several potential events in this market. First, be cautious if you talk about buying all through the negotiation process only to be offered a lease at the last minute. The monthly charge will be lower and you may be tempted to sign a deal that really costs considerably more. Second, make sure that all oral agreements related to trade-in value,

Comparing Automobile Financing and Leasing

The worksheet below can be used to compare leasing and borrowing to buy a vehicle. Remember that the cost of credit is the finance charge—the extra that you pay because you borrowed. Leases also carry costs, but they are hidden in the contract, and some remain unknown until the end of the lease period. These items, which are indicated by an asterisk below, are defined in the text. Ask the dealer for the amount of each cost as these fees must be disclosed by dealers. Then complete the worksheet and compare the dollar cost of leasing with the finance charge on a loan for the same time period.

To make the comparison accurately, you must know the underlying price of the vehicle as if you were purchasing it. Often you are not told this value in a lease arrangement, so you must negotiate a price for the vehicle before mentioning the lease option.

You should shop for a lease through various dealers and through independent leasing companies because costs vary considerably. Finally, if you do choose a leasing option, the goal should be to lower your monthly cost rather than to buy more car. Otherwise, in just a few years, you will find yourself having spent big bucks for a vehicle you no longer have. This worksheet can be found on the *Garman/Forgue* Web site.

Step	Example	Your Figures
1. Monthly lease payment	$ 9,900	_____
(36 payments of $275, for example)		
2. Plus acquisition fee* (if any)	300	_____
Plus disposition charge* (if any)	300	_____
Plus estimate of excess mileage charges* (if any)	0	_____
Plus projected residual value* of the vehicle	4,500	_____
3. Amount for which you are responsible under the lease	15,000	_____
4. Less the capitalized cost* after taking capitalized cost reductions*	12,600	_____
5. Dollar cost of leasing to be compared with a finance charge	2,400	_____

mileage charges, and rebates are included in the lease contract. Third, watch out for additional fees being assessed, especially near the very end of the negotiations or in the final written lease.

◄ DECISION-MAKING ► Worksheet
Choosing between Low-Interest-Rate Dealer Financing and a Rebate on a New Vehicle

It is not uncommon to see ads for new vehicles offering low APRs for dealer-arranged loans. For buyers that arrange their own financing or pay cash, a cash rebate of $500 to $2000 (or more) off the price of the car is sometimes offered as an alternative to the low interest rate. If you intend to pay cash, obviously the cash rebate represents the better deal. But which alternative is better when you can arrange your own financing? You can't simply compare the dealer APR to the APR that you arranged on your own.

To compare the two APRs accurately, you must add the opportunity cost of the foregone rebate to the finance charge of the dealer financing. The worksheet below provides an example of this process. Suppose your dealer offers 4.79 percent financing for three years with a $906 finance charge; alternatively, you can receive a $1500 rebate if you arrange your own financing. The price of the car before the rebate is $14,000. Assume you can make a $2000 down payment and that you can get a 9.5 percent loan on your own. This worksheet can be found on the *Garman/Forgue* Web site.

Step	Example	Your Figures
1. Determine the dollar amount of the rebate.	$1500	_____
2. Add the rebate amount to the finance charge for the dealer financing (dollar cost of credit).	+ $ 906	_____
3. Use the n-ratio APR formula from Chapter 7 (Equation 7.3 on page 194 and replicated here as Equation 8.1) to calculate an adjusted APR for the dealer financing.		

$$APR = \frac{Y(95P + 9)F}{12P(P + 1)(4D + F)} \qquad (8.1)$$

where

APR = **annual percentage rate**
Y = number of payment periods in 1 **year**
F = **finance charge** in dollars
D = **debt** (amount borrowed)
P = total number of scheduled **payments**

$$APR = \frac{(12)[(95 \times 36) + 9]($906 + $1500)}{(12 \times 36)(36 + 1)[(4 \times $12,000) + ($906 + $1500)]} = 12.3\% \quad \underline{\hspace{1cm}}$$

4. Write in the APR that you arranged on your own.	9.5%	_____

The lower value obtained in steps 3 and 4 is the better deal. In this instance, the financing that you arranged on your own is more attractive. In fact, any loan you arrange that carries an APR lower than 12.3 percent compares favorably with the dealer-arranged financing in this case.

Be Alert to Balloon Financing

Bank lenders have seen the demand for automobile loans slacken because of the growing popularity of automobile leasing. In response, many have developed balloon automobile loans. With a **balloon automobile loan**, the last monthly payment equals the projected residual value of the vehicle at the end of the loan period. Basically, the amount borrowed represents the difference between the selling price and the vehicle's expected value at the end of the loan period. This value is the balloon payment. This arrangement effectively lowers the other monthly payments to make them more competitive with lease payments. For example, borrowing $12,400 to buy a car at 8.9 percent APR for 48 months would require a payment of $308 per month. A balloon auto loan to finance the same amount at the same interest rate for 48 months might require 47 monthly payments of $266 and a final "balloon" payment of $2666. When the final balloon payment is due, the borrower generally has three options: (1) sell the car and pay the balloon payment with the proceeds (with luck, the vehicle will sell for a high-enough amount); (2) pay the balloon payment and keep the vehicle; or (3) return the vehicle to the lender. Before arranging financing on any vehicle, it would be wise to review the material on installment loans provided in Chapter 7, "Planned Borrowing."

Negotiate and Decide upon the Best Deal

4 Negotiate effectively and make intelligent decisions when undertaking major expenditures.

Negotiating and decision making follow comparison shopping in the buying process. Moving through these steps too quickly is an invitation to pay too much when making major purchases such as vehicles. Remember that sellers of such products sell every day, and they are highly skilled; in contrast, consumers are amateurs.

Successful Negotiations Require Information

Negotiating (or **haggling**) is the process of discussing the actual terms of an agreement with a seller. We skip this step in most purchases because prices are firm. With "big ticket" items—especially appliances, furniture, fine jewelry, and vehicles—there is an opportunity, and often an expectation, that offers and counteroffers will be made before arriving at the exact price.

Negotiating is especially difficult when buying vehicles because so many variables must be considered, including the price of the vehicle, the trade-in value, the possibility of a rebate, the prices of options, the interest rate, and possibly a service contract. The dealer can appear to be cooperative on one aspect and make up the difference elsewhere. Many times the vehicle comes with a number of manufacturer- or dealer-installed options, such as special striping, tinted windows, and fabric finish protection. The key to successful negotiation is to be armed with accurate information on all of these variables. New vehicle buying services are particularly important in that respect. A number of vehicle manufacturers (Saturn was the first) and dealers have moved to a haggle-free pricing policy by setting one price and sticking to it. These prices must still be compared to those of their competitors that still employ the haggle method.

The key to success when negotiating a vehicle purchase is to obtain a firm price from a dealer for the vehicle and optional equipment desired before discussing *any other* aspects of the deal. Do not discuss anything about a loan or a trade-in until you have pinned the salesperson down to a price. You should know from your preshopping research and comparison shopping what a good price for the vehicle in question would be (see the "How to" box on page 210). You should obtain prices from several dealers and let each know that you have done so and whether their price is low compared with the others. The dealer will then have the chance to reduce the asking price to meet the competition. This strategy pressures the dealer to meet your needs rather than the other way around.

Consider the case of Gary Joseph, a production manager from Northville, Michigan. Gary had narrowed his choice of cars down to one model and two dealerships. Gary presented his list of desired options to the first dealer and was shown a suitable car on the lot. He had arranged his own financing and, therefore, was interested in only price and whether the dealer could offer an even lower APR. When Gary inquired about price, the salesperson asked what monthly payment Gary could afford. Gary countered that his budget was not important and that he wanted to know the price. When the salesperson responded that it was policy to get the affordable payment before answering any questions, Gary walked out of the dealership with the salesperson in pursuit seeking to continue the sale. The next day the salesperson called Gary at home, saying that he would lose his job if he quoted a price before getting an affordable monthly payment amount. By then, however, Gary had already bought his car at the other dealership. Had Gary responded to the questions, the salesperson could have tailored the price to Gary's figure, which likely would not have been the lowest price that the dealership would have accepted. A key to all negotiations is to be prepared to say "no" and go elsewhere if the terms are not satisfactory.

Make the Decision

Most people make buying decisions for "big ticket" purchases inside a retail store or showroom. These are not the best places to decide because of pressures to buy that may be applied by the seller or by a customer's desire to complete the process. It is better to wait until you get home to make the final decision. There, you can rationally retrace your steps through the buying process, making sure that the decision is based on the proper facts and logic. After making your decision, you can return to the dealer's showroom and close the sale.

Some people use a decision-making grid that allows them to visually and mathematically weigh the decision they are about to make. Such a grid is illustrated in Table 8.2 for someone who might be deciding among three different washing machines. The first task in developing such a grid is to determine the various criteria for making the decision. Factors such as price, durability, and styling are used in Table 8.2. Each criterion is assigned a weight that reflects the importance each has in the mind of the purchaser. Each brand and model under consideration is then given a score (from 1 to 10 in this case) that indicates how well the brand/model performs on that criterion. The score (*S*) is multiplied by the weight (*W*) to obtain a weighted score. The total of the weighted scores for each brand/model can be compared with the totals for the others to determine which "wins." In this example, Appliance C, which has a total score of 8.0,

Table 8.2

Decision-Making Grid (Illustrated for a Washing Machine)

Criteria	Decision Weight (W)	Appliance A		Appliance B		Appliance C	
		Score (S)*	W × S	Score (S)	W × S	Score (S)	W × S
Price	30%	9	2.7	7	2.1	5	1.5
Durability	25%	6	1.5	8	2.0	10	2.5
Features	20%	6	1.2	8	1.6	10	2.0
Warranty	15%	6	0.9	10	1.5	8	1.2
Styling	10%	10	1.0	6	0.6	8	0.8
TOTAL	100%		7.3		7.8		8.0

* Using a 10-point scale.

Buy a Used Vehicle

The average new vehicle now sells for more than $20,000. For many people, such prices are simply more than they are able or willing to pay. Consequently, more than three times as many used vehicles are sold each year as new cars. For buyers on a tight budget, a good, reliable used car or pickup can do very nicely. You need to be careful when buying a used vehicle, however. Following some basic steps can help you avoid getting a vehicle with excessive mechanical problems.

1. *Decide on features and options.* First, select the features you want, such as power steering, air conditioning, and stereo. You do not need to be as careful about distinguishing between the options you need or want as you would be when buying a new vehicle. If you want an option, you can usually obtain it without spending more simply by choosing an older model. Because you have many vehicles from which to choose, this task should not be difficult.

2. *Decide how much you can afford to spend.* You can purchase a used vehicle for as little as $500 or as much as $20,000 or $30,000. Decide in advance how much you can afford, and then search for vehicles in your price range.

3. *Select several reliable makes and models in your price range.* The National Automobile Dealers Association (NADA) publishes weekly reports on the average retail and wholesale prices of various makes and models of used vehicles. The Internet is an excellent source of used car pricing information. The classified advertisements in your local newspaper and used-vehicle advertising tabloids distributed at supermarkets and convenience stores also can be a source of price information. In addition, you should consult the most recent April issue of *Consumer Reports* for its lists of recommended used vehicles in various price ranges. The same issue also lists the frequency-of-repair histories for most makes and models as reported by the magazine's readers. Although these histories and price-range recommendations go back only six years, you can consult the April issues from previous years to get information for the past ten or more years. You can also use the *Consumer Reports* Used Car Price Service [(900) 446-0500; $1.75 per minute, typical call five minutes or more].

would be chosen. Note that each purchaser would arrive at different scores as the weights assigned and the scores awarded will differ according to individual tastes and preferences. Someone who weighted "price" very high might purchase Appliance A, as it has the highest rating on that criterion. Similarly, each person would differ in how he or she scores an appliance's "styling" even if everyone weighted that criterion in the same way. Nonetheless, a grid of this type helps add objectivity to the decision-making process and can be of great benefit especially for "big ticket" items.

Be wary of a sales technique called **lowballing**, which involves an attempt to raise an orally negotiated price when it comes time to finalize the written contract. For example, after agreeing on the price of a vehicle with a buyer, the salesperson might write up the sale on the appropriate forms. Just before it is time to sign, the salesperson states that, as a formality, the approval of a manager is necessary. While the buyer is dreaming of driving home in the new car, the salesperson and the manager are talking about how much more they can get for the vehicle. When the salesperson returns, he or she indicates that some problem or

4. *Start your search.* Armed with your list of reliable makes and models in your price range, you can start looking for specific vehicles for sale. You may purchase a used vehicle from a new car dealership, a used car dealership, a rental car company, a private individual, or even a repossession auction. New car dealerships tend to offer the nicer, more reliable, and more expensive vehicles. Used car dealerships, on the other hand, tend to have the widest range of quality. Some used car dealerships deserve the negative image with which they are sometimes tagged, so be careful. Private individuals deserve your attention because they usually own the vehicle personally and know its history. Used cars sold by rental agencies such as Hertz and Avis can be a good choice because they have been regularly maintained. Regardless of the source, immediately rule out any vehicle that seems to have a problem or raises a question in your mind. Do the same for sellers who do not seem cooperative. There are too many vehicles available to waste time with vehicles of poor quality or uncooperative sellers.

5. *Check your selections carefully.* By now you should have narrowed your choice to two or three specific vehicles. Inspect them inside and out. Take along a friend who is knowledgeable about cars if you are less car-savvy. Test-drive the vehicle and test all of its functions. Ask for maintenance records if the seller is an individual or a rental company. Ask the dealer for the name and address of the previous consumer owner and give that person a telephone call. Before you agree to buy any vehicle, have it examined by a mechanic; although the examination may cost $30 to $50, it may help you avoid purchasing a vehicle with problems and save hundreds of dollars in repairs later.

6. *Negotiate and decide.* Never pay the asking price for a used vehicle. Sellers expect to negotiate and set a price higher than required to give room for bargaining. Get all verbal promises and guarantees in writing. If a seller will not put his or her words in writing, shop elsewhere. Finally, return to the quiet of your home to consider your alternatives and to make your final decision. If necessary, put down a small deposit to hold the vehicle for a day or two while you make your decision.

mistake has occurred, and that the price has to be "X amount" higher. Perhaps the trade-in value is too high, or the sticker price can't be discounted by quite as much as planned, or the price of a certain option has increased. In reality, of course, lowballing is a ruse for the dealer to get more money. Sign only a **buyer's order** that names a specific vehicle and all charges. If you ever encounter lowballing, leave quickly without signing anything. Do not look back, and do not apologize.

Evaluate Your Decision

5 Evaluate your purchase decision as a guide for future behavior.

The wise buying process comes full circle when you evaluate your decision. The purpose of this step is to determine where things went well and where they went less smoothly. The lessons learned will prove useful when you need to make a similar purchase in the future. Sometimes the process was so successful that you will want to compliment the seller. In other cases, you may want to complain about the product or service so as to obtain **redress**—that is, to right the wrong. This process should always start with the actual seller as indicated in Table 8.3, which shows the five channels of complaining: to the local business, to the manufacturer, to self-regulatory organizations, to consumer-action agencies, and to small claims and civil courts. It is important to begin sequentially, with the local

Get the Most for Your Car-Buying Dollar

The following points are designed to help you get the most for your transportation dollar:

1. ***Buy used vehicles.*** New cars lose 20 to 40 percent of their value as a result of depreciation in the first two years after purchase. Let someone else pay for this decline in value.

2. ***Buy used vehicles from private owners.*** Why pay retail prices when you can obtain a price closer to wholesale? In addition, you will be dealing with someone closer to your level of expertise.

3. ***Visit dealerships three times before actually signing a deal.*** The first trip is for preshopping research, the second is for comparison shopping, and the third is for negotiation. Even then, you should go home to make the final decision.

4. ***Negotiate price first.*** The bottom line in any deal is the price of the vehicle itself. Never discuss your affordable monthly payment with a dealer. The full purchase price should be determined before even mentioning that you might have a trade-in, need a loan, or are considering leasing. Then comparison shop and negotiate each of these items separately.

5. ***Consider leasing.*** Leasing is becoming an increasingly attractive option, especially for the person who intends to buy a new vehicle every two to four years.

6. ***Use your vehicles up.*** The best way to realize the full value of a vehicle is to keep it for its entire lifetime. Vehicles built today should last 12 years or 150,000 miles (or more) with proper maintenance. The repairs to an older vehicle cost less than the depreciation on a new vehicle.

Table 8.3

Complaint Procedure (Levels and Channels of Complaining)

Levels to Bring Your Complaint	Channels for Complaint
1. Local business	Salesperson → supervisor → manager/owner
2. Manufacturer	Consumer affairs department → president/chief executive officer
3. Self-regulatory organizations	Better Business Bureau → county medical societies → consumer action panels
4. Consumer-action agencies	Private consumer-action groups → media action lines → government agencies
5. Small claims or civil court	Small claims court → civil court

merchant, before moving to other channels. For example, a complaint not resolved satisfactorily with an auto dealer could be brought to the attention of the manufacturer's regional consumer affairs department before communicating with the manufacturer's president. Seeking redress through the first three channels in the complaint procedure given in Table 8.3 can rectify almost all consumer complaints.

Sometimes the first efforts at redress are not successful. As a result, the wronged person might then consider legal action against the business. While many people consider legal costs to be too high, costs depend on the case and the type of court chosen.

A **civil court** is a state court in which numerous civil matters are resolved and a written record is made of the testimony. The proceedings are completed with the assistance of attorneys, witnesses, a judge, and sometimes a jury. The wronged person generally must hire an attorney and pay additional fees. It is not unusual to spend $500 to $1000 resolving an issue in a civil court.

A **small claims court** is a state court with no written record of testimony in which civil matters are often resolved without the assistance of attorneys (in some states, attorneys are actually prohibited from representing clients in small claims courts). This court is also known as a **court not of record.** It is designed to litigate small civil claims, with legal maximums typically ranging from $500 to $2500. Cases for amounts exceeding the small claims court maximum must be filed in a regular civil court.

To file a small claims court action, go to the courthouse and ask which court hears small claims. A small fee (often $15 or less) is required, along with a small fee (e.g., $3) for each **court summons** (also called a **subpoena**) for each witness. In completing the necessary forms, it is important to fill out the full legal name of the **defendant** (the person who allegedly committed the wrong deed and is the subject of the litigation) and to describe carefully the action with which the lawsuit is concerned. The court will subpoena all necessary witnesses and the defendant for the day of trial. On the day that the case is heard, the **plaintiff** (the person who has filed the case and is suing the defendant), should be well prepared with all relevant documentation and have a clear understanding of the sequence of events that led up to the claim. A written record of the court is not kept, and in most courts the decision of the judge can be appealed by the loser to a higher court (which, of course, may result in considerable attorney fees and

The Best Way to Designate Vehicle Ownership

One consideration when buying a vehicle is the name that should go on the title. Couples may be tempted to put major assets in both names, and often that is the best way to go. For automobiles, however, the story is more complicated. The owner of a vehicle is legally liable for accidents caused by the driver. If both partners own an automobile, both could be sued. Thus, it is best to put an automobile in only one name. For couples with two vehicles, each should be owned separately.

related costs). Most small claims court decisions are won by the plaintiff and are not appealed.

Alternative dispute resolution programs are industry- or government-sponsored programs that provide an avenue to resolve disputes outside the formal court system. **Mediation** is a procedure in which a neutral third party works with the parties involved in the dispute to arrive at a mutually agreeable solution. In **arbitration**, a neutral third party hears (or reads) the claims made and positions taken by the parties to the dispute and issues a ruling that is binding on one or both parties. Most automobile manufacturer warranty programs provide an opportunity for mediation and arbitration of warranty disputes.

Most states have enacted **new-vehicle lemon laws** that provide guidelines for arbitrators to use to order a buy-back of a vehicle that is considered a "lemon." A common definition of a lemon is a vehicle that was in the shop for repairs four times for the same problem in the first year after purchase. To enforce a lemon law, the buyer must go through the prescribed warranty process specified in the owner's manual. Eventually, if the problem is not resolved, an arbitration hearing will be held through which the owner can request a buy-back. Some states have also enacted used-vehicle lemon laws.

Summary

1. You can save money by following the basic rules of wise buying: control buying on impulse, pay cash when possible, buy at the right time, avoid paying extra for a "name," avoid the high price of convenience, and use life-cycle planning for major purchases.

2. The planned buying process includes three steps that occur prior to interacting with sellers: prioritizing wants, obtaining information during preshopping research, and fitting the planned purchase into the budget. These steps represent the homework needed when preparing to buy.

3. To interact effectively with sellers, you should comparison shop to find the best buy. When purchasing vehicles, this shopping process includes comparing warranties

and service contracts, comparing leasing to buying, and being alert to balloon financing.

4. For expensive purchases, the next step after comparison shopping is negotiating with the seller, especially with items such as automobiles where price haggling is generally expected. The final decision should be made at home, however.

5. The final step in wise buying occurs after the purchase is made and entails evaluating the decision and seeking redress, if needed.

Key Words & Concepts

arbitration   *226*
best buy   *214*
civil court   *225*

Questions for Thought & Discussion

1. Describe the guidelines that people can follow to save money on major expenditures.

2. List the seven steps in the buying process.

3. Describe the steps in the buying process that occur prior to interacting with sellers.

4. Distinguish between needs and wants and explain why it may be better to act as if no needs exist.

5. Explain how preshopping research can help you save money.

6. Explain why magazines that accept advertising for products that they rate for quality do not always provide reliable product information. Which magazine is the most objective in assessing product quality?

7. Describe the three steps in the buying process that involve direct interaction with sellers.

8. Why doesn't obtaining the lowest price for a product ensure that you receive the best buy?

9. Explain the difference between an implied warranty and an express warranty.

10. Distinguish between full and limited warranties as defined by the Magnuson–Moss Warranty Act.

11. What is the purpose of a service contract? What is a disadvantage of such a contract?

12. How do buyer protection plans and service contracts differ?

13. Explain why lease payments for a new vehicle are lower than loan payments for the same vehicle.

14. Explain the relative benefits of open-end versus closed-end leases.

15. Compare and contrast balloon auto loans with vehicle leasing.

16. Describe three keys to success in negotiating the price of a new vehicle.

17. Where could a new car buyer obtain assistance when searching for a new car, and what services might the buyer receive?

18. In what physical location should you make major buying decisions? Why?

19. Define the word "redress" and the complaint procedure a consumer could use to obtain redress.

20. Distinguish between civil courts and small claims courts as mechanisms for obtaining consumer redress.

21. Distinguish between mediation and arbitration as alternative dispute resolution programs.

22. How might a car buyer proceed to make use of a new-vehicle lemon law?

DECISION-MAKING CASES

Case 1   Purchase of a New Refrigerator

Tracy Sullivan, a financial consultant from Ames, Iowa, who lives alone, is remodeling her kitchen. She has decided to replace her refrigerator with a new model that offers more conveniences. She has narrowed her choices to models that are about 19 cubic feet in size and have a top freezer. Quality models in this size cost about $750. Tracy has drawn up a list of possible convenience options and their prices: automatic defrost, $125; ice maker, $50; textured enamel surface, $75; glass shelving, $30; and ice-water port, $95. Tracy's credit union will loan her the necessary funds for one year at 12 percent APR on the installment plan. Following is her budget, which includes $1115 monthly take-home pay.

Food	$ 150
Entertainment	75
Clothing	50
Gifts	50
Car payment	232
Personal care	40
Automobile expenses	75
Savings	75
Housing	325
Miscellaneous	43
TOTAL	$1115

(a) What preshopping research should Tracy do to select the best brand of refrigerator?

(b) Advise Tracy on which convenience options you think she should regard as high priority and which she should consider as low priority.

(c) Using the information in Table 7.3 or the *Garman/Forgue* Web site, determine Tracy's monthly payment for (1) the basic model, (2) the basic model with high-priority options, and (3) the basic model with high- and low-priority options.

(d) Fit each of the three monthly payments into Tracy's budget.

(e) Advise Tracy on her decision.

Case 2   A Dispute over New-Car Repairs

David Hardison, a high school football coach from Oklahoma City, Oklahoma, purchased a new automobile for $18,000. He used the car often, and in less than nine months had put 14,000 miles on it. A 24,000-mile, two-year warranty was still in effect for the power-train equipment, although David had to pay the first $100 on each repair. At 16,500 miles and in month 11 of driving, the car experienced some severe problems with the transmission. David took the vehicle to the dealer for repairs. A week later he picked the car up, but some transmission problems remained. When David took the car back to the dealer, the dealer said that no further problems could be identified. David was sure the problem was still there, however, and he was amazed that the dealer would not correct it. The dealer told him he would take no other action.

(a) Was David within his rights to take the car back for repairs? Explain why or why not.

(b) What logical steps would David follow if he continues to be dissatisfied with the dealer's unwillingness or inability to repair the car?

(c) Should David seek any help from the court system? If so, describe what he could do without spending money on attorney's fees.

Financial Math Questions

1. Diana Forsythe of Desitin, Florida, must decide whether to buy or lease a car she has selected. She negotiated a purchase price of $14,700 and could borrow the money to buy from her credit union by putting $1000 down and paying $338 per month for 48 months. Alternatively, she could lease the car for 48 months at $260 per month by paying $500 capital cost reduction and a $350 disposition fee on the car, which is projected to have a residual value of $4100 at the end of the lease. Use the decision-making worksheet on page 218 to advise Diana whether she should buy or lease the car.

2. Tom Parker of Fayetteville, Arkansas, has been shopping for a new car for several weeks and has negotiated a price of $17,000 on a model that carries a choice of a $1250 rebate or dealer financing at 4.5 percent APR. The dealer loan would require a $1000 down payment and a monthly payment of $365

for 48 months. Tom also had arranged for a loan from his bank with an 8.5 percent APR. Use the decision-making worksheet on page 219 to advise Tom on whether he should use the dealer financing or take the rebate and use the financing from the bank.

MONEY MATTERS: LIFE-CYCLE CASES

Victor and Maria Hernandez Buy a Third Car

The Hernandezes' older son has reached the age at which it is time to consider purchasing him a car. Victor and Maria have decided to give Maria's old car to their son Hector and buy a later-model used car for Maria. Hector wants to do most of the preshopping research and comparison shopping himself. Maria will then assist with the negotiations.

1. What sources of information can Hector use to access price and reliability information on various makes and models of used cars?

2. What sources of used cars might be available to Hector, and what differences might exist among them?

3. How might Hector check out the cars in which he is most interested?

4. What strategies might Hector and Maria employ when they negotiate the price for the car they select?

The Johnsons Decide to Buy a Car

It is now October, and the Johnsons have decided to move out of their apartment and into some form of owned housing. Although they have not decided on what type of housing they will buy, they know that Belinda will no longer be able to ride the bus to work. Thus, they are in the market for another car. They have decided not to buy a new car, and the Johnsons think they have some room in their budget for a used car, given the raises each has received this year (see Table 4.3 on page 107). They estimate that they could afford to spend about $3200 on a used car by making a down payment of $600 and financing the remainder over 24 months at $120 per month.

1. Make suggestions about how the $120 might be integrated into the Johnsons' budget (Table 4.3) without changing the amount left over at the end of each month. Harry and Belinda want to retain that extra money to help defray some of the added expenses of home ownership.

2. Which sources of used cars should they consider? Why?

3. Assume that the Johnsons have narrowed their choices to two cars. Both have air conditioning, AM/FM radio, and automatic transmission. The first car is a six-year-old Chevrolet Lumina with 62,000 miles, being sold for $3400 by a private individual. The hatchback-style car has a six-cylinder engine, and the seller has kept records of all repairs, tune-ups, and oil changes. The car will need new tires in about six months. The second car is a five-year-old, two-door Ford Taurus with 66,000 miles, being sold by a used car dealership. It has a four-cylinder engine. Harry contacted the previous owner and found that the car was given in trade on a new car about three months ago. The previous owner cited no major mechanical problems but simply wanted a bigger car. The dealer is offering a written 30-day warranty on parts only. The asking price is $3200. Which car would you advise that they buy? Why?

Exploring the World Wide Web of Personal Finance

To complete these exercises, go to the *Garman/Forgue* Web site at

www.hmco.com/college/business/

Select Personal Finance. Click on the exercise link for this chapter and answer the questions that appear on the Web page.

1. Visit the Web site of the Consumer Information Center in Pueblo, Colorado, where you will find an on-line copy of the *Consumer Resource Handbook*. Download or order the

handbook. How might having the handbook help you obtain redress in the marketplace?

2. Visit the Web site of IntelliChoice, where you will find a series of auto reports. Select a *Face-Off Report* on four automobile makes and models that interest you. View the results of the on-line comparisons of these vehicles. What value do you see in such comparisons?

3. Visit the Web site of the Federal Reserve Board, where you will find a Web page entitled "Keys to Vehicle Leasing" that expands upon the information in this book. Use the information to generate a list of pros and cons of leasing versus purchasing a vehicle. By clicking on "sample leasing form" on this Web page, you can view and print a copy of the required vehicle leasing disclosure form.

4. Visit the Web site of *Consumer Reports* magazine, where you will find tips on buying used cars. In what ways are the strategies similar and in what ways do they differ from the tips offered in this book for buying a new car?

5. Visit the *Consumer Reports* Web site. Review the information describing how the magazine staff goes about testing products to be rated. What steps are particularly important for ensuring that the ratings are as unbiased as possible?

6. Visit the Web site for the Bank Rate Monitor Info Bank, where you will find information on vehicle loan interest rates around the United States. View the information for the lenders in a large city near your home. How do the rates in the city you selected compare with average national rates? Use the links provided for one or two vehicle manufacturer sites to compare bank lending rates to manufacturer financing offers. Why are the bank rates and manufacturer rates not directly comparable, and how should you calculate comparable rates?

The Housing Expenditure

9

OBJECTIVES

After reading this chapter, you should be able to:

1 Examine the options available for rented and owned housing and whether renters or owners pay more for housing.

2 Determine how much buyers can afford for housing.

3 Describe the various mechanisms for financing a home.

4 Identify the numerous costs of buying a home, including principal, interest, and closing costs.

5 List and describe the steps in the home-buying process.

6 Identify some important concerns in the process of selling a home.

The four major areas of personal expenditures are housing, food, transportation, and insurance. Of these areas, the greatest expenditure is usually for housing, which often consumes as much as 40 percent of disposable income. As a result, housing represents one of the most important components of personal financial planning.

This chapter begins with a discussion of the question of renting versus buying and describes how to calculate the amount you can afford for housing. Next, we discuss how to finance the purchase of a home and explain how to estimate total home-buying costs, including real estate taxes. The chapter ends with a look at the processes of buying and selling a home. The important topic of real estate as an investment is covered in Chapter 17, "Real Estate and Advanced Portfolio Management."

Renting versus Owning Your Home

1 Examine the options available for rented and owned housing and whether renters or owners pay more for housing.

A wide variety of rented and owned housing is available, depending on your wants and needs and the amount allocated to your housing budget. When making your choice, you must determine which costs more—renting or buying. Each has special considerations, which are discussed in the following paragraphs.

Rented Housing

There are several reasons people may choose to rent housing. They may not have the funds for the down payment and high mortgage costs associated with buying a home. Alternatively, they may prefer the easy mobility of renting or may prefer to avoid many of the responsibilities associated with buying. Prospective renters need to consider the monthly rental fee and related expenses, the lease agreement and restrictions, and tenant rights.

Rent, Deposit, and Related Expenses   **Rent** is the cost of using an apartment or other housing space. It is usually due on a specific day each month, with a late penalty being assessed if the tenant is late in making the payment. Other fees could be assessed for features such as rental of a clubhouse and use of a pool, exercise facilities, cable television, and space for storage and for parking.

The **security deposit** is an amount paid in advance to a landlord to pay for repairing the unit beyond the damage expected from normal wear and tear. It is often charged before the tenant moves in, along with prepayment of the first and last months' rent. Thus, an apartment with a monthly rent of $800 might require prepayment of the first and last months' rent ($1600 total), plus a security deposit (perhaps $400).

Lease Agreement and Restrictions   If you rent a unit without signing any legal contract, you may have few legal protections. As an alternative, you could sign a **lease,** which is a contract specifying the legal responsibilities of both the tenant and the landlord. It identifies the amount of rent and security deposit, the length of the lease (typically one year), payment responsibility for utilities and repairs, penalties for late payment of rent, eviction procedures for nonpayment of rent, and what is to happen when the lease ends.

There are two types of leases. One type provides for **periodic tenancy** (e.g., week-to-week or month-to-month), where the agreement can be terminated by either party if they give proper notice in advance (e.g., one week or one month). Without such notice, the agreement stays in effect. This arrangement also typically applies in situations where no written lease is established. The second type of lease provides for **tenancy for a specific time** (e.g., one year), after which the agreement terminates unless notice is given by both parties that the agreement will be renewed. Leases often state whether the security deposit accumulates interest, how soon the unit must be inspected for cleanliness after the tenant vacates, and when the security deposit (or the balance) will be forwarded to the tenant. Local laws may also address these issues.

Lease agreements may contain a variety of restrictions that are legally binding on tenants. Pets may or may not be permitted; when they are permitted, a larger security deposit is often required. Excessive noise from stereos, televisions,

Make Sure Your Security Deposit Is Returned

If you leave a rental unit clean and undamaged, you have the legal right to a refund of your security deposit when you move out. Several steps will help ensure you receive a full refund.

- Make a list of all damages and defects *before* moving into the unit. Have the landlord sign this list.
- Maintain the unit and keep it clean. Notify the landlord promptly (in writing if necessary) of any maintenance problems and malfunctions.

- Give proper written notice of intent to move out at least 30 days in advance of lease expiration.
- Make a written list of all damages and defects *after* moving out but prior to turning over the keys. Have the landlord sign this second list.
- Use certified mail (with a return receipt) to request return of your security deposit and to inform the landlord of your new address.
- Use small claims court (see Chapter 8), if necessary, to obtain a court-ordered refund.

or parties may be prohibited as well. To protect other renters from overcrowding, a clause may limit the number of overnight guests. An important restriction applies to **subleasing** (leasing the property from the original tenant to another tenant). A tenant who moves before the lease expires may need to obtain the landlord's permission before someone else can take over the rental unit. The new tenant may even have to be approved, and the original tenant may retain some financial liability until the term of the original lease expires.

Tenant Rights Tenants have a number of legal rights under laws in most states and many local communities. Some important rights are as follows:

- Prohibitions against harassment in the form of rent increases, eviction, or utility shut-off for reporting building-code violations or otherwise exercising the tenant's legal rights.

- Assurances of some legally prescribed minimum standard of habitability for items such as running water, heat, and a working stove and of the safety of access areas such as stairways.

- The right to make minor repairs and deduct the cost from the tenant's next rent payment. This right is subject to certain restrictions, such as giving sufficient prior written notification to the landlord.

- Prompt return of security deposits with limits on the kinds of deductions that can be made. Landlords must explain specific reasons for deductions. In some states, laws require that interest be paid on security deposits.

- The right to file a lawsuit against a landlord for nonperformance. All states give this right to tenants. Such suits can be brought in a small claims court.

Owned Housing

Americans have historically favored single-family dwellings to satisfy their owned-housing needs. Because of rising construction and interest costs, however, less expensive alternatives such as condominiums, cooperatives, manufactured housing, and mobile homes have increased in popularity.

Single-Family Dwellings   A housing unit that is detached from other units constitutes a **single-family dwelling.** Such units are traditionally located in residential neighborhoods. In addition to choice of style, buyers face a choice between new and older homes. Some people prefer the modern kitchens and other features found in newer homes; others prefer the larger rooms, higher ceilings, and completed landscaping of older homes. Buyers considering an older residence should order inspections for termite infestation, wood rot, and radon gas, as well as a general inspection of its condition.

Condominiums and Cooperatives   The terms "condominium" and "cooperative" describe forms of ownership rather than types of buildings. These "owned apartments" are located in multi-unit structures and multiplex units, as well as in townhouses and rowhouses. Some people prefer these forms of ownership because they usually carry lower purchase prices than single-family dwellings, offer recreation facilities, and reduce maintenance obligations.

With a **condominium,** the owner holds legal title to a specific housing unit within a multi-unit building or project and owns a proportionate share in the common grounds and facilities. The entire complex is run by the owners through a homeowner's association. Use of the property must be in accordance with the association's bylaws. Besides making monthly loan payments, the condominium owner must pay a monthly **homeowner's fee** that is established by the **homeowner's association.** This fee covers expenses related to the management of the common grounds and facilities and insurance on the building. Insurance on the personal property and contents is the responsibility of the condominium unit owner. Some areas of concern for the potential buyer include potential increases in homeowner's fees and limited resale appeal of the unit.

With a **cooperative,** the owner holds a share of the corporation that owns and manages the group of housing units. The value of the share is equivalent to the value of the owner's particular unit. The owner also holds a proportional interest in all common areas. A monthly fee for the cooperative covers the same types of items as does a condominium fee but also includes an amount to cover the professional management of the complex and payments on the cooperative's mortgage debt. (The pro rata share for interest and property taxes is deductible on each shareholder's income tax return.) The corporation holds legal title to the apartments and leases specific units to each buyer. The shareholders have some input in creating the rules and regulations of the corporation and usually can change management firms if they desire.

Manufactured Housing and Mobile Homes   **Manufactured housing** consists of fully or partially factory-built housing units designed to be transported (often in portions) to the home site. Final assembly and readying of the housing for occupancy occurs at the home site.

Mobile homes, in contrast, are fully factory-assembled housing units that are designed to be towed on a frame with a trailer hitch. Mobile homes are often sold complete with appliances, furniture, carpeting, and curtains. The building cost per square foot for such a unit is about half that of a single-family dwelling.

Of utmost importance is the quality of the mobile home park in which the home may be located or the local zoning requirements if the mobile home will be moved to the buyer's own property. Mobile homes rarely appreciate in value like other forms of housing; in fact, they often depreciate.

Who Pays More—Renters or Owners?

According to conventional wisdom, homeowners enjoy a financial advantage over renters when total housing costs are calculated over many years. Renters generally pay out less money in terms of annual cash flow, but owners usually see an increase in the value of their homes over time and receive some income tax advantages that eventually improve their financial situation. Nearly 90 percent of the households headed by persons under age 25 are rental households compared with slightly less than 20 percent of those headed by persons aged 55 to 64.

 Did You KNOW?

The Advantages and Disadvantages of Renting and Buying

	Advantages	Disadvantages
Renting	Low moving-in costs; easy mobility Apartment amenities (pool, tennis courts, party rooms, laundry facilities) Lifestyle requires fewer responsibilities No maintenance or repairs Fixed monthly housing expenditure (rent) makes it easy to budget No chance for financial loss (beyond the amount of the lease) Proximity of neighbors gives sense of security Opportunity to look over the community and move again	No special tax deductions No potential gain from the rising value of property Usually less space for the money Alterations cannot be made Rent rises with inflation Many restrictions on noise level, pet ownership, and children No pride of ownership
Buying	Pride and higher status of ownership Improves the buyer's credit rating Monthly payment usually remains relatively constant for many years Income tax deduction for mortgage interest and real estate property taxes Potential for home to increase in value Owner can borrow against owner's equity as value of home increases More space available Freedom to make home improvements	Substantial down payment and move-in costs needed A big commitment in time, emotions, and money must be made Possibility that the home will decrease in value Limited liquidity because owner's money is tied up in the home Cost of repairs and maintenance Difficulty in budgeting for repair, maintenance, and home improvements Possibility that real estate property taxes could increase dramatically

Based on Cash Flow, Renters Appear to Win   To compare renting and buying fairly, we must assess comparable forms of housing. Comparing a house with an apartment is not a fair comparison, as differences are likely to exist in privacy, square footage, and neighborhood. The Decision-Making Worksheet, "Should You Buy or Rent?," illustrates a comparison between a small condominium and an apartment with similar space and amenities. For the apartment, rent would total $600 per month. Assume you could buy the condominium for $80,000 by using $15,000 in savings as a down payment and borrowing the remaining $65,000 for 25 years at 9 percent interest. As the worksheet shows, renting would

Should You Buy or Rent?
(Based on Costs for the First Year)

This worksheet can be used to estimate whether you would be better off continuing to rent housing or to buy. If you are renting an apartment and planning to buy a house, qualitative differences should also enter into the decision. Using the worksheet alone will put the financial picture into focus, however.

Costs	Example Amounts		Your Figures	
	Rent	Buy	Rent	Buy
Annual cash-flow considerations				
Annual rent ($600/month) or mortgage payments ($545.48/month)*	$7200	$6546	_____	_____
Property and liability insurance	270	425	_____	_____
Real estate taxes	0	2000	_____	_____
Maintenance	0	320	_____	_____
Other housing fees	0	480	_____	_____
Less interest earned on funds not used for down payment (at 5%)	−750	0	_____	_____
CASH-FLOW COST FOR THE YEAR	$6720	$9771	_____	_____
Tax and appreciation considerations				
Less principal** repaid on the mortgage loan	n/a	−$ 725	n/a	_____
Plus tax on interest earned on funds not used for down payment (28% marginal tax bracket)	210	n/a	_____	n/a
Less tax savings due to deductibility of mortgage interest† (28% marginal tax bracket)	0	−1630	_____	_____
Less tax savings due to deductibility of real estate property taxes (28% marginal tax bracket)	0	−560	_____	_____
Less appreciation on the dwelling (2% annual rate)	0	−1600	_____	_____
NET COST FOR THE YEAR	$6930	$5256	_____	_____

* Calculated from Table 9.4.
** Calculated according to the method illustrated in Table 9.2.
† Mortgage interest tax savings equal total mortgage payments minus principal repaid multiplied by the marginal tax rate.

have a cash-flow cost of $6720 after a reduction for the interest that could be earned on your savings. Buying requires several expenses beyond the monthly mortgage payment, including a $480 annual homeowner's fee. In this case, the cash-flow cost of buying is $9771, or $3051 more than renting.

After Taxes and Appreciation, Owners Usually Win To make the comparison more accurate, we need to consider the tax and appreciation aspects of the two options. If you buy the condominium, $725 of the $6546 in annual mortgage payments will go toward the principal of the debt. Both mortgage interest and real estate property taxes qualify as income tax deductions. If you are in the 28 percent marginal tax bracket, you would lower your taxes $1630 [($6546 − $725) × 0.28] as a result of deducting the mortgage interest and the real estate tax of $560 ($2000 × 0.28). Condominiums also carry the likelihood of **appreciation**, or increase, in the home's value. A conservative assumption would be that the condominium will increase in value by 2 percent a year. A home valued at $80,000 would, therefore, be worth $81,600 ($80,000 × 1.02) after one year, a gain of $1600. If you rent, however, you would pay $210 ($750 × 0.28) in income taxes on the interest on the amount in your savings account ($15,000) not used for your down payment. In this case, buying is financially better than renting by approximately $1674 ($6930 − $5256).

The appreciation on a home does not become money in your pocket until the unit is sold. Until then, it is only a "paper profit." When you sell a home, you will likely pay a commission of 6 percent if a real estate agent handles the sale. In the first few years, any appreciation likely will be offset by the anticipated sales commission. Thus, appreciation benefits of home ownership generally do not begin to be realized until three to five years after purchase.

How Much Can You Afford for Housing?

2 Determine how much buyers can afford for housing.

Your housing decision should be based on a careful cost analysis. Too often an individual takes the first reasonably priced apartment or quickly accepts an offer to share expenses with a friend. Two important considerations when determining housing affordability are (1) setting up a housing budget and (2) understanding the appropriate rules of thumb when borrowing to buy housing.

Your Housing Budget

Housing costs generally have risen and will probably continue to rise in most areas of the United States, as indicated in Table 9.1 on the following page, although some exceptions are likely to emerge. Your task is to calculate your housing budget using some of the budgeting tactics described in Chapter 4. Add up your living expenses *other than* those for housing to determine how much income is left for this expenditure. Note that such calculations give you the maximum amount available for housing, assuming that expenses other than housing costs do not rise. Because such expenses often do increase, however, good planning dictates that you initially pay less than the maximum amount available, if possible. Families buying housing today may well spend 40 percent of their total income on the mortgage payment, taxes, insurance, and utilities.

Table 9.1

Changes in the Median Price of Existing Homes in the Most and Least Expensive Metropolitan Areas

Metropolitan Area*	1993	1996	1998	1999†
Ocala, FL	$57,800	$63,600	$69,900	$65,700
Waterloo / Cedar Falls, IA	50,500	60,600	69,300	70,300
El Paso, TX	n/a	76,200	78,100	75,300
Davenport / Moline / Rock Island, IL	58,300	69,400	78,600	75,400
Saginaw / Bay City, MI	58,300	66,400	78,100	78,200
Syracuse , NY	n/a	79,100	79,600	78,600
Amarillo, TX	n/a	73,700	79,300	78,700
National Average	**106,000**	**118,200**	**130,600**	**131,600**
Newark, NJ	185,100	n/a	199,200	192,000
San Diego, CA	n/a	174,500	207,100	214,700
Boston, MA	173,200	189,300	212,600	216,000
Bergen / Passiac, NJ	188,400	199,400	213,500	227,800
Orange County, CA	217,200	213,400	261,700	245,700
Honolulu, HI	358,500	335,000	288,500	n/a
San Francisco Bay Area, CA	254,400	266,700	321,700	331,100

* Metropolitan area includes central city and surrounding areas.
† Preliminary figures for first quarter 1999.
Source: National Association of Realtors®, *Real Estate Outlook: Market Trends and Insights.*

Rules of Thumb

Lenders use two rules of thumb to estimate the maximum affordability of housing expenses. The first is sometimes referred to as the front-end ratio, while the second is known as the back-end ratio.

The **front-end ratio** compares the total annual expenditures for housing (the principal and interest on the mortgage plus the real estate taxes and insurance) with the loan applicant's gross annual income. Generally, the total annual expenditures should not exceed 25 to 29 percent of gross annual income. Applying a 28 percent front-end ratio, a couple with a gross annual income of $43,000 could qualify for a mortgage requiring total annual expenditures of less than $12,040 (0.28 × $43,000), or $1003 per month.

The **back-end ratio** compares the total of all monthly debt payments (for the mortgage, real estate taxes, and insurance, plus auto loans and other debts) with gross monthly income. Generally, lenders require that monthly debt payments do not exceed 33 to 41 percent of gross monthly income. Applying a back-end ratio of 36 percent, the same couple could qualify for any loan that does not result in monthly debt repayments exceeding $1290 (their monthly income of $3583 × 0.36).

TAX Considerations & Consequences — *Housing*

A big tax break offered to U.S. taxpayers is the deductibility of both mortgage interest and real estate taxes. These amounts usually exceed the IRS's standard deduction (see Chapter 3), thereby making it advantageous to itemize your other deductions. You can then take advantage of even more deduction opportunities available to taxpayers who itemize. As the following example illustrates, middle-income individuals and families can usually save $1000 or $2000 per year in taxes because of these deductions (calculations from Table 3.2).

	Couple A (Renters)	Couple B (Home Buyers)
Adjusted gross income	$39,850	$39,850
Standard deduction	−7,200	itemized
Mortgage interest	0	−7,500
Real estate taxes	0	−1,300
Other deductions	0	−5,200
Exemptions	−5,500	−5,500
Taxable income	$27,150	$20,350
Tax liability	$4,072	$3,052

Couple B saves $1020 ($4072 − $3052) on their federal income taxes because they can deduct housing-related interest and taxes and itemize other deductions, possibly for health care expenses, state and local income taxes, charitable contributions, and miscellaneous deductions. The actual savings would be even greater for couple B because their state income taxes would likely be lower, too.

If you sell a home for more than you originally paid, you will have a capital gain. Any capital gains tax liability may be lowered if you maintained accurate records of **home improvements** made over the years (such as constructing a new garage) that add to its value, prolong its useful life, or adapt it to new uses. These expenses can be subtracted from taxable gains possible from the sale of a home. The IRS requires proof of tax-deductible expenses, so accurate records must be kept for a long time.

Tax law changes implemented in 1998 have greatly reduced the likelihood that capital gains on home sales will be taxed. Homeowners with appreciated principal residences can avoid tax on gains of up to $500,000 if married and filing jointly, and up to $250,000 if single. To realize this benefit, the home must have been owned and used as the principal residence for two of the last five years preceding the date of the sale; the seller does not need to purchase a replacement property. You can take advantage of this exclusion as often as desired as long as you meet the two-year out of five-year residency requirement.

Beginning in 1998, individuals can establish new Roth IRAs (see Chapter 18). Once such an account is five years old, as much as $10,000 may be withdrawn tax- and penalty-free, provided that the qualifying first-time home buyer uses the funds for home-buying costs. Funds must be used within 120 days of withdrawal. A qualifying first-time home buyer is someone who has not owned a principal residence in the two-year period prior to acquiring the new home. The person withdrawing the funds can be the home buyer or his or her spouse, parent, or grandparent. Hence, this mechanism allows parents or grandparents to make withdrawals from Roth IRAs (up to $10,000) to help young family members buy their first home.

The Income Needed to Qualify to Buy a Home

The table at right will give you a quick idea of how much income you need to buy a home at a certain price using a front-end ratio of 28 percent. The illustration is for a 30-year loan with a 20 percent down payment. For each home price, the *top* figure in each row shows the monthly payment for principal, interest, real estate taxes, and homeowner's insurance for the interest rates; the *bottom* figure shows the required gross annual income to qualify for the loan. For example, a 7 percent loan on a $100,000 home requires a monthly payment of $615 plus an income of $26,357 to qualify. Taxes and insurance are assumed to be 1 percent of the purchase price (divided by 12 months). Visit the *Garman/Forgue* Web site to perform these calculations for a variety of home prices and interest rates.

Interest Rate	Price of Home				
	$60,000	$80,000	$100,000	$120,000	$140,000
4.0%	$ 279	$ 371	$ 465	$ 558	$ 651
	11,957	15,900	19,929	23,914	27,900
5.0	308	410	513	615	718
	13,200	17,571	21,985	26,357	30,771
6.0	338	450	563	676	788
	14,486	19,286	24,129	28,971	33,771
7.0	369	493	615	739	862
	15,814	21,129	26,357	31,671	36,943
8.0	402	536	670	804	938
	17,229	22,971	28,714	34,457	40,200
9.0	436	582	727	872	1,018
	18,686	24,943	31,157	37,371	43,629
10.0	471	628	785	942	1,099
	20,186	26,914	33,643	40,371	47,100

Financing a Home

3   Describe the various mechanisms for financing a home.

Buying a home represents the largest expenditure most people ever make. You can use several tactics to obtain the money for this purchase. Many people establish a "home savings" fund while renting. Some must rent for five years or more before they are able to save enough to purchase a home. Some couples postpone having children, while other people cut back on entertainment and vacations and put off making major purchases. You also can prepare for home ownership by renting a home with an option to purchase it. Ultimately, however, you must become knowledgeable about mortgage loans and how they work to purchase a home.

Mortgage Loans

A **mortgage loan** is a loan to purchase real estate in which the real estate itself serves as collateral. Mortgage loans are available from depository institutions (savings and loan associations, mutual savings banks, commercial banks, mort-

Table 9.2

Amortization Effects of Monthly Payment of $733.76 on a $100,000, 30-Year Mortgage Loan at 8 Percent

First Month

$100,000 × 8% × $^1/_{12}$ =	$	666.67	Interest payment
$733.76 − 666.67 =		67.09	Principal repayment
$100,000 − 67.09 =		$ 99,932.91	Balance due

Second Month

$99,932.91 × 8% × $^1/_{12}$ =	$	666.21	Interest payment
$733.76 − 666.21 =		67.55	Principal repayment
$99,932.91 − 67.55 =		$99,865.36	Balance due

Third Month

$99,865.36 × 8% × $^1/_{12}$ =	$	665.76	Interest payment
$733.76 − 665.76 =		68.00	Principal repayment
$99,865.36 − 68.00 =		$99,797.36	Balance due

gage finance companies, and credit unions, as described in Chapters 5 and 7) and through **mortgage brokers** that, for a fee, will shop and arrange financing for the prospective buyer. In exchange for the loan, the lender (*mortgagee*) has a **lien** on the real estate—that is, the legal right to take and hold property or to sell it in the event the borrower (*mortgagor*) defaults on the loan. **Foreclosure** is the process in which the lender sues the borrower to prove default and asks the court to order the sale of the property to pay the debt.

The term "mortgage" receives its name from the concept of **amortization**, which is the process of gradually paying off a loan through a series of periodic payments to a lender. Each payment is allocated in two ways. First, a portion goes to pay simple interest on the debt based on a monthly interest rate applied to the outstanding debt. The remainder goes to repay the **principal**, which is the debt remaining from the original amount borrowed. As the principal is paid down, increasingly lower portions of the payments will be required to pay interest while payments devoted to the principal accelerate. At any point, the amount that has been paid off (including the down payment) plus any appreciation in the value of the home represents the homeowner's **equity** (the dollar value of the home in excess of the amount owed on it). Additional payments can be directed toward the principal at any time to reduce it and increase equity.

Necessarily, most of each monthly payment during the early years of a mortgage loan is allocated to interest because the debt outstanding remains very high. Table 9.2 shows the interest and principal payment amounts for the first three months of a $100,000, 30-year, 8 percent mortgage loan. For the first month, $666.67 goes for interest costs, and only $67.09 goes toward retirement of the principal of the loan. The monthly principal-repayment portion increases very slowly over the life of a loan, as shown in the partial amortization schedule in Table 9.3 on the following page. An **amortization schedule** lists each monthly payment, the portion that will go toward interest and principal, and the debt remaining after the payment is made. Many years must typically pass before the monthly payment significantly reduces the outstanding balance of the loan.

Three Factors Affecting the Monthly Payment on a Mortgage

Three basic factors affect the monthly payment on a mortgage loan: the amount borrowed, the interest rate charged, and the time period of the loan.

Table 9.3

Partial Amortization Schedule for a $100,000, 30-Year (360-Payment) Mortgage Loan at 8 Percent

Payment Number (Month)	Monthly Payment Amount	Portion to Principal Repayment	Portion to Interest	Total of Payments to Date	Outstanding Loan Balance
1	$733.76	$ 67.09	$666.67	$ 733.76	$99,932.91
2	733.76	67.55	666.21	1,467.52	99,865.36
3	733.76	68.00	665.76	2,201.28	99,797.36
4	733.76	68.44	665.32	2,935.04	99,728.91
5	733.76	68.91	664.85	3,668.80	99,660.00
6	733.76	69.36	664.40	4,402.56	99,590.64
7	733.76	69.83	663.93	5,136.32	99,520.81
8	733.76	70.29	663.47	5,870.08	99,450.52
9	733.76	70.76	663.00	6,603.84	99,379.76
10	733.76	71.23	662.53	7,337.60	99,308.53
11	733.76	71.71	662.05	8,071.36	99,236.82
12	733.76	72.19	661.57	8,805.12	99,164.63
24	733.76	78.18	655.58	17,610.24	98,259.94
60	733.76	99.30	634.46	44,025.60	95,069.85
120	733.76	147.95	585.81	88,051.20	87,724.70
180	733.76	220.42	513.34	132,076.80	76,781.55
240	733.76	328.38	405.38	176,102.40	60,477.95
300	733.76	489.25	244.51	220,128.00	36,188.09
360	733.76	728.90	4.86	264,153.60	0

The Amount Borrowed The payment schedule illustrated in Table 9.4 gives the monthly payment required for each $1000 of a mortgage loan at different interest rates. Using this table, you can calculate the monthly payment for mortgage loans of different amounts. For example, the $100,000 mortgage loan described earlier at 8 percent for 30 years costs $7.3376 per $1000 per month. Thus, 100 × $7.3376 equals $733.76. If the loan amount was $120,000, then the monthly payment would be $880.40 (120 × $7.3367).

The amount borrowed is determined in part by the down payment required by the lender. The minimum down payment is based on the lender's desired **loan-to-value ratio**, which is calculated by dividing the maximum amount the lender will loan on a piece of property by the property's purchase price. The lender limits the amount that it will risk on a mortgage to ensure that it can recover the debt if the loan goes into default. For example, a home with a value of $120,000 for which a lender desires the standard loan-to-value ratio of 0.80 will have a maximum loan of $96,000 (0.80 × 120,000). Thus, the lender would require a down payment of $24,000 ($120,000 − $96,000), or 20 percent.

Table 9.4

Estimating Mortgage Loan Payments for Principal and Interest
(Monthly Payment per $1000 Borrowed)

Interest	Payment Period (Years)			
Rate (%)	15	20	25	30
4.5	$7.6499	$6.3265	$5.5583	$5.0669
5.0	7.9079	6.5996	5.8459	5.3682
5.5	8.1708	6.8789	6.1409	5.6779
6.0	8.4386	7.1643	6.4430	5.9955
6.5	8.7111	7.4557	6.7521	6.3207
7.0	8.9883	7.7530	7.0678	6.6530
7.5	9.2701	8.0559	7.3899	6.9921
8.0	9.5565	8.3644	7.7182	7.3376
8.5	9.8474	8.6782	8.0523	7.6891
9.0	10.1427	8.9973	8.3920	8.0462
9.5	10.4422	9.3213	8.7370	8.4085
10.0	10.7461	9.6502	9.0870	8.7757

Note: To use this table to figure a monthly mortgage payment, divide the amount borrowed by 1000 and multiply by the appropriate figure in the table for the interest rate and time period of the loan. For example, an $80,000 loan for 20 years at 9 percent would require a payment of $719.78 [($80,000 ÷ 1000) × 8.9973]; over 30 years, it would require a payment of $643.70 [($80,000 ÷ 1000) × 8.0462]. For calculations for different interest rates, visit the *Garman/Forgue* Web site.

A borrower may want to make only the minimum down payment required by the lender's loan-to-value ratio. For persons with limited cash, this assumption may be appropriate, but for borrowers with an extra $5000 or $10,000 available, the situation differs. Making a down payment that is larger than required lowers the borrower's monthly payments. A smaller loan also carries lower total interest costs.

Table 9.5 shows the progressively smaller monthly payments associated with increased down payments. At 7 percent interest, a 20-year loan of $95,000 costs $736.53 per month. Increasing the down payment by $5000 reduces the monthly payment to $697.77, and an additional $5000 reduces it even further to $659.00.

Low- and moderate-income families often find it difficult to save the 20 percent down payment required by most lenders. FHA and VA loans (discussed later) provide some opportunity for low down payments but are not available to all borrowers or on all homes. Other programs have been developed for lower-income buyers and people buying homes for the first time. Lenders in your area can provide you with information about programs that target these special-needs groups. It may be possible to buy a home with a low (or no) down payment and at a low, government-subsidized interest rate.

Table 9.5

Effect of Down Payment Size on Monthly Payment for a $100,000 Home
(7 Percent Mortgage Loan for 20 Years)

Down Payment	Amount of Loan	Monthly Payment
$ 5,000	$95,000	$736.53
10,000	90,000	697.77
15,000	85,000	659.00
20,000	80,000	620.24
25,000	75,000	581.48

The Interest Rate The higher the interest rate, the higher the monthly payment on a mortgage loan (see Table 9.4). For example, a $733.76 monthly payment is required for a $100,000 mortgage loan taken out for 30 years at 8 percent. If the interest rate were 9.5 percent, the monthly mortgage payment would be $840.85 (100 × $8.4085), an increase of more than $100. The impact is even greater on the total payback and the total interest paid over the life of the loan. The 8 percent loan will have total payments of $264,153.60 (360 × $733.76) with total interest of $164,153.60 ($264,153.60 − $100,000.00). For the 9.5 percent loan, total payments are $302,706.00 (360 × $840.85) and total interest is $202,706.00 ($302,706.00 − $100,000.00). Thus, the added cost for the 30-year loan at 9.5 percent is $38,552.40 over the life of the loan.

Homeowners may find it advantageous to refinance a mortgage when interest rates decline. In **mortgage refinancing**, a new mortgage is obtained to pay off and replace an existing mortgage. Most often it is undertaken to lower the monthly payment on the home via a lower interest rate. It may also be possible to borrow more than the current balance on the existing loan, thereby utilizing some of the equity built up in the home. Borrowers refinancing for more than the amount owed should understand that rebuilding the equity to its previous level may take many years.

Length of Maturity Table 9.6 illustrates the relationships among maturity length, monthly payment, and interest cost for a $70,000 loan at various interest rates. For loans with the same interest rate, a longer term of repayment results in a smaller payment. Ironically, more total interest is paid over the longer repayment time period despite the lower monthly payment. For example, the monthly payment on an 8 percent loan is $586 for 20 years but only $514 for 30 years. When the loan is paid back in 20 years, the total interest costs are much lower ($71,000 rather than $115,000, for a savings of $44,000).

Some borrowers opt for a mortgage loan with a comparatively short 15-year maturity. Its advantages include a faster build-up of equity, lower total interest,

Table 9.6

Monthly Payment and Total Interest to Repay a $70,000 Loan

Length of Loan	Interest Rate (%) 6	8	10	12
30 years	$ 420	$ 514	$ 614	$ 720
	81,000	115,000	151,000	189,000
25 years	451	540	636	737
	65,000	92,000	121,000	151,000
20 years	502	586	676	771
	50,000	71,000	92,000	115,000
15 years	591	669	752	840
	36,000	50,000	65,000	81,000

Note: Figures are rounded. The top figure in each pair is the monthly payment, and the bottom figure is the total interest paid rounded to the nearest $1000.

and a quicker payoff of the loan. These advantages can also be gained with a 20- or 30-year mortgage by simply paying additional amounts toward the principal during the time period of the loan. Because mortgage loans are simple-interest loans in which no penalty is incurred for occasionally (or regularly) making larger-than-necessary payments, it is generally wise to take a longer repayment period even if you plan to pay off in 15 (or fewer) years. With that strategy, the faster payoff is optional rather than mandatory.

The Conventional Mortgage Loan

A **conventional mortgage** is a fixed-rate, fixed-term, fixed-payment mortgage loan. For example, an $80,000 loan could be granted at a 9 percent annual interest rate over a period of 30 years with a monthly payment of $643.70. Because the lender's only protection against possible default is the home itself, a down payment of 20 percent of purchase price (a loan-to-value ratio of 80 percent) is standard practice. On a $100,000 home, for example, a lender would likely lend only $80,000. Should the borrower default, the lender could probably sell the home for at least the amount of the outstanding loan balance. Lenders feel more secure with substantial down payments and often offer slightly reduced interest rates in return for higher down payments. With a down payment of 30 percent, for example, a lender might offer an interest rate 0.25 or 0.5 percentage points lower than the interest rate for a loan with a 20 percent down payment. Note, however, that lenders may accept as little as 3 percent down if the mortgage is insured. Mortgage insurance is discussed later in this chapter.

The Adjustable-Rate Mortgage Loan

With an **adjustable-rate mortgage (ARM)**—sometimes called a **variable-rate mortgage**—a borrower's interest rate will fluctuate according to some index of interest rates based on the performance of the economy as a whole. Thus the monthly payment could increase or decrease, usually on an annual basis, but sometimes monthly. Lenders offer ARM rates at 1 to 3 percent (or more) below conventional mortgage rates. With all ARMs, a decline in the rate will cause the monthly payment to drop. Conversely, future increases in the rate may increase monthly payments, perhaps making them unaffordable and forcing some borrowers to sell. Borrowers with ARMs should always determine the "worst case" scenario for interest rate increases under their loan contract and calculate the monthly payment that would result.

Sometimes ARM lenders will offer a **teaser rate** to encourage people to borrow. Such a loan will carry an interest rate for the first year or so that may be 2 to 4 percentage points below regular ARM loan rates. Most ARMs have **interest-rate caps** that limit the amount that the interest rate can increase (perhaps no more than 2 percent per year and no more than 5 percent over the life of the loan). **Payment caps**, in turn, limit the amount that the payment can vary on an ARM. Having a loan with a payment cap but without an equivalent interest-rate cap is an invitation to **negative amortization**, which occurs when monthly payments are actually smaller than necessary to pay the interest. This practice will result in a principal loan balance that actually rises.

For example, consider an ARM initially written at 6.0 percent for a 30-year, $100,000 mortgage with a $650 payment cap. The initial monthly payment would be $599.55 (from Table 9.4; 100 × 5.9955)—more than enough to pay the interest owed each month. Should the rate rise to 8 percent after one year, $658.48 would be needed just to pay the interest for the first month after the rate went up.* Because the monthly payment was capped at $650, the principal balance owed would actually increase $8.48 in the first month after the rates rose. This shortfall would increase each month as the principal owed grew. Higher payments, perhaps of $800 or $900, would be required in later years to pay off the loan because of this negative amortization.

Four innovations in ARMs have been developed. The first is the **convertible adjustable-rate mortgage**, which allows conversion of an ARM to a fixed-rate mortgage, usually during years 2 through 5 of the ARM. The second innovation, the **reduction-option loan**, begins as a fixed-rate loan that allows a one-time optional adjustment in the interest rate to current rates, perhaps during years 2 through 6 of the original loan. If rates drop, you can take the option and reduce your payments. If rates do not drop, you simply choose not to exercise your option. The third innovation is a **price-level-adjusted mortgage**. Its initial rate is extremely low, perhaps 4 percent, and amortization occurs. The interest rate and monthly payment are subsequently adjusted according to the inflation rate over the years. Over a 20-year period, the monthly payment could triple or even quadruple. In such a case, the borrower would hope that his or her income keeps pace with inflation, maintaining the affordability of the loan payments. In the fourth innovation, which is known as a **two-step mortgage**, the interest is adjusted just once, usually at the end of the seventh year. Thus, in the first step, the mortgage has the original interest rate; the second step applies the current rate available in the market at the end of the seventh year. This option offers the benefit of a fixed monthly payment in the early years.

Alternative Mortgage Loans

A number of alternative mortgage approaches have emerged in response to interest rate fluctuations and increasing costs for housing. In general, most alternative lending approaches aim to keep the monthly payment as low as possible, especially in the early years of the loan for first-time and lower-income buyers. The lower payments also permit borrowers to purchase larger, more expensive homes than they could afford with a traditional loan. A number of these alternative mortgages are described in the following paragraphs.

Graduated-Payment Mortgage Smaller-than-normal payments are required in the early years but gradually increase to larger-than-normal payments in later years with the **graduated-payment mortgage**. It makes the assumption that increased income will be available for the higher payments. The interest rate is fixed, but payments early in the mortgage may be lower than necessary to pay even the interest. Payments could then increase each year. When payments in the beginning are less than the interest owed, negative amortization results.

---

* The logic of Table 9.2 would show that the loan balance after the first year would be $98,771.99. This amount would be amortized over the remaining 29 years at the new 8 percent rate, and $658.48 would go to interest [($98,771.99 × 0.08) ÷ 12] in the first month after the rate went up.

Lender Buy-Down Mortgage With the **lender buy-down mortgage**, the interest rate changes, triggering corresponding changes in the monthly payments. First-time home buyers often use buy-down mortgages to take advantage of lower monthly payments in early years of the loan. A base interest rate is set, usually 0.5 percentage points above current fixed rates. For the first year, the borrower pays a rate 2 percentage points *below* the base rate. In the second year, the rate is 1 point below the base. In the third and future years, the base rate would be charged. Unlike with an adjustable-rate mortgage, these changes are known in advance and are contractual. Negative amortization does not occur with a buy-down mortgage.

Rollover, or Renegotiable-Rate, Mortgage A **rollover mortgage** consists of a series of short-term loans for two- to five-year time periods, but with total amortization spread over the usual 25 to 30 years. The loan is renewed for each time period at the market interest rates that prevail at the time of the renewal.

Shared-Appreciation Mortgage With a **shared-appreciation mortgage**, the lender offers an interest rate about one-third less than the market rate. In exchange, the lender gains the right to receive perhaps one-third of any appreciation in the home's value when the home is sold or ten years after the time of the loan.

Growing-Equity Mortgage The **growing-equity mortgage (GEM)** is meant for people who design their loan in advance to reduce interest costs by paying off the mortgage loan early. The payments on the fixed-interest loan are scheduled to increase by a predetermined amount each year, perhaps 2 to 7 percent. The larger amounts go toward reducing the principal owed—thus, a 30-year mortgage may be paid off in less than 20 years. As illustrated below, the GEM's major advantage is a significantly reduced total payout for interest on the loan.

One form of GEM is the **biweekly mortgage**, which calls for payments every two weeks that represent half of the normal monthly payment. The borrower, therefore, makes 26 payments per year. For example, an $80,000, 9 percent, 30-year loan requires a $643.70 monthly payment for a total of $7724.40 (12 × $643.70) paid in one year. On a biweekly basis with payments of $321.85 ($643.70 ÷ 2), the total amount paid each year would be $8368.10 ($321.85 × 26). The difference of $643.70 ($8368.10 − $7724.40) is equivalent to one extra monthly payment per year and is applied to the principal of the loan. Under the biweekly repayment plan, a loan may be repaid in approximately 20 years, rather than the 30 years dictated by the monthly payment plan. Almost all mortgage lenders permit payment of additional amounts toward principal at any time. For example, paying an additional $50 per month on an $80,000, 9 percent, 30-year loan (that is, paying $693.70 rather than $643.70) would cause the loan to be paid off in 22 years, four months, and would save $45,821 in interest costs.

Assumable Mortgage It may be possible to assume—or take over—the original mortgage taken out by the seller of a home. With an **assumable mortgage**, the buyer pays the seller a down payment generally equal to the seller's equity in the home and takes over the mortgage loan payments for the remaining term of the loan. The buyer's goal is to obtain the loan at the original interest rate, which is below current market rates.

The down payment for an assumable mortgage may be large because the home will have increased in value and the principal of the loan will have been reduced over the years. To assume an existing mortgage, the buyer sometimes must obtain a second mortgage to cover a portion of the down payment. A **second mortgage** is an additional loan on a residence besides the original mortgage. In case of default, the amount owed on the original mortgage must be paid first. With this additional risk, the interest rate on a second mortgage is often 2 to 5 percentage points higher than current market rates for first mortgages. For example, suppose Robert and Louise Bond, a dual-earner family from Van Nuys, California, wish to buy a $250,000 home from the Roget family. The Bonds want to assume the Rogets' remaining mortgage of $170,000, but they have only $50,000 available to pay the Rogets for their equity of $80,000 ($250,000 − $170,000). A lender (maybe the Rogets'?) that thinks the Bonds can afford to make two mortgage payments might give them a second mortgage loan of $30,000 to make up the difference. Second mortgages often run from three to ten years in length, so the Bonds can look forward to having only one mortgage payment at some point. Of course, they may face considerable budget stress while paying on both mortgages at the same time.

Seller Financing   **Seller financing** occurs whenever the seller of a home agrees to accept all or a portion of the purchase price in installments rather than a lump sum. The Bond family in the preceding example could have used seller financing if the Rogets agreed to accept installment payments on the $30,000 the Bonds lacked for the equity. Such a case would be labeled a "seller-financed second mortgage." Other variations also exist. For example, a seller may be willing to finance the entire purchase price for 20 or 30 years with a 10 or 20 percent down payment, thereby acting much like a mortgage lending institution. Usually seller financing is a short-term arrangement, however, with payments based on amortization occurring over perhaps 20 years and a balloon payment due after perhaps five years. Thus, all principal not paid after five years would be due. This extremely large sum would typically require refinancing via a mortgage from a financial institution. Such a loan should not be difficult to obtain assuming that equity has built up in the property. Interest rates could have risen dramatically, however, making it difficult for the buyer to budget the new, larger mortgage payments. In most seller financing, the buyer obtains the title to the property when the deal is closed and the contract signed. A **land contract** (or **contract for deed**), in contrast, brings greater risk for the buyer because all terms in the contract (including payment of the debt) must be satisfied before obtaining title. As a result, if you move before paying off the contract in full, you forfeit all money paid in installments to the seller and any appreciation in the home's value. You build no equity until the contract is completed.

Reverse Mortgage   A **reverse mortgage**, also known as a **home-equity conversion loan**, allows a homeowner over age 61 to borrow against the equity in a home that is fully paid for and to receive the proceeds in a series of monthly payments, often over a period of five to 15 years or for life. The contract allows the person to continue living in the home. Essentially, the borrower trades his or her equity in the home in return for either a fixed monthly income or a line of credit that can be drawn upon at the option of the homeowner. The most likely prospects for such loans are elderly persons who have paid off their mortgages but are strapped for income. The mortgage does not have to be paid back until the last surviving owner sells the house, moves out permanently, or dies. Instead of "interest," these loans carry various fees and charges. Lenders must disclose these fees in a uniform way so that borrowers can compare among lenders for the most economical choice. Generally, the longer the owner lives in the home after the mortgage begins, the less it costs on an annualized basis because fees assessed up front can be spread out over many years.

Second Mortgage A second mortgage is a loan exceeding the amount owed on the first mortgage, with the mortgaged property serving as collateral. Second mortgages allow borrowers to access their home equity. Although the property serves as collateral for both loans, the claim of the first mortgage lender is primary. Thus, if the home is sold or if either loan goes into foreclosure and the home must be sold at auction, the proceeds of the sale will be first applied to the first mortgage and only then to the second loan. Historically, people have used second mortgages to pay for major remodeling projects, finance college costs for children, pay off medical bills, or start a business. Today, some people use these funds for everyday living expenses, an unwise practice dubbed "eating one's house."

Two types of second mortgages exist. With a **home-equity installment loan**, a specific amount of money is borrowed for a fixed time period with fixed monthly payments. With a **home-equity line of credit**, a maximum loan amount is established and the loan operates as open-ended credit, much like a credit card account. These line-of-credit loans often have a variable interest rate and a flexible repayment schedule.

The credit limit on a second mortgage loan is usually set at 75 to 80 percent of the home's appraised value minus the amount owed on the first mortgage. For example, a person with a home appaised at $200,000 with a balance owed of $100,000 on a first mortgage might be allowed to take out a $60,000 second mortgage [($200,000 $\times$ 0.80) $-$ $100,000]. The interest rate on a second mortgage is usually 1.5 to 2.0 percentage points higher than the prevailing first mortgage rates in the market. Generally, the interest can be used as a deduction on state and federal income tax forms.

What Does It Cost to Buy a Home?

4 Identify the numerous costs of buying a home, including principal, interest, and closing costs.

Some prospective home buyers look at homes that are too expensive but end up buying them anyway. Such buyers will have nice homes but could be called "house poor" because they will spend such a great proportion of income on housing costs that very little money will be left over for other items. To avoid becoming house poor, the wise financial planner carefully estimates all initial and subsequent costs of housing and thus makes more knowledgeable decisions. In the discussion that follows, we assume that the prospective homeowner has $15,000 to use as a down payment on a $115,000 vacation home. All other costs are described in the following sections, and Table 9.7 on the following page shows a summary of estimated costs.

Table 9.7

Estimated Buying and Closing Costs
(Purchase Price of a Vacation Home, $115,000 with $15,000 Down; Closing on July 1)

Home Buying Costs	At Closing	Monthly
Down payment	$15,000	—
Points (2)	2,000	—
Loan application fee	100	—
Principal and interest (from Table 9.4 for a $100,000 loan for 30 years at 8%)	—	$733.76
Property taxes (for first half-year, then monthly)	750 *	125.00
Homeowner's insurance (for first half-year, then monthly)	480 †	40.00
Mortgage insurance	—	41.67
Loan origination fee	500	—
Title search	100	—
Title insurance (to protect lender)	200	—
Title insurance (to protect buyer)	200	—
Attorney's fee	300	—
Credit reports	25	—
Recording fees	20	—
Appraisal fee	150	—
Termite and radon inspection fee	130	—
Survey fee	100	—
Notary fee	50	—
SUBTOTAL	$20,105	$940.43
Less amount owed by seller	−750 *	—
SUBTOTAL	$19,355	
Warranty insurance (optional)	240	20.00
TOTAL	$19,595	$960.43

* Would be received from seller who legally owes these taxes, and then deposited in escrow account.

† Would be paid to escrow account.

Principal and Interest

A mortgage loan requires repayment of both principal (P) and interest (I), which are the first two letters of the popular abbreviation **PITI**, which real estate agents and lenders often use to indicate a mortgage payment that includes principal, interest, real estate taxes, and insurance. The monthly payment schedule in Table 9.4 gives the amount needed per month to repay each $1000 of mortgage loan at different interest rates. For our 30-year, 8 percent loan, the amount in the table is $7.3376. In our example, the loan amount is $100,000 ($115,000 − $15,000); multiplying 100 by $7.3376 gives a monthly payment of $733.76 to repay the principal and interest.

Taxes and Insurance

Taxes (T) and insurance (I) represent the last two letters of PITI. Real estate property taxes must be paid to local and state governments. The amount varies by community, but usually ranges from 1 to 4 percent of the value of the home. The total amount ($1500 in our example) is due once each year when the government sends out its tax bill. When an escrow account is used, lenders require that the borrower deposit in advance a pro rata share (one-twelfth) of the estimated real estate taxes each month ($125 in our example). An **escrow account** is a special reserve account at a financial institution (in this case, the lender) where funds are held until they are paid to a third party (in this case, the taxing agency and the insurance company). If a buyer takes possession at the midpoint of the tax year, the seller, who owes those taxes, should make one-half ($750 here) of the taxes due available out of the escrow account to the buyer on the day of the **closing.** Closing takes place when the home is financially and legally transferred to the new buyer and usually occurs in the office of the lender or an attorney.

Lenders always require homeowners to insure the home itself in case of fire or other calamity. In contrast, insurance on the contents of the home is the responsibility of the homeowner. Both the home and its contents can be covered in a typical homeowner's insurance policy. (Chapter 10 covers this information in detail.) The annual premium for such insurance must be paid each year in advance. Most lenders require prepayment of a pro rata share (one-twelfth) each month ($40 here) of the next year's estimated insurance premium. In addition, on closing day the purchaser must be prepared to prepay one year's premium ($480 here) in advance.

Mortgage Insurance

When a buyer makes a down payment that is less than 20 percent of the home's purchase price, the lender almost always requires that the borrower obtain mortgage insurance. **Mortgage insurance** typically insures the first 20 percent of a loan in case of default. In our example, the lender is willing to loan $100,000 even though the $15,000 down payment is less than the standard 20 percent. The mortgage insurance company would insure 20 percent, or $20,000 ($100,000 × 0.20), of the debt. The lender would be assured of payment of the loan balance if the home were later repossessed for default and sold for less than the amount owed. In this example, assume a premium charge totaling 0.5 percent of the mortgage loan, or $500 (0.005 × $100,000) annually, to be paid monthly ($41.67) to the lender, which forwards it to the mortgage insurance company. Mortgage insurance may be obtained from several sources.

Private Mortgage Insurance **Private mortgage insurance (PMI)** is mortgage insurance obtained from a private company rather than a government agency. The largest private mortgage insurer is the Mortgage Guaranty Insurance Corporation (MGIC, pronounced "magic"). The cost of PMI varies from 0.25 to 2.0 percent of the debt, depending on how far below 20 percent the down payment falls. PMI premiums must be paid until the unpaid balance drops to 80 percent of the home's value. At that point it may be possible to cancel the insurance, but the borrower must request the cancellation in writing.

About Real Estate Property Taxes

Real estate property taxes are based on the value of buildings and land. Local government officials establish a **fair market value** for the owner's home and land. Next, the **assessed value** of the property is calculated. This value is established by the local tax assessor or by law as a fixed percentage of fair market value (perhaps 50, 60, or 100 percent). A home with a fair market value of $100,000, for example, might have an assessed value of $60,000. The real estate tax on an assessed valuation of $60,000 at a tax rate of 30 mills (each mill represents one one-thousandth of a dollar) would be $1800 ($60,000 × 0.030).

Although you can do little to affect the tax rate on real estate property, you can claim that the assessed valuation on your home is too high. If your appeal is successful, your tax bill will be lowered accordingly. On a national basis, about one-half of all appeals are successful.

Instead of making monthly payments for PMI, it may be possible to obtain lender-paid mortgage insurance. In such a case, the lender pays the mortgage insurance premium and in return charges a higher interest rate on the loan of perhaps an additional 1/4 to 3/4 of a percentage point. The mortgage insurance premium is tax-deductible because it represents part of the interest payments, but the insurance cannot be dropped without completely refinancing the loan.

FHA Mortgage Insurance   Many borrowers seek government mortgage insurance and guarantees instead of private mortgage insurance. To encourage lending, the **Federal Housing Administration (FHA)** of the U.S. Department of Housing and Urban Development (HUD) insures loans that meet its standards. The borrower must be creditworthy, and the home must meet the FHA's minimum-quality standards.

An **FHA mortgage** is granted by a mortgage lender such as a bank, which is insured against borrower default by the federal government. Like private mortgage insurers, the FHA charges the borrower a mortgage insurance premium. This premium may be paid as a single up-front, lump-sum payment, or it may be financed and paid in monthly amounts like private mortgage insurance.

Usually, only a very small down payment is required on an FHA-insured mortgage because the loan is backed by the federal government. Down-payment minimums are calculated as follows: the lesser of 2.25 percent of the appraised value *or* 3 percent on the first $25,000, 5 percent on amounts between $25,000 and $125,000, and 10 percent on amounts over $125,000. Mortgage loans insured by FHA can be made on homes that do not exceed FHA lending limits, which change frequently and vary across the country according to local housing market prices. Terms can be up to 30 years, and the time to process an application is often 60 to 90 days.

VA Mortgage Insurance   The federal Department of **Veterans Affairs (VA)** promotes home ownership among military veterans (active-duty, reserve, and

National Guard veterans may qualify) by providing the lender with a guarantee against buyer default. In effect, the VA guarantee operates much like FHA or private mortgage insurance because the lender is protected for a portion of the loan's value in the event that the home must be repossessed and sold. Homes must meet VA standards of construction, but mobile homes also qualify for these loans. Little or no down payment is required on VA loans, and lending limits are set by the VA. Usually 60 to 90 days are needed to approve an application.

Points

A **point** is a fee equal to 1 percent of the total loan amount, and any charge for points must be paid in full when the home is bought. **Interest points** increase the return to the lender. In our example, the lender charged 2 points on the $100,000 loan, resulting in a charge of $2000. By law, interest points do not have to be included in calculating the annual percentage rate (APR) for the loan. Each point charged would increase the annual percentage rate approximately 0.125 percent, however. Many lenders charge interest points, which are deductible on federal income tax returns.

Lenders most often charge interest points to increase the yield on FHA and VA mortgage loans to the level that market conditions demand. These government-regulated loans have interest rate ceilings that are often set lower than prevailing conventional mortgage interest rates. For example, if interest rates on conventional mortgage loans average 8 percent, FHA and VA loans will probably carry a rate of approximately 7 percent. Lenders must be encouraged to make such below-market-rate loans. Accordingly, the lender charges the seller or the buyer of a home one or more points. Sellers of FHA and VA homes who pay points (FHA insurance premiums are usually 2.25 points) typically increase the sales price of their homes by an equivalent amount when negotiating prices with purchasers who intend to use FHA or VA mortgage assistance. A home purchaser is protected to some extent from an inflated price because the FHA and VA will not insure a loan for more than the appraised value of the home.

Points are also sometimes charged in connection with a **loan origination fee.** Lenders charge borrowers these noninterest points for doing all of the paperwork and setting up the mortgage loan. The fee usually ranges from 0.5 to 2.0 percent of the amount of the loan, or 0.5 to 2 points. In our example, a $500 loan origination fee is assessed as shown in Table 9.7.

Title Insurance

The **title** to real property is the legal right of ownership interest. In real estate transactions, the title is transferred to a new owner through a **deed,** which is a written document used to convey real estate ownership. Usually with the assistance of an attorney at closing, the buyer reviews various documents to ensure having as clear a title as possible. Examples of claims against property include electrical work for which a previous owner never paid and the sale of mineral rights perhaps 75 years ago. Four types of deeds are used:

1. A *warranty deed* is the safest, as it guarantees that the title is free of any previous mortgages.

2. A *special warranty deed* guarantees only that the current owner has not placed any mortgage encumbrances on the title.

3. A *quitclaim deed* transfers whatever title the current owner had in the property with no guarantee.

4. A *deed of bargain and sale* conveys title with or without a guarantee that the seller had an ownership interest.

If the quality of the deed is suspect, a title search and the purchase of title insurance can offer better protection. An attorney or title company can inspect court records and prepare a detailed written history of property ownership called an **abstract**. In a **title search**, an attorney examines the abstract and other documents and may issue a **certificate of title**. This legal opinion (not a guarantee) of the status of the title is often provided when an abstract is unavailable or lost. The seller normally pays the fees for preparation of these documents.

A lender often requires a buyer to purchase **title insurance** because it protects the lender's interest if the title is later found faulty. A *separate* title insurance policy must be purchased by homeowners who wish to insure their own interest. Policies for homeowners usually cover only the amount of the down payment (the beginning equity) rather than any appreciating equity occurring over the years. Premiums for title policies vary among title companies. The one-time charge at closing may amount to 0.25 percent of the amount of the loan for each policy ($200 in our example).

In areas where real estate transfers are frequent, the wise money manager might want to ask a title insurance company about a **reissue rate.** This type of policy carries a lower-rate premium because the property history has been checked in recent years. Some homeowners do not purchase title insurance for themselves, assuming that the title insurance company will successfully fight any claims; this assumption may not be correct, however.

The Services of an Attorney

About half of all home buyers hire an attorney to represent them during closing to review all documents and provide advice. Attorney fees commonly amount to 0.5 percent of the purchase price of the home, although some attorneys do this work for as little as 0.25 percent. (The attorney's fee is $300 in our example.)

Miscellaneous Costs

When a prospective mortgage borrower applies for a loan, the lender may charge a **loan application fee** to process the application. In addition, a credit report normally must be compiled before a home buyer can obtain a loan; the borrower pays the fee for this report. **Recording fees** are charged to transfer ownership documents in the county courthouse. An **appraisal fee** may be required for a professionally prepared, fair market estimate of the value of the property by an objective party. If you are charged an appraisal fee, you have the right to receive a copy of the appraisal. A **survey** is sometimes required to certify the specific boundaries of the lot. Occasionally, fees may be charged for termite and radon inspections. Finally, separate **notary fees** may be charged for the services of those legally qualified to certify (or notarize) signatures.

Numerous miscellaneous expenses are involved in buying a home and paying the many service providers who take part in the transaction. The real estate agent often makes the arrangements for these service providers in return for a referral fee. Always ask the agent about the nature of such relationships. You are under no obligation to use a service provider arranged by the agent. The costs for most home-buying expenses are subject to negotiation, and the wise financial manager shops for better prices whenever possible. (Table 9.7 shows sample fee amounts.)

The federal Real Estate Settlement Procedures Act requires that the borrower be given a "good faith estimate" of all specific closing costs within three days of making a mortgage loan application. Each borrower also must receive a settlement information booklet that explains many details of the closing process. Depending on state laws, closing costs may vary from 1 percent of the mortgage loan amount up to 4 or 5 percent.

Home Warranty Insurance

All homes for sale carry some type of implied warranty giving an unspoken and unwritten assurance of a certain level of quality and functionality that an ordinary buyer has a right to expect. In some states, home sellers must complete a form verifying the condition of home features and major mechanical equipment. Although the heating unit and air conditioner should work at the time the buyer purchases the home, for example, completion of this form does not mean that they must still be working two years later. A seller who knowingly hides serious defects might be liable, but the buyer will have to hire an attorney and sue to prove this point. Many home builders provide an express warranty for one year on the new homes they sell. If the builder goes out of business or becomes bankrupt, however, the buyer may have little recourse in enforcing any warranty, whether implied or expressed.

Home warranty insurance provides another option for the homeowner and operates much like a service contract (discussed in Chapter 8). Home warranty insurance on existing homes is sold by insurance companies through real estate agents for a one-time premium of perhaps $200 to $800. For new homes, both builders and insurance companies may offer home warranty insurance. Participating builders pay an initial warranty insurance premium (usually for the first two years) on all of their homes, plus a service fee for each year that the warranty remains in effect. These costs are incorporated into the sale price of each home. The builder is responsible for repairs during the first year or two, and the insurance company is responsible for the remaining term (usually eight more years). Usually the homeowner must pay the first $35–$200 of any repair. Like service contracts, these home warranties are only as good as the financial condition of the builder and insurance company. As little as 30 cents of the average premium dollar actually goes toward paying for repairs. A little-known benefit of having a mortgage loan insured by the FHA or guaranteed by the VA is that newly built homes have a one-year warranty against the builder failing to meet specifications. Furthermore, defects that seriously affect livability can be repaired at government expense during the first four years of ownership.

Special Considerations in Home Buying

A **real estate broker (agent)** is a person licensed by a state to provide advice and assistance, for a fee, to buyers or sellers of real estate. Real estate brokers who are members of the National Association of Realtors® often use the registered trademark of **Realtor®** to describe themselves. If you are unfamiliar with housing in an area or if you need special financing arrangements to pay for your housing, the services of a Realtor could prove invaluable. In addition, real estate brokers and agents often represent good sources of information about rental housing.

Brokers typically earn a commission of 5 to 7 percent on the sale price of a home. Recently **flat-fee brokers,** who charge a flat fee for their services rather than a percentage commission, have emerged in the real estate market. The seller—not the buyer—typically pays the commission or fee.

Almost any agent can show you housing that is **listed** (under contract with the seller and the broker) by the realty firm. In addition, many communities have a **multiple-listing service,** which is an information and referral network among real estate brokers allowing properties listed with a particular broker to be shown by all other brokers.* (This service also may be called an **open listing**.) The broker's legal obligation is to the party that will pay his or her fee or commission (generally the seller). Buyers should be aware of this potential conflict of interest, and hire their own broker if they need such services.

The steps in home buying closely resemble the planned buying steps outlined in Chapter 8. The actual search may take several months. Special emphasis should be paid to finding a home that represents a good value and that has solid market potential for many years to come. Special attention will also need to be paid to five steps: (1) shopping for a mortgage; (2) fitting the cost of buying into your budget; (3) negotiating; (4) shopping for a mortgage loan; and (5) signing your name on closing day.

Shopping for a Mortgage

At the same time you are shopping for the home itself, you should be talking with lenders to get a good idea of the mortgage terms available in your community. At this stage, a goal of shopping for a mortgage is to determine if you qualify for credit in the price range of homes that you desire given your intended down payment (see the box on page 240). A second goal is to find the lowest APR for loans available to you.† Although real estate agents often recommend lenders, they may be receiving a referral fee for steering potential buyers to a specific lender. Mortgage brokers arrange about one-half of all mortgage loans today. The fee charged by the broker may be paid by the lender or, if paid by the borrower, is offset generally by lower closing costs assessed by the lender.

---

* Multiple-listing information for communities is increasingly being posted to the Internet, complete with photographs of the homes. You can access these postings at *www.realtor.com*.

† At least two services providing information on sources of low APR loans are available: HSH Associates [(800) 873-2837, *www.hsh.com*] and Mortgage Market Information Services [(800) 509-4636, *www.interest.com*].

The Best Way to Designate Home Ownership

When buying a home, it is important to consider the names that should go on the title. Couples buying a home should generally put the ownership in both names, in an arrangement known as **joint tenancy with right of survivorship.** This form of ownership means that if one of the parties should die, the other would have clear title to the entire property. Otherwise, the home could be tied up in probate. Joint ownership is also important in case of divorce because the home can automatically become part of the marital property subject to court action to arrive at a fair property settlement. An exception occurs in cases where one or both spouses bring prior ownership of housing into a marriage. Premarital assets are considered separable property in the event of a divorce. When a home is a premarital asset, it is wise to seek legal advice. It may be appropriate to use a prenuptial agreement to clearly establish inheritance interests in the event of the death of the owner or a divorce.

Fitting the Home to Your Budget

The wise financial manager adds a few more budget items when considering buying a home. For starters, some estimate ought to be made for maintenance, which could range from $15 to $20 monthly for a small owned apartment to $100 or more for a single-family dwelling. Buyers of new homes pay on average more than $7000 and buyers of existing homes more than $2500 on such things as furnishings and yard improvements in the first year. It may be helpful to estimate the costs of utilities as well. The previous owner may agree to show you utility receipts for the past year or two with which to develop your estimates.

Negotiating

It is essential that you be prepared to negotiate the terms of a home purchase. Sellers generally put a price on the property that is 5 to 10 percent higher than what they expect to receive. Therefore, you probably should make an offer to buy that is somewhat lower than the asking price. Perhaps $10,000 to $20,000 is at stake here.

Make an Offer to Buy Once you have selected the home you wish to purchase, you will make an offer to the seller. The written offer to purchase real estate is called a **purchase offer,** or an **offer to purchase.** Of course, you will specify a price, but other aspects of the sale may be included in your offer as well. Examples of conditions you might want to list include: seller-paid termite and radon inspections; certification of the plumbing, heating, cooling, and electrical systems; inclusion of the living room drapes and kitchen appliances; and, most importantly, financing terms approved by your lender.

When you make an offer, you need to give the seller some **earnest money** as a deposit to ensure that the seller will not sell the house to someone else while you are negotiating. Make sure that your earnest money is protected by a **contingency clause** in the purchase offer that stipulates that the seller refund the earnest money if you cannot obtain satisfactory financing within a specified time period, usually 30 days. This clause protects you if lending conditions suddenly become unfavorable or if you are turned down for a loan. Earnest money is usually kept in an escrow account. Of course, if you simply change your mind about buying, you may forfeit your earnest money.

Respond to a Counteroffer   Most people who sell their homes do not accept the first offer. They assume that if a buyer is willing to make a formal offer, then he or she may be willing to pay a few thousand dollars more. The seller might make you an official **counteroffer**, which is a legal offer to sell (or buy) a home at a different price and perhaps with conditions different from those of the original offer. If a seller is willing to make a counteroffer, then he or she may also be willing to sell at a slightly lower price. Thus, if you then make a counteroffer falling between the two prices, a sale will usually result. On the other hand, if you push the seller too far, you risk having the seller back out of the negotiations altogether. Remember that while such dickering is going on, the seller could be receiving offers from other prospective buyers. In any event, the seller may want you to believe that other offers are forthcoming.

Sign a Purchase Contract   A **purchase contract** or **sales contract** is the formal legal document that outlines the actual agreement that results from the real estate negotiations. It includes the agreed-on price and a list of conditions that the seller has agreed to accept. It is wise to use preprinted forms available from real estate professionals and attorneys because they often include protective clauses (e.g., another contingency clause). When the purchase contract is signed, a seller may request additional earnest money because he or she has agreed to take the home off the market and sell to you. All earnest money will be applied to the down payment on the home at closing.

Applying for a Mortgage Loan

Only after you sign a purchase contract will you formally apply for a mortgage loan on the specific home you have selected. At that point you must be given a **good-faith estimate** of all of the points, fees, and charges that will be required when the deal is finally closed. The financial institution usually approves or disapproves the loan within a few days. Your exact interest rate may be the current rate at the time of application or the rate at the time of closing.

If you expect rates to rise between the time you apply for the loan and the actual closing, you may wish to obtain a **mortgage lock-in**. This agreement includes a lender's promise to hold a certain interest rate (and possibly the number of points) for a specified period of time. It may be part of, but is not the same as, a **loan commitment**, which is a lender's promise to grant a loan.

The same legal protections against unfair discrimination that apply to credit in general (see Chapter 6) also apply to mortgage lending. The Federal Community Reinvestment Act dictates that most lenders meet guidelines requiring that a portion of the loans granted serve the local community. As with other types of credit, lenders increasingly use credit scoring to decide among applicants. Different scoring programs are used, however, because the characteristics of persons who tend to default on mortgages are somewhat different than for other types of loans. It is a good idea to obtain copies of your credit report from the major credit reporting agencies at the start so you can clear up any errors before the loan application process begins. Some lenders offer so-called **performance loans** to borrowers with less-than-optimal credit records. Under this arrangement, the mortgage loan is granted at a slightly higher interest rate that will be lowered if the borrower shows good repayment behavior after two years.

Signing Your Name on Closing Day

The buyer and seller and their representatives generally meet in the lender's office on closing day and sign all required documents. A key item is the **uniform settlement statement**, which lists all of the fees to be paid at the closing. You have the right to see this statement one business day before the closing so that you can avoid surprises and can compare the fees with the good-faith estimate provided earlier. Challenge all discrepancies. The buyer must be prepared to write several checks, including one for the purchase price itself. The middle column of Table 9.7 lists all of the items that are addressed during the closing. Closing costs (plus the $15,000 down payment) in the illustration amounted to $19,595.

Selling a Home: A Lesson in Role Reversal

> **6** Identify some important concerns in the process of selling a home.

Although most of this chapter deals with buying a home, important considerations also arise when selling a home. Generally it helps to do some minor painting, cleaning, and repairing before listing your home for sale. It is important to understand that sellers must disclose known defects in their home to their real estate agent and to potential buyers. In the following discussion, we will examine the pros and cons of listing your home with a broker, note some of the costs of selling, highlight some dangers of seller financing, and consider when it is smart to refinance a mortgage.

Should You List with a Broker or Sell a Home Yourself?

Knowing that the sales commission to a broker on a $100,000 home could easily be $6000 provides motivation for some homeowners to consider selling the home themselves. The key is to know what price to ask for your home. Asking too little could cost you much more than the commission paid to a broker.

Many homeowners begin by contacting a few brokers to get their opinions on how much the home is worth. Brokers are often quite willing to give their opinions, because the homeowner might list the home with them if it does not sell quickly. A for-sale sign on your lawn and about $200 in advertising should keep your telephone ringing for a month or so with all types of inquiries. If your home does not sell by then, you might consider listing it with a broker.

Brokers require that homeowners sign a **listing agreement** permitting them to list the property exclusively or with a multiple-listing service. A multiple-listing service may work best because it allows every broker in the community to show and sell the home. Brokers are invaluable in **qualifying prospective buyers**—keeping people away who want to visit homes they simply cannot afford and distinguishing between serious buyers and people who are just looking. If your broker cannot find a buyer within 60 days, you should consider signing an agreement with another broker who might be more aggressive in advertising and selling your property. If a sale occurs (or begins) during the time period of the listing agreement, you must pay a commission to the broker for any sale to a buyer not listed as an exception in the listing agreement.

Selling Carries Its Own Costs

The largest selling cost is the broker's commission. Sellers typically are unaware that many brokers will negotiate their commission. Most sellers also pay for a title search, and some may pay for a professional appraisal as well.

Many home sellers have an existing loan that carries an interest rate below current market rates. A low rate could make it much easier to sell a home through loan assumption rather than making the buyer obtain his or her own mortgage, but only if the original mortgage loan agreement does not include a **due-on-sale clause.** Such a clause requires that the mortgage loan be paid off if the home is sold. It can impose a burden on the seller because it prohibits a buyer from assuming the mortgage loan. Avoid this clause, if possible, when buying because it eliminates one selling option. If you are unclear about your present mortgage loan clause, ask your lender for clarification.

 The Different Types of Real Estate Agents

Most home buyers use a real estate agent in their search for a home. Buyers should understand that a real estate agent can play three possible roles.

The **listing agent** is the party with whom the seller signs the listing agreement. The listing agent advertises the property, shows it to prospective buyers, and assists the seller in negotiations. He or she receives a commission when the home is sold and owes the seller undivided loyalty.

A **selling agent** is any real estate agent that seeks out buyers for a home. Obviously, listing agents play this role, but any real estate agent can search for buyers for a property. Buyers who approach a real estate agent to help them look for a house need to understand that they are working with a selling agent, because selling agents share in the commission paid to the listing agent. Because the home seller pays this commission, the selling agent owes the *seller* undivided loyalty.

Home buyers who seek those same obligations from their agent require the services of a **buyer's agent** (or **broker**) who serves as the buyer's representative in the real estate negotiations and transaction.

Why is this distinction important? Consider the example of a buyer who has asked a selling agent to help him find a house. During negotiations, the potential buyer decides to offer $175,000 for a house with an asking price of $189,000 but tells the selling agent that he would be willing to go as high as $180,000. The selling agent would be *legally obligated* to tell the seller of this $180,000 figure.

A **prepayment fee** may be required for some mortgages. This fee is designed to discourage people from refinancing a mortgage every time that interest rates drop. Most mortgage loans are paid off before maturity because people move and must sell their homes. Some mortgage loan contracts include a clause that specifies a prepayment fee or penalty, which can range 1 to 3 percent of the original mortgage loan. On an $80,000 mortgage loan, for example, the charge might vary from $800 to $2400.

Many local communities assess **real estate transfer taxes.** These special taxes are assessed on the seller and possibly the buyer based on the purchase price of the home or the equity the seller has in the home. Tax rates can be as

---

When Is It Smart to Refinance a Mortgage?

The following example illustrates how to determine whether mortgage refinancing is wise. The original mortgage for $89,000 was obtained ten years ago at an 11 percent interest rate for 30 years. The monthly payment is $847.57. After ten years the principal owed has declined to $82,113.67. If interest rates for new mortgages are now 9 percent, the owner could take out a new mortgage at the lower rate. Borrowing $82,113.67 for 20 years at 9 percent saves approximately $109 per month ($847.57 − $738.80). Note, however, that refinancing brings up-front costs, including a possible prepayment penalty on the old mortgage and closing costs for the new mortgage. The question then becomes whether these costs would be more than offset by the monthly savings.

The following worksheet provides a means for estimating whether refinancing offers an advantage. The worksheet compares the future value of the reduced monthly payments (line 5) with the future value of the money used to pay the up-front costs of refinancing (line 8). The homeowner would need to estimate the number of months he or she expects to own the home after refinancing. Given an estimate of four years in this example, net savings would be $743 (subtracting line 8 from line 5), and it would appear that refinancing would benefit the owner.

Decision Factor	Example Amounts	Your Figures
1. Current monthly payment	$ 848	_____
2. New monthly payment	739	_____
3. Annual saving (#1 − #2 × 12)	1308	_____
4. Additional years you expect to live in the house	4	_____
5. Future value of an account balance after 4 years if the annual savings were invested at 3% after taxes (using Appendix A.3)	5472	_____
6. Prepayment penalty on current loan (if any)	1000	_____
7. Closing costs for new loan	3200	_____
8. Future value of an account balance after 4 years if the prepayment penalty and closing costs ($4200) had been invested instead at 3% after taxes (using Appendix A.1)	4729	_____
9. Net saving after 49 months (#5 − #8)	743	_____

high as 4 percent. When paid by the seller, they may affect the price that the seller is willing to accept for the home.

Be Wary of Seller Financing

Some sellers who have had trouble marketing their homes have successfully resorted to many variations of seller financing, although difficulties can arise with these options. Suppose you have a home worth $100,000 with a mortgage loan balance of $45,000 and equity of $55,000. The buyer assumes the existing mortgage loan, puts up $20,000 in cash, and takes out a second mortgage from you of $35,000 for five years. At closing, the broker receives a commission of $6000, and you come away with only $14,000 cash—a small sum to use in making a down payment on another home. Also, seller financing carries a risk that the buyer may not be able to make the second mortgage payments to you and could potentially default on the loan.

Summary

1. Renters must consider the costs of rent, a security deposit, and related items. Home buyers can choose among single-family dwellings, condominiums, cooperative housing, manufactured housing, and mobile homes. Renters generally pay out less money in terms of cash flow in the short run, while owners have tax advantages and generally see an increase in the market value of their homes, making them better off financially in the long term.

2. The decision to spend a certain amount of money on housing should be based on careful budget analysis and an understanding of the rules of thumb used to determine the amount one can afford to spend on purchasing housing.

3. Mortgage loans for homes are amortized. Amortization is the process of gradually paying off a mortgage through a series of periodic payments to a lender, with a portion of each payment going to pay off the principal and another portion to pay interest owed. Conventional mortgages and adjustable-rate mortgages are the most common types of housing loans. Numerous alternative types of mortgages are available that have reduced the importance of the long-term, fixed-rate mortgage loan in addition to providing ways to keep the monthly payment as low as possible.

4. The mathematics of buying a home shows that you must consider more than just the down payment and monthly mortgage payment. A number of additional costs are involved at the point of the closing and every month, including taxes and insurance, title insurance, and closing costs. The wise financial planner tries to avoid becoming "house poor" by carefully estimating all housing costs.

5. Four steps that expedite the process of buying a home include: (1) fitting the cost of buying into your budget, (2) negotiating, (3) shopping for a mortgage loan, and (4) signing your name on closing day.

6. When selling a home, it is wise to consider the pros and cons of listing with a real estate broker versus selling the home yourself, the extent of selling costs, the dangers of seller financing, and the impact of income taxes.

Key Words & Concepts

adjustable-rate mortgage (ARM)   *245*
amortization   *241*
closing   *251*

Questions for Thought & Discussion

1. Why do landlords require that renters pay a security deposit?

2. Explain the purpose and value of a lease.

3. List some tenant rights, and explain how they work to the advantage of the tenant.

4. Distinguish among the types of owned housing.

5. List the purposes of the homeowner's fee associated with condominium ownership.

6. Distinguish between manufactured housing and mobile homes.

7. Define the term "amortization."

8. Illustrate how housing buyers pay less than renters when taxes and appreciation of housing values are considered.

9. Give supporting evidence for the statement, "Renters do better financially on an annual cash-flow basis than home buyers."

10. What are the two rules of thumb for purchased housing affordability?

11. Illustrate the two ways that homeowners build equity in their homes.

12. Explain how the principal of a home loan is reduced as a result of monthly payments made over several years. In your explanation, describe what happens to principal and interest amounts with each subsequent payment.

13. Give one reason for and one reason against using a longer maturity period to extend payback of a housing loan.

14. Describe the conventional mortgage.

15. Why have adjustable-rate mortgages become so popular?

16. What are the consequences of negative amortization?

17. Who might benefit most from a reverse-annuity mortgage?

18. Describe what happens when a home is purchased with an assumable mortgage.

19. Distinguish between a home-equity line of credit and a home-equity installment loan.

20. What are the benefits and pitfalls of seller financing?

21. Identify the components of PITI.

22. Who is protected by private mortgage insurance?

23. Explain why lenders use points in home loans. Who is responsible for paying points?

24. Distinguish between the four types of deeds used to transfer the title to real property.

25. Explain the purpose of warranty insurance.

26. What benefit does a seller receive from using a multiple-listing service?

27. Besides the price, what other items might be included in an offer to purchase real estate?

28. Define a real estate purchase contract.

29. What occurs at a real estate closing?

30. Give one reason for and one reason against a homeowner selling a home personally rather than through a real estate broker.

31. What disadvantage is there to home buyers who use a listing agent or selling agent to look for a home? How can they overcome this disadvantage?

DECISION-MAKING CASES

Case 1   Grant and Richard Weigh the Benefits and Costs of Buying versus Renting

Grant Higginbott and Richard Van Ness of Binghamton, New York, are trying to decide whether they should rent or purchase housing. Both men are single. Grant favors buying and Richard leans toward renting, and both seem able to justify their particular choice. Grant thinks that the tax advantage is a very good reason for buying. Richard, however, believes that cash flow is so much better when renting. See if you can help them make their decision.

(a) Does the home buyer enjoy a tax advantage? Explain.

(b) Discuss Richard's belief that cash flow is better with renting.

(c) Suggest some reasons why Grant might consider renting rather than purchasing housing.

(d) Suggest some reasons why Richard might consider buying rather than renting housing.

(e) Is there a clear-cut basis for deciding either to rent or to buy housing? Why or why not?

Case 2   Patricia Chooses among Alternative Mortgage Options

Patricia Rafferty of Boston, Massachusetts, has examined several options for new home financing. She has been favoring alternative mortgage plans because of the current high mortgage rates. Patricia hopes that the market rate will drop in a couple of years.

(a) What broad concerns are present with alternative mortgages?

(b) What financing option would you suggest for Patricia, assuming she is able to use any type of mortgage available? Why?

Case 3   Jeremy Decides to Sell His Home Himself

Jeremy Jorgensen of Salt Lake City, Utah, is concerned about the costs involved in selling his home, so he has decided to sell his house himself rather than pay a broker to do it.

(a) What challenges will Jeremy encounter, if any, when selling his own home?

(b) How would you advise Jeremy if he asked you whether he should sell the house himself or list with a broker? Explain your answer.

(c) Would Jeremy really save money by selling his home himself if he considers his time as part of his costs? Why or why not?

(d) Can you suggest any ways that Jeremy could reduce the selling costs without doing the selling himself? Explain.

Financial Math Questions

1. Walt and Mary Jensen of Atlanta, Georgia, both of whom are in their late twenties, currently are renting an unfurnished two-bedroom apartment for $500 per month, with an additional $80 for utilities and $10 for insurance. They have found a condominium they can buy for $100,000 with a 20 percent down payment and a 30-year, 7 percent mortgage. Principal and interest payments are estimated at $532 per month with property taxes of $800 per year and a homeowner's insurance premium of $250 per year. Closing costs are estimated at $2400. The monthly homeowner's association fee is $75, and utility costs are estimated at $100 per month. The Jensens have a combined income of $35,000 per year, with take-home pay of $2100 per month. They are in the 28 percent tax bracket, pay $225 per month on an installment contract (ten payments left), and have $39,000 in savings and investments.

   (a) Can the Jensens afford to buy the condo? Use the results from the *Garman/Forgue* Web site or the information on page 240 to support your answer. Also, consider the effect of the purchase on their savings and monthly budget.

(b) Walt and Mary think that their monthly housing costs would be lower the first year if they bought the condo. Do you agree? Support your answer.

(c) If they buy, how much will Walt and Mary have left in savings to pay for moving expenses?

(d) Available financial information suggests that the mortgage rates might drop over the next few weeks. If the Jensens wait until the rates drop to 6.0 percent, how much will they save on their monthly mortgage payment? Use the information in Table 9.4 or the *Garman/Forgue* Web site to calculate the payment.

2. Steve and Marcie Moore of Holyoke, Massachusetts, have an annual income of $60,000.

(a) Using a 28 percent front-end ratio, what is the total annual and monthly expenditures for which they would qualify?

(b) Using a 41 percent back-end ratio, what is the monthly mortgage payment they could afford given that they have an automobile loan payment of $269, a student loan payment of $150, and credit card payments of $100? (Hint: Subtract these amounts from the total monthly affordable payments for their income to determine the amount left over to spend on a mortgage.)

(c) If mortage interest rates are around 8 percent and the Moores want a 30-year mortage, use Table 9.4 on page 243 to estimate how much they could borrow given your answer to (b).

3. Phillip Guadet of Monroe, Louisiana, has been renting a two-bedroom house for several years. He pays $650 per month in rent for the home and pays $200 per year in property and liability insurance. The owner of the house wants to sell it, and Phillip is considering making an offer. The owner wants $78,000 but Phillip thinks he could get the house for $75,000 and could use his $15,000 in 6 percent certificates of deposit that are ready to mature for the down payment. Phillip has talked to his banker and

could get a 7.5 percent mortgage loan for 25 years to finance the remainder of the purchase price. The banker advised Phillip that he would reduce his debt by $850 during the first year of the loan. Property taxes on the house are $1400 per year. Phillip estimates that he would need to upgrade his property and liability insurance to $390 per year and would incur about $1000 in costs the first year for maintenance. Property values are increasing at about 1.5 percent per year in the neighborhood. Phillip is in the 28 percent marginal tax bracket.

(a) Use Table 9.4 to calculate the monthly mortgage payment for the mortgage loan that Phillip would need.

(b) How much interest would Phillip pay during the first year of the loan?

(c) Use the Decision-Making Worksheet "Should You Buy or Rent?" on page 236 to determine whether Phillip would be better off buying or renting based on cash flow.

(d) Use the Decision-Making Worksheet "Should You Buy or Rent?" on page 236 to determine whether Phillip would be better off buying or renting after considering the effect of taxes and appreciation.

4. Kevin Raymond of Rochester Hills, Michigan, has owned his home for 15 years and expects to live in it for five more years. He originally borrowed $105,000 at 10 percent interest for 30 years to buy the home. He still owes $85,750 on the loan. Interest rates have fallen to 7.5 percent, and Kevin is considering refinancing the loan for 15 years. He would have to pay 2 points in closing costs on the new loan with no prepayment penalty on the current loan.

(a) What is Kevin's current monthly payment?

(b) Calculate the monthly payment on the new loan.

(c) Advise Kevin on whether he should refinance his mortgage using the Decision-Making Worksheet "When Is It Smart to Refinance a Mortgage?" on page 261.

MONEY MATTERS: LIFE-CYCLE CASES

Victor and Maria Hernandez Learn about Real Estate Agents

Victor and Maria have been thinking about selling their home and buying a house with more yard space so that they can indulge their interest in gardening. Before they make such a decision, they want to explore the market to see what might be available and in what price ranges. They will then list their house with a real estate agent and begin searching in earnest for a new home.

1. What services could a real estate agent provide for the couple, and what types of agents would represent them as they sell their current home?

2. A friend has advised them that they really need a buyer's agent for the purchase of the new home. Explain to the Hernandezes the difference between buyer's and seller's agents.

The Johnsons Decide to Buy a Condominium

Belinda Johnson's parents and maternal grandmother have combined their finances and presented Harry and Belinda with $15,000 with which to purchase a condominium. The Johnsons have shopped and found two that they like very much. The financial alternatives are presented below, and data for condo 1 are summarized in the accompanying table on page 267.

1. Study the financial information for condo 1 in the table and create a similar table for condo 2 using the financial information given.

2. Which plan has the lowest total closing costs? The highest?

3. If the Johnsons had enough spare cash to make the 20 percent down payment (which they do not), would you recommend lender C or D? Why?

4. Assuming that the Johnsons will need about $2500 for moving-in costs (in addition to closing costs) and they must choose between developers A and B, which would you recommend? Why?

5. Choose the best option for the Johnsons, and explain briefly why you recommend that developer or lender.

6. Assume that after five years the interest for the Johnsons' ARM has jumped to the maximum of 13 percent with a remaining balance of $74,500 for 25 years. Use the information in Table 9.4 or on the *Garman/Forgue* Web site to calculate their monthly payment. What would the payment be if the rate dropped to 7 percent?

Financing Details on Two Condominiums Available to the Johnsons

Condo 1: Price, $85,000 Developer A will finance with a 10 percent down payment and a 30-year, 8 percent ARM loan with 2 points as a loan origination fee. The initial monthly payment for principal and interest is $561.33 ($76,500 after the down payment; 76.5 × $7.3376). After one year, the rate rises to 9 percent, with a principal plus interest payment of $614.59.* At that point, the rate can go up or down as much as 2 percent per year, depending on the cost of an index of mortgage funds. There is a cap of 5 percent over the life of the loan. Taxes are estimated to be about $600, and the homeowner's insurance premium should be about $240 annually. A mortgage insurance premium of $48 per month must be paid monthly.

Condo 2: Price, $81,000 Developer B will finance with a 5 percent down payment and a conventional 30-year, 9 percent loan with 3 points as a loan origination fee. The monthly payment for principal and interest is $619.18. Taxes are estimated at about $552, and the homeowner's insurance premium should be about $240 annually. A

---

* Note that the loan balance would be $78,861 at the end of the first year. Thus, the payment would be slightly less than that required to pay $76,500 at 9 percent over 29 years or even 30 years.

Condo 1: Price, $85,000; Taxes, $600; Insurance, $240

	Developer A	Lender C	Lender D	Lender E
Loan Term and Type	30-year ARM	30-year CON	15-year CON	20-year REN*
Interest Rate	8%	10%	9%	7.5%
Down Payment	$ 8,500	$17,000	$17,000	$ 8,500
Loan Amount	$76,500	$68,000	$68,000	$76,500
Points	$1,530	$ 680	$ 680	$2,295
Other Closing Costs	—	—	—	—
Total Closing Costs	$10,030	$17,680	$17,680	$10,795
P&I Payment	$561.33	$596.75	$689.70	$616.28
PMI	$48	$ 0	$ 0	$44
Taxes	$50	$50	$50	$50
Insurance	$20	$20	$20	$20
Total Monthly Payments	$679.33	$666.75	$759.70	$730.28

* Renegotiable every five years.

mortgage insurance premium of $385 must be paid in full at the closing.

Other Lenders   Lender C offers a conventional 30-year mortgage loan at 10 percent with a 20 percent down payment on either condo and a 1 point loan origination fee. On condo 1, the monthly payment for principal and interest will be $596.75. On condo 2, it amounts to $568.67. Lender D offers a 15-year mortgage loan at 9 percent with a 20 percent down payment on either condo and a 1 point loan origination fee. On condo 1, the monthly payment will amount to $689.70; on condo 2, it will be $657.24. Lender E offers a 20-year mortgage with a renegotiable rate (every five years) at 7.5 percent with a 10 percent down payment on either condo and a 3 point loan origination fee. Initial monthly payments would be $616.28 on condo 1 and $578.28 on condo 2.

Exploring the World Wide Web of Personal Finance

To complete these exercises, go to the *Garman/Forgue* Web site at

www.hmco.com/college/business/

Select Personal Finance. Click on the exercise link for this chapter and answer the questions that appear on the Web page.

1. Visit the Web site for Hugh Chou of Washington University in St. Louis, where you will find a calculator that determines the monthly payment for any mortgage loan given the time period, interest rate, and loan amount. Assume you wish to borrow $100,000 to buy a home. Vary the time period and interest rate of the loan to see how these variations affect your monthly payment.

2. Visit the Web site for the Bank Rate Monitor, where you will find information on mortgage interest rates around the United States. View the information for the lenders in a

large city nearest your home. How does the information compare with your current credit card account(s)? How do the rates in the city you selected compare with other rates found in the United States?

3. Visit the Web site for Hugh Chou of Washington University in St. Louis, where you will find a calculator to convert a mortgage interest rate to an after-tax rate to adjust for the tax deductibility of mortgage interest. Calculate the effective after-tax interest rate for the best mortgage rate you found in Exercise #2. If you did not complete that exercise, use an 8 percent rate and your state and federal marginal tax rates.

4. Visit the Web site for HomePath, where you will find a Web page calculator that helps you determine the amount you can afford for the purchase of a home given your income and funds available for a down payment, closing costs, and other home-buying expenses. Enter the data requested for your current situation. What does the calculator tell you about your housing affordability? Change the entered data for some point in the future when you project a better finan-

cial situation for yourself. How do the results change?

5. Visit the Web site for Legg Mason, where you will find a Web page that allows you to generate an amortization schedule for a mortgage loan. Enter a loan amount, interest rate, time period, and other data to generate a schedule for a hypothetical or real loan.

6. Visit the Web site for *Kiplinger's Personal Finance* magazine, where you can compare two loans with varying interest rates, time periods, closing costs, points, and other variables. Compare two hypothetical loan situations.

7. Visit the Web site for the National Association of Realtors, where you can search for owned housing in various locales around the United States. Look for housing in your local area of a type that would interest you and in your price range. Were you able to find housing that meets your criteria? Also search for similar housing in one of the high- and low-cost metropolitan areas as indicated in Table 9.1 and compare the results to the housing found in your area.

PART THREE

Income and Asset Protection

Risk Management and Property / Liability Insurance

10

OBJECTIVES

After reading this chapter, you should be able to:

1 Define risk and apply the risk-management process to personal financial affairs.

2 Define insurance terminology and explain the relationship between risk and insurance.

3 Design a homeowner's insurance program to meet your needs and keep the cost of the plan to a minimum.

4 Design an automobile insurance program to meet your needs and keep the cost of the plan to a minimum.

5 Describe property and liability insurance policies designed to meet needs other than those related to housing and automobiles.

6 Outline the steps to make a claim against a property or liability insurance policy.

To this point, we have focused on ways to maximize financial resources and use such resources to achieve personal goals. The next step is to protect the resources and assets you attain from the possibility of financial loss. You can achieve some of this protection by locking doors, minimizing fire hazards, and driving safely. Nevertheless, you need additional protection from the risk of financial loss associated with owning an automobile and home, health care, financially supporting yourself and dependents, and many other aspects of life.

This chapter begins by discussing the topic of risk management, of which insurance represents just one component. Next we cover the concept of insurance—its definition and its associated terminology. Central to this discussion is the relationship between risk and insurance. We then discuss two major forms of property and liability insurance—homeowner's insurance and automobile insurance—before turning to several specialized types of property and liability insurance. The final section examines the process of collecting from an insurance company when a property or liability loss occurs.

Risk and Risk Management

Risk is uncertainty about the outcome of a situation or event. It arises out of the possibility that the outcome will differ from what is expected. In the area of potential financial losses, risk consists of uncertainty about whether the financial loss will occur and how large the loss will be.

The Nature of Risk

Two types of risk exist. **Speculative risk** is present when a situation offers a potential for gain as well as loss. Investing involves speculative risk. **Pure risk** exists when there is no potential for gain, only a possibility of loss. Fires, automobile accidents, illness, and theft are examples of events involving pure risk. Insurance can be bought to reduce pure risk but not to address speculative risk.

Defining risk as uncertainty differs somewhat from the more common definition of risk as odds, chance, or probability. This difference is subtle but very important. An event with a 95 percent chance of occurring is highly likely to occur. Thus, both uncertainty and risk are low. An event with a 0.000001 percent chance of occurring is highly likely *not* to occur. Thus, both uncertainty and risk are low. When an event has a moderate chance of occurring—5 percent, for example—the uncertainty and risk are relatively high, because it is difficult to predict the one person in 20 who will experience the event. In such cases, insurance often represents a wise choice for reducing risk.

People usually have one of three personal reactions to risk. Some people are **risk takers** who are not upset by uncertainty and may even enjoy risky situations. Others are **risk-neutral**, neither fearing nor enjoying risk. Still others are **risk-averse**, being very uncomfortable with risk and avoiding it whenever possible. Chapters 10 through 12, which focus on various types of insurance, will start you on your way to becoming a successful risk manager who keeps a wary eye on both current and future risks.

The Risk-Management Process

Insurance is only one of many ways of handling risk, and it is not always the best choice. **Risk management** is the process of identifying and evaluating situations involving pure risk to determine and implement the appropriate means for its management. The goal is to minimize any risk or potential for risk through advanced awareness and planning. Risk management is designed to make the most efficient before-loss arrangements so as to minimize any after-loss impact on one's financial status. It is an important part of overall personal financial management, in that it preserves the results of other financial-planning efforts. The risk-management process involves five steps: (1) gather information to identify risk exposures and potential losses; (2) evaluate the potential losses; (3) decide on the best ways to handle risk and losses; (4) administer the risk-management program; and (5) periodically evaluate and adjust the program. Table 10.1 on the following page illustrates the steps in the risk-management process.

Step 1: Gather Information to Identify Risk Exposures Sources of risk, called **exposures**, are the items you own and activities in which you engage that

Table 10.1

The Risk-Management Process

Step 1: Gather information to identify your exposures to risks. Determine the source of risk:			
	Possession	**Activity**	**Accompanying Peril**
	Vehicle	Driving	Accident
	House	Smoking	Fire
	Jewelry	Traveling	Theft

Step 2: Evaluate risk and potential losses.	(a) Determine the likely frequency of losses associated with each exposure. (b) Determine the potential severity and magnitude of losses associated with each exposure.
Step 3: Choose among mechanisms for handling the risk exposures and losses.	(a) Avoid risk. (b) Retain risk. (c) Control losses. (d) Transfer risk. (e) Reduce risk.
Step 4: Implement and administer your overall risk-management plan.	(a) Refrain from certain activities. (b) Take extra precautions. (c) Buy insurance.

Step 5: Periodically evaluate the risk-management plan and adjust if necessary.

expose you to potential financial loss. Owning an automobile is a very common exposure. In risk management, you should take an inventory of what you own and what you do to identify your exposures to loss.

You also need to identify the perils that you face. A **peril** is any event that causes a financial loss. Some perils are associated more closely with certain exposures than with others. For example, the theft peril does not apply to a dwelling, but it does apply to the contents of a dwelling.

Step 2: Evaluate Risk and Potential Losses Once you have identified your exposures to risk, you should estimate both loss frequency and loss severity. **Loss frequency** refers to the likely number of times that a loss might occur over a period of time. **Loss severity** describes the potential magnitude of the loss that may occur. An important consideration is the range of potential losses. The average driver will be involved in an accident approximately once every seven years, and the severity of accidents can range from a small "fender bender" to a catastrophic collision with losses in the hundreds of thousands of dollars. The maximum possible loss is an important figure because it can be used to guide the dollar amount of coverage to buy. Figure 10.1 illustrates the relationship between loss frequency and loss severity in risk management.

Step 3: Choose among the Mechanisms for Handling Risk The risk of loss may be handled five major ways: risk avoidance, risk retention, loss control, risk transfer, and risk reduction. Each strategy may be appropriate for some circumstances, and the mix that you choose will depend on the source of the risk, the

Figure 10.1

The Relationship between Severity and Frequency of Loss

	HIGH SEVERITY	LOW SEVERITY
LOW FREQUENCY	Purchase insurance to cover the potentially large losses. Their infrequency will make premiums affordable.	Consider retaining risk because the frequency and severity of loss are both low.
HIGH FREQUENCY	Purchase insurance. Loss control efforts can be useful in reducing the necessarily high premiums.	Retain risk but also budget for losses that are likely to be frequent.

size of the potential loss, your personal reactions to risk, and the financial resources available to pay for losses.

• *Risk Avoidance.* The first, and simplest, way to handle risk is to avoid it. With this approach, you must refrain from owning items or engaging in activities that expose you to possible financial loss. For example, choosing not to own an airplane or not to skydive limits your exposure. Avoiding risk is not always practical, however. You can avoid some of the risk associated with home ownership by renting, for example, but you will lose the benefits of owning a home.

• *Risk Retention.* A second way to handle risk is to retain or accept it while recognizing that certain risks and potential losses are part of everyday life. The risk that your shrubbery may die during a dry spell is such a retained risk. Although this approach might seem somewhat fatalistic, risk retention has an important role to play in risk management. It should be considered when no other method is available, when the worst possible loss is not serious, and when both frequency and severity of losses are highly predictable.

Risk retention is clearly inappropriate in two cases. The first is risk retention because of ignorance. If people do not understand the risks they face, they take no action and engage in risk retention by default. The second is risk retention because of inaction. As an example, many people put off the purchase of life insurance because they consider it to be a morbid, unpleasant task. Such poor uses of risk retention are the opposite of effective risk management.

• *Loss Control.* **Loss control**, the third method of handling risk, is designed to reduce loss frequency and loss severity. For example, installing heavy-duty locks and doors will reduce the frequency of theft losses. Installing fire alarms and smoke detectors cannot prevent fires but will reduce the severity of losses from them. Insurance companies often require loss-control efforts or give discounts to insureds who implement them.

• *Transferring Risk.* A fourth way to handle risk is to transfer it. A **risk transfer** is any arrangement where an insurance company agrees to reimburse you for a financial loss. For example, a professional football team's star running back might take out an insurance policy on his legs. The uncertainty is simply transferred (for a not-so-small fee) from the running back or his team to an insurance company. Insurance represents one method of transferring risk, although not all risk transfers can be classified as insurance. Insurance goes beyond mere risk transfer to the actual reduction of risk.

• *Risk Reduction.* The fifth way to handle risk is to reduce it to acceptable levels. Insurance is used by individual insureds to transfer a substantial portion of their risk to an insurance company, thereby reducing their own level of risk.

Step 4: Administer the Risk-Management Program The fourth step in risk management is to implement and administer the methods you have chosen. For most households, the most significant aspect of risk management is the transfer and reduction of risk through insurance. Types of policies and coverage, dollar amounts of coverage, and sources of insurance protection will form an important part of administering the insurance program.

Personal risk managers often wonder which insurance coverages are the most important. The answer depends on individual circumstances, of course, but some general guidelines do apply. First, never risk a lot for a little. That is, you should not let a large potential loss go uncovered by insurance just to save a few premium dollars. Second, never risk more than you can afford to lose. Insurance coverage can be classified according to the following descriptions:

- *Necessary insurance.* Insurance is a necessity when the potential loss could lead to bankruptcy, destroy accumulated wealth, or destroy one's ability to build wealth. Automobile liability insurance is necessary.

- *Important insurance.* Insurance is important if the potential losses would require the insured to borrow or use a line of credit to pay the loss.

- *Optional insurance.* Insurance could be deemed optional if the likely losses could be covered with current earnings or savings earmarked for emergencies.

Step 5: Evaluate and Adjust the Program The fifth step in risk management is regular review of risk-management efforts. The risks people face in their lives change continually. Therefore, no risk-management plan should be put in place and left alone for long periods of time. For certain exposures, such as ownership of an automobile, an annual review is appropriate. For areas involving life insurance, a review should occur about once every three to five years or whenever family structure and employment situations change. The necessary adjustments should be implemented promptly to reflect the changing scenarios. In reality, a complex pattern of risk-management techniques is used that evolves over the life cycle.

What Is Insurance?

2 Define insurance terminology and explain the relationship between risk and insurance.

Insurance is a mechanism for transferring and reducing pure risk through which a large number of individuals share in the financial losses suffered by members of the group. Insurance protects each individual in the group by replacing an uncertain—and possibly large—financial loss with a certain but relatively small fee. This fee, called the **premium**, includes the individual's share of the group's losses, insurance company reserves set aside to pay future losses, a proportional share of the expenses of administering the insurance plan, and, when the plan is administered by a profit-seeking company, an allowance for profit.

When you purchase insurance, you are buying an insurance policy. An **insurance policy** is a contract between the person buying insurance (the **insured**) and the insurance company. The policy contains language that describes the rights and responsibilities of both parties. To understand the policy, you will need to comprehend its contractual nature and its various sections. It is also necessary to know that different types of losses are covered by different types of insurance policies.

Modern insurance provides a vast and complicated assortment of products designed to protect assets and income. Despite its widespread availability, however, insurance remains one of the least understood purchases most people make. A sound understanding of insurance requires a knowledge of its basic terms and concepts. These meanings will bring insurance into a sharper focus and clarify its role as a protection from financial loss.

Hazards

A **hazard** is any condition that increases the probability that a peril will occur. Driving under the influence of alcohol represents an especially dangerous hazard. Three types of hazards are important in insurance. First, a **physical hazard** is a particular characteristic of the insured person or property that increases the chance of loss. An example of a physical hazard is high blood pressure in a person covered by health insurance. Second, a **morale hazard** exists when a person is indifferent to a peril or does not care if it occurs. For example, such a hazard exists if the insured party, knowing that theft insurance will pay the loss, becomes careless about locking doors and windows. Third, a **moral hazard** exists when a person wants and causes a peril to occur. An example of a moral hazard would include the temptation to cause a loss intentionally so as to collect on an insurance policy. Insurance companies often limit or deny coverage if a loss occurs as a result of a morale or moral hazard.

Financial Loss

A **financial loss** is any decline in the value of income or assets in the present or future. Certain minimum requirements must be met for a financial loss to be insurable—in particular, the loss must be fortuitous, financial, and personal. **Fortuitous losses** are unexpected in terms of both their timing and their magnitude. A loss caused by lightning is fortuitous; a loss caused by a decline in the value of a corporate common stock is not, because it is reasonable to expect stock values to rise and fall. **Financial losses** can be measured objectively in dollars and cents. When you become sick, you suffer as a result of the discomfort, inconvenience, lost wages, and medical bills. Insurance will cover only the lost wages and medical bills, however, because only these losses can be objectively measured. Finally, **personal losses** can be directly attributable to specific individuals or organizations. No insurance is possible to protect against losses affecting society as a whole.

Insurable Interest

To buy insurance, an individual or organization must have an **insurable interest** in the property or person insured. Such an interest exists when a person or organization stands to suffer a financial loss resulting directly from a peril. Thus, you can buy fire insurance on your own home, but you cannot buy it on a friend's home. Nor can you purchase life insurance on a total stranger.

Insurable interest separates insurance and gambling. If you bought insurance on a friend's house, you would actually be gambling because you would gain if the home burned down. Insurance is not gambling because you can buy it only if you stand to suffer a loss—that is, if you have an insurable interest.

The Principle of Indemnity

The **principle of indemnity** states that insurance will pay *no more* than the actual financial loss suffered. For example, an automobile insurance policy will pay only the actual cash value of a stolen automobile. This principle prevents a person from gaining financially from a loss. Thus, if a windstorm causes $500 in damage to a home, the homeowner should not receive more than $500.

The principle of indemnity does not guarantee that insured losses will be totally reimbursed, however. Insurance policies are not open-ended agreements to pay. Every policy includes **policy limits**, which are the maximum dollar amounts that will be paid under the policy. Insurance purchasers must be careful that the policy limits are sufficient to cover potential losses.

Factors That Affect the Cost of Insurance

Specific features of insurance policies are available that can lower your premiums without significantly lowering protection. These features include deductibles, coinsurance, hazard reduction, and loss reduction.

Deductibles are requirements that you pay an initial portion of any loss. For example, automobile collision insurance often includes a $200 deductible. The first $200 of loss to the car must be paid by the insured. The insurer then pays the remainder of the loss, up to the limits of the policy. Most health and property insurance policies also include deductibles. They are sometimes required and sometimes optional, and you usually have a choice of deductible amounts. The higher the deductible, the lower the premium will be. Insurance buyers should seek to obtain protection from large, infrequent losses, not small, predictable losses. Therefore, you should choose the highest deductible that you can afford to cover should a loss occur. The premium saved by selecting a higher deductible can be used to pay for higher policy limits.

Coinsurance is a method by which the insured and the insurer share proportionately in the payment for a loss. For example, health insurance commonly requires that the insured pay 20 percent of a loss and the insurer pay the remaining 80 percent. Substantial premium reductions can be realized through coinsurance, but you must be prepared to pay your share of losses. The following **deductible and coinsurance reimbursement formula** can be used to determine the amount of a loss that will be reimbursed when the policy includes a deductible and a coinsurance clause:

$$R = (1 - CP)(L - D) \qquad (10.1)$$

where

R = **reimbursement** (i.e., the amount the insurance company will pay)
CP = **coinsurance percentage** required of the insured
L = **loss**
D = **deductible**

Assume a health insurance policy with a $100 deductible per hospital stay and a 20 percent coinsurance requirement. If the hospital bill is $1350, the reimbursement will be $1000, calculated as follows:

$$
\begin{aligned}
R &= (1.00 - 0.20)(\$1350 - \$100) \\
&= (0.80)(\$1250) \\
&= \$1000
\end{aligned}
$$

Hazard reduction is action by the insured to reduce the probability of a loss occurring. Insurance companies often offer reduced premiums to insureds who practice hazard reduction—for example, to nonsmokers.

Who Sells Insurance

Sellers of insurance, called **insurance agents**, represent one or more insurance companies. They have the power to enter into, change, and cancel insurance policies on behalf of companies. There are two types of insurance agents: independent agents and exclusive agents.

Independent insurance agents represent two or more insurance companies. They are independent businesspersons who act as third-party links between insurers and insureds. Such agents earn commissions from the companies they represent and will place each insurance customer with the company that they feel best meets the customer's needs. Insurance companies that rely on a sales force of independent insurance agents are called **agency companies.**

Exclusive insurance agents represent only one insurance company for a specific type of insurance. They are often employees of the insurance company they represent. Life insurance, for example, is often sold through exclusive insurance agents.

Not all insurance is sold and serviced through agents. A number of companies are **direct sellers**, marketing their policies through salaried employees, mail-order marketing, newspapers, and even vending machines. Any type of insurance can be sold directly. For the risk manager who knows what coverage he or she needs, some of the lowest insurance premiums can be found with direct sellers.

Choosing among independent agents, exclusive agents, and direct sellers is not an easy task. Each type of seller presents both advantages and disadvantages. Independent agents may provide more personalized service and they can select among several companies to meet a customer's needs. Exclusive agents can provide personalized service as well, but are limited to the policies offered by the one company they represent. Nonetheless, premiums may be lower through exclusive agents because sales commissions tend to be lower.

Many agents have received training and taken tests to receive professional designations such as Chartered Life Underwriter (CLU) in life insurance and Chartered Property and Casualty Underwriter (CPCU) in automobile and homeowner's insurance. These designations can indicate a high level of expertise and professionalism.

Loss reduction is action by the insured to lessen the severity of loss should a peril occur. Smoke alarms and fire extinguishers in the home are examples of loss reduction efforts. These items will not prevent fires, but they may lessen the severity of the loss. Many property insurers offer reduced premiums to insureds who practice loss reduction.

Types of Insurers

An **insurer** is any individual or organization that provides insurance coverage. The major function of an insurer is to combine the premiums paid by the insureds into a fund for the payment of losses. Some insurers seek to make a profit; others operate on a not-for-profit basis.

Make Sense of an Insurance Policy

Insurance policies do not invite casual reading. Consequently, many people fail to read their policies until a loss occurs, only to find that they had misunderstood the terms of the agreement. You can avoid such problems by carefully and systematically reading a policy before you purchase it. Your understanding of the policy provisions can be enhanced if you focus on eight key points:

1. **Perils covered.** Some policies list only the perils that are covered; others cover all perils except those listed. The definition of certain perils may differ from that used in everyday language.

2. **Property covered.** Like perils, the property covered under a policy may be listed individually, or only the excluded property may be listed. When the property is listed individually, any new acquisitions must be added to the policy.

3. **Types of losses covered.** Three types of property losses can occur: (1) the loss of the property itself, (2) extra expenses that may arise because the property is unusable for a period of time, and (3) loss of income if the property was used in the insured's work.

4. **People covered.** Insurance policies may cover only certain individuals. This information is usually contained on the first page of the policy but may be changed subsequently in later sections.

5. **Locations covered.** Where the loss occurs may have a bearing on whether it will be covered. It is especially important to know which locations are not covered.

6. **Time period of coverage.** Policies are generally written to cover specific time periods. Restrictions may exclude coverage during specific times of the day or certain days of the week or year.

7. **Loss control requirements.** Insurance policies often stipulate that certain loss control efforts must be maintained by the insured. For example, coverage on a restaurant may be denied if the owner fails to maintain an adequate fire-extinguishing system.

8. **Amount of coverage.** All insurance policies specify the maximum amount the insurer will pay for various types of losses.

Finally, note that the information on these eight points may be spread throughout a policy. In fact, coverage that appears to be provided in one location actually may be denied elsewhere. Study the entire policy to determine the protection that it actually provides. If necessary, telephone the salesperson or company for clarification.

Stock insurance companies are owned by their stockholders and provide insurance coverage in return for the opportunity to earn a profit for their owners. They sell stock to raise capital, use the proceeds to sell a product or service, and distribute any profits to the owners. These distributed profits are called **investment dividends**.

How Insurance Companies Select from among Applicants

The insurance process begins with an offer by the purchaser in the form of a written or oral application for coverage. Generally, an oral application is followed by a written application. The insurer typically gives temporary acceptance when an applicant submits full or partial payment of the initial premium. This temporary insurance contract, called a **binder**, is either replaced at a later date with a written contract (the policy) or allowed to expire. The application then goes through a process of **underwriting**—that is, the insurer's procedure for deciding which insurance applicants to accept. To describe the process of underwriting, we must first discuss how insurance rates are set.

An **insurance rate** is the price charged for each unit of insurance coverage. Units are usually stated in dollars of coverage, but they may also apply to individual pieces of property to be covered. Rates represent the average cost of providing coverage to various groups of insureds. These groups, called **classes**, consist of the insureds who share characteristics that are associated with the potential for suffering losses. For example, automobile insurance policyholders may be classified by age, gender, marital status, and driving record, as well as by the make and model of vehicle that they drive. Insurance companies use statistical information about losses to establish rates for the various classes of insureds. Note that it is becoming common for insurance companies to use an applicant's credit report to provide information in underwriting.

When underwriters receive an application for insurance, they assign the applicant to the appropriate class based on his or her relevant characteristics. They then determine whether the rates established for that class are sufficient to provide coverage for that applicant. Because some applicants will

generate higher-than-average or lower-than-average loss expectancies for their class, underwriters divide insurance applicants into four groups. The first group—"preferred" applicants—have lower-than-average loss expectancies and may qualify for lower premiums. The second group consists of "standard" applicants with average loss expectancies for their class. The first two groups are accepted for coverage. The third group has loss expectancies projected to be slightly above average. Although they are accepted, these "substandard" applicants may be charged higher premiums and have restrictions placed on the types or amounts of coverage they may purchase. The fourth group, "unacceptable" applicants, have loss expectancies that are much too high; they are rejected.

Many people wonder how some "bad" drivers get insurance while "good" drivers are canceled or turned down for insurance. The key to acceptance or rejection lies in the loss expectancies for the groups into which people are categorized. Some groups, such as those with more experienced drivers, have a low loss expectancy as a group. Thus, someone in that group who has two or more at-fault accidents might be deemed "unacceptable" for that group. In contrast, some groups might be made up primarily of individuals with poor driving records. Thus, someone with an even worse driving record would be the norm for that group and would be deemed "standard." While the premiums for the latter group would be much higher than the premiums for the former group, at least the person would be insured. When a person is turned down or canceled as unacceptable in one class, insurance will usually remain available, but at a much higher price in another class.

Mutual insurance companies are owned by their policyholders and operate on a not-for-profit basis. Funds remaining after expenses and losses have been paid are returned to the policyholders as **insurance dividends**. In addition to receiving insurance dividends, the policyholders of a mutual company maintain voting control over the company. To be competitive, some stock companies pay insurance dividends to policyholders even though the policyholders have no voting privileges.

The Essence of Insurance

Insurance consists of two basic elements: the reduction of risk and the sharing of losses. Each insurance customer who exchanges the uncertainty of a potentially large financial loss for the certainty of a fixed insurance premium reduces his or her risk. Risk is reduced for the insurer as well through the **law of large numbers**, which states that as the number of members in a group increases, predictions about the group's behavior become increasingly accurate. The greater accuracy decreases uncertainty and therefore risk. For example, consider a city of 100,000 households in which the probability of a fire striking a household is 1 in 1000, or 0.1 percent. If we focus on groups of ten or even 100 households at a time, we cannot predict very accurately whether a fire will strike a house in a given group. Some groups might have two or three fires, while others might have none. If we combine all the households into one group, however, we can more accurately predict that 100 fires will occur (100,000 × 0.001). Even if 103 fires occurred, our prediction would be in error by only a small percentage. Insurance companies, which may have millions of customers, can be even more accurate in their group predictions.

When viewed in this way, the essence of insurance becomes clear: Individual insurance purchasers benefit regardless of whether they suffer a loss. The reduction of risk itself provides a benefit. Reduced risk gives one the freedom to drive a car, own a home, and plan financially for the future with the knowledge that some unforeseen event will not result in financial disaster. Society also benefits from insurance. No major business activity—whether the construction of a house, the drilling of an oil well, or the establishment of a law firm—is undertaken without insurance protection. Without insurance, the only way to handle risk with confidence is to avoid risky situations.

Homeowner's Insurance

3 Design a homeowner's insurance program to meet your needs and keep the cost of the plan to a minimum.

Whether you own or rent housing, you face the possibility of suffering property and liability losses. **Homeowner's insurance** combines liability and property insurance coverage needed by homeowners and renters into a single-package policy. **Property insurance** protects you from financial losses resulting from the damage to or destruction of your property or possessions. **Liability insurance** protects you from financial losses suffered when you are held liable for the losses of others. There are four types of homeowner's insurance for people who own a house, one type for the owners of condominiums, and another type for those who rent housing.

The Coverages

The standard homeowner's insurance policy is divided into two sections. Section 1 provides protection from various types of property damage losses, including: (1) damage to the dwelling; (2) damage to other structures on the property; (3) damage to personal property and dwelling contents; and (4) expenses arising out of a loss of use of the dwelling (for example, food and lodging). Additional coverages are usually provided for such items as debris removal, trees and shrubs, and fire department service charges.

An important variable related to Section 1 of a policy involves the number of loss-causing perils that are covered. **Named-perils policies** cover only those losses caused by perils that are specifically named in the policy. **All-risk (or open-perils) policies** cover losses caused by all perils *other than* those specifically excluded by the policy. All-risk policies provide broader coverage because hundreds of perils can cause property losses, but only a few would be excluded.

Section 2 deals with liability insurance. **Homeowner's general liability protection** applies when you are legally liable for the losses of another person. Whenever a homeowner is negligent or otherwise fails to exercise due caution in protecting visitors, he or she may potentially suffer a liability loss.

Homeowners often wish to take responsibility for the losses of another person regardless of the legal liability. Consider, for example, a guest's child who suffers burns from touching a hot barbecue grill despite warnings that the grill was hot. **Homeowner's no-fault medical payments protection** will pay for bodily injury losses suffered by visitors regardless of who was at fault. Such coverage would help pay for the medical treatment of the visitor's burns. Members of the insured's immediate family are not covered under no-fault medical payments; they should be covered by health insurance instead (see Chapter 11). **Homeowner's no-fault property damage protection** will pay for property losses suffered by visitors to your home. An example of such a loss might be damage to a friend's leather coat that was chewed by your dog.

Types of Homeowner's Insurance

There are six distinct types of homeowner's insurance policies: HO-1 through HO-4, HO-6, and HO-8. They are described in detail in Table 10.2 and more generally in the sections that follow. The terms and numbers used to identify these policies are generally used by most insurance companies.

Basic Form (HO-1) The **basic form (HO-1)** is a named-perils policy that covers 11 property-damage-causing perils and provides three areas of liability-related protection: personal liability, property damage liability, and medical payments. The most common perils that can cause property damage—fire and lightning, windstorm, theft, and smoke—are covered in the basic homeowner's policy.

Broad Form (HO-2) The **broad form (HO-2)** is a named-perils policy that covers 18 property-damage-causing perils and provides protection from the three liability-related exposures.

Special Form (HO-3) The **special form (HO-3)** provides open-perils protection (except for commonly listed perils of war, earthquake, and flood) for four

Table 10.2

Summary of Homeowner's Insurance Policies

	HO-1 (Basic Form)	HO-2 (Broad Form)	HO-3 (Special Form)
Perils covered (descriptions are given below)	Perils 1–11	Perils 1–18	All perils except those specifically excluded for buildings; perils 1–18 on personal property (does not include glass breakage)
Property coverage/limits			
House and any other attached buildings	Amount based on replacement cost, minimum $15,000	Amount based on replacement cost, minimum $15,000	Amount based on replacement cost, minimum $20,000
Detached buildings	10 percent of insurance on the home (minimum)	10 percent of insurance on the home (minimum)	10 percent of insurance on the home (minimum)
Trees, shrubs, plants, etc.	5 percent of insurance on the home, $500 maximum per item	5 percent of insurance on the home, $500 maximum per item	5 percent of insurance on the home, $500 maximum per item
Personal property	50 percent of insurance on the home (minimum)	50 percent of insurance on the home (minimum)	50 percent of insurance on the home (minimum)
Loss of use and/or add'l living expense	10 percent of insurance on the home	20 percent of insurance on the home	20 percent of insurance on the home
Credit card, forgery, counterfeit money	$1000	$1000	$1000

Liability coverage/limits (for all policies)

Comprehensive personal liability	$100,000
No-fault medical payments	$1000
No-fault property damage	$500

Special limits of liability

For the following classes of personal property, special limits apply on a per-occurrence basis (e.g., per fire or theft): money, coins, bank notes, precious metals (gold, silver, etc.), $200; securities, deeds, stocks, bonds, tickets, stamps, $1000; watercraft and trailers, including furnishings, equipment, and outboard motors, $1000; trailers other than for watercraft, $1000; jewelry, watches, furs, $1000; silverware, goldware, etc., $2500; guns, $2000.

List of perils covered

1. Fire, lightning
2. Windstorm, hail
3. Explosion
4. Riots
5. Damage by aircraft
6. Damage by vehicles owned or operated by people not covered by the homeowner's policy
7. Damage from smoke
8. Vandalism, malicious mischief
9. Theft
10. Glass breakage
11. Volcanic eruption
12. Falling objects (external sources)
13. Weight of ice, snow, sleet
14. Collapse of building or any part of building (specified perils only)
15. Leakage or overflow of water or stream from a plumbing, heating, or air-conditioning system
16. Bursting, cracking, burning, or bulging of a steam or hot water heating system, or of appliances for heating water
17. Freezing of plumbing, heating, and air-conditioning systems and home appliances
18. Injury to electrical appliances and devices (excluding tubes, transistors, and similar electronic components) from short circuits or other accidentally generated currents

Note: This table describes the standard policies. Specific items differ from company to company and from state to state. When you want a limit that exceeds the standard limit for your company, you usually can increase the limit by paying an additional premium.

HO-4 (Renter's Contents Broad Form)	HO-6 (For Condominium Owners)	HO-8 (For Older Homes)
Perils 1–9, 11–18	Perils 1–18	Perils 1–11
10 percent of personal property insurance on additions and alterations to the apartment	$1000 on owner's additions and alterations to the unit	Amount based on actual cash value of the home
Not covered	Not covered (unless owned solely by the insured)	10 percent of insurance on the home (minimum)
10 percent of personal property insurance, $500 maximum per item	10 percent of personal property insurance, $500 maximum per item	5 percent of insurance on the home, $500 maximum per item
Chosen by the tenant to reflect the value of the items, minimum $6000	Chosen by the homeowner to reflect the value of the items, minimum $6000	50 percent of insurance on the home (minimum)
20 percent of personal property insurance	40 percent of personal property insurance	20 percent of insurance on the home
$1000	$1000	$1000

property coverages: losses to the dwelling, losses to other structures, landscaping losses, and losses generating additional living expenses. Contents and personal property are covered on a named-perils basis for 17 of the 18 major homeowner's perils (the exception is glass breakage). In terms of liability protection and in all other respects, the coverage under HO-3 is the same as under HO-2.

Renter's Contents Broad Form (HO-4)   The **renter's contents broad form (HO-4)** is a named-perils policy that protects the insured from losses to the contents of a dwelling rather than the dwelling itself. It covers 17 major perils and provides liability protection. HO-4 is ideal for renters because it provides protection from losses to dwelling contents and personal property and provides for additional living expenses if the dwelling is rendered uninhabitable by one of the covered perils. Although insurance is relatively inexpensive, only one-fourth of all renters carry HO-4 protection.

Condominium Form (HO-6)   The **condominium form (HO-6)** is a named-perils policy protecting condominium owners from the three principal losses they face: losses to contents and personal property, losses due to the additional living expenses that may arise if one of the covered perils occurs, and liability losses. (The building itself is insured by the management of the condominium.) Two additional coverages are included in the HO-6 policy as necessary to meet the specific needs of the condominium unit owner. The first is protection against losses to the structural alterations and additions that condominium owners sometimes make when they remodel their units. The second is supplemental coverage for the dwelling unit to protect the condominium owner if the building is not sufficiently insured.

Older Home Form (HO-8)   The replacement value for an older home may be much higher than its market or actual cash value. The **older home form (HO-8)** is a named-perils policy that provides actual-cash-value protection on the dwelling. It does not provide that the dwelling be rebuilt to the same standards of style and quality, as those standards may be prohibitively expensive today. Instead, the policy provides that the dwelling be rebuilt to make it serviceable.

Buying Homeowner's Insurance

You can purchase homeowner's insurance with varying coverage amounts, exclusions, and limitations. Basically, three areas of concern arise when buying a policy. First, how much coverage will you need to replace the dwelling itself? Second, how much coverage will you need on the contents and personal property in general and for expensive items such as jewelry or antiques in particular? Third, how much coverage will you need for liability protection?

Determining the Coverage Needed on Your Dwelling

Both property and liability losses can occur to owners or renters of housing. Your first step is to determine the dwelling's replacement value. You could either use the services of a professional liability appraiser or consult with your insurance agent to determine replacement value.

Homeowner's insurance policies usually contain a **replacement-cost requirement** that stipulates that a home must be insured for 80 (or perhaps 100) percent of its replacement value in order for the policy to fully reimburse (after payment of the deductible by the policyholder) any losses to the dwelling. Thus, a home with a replacement value of $100,000 would need to be insured for $80,000 or $100,000, and this amount would be the maximum that the insurance company would be obligated to pay for any loss. If you fail to meet your replacement-cost requirement, you will not be considered fully insured because you will, by default, be using a form of coinsurance. The amount of reimbursement for any loss will be calculated using the **replacement-cost-requirement formula**:

$$R = (L - D) \times \frac{I}{(RV \times 0.80 \text{ or } 1.00)} \qquad (10.2)$$

where

R = **reimbursement** payable
L = the amount of **loss**
D = **deductible**, if any
I = amount of **insurance** actually carried
RV = **replacement value** of the dwelling

Many homeowner's policies include a clause that automatically raises the policy coverage amount each year to keep pace with inflationary increases in the cost of replacing the dwelling. Although a loss in excess of replacement cost is rare, such losses do occur. Thus, carrying only the required percent would not fully cover such a loss because the policy limit would be reached before providing the full replacement value. The requirement enables you to avoid coinsurance on small losses but might result in inadequate coverage on large losses. Thus, it is wise to insure your dwelling for 100 percent of its replacement cost. Indeed, in such cases your insurance company will fully cover a loss even if it costs 20 to 25 percent more than the replacement cost to repair or rebuild the dwelling.

Determining the Coverage Needed on Your Personal Property   Making an inventory of, and placing a value on, all the contents of your home are time-consuming but important tasks. Table 10.3 shows the inventory and valuation for the contents of and personal property in a typical living room. You should conduct such an inventory for each room, the basement, garage, shed, and yard possessions. When totaled, the values enable you to select proper policy limits.

Most homeowner's policies will automatically cover contents and personal property for up to 50 percent of the coverage on the home. Thus, if your home is insured for $140,000 but contains $75,000 of personal property, you probably

Table 10.3

Personal Property Checklist: Living Room

Item	Date Purchased	Purchase Price	Actual Cash Value	Replacement Cost
		Valuation		
Furniture				
Sofa	8/95	$ 750	$ 375	$ 950
Chair	11/93	250	100	375
Lounger	12/96	575	300	695
Ottoman	12/96	100	50	120
Bookcase	4/98	275	225	300
End table (2)	7/99	300	250	300
Appliances				
TV	1/99	550	500	600
VCR	6/98	400	300	400
Wall clock	7/93	60	10	100
Furnishings				
Carpet	6/92	375	50	600
Painting	12/96	125	225	225
Floor lamp	4/94	150	50	225
Art (three items)	10/98	600	600	800
Table lamp	4/94	75	40	100
Table lamp	5/98	125	100	135
Throw pillows	7/95	45	20	60
TOTAL		$4755	$3195	$5985

need to purchase an extra $5000 in contents coverage. Furthermore, some specified items of personal property may have specific policy limits. For example, a homeowner's insurance policy might provide a maximum of $200 coverage for cash, $5000 for personal computers, and $1000 for jewelry. If your inventory reveals a higher valuation on such items, an endorsement providing extra coverage might be a wise choice.

Notice that Table 10.3 lists three estimates for the value of the contents of a room: the purchase price, the actual cash value, and the replacement cost. Historically, property insurance policies paid only the **actual cash value** of an item of personal property, which represents the purchase price of the property less depreciation. The **actual-cash-value (ACV) formula** is

$$ACV = P - [CA \times (P \div LE)] \tag{10.3}$$

where

$$P = \text{purchase \textbf{price} of the property}$$
$$CA = \textbf{current age} \text{ of the property in years}$$
$$LE = \textbf{life expectancy} \text{ of the property in years}$$

Consider the case of Ann Jones, a bartender from Telluride, Colorado, whose eight-year-old color television set was stolen. The TV cost $500 when new and had a total life expectancy of ten years. Its actual cash value when it was stolen was

$$\begin{aligned} ACV &= \$500 - [8 \times (\$500 \div 10)] \\ &= \$500 - (8 \times \$50) \\ &= \$100 \end{aligned}$$

Ann would find it very difficult to replace the TV for $100. A more realistic replacement cost for the TV might be $600. **Contents replacement-cost protection** is an option available in most homeowner's insurance policies (including the renter's form) that pays the full replacement cost of any personal property. The standard limitation that applies to contents (50 percent of insured value of the dwelling) remains in effect if contents replacement-cost protection is purchased. Thus, the overall limit on contents may need to be raised, since it is easier to reach the 50 percent figure when replacement-cost valuation is used.

Coverage for Liability Losses   Standard homeowner's policies typically provide $100,000 of personal liability coverage, $1000 of no-fault medical expense coverage, and $250 of no-fault property damage coverage. Wise risk managers consider increasing the policy limits for all three of these coverages. The extra cost is small and the rule "never risk a lot for a little" applies.

How Homeowner's Insurance Is Priced   Many factors affect the pricing of homeowner's insurance, with the most important being the amount and type of coverage and the number of perils covered. Insurance companies vary their premiums based on the adequacy of the fire-fighting system in a town or city. Even the distance of the home from a fire hydrant can influence the premium. The type of construction used to build a house may affect the homeowner's insurance premium as well. In addition, the loss experience of the company may alter the premium because the company must collect sufficient premiums to pay the loss claims made by its customers.

What Happens When You Fail to Fully Insure Your Home

Twin brothers, Chris and Colin Shearer, are circus clowns from Sarasota, Florida. Each owns a home with a replacement value of $100,000, and each home suffers a $40,000 fire loss over and above the deductible. Chris, who took a personal finance class in college, had insured his home for $80,000. Colin, in an attempt to save some money, had insured his home for $72,000. Applying Equation (10.2), each brother determines the amount he will be reimbursed for the loss to his dwelling.

Chris's calculations are

$$R = \$40,000 \times \frac{\$80,000}{(\$100,000 \times 0.80)}$$

$$= \$40,000 \times \frac{\$80,000}{\$80,000}$$

$$= \$40,000$$

Thus, Chris will be fully covered for his loss.

Colin's calculations are

$$R = \$40,000 \times \frac{\$72,000}{(\$100,000 \times 0.80)}$$

$$= \$40,000 \times \frac{\$72,000}{\$80,000}$$

$$= \$40,000 \times 0.90$$

$$= \$36,000$$

Thus, Colin will be reimbursed for only $36,000 of his loss. His failure to insure his house for 80 percent of its replacement cost, or $80,000 = ($100,000 × 0.80), means he will be covered for only 90 percent ($72,000 ÷ $80,000), and he must pay 10 percent of any loss—in this case, $4000. All of this extra expense occurs because he tried to save about $50 per year in insurance premiums.

Automobile Insurance

4 Design an automobile insurance program to meet your needs and keep the cost of the plan to a minimum.

Both owning and driving an automobile expose you to the risk of devastating financial losses. A split-second error in driving judgment or simple bad luck can result in a loss of thousands of dollars in property damage and personal injury. **Automobile insurance** combines the liability and property insurance coverages needed by automobile owners and drivers into a single-package policy. More than 30 states require automobile owners to purchase automobile insurance, and the remainder require automobile owners to show, in advance, financial responsibility for any accident that might occur. This requirement is most commonly satisfied through the purchase of automobile insurance.

Losses Covered

Automobile insurance combines four distinct types of coverage: (A) liability insurance; (B) medical payments insurance; (C) protection against uninsured (and sometimes underinsured) motorists; and (D) insurance for physical damage to the insured automobile. Each coverage has its own policy limits, conditions, and exclusions. Table 10.4 summarizes the coverage provided by automobile insurance coverage for persons not specifically excluded in the policy.

Table 10.4

Summary of Automobile Insurance Coverages

Section	Type of Coverage	Persons Covered	Property Covered	Recommended Limits
A	LIABILITY INSURANCE			
	(1) Bodily injury liability	Relatives living in insured's household driving an owned or nonowned automobile	Not applicable	At least legally required minimums or $250,000/$500,000, whichever is greater
	(2) Property damage liability	Relatives living in insured's household driving an owned or nonowned automobile	Automobiles and other property damaged by insured driver while driving	At least legally required minimum or $100,000, whichever is greater
B	MEDICAL PAYMENTS	Passengers in insured automobile or nonowned automobile driven by insured family member	Not applicable	$50,000 or higher
C	UNINSURED AND UNDERINSURED MOTORISTS	Anyone driving insured car with permission and insured family members driving nonowned automobiles with permission	Not applicable	$50,000/$100,000 or higher, if available
D	PHYSICAL DAMAGE			
	(1) Collision	Anyone driving insured car with permission	Insured automobile	Actual cash value less deductible
	(2) Comprehensive	Not applicable	Insured automobile and its contents	Actual cash value less deductible

Liability Insurance (Coverage A)   Liability insurance covers the insured when he or she is held responsible for losses suffered by others. Two types of liability can arise out of the ownership and operation of an automobile. First, **automobile bodily injury liability** occurs when a driver or car owner is held legally responsible for bodily injury losses suffered by other persons, including pedestrians. Second, **automobile property damage liability** occurs when a driver or car owner is held legally responsible for damage to the property of others. Such damage can include damage to another vehicle, a building, or roadside signs and poles. The typical bodily injury liability claim is more than five times the average property damage liability claim. Furthermore, the cost of insurance claim settlements and court awards resulting from automobile accidents has risen steadily in recent years.

The policy limits for automobile liability insurance are usually quoted with three figures, such as 100/300/50, with each figure representing a multiple of $1000 (Figure 10.2). The first of the three figures is the maximum that will be paid for liability claims for *one* person's bodily injury losses resulting from an automobile accident ($100,000 in our example). The middle figure represents the overall maximum that will be paid for bodily injury liability losses to *any*

Figure 10.2

Automobile Liability Insurance Policy Limits

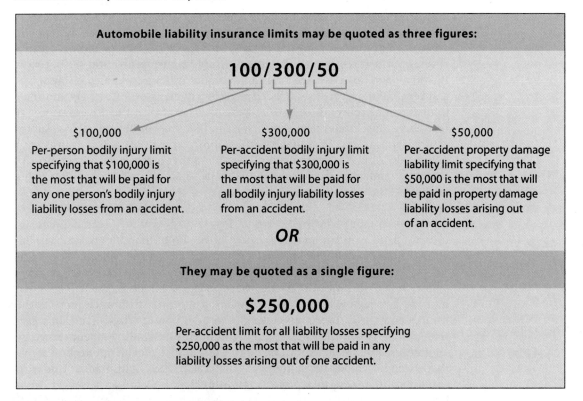

number of persons resulting from an automobile accident ($300,000 in our example). The third figure represents the maximum that will be paid for property damage liability losses resulting from an accident ($50,000 in our example).

In some policies, the liability limits are stated as a single figure, such as $250,000. Under such policies, all property and bodily injury liability losses from an accident would be paid until the limit is reached.

Liability insurance covers the insured for losses suffered by others; it cannot be used to pay for bodily injury losses suffered by the insured or for property damage to that driver's car. Injured passengers of the at-fault driver may collect under the driver's liability coverage, but only after exhausting the coverage provided under medical payments (discussed below) and only after reimbursement is made to persons injured in other vehicles or as pedestrians.

Medical Payments Insurance (Coverage B) **Automobile medical payments insurance** covers bodily injury losses suffered by the driver of the insured vehicle and any passengers regardless of who is at fault. Medical losses occurring within one year and as a direct result of an accident will be reimbursed up to the limits of the policy. Automobile medical payments insurance also covers insured family members who are injured while passengers in any car, or who are injured by a car when on foot or riding a bicycle. Medical payments coverage is subject to a single policy limit, which is applied per person per accident.

A number of states have adopted some type of no-fault automobile insurance mechanism. In such states, insureds collect first (and possibly only) from their own insurance company for bodily injury losses resulting from an automobile accident, regardless of who was at fault. In these states, the medical payments coverage, which is often referred to as **personal injury protection (PIP)**, covers the driver and any passengers for bodily injury losses as well as possibly wages and rehabilitation expenses. Under medical payments or PIP, drivers and their injured parties collect directly from the driver's insurer. If the driver was not at fault, his or her insurer pays the claims and then may be able to exercise subrogation rights against the at-fault party. **Subrogation rights** allow an insurer to take action against a negligent third party (and that party's insurance company) to obtain reimbursement for payments made to an insured. Subrogation rights are limited in no-fault states.

Uninsured and Underinsured Motorist Insurance (Coverage C)   Sometimes the driver at fault in an automobile accident carries no insurance or insufficient liability insurance. To protect against such losses, an insured can purchase uninsured and underinsured motorist insurance as part of the automobile insurance policy. When the medical payments coverage is exhausted, such uninsured motorist coverage will take over. **Uninsured motorist insurance** protects the insured and the insured's passengers from bodily injury losses (and, in a few states, property damage losses) resulting from an automobile accident caused by an uninsured motorist. Uninsured motorist insurance provides protection above that extended under the automobile medical payments insurance. **Underinsured motorist insurance** protects the insured and his or her passengers from bodily injury losses (and, in some cases, property damage losses) when the at-fault driver has insurance but coverage is insufficient to reimburse the losses. The limits for uninsured motorist insurance are quoted in a manner similar to that for automobile liability insurance. For example, uninsured motorist protection with limits of 50/100 would provide up to $50,000 for any one injured person and up to $100,000 for multiple bodily injury losses in one accident. Most states require insurers to offer uninsured and underinsured motorist insurance. Such insurance is a wise risk-management choice and carries a very low premium—often less than $25 per year.

Physical Damage Insurance (Coverage D)   A number of perils can cause property losses to an insured automobile. **Automobile physical damage insurance** provides protection from losses due to damage to your car from collision, theft, and other perils. The most common peril is, of course, a collision with another vehicle or an object. In general, the cars with the highest collision losses per vehicle tend to be smaller, sportier models. The other most common peril is theft. Again, sportier models are often associated with a greater frequency of theft claims.

Collision insurance reimburses an insured for losses resulting from a collision with another car or object or from a rollover. The insurer pays the cost of repairing or replacing the insured's car regardless of fault. When the other driver is at fault, subrogation rights allow the insurer to obtain reimbursement through that driver's property damage liability protection. Collision insurance is written with a deductible that usually ranges $100 to $1000. If you carry collision insurance coverage on your own car, you are generally covered when you drive someone else's car with their permission.

Driving a rental car exposes you to the same potential liabilities as driving your own vehicle. If you have automobile liability insurance, such liabilities will be covered while you drive a rented car. But what about the damages to the rented car? The answer hinges on whether you carry collision coverage on your car and whether that coverage extends to rented vehicles. Most automobile insurance policies provide such coverage. The rental company may also seek to hold you liable for the lost rental fees while the car undergoes repairs, however. Check with your insurance agent before renting a car to find out if you are protected. If so, you can decline the offer of collision damage waiver (CDW) and loss damage waiver (LDW) insurance from the rental company. These might add $25 per day to the cost of renting while duplicating your existing protection.

Comprehensive automobile insurance protects against property damage losses caused by perils other than collision and rollover. Covered perils include fire, theft, vandalism, hail, and wind, among many others. Comprehensive insurance is written on an open-perils basis, and often includes a deductible ranging from $100 to $500.

When you have a loss that qualifies under collision and comprehensive insurance, an estimate of the repair cost will be made. If the estimate exceeds the book value of the car, the lower of the two figures is paid, less any deductible. The **book value** of a car is based on the average current selling price of cars of the same make, model, and age. Many automobile insurance purchasers drop collision insurance on cars that have lost much of their resale value.

Other Protection Two other inexpensive, but sometimes important, coverages are also available to automobile insurance buyers. **Towing coverage** pays the cost of having a disabled automobile transported for repairs. It usually pays only the first $25 or $50 per occurrence but will cover *any* towing need—not just one due to an accident. **Rental reimbursement coverage** provides a rental car when the insured's vehicle is being repaired after an accident or has been stolen. It often has a daily limit of $20 to $30 and, therefore, provides only part of the funds needed to obtain replacement transportation.

Types of Automobile Insurance Policies

The **family automobile policy (FAP)** and the **personal automobile policy (PAP)** are the types of automobile insurance most commonly selected by individual consumers and households. The FAP is designed for automobiles owned by families that include several persons who might drive the car. The family automobile policy provides coverage for the owner, relatives living in the owner's household unless specifically excluded, and persons who have the owner's permission to operate the insured vehicle. If a friend loans you his or her car, your relatives living in your household and other persons acting on your permission also will be covered under your family automobile policy when driving that borrowed car. In contrast, the PAP is designed for automobiles owned by an individual who is likely to be its only driver.

Apply Automobile Insurance to a Serious Auto Accident

Just how the many provisions in an automobile insurance policy apply to a specific accident is a mystery to many people. As a result, the claims process may generate considerable dissatisfaction after an accident. The example given here and outlined in the following chart are intended to clarify the application of the multiple coverages and limits.

In September of last year, Donna Redman, a college student from Greenville, South Carolina, caused a serious accident when she failed to yield to an approaching vehicle while attempting to make a left turn. Donna suffered a broken arm and facial cuts, resulting in medical costs of $1254. Her passenger, Philip Windsor, was seriously injured, with head and neck wounds requiring surgery, a two-week hospital stay, and rehabilitation. Philip's injuries generated medical costs of $17,650. The driver of the other car, John Monk, suffered serious back and internal injuries and facial burns that resulted in some disfigurement. His medical care costs totaled $22,948. His passenger, Annette Combs, suffered cuts and bruises requiring minor medical care at a cost of $423. Both cars were completely destroyed. Donna's ten-year-old Buick was valued at $2150. John's Mazda Miata was valued at $19,350. The force of the impact spun John's car around, causing it to destroy a traffic-signal control box (valued at $3650).

Both Donna and John were covered by family automobile policies. In our example, both Donna's and John's automobile insurance policies had liability limits of $20,000/$50,000/$15,000 and medical payments limits of $5000 per person. Donna and Philip were reimbursed for their medical losses by Donna's medical payments coverage. Because Philip's losses ($17,650) exceeded Donna's medical payments policy limits, he also made a liability claim against her policy. John Monk's policy also comes into play here. Remember that medical payments insurance will pay regardless of who is at fault for an accident. Therefore, John and Annette were initially reimbursed by John's policy for $5000 (the policy limit) and $423, respectively. John then made a claim against Donna's insurance company to be reimbursed for the remainder of his bodily injury losses. Also, John's insurer exercised its subrogation rights and made a claim against Donna's insurer to collect the $5000 it had paid John and the $423 it had paid Annette. Donna's policy paid $20,000 (the per-person policy limit) toward John's injuries ($15,000 to John and $5000 to his insurance company) and to Philip for the $12,650 in bodily injury losses not covered by her medical payments protection.

John's collision insurance covered the damage to his vehicle less his $100 deductible. John's insurance company then applied its subrogation rights for the entire amount of the loss (including the deductible) against Donna's property damage liability coverage. Because Donna's policy had a maximum of $15,000 in property damage liability losses, she was required to pay the excess out of her own pocket. Donna collected $2050 for her car under her collision coverage, which carried a $100 deductible.

Automobile Insurance Plans

It is illegal to operate a motor vehicle without being financially responsible for losses you might cause. To address this need, most states have established a mechanism to provide coverage for drivers who may find it difficult—if not impossible—to obtain insurance coverage at any price. These **automobile insurance plans (AIPs)** for high-risk drivers assign a proportional share of uninsurable drivers to each company writing automobile insurance policies in the state. The proportion is based upon the company's share of the total automobile insurance policies written in that state. Not surprisingly, the premiums for such coverage are extremely expensive, and coverage is usually limited to the minimum liability insurance limits. Drivers assigned to one of these plans should check with several insurers to compare prices.

In total, Donna had to pay $11,048 out of her own pocket, as the policy limits were exceeded by John's medical costs and the property damage. If she had a single-limit personal automobile policy for $65,000 (the total of her $50,000 per accident bodily injury liability and $15,000 per accident property damage liability), she would have had no out-of-pocket liability losses.

An additional point needs to be raised concerning situations in which an accident victim suffers serious, permanent injuries that are not fully reimbursed by the insurance policy protecting the driver at fault. In our example, John suffered very painful injuries resulting in permanent disfigurement. He may wish to sue Donna for his pain and suffering and his unpaid medical expenses. If he were to file such a suit, Donna would be provided legal assistance by her insurance company. Any judgment that exceeds the policy limits (remember that Donna's per-person policy limit has already been reached) will be Donna's responsibility, however. Obviously, both Donna and John were underinsured.

Donna Redman's Accident: Who Pays What?

Coverage	Donna's Policy	John's Policy
Liability (limits)	(20/50/15)	(20/50/15)
Bodily injury:		
John Monk	$20,000	
Annette Combs	423	
Philip Windsor	12,650	
Property damage:		
John Monk's car	15,000	
Medical payments (limits):	($5,000)	($5,000)
John Monk	5,000 *	
Annette Combs	5,000 *	
Donna Redman	1,254	
Philip Windsor	5,000	
Collision coverage (limits):	(ACV, $100 deductible)	(ACV, $100 deductible)
Donna's car	2,050	
John's car	19,250 *	
Donna's out-of-pocket expenses:		
John Monk's bodily injury	2,948	
John Monk's car	4,350	
Traffic-signal control box	3,650	
Collision insurance deductible	100	
TOTAL	$11,048	

* Also included in Donna's column, as John's company filed a claim against Donna by exercising its subrogation rights.

Buying Automobile Insurance

The wise risk manager should shop carefully for automobile insurance because of its high cost. The task is to select the proper automobile insurance program while keeping premiums as low as possible. Because coverages are fairly standardized and premiums vary widely, comparison shopping for premium prices often saves considerable money.

Determining Coverages and Policy Limits   The first step toward designing an adequate automobile insurance program involves identifying the types of losses that might occur. This task is not difficult because the standard policies cover most of the losses that you can reasonably expect to face as a result of owning and driving a car.

Next, you must determine the amount of coverage you need. At a minimum, you must conform to the financial responsibility requirements in your state. Even in states that do not require automobile insurance, most automobile owners choose automobile insurance as the means to show the required financial

Buying Automobile Insurance

Even though automobile insurance premiums can vary hundreds of dollars annually among companies, only about 40 percent of consumers shop around when they buy or renew coverage.

The following worksheet can be used to record automobile insurance premium quotations obtained from insurers. Remember to add surcharges for previous claims and other factors and to subtract discounts for which you might qualify. If you must join an organization (e.g., American Automobile Association) to obtain coverage from an insurer, add the membership fees to the final premium.

| | | | Premium* | |
Coverage Type	Coverage/Amount of Deductible	Company A (example)	Company B (your figures)	Company C (your figures)
A. Liability insurance				
Bodily injury	250/500	$132	_____	_____
Property damage	100	$58	_____	_____
B. Medical payments/personal injury protection				
Medical payments	100	$ 51	_____	_____
PIP (no-fault states)	n/a	n/a	n/a	n/a
C. Uninsured/underinsured motorist protection				
Uninsured motorist	50/100	$ 28	_____	_____
Underinsured motorist	50/100	$ 17	_____	_____
D. Physical damage protection				
Collision coverage	$100 deductible	$126	_____	_____
	$200 deductible	$111	_____	_____
	$500 deductible	$ 88	_____	_____
	$1000 deductible	$ 62	_____	_____
Comprehensive	no deductible	$ 59	_____	_____
	$50 deductible	$ 48	_____	_____
	$200 deductible	$ 34	_____	_____
	$500 deductible	$ 24	_____	_____
Total premium		**$438**	_____	_____
Plus surcharges		n/a	_____	_____
Less discounts		$33	_____	_____
Final premium*		**$405**	_____	_____

*Premium for six months for a midsize car in a medium-size city based on a $200 collision deductible and a $100 comprehensive deductible.

responsibility. Because health care and automobile repair costs can be enormous, it is wise to buy as much liability coverage as you can afford. Minimum limits of $250,000/$500,000/$100,000 are commonly recommended. High limits for uninsured and underinsured motorist coverage are also advisable. Limits recommended for automobile medical expense coverage are a minimum of $50,000 per person.

It may be tempting to skip some of the coverages provided in a policy to reduce the overall premium. A reduction in premiums may be obtained by eliminating collision coverage, as the premium for such collision coverage typically represents 30 to 40 percent of the total automobile insurance premium. This strategy is generally recommended only for cars having a book value of less than $1000. Elimination of other nonessential coverages (e.g., comprehensive or uninsured/underinsured motorist insurance) would yield little savings and would sharply reduce protection.

How Automobile Insurance Is Priced The premium charged for an automobile insurance policy is based on as many as 52 characteristics that describe the driver, the car itself, and the usage of the car. These characteristics are used to place the insured in one of more than 160 classes. Members of the same class have a similar probability of loss. The same price per unit of insurance is assigned to each member of the class and then adjusted to account for the individual driver's accident and traffic violation experience, as well as any discounts for which the driver qualifies. The resulting price per unit is then multiplied by the number of units applicable to the selected coverage to obtain the premium.

Other Property and Liability Loss Exposures

5 Describe property and liability insurance policies designed to meet needs other than those related to housing and automobiles.

Many individuals need protection against property and liability losses that are not covered by homeowner's or automobile policies. This section will discuss some of the less well-known, but still important, property and liability policies.

Floater Policies

Floater policies provide all-risk protection for accident and theft losses to movable personal property (such as cameras, sporting equipment, and clothing) regardless of where the loss occurs. Although floater protection is part of the standard homeowner's insurance policy, additional coverage can be added to a homeowner's policy or purchased as a separate policy. **Scheduled floater policies** provide insurance protection for specifically identified items of personal property. **Unscheduled floater policies** provide insurance protection for certain classes of property or all movable property owned by the insured.

Many items of personal property are transported in automobiles and kept at temporary residences such as motel rooms and college dormitories. Automobile insurance policies do not cover portable personal property. If covered under a homeowner's policy while in the home, however, personal property will be covered elsewhere under the standard floater protection provided by the homeowner's policy. For example, a compact disc player permanently installed in a car would not be considered portable and thus would be covered by the automobile policy. If it can be removed for use indoors, the CD player would be covered under the homeowner's (or renter's) policy. Claims for losses can be made up to one year after the date of the loss. Theft and vandalism losses can best be documented with a police report.

Professional Liability Insurance

Professionals, such as surgeons, dental hygienists, and accountants, can be held legally liable for losses suffered by their patients or clients. **Professional liability insurance** (sometimes called **malpractice insurance**) protects individuals and organizations that provide professional services when they are held liable

 Save Money on Property and Liability Insurance

The buyer of property and liability insurance must be careful to buy adequate coverage while keeping insurance expenditures to a minimum. Some suggestions for reaching this goal follow:

Shop around for the lowest-cost coverage.
Considerable savings can be realized by seeking quotes from several agents and direct sellers. To obtain a quote, simply telephone an agent or direct seller and provide some basic descriptive information. Insurance premiums can vary by 100 percent or more for essentially the same coverage. Most agents will provide quotes over the telephone, so don't hesitate to use the yellow pages when considering a new policy or renewal of an existing policy. Insurance ads provide little useful information to insurance purchasers, especially cost information. The insurance regulatory agency in your state may publish more helpful **insurance buyer's guides** that discuss how to buy specific types of insurance, compare premiums, and rate the companies providing such insurance. *Consumer Reports* magazine periodically publishes feature articles that discuss insurance.

Select appropriate coverages and limits.
Buy only needed coverages and select policy limits appropriate for the largest potential losses.

Assume risks that are affordable.
Assume risks that you can afford—by raising a deductible, for example—and insure against losses

that would be financially unaffordable. Buy the highest liability limits (such as 250/500/100 for automobile liability), and pay for them with the savings gained from choosing a high collision deductible (e.g., $500).

Take advantage of discounts.
Most insurance companies offer discounted premiums for policyholders who buy several types of insurance (e.g., both automobile and homeowner's insurance) from them. A discount is common for a college student listed on a parent's policy if the student does not have a car at school and the school is at least 100 miles from the parent's home.

Engage in loss control.
Many companies charge lower premiums to policyholders who take steps to reduce the probability or severity of loss. For example, discounts are available if you install dead-bolt door locks or a fire extinguisher in your home. Ask your agent what you need to do to qualify.

Make sure you are properly classified.
You can save money by making sure that you have been placed in the proper class for premium-determination purposes. Verifying that you are in the proper class is also important because a claim may be denied if premiums were based on an inappropriate classification.

for the losses of their clients. Policy limits, deductibles, premiums, and other characteristics of such policies vary widely depending on the profession involved. Generally, professional liability policies are written with policy limits of $250,000 or more. A $1 million professional liability policy written for a family therapist may cost as little as $300 per year; in contrast, some surgeons pay $60,000 or more per year for professional liability insurance.

Comprehensive Personal Liability Insurance

Owning a home and driving a car are not the only sources of potential liability you may face. Consider, for example, the case of Bill Crain, a pharmacist from Golden, Colorado. While climbing in a restricted area, he accidentally loosened some rocks, which fell down the slope and seriously injured hikers below. Because Bill was in a restricted area and had failed to warn the hikers of his presence, he was held liable for their injuries and was ordered to pay a court judgment of $78,000. Fortunately for Bill, he was protected by a **comprehensive personal liability insurance policy,** which provides protection from liability losses that might arise out of activities that are unrelated to business or the use of an automobile. Recall that the standard homeowner's insurance policy provides comprehensive personal liability insurance up to a specified limit. Individuals who lack such coverage or who desire higher limits can purchase a separate comprehensive personal liability policy.

Umbrella Liability Insurance

It is possible to lose one's entire life savings as a result of a single liability loss. Thus, persons who are risk-averse and those with a high degree of exposure to such a catastrophe may want to buy broad liability protection with a policy limit of $1 million or more. **Umbrella liability insurance** is a personal catastrophe liability policy that covers both general and automobile liability protection. Professional liability can also be included if the insured also carries a basic professional liability insurance policy. Umbrella liability policies provide two benefits. First, the types of losses covered are broader than those recognized by more narrowly defined policies. Second, these policies provide for high dollar amounts of coverage over and above the basic policies. To be covered for these higher limits, you must carry the basic coverages as well.

Figure 10.3 provides an illustration of how umbrella policies work. In this case, the insured has an automobile insurance policy with total liability limits of $130,000 (the total liability coverage for one accident is $100,000 per

Figure 10.3

How Umbrella Policies Work

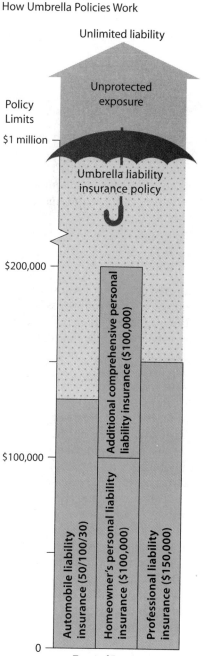

Types of Exposures

Umbrella policies generally exclude automobile, aircraft, watercraft, and professional liability exposures unless these are included in one of the basic plans.

bodily injury plus $30,000 for property damage), a homeowner's insurance policy with liability protection of $100,000 supplemented by a $100,000 comprehensive personal liability policy, and a $150,000 professional liability insurance policy. If the insured bought an umbrella policy with a $1 million limit and then experienced a $750,000 professional liability loss, the umbrella policy would provide protection of $600,000 after the professional liability policy limits were exceeded. Umbrella policies are relatively low in cost when purchased to supplement basic policies (perhaps $150 per year for $1 million of protection) and protect against virtually all major liability exposures one might face.

Collecting on Your Property and Liability Losses

6 Outline the steps to make a claim against a property or liability insurance policy.

A tangible benefit of owning insurance becomes evident when a loss occurs and reimbursement is obtained. After a loss, you first contact your insurance agent or company claims representative. Take this step as soon as possible. Then keep the company informed of everything relevant to the loss, even if it requires daily or weekly contact until the claim is settled. The tenacious claimant is most likely to collect fully on a loss.

Document Your Loss

You carry the burden of proof whenever a property or liability loss occurs. Adequate documentation of the circumstances and the amount of the loss is essential. In the absence of such documentation, the insurance company will generally interpret the situation in the manner favorable to its interests, not yours. While essentially the same in principle, the documentation needed for homeowner's and automobile insurance differs in detail.

The best way to document a theft, fire, or other personal property loss is with pictures. Photograph or videotape all valuable property in your home when you purchase it or when you obtain insurance coverage. Write the date of purchase, price paid, description, model name and number, and serial number (if any) of the property on the back of the photograph or verbally record it on the videotape. Prepare a list describing any items not photographed or videotaped. Keep such records in a safe-deposit box, in a file cabinet at work, or with a relative. If a loss occurs, file a report with the police or fire department, and then present a *copy* of your documentation to the agent or insurance company.

You should always file a police report when involved in an automobile accident or have an automobile (or property in the automobile) stolen. Insureds also should prepare written documentation of any automobile accident for their own records. This documentation should include a diagram of the accident scene showing the location of the vehicles before, during, and after the time of impact, plus the location of traffic lights and signs and any landmarks (for example, road construction or repairs). The description includes a written narrative giving the time and place of the accident, the direction of travel and estimated speed of the cars involved, road and weather conditions, and behavior of the parties involved. If possible, obtain the names and addresses of any witnesses. Detailed notes will help prove your claim in the event of later litigation.

File Your Claim

An **insurance claim** is a formal request to the insurance company for reimbursement for a covered loss. All of the documentation and information will be requested by the insurance agent or **claims adjuster**, who is the person designated by the insurance company to assess whether the loss is covered and to determine the dollar amount that the company will pay. A claims adjuster can be an employee of the insurance company or someone who provides these services to an insurance company for a fee. Generally, the insurance agent oversees the settlement process. Insurance companies require that claims be made in writing, although the adjuster may assist in completing the necessary forms.

Sign a Release

The final step in the claims-settlement process is the signing of the **release**, which is an insurance document affirming that the dollar amount of the loss settlement is accepted as full and complete reimbursement and that the insured will make no further claims for the loss against the insurance company. Signing the release absolves the insurance company of any further responsibility for the loss. Never sign a release prematurely, because the full extent of the loss may not manifest itself until some time after the loss occurs—a particularly important concern when bodily injury losses are involved. Sometimes the insured is pressured into signing the release quickly to receive payment, but you should resist the temptation to give in to such pressure. When dealing with an insurance company, gently—but firmly—insist that adequate time elapse so that the full magnitude of the loss has a chance to become evident.

 Who Decides Who Will Fix Your Car

When a car was damaged, the insured traditionally obtained repair estimates from two shops and presented them to the claims adjuster, who generally agreed to pay the lowest estimate as settlement for the claim. The insured then took responsibility for having the car fixed. If the estimate proved to be too low or the car was taken to a repair shop other than the one with the lowest estimate, the insured might have had to pay the difference.

Increasingly, insurance companies are experimenting with plans that allow the company to participate in the decision of where the car will be repaired. One such plan is known as a **direct repair plan (DRP)**. With a DRP, the insurer provides a list of repair shops that it has prescreened for quality and with which it has negotiated price agreements. If the insured chooses a repair shop from this list, the insurer will cover all costs above the deductible and may even guarantee the work. The insured can choose a repair shop not on the list but must make all of the arrangements and bear the risk that the repairs may cost more than the settlement. A variation of the DRP is the **car maintenance organization (CMO)** in which the insured must (or may) choose a repair shop from a list established by the insurer to be reimbursed for car repairs. In return for giving up the right to choose a repair shop not on the list, the insured may be charged a reduced premium for the policy or might have all or a portion of the deductible waived.

Summary

1. Personal financial managers must practice risk management to protect their present and future assets and income. Risk management entails identifying the sources of risk, evaluating risk and potential losses, selecting the appropriate risk-handling mechanism, implementing and administering the risk-management plan, and evaluating and adjusting the plan periodically.

2. Insurance is a mechanism for reducing pure risk by having a larger number of individuals share in the financial losses suffered by all members of the group. It cannot be used to protect against a speculative risk, which carries the potential for gain as well as loss. Nor can insurance be used to provide payment in excess of the actual financial loss suffered. Insurance consists of two elements: (1) the reduction of pure risk through application of the law of large numbers, and (2) the sharing of losses.

3. Homeowner's insurance is designed to protect homeowners and renters from property and liability losses. Six different types of homeowner's insurance are available, including one for renters. Homeowner's policies can be purchased on a named-perils or open-perils basis.

4. Automobile insurance is designed to protect the insured from property and liability losses arising from use of a motor vehicle. Policies typically provide liability insurance (both bodily injury and property damage liability), medical payments or personal injury protection insurance, property insurance on your car, and underinsured and uninsured motorist insurance. The most commonly purchased type of automobile insurance is the family automobile policy. The premium for automobile insurance is based on the characteristics of the insured driver, including age, gender, marital status, and driving record.

5. Other important types of property and liability insurance include floater policies to protect personal property regardless of its location and professional liability insurance.

6. The insured is responsible for documenting and verifying a loss. Photographs or videotapes of the insured property are ideal for documenting losses under a homeowner's insurance policy. A police report provides the best documentation for losses under an automobile insurance policy.

Key Words & Concepts

actual cash value   *286*

automobile insurance   *287*

claims adjuster   *299*

collision insurance   *290*

deductibles   *276*

homeowner's insurance   *280*

insurable interest   *276*

insurance   *274*

insurance agents   *277*

insurance claim   *299*

liability insurance   *280*

peril   *272*

policy limits   *276*

principle of indemnity   *280*

professional liability insurance   *296*

property insurance   *280*

risk   *271*

risk management   *271*

umbrella liability insurance   *297*

underwriting   *279*

Questions for Thought & Discussion

1. Define risk, and distinguish it from odds or chance.

2. Describe three personal reactions to risk.

3. Describe the five steps of risk management.

4. Distinguish between loss frequency and loss severity.

5. Describe the mechanisms available for handling risk.

6. Define insurance.

7. Describe how insurance serves to reduce pure risk.

8. Distinguish between perils and hazards.

9. Differentiate among the three types of hazards.

10. Describe the three characteristics of financial losses required to make them insurable.

11. How does the requirement of insurable interest affect your ability to buy insurance?

12. Why is the principle of indemnity so important to insurance sellers?

13. Describe the two-part essence of insurance.

14. What is an insurance policy?

15. On what key factors should you focus in an attempt to make sense of an insurance policy?

16. Distinguish between the two types of insurance agents.

17. How might an insurance buyer use deductibles, coinsurance, hazard reduction, and loss reduction to lower the cost of insurance?

18. Distinguish between property and liability insurance.

19. Explain why you would purchase property and liability insurance.

20. Define homeowner's insurance.

21. Name the five types of losses covered under the property insurance portion of a homeowner's policy.

22. Distinguish between a named-perils policy and an open-perils policy.

23. Give an example of a homeowner's liability loss that could be covered under general liability insurance.

24. Briefly describe the six types of homeowner's insurance policies identified as HO-1 through HO-4, HO-6, and HO-8.

25. What is the result when an insured fails to insure the home for the amount indicated by the replacement-cost requirement?

26. In most homeowner's insurance policies, contents and personal property are covered up to what percentage of the coverage on the dwelling itself?

27. Distinguish between actual cash value and contents replacement-cost policies.

28. Define automobile insurance.

29. Distinguish between the two types of losses covered by automobile insurance.

30. Identify the two automobile insurance policies most often purchased by individuals or families, and name their four parts.

31. Many automobile insurance policies identify dollar coverage for the insured with three figures such as $100,000/$300,000/$50,000. Explain what each figure means.

32. Explain the type of coverage provided under automobile medical payments insurance.

33. How do subrogation rights come into play in automobile insurance?

34. Distinguish between collision and comprehensive automobile physical damage insurance coverage.

35. What type of property loss would a floater policy cover?

36. How might a personal risk manager use an umbrella liability policy to enhance his or her insurance protection?

37. What is the best way to document a theft, fire, or other personal property loss in the home?

38. Describe what you should do to file a claim most effectively when involved in an automobile accident.

DECISION-MAKING CASES

Case 1   The Smiths' Auto Insurance Is Not Renewed

Harold and Katrina Smith are faced with a crisis. Their automobile insurance company has notified them that their current coverage expires in 30 days and will not be renewed. Both Harold and their younger son have had minor, at-fault accidents in the past year. The children are otherwise good drivers, as are their parents. They are confused because they know families whose members have much worse driving records but still have insurance.

(a) Explain to Harold and Katrina why their policy might have been canceled.

(b) Use the box on page 294 to give Harold and Katrina some pointers on how to save money on their new policy.

Case 2   Abigail Contemplates a New Homeowner's Insurance Policy

Abigail Elizabeth Proctor of Bedford, Oregon, recently bought a home for $100,000. The previous owner had an $80,000 HO-1 policy on the property, and Abigail can simply pay the premiums to keep the same coverage in effect. Her insurance agent called her and cautioned that she would be better off to upgrade the policy to an HO-2 or HO-3 policy. Abigail has turned to you for advice. Use the information in Table 10.2 to advise Abigail.

(a) What additional property protection would Abigail have if she purchased an HO-2 policy?

(b) What additional property protection would Abigail have if she purchased an HO-3 policy?

(c) What property protection would remain largely the same whether Abigail had an HO-1, HO-2, or HO-3 policy?

(d) Advise Abigail on what differences in liability protection, if any, exist among the three policies.

Case 3   A Student Buys Insurance for a Used Car

Makiko Iwanami, a student from Osaka, Japan, is a member of your history class. She is considering the purchase of a used car and has been told that she must buy automobile insurance to register the car and obtain license plates. She has come to you for advice, and you have decided to focus on three aspects of automobile insurance.

(a) Explain how liability insurance works in the United States. Advise Makiko about which liability insurance limits she should select.

(b) Makiko is especially impressed that automobile insurance includes medical payments coverage because she has no health insurance. Explain why the medical payments coverage does not actually solve her health insurance problem and describe the type of coverage it provides.

(c) Makiko is going to pay cash for the car and doesn't plan to spend more than $2000. Outline the coverage provided by collision insurance and factors that might make such coverage optional for Makiko.

Case 4   An Argument about the Value of Insurance

You have been talking to some friends about how much you know about insurance. One young married couple in the group believes that insurance is really a waste of money in most cases. They argue that "the odds of most bad events occurring are so low that you need not worry." Furthermore, they say that "buying insurance is like pouring money down a hole; you rarely have anything to show for it in the end." Based on what you learned from this chapter, how might you argue against this couple's point of view?

Financial Math Questions

1. Roseanne and Dan Connor of Chicago, Illinois, recently suffered a fire in their home. The fire began in a crawl space at the back of the house, causing $24,000 of damage to the

dwelling. The garage, valued at $8400, was totally destroyed but did not contain a car at the time of the fire. Replacement of their personal property damaged in the home and garage totaled $18,500. In addition, $350 in cash and a stamp collection valued at $3215 were destroyed. While the damage was being repaired, the Connors stayed in a motel for one week and spent $1350 on food and lodging. The house had a value of $95,000 and was insured for $68,400 under an HO-3 comprehensive-form homeowner's policy with a $250 deductible. Use Table 10.2 to answer this case. (Hint: You must first determine whether the Connors have adequate dwelling replacement coverage and, if not, what percentage of the necessary 80 percent coverage they do have. The resulting answer will determine the percentage of the loss to the dwelling covered, and consequently the amount to be reimbursed by the insurance company.)

(a) Assuming that the deductible was applied to the damage to the dwelling, calculate the amount covered by insurance and the amount that the Connors must pay for each loss listed: the dwelling, the garage, the cash and stamp collection, and the extra living expenses.

(b) How much of the amount of the personal property loss would be covered by the insurance? Paid for by the Connors?

(c) Assuming contents replacement-cost protection on the personal property, what amount and percentage of the total loss must be paid by the Connors?

2. Clyde Barrow of Independence, Missouri, has owned his home for ten years. When he purchased it for $78,000, Clyde bought a $78,000 homeowner's insurance policy. He still owns that policy even though the replacement cost of the home is now $110,000.

(a) If Clyde suffered a $20,000 fire loss to the home, what percentage and dollar amount of the loss would be covered by his policy?

(b) How much insurance on the home should Clyde carry to be fully reimbursed for a fire loss?

3. Louise Miller of Denver, Colorado, drives a three-year-old Plymouth valued at $5600. She has a $75,000 personal automobile policy with $10,000 per person medical payments coverage and both collision ($200 deductible) and comprehensive. David Smith of Fort Collins, Colorado, drives a two-year-old Chevrolet Lumina valued at $8500. He has a 25/50/15 family automobile policy with $20,000 in medical payments coverage and both collision ($100 deductible) and comprehensive. Late one evening, while he was driving back from Rocky Mountain National Park, David's car crossed the center line of the road, striking Louise's car and forcing it into the ditch. David's car also left the road and did extensive damage to the front of a roadside store. The following table outlines the damages and their dollar amounts.

Item	Amount
Bodily injuries suffered by Louise	$ 6,800
Bodily injuries suffered by Fran, a passenger in Louise's car	28,634
Louise's car	5,600
Bodily injuries suffered by David	2,700
Bodily injuries suffered by Cecilia, a passenger in David's car	12,845
David's car	8,500
Damage to the roadside store	14,123

Complete the chart below and use the information to answer the following questions:

(a) How much will Louise's policy pay Louise and Fran?

(b) Will subrogation rights come into play? In what way?

(c) How much will David's bodily injury liability protection pay?

(d) To whom and how much will David's property damage liability protection pay?

(e) To whom and how much will David's medical protection pay?

(f) How much reimbursement will David receive for his car?

(g) How much will David be required to pay out of his own pocket?

David Smith's Accident: Who Pays What?

Coverage	David's Policy	Louise's Policy
Liability (limits)	_____	_____
Bodily injury	_____	_____
Louise	_____	_____
Fran	_____	_____
Cecilia	_____	_____
Medical payments (limits)	_____	_____
David	_____	_____
Louise	_____	_____
Fran	_____	_____
Cecilia	_____	_____
Collision coverage (limits)	_____	_____
David's car	_____	_____
Louise's car	_____	_____
David's out-of-pocket expenses	_____	_____
Fran's bodily injury	_____	_____
Excess property damage losses	_____	_____
Collision insurance deductible	_____	_____
TOTAL	_____	_____

4. Cindy Cassady of Terre Haute, Indiana, recently had a hospital stay for removal of her appendix. Her hospital insurance policy has a $250 deductible per year and a coinsurance requirement that she pay 20 percent and her insurance company pay 80 percent of any loss. This event was her only hospitalization for the year.

    (a) How much of the loss was paid by Cindy?

    (b) How much of the loss was paid by her insurance company?

MONEY MATTERS: LIFE-CYCLE CASES

The Hernandezes Consider Additional Liability Insurance

Victor and Maria's next-door neighbor, Joan Saunders, was recently sued over an automobile accident and was held liable for $437,000 in damages. Joan's automobile policy limits were 100/300/50. Because of the shortfall, she had to sell her house and move into an apartment. Victor and Maria are now concerned that a similar tragedy could potentially befall them. They have a homeowner's policy with $100,000 in comprehensive personal liability coverage, an automobile policy with 50/100/25 limits, and a small ($100,000) professional liability policy through Maria's employer.

1. How might Victor and Maria more fully protect themselves through their homeowner's and automobile insurance policies?

2. What additional benefits would they receive in buying an umbrella liability policy?

The Johnsons Decide How to Manage Their Risks

The financial affairs of the Johnsons have become much more complicated since we began following them in Chapter 2. Both Harry ($75 per month) and Belinda ($200 per month) have been given raises at work. They have purchased a $125,000 condominium that has added about $400 per month to their housing expense. They have purchased a $3200 used car, adding about $120 per month to their expenses. As a result of these changes, Harry and Belinda realize that they now face greater risks in their financial affairs. They have decided to review their situation with an eye toward managing their risks more effectively. Use Table 10.1, their net worth and income and expense statements at the end of Chapter 2, and other information in this chapter to answer the following questions:

1. What are Harry and Belinda's major sources of risk from home and automobile ownership, and what is the potential magnitude of loss from each?

2. Given the choices listed in Step 2 of Table 10.1, how would you advise that the Johnsons handle the sources of risk listed in question 1?

Exploring the World Wide Web of Personal Finance

To complete these exercises, go to the *Garman/Forgue* Web site at

www.hmco.com/college/business/

Select Personal Finance. Click on the exercise link for this chapter and answer the questions that appear on the Web page.

1. Visit the Web site for the National Association of Insurance Commissioners, where you will find a map of the United States through which you can link to your state insurance regulator's Web site. If available, obtain an insurance buyer's guide for automobile and homeowner's insurance that describes policy provisions and compares insurance rates. Use these rate comparisons to select two automobile insurance companies that would be appropriate for your needs. Write or telephone the companies to obtain specific premium quotations for the desired insurance protection. Do the same for single-family dwelling, condominium, or renter's insurance, depending upon your circumstances.

2. Visit the Web site for the Insurance News Network. Check the minimum automobile liability insurance requirements for your state.

3. Visit the Web site for A. M. Best, Inc. For your automobile and homeowner's insurance providers (and perhaps one or two others that you have seen advertised), determine the current rating for each company on the basis of its financial strength. When you have found the rating for the first company, click "ratings category" to see an explanation of the ratings given by A. M. Best. Check Standard & Poor's, which also provides such ratings. Compare the ratings given by the two organizations.

4. Visit the Web site for the Highway Loss Data Institute. For your own vehicle and one or two you would like to own, check on how the vehicles stack up against the competition in terms of injury and collision and theft losses. For additional information along these lines, visit the Web site of the Insurance Institute for Highway Safety.

5. Visit the Web site for the Insurance News Network, where you will find an explanation of the coverages provided by the various forms of homeowner's insurance. How are special cases such as flood, earthquake, and windstorm handled under these policies?

Health Care Planning

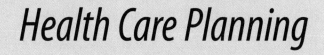

11

OBJECTIVES

After reading this chapter, you should be able to:

1 Identify the major sources of health care plans.

2 Describe the major types of coverage provided by health care plans.

3 Explain the major provisions of health care plans and insurance policies.

4 Describe the purpose and major features of disability income insurance.

Four types of losses can result from an injury or illness. The most obvious is the expense for direct medical care. The other three types are often overlooked, although they may result in large dollar losses as well. They are losses resulting from the need for recuperative care, for rehabilitation, and for replacement of income lost while the patient is unable to work. To protect themselves from these losses, approximately 85 percent of Americans are covered by some form of **health care** (or simply **health**) **plan**—that is, health insurance or another program that pays for or provides reimbursement for health care expenditures and/or losses. This chapter is designed to improve your understanding of these plans. We first address the major sources of health care plans. A thorough examination of the types of coverage provided by health care plans follows. The next section covers important contractual provisions of health care plans and health insurance policies. The final section covers the important topic of disability income insurance.

Providers of Health Care Plans

> **1** Identify the major sources of health care plans.

You can obtain health care benefits as an individual or as a member of a group. A **group health care plan** is sold collectively to an entire group of persons rather than to individuals. Group plans may be more desirable than obtaining health care benefits individually for three reasons. First, a participant *may* be able to obtain group coverage at lower rates. Second, employers often provide group coverage as an employee benefit for their workers. Third, persons who have existing health problems may find it easier to obtain group coverage as the underwriting is based on the entire group rather than an individual. Note that group health care plans generally have an **open enrollment period** annually for about one month during which one might begin or make changes in coverage or switch among alternative plans. Only minimal changes are allowed outside this time period.

Private Insurance Companies

Health insurance provides protection against financial losses resulting from illness, injury, and disability. It may cover hospital, surgical, dental, and other medical expenditures. Because so many different companies exist, do not trust advertising to provide the necessary information as it rarely mentions the exclusions that can reduce benefits.

Managed Care Plans

A **managed care plan** is any health care plan that pays or reimburses for health care expenditures and exerts significant control over the conditions under which health care can be obtained. The two most common forms of managed care plans are preferred provider organizations (PPOs) and health maintenance organizations (HMOs). Examples of controls can range from preapproval of hospital admissions to restrictions on which hospital or doctor can be used. Today more than three-fourths of U.S. workers with health benefit plans are covered by a managed care plan.

Preferred Provider Organization A **preferred provider organization (PPO)** is a group of medical care providers (doctors, hospitals, and other health care providers) who contract with a health insurance company to provide services at a discount. The discount is then passed along to the policyholders in the form of reductions or elimination of deductibles and coinsurance requirements if they choose the PPO providers for their medical care. The discounts do not apply if the policyholders receive health care from non-PPO members. Should the fee charged by a nonmember exceed the amount that the insurer considers reasonable, policyholders must pay the excess.

Consider the case of Earl Fletcher, who works for a large engineering firm in Birmingham, Alabama. His firm's health insurance plan has contracted with a PPO representing a local university's teaching hospital and its affiliated physicians. Because Earl chose the university hospital for treatment of a broken ankle, he saved $150 on the $250 deductible and did not have to pay the usual

20 percent coinsurance share of the bill. Of course, he gave up the right to go to his family doctor, who is not a PPO member, although he could still see that physician for other health care needs in the future.

Provider Sponsored Networks

A **provider sponsored network (PSN)** (also called a provider sponsored organization) consists of a group of cooperating physicians and hospitals who band together to provide health insurance contracts. They operate primarily in rural areas where access to HMOs may be limited. As a group, a PSN coordinates and delivers health care services and manages the insurance plan financially. They contract with outside providers for medical services not available through members of the group. Contracts are marketed to firms wishing to provide health care plans to their employees, to individuals, and as options for those persons covered by government health care plans discussed below.

Health Maintenance Organizations

Health maintenance organizations (HMOs) provide a broad range of health care services to members on a prepaid basis. They do not provide health insurance, but rather health care. Services are available both to groups and individuals. For a specific monthly fee, HMO members receive a wide range of health care services, including hospital, surgical, and preventive medical care. Many HMOs also provide eye examinations, psychiatric care, and ambulance service. If an HMO cannot provide certain types of care, it contracts with a local hospital or clinic for those services. Typically, HMOs operate out of one building or a cluster of buildings housing physicians' offices, treatment rooms, laboratories, and so forth.

A variation is the **individual practice association (IPO)**, a structure in which the HMO contracts with, rather than hires, groups of physicians who maintain their own offices in various locations around town. Another variation is a **point-of-service plan (POS)**, which combines features of PPOs and HMOs. The covered party chooses a primary physician from an approved list who either provides treatment or refers the patient to other approved providers. Unlike HMOs, POS plans allow the patient to choose another provider in return for paying much higher deductibles and copayments.

HMOs generally do not charge for services over and above the monthly fee, although some plans require a small copayment of $5 to $20 for each office visit. A goal of HMOs is to catch problems early, thereby reducing the probability of subsequent high-cost medical treatment. Because HMOs collect only the monthly fee, they have an incentive to keep costs and unnecessary procedures to a minimum. Some critics of HMOs argue that cost-cutting measures lead to a reduction in the quality of services provided. Another common criticism relates to the reduced freedom of choice among physicians. Members are assigned a primary-care physician by the HMO, but they are seen by another physician if their primary-care physician is not on duty when they seek treatment. The primary-care physician must order or approve referrals to health care specialized providers within the HMO.

Federal law requires that employers of more than 25 workers that provide group health insurance benefits to their employees also offer HMO membership as an alternative if an HMO in the area has solicited their business. It would certainly pay to investigate the HMO alternative if it is available to you either through a group or as an individual. While the monthly HMO fee may be slightly higher than the group or individual health insurance premiums, the avoidance of deductibles and coinsurance costs can more than offset the extra monthly cost. When considering an HMO, ask questions about turnover rates among the physicians (high is bad, low is good), the level of satisfaction among current members, reimbursement policies for medical expenses incurred when you are out of town, and the waiting time for a nonemergency appointment (ten to 14 days should be the maximum).*

Government Health Care Plans

The government operates two major health care programs: Medicare and Medicaid. **Medicare** is a program administered by the Social Security Administration that provides payment for hospital and medical expenses of persons aged 65 and over and some others. **Medicaid** is a program of health care for the poor that is jointly administered and funded by the federal and state governments. In addition, military veterans are eligible for free or low-cost health care provided at **Veterans Administration (VA) medical centers**.

Medicare Medicare is funded by means of the Social Security payroll tax. Medicare beneficiaries include persons aged 65 and older who are eligible for Social Security retirement benefits, federal civilian employees aged 65 and older who retired after 1982, persons who are eligible for Social Security disability benefits, and individuals with kidney disorders that require kidney dialysis treatments.

Medicare is divided into two parts. **Medicare Part A** is the hospitalization portion of the program and requires no premium. **Medicare Part B** is the supplementary medical expense insurance portion of the Medicare program. This optional program is open to all Part A recipients and to anyone else age 65 or older. Those choosing Part B pay a monthly premium ($45.50 in 1999) that is adjusted annually.

Medicare Part A will pay benefits for up to 90 days of hospitalization per benefit period. A benefit period begins on the first day of any hospitalization and lasts until the patient goes 60 consecutive days without hospitalization. No limits are placed on the number of benefit periods that a person may use. For a longer hospital stay, a patient may draw on a lifetime maximum of 60 reserve days of benefits.

Medicare Part B will pay benefits for medical expenses related to outpatient care, doctor office visits, or certain other services. It requires the payment of an annual deductible that is adjusted annually and is now over $100; it also includes an 80 percent/20 percent coinsurance requirement. Thus, Part B will reimburse 80 percent of the reasonable approved charge for covered expenses.

Medicare recipients must select among six approaches for managing their Medicare plan. The first approach is the traditional Medicare option, called Original Medicare, which operates much like the Part A/Part B plan. The second approach involves a Medicare HMO option with the HMO being operated by a

---

* The National Committee for Quality Assurance maintains a Web site on the Internet that is used to publish its ratings of HMOs *(www.ncqa.org)*.

private health insurance or HMO organization. The third choice is a Medicare PPO that provides more options for care providers than are available under the HMO option. The fourth approach is an HMO run by a network of local physicians and hospitals that must charge fees within Medicare Administration guidelines. The final two plans—private health insurance subsidized by Medicare and a medical savings account option—are designed for higher-income recipients who wish to chip in their own funds to enhance the coverage provided by Medicare.

Medicaid Eligibility for Medicaid is based on household income and net worth. Health services provided through Medicaid vary from state to state, but generally include hospital, surgical, and medical care. In some states, dental care for children may be covered as well. A key feature of Medicaid is its coverage of custodial long-term and nursing home care. Elderly who have spent down their assets on long-term care may be eligible to receive Medicaid coverage.

Coverages Provided by Health Care Plans

2 Describe the major types of coverage provided by health care plans.

The term "health care plan" is a general name for a wide variety of health insurance policies and other plans that protect against health care losses. No one policy or plan provides coverage for all types of losses. The purchaser of a health care plan faces a situation not unlike that of a diner who must choose from an à la carte menu—that is, he or she must select coverages for medical expenses, recuperative care, and rehabilitative care. The following sections discuss the health benefits "menu" from the perspective of private health insurance, but HMOs and government health care plans also follow a very similar pattern of benefits. These plans are also summarized in Table 11.1.

Hospital Coverage

Hospital (or **hospitalization**) **coverage** protects you from the costs arising out of a stay in a hospital, including room and board charges, routine laboratory expenses, general nursing services, basic supplies, and drugs. Approximately 80 percent of all Americans are covered by some form of hospital coverage, although many have inadequate protection.

In insurance plans, there are three types of hospital coverage: (1) hospital expense insurance, (2) hospital-service-incurred plans, and (3) hospital indemnity insurance. **Hospital expense insurance** provides cash reimbursement for specific hospital expense items incurred during a hospital stay. These expenses include the per-day hospital room charges and miscellaneous hospital expenses (e.g., drugs, supplies, and so on). A **hospital-service-incurred** (or **fee-for-service) plan** pays the hospital directly for the covered services rather than providing a cash reimbursement to the insured for hospital expenses. **Hospital indemnity insurance** provides a cash payment of a specific amount per day of hospitalization. No attempt is made to match the payment to a specific item of expense. Such a plan might pay up to $200 per day of hospitalization, up to a maximum number of days.

Table 11.1

Recommended Criteria for Health Care Plans

Plan*	Policy Limits	Deductible	Coinsurance/ Copayment	Coordination of Benefits	Exclusions
Hospital coverage	Should pay usual, reasonable, and customary charges for a period of 180 days per episode; semiprivate room recommended	Small deductible ($200) can be used to lower premium; deductible should apply on an annual basis	None	Primary	Exclusions should be kept to a minimum; maternity benefits can be excluded, as can mental illness benefits and hospitalization for elective cosmetic surgery
Surgical coverage	Should pay usual, reasonable, and customary charges with no limit	None	None	Primary	Should be few exclusions; elective cosmetic surgery can be excluded; outpatient and doctor's office surgical procedures should not be excluded
Medical expense coverage					
Drugs	$1000 annually	$100 annually	$5 or $10 copayment recommended	Primary	Drugs provided during hospitalization should be covered under hospital coverage; will not cover nonprescription drugs and medicines
Home nursing care	Full payment for 30 days per episode	None	None	Supplement to hospital coverage	None
X rays	$500 annually	$50 annually	$10 copayment per X ray may help lower premium	Supplement to hospital coverage	None
Maternity	Maternity protection should treat a maternity event like any other hospitalization episode and surgical procedure				
Major medical	$500,000 per episode	$500 annually	20 percent/ 80 percent with $10,000 cap	Supplemental to basic plans	Very few exclusions recommended, such as cosmetic surgery
Comprehensive	Any comprehensive plan chosen should have at least the same features as the combined basic and major medical plans outlined above				
Dental	$3000 annually	$100 annually	10 percent or 20 percent coinsurance would help lower premium	Primary	Exclusion of orthodontic procedures may help reduce premiums; cleaning and other preventive care should not be excluded
Vision care	Not recommended				
Supplemental					
Dread disease	Not recommended				
Accident	Not recommended				
Medigap	See major medical recommendations				

* All policies should be written on a guaranteed renewable basis.

Surgical Coverage

Surgical coverage protects you from the expenses of surgical procedures. A **surgical-service-incurred** (or **fee-for-service**) **insurance plan** pays the surgical service providers—the surgeon, anesthesiologist, hospital, and others—directly for their services. Surgical-service-incurred plans usually pay the **usual, customary, and reasonable (ucr)** charge, based on what most service providers charge for similar services within your specific geographic area. If your surgeon charges more than the plan's allowable charge, you may be liable for the difference, especially if you choose a care provider who is not an approved provider under your plan. Surgical plans may have deductible and coinsurance requirements.

Medical Expense Coverage

Medical expense coverage provides reimbursement for physician and medical services other than those directly connected with surgery. It may pay for non-surgical outpatient procedures, X rays, doctor's visits, prescription drugs, and other bills. Such plans usually include a dollar maximum per year, as well as a coinsurance clause and a deductible clause. The deductible clause is often written on an item basis rather than in terms of an annual dollar amount.

Major Medical Expense Insurance

The three types of health care coverage discussed thus far are sometimes referred to as providing "first dollar" protection. They will pay the first dollar (or nearly so) of a covered health care expense. If you rely solely on hospital, surgical, and medical expense coverage, however, you may be reimbursed for small losses but could be wiped out by a serious illness whose costs go beyond the limits of your protection.

Major medical expense insurance provides reimbursement for a broad range of medical expenses, including hospital, surgical, and medical expenses, and may have policy limits as high as $1 million and annual deductibles as high as $1000. It is often used as a supplement to hospital, surgical, and medical expense coverage. Thus, major medical insurance will cover expenses beyond those covered by the more basic plans but only after its deductible has been met.

Most major medical policies include a coinsurance clause, which requires you to pay a percentage (usually 20 percent) of health care expenses (up to some limit) once the deductible is met. Table 11.2 shows how a supplemental major medical plan might apply to a $200,000 health care emergency incurred by Joe Preston, of Boise, Idaho. Even with a $150,000 limit on the major medical policy and reimbursement from hospital, surgical, and medical expense insurance, Joe will still face out-of-pocket expenses of $26,600. Given today's rising health care costs, a major medical policy with an overall limit of $500,000 may not be sufficient.

Comprehensive Health Insurance

A **comprehensive health insurance** plan combines the protection provided by hospital insurance, surgical insurance, medical expense insurance, and major medical expense insurance into a single policy. Such a package of protections

Table 11.2

**Major Medical Expense Insurance
Applied to Joe Preston's Stroke and Neurosurgery**

	Total Expenses $200,000	
	Paid by Joe	Paid by Insurer
Items covered by "first-dollar" protection (hospital, surgical, and medical expense insurance)	$ 0	$ 23,400
Major medical deductible	500	
Portion of the loss subject to major medical coinsurance clause	2,000	8,000
Remainder covered by major medical insurance		142,000
Expenses beyond major medical policy limit	24,100	0
TOTALS	$26,600	$173,400

$150,000 aggregate policy limits, $500 deductible, 20 percent/80 percent coinsurance requirement, $2000 out-of-pocket coinsurance cap.

provides both the coverage of the basic plans and the broad, high-limit coverage of major medical insurance. Comprehensive health insurance plans usually include a $100 or $200 annual deductible and a 20 percent coinsurance requirement for all expenses up to the coinsurance cap. Policy limits of $1 million or more are common. A benefit of a comprehensive policy is that you do not need to determine which policy applies to a given expense. Comprehensive health insurance plans are primarily available on a group basis, and many employers who wish to provide a full line of health insurance coverage to workers take the approach of offering one comprehensive policy.

Dental Expense and Vision Care Insurance

Dental expense insurance provides reimbursement for dental care expenses. It is similar to other forms of health insurance in that it includes deductibles, coinsurance requirements, maximum payments for specific procedures, and overall policy limits. Oral surgery is often excluded from such policies but may be covered under surgical expense insurance. Most dental expense insurance is written on a group basis as an employment benefit.

Vision care insurance provides reimbursement for the expenses related to the purchase of glasses and contact lenses. Such a policy would cover eye examinations, refraction tests, fitting of the lenses, and the cost of the lenses and frames. Most vision care insurance is written on a group basis as an employment benefit. For an individual, vision care insurance is probably not a good buy. The cost of glasses is not so high nor the risk great enough to prevent such expenses from being paid out of the regular budget. Furthermore, the highest expenses for eye care arise out of diseases and injuries to the eyes, which would be covered under general health insurance plans.

Medicare Supplement (Medigap) Insurance

Medicare supplement insurance (sometimes called **Medigap insurance**) is intended to broaden and supplement the protection provided by Medicare. Medicare has certain deductibles and coinsurance requirements that may make the purchase of a supplemental policy desirable. According to federal law, only ten variations (Plans A through J) may be sold to supplement Medicare. These variations range from a basic plan covering Medicare Part A per-day coinsurance and Medicare Part B coinsurance only (Medigap Plan A) to one that covers virtually all medical care costs not covered by Medicare (Medigap Plan J). Only one Medigap policy is needed by an individual because Plan B contains the essential elements of Plan A, and Plan C contains the essential elements of Plan B, and so on. Each plan (A through J) is virtually identical across all insurance companies, making it easier to compare premium quotes for a specific plan. Note that Medigap policies generally will not cover the full cost of custodial nursing home care or physician charges that exceed those accepted by Medicare. Medigap policies are not needed by people eligible for Medicaid; such persons should contact their local Medicaid office to inquire about information on special benefits that supplement Medicare.

 How Dual-Income Families Select Health Care Fringe Benefits

You may be understating your true income by thousands of dollars if you think of your salary as your only payment for employment. An **employee benefit** is any payment for employment that is not provided in the form of wages, salary, or commissions. Many employees receive 40 to 50 percent over and above their salary in the form of employee benefits. Some of the most common benefits include fully paid or subsidized group health insurance, group life insurance, retirement programs, savings programs, tuition subsidies, unemployment insurance, child care, clothing allowances, and employee discounts. The value of these benefits becomes even greater when you consider that the income they represent is often non-taxable or tax-deferred.

Dual-income households often experience duplication of some benefits. For example, both Harry and Belinda Johnson's employers provide partially subsidized family health insurance plans as employee benefits. The Johnsons chose to be covered under Belinda's policy because it provides more protection and is less expensive.

Harry's employer offers a flexible approach toward providing employee benefits. Employees are provided with a maximum dollar amount to be used for benefits. They then choose from a "menu" of employee benefits. Harry has decided to forgo his health insurance to receive tuition support for his master's degree and some additional life insurance protection. He has decided not to take the employer-provided disability income insurance and will seek a policy on his own. This choice may turn out to be advantageous because disability benefits are subject to income taxation if paid from employer-provided plans; by paying the premiums himself, Harry can avoid taxes on the disability income should he become disabled.

Long-Term Care Insurance

Many health care episodes are followed by a period of time where the patient no longer needs skilled medical care but does need assistance to a degree that requires confinement in a nursing home or special help at home. This need is especially prevalent with the extremely elderly (over age 85) and patients with Alzheimer's disease. Such costs are not covered by health insurance, PPOs, HMOs, or Medicare because the care is not *medically* necessary. Nevertheless, this long-term care may cost more than $30,000 per year.

Long-term care insurance provides reimbursement for costs associated with intermediate and custodial care in a nursing facility or at home. Key features to assess when considering such a policy include the following:

- *The type of care covered.* While the largest expenses related to long-term care result from a stay in a nursing home, many people are able to remain in their homes with the assistance of visiting nurses, therapists, and even house-keepers. Long-term care policies can be written to cover such in-home care.

- *Your age.* The younger you are when you take out your policy, the lower the premium. This difference arises because premiums can be collected for many years before long-term care is needed at an advanced age. The trade-off lies between buying young and paying premiums for many years versus waiting to purchase a policy, at which time it may be difficult to buy coverage because of the preexisting condition exclusion.

Did You KNOW ? *Ways People Address Their Need for Long-Term Care*

About 40 percent of the over-65 population can expect to spend time in a nursing home, although less than 20 percent will stay there more than one year. Although Medicaid covers purely custodial (nonmedical) care, the program is meant for the poor, and income and wealth must be extremely low to qualify. How do those elderly who have built up considerable retirement funds intended for both the person who needs the long-term care and for his or her surviving spouse handle this dilemma? Must they have their wealth virtually eroded by the cost of long-term care before they can qualify for Medicaid?

In one sense, the answer is yes. It is also possible for the wealth to be given away to relatives through gifts and through irrevocable trusts (covered in Chapter 19) to bring wealth down to a level that allows one to qualify for Medicaid. Such techniques require the services of a lawyer specializing in estate planning. They also pose a moral quandary. Is it right to "hide" wealth by giving it away to close relatives solely to qualify for a government program intended for the poor? Many people recoil from such techniques out of a sense of justice or a desire to avoid the stigma of taking a handout. Of course, you may also pay your own long-term care expenses until most wealth is depleted and only then seek Medicaid assistance. One way to plan for this event is to set up an investment fund during middle age. The amount going into the fund could be roughly equivalent to the premiums you might pay for a long-term care health insurance policy. Over 20 to 30 years, the fund could grow to a substantial amount.

- *The benefit amount.* Long-term care plans are generally written to provide a specific dollar benefit per day of care. If the cost per day for nursing homes in your area is typically $140, you might buy a policy for $110 per day, thereby coinsuring for a portion of the expenses.

Shop for a Private Health Care Plan

Shopping for a health care plan requires a comparison of the many options available. You should focus your attention on three areas: (1) the cost, (2) the company, and (3) the plan itself.

The Cost

A sound health insurance program purchased outside of a group for the typical family of four can easily cost more than $500 per month. When you apply for an individual health care plan, the decision of whether to accept you is based on a number of underwriting factors, including your age, gender, occupation, family and personal health history, and physical condition. Each of these factors has a bearing on the likelihood of health-related expenditures. A Medical Information Bureau (similar to a credit bureau) also maintains files on insurance applicants.* Both medical and nonmedical information are maintained in these files. If you are charged more or turned down for credit or insurance because of information in such a file, you must be told that the information came from such a file and you can request a copy of the report to verify the accuracy of the information. (Group health care plans, on the other hand, are likely to accept all applicants who qualify as members of the group.)

The Company

Health care companies can also serve as sources of information. Wise financial planners always ask about the percentage of premiums collected by an insurance company that is subsequently paid out to reimburse the losses of the participants. The **claims ratio (payout ratio) formula** is

$$\text{Claims ratio} = \frac{\text{losses paid}}{\text{premiums collected}} \qquad (11.1)$$

Blue Cross/Blue Shield companies typically have claims ratios that exceed 90 percent. At the other extreme are companies (especially those that sell hospital indemnity and dread disease insurance by mail, over the phone, or through newspaper inserts) that have claims ratios of less than 25 percent. The lower the claims ratio, the lower the return (the actual benefits) to the policyholder on the premium dollar paid.

The Plan

The most effective way to compare health care plans is to set some criteria for judging whether a policy provides the needed coverage. The plans that do provide the needed coverage can then be compared on a price basis. Table 11.1 outlines a set of criteria to use in judging the merits of various types of plans, including the plan limits you need to obtain adequate coverage and keep the cost affordable. Many plans will greatly exceed the criteria in this table, but you may not be willing to pay the prices that they charge. Similarly, you may find lower-priced plans, but the lower price may come at the expense of adequate coverage.

Pay special attention to the purchase of any health care plan offered through the mail or in newspapers. The advertising for such plans cannot possibly detail the exact extent of coverage. No plan should be purchased "sight unseen." If an agent or company will not allow you to study a plan for a few days, buy your policy elsewhere.

---

* To obtain a copy of your report ($8 or free within 30 days of an adverse report), write the Medical Information Bureau at P.O. Box 105, Essex Station, Boston, MA 02112, or call (617) 426-3660 for an application or visit *www.mib.com*.

- *The benefit period.* Although it is possible to buy a policy with lifetime benefits, this option can be very expensive. The average nursing home stay is about two and one-half years. A policy with a three-year limit might cost one-third less than a policy with a lifetime benefit period.

- *The waiting period.* Policies can pay benefits from the first day of nursing home care or can include a waiting period. Selecting a 30-day or 90-day waiting period can significantly reduce premiums.

- *Inflation protection.* If you buy a policy prior to age 60, you face a significant risk that inflation will render your daily benefit woefully inadequate when care is ultimately needed. Some policies increase the daily benefit 4 or 5 percent per year to adjust for inflation, but this protection adds considerably to the premium. The younger your age when a policy is purchased, the more you might need inflation protection. Persons over age 65 or so are less likely to benefit from this protection.

Accident and Dread Disease Health Insurance

Accident and dread disease health insurance are two prominent examples of **supplemental health insurance** plans. They are designed to fill the gaps in coverage of the standard health insurance plans or to provide reimbursement in addition to that provided by the standard plans. Most of these plans are overpriced and are not as generous as implied in their sales promotions. Typically you are covered for a narrow range of services and are paid only a small portion of the expenses supposedly "covered." Purchasers often remain unaware of these limitations until they request reimbursement.

Accident insurance pays a specific amount per day—for example, $100 for a hospital stay arising out of an accident—or a specific amount for the loss of certain limbs or body parts—for example, $2000 for the loss of a finger or an arm. The premium for such a policy is very low, and the benefits are relatively small, perhaps $100 per day. Such per-day hospitalization benefits are far too low to be helpful, and reimbursement usually begins only after the hospitalization exceeds seven, ten, or 14 days. The inadequacy of accident insurance becomes evident when you consider that the average cost of a semiprivate hospital room in the United States is more than $400 per day (room charges only) and the average hospital stay is two or three days.

Dread disease insurance provides reimbursement for medical expenses arising out of the occurrence of a specific disease, most commonly cancer. The fear of cancer and the staggering costs of its treatment lead many people to consider buying dread disease insurance, even though this purchase represents a poor use of scarce funds. Like accident insurance,

Who Pays If You Are Hurt on the Job

If you are injured on the job or become ill as a direct result of employment, state law requires your employer to pay any resulting medical costs. **Workers' compensation insurance** covers employers for liability losses for injury or diseases suffered by employees that result from employment-related causes. The benefits to the employee include health care, recuperative care, replacement of lost income, and, if necessary, rehabilitation. Thus, workers' compensation insurance covers the full range of health-related losses. Because only those losses resulting from work-related accidents are covered and benefits are limited, workers' compensation can only supplement your total health insurance plan.

the benefits of dread disease insurance are minuscule compared with the premiums paid. It is much wiser to put the funds toward the purchase of a major medical policy with high limits. Purchasers of accident and dread disease insurance often lack adequate information about medical care costs and the benefits that traditional health care plans may provide.

Making Sense of Your Health Benefits

3 Explain the major provisions of health care plans and insurance policies.

If you are covered by individual health insurance, the insurance policy outlines the general benefits and includes the limitations and conditions that affect the amount reimbursed. If you are covered by group health insurance, you will receive a **certificate of insurance**—a document that outlines the benefits and policy provisions for the participants. If you are covered by an HMO, either as an individual or a member of a group, the HMO (or your employer, if the plan is considered an employee benefit) can provide you with a description of benefits, costs, and procedures for obtaining care. This section describes the important provisions of health care plans and is applicable to health insurance, managed care, and government plans.

General Terms and Provisions

It is important to understand the definitions of terms used in a plan, who is covered by the plan, and the time period of the protection.

Definitions The definitions of the terms used in the plan are of vital importance. For example, a plan may promise to pay $100 for each day of a hospital stay. But what is a hospital? Would such a plan cover nursing home care? Probably not. Would it cover a stay in an osteopathic hospital? Maybe. Two critical definitions contained in a health insurance policy are those for injury and illness. Expenses resulting from an injury may be covered to a greater or lesser degree than those resulting from an illness.

Who Is Covered Health insurance policies can be written to cover an individual, a family, or a group. Few misunderstandings arise when an individual is the focus of the coverage, but family policies can be more complex. Generally, a family consists of a parent or parents and dependent children. Are children who are born while the plan is in effect automatically covered from the moment of birth? What about stepchildren? At what age are children no longer covered? These questions must be answered to ensure that all family members receive adequate protection.

The question of who is covered under a group plan is also very important. All group members are usually covered, but new members may experience a waiting period before receiving protection. If the group consists of the employees of a business, different protection may be offered for full-time and part-time employees. The family of the group member may be covered but, once again, the definition of family must be considered.

The Time Period Individual and group health insurance plans are usually written on an annual basis. An annual plan beginning on January 1 will start at 12:01 A.M. that day and end at 12:01 A.M. on January 1 of the following year. Any illness that begins during the year will be covered. But will coverage end if the plan expires while you are in the hospital? The answer is usually no. Similarly, a surgical procedure performed after a plan expires but for an illness or injury for which treatment was sought during the plan period may be covered.

Payment Limitations

Health care plans contain provisions that specify the level of payments for covered expenses. These provisions include policy limits, deductibles, copayment and coinsurance requirements, and coordination-of-benefits requirements.

Policy Limits **Policy limits** are the maximum amounts that a plan will pay to reimburse a covered loss. Health care plans may employ as many as four types of policy limits. To illustrate these limits, we will consider the case of Karl Gruenfeld, an unmarried electrician from Parma, Ohio, who has a hospitalization policy.

Item limits specify the maximum reimbursement for a particular health care expense. Karl's policy contains a $500 maximum for X rays. Karl suffered a heart attack and had X-ray expenses of $617. The policy will pay $500 of this expense, and Karl will pay the remainder.

Episode limits specify the maximum payment for health care expenses arising from a single episode of illness or injury, with each episode being considered separately. Karl's policy contains an episode limit of $10,000 for hospitalization expenses. After his heart attack, Karl was hospitalized for two weeks and incurred $11,223 in hospital charges. His policy will pay $10,000 of these charges. One month later, Karl suffered burns in a cooking accident at his home and was hospitalized for two days, incurring hospital care costs of $1310. His policy will pay these expenses in full because the second hospitalization is considered a separate episode.

Time period limits specify the maximum payment for covered expenses occurring within a specified time period, usually one year. Consider Karl's heart attack and burn hospitalizations. If his policy had contained a $10,000 annual time period limit rather than an episode limit, the hospital expenses from Karl's second hospitalization would not have been covered.

Aggregate limits place an overall maximum on the total amount of reimbursement available under a policy. If Karl's policy has an aggregate limit of $100,000, no more than $100,000 will be reimbursed for hospitalization expenses Karl incurs during the life of the policy.

Aggregate dollar limits are always higher than time period limits, which are higher than episode limits. A policy with high aggregate limits may seem attractive, but it may not be a good buy if the episode limits are too low. Analyze each limit separately to determine whether it provides sufficient protection.

Deductibles and Copayments **Deductibles** are clauses in health care plans that require you to pay an initial portion of losses before receiving reimbursement. They may apply to specific types of expense items. For example, a medical expense plan may require you to pay the first $50 of total X-ray expenses during the course of a year. Deductibles also may apply to each episode of illness or injury. For example, a plan might require you to pay the first $500 of expenses from a hospital stay. If you are hospitalized three times during a year, you would have to pay the deductible each time, for a total of $1500. Deductibles may apply for a certain time period, typically one year.

Family plans warrant special attention. Generally, they include a deductible for each family member (perhaps $200 per year) with a maximum family deductible (perhaps $500 per year). Once the deductible payments for individual family members reach the family deductible ($500 in this example), further individual deductibles will be waived.

A **copayment clause**, which is a variation of a deductible, requires you to pay a specific dollar amount each time you have a specific covered expense item. Copayment is often required for doctor's office visits and prescription drugs. For example, you might have to pay $10 for each prescription, with the insurer paying the remainder. A copayment differs from a deductible in that a deductible might require that you pay the first $100 of X-ray expenses during a year, while a copayment clause might require that you pay the first $25 of *each* X ray.

Coinsurance   A **coinsurance clause** requires you to pay a proportion of any loss suffered. The typical share is 80/20, with the insurer paying the larger percentage. Usually, a **coinsurance cap** limits the annual out-of-pocket payments made by the patient when meeting the coinsurance. The following example illustrates how a deductible of $250 and an 80/20 coinsurance provision with a $1000 coinsurance cap work together to effect the coverage for an $8760 health care bill. As the deductible is the responsibility of the insured party, the patient pays the first $250. The coinsurance ratio is applied to the remaining $8510 ($8760 − $250) until the portion paid by the patient reaches the coinsurance cap. Thus, $1000 is covered by the insured and $4000 by the insurer. The additional expenses of $3510 ($8510 − $1000 − $4000) are covered 100 percent by the insurance company up to the overall limits of coverage (perhaps $100,000). In this example, the insured party will pay $1250 ($250 deductible + $1000 coinsurance) and the insurer will pay $7510 ($4000 coinsurance + $3510 remaining charges).

Coordination of Benefits   The **coordination-of-benefits clause** prevents you from collecting insurance benefits that exceed the loss suffered. Such a clause designates the order in which plans will pay benefits if multiple plans are applicable to a loss. The primary plan is the first applied to any loss when more than one plan provides coverage. If the primary plan fails to reimburse 100 percent of the loss, any secondary (or excess) plans will be applied in order until the loss is fully paid or benefits are exhausted, whichever occurs first.

Coverage Limitations

In addition to limits on the dollar amounts reimbursed, health care plans may contain a number of provisions that limit the types of expenses covered by the plan. Three categories of common coverage limitations exist: (1) limitations based on timing of the loss; (2) general exclusions; and (3) maternity benefits.

Limitations Based on Timing of the Loss For losses to be insurable, they must be unexpected. Imagine that you develop a serious ulcer and are told by your doctor that surgery will be needed. You might be tempted to buy surgical insurance before having the surgery if you were not already insured. Because the surgery is expected, however, the new policy would not cover its expense. Health plans usually contain provisions that prohibit coverage for **preexisting conditions**, which are medical conditions or symptoms that were known to the participant or diagnosed within a certain time period, usually one or two years, before the effective date of the plan. Group plans exclude fewer preexisting conditions than individual plans.

Disputes sometimes arise over whether a medical loss actually results from a preexisting condition. To clarify matters and to prevent such disputes, insurance plans may dictate waiting periods for specific types of expenses. For example, a "one-year waiting period" is often required for maternity benefits to be covered under a new health insurance plan.

Disputes also arise when episode deductibles and limits are applicable under a plan. The dispute may center on whether a recurrence of an illness represents a separate episode. If the recurrence is considered a separate episode, the deductible must be paid, but reimbursement will be available up to the full episode limits. If the recurrence is considered a continuation of the original episode, the second deductible will not apply, but the loss may exceed the episode limit. A **recurring clause** clarifies whether a recurrence of an illness is considered a continuation of the first episode or a separate episode. Such clauses often stipulate a minimum number of days between hospital stays for a recurrence to be considered a separate episode. Usually, the best recurring clause requires a short waiting period before a recurrence is considered a separate episode, because it is typically less expensive to pay a deductible than to pay expenses exceeding the episode limit. Nonetheless, you should judge each policy individually in terms of the recurring clause, the amount of the deductible, and the amount of the episode limit.

General Exclusions **Exclusions** narrow the focus of and eliminate specific coverage provided in a plan. Losses resulting from war, riot, and civil disturbance may be excluded from health care plans. Most policies exclude expenses for voluntary cosmetic surgery, and many deny coverage if the illness or injury occurs outside the United States. Expenses resulting from self-inflicted wounds are commonly excluded during the first two years of the policy.

Maternity Benefits Maternity benefits are often considered separately from other benefits in a health care plan, and specific limits and exclusions may apply. The best coverage treats maternity care in the same way as any other health care episode. A common limitation on maternity-related benefits restricts payment for hospitalization of the newborn after the mother has been discharged from the hospital.

Nonmedical Provisions

Health care plans contain important provisions that regulate the payment of premiums and the terms under which the plan may be renewed and canceled. These nonmedical provisions include continuation provisions, grace periods, and convertibility.

Continuation Provisions   Health insurance and disability income insurance policies usually expire after one or five years, at which time they can be renewed, changed, or dropped. During the policy period, they may even be canceled. The following terms apply to the continuation of health insurance policies:

- **Cancelable policies** may be canceled or changed at any time at the option of the insurer. Such policies are no longer common and should be avoided.

- **Optionally renewable policies** may be canceled or changed by the insurer, but only at the time of expiration and renewal.

- **Guaranteed renewable policies** must be continued in force as long as the participant pays the required premium. Premiums may change, but only if the change applies to an entire class of participants rather than to an individual participant. This requirement prevents the company from raising the premium for a specific individual to force him or her to cancel. This type of health insurance policy is the most common and desirable.

- **Noncancelable policies** must be continued in force without premium changes up to age 65 as long as the participant pays the required premium. Noncancelable policies are recommended when buying disability income insurance (discussed later in this chapter).

Grace Period   Health insurance policies may contain provisions for a grace period (commonly 31 days), which prevents the lapse of a policy if a payment is late. The policy remains fully in force during the grace period, but only if the insured pays the premium before the end of the grace period.

Convertibility and Portability   Many people are covered by group health insurance through their employers. The **Comprehensive Omnibus Budget Resolution Act (COBRA)** of 1985 (and subsequent amendments) requires that employers with more than 20 employees who offer group health insurance continue to offer group coverage for 18 months after an employee has quit or been laid off. The option to continue group coverage must be offered to the former employee and to any dependents who had been covered under the employer's group plan. Under COBRA, widows, widowers, divorced spouses, and dependents of terminated employees must be given this option for 36 months. The employee or dependents desiring to maintain the coverage must indicate this fact within 60 days of the termination of employment and generally must pay the full premiums (including the employee and employer's portion) plus a 2 percent fee. Thus, the employer is not required to pay for the coverage, only to maintain the former employee's eligibility as a member of the group. Eventually, eligibility to remain under the group plan may run out. The 1996 health insurance law requires a **portability option**

HOW to... Maintain Health Coverage When Changing Jobs

The COBRA law is intended to protect workers' health care benefits in the event of a time lag between jobs. COBRA also can be beneficial for people changing jobs without a time lag, especially those whose health problems subject them to a waiting period under preexisting condition clauses in their new coverage. For example, a worker with diabetes who does not qualify for immediate benefits under his or her new employer's health care plan could elect COBRA continuation rights under the previous employer's plan. This coverage could provide protection during the waiting period for the new plan. The worker would be required to pay the premium for this coverage but would be covered in the interim should a health care episode occur.

that allows the insureds to convert their group coverage to individual coverage when they lose company-sponsored group health insurance. The individual policy premium may be higher but the waiting period and preexisting condition provisions will not apply.

Disability Income Insurance

4 Describe the purpose and major features of disability income insurance.

A number of sources are available for income protection during a period of disability. Many U.S. workers have sick pay benefits that can help ease the burden of a short period of disability. Some employers offer group disability income insurance, although typically the coverage lasts for only a short term (less than two years). In addition, many pension plans provide benefits to workers who become disabled while still employed. Such benefits plans, however, often fall far short in meeting the needs of young and middle-aged workers, who may have accumulated only a small amount of retirement funds.

Disability income insurance replaces a portion of the income lost when you cannot work because of illness or injury. It is probably the most overlooked type of insurance, but is vitally important for all workers. For example, a 22-year-old without dependents would probably need no life insurance, but would likely need disability insurance to support himself or herself during a period of disability. Furthermore, at age 22, the chances of becoming disabled for at least three months are seven times greater than the chances of death. (The probability of death for a male aged 22 is 18.9 per 10,000; the likelihood of disability is 142.8 per 10,000.)

Social Security disability income insurance provides benefits that will help replace the lost income of eligible disabled workers. This insurance provides eligible workers and their dependents with income during a period of disability expected to last at least 12 full months or until the worker's death. Benefits begin after a five-month waiting period, and the disability must be total. That is, the recipient must not be able to engage in any substantial, gainful activity. If he or she can perform any work for pay, benefits will not be paid. Social Security disability income protection may provide more than $20,000 in tax-free income to the family of a fully insured disabled worker. See Appendix B for an illustration of how to estimate these benefits.

Level of Need

The first question to ask when contemplating disability income insurance is, "How much protection do I need?" The dollar limits on disability income policies are written either in increments of $100 per month or as a percentage of monthly income. Most companies will not write policies for more than 60 to 80 percent of the insured's after-tax earnings. Major factors affecting the premiums charged include: the amount of coverage desired; your age, health status, occupation, and gender; and whether the policy is noncancelable or guaranteed renewable (the more commonly available choice).

Determining the amount of protection needed may be difficult because some sources of help may not actually be available for all disabilities. For example, recall the five-month waiting period and total disability requirements (for which

Determining Disability Income Insurance Needs

The determination of disability income insurance needs begins with your current monthly after-tax income. From this figure, subtract the amounts you would receive from Social Security disability benefits and other sources of disability income. As shown below, the resulting figure would provide an estimate of extra coverage needed.

Decision Factor	Example	Your Figures
1. Current monthly after-tax income	$2100	_____
2. Minus previous established disability income protections		
(a) Estimated monthly Social Security benefits	750	_____
(b) Monthly benefit from employer-provided disability insurance	600	_____
(c) Monthly benefit from private disability insurance	—	_____
(d) Monthly benefit from other government disability insurance	—	_____
(e) Reduction of monthly life insurance premiums due to waiver of premiums on these policies	—	_____
Total Subtraction	−1350	_____
3. Estimated monthly disability income insurance needs	$ 750	_____

70 percent of all applicants are rejected) under Social Security. A disability that does not qualify for Social Security disability income insurance may create a need for more disability insurance than a more severe disability that does qualify for Social Security.

In addition, some disability benefits may cover short-term, but not long-term, disability. Nevertheless, it would be wise to complete the calculations in the Decision-Making Worksheet, "Determining Disability Income Insurance Needs." You can use the figure obtained in the worksheet as a starting point when shopping for disability income insurance protection.

Important Disability Income Insurance Policy Provisions

Once you have estimated your level of need, you can begin the search for a disability income insurance policy. Look first for the major policy provisions that meet your needs. The following paragraphs discuss these important policy provisions.

Elimination Period The **elimination period (waiting period)** in a disability income policy is the time period between the onset of the disability and the date that disability benefits begin. The longer the elimination period, the lower the premium will be. Increasing the disability period from 30 to 90 days can reduce the premium by as much as one-third, for example. If your employer offers sick pay benefits, you can coordinate the elimination period in a policy with the number of sick days you have accrued. Alternatively, if you have some savings set aside as an emergency fund to carry you through several months without income, your elimination period can be lengthened. Note that because disability income benefits are paid monthly, the first check will not arrive until 30 days after the end of the elimination period.

Benefit Period The **benefit period** in a disability income policy is the maximum period of time for which benefits will be paid. It begins when the elimination period ends. The benefit period is usually stated in years and may vary from one year to "to age 65." Most disability income policies will not pay past age 65.

Degree of Disability Policies can be written on an "own-occupation" or "any-occupation" basis. An **own-occupation policy** will provide benefits if you can

How Much Disability Income Insurance Costs*

Fewer than one in four U.S. workers is covered by **long-term disability insurance** (disability income insurance that has a benefit period of more than two years). Yet such a period of disability could destroy your financial security for life. How does the wise purchaser of disability income insurance obtain long-term coverage and keep the premiums affordable? The answer lies in an analysis of the following table. For each waiting period, the premium increases as the length of the benefit period increases. With a seven-day waiting period and benefits to age 65, the illustrated policy would cost $1022 per year. This premium could be cut by more than one-half with the selection of a 60- or 90-day waiting period. The extra premium required can be offset by choosing a longer waiting period. Again we see an application of the rule that says, "Insure the losses you cannot afford (in this case, a long-term disability) and assume the losses that you can reasonably afford (the first few months of a disability)."

* Direct sellers of disability income insurance include the Wholesale Insurance Network at (800) 808-5810 and Fee for Service at (800) 874-5662.

Illustrative Disability Income Insurance Premiums

Waiting Period	Maximum Benefit Period			
	1 Year	3 Years	5 Years	Age 65
7 days	$586	$653	$709	$1022
14 days	463	553	608	910
30 days	269	334	378	604
60 days	184	242	285	498
90 days	—	194	237	446
1 year	—	—	207	370

Note: Illustrative annual premium for a $2000 per month disability income policy for a 35-year-old male in a white-collar occupation. For different dollar amounts, adjust proportionately.

no longer perform the occupation you had at the time you became disabled. An **any-occupation policy** will provide benefits only if you cannot perform any occupation. In effect, an any-occupation policy is an income replacement policy, as it makes up a portion of the difference between what you were earning prior to becoming disabled and what you can earn while disabled. Own-occupation policies are more generous and, therefore, cost more. Some policies provide own-occupation coverage during the first two years of a disability and then switch to an any-occupation basis with income replacement for the remaining years of the benefits. Such **split-definition policies** are likely to provide benefits for rehabilitation and retraining at company expense.

Residual Clause   A **residual clause** is a feature of own-occupation policies that allows for some reduced level of disability income benefits when a partial—rather than full—disability strikes. Consider the case of Francoise LaDeux, a criminal lawyer in Shreveport, Louisiana, who had purchased a disability policy with a benefit of $3000 per month. Francoise later suffered from extremely high blood pressure and was forced to cut back her workload by 50 percent, thereby taking a 50 percent pay cut. Her disability policy had a residual clause, so she received $1500 (0.50 × $3000 per month) during her disability.

Social Security Rider   If you have figured your disability income insurance needs assuming that you would receive Social Security benefits, you will find yourself with inadequate protection if your Social Security application is denied. To provide an extra dollar amount of protection should you fail to qualify for Social Security disability benefits, a **Social Security rider** may be added to your policy. Consider the case of Karen Gifford, a florist from Urbana, Illinois. Karen determined that her disability insurance needs would be $1400 after assuming

TAX Considerations & Consequences   *Health Care*

Self-employed people may deduct as a business expense a portion of the cost of medical expense premiums for themselves and dependents. Other people may save on taxes when they pay health care costs using a *flexible spending account* through their employers (see Chapter 1). Under such a plan, your employer deducts a portion of your salary and puts it into an account that is used to pay some of your health care expenditures. This money is not included in your taxable income. For example, if you are in the 28 percent marginal income tax bracket and set aside $100 per month (or $1200 for the year), you could save $336 ($1200 × 0.28) in federal income taxes.

Medical savings accounts allow individuals to set up their own tax-deductible savings accounts to be used to pay future health-related expenses. This experimental program is an alternative to group health insurance for those who are self-employed or who work for small firms with high-deductible plans.

In addition, recall from Chapter 3 that health care expenditures (including a portion of certain long-term care insurance premiums) are itemized deductions on one's income tax return. However, only the amount that exceeds 7.5 percent of the adjusted gross income are deductible.

that she would receive $1000 from Social Security if she were to become disabled. She could have purchased a $2400-per-month policy and removed all uncertainty, but the premium would have been more than she could afford. Instead, she bought a $1400 policy with a $1000 Social Security rider for a premium savings of 30 percent.

Cost-of-Living Adjustments You might want to seek out policies with a **cost-of-living clause**, which will increase your benefit amount to keep up with inflation. You might also consider buying a policy that limits benefits to a percentage of income rather than a specific dollar amount per month. With such a policy, your potential monthly benefit would increase automatically as your income increases.

Summary

1. Providers of health care loss protection include private health insurance, managed care plans, and government programs. Private health insurance and managed care plans can be obtained individually or on a group basis.

2. The major benefits provided by health care plans are hospital, surgical, medical expense, major medical expense, comprehensive coverage, dental expense benefits, and vision care benefits.

3. Health care plans contain language that outlines coverage in general and, more importantly, describes the limitations and conditions that determine the level of protection under the plan. Some of the more important plan provisions include definitions of terms used in the plan, who is covered under the plan, and the time period for the coverage. Important limitations include deductibles and copayments, coinsurance requirements, and limitations on the types of losses covered.

4. Disability income insurance replaces a portion of the income lost when you cannot work as a result of illness or injury. The amount you need is equal to your monthly after-tax income less any benefits to which you are entitled (e.g., Social Security). By selecting among various policy provisions, you can tailor a policy that fills the gaps in your existing disability protection.

Key Words & Concepts

Questions for Thought & Discussion

1. Categorize the losses that can result from an injury or illness.

2. Distinguish among private health insurance, managed care plans, and government health care programs.

3. Identify one positive aspect of group health care plans.

4. Distinguish between PPOs and HMOs.

5. Distinguish between Medicare and Medicaid.

6. Describe the differences among the three types of hospital insurance.

7. Define medical expense insurance.

8. How does major medical insurance differ from the three types of "first-dollar" health coverage?

9. Describe comprehensive health insurance.

10. What is Medicare supplement insurance and how many different plans meet its standards?

11. Define long-term care insurance and describe four considerations you must keep in mind when selecting this type of insurance.

12. On what three areas should you focus when shopping for health insurance coverage?

13. What valuable piece of information is conveyed by an insurance company's claims ratio?

14. Describe the type of insurance that protects you if you are hurt while on the job.

15. Explain the purpose of a certificate of insurance.

16. Distinguish among item limits, episode limits, time period limits, and aggregate limits as used in health insurance policies.

17. What are the differences between a deductible and a copayment?

18. Explain the purpose of a coordination-of-benefits clause.

19. What is a preexisting condition, and how does it relate to a recurring clause in a health insurance policy or health care plan?

20. Explain the various continuation provisions typically used in health insurance policies.

21. Define disability income insurance and explain how you determine your level of need for such insurance.

22. Identify the major policy provisions to consider when purchasing disability income insurance.

DECISION-MAKING CASES

Case 1   A New Employee Ponders Disability Insurance

Jim Napier of Bethlehem, Pennsylvania, recently took a new job as a manufacturer's representative for an aluminum castings company. While looking over his employee benefits materials, he discovered that his employer would provide ten sick days per year. Jim can accumulate a maximum of 60 sick days if any go unused in a given year. In addition, his employer provides a $1000-per-month, short-term, one-year total disability policy. After calling the employee benefits office, Jim found that he might qualify for $400 per month in Social Security disability benefits if he became unable to work. Jim also knew that he could cease paying $50 per month in life insurance premiums if he became disabled under a waiver-of-premium option in his life insurance policy. Jim earns a base salary of $1500 per month and expects to earn about that same amount in commissions, for an average after-tax income of $2100 per month. After considering this information, Jim became understandably concerned that a disability might destroy his financial future.

(a) What is the level of Jim's short-term, one-year disability insurance needs?

(b) What is the level of Jim's long-term disability insurance needs?

(c) Help Jim select from among the important disability insurance policy provisions (on pages 324–327) to design a disability insurance program tailored to his needs.

Case 2   A CPA Selects a Health Insurance Plan

Your friend Taliesha Jackson of Tulsa, Oklahoma, recently started a new job in a moderate-size CPA firm. Knowing that you were taking a personal finance course, she asked your advice about the selection of her health insurance plan. Her employer offered four options:

• *Option A* A package of hospital, surgical, and medical expense insurance plus a major medical policy. The "first-dollar" coverages provide for 45 days per year of hospitalization and otherwise would pay the usual, customary, and reasonable charges for almost any event, including maternity. The major medical policy has a $500 annual deductible and an 80 percent/20 percent coinsurance clause with a $20,000 coinsurance cap. The major medical policy has a $100,000 aggregate limit.

• *Option B* A comprehensive health insurance policy with a $250 annual deductible, an 80 percent/20 percent coinsurance clause with a $10,000 coinsurance cap, and a $250,000 aggregate limit.

• *Option C* Same as option B except that a PPO is associated with the plan. If Taliesha agrees to have services provided by the PPO, her annual deductible drops to $100 and the coinsurance clause is waived. As an incentive to get employees to select option C, Taliesha's employer will provide dental expense insurance worth about $20 per month.

• *Option D* Membership in an HMO. Taliesha would have to contribute $25 extra each month if she chose this option.

(a) Explain to Taliesha why her employer requires her to pay extra if she joins the HMO.

(b) Why might Taliesha's employer provide an incentive of dental insurance if she chooses option C?

(c) To help her make a decision, Taliesha has asked you to make a list of three positive and three negative points about each plan. Prepare such a list.

Financial Math Questions

1. Bernard Haley of Rockford, Illinois, aged 61, recently suffered a severe stroke. He was in intensive care for 12 days and was hospitalized for 18 more days. After being discharged from the hospital, he spent 45 days in a nursing home for medically necessary nursing and rehabilitative care. Bernard had hospital, surgical, and medical expense insurance through his employer. He had also purchased major medical insurance through a group plan with a $1000 deductible and $50,000 episode and $250,000 aggregate limits. The major medical policy had an 80/20

coinsurance clause with a $2000 coinsurance cap. All of Bernard's policies covered medically necessary services performed in a nursing home setting. His total medical bill was $125,765, and his insurance from his employer covered $42,814 of these charges.

(a) Of the remainder, how much did the major medical policy pay?

(b) How much did Bernard pay?

2. Michael Howitt of Berkley, Michigan, recently had his gallbladder removed. His total bill for this event, which was his only health care expense for the year, came to $13,890. His health insurance plan has a $500 annual deductible and a 75/25 coinsurance provision. The cap on Michael's coinsurance share is $2000.

(a) How much of the bill will Michael pay?

(b) How much of the bill will be paid by Michael's insurance?

3. Marjorie Wolfstead, a mortgage broker in Tucson, Arizona, had heart bypass surgery last year. Marjorie was covered by both Parts A and B of Medicare with the following information applicable at that time.

Part A annual deductible:	$716
Part B annual deductible:	$100

Part A coinsurance:
For each day hospitalized over 60 and up to 90 days	$179/day
For days 1–20 for skilled nursing home care	20%
For days 21–100 for skilled nursing home care	$89.50/day
For nonskilled approved home health care	20%
For approved durable medical equipment	20%

Part B coinsurance:
For Medicare-approved services	20%

Given this information and the additional billing information for Marjorie's surgery and recovery, calculate her share of each component.

(a) The hospital bill:

7 days in intensive care at $700 per day	$ 4,900
14 days in a regular room at $350 per day	4,900
Operating room, X rays, tests	5,000
Total	$14,800

(b) The physician's bills:

Cardiologist for surgery and follow-up	$ 3,000
Anesthesiologist	1,000
Primary-care physician for hospital visits	1,320
Total	$5,320

(c) Recovery expense bills after the hospital stay:

Skilled nursing home care for 30 days at $300 per day	$ 9,000
Nonskilled home health care for 14 days at $100 per day	1,400
Total	$10,400

(d) What was the total amount paid by Marjorie?

MONEY MATTERS: LIFE-CYCLE CASES

The Hernandezes Face the Possibility of Long-Term Care

Victor Hernandez has recently learned that his uncle has Alzheimer's disease. After discussing this tragedy with Maria, he has realized that two of his grandparents probably had the disease, although no formal diagnosis was ever made. As a result, Victor and Maria have become interested in how they might protect themselves from the financial impact of long-term health care.

1. What factors should the Hernandezes consider as they shop for long-term care protection?

2. Victor is still in his forties. How does his age affect their decisions related to long-term care protection?

The Johnsons Consider Buying Disability Insurance

Although Belinda receives a generous employee benefit program, it does not provide disability income protection other than eight sick days per year that may accumulate to 20 days if she does not use them. Harry also has no disability income insurance. Although both have worked long enough under Social Security to qualify for disability benefits, Belinda has estimated that Harry would receive about $640 and she would receive about $800 per month if they qualified for Social Security. Harry and Belinda realize that they could not maintain their current living standards on only one salary. Thus, the need for some disability income insurance has become evident even though they probably cannot afford such protection at this time. In fact, they chose not to purchase the disability waiver of premium option when they purchased their life insurance. Advise them on the following points:

1. Use the Decision-Making Worksheet on page 324 to determine how much disability insurance Harry and Belinda each need. Use the December salary figures from Table 4.3. To determine the amount of taxes and Social Security paid by each, assume that Harry, whose salary represents approximately 42 percent of their total income, paid a comparable percentage of the taxes.

2. Use the information on pages 324–327 to advise the Johnsons about their selections related to the following major policy provisions:

   (a) elimination period

   (b) benefit period

   (c) residual clause

   (d) Social Security rider

   (e) cost-of-living adjustments

Exploring the World Wide Web of Personal Finance

To complete these exercises, go to the *Garman/Forgue* Web site at

www.hmco.com/college/business/

Select Personal Finance. Click on the exercise link for this chapter and answer the questions that appear on the Web page.

1. Visit the Web site for the National Committee on Quality Assurance, where you will find information assessing the quality of and accreditation status of health care plans. If you are covered by a health care plan, search for information on your plan. If you are not covered or if data are not available on your plan, select a major city and obtain the report on a plan in that city. What information, criteria, and other data in the report might assist you in assessing the quality of any plan? Also print a copy of NCQA's consumer brochure.

2. On the *Garman/Forgue* Web site, you will find the Decision-Making Worksheet on page 324 to calculate your disability income insurance needs. Call an insurance agency and a direct seller (see footnote on page 325) to obtain policy information and premium quotations on policies that would fit your needs.

3. Visit the Web site of the Insurance News Network, where you will find tips for buying health insurance for people who are not part of a group plan. List four suggestions for saving money on individual health plans.

4. Revisit the Web site for the Insurance News Network. Determine the mandatory coverages in your state for various types of health procedures and providers. How does your state compare with others in the breadth and depth of mandated coverages?

Life Insurance Planning

12

OBJECTIVES

After reading this chapter, you should be able to:

1 Identify the purpose of life insurance and the reasons for buying it.

2 Recognize that the need for life insurance varies over the course of one's life and identify the procedures used to calculate life insurance needs.

3 Distinguish among the various types of term and cash-value life insurance policies.

4 Describe and explain the purpose of the major provisions of life insurance policies.

5 Discuss important points to consider when choosing and buying life insurance.

Although death is certain, when it will occur is not. With this uncertainty comes the risk of financial losses. **Life insurance** is an insurance contract that protects against financial losses resulting from death. This chapter examines the role of life insurance in your overall personal risk-management plan. Topics covered include reasons for buying life insurance, ways to determine your insurance needs, the many types of life insurance, the life insurance policy and its major provisions, and strategies for buying life insurance.

Why Buy Life Insurance?

1 Identify the purpose of life insurance and the reasons for buying it.

In a sense, the term "life insurance" is a misnomer. The person on whose life an insurance policy is issued will not be protected from death, nor will he or she benefit financially when the proceeds of the policy are paid. The primary reason for buying life insurance is to obtain financial protection for others when the insured party dies—thus, perhaps it should more accurately be called "death insurance." In another sense, however, life insurance is appropriately named. Life insurance can allow the survivors and heirs of the deceased to continue with their lives free from the financial burdens that death can bring. Home ownership can be safeguarded, and a surviving parent of young children may be able to stay at home rather than work for money income at least for a time. College or other educational plans can remain intact, and retirement income can be made available for the surviving spouse.

Insurance companies employ **actuaries**, who calculate the probabilities of death for individuals based on such characteristics as age, health, and lifestyle; these probabilities are then used to establish the rates that an individual must pay for life insurance. The **death rate** represents the probability that an individual will die at a given age. As you would expect, it increases as a person grows older. In recent years, death rates for most age groups have declined due to medical advances in the treatment of heart disease, stroke, and cancer. Although most people live to at least retirement age, approximately 25 percent of today's adults will die during their working years. Life insurance purchased as part of one's overall financial plan enables people to deal with this potential financial loss.

How to Determine Your Life Insurance Needs

2 Recognize that the need for life insurance varies over the course of one's life and identify the procedures used to calculate life insurance needs.

Life insurance needs are highly individualized and can vary from zero to more than $1 million. The individual's stage in the life cycle is a key factor, as are relevant financial factors. After discussing these factors, this section presents two methods for calculating life insurance needs.

Life Insurance Needs over the Life Cycle

The need for life insurance varies over the life cycle. During childhood and while single, our need for life insurance is nonexistent or very small, because few, if any, other people rely on our income. With marriage comes the increased responsibility for another person, although life insurance needs will probably remain low because each spouse usually has the potential to support himself or herself if the other partner were to die. The arrival of children, however, triggers a sharp increase in life insurance needs except in the rare circumstances where sufficient amounts of other financial resources are available. Children often require as many as 25 years of parental support, during which time they have little ability to provide for themselves. As children grow older, the number of years of remaining dependency declines. Most parents eventually see a reduced need for life insurance once their children become independent, in part because parental responsibility for children declines and in part because the parent's investment program may have grown large enough to be used for income. Retirement and the likelihood of another period of singlehood reduce the need for life insurance even further—or may even eliminate it altogether.

Financial Factors Affecting Life Insurance Needs

In addition to grief over the personal loss involved in the death of a loved one, survivors may experience severe financial losses. These losses can include the lost income of the deceased and expenditures for final expenses, a readjustment period, debt repayment, and education for children. Existing life insurance, financial assets, and Social Security may partially offset such losses.

Income-Replacement Needs The major financial loss resulting from premature death is the lost income of the deceased—that is, the money used to pay for the household's ongoing needs. Included in this lost income is the value of any essential employment fringe benefits, such as health plan benefits for dependents. Similarly, the household work of family members should not be overlooked. The best way to calculate the value of household work is to estimate the annual cost of hiring the lost services. In addition, many dual-earner families require both incomes to maintain the desired level of living. Thus, life insurance needs should be calculated for all family income providers. Some people may also provide income for their parents, and this flow of income must be protected as well.

Final-Expense Needs **Final expenses** are those one-time expenses occurring just prior to or after a death. Probably the greatest of these expenses relates to the funeral, which often costs more than $5000. Travel expenses for family members during a terminal illness and to attend a funeral can be quite high. Likewise, food and lodging expenses for mourners are often substantial. Severe and costly disruptions of family life can last up to a month or more.

Readjustment-Period Needs A period of readjustment is often necessary after the death of a loved one. This period may last for a few years and may have financial aspects that require substantial life insurance proceeds. For example, the death of a parent with young children may be such a shock that the surviving spouse chooses to forgo employment for a while. Similarly, a working spouse may need to take time off from a job to obtain further education.

Debt-Repayment Needs Many people expect life insurance proceeds to pay off installment loans, personal loans, and the outstanding balance on the home mortgage should a family income provider die. Actually, a family that has provided adequately for the replacement of lost income probably will not need to make specific insurance provisions for the repayment of debts. It is sometimes helpful, however, to create a plan to pay off all debts other than the mortgage for no other reason than to simplify the financial life of the survivors.

College-Expense Needs Many families with small children have a college savings plan in place. Adequate provision to replace lost income should allow continuation of the plan. However, most families will also use current income to handle expenses when the children are in college, and the death of a family income provider may, therefore, impede the ability to meet the need. The solution is to earmark a dollar amount of life insurance proceeds for future college expenses.

Other Special Needs Many families have special needs that require consideration in the life insurance planning process. Wealthier families might need extra life insurance to pay federal estate and state inheritance taxes (covered in Chapter 19). A family with a disabled child might have special needs if that child is likely to require medical or custodial care as an adult.

Government Benefits Widows, widowers, and their dependents may qualify for various government benefits, most notably **Social Security survivor's benefits** that are paid to a surviving spouse and children. The level of benefits depends on the amount of Social Security taxes paid by the deceased during his or her life. (Details on estimating Social Security benefits are provided in Appendix B.) If eligible, a family can receive as much as $25,000 per year, but these benefits generally cease when the youngest child reaches age 18 and do not begin again until the surviving spouse nears retirement age. This period of ineligibility for Social Security benefits, called the **Social Security blackout period,** ends when the surviving spouse reaches the age of 60. The surviving spouse may then collect survivor's benefits until age 62 when he or she may begin collecting Social Security retirement benefits from the individual's Social Security retirement account or from the spouse's account, whichever provides the higher payment.

Existing Insurance and Assets Employers often provide life insurance to their employees as an employee benefit. In addition, many people have existing life insurance that was purchased for them as children or that they themselves purchased prior to employment. These coverages can reduce the need for additional life insurance purchases.

   As time passes, individuals and families usually acquire at least a minimal amount of savings and investments. The funds held in savings accounts, certificates of deposit, stocks, bonds, and mutual funds often are specifically earmarked for some special goal, such as retirement, travel, or college for children. In the event of a premature death, they could be used to meet final and readjustment expenses as well as to replace lost income, even though it may be wiser to use these funds for their originally intended purpose. Pension funds and retirement plans of the deceased, such as 401(k) and 403(b) plans and IRAs (discussed in Chapter 18, "Retirement Planning"), are sometimes viewed as resources. Younger families should be wary of using retirement money for living expenses after the death of an income provider, however, as this strategy may jeopardize the surviving spouse's retirement. As a general rule, life insurance needs decrease and assets increase over the course of one's life. At some point, savings and investments may exceed potential losses and eliminate the need for life insurance—especially after age 60, when retirement is imminent or has arrived.

Calculating the Dollar Amount of Loss

Determining the magnitude of the possible losses resulting from a premature death can be complicated. One calculation method involves an attempt to put a dollar value on the life to be insured based on some notion of the psychological loss that would be felt. This approach is particularly inadequate and hazardous because it has no connection to the actual financial loss that will be suffered.

The Multiple-of-Earnings Approach Some people use a **multiple-of-earnings approach** to estimate how much life insurance they need. This method consists of multiplying one's income by some factor to derive a final figure. For example, one simple rule-of-thumb multiple-of-earnings approach is to have life insurance five or six times one's annual income. One could also use the interest factors from Appendix A.4 for a given after-tax, after-inflation interest rate and given number of years of need. For example, someone who wishes to replace $36,000 for 20 years at an interest rate of 4 percent would need to have $489,240 of life insurance protection.

Note that the multiple-of-earnings approach addresses only one of the factors affecting life insurance needs—income-replacement needs. It does not take into consideration such factors as age, family situation, and losses other than income that can occur when someone dies. Thus, it is an imprecise (although relatively easy-to-use) method for determining life insurance needs.

The Needs Approach The **needs approach** to estimating life insurance needs considers all of the factors that might affect the level of need. It improves upon the calculations of a multiple-of-earnings approach by including a more accurate assessment of income replacement need and considers factors that add to and reduce the level of need. The Decision-Making Worksheet "The Needs Approach to Life Insurance" illustrates calculations made via the needs approach. Consider the example of Zoel Raymond, a 35-year-old factory foreman from Holyoke, Massachusetts, who has a spouse (aged 30) and three sons (aged eight, seven, and two years). Zoel earns $36,000 and desires to replace his income for 30 years, at which time his spouse would no longer need to support her children financially. The middle column of the worksheet expands on the situation faced by Zoel.

1. *Income-replacement needs.* Zoel's income of $36,000 is multiplied by 0.75 and the interest factor of 17.292. This factor was used because Zoel decided that it would be best to replace his lost income for 30 years or until Mary, his wife, reached age 60 and passed through the Social Security blackout period. Zoel and Mary are moderate-risk investors and believe that she could earn a 4 percent after-tax, after-inflation rate of return on life insurance proceeds. Income replacement needs based on these conditions amount to $466,884.

2. *Final-expense needs.* Zoel estimates his final expenses for funeral, burial, and other expenses at $10,000.

3. *Readjustment-period needs.* Mary has a career as a columnist for a local newspaper, which earns her an annual income of $38,000. Allocating $19,000 for readjustment-period needs would allow her to take a six-month leave of absence from her job or meet other readjustment needs.

4. *Debt-repayment needs.* Zoel and Mary owe $10,000 on various credit cards and an auto loan. They also owe about $78,000 on their home mortgage. Mary would like to pay off all debts except the mortgage debt should Zoel die. The mortgage debt would be affordable if Zoel's income was replaced.

◀ DECISION- ▶
MAKING
Worksheet

The Needs Approach to Life Insurance

This worksheet provides a mechanism for estimating life insurance needs using the needs approach. The amounts needed for income replacement, final expenses, readjustment needs, debt repayment, college expenses, and other special needs are calculated and then reduced by funds available from government benefits and any current insurance or assets that could cover the need. This worksheet is reproduced on the *Garman/Forgue* Web site.

Factors Affecting Need	Example	Your Figures
1. Income-replacement needs		
Multiply 75 percent of annual income* by the interest factor from Appendix A.4 that corresponds with the number of years that the income is to be replaced and the assumed after-tax, after-inflation rate of return.		
($27,000 × 17.292 for 30 years at a 4% rate of return)	$466,884	$ _____
2. Final-expense needs	+ 10,000	+ _____
Includes funeral, burial, travel, and other items of expense just prior to and after death.		
3. Readjustment-period needs	+ 19,000	+ _____
To cover employment interruptions and possible education expenses for surviving spouse and dependents.		
4. Debt-repayment needs	+ 10,000	+ _____
Provides repayment of short-term and installment debt, including credit cards and personal loans.		
5. College-expense needs	+ 75,000	+ _____
To provide a fund to help meet college expenses of dependents.		
6. Other special needs	+ 0	+ _____
7. Subtotal (combined impact of items 1–6)	+ $580,884	+ _____
8. Government benefits		
Present value of Social Security survivor benefits and other benefits.		
Multiply monthly benefit estimate (from Appendix B) by 12 and use Appendix A.4 for the number of years that benefits will be received and the same interest rate that was used in item 1.		
($1933 × 12 × 11.118 for 15 years of benefits and a 4% rate of return)	− 257,893	− _____
9. Current insurance assets	− 95,000	− _____
10. Life insurance needed	$ 227,991	_____

* Seventy-five percent is used because about 25 percent of income is used for personal needs.

5. *College-expense needs.* Zoel estimates that it would currently cost $25,000 for each of his sons to attend the local campus of a public university. Should he die, $75,000 of the life insurance proceeds could be invested until each son goes to college. If invested appropriately, the funds would grow at a rate sufficient to keep up with increasing costs of a college education.

6. *Other special needs.* Zoel and Mary do not have any unusual needs related to life insurance planning and entered $0 for this factor.

7. *Subtotal.* The Raymonds total items 1 through 6 on the worksheet and determine that financial needs arising out of Zoel's death would total $580,884. Although this sum seems large to them, they have access to two resources that can reduce this figure, as indicated in items 8 and 9.

8. *Government benefits.* Zoel estimates that his family would qualify for monthly Social Security survivor's benefits of $1933 (estimated from Appendix B). These benefits would be paid for 15 years, until his youngest son turns 18. The present value of this stream of benefits is $257,893 from Appendix A.4, assuming a 4 percent return for 15 years.

View Life Insurance If You Are a Young Professional

When people graduate from college, their names and accomplishments may become known to many people through announcements in hometown newspapers. Life insurance agents use such lists to obtain sales prospects, who are solicited by mail or by telephone for a life insurance "consultation."

For example, Irene Leech of Monterey, California, recently graduated with a degree in tourism management and has accepted a position paying $33,000 per year in gross salary. Irene is single and lives with her sister. She owes $9500 on a car loan as well as $11,800 in education loans. She has about $4000 in the bank. Among her employee benefits is an employer-paid term insurance policy equal to her annual salary.

Irene has been approached by a life insurance agent whose calculations suggest that she needs $165,000, or five times her income. Does she? If we apply the needs approach to Irene's situation, we see the following:

- Because Irene has no dependents, she needs no insurance for income replacement, readjustment-period needs, college-expense needs, or other special needs. Items 1, 3, 5, and 6 in the needs approach worksheet on page 337 are $0.

- Irene's survivors will not qualify for any government benefits, so item 8 will also be $0.

- Irene estimates her burial costs at $6000, which she entered for item 2.

- Irene would like to see her $9500 in automobile and $11,800 in education loans repaid in the event of her death. She feels better knowing that her younger sister could inherit her car free and clear. She entered $19,300 for item 4.

- Irene has combined life insurance and assets of $37,000 and entered that amount for item 8.

The resulting calculations show that Irene needs no additional life insurance ($6000 + $21,300 − $37,000 = −$9700). When her circumstances change, Irene could reappraise her needs.

9. *Current insurance and assets.* Zoel has a $50,000 life insurance policy purchased five years ago. His employer also pays for a group policy equal to his $45,000 gross annual income. Zoel's major assets include his home and his retirement plan. Because he does not want Mary to have to liquidate these assets if he dies, he includes only the $95,000 insurance coverage in item 9.

10. *Life insurance needed.* After subtracting worksheet items 8 and 9 from the subtotal, Zoel estimates that he needs an additional $227,991 in life insurance.

Because Mary earns an income similar to that of Zoel's, her life insurance needs may be similar; to determine the specific amount, however, the couple must complete a worksheet for her as well. Next, the Raymonds will need to decide what type of life insurance is best and from whom to buy additional life insurance. The remainder of this chapter covers these topics.

Types of Life Insurance

> **3** Distinguish among the various types of term and cash-value life insurance policies.

Although many people are confused by the variety of life insurance policies, in reality there are only two types of life insurance: term life insurance and cash-value life insurance. **Term life insurance** is often described as "pure protection" because it pays benefits only if the insured person dies within the time period (term) of the policy. The policy must be renewed if coverage is desired for another time period. **Cash-value life insurance** pays benefits at death and includes a savings/investment element that can provide benefits to the policyholder. Cash-value insurance is sometimes called **permanent insurance** because it does not need to be renewed. Due to its investment aspect, cash-value life insurance costs more than term insurance.

Term Life Insurance

Term life insurance contracts are most often written for time periods of one, five, ten, or 20 years. If the insured survives the specified time period, the beneficiary receives no monetary benefits. Term insurance can be purchased in contracts with face amounts in multiples of $1000, usually with a minimum face amount of $50,000. The **face amount** is the dollar value of protection as listed in the policy and used to calculate the premium.

Unless otherwise stipulated by the original contract, you must apply for a new contract and may be required to undergo a medical examination to renew the policy. The premium will increase, reflecting your older age and greater likelihood of dying while the new policy remains in force. If you have a health problem, you may be denied a new policy or be asked to pay higher premiums. Thus, term insurance premiums rise with each renewal. For example, a $100,000 five-year renewable term policy for a man aged 25 might have an annual premium of $110; at age 35, the policy might cost $165; and at age 45, it might cost $230. Nonetheless, term policies are less expensive than cash-value policies because they do not include a savings/investment element.

Guaranteed Renewable Term Insurance Proving insurability may be difficult should you develop a health problem during the period of a term policy. Term life insurance policies, however, are usually written as **guaranteed renewable term insurance**. If designed to be renewed annually, such policies are called **annual renewable term (ART)**. In a sense, the renewability option insures against the possibility of becoming uninsurable. The number of renewals you can make without proving insurability may be limited, and a maximum age may be specified for these renewals (usually age 65 or 70). Unless you are positive that you will not need a renewal, guaranteed renewable term insurance is recommended.

Level-Premium Term Insurance You can partially avoid term insurance premium increases as you grow older by buying **level-premium** (or **guaranteed-premium) term insurance**, which is a term policy with a long time period of perhaps five, ten, or 20 years. Under such a policy, the premiums remain constant, possibly throughout the entire life of the policy; more likely, however, they remain constant for a five- or ten-year interval, at which time they might increase to a new constant rate for another five- or ten-year interval. Premiums charged in early years are higher than necessary to balance out the lower-than-necessary premiums in later years. Level-premium policies may include a *re-enter provision*, requiring proof of good health at the beginning of each interval. If health status changes, the insured must re-enter the policy at higher rates than originally anticipated. Be wary of policies with such a provision, especially if you anticipate needing coverage beyond the initial level-premium interval.

Decreasing Term Insurance With **decreasing term insurance**, the face amount of coverage declines annually, while the premiums remain constant. The owner chooses an initial face amount and a contract period, after which the face amount of the policy gradually declines (usually each year) to some minimum (such as $50,000) in the last year of the contract. For example, a woman aged 25 might buy a 30-year $200,000 decreasing term policy that declines by $5000 each year. The major benefit of decreasing term policies is that they attempt to fit one's changing insurance needs.

Credit Term Life Insurance **Credit term life insurance** will pay the remaining balance of a loan if the insured dies before repaying the debt. Basically, it represents a decreasing term insurance policy with the creditor named as beneficiary. Though this type of insurance is seriously overpriced, individuals who have health problems that make life insurance expensive or difficult to obtain might use this option to help meet a portion of their overall life insurance needs.

Group Term Life Insurance Group term life insurance is issued to people as members of a group rather than individually. Most such policies are written for a large number of employees, with premiums paid in full or in part by the employer. Group life insurance premiums are average rates based on the group's characteristics. Unlike with health insurance, group life insurance rates are *not* consistently lower than individual rates. If you are a good risk, you usually can do better buying life insurance on your own. If you are insured under a group plan, you need not prove your insurability, and you can usually convert the policy to an individual basis without proof of insurability if you leave the group. Such convertibility represents a major benefit for persons whose health status makes individual life insurance unaffordable or unattainable.

Convertible Term Insurance **Convertible term insurance** offers the policyholder the option of exchanging a term policy for a cash-value policy without evidence of insurability. Usually, this conversion is available only in the early years of the term policy. Some policies provide for an automatic conversion from term to cash-value insurance after a specific number of years.

There are two ways to convert a term policy to a cash-value policy. First, you can simply request the conversion and begin paying the higher premiums required for the cash-value policy. The savings/investment element of the cash-value policy will begin accumulating as of the date of the conversion. Second, you can give the company the money that would have built up had the policy originally been written on a cash-value basis. Although this lump sum may be a considerable amount, it does represent an asset for the policyholder. Furthermore, the new premiums will be based on your age at the time you bought the original term policy. This may result in lower premiums.

Cash-Value Life Insurance

Cash-value life insurance pays benefits upon the death of the insured and also incorporates a savings/investment element that allows the payment of benefits prior to death. Thus, it includes a **cash value** representing the value of the investment in the life insurance policy. This cash value belongs to the owner of the policy and not to the beneficiary (unless, of course, they are the same person). While the insured is alive, the owner may obtain the cash value by borrowing from the insurance company or by surrendering and canceling the policy. Such insurance is sometimes called whole life insurance because coverage is maintained for the entire life of the insured. You do not need to renew the policy or prove your insurability again, and the annual premiums for cash-value policies usually remain constant.

Parties to the Contract

Several parties will be named in the life insurance contract (policy). The **owner** (also called the **policyholder**) retains all rights and privileges granted by the policy, including the right to amend the policy and the right to designate who receives the proceeds. The **insured** is the person whose life is insured. The **beneficiary** is the person or organization named in the policy that will receive the life insurance or other benefit payment in the event of the insured's death. The **contingent beneficiary** becomes the beneficiary if the original beneficiary dies before the insured. Although the owner and the insured are often the same person, it is possible for four different people to be named.

Figure 12.1

Comparison of Premium Dollars for Life Insurance

For example, for a 25-year-old female, the annual premium might be $800 for a $100,000 cash-value policy, but only $120 for a $100,000 term policy.

Cash-Value Policy	Term Policy
Premium to pay for insurance protection, sales commissions, and company expenses	Premium to pay for insurance protection, sales commissions, and company expenses
Premium to provide for the building of cash value and related company expenses	Dollars not spent on life insurance and available to spend, save, or invest

Figure 12.2

The Essence of Cash-Value Life Insurance

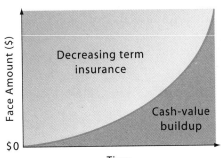

The premiums for cash-value policies are always higher than those for term policies providing the same amount of coverage, because only a portion of the premium is used to provide the death benefit and the remainder is used to build the cash value. Figure 12.1 illustrates the premium differences between cash-value and term life insurance policies.

Cash-value life insurance actually represents a combination of decreasing term insurance and an investment account that adds up to the face amount of the policy. Figure 12.2 illustrates this concept. Initially, for example, you might have $100,000 of insurance and no savings. Several years later, you might have built up $2000 in savings within the policy. In the event of your death, your beneficiary would collect $100,000, of which $2000 would be your own money. If you lived long enough, the cash value could equal—and might surpass—the $100,000 figure. In effect, your beneficiary would then collect your "savings account" rather than an insurance payment.

The rate at which the cash value accumulates in a policy depends on the rate of return earned. Most cash-value policies have a guaranteed minimum rate of return, often 2 to 4 percent. The second column of Table 12.1 shows the cash-value accumulations for a typical cash-value policy with a guaranteed rate of return of 4 percent.

Even though the cash value of a life insurance policy accumulates throughout your life, only the face amount of the policy will be paid upon your death. Prior to death you may cash in the policy for the accumulated cash value, which cancels your insurance coverage, or you may borrow all or part of the cash value. You must repay the amount borrowed with interest, and any amount owed will be subtracted from the face amount of the policy should you die while the debt remains outstanding. (The specifics of cashing in a policy and borrowing cash values will be discussed in more detail later in this chapter.) In many ways, cash values represent a kind of forced saving that allows funds to build up while you buy life insurance. Several different types of cash-value life insurance are available.

Whole Life Insurance **Whole life insurance** is a form of cash-value life insurance that provides lifetime life insurance protection and expects you to pay premiums for life. **Straight life** and **ordinary life** are labels sometimes used interchangeably with "whole life."

Limited-Pay Whole Life Insurance **Limited-pay whole life insurance** is whole life insurance that allows premium payments to cease before you reach the age

Table 12.1

Cash-Value Buildup—Guaranteed versus Current Rates

Figures are illustrative for a $50,000 universal life policy; the annual premium is $684.

Policy Year	"Guaranteed" Cash-Surrender Value (4.0% rate)*	"Current Rate" Cash-Surrender Value (7.6% rate)*
1	$ 0	$ 0
2	0	236
3	585	886
4	1,280	1,577
5	1,993	2,377
6	2,723	3,187
7	3,470	4,212
8	4,234	5,258
9	5,016	6,302
10	5,816	7,419
15	10,089	14,748
20	14,738	25,812
25	19,888	39,419

* The policy has a back-end load that reduces buildup of cash-surrender values in early years.

of 100. Two common examples are **twenty-pay life** policies, which allow premium payments to cease after 20 years, and **paid-at-65** policies, which require payment of premiums only until the insured turns 65. Although premiums need be paid only for the specified time period, the insurance protection lasts for your entire life. An extreme version of limited-pay life insurance is the **single-premium** life insurance policy, in which the premium is paid once in the form of a lump sum. As you might expect, the annual premiums for limited-pay policies are higher than for whole-life policies because the insurance company has fewer years to collect premiums. Limited-pay policies are said to be **paid up** when the owner can stop paying premiums. Paid-up policies continue to accumulate cash values but at a slower rate because a portion of the earnings go to pay the premiums no longer being paid by the owner.

Life insurance agents often pitch **vanishing premium life insurance** designed to allow policyholders to cease making premium payments after just a few years. In these plans, cash-value accumulations are supposedly used to pay premiums. While attractive at first glance, these policies contain a significant hazard. If the growth in cash-value accumulations proves insufficient to pay the premium, the owner of the policy will be charged the premium shortfall—possibly after many years of having not paid premiums. Look in the policy for a clause indicating that such a charge can be imposed. Always assume any life insurance charge that *can* be imposed *will* be imposed.

Adjustable Life Insurance The three cornerstones of cash-value life insurance are the premium, the face amount, and the rate of cash-value accumulation.

Life Insurance

Cash-value accumulations in life insurance in excess of premiums paid are not taxable as they are earned, but will be taxed if the policy is cashed in prior to the death of the insured. Using cash-value insurance as an investment vehicle has tax-shelter benefits, meaning that the income remains exempt from current income taxes as it accumulates. Thus, the investments grow and compound in value tax-free. The additional benefit of tax deductibility of payments into the investment—available for many retirement savings programs, as discussed in Chapter 18—is not permitted for life insurance. Thus, you should not use life insurance as a tax shelter for cash-value accumulations until you have taken all possible steps involving qualified retirement plans to shelter both payments into and income growing within those plans.

The death benefit of a life insurance policy is generally not subject to federal and state income taxes for the beneficiary, the insured, or the owner. Once the death benefit has been paid, however, the income from the proceeds (e.g., interest from a bank account) becomes taxable income for the beneficiary. To avoid paying federal gift and estate taxes on life insurance proceeds, see the suggestions in Chapter 19, "Estate Planning."

Adjustable life insurance allows you to modify any of the three with corresponding changes in the other two. Adjustable life insurance that pays a fixed rate of return was created in response to policyholder demands for more flexibility in policies. For example, you may feel that inflation has increased your need for life insurance. Adjustable life insurance would allow you to increase the face amount. In return, your premiums could increase or the cash-value accumulation could slow, or some combination of the two. With traditional life insurance policies, these changes can be made only if you purchase a new policy or cash in an existing one. In addition, these changes may be made without providing new proof of insurability.

Modified Life Insurance   **Modified life insurance** is whole life insurance with reduced premiums in the early years and higher premiums thereafter. The premiums are lower in early years because some of the protection during the early years is provided by term insurance. The period of reduced premiums can vary from one to five years. Modified life insurance is primarily designed for people whose life insurance needs are high (young parents, for example) but who cannot immediately afford the premiums required for a cash-value policy. Because it uses term insurance in the early years, modified life insurance accumulates cash value very slowly.

Endowment Life Insurance   **Endowment life insurance** pays the face amount of the policy either upon the death of the insured or at some previously agreed-upon date, whichever occurs first. The date of payment, called the **endowment date,** is commonly some specified number of years after issuance of the policy (e.g., 20 or 30 years) or some specified age (such as 65). Because of recent changes in U.S. tax laws, few of these policies are now written.

Table 12.2

Comparisons of Three Popular Life Insurance Policies

Feature	Term Insurance	Whole Life Insurance	Interest-Sensitive Life Insurance
Face amount	Fixed or declining during term of the policy; changeable at renewal	Fixed	Variable
Premiums	Low with increases at renewal	High and fixed	High but variable within limits
Cash-value accumulation	None	Fixed rate of accumulation	Variable accumulation as premium and interest rates vary
Rate of return paid on cash accumulations	Not applicable	Fixed	Variable with interest rates in the economy or as specified by company
Cost of the death benefit portion	Low, with interest at renewal	Unknown	Known but can vary and may hide some expense charges
Company expense charges	Low but unknown; hidden in premium	Unknown; hidden in premium	Known; may be high

Interest-Sensitive Life Insurance

The cash-value life insurance policies discussed to this point usually pay a fixed, guaranteed rate of return on the accumulated cash value. **Interest-sensitive life insurance** employs rates of return that vary according to changing interest rates and investment returns. Pressures for such changes in life insurance have come from investors who criticized the low yields paid on traditional cash-value life insurance and advised buyers to "buy term and invest the difference" in ways that pay a better rate of return.

An examination of interest-sensitive life insurance requires an understanding of the premium, the cost of the insurance protection portion, the rate of return on the invested funds, and the company expense charges. Table 12.2 compares these elements for term, whole life, and interest-sensitive life policies. Literally thousands of variations exist among these life policies, so comparisons are extremely difficult.

Initially, the purchaser selects a face amount, and the company quotes an annual premium. The annual premium goes into the cash-value fund,* from which the insurer deducts the cost of providing the insurance protection and charges for company expenses. As time goes by, the insured may reduce or increase the premium, with corresponding changes incurred in the insurance protection or amount added to cash value. If premiums drop below the amount necessary to cover the insurance protection and expenses, funds are removed

---

* Some interest-sensitive life policies pay both the face amount and the accumulated cash value upon the death of the insured party, thereby completely separating the insurance from the investment element.

from the cash-value account to cover the shortfall. Sometimes these life policies are promoted as allowing the cessation of premium payments after five, seven, or ten years, but the funds that support these unpaid premiums come at the expense of cash-value accumulation.

The portion of the premium necessary to provide the death benefit is clearly disclosed in interest-sensitive life insurance policies, unlike with whole life and other traditional cash-value policies. This disclosure allows the insured to compare the cost of protection with other cash-value life policies and, more importantly, with a similar amount of term insurance. Most policies include two tables of premiums for various death benefit amounts: one listing the premiums that are currently being assessed to purchasers, and a second listing the maximum premium that can be charged for various death benefit levels. Most companies charge less than the maximum, and agents typically emphasize the lower premium, but the company has the right to raise the premiums for death benefits up to the maximum in the contract.

The company expense charges are the last elements necessary for an understanding of interest-sensitive life insurance. Like the rate of return and the death benefit premiums, the company expense charges are disclosed clearly in the policy. The most typical of these fees involves a deduction of 5 to 10 percent from each annual premium.

Did You KNOW ?   *About Life Insurance Sales Commissions and Loads*

Sales commissions typically represent 20 to 100 percent of the first-year premium paid for a life insurance policy. The lowest commissions are paid on term insurance, and the highest are paid on limited-pay and endowment life insurance policies. Commissions are paid every year that the policy remains in force, although they drop steadily in succeeding years. Insurance buyers rarely realize that so much of their premium comprises the commission paid the agent. The commission is included in the **load**, which also includes company marketing and overhead costs.

Low-load life insurance does not involve payment of a commission by the insurer to an insurance agent. Low-load insurers market their products directly to consumers (e.g., by mail) or through fee-only financial planners and fee-for-service insurance agents. Thus, their marketing costs and overhead are also low. Cash values begin building in the very first year, and cashing them in during the first few years is, therefore, not as detrimental as it is for policies bought from companies that market their products in more traditional ways.

Unfortunately, many so-called low-load plans charge annual fees that may prove difficult for buyers to understand. Some companies also charge a **back-end load** or **surrender charge**, which is a fee assessed if you withdraw some or all of the cash value accumulated. This charge is often highest in the early years of the policy and may be eliminated in later years. Ask about loads whenever shopping for life insurance. The policy illustrated in Table 12.1 has a back-end load in the first few years that accounts for the initially low cash-surrender values. Be wary of policies that have both commissions and back-end loads.

About Buying Term Insurance and Investing the Difference

The principle underlying "buy term and invest the difference" is simple: If you invest the money difference between the cost of term insurance and that of another type of policy, you will *always* be ahead financially. For example, consider the first year of estate buildup in the following table for a life insurance purchase by a 29-year-old. Instead of purchasing a $100,000 whole life policy with an annual premium of $870, the person pays $160 for the first year's premium of a $100,000 annual renewable term policy and puts the difference of $710 ($870 − $160) in a mutual fund account. If the person dies tomorrow, the estate is already ahead because of the money just deposited; upon death, the beneficiary would receive both the $100,000 in insurance and the $710 in savings. After one year (age 30), the $710 in savings would have grown to $746. If the person dies years into the future, the estate is even further ahead because of the growing principal in the account.

What the data show is that "buy term and invest the difference" is the preferred approach when adding another policy to your holdings. Such data are sometimes incorrectly described by unscrupulous life insurance agents in an effort to persuade owners of cash-value policies to cash in their policies and buy a new term policy or a higher-yielding cash-value policy. Cash-value policies that are seven to ten years old (or older) might best be held, however, as the return has finally begun to be competitive. The first few years of cash-value policies are the most detrimental to policyholders because so much of the premium goes for agent commissions. In addition, many cash-value policies require payment of surrender charges if they are cashed in prior to being held for seven to ten years. It likely will not pay to surrender one cash-value policy to buy another, thereby paying the commissions twice.

Estate Buildup if a Term Life Insurance Buyer Invests the Difference

Age	Premium for Annual Renewable Term	Difference (Not Spent on Whole Life)	Total Investment and Earnings* at 5%	Total Estate
30	$ 160	$ 710	$ 746	$100,746
35	180	690	5,004	105,004
40	200	670	10,323	110,323
45	225	645	16,977	116,977
50	250	620	25,326	125,326
55	640	230	34,751	134,751
60	1,320	− 450	43,575	143,575
65	2,700	−1,830	48,924	148,924

* This illustration makes the following assumptions: The whole life policy premium for the same $100,000 in coverage is $870 every year, the buyer pays the annual renewable term premium at the beginning of each year, and the difference is invested. Those amounts stay in the investments account all year, as does the previous year's ending balance. Investments are compounded annually at a 5 percent after-tax rate. To make the calculations for one year, such as beginning at age 30, simply take the difference not spent on the whole life policy ($870 − $160 = $710) and multiply it times 1.05 (for 5 percent interest), which yields the total investment ($746 by the end of the year), including interest earned for the year. Upon death at a certain age, the beneficiary would receive the $100,000 face amount of the term life insurance policy plus the amount built up in the investment account earning 5 percent.

Universal Life Insurance   **Universal life insurance** provides both the pure protection of term insurance and the cash-value buildup of whole life insurance, along with variability in the face amount, rate of cash-value accumulation, premiums, and rate of return. Essentially, universal life insurance combines annual term insurance with an investment program. Universal life policies are usually available in initial face amounts of $100,000 or more. The rate of return is tied to some interest rate prevailing in the financial markets or is dictated by the insurance company. In either case, the rate of return usually exceeds those available under other types of cash-value policies.

Variable Life Insurance   **Variable life insurance** allows you to choose the investments made with your cash-value accumulations and to share in any gains or losses. The face amount of your policy and the policy's cash value may rise or fall based on changes in the rates of return on the invested funds. The face amount of the policy usually will not drop below the originally agreed-upon amount. Instead, the cash value will fluctuate. Because you pay premiums on an ongoing basis, the cash value will increase, but it may increase slowly if investments perform poorly.

Holders of variable life insurance policies can exert some control over the types of investments made with their premiums. If you are unfamiliar with markets for corporate stocks and bonds and mutual funds, you should probably avoid variable life insurance. Many variable life insurance policies contain provisions calling for the payment of fees and sales charges *before* the policyholders can share in any investment returns. Variable life insurance policies should be read and analyzed very carefully before purchase.

Variable–Universal Life Insurance   **Variable–universal life insurance** is a form of universal life insurance that gives the policyholder some choice in the investments made with the cash value accumulated by the policy. It is sometimes called **universal life II** or, if the owner can vary the premium, **flexible-premium variable life insurance.** This life insurance product most closely embodies the philosophy of "buy term and invest the difference." Because you select the investment vehicles (a combination of stocks, bonds, or money market mutual funds), a higher rate of return can potentially be realized than under a universal life policy. With this flexibility comes the risk of a lower rate of return, however. As a result, variable–universal life policies usually provide no minimum guaranteed rate of return. It is possible that you might lose the cash value and perhaps be required to pay a higher premium to keep the policy in effect. Prospective purchasers of variable–universal life insurance need to consider carefully how much risk they are willing to accept in their life insurance program. Variable–universal life insurance also carries higher commissions and is more likely to require annual fees than other forms of life insurance. A 2 percent annual fee would change a policy with an annual return of 7 percent on its investments to one with a net 5 percent return. You should also evaluate the investment component against other alternative investments. (Investments are covered in Part 4 of this book.)

Understanding Your Life Insurance Policy

4 Describe and explain the purpose of the major provisions of life insurance policies.

A **life insurance policy** is the written contract between the insurer and the policyholder. The policy contains all of the information relevant to the agreement. Although individual policies vary somewhat, it is helpful to focus on four features: (1) the organization of the policy, (2) terms and provisions unique to life insurance, (3) special features of cash-value policies, and (4) settlement options.

Organization of an Insurance Policy

You can best comprehend any insurance policy by dividing it into its component parts and examining each part separately. All insurance policies include five basic components, each of which serves a specific purpose and provides specific information. These five elements, in order of their usual location in the policy, are as follows: declarations, insuring agreements, exclusions, conditions, and endorsements.

Declarations **Declarations** provide the basic descriptive information about the insured person or property, the premium to be paid, the time period of the coverage, and the policy limits. Also included may be promises by the insured to take steps to control the losses associated with a specific peril. For example, a life insurance purchaser may promise not to smoke in exchange for paying a discounted premium. The information in the declarations is used to help determine the premium and for identification purposes.

Insuring Agreements The **insuring agreements** are the broadly defined coverages provided under the policy. The insurer makes these promises in return for the premium paid by the insured. For example, in life insurance, the insurer will promise to pay the death benefit amount to the beneficiary in the event of the insured's death. In automobile insurance, the insuring agreements will often include definitions of a motor vehicle or insured premises to clarify the promises made.

Exclusions **Exclusions** narrow the focus and eliminate specific coverages broadly stated in the insuring agreements. The insurer makes no promise to pay for these exceptions and special circumstances. For example, suicide is commonly excluded during the first two years of a life insurance policy. A common automobile insurance exclusion denies coverage under a family policy if the car is used primarily for business purposes. People who do not understand the exclusions in their policies often believe they are covered for a loss when, in fact, they are not.

Conditions **Conditions** impose obligations on both the insured and the insurer by establishing the ground rules of the agreement. Such conditions might include the procedures for making a claim after a loss, rules for cancellation of the policy by either party, and procedures for changing the terms of the policy. The insured who fails to adhere to procedures or obligations described in the conditions may be denied coverage when a loss occurs.

Endorsements Endorsements (or **riders,** as they are sometimes called in life insurance) are amendments and additions to the basic insurance policy that can both expand and limit coverage to accommodate specific needs. When the terms of an endorsement or rider differ from the terms of the basic policy, the endorsement will be considered valid. Endorsements may be added at any time during the life of the policy to expand coverage, raise the policy limits, and make other changes.

Terms and Provisions Unique to Life Insurance

Life insurance policies define the terminology used in the policy and outline the basic provisions. Such information serves to clarify the meaning of the policy and the protection afforded the insurer and the policyholder.

The Application The **life insurance application** is the policyholder's offer to purchase a policy. The application provides information and becomes part of the life insurance policy. Any errors or omissions in the application may allow the insurance company to deny a request for payment of the death benefit.

Lives Covered Most life insurance policies cover the life of a single person—the insured. It is also possible to cover two or more persons with one policy, however. **First-to-die policies** cover more than one person but pay only when the first insured dies. These policies are less costly than separate policies written on each person, but, of course, the survivor then has no coverage after the first person dies. An alternative is the **survivorship joint life policy,** which pays when the last person covered dies.

The Incontestability Clause Life insurance policies generally include an **incontestability clause** that places a time limit—usually two years after issuance of the policy—on the right of the insurance company to deny a claim. This clause addresses the problems arising out of questionable insurable interest and false statements in the application.

The Suicide Clause Life insurance policies generally include a **suicide clause** that allows the life insurance company to deny coverage if the insured commits suicide within the first few years after the policy is issued. If the specified number of years (usually two) has elapsed, the full death benefit will be paid. If not, only a refund of the premiums paid up to that point will be payable.

Cash Dividends **Insurance dividends** are defined legally by the Internal Revenue Service as a return of a portion of the premium paid for a life insurance policy; they are not considered income. They represent the surplus earnings of the company that reflect the difference between the premium charged and the cost to the company of providing insurance. Policies that pay dividends are called **participating policies,** and policies that do not pay dividends are called **nonparticipating policies.** Both term and cash-value policies may pay dividends. Owners of participating policies may receive dividends as a cash payment, which can be maintained with the insurance company to earn interest, or they may use the dividends to purchase small amounts of paid-up life insurance.

Death Benefit The **death benefit** of a life insurance policy is the amount that will be paid upon the death of the insured person. The amount of the death benefit may differ somewhat from the face amount. The face amount may be increased (to allow for such items as earned dividends not yet paid or premiums paid in advance) or decreased (for outstanding policy loans or unpaid premiums) to calculate the death benefit. Consider a $100,000 participating whole life policy with annual premiums of $1380. If the insured died halfway through the policy year, with an outstanding cash-value loan of $5000 and earned but unpaid dividends of $4000, the death benefit would be $99,690, calculated as follows:

$100,000	Face amount
4,000	Unpaid dividends
+ 690	Premiums paid in advance (one-half year)
$104,690	Subtotal
− 5,000	Outstanding cash-value loan
$ 99,690	Death benefit

Grace Period Prompt payment of the premium is crucial to the continuation of coverage provided by any insurance policy. A **lapsed policy** is one that has been terminated because of nonpayment of premiums. More than one-half of all whole life policies lapse within ten years of being issued. If your life insurance policy lapses, you must prove insurability and pay any missed premiums, plus interest, to be reinstated. Alternatively, you might pay a higher premium for a new policy, reflecting your current age.

To help prevent a lapse, state laws generally require that cash-value and multiyear term policies include a **grace period**—that is, a period of time (usually 31 days following each premium due date) during which an overdue premium may be paid without a lapse of the policy. During the grace period, all provisions of

---

Who Should Own Your Life Insurance Policy

The ownership of a life insurance policy can have considerable impact on the potential for federal estate taxation. If the owner and the insured are the same person, the proceeds will be counted in the insured's estate at death and can be subject to estate taxes at rates as high as 55 percent. For this reason, individuals with an estate (including the face amount of owned policies on their life) amounting to more than $650,000 should not own the life insurance on their own lives. Instead, the beneficiary generally should be designated as the owner if he or she is not the spouse of the insured.

If the beneficiary is the spouse of the insured, the death benefit becomes part of the spouse's estate and may be subject to estate taxation at his or her death. Thus, many people establish an irrevocable life insurance trust so that the spouse can receive the income earned from the death benefit but with the trust going to some other person (e.g., a son or daughter) upon the death of the second spouse. In this way, both the insured and the spouse avoid estate taxes. (Estate taxation and trusts are covered more fully in Chapter 19.)

The Two Ways Insurance Companies Make Money

Insurance companies make money in two ways. First, they make **underwriting profits**, which result when the premiums collected exceed the expenses of providing coverage plus the losses paid by the company. Note that insurance companies do not simply hold the premiums that they collect until it is used to pay for the losses of their customers. Rather, they invest this money until it is needed.

These investments provide **investment profits**, which result from the return on the investments made with premiums collected from the insureds. Insurers need not make an underwriting profit to be profitable. For example, the underwriting losses of automobile insurers are often more than offset by their investment profits. The diagram below shows the sources of insurance company profits.

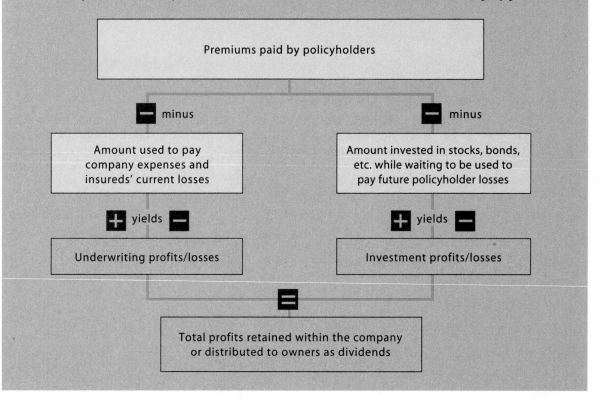

the policy remain intact, but only if payment is made before the grace period ends. Assume, for example, that payment was due but not paid on January 1. If the insured were to die on January 15, the policy could be reinstated as long as payment was made by January 31, given a 31-day grace period. It also may be possible to "buy back" a lapsed cash-value policy by paying any missed premiums and the cash-value that would have accumulated while the policy was lapsed. Insurance agents will rarely suggest this option because they make more commission from new policies.

Multiple Indemnity A **multiple indemnity clause** provides for a doubling or tripling of the face amount if death results from certain specified causes. This type of clause is most often used to double the face amount if death results from an accident. A multiple indemnity clause is often included automatically as part of the policy at no extra cost, but sometimes a charge is assessed. If you are adequately insured, such a clause is unnecessary.

Settlement Options

Settlement options are the choices the life insurance beneficiary or policyholder has concerning the payment of the death benefit from a life insurance policy. The option may be chosen by the owner before death or selected by the beneficiary after the insured's death. The appropriateness of an option depends upon the financial situation faced by the beneficiary. The five settlement options are as follows: ·

1. **Lump sum.** The death benefit may be received as a lump-sum cash settlement immediately after death. Often this lump-sum is used to purchase an annuity (see Chapter 18, "Retirement Planning").

2. **Interest income.** The beneficiary can receive the annual interest earned from the death benefit. For example, the beneficiary would receive $4000 each year from a $100,000 death benefit earning 4 percent interest. The $100,000 principal would remain intact and would continue to earn interest until the death of the beneficiary, when it becomes part of his or her estate.

3. **Income for a specific period.** The beneficiary may receive an income from the death benefit for a specific number of years. For example, a widow with small children may choose to receive an income for 18 years. The insurance company would calculate a level of income that would allow for equal proceeds each year, with all funds, including interest, being exhausted at the end of the eighteenth year.

4. **Income for life.** The beneficiary can elect to receive an income for life. The insurance company would use the life expectancy of the beneficiary to calculate the level of income that would allow for equal annual payments so that funds would be exhausted by the expected date of the beneficiary's death. If the beneficiary lives longer than expected, the income payments will continue.

5. **Income of a specific amount.** The beneficiary may receive a specific amount of income per year from the death benefit. Under this option, payments cease when the death benefit and interest are exhausted. For example, a $100,000 death benefit earning 4 percent interest would provide a $15,000 annual income for approximately eight years.

Special Features of Cash-Value Life Insurance Policies

Cash-value life insurance policies carry special features that relate to the cash values built up in the policies.

The Illustration Cash-value life insurance policies generally provide a **policy illustration** that charts the projected growth in the cash value for given rates of return. Two rates are usually quoted: the **guaranteed minimum rate of return**

(the minimum rate that, by contract, the company is legally obligated to pay), and the **current rate** (the rate of return recently paid by the company to policyholders). Agents typically emphasize the current rate, perhaps by presenting a table that illustrates the rate of cash-value accumulation resulting from the two rates. Table 12.1 provides an example of such a table. Note the differences in the two cash-value columns—it is easy to understand why the agent would emphasize the current rate. Policy illustrations can easily be made to look much more optimistic than it is reasonable to expect. Only after the policy is in force for perhaps ten to 20 years can an accurate picture be drawn. It is wise to periodically ask your agent for an **in-force illustration** that shows the cash-value status of the policy and projections for future years given the rate of return current at the time of the illustration (rather than the rate used at the inception of the policy). People who bought such policies in the early 1980s have learned this lesson all too well, as current rates were high at the time of purchase but much lower rates now prevail.

Nonforfeiture Values   **Nonforfeiture values** are clauses in the insurance contract that protect the value, if any, in the event that the policyholder chooses not to pay or fails to pay the required premiums. The policy owner can receive the accumulated cash-value funds in one of three ways. First, he or she may simply surrender the policy and receive the **cash surrender value**, which represents the cash value minus any back-end load surrender charges. In reality, the true measure of the cash value of a policy is its cash surrender value (the amount received when the policy is canceled). Second, the policy owner may continue the policy with the original face amount but for a time period shorter than the original policy. Third, the policy may be continued on a paid-up basis, and a new and lower face amount will be established based on the amount that can be purchased with the accumulated funds. Table 12.3 illustrates the nonforfeiture options for a paid-at-65 cash-value policy. Note that a cash-value policy has very little cash surrender value unless you have held it for a number of years.

What Questions to Ask about a Policy Illustration

Policy illustrations can be helpful in many cases—but can also be written in such a way as to make the policy look better than it really is. Asking a few pertinent questions can help cut through some of the misconceptions:

1. Is the "current rate" illustrated actually the rate paid recently? What was the current rate in each of the last five years?

2. What assumptions have been used regarding company expenses, dividend rates, and policy lapse rates?

3. Does all of my cash value earn the current rate? (If not, the current rate is misleading.)

4. Is the illustration based on the "cash surrender value" or the "cash value"? (Cash surrender value is usually the lower value and reflects what will actually be paid if the policy is canceled.)

Policy Loans The owner of a cash-value policy may borrow all or a portion of the accumulated cash value. Interest rates charged for the loan will range from 2 to 8 percent, depending on the terms of the policy. In addition, the interest rate earned on the remaining cash value typically reverts to the guaranteed minimum rate while the loan is outstanding. As a result, the cash value ultimately accumulated may be significantly reduced.

Automatic Premium Loan An **automatic premium loan** provision allows any premium not paid by the end of the grace period to be paid automatically with a policy loan if sufficient cash value or dividends have accumulated. In the first few years of a policy, this provision may not offer much benefit because cash value and dividends accumulate slowly. Eventually these funds may grow enough to pay premiums for a considerable length of time, thereby effectively preventing the lapse of the policy.

A growing number of life insurance companies now make a policy's death benefit available to a terminally ill insured. Some companies provide this benefit for policies already in effect, while others offer a **living benefit clause** that allows the payment of all or a portion of the death benefit prior to death if the insured contracts a terminal illness. These early payments are not cash-value loans, so it is possible to obtain more than the cash value accumulated in the policy. In addition, **viatical companies** specialize in buying life insurance policies from insureds for $0.50 to $0.80 per $1 of death benefit in return for being named beneficiary on the policy.

Table 12.3

Table of Nonforfeiture Values (Policyholder Can Choose A, B, or C)
For a $10,000 paid-at-65 limited-payment cash-value life insurance policy for a male aged 25. The annual premium is $180.

Policy Year	A Cash or Surrender Value*	B Period of $10,000 Term Insurance Years	Days	C Face Value of Term Insurance Paid Up for Life*
0	$ 0	0	0	$ 0
2	0	0	0	0
3	60	2	81	240
4	190	7	35	720
5	310	10	282	1,140
10	1,000	19	351	3,160
15	1,790	22	346	4,900
20	2,690	23	122	6,410
30	4,350	21	228	8,260
35	5,390	20	286	9,140
40	6,520	For life	—	10,000
45	7,110	For life	—	10,000

* The policy has a back-end load that reduces buildup of cash value in early years.

Waiver of Premium   A **waiver of premium** sets certain conditions under which an insurance policy would be kept in full force by the company without the payment of premiums. It usually applies when a policyholder becomes totally and permanently disabled, but it may also apply under other conditions, depending on the policy provisions. In effect, the waiver-of-premium option (for an extra cost) protects against the risk of becoming disabled and being unable to pay premiums. This option can be expensive and may account for as much as 10 percent of the policy premium. If you are adequately covered by disability income insurance (see Chapter 11), you might want to dispense with this option.

Guaranteed Insurability   The **guaranteed insurability option** permits (for an extra cost) the cash-value policyholder to buy additional stated amounts of life insurance at stated times in the future without evidence of insurability. This option differs from the guaranteed renewability option for term insurance in that it enables the owner to increase the face amount of the policy or to buy an additional policy. The policy might allow the exercise of these options when the insured turns 30, 35, or 40, or when he or she marries or has children.

Strategies for Buying Life Insurance

5 Discuss important points to consider when choosing and buying life insurance.

In a recent year, more than 18 million new individual life insurance policies were purchased in the United States. Did each individual really need to be covered by life insurance? Was the policy purchased the right one, and was it purchased from a reputable company and agent? Did the buyer pay the right price? This section will help you, as an insurance purchaser, answer these questions.

Should Your Life Be Insured at All?

Anyone whose death will result in financial losses to others should be covered by life insurance unless sufficient resources are available to cover the losses. Most U.S. families do not own enough life insurance. The bulk of any family's life insurance expenditures and protection should be concentrated on the primary income earners. If other workers provide income on which the family depends, they should also be covered to protect that income. People who generally do not need life insurance include children, singles with no dependents, and married people with no dependents who have sufficient individual income and no desire to leave an estate. People who are sometimes unnecessarily insured include the elderly, who may have already built up assets sufficient to provide for income for the survivor and cover burial expenses. If they have not achieved this financial status, the high cost of life insurance premiums for people over the age of 60 means they might be better off by purchasing only a small policy for funeral expenses and using their scarce funds to support their living expenses.

If you receive income from a former spouse either through alimony or child support, you will need to protect that source of income flow. Therefore, life insurance on that person is advisable. If a policy purchased while married remains in effect, it is wise to keep it. To be certain that the correct beneficiary is named, have that requirement stated in a court order or made part of the divorce decree. The custodial parent should then be named as owner of the policy, thereby preventing the noncustodial parent from making any changes in the policy. Noncustodial parents will also need life insurance on their former spouses because they will probably receive custody of the children if the former spouse dies and may need additional income to support them.

Choosing the Right Type of Life Insurance

A fundamental decision to make when buying life insurance is whether to purchase term insurance or cash-value insurance. Cash-value policies are often recommended by life insurance agents because the premiums usually stay the same over time, they provide protection for life, and they include a savings/investment element. Such recommendations from sales agents are not too surprising, however, as cash-value policies are much more profitable for them than term policies.

Independent financial advisors consistently advise people to "Buy term and invest the difference." In fact, more than 70 percent of all new policies consist of term insurance. Of course, this decision requires some planning and action on your part.

Although term insurance provides more coverage for the same premium than cash-value insurance, term policies do have some negative features. You may avoid these drawbacks by purchasing guaranteed renewable and convertible term insurance, which ensures that convertibility remains an option and is not required at some future date.

Choosing a Company

The most important feature of a life insurance company is its ability to pay its obligations. The company must have the stability and financial strength to survive for the many years your policy will remain in force. Banks that sell life insurance do so through subsidiary companies that are not federally insured. Thus, these subsidiary insurance companies should be just as financially strong as traditional insurance companies.

The *Insurance Forum* (P.O. Box 245-J, Ellettsville, IN 47429) publishes a summary of ratings (available for a fee of $15) from various insurance rating organizations on more than 1000 life and health insurance companies. Links are provided to additional sources on the *Garman/Forgue* Web site.

Choosing an Agent

The most obvious source of information about the cost of life insurance is the agent selling the policy. An **insurance agent** is an authorized representative of an insurance company who sells, modifies, services, and terminates insurance contracts. In the United States, life insurance is typically sold through **exclusive agents** who represent only one company, although some **independent agents** represent more than one company. Some life insurance companies also sell policies directly through the mail, usually with the help of a toll-free number. The life insurance agent must be qualified to design a program tailored to your spe-

Why People Buy the Wrong Amount and Types of Life Insurance

A recent poll conducted by ICR Survey Research Group of Media, Pennsylvania, provides some interesting insights into why people often buy the wrong amount and types of life insurance. When asked basic questions about life insurance, the respondents flunked the knowledge quiz. Only 4 percent could define term, whole life, variable life, and universal life insurance, and 30 percent could not identify even one of these types of insurance. Only about one-third knew that term insurance paid the highest death benefit per premium dollar, and more than one-fourth thought whole life insurance did so. Nearly 40 percent of respondents believed that agent commissions for whole life

insurance accounted for less than 10 percent of premiums in the first year, and only 14 percent knew that commissions average more than 50 percent of first-year premiums.

Perhaps overconfidently, more than two-thirds of the respondents said they understood the last policy they purchased. Moreover, the poll indicates a curious mix of too little knowledge and too much trust—certainly a recipe for bad decisions. When buying a car, most people would never ask the salesperson what type of car they should buy and how much they should pay, but many people do exactly that when buying life insurance.

cific needs and should understand the dynamics of family relationships, which influence all life insurance needs. The agent should have earned a professional designation, such as **chartered life underwriter (CLU)**. To earn the CLU, an agent must have three years of experience and pass a ten-course program in life insurance counseling. Some agents also may have earned the **certified financial planner (CFP)** or **chartered financial consultant (ChFC)** designation (see pages 47–48).

Your agent should be willing to take the time to provide personal service and to answer all questions about the policy both before and after you purchase it. Always ask an agent about the first-year commission on any policies you are considering. You should check your agent's reputation with your state's insurance regulatory agency. Although this agency will not tell you about consumer complaints or pending disciplinary action, it will notify you of formal disciplinary actions that may have already been taken. Because many life agents sell variable life insurance, they must have securities dealer licenses; thus, you can also contact your state's securities regulatory department for information. Such agencies generally provide more information than an insurance regulatory agency.

Making Cost Comparisons in Life Insurance

The price people pay for life insurance depends on their age, health, and lifestyle. Age is important, of course, because the probability of dying increases with age. A person who has a health problem such as heart disease or diabetes may pay considerably higher rates for life insurance or may not be able to obtain coverage at any price. People with hazardous occupations (police officers) or dangerous hobbies (skydivers) are sometimes required to pay higher life insurance premiums as well. Life insurance companies typically offer their lowest prices to "preferred" applicants whose health status and lifestyle (e.g., non-smokers) suggest longevity. "Standard" and "impaired" applicants would pay more. Companies differ on how they assign these labels to applicants, so you should shop around for the best treatment. Some companies even specialize in insurance for persons with certain types of medical conditions, such as diabetes.

Popular magazines such as *Kiplinger's Personal Finance Magazine, Consumer Reports,* and *Money* regularly publish articles that give average or typical premiums for different types of policies. In addition, your state department of insurance may publish life insurance buyer's guides containing price guidelines that may prove useful in selecting companies with the lowest prices. Premium-quote services that do not charge a fee but receive a commission if you buy from a recommended company include Master Quote [(800) 337-5433], LifeRates of America [(800) 457-2837], TermQuote [(800) 444-8376], Quotesmith [(800) 431-1147], SelectQuote [(800) 343-1985], and Insurance Quote Services [(800) 972-1104]. In addition, the Wholesale Insurance Network [(800) 808-5810] is a discount broker for low-load cash-value life insurance and will provide quotes.

Comparing Term Insurance Policies You may save a substantial amount on term life insurance premiums by using a **premium quote service**, which is an independent life insurance agent or group of agents who concentrate on one thing—low rates. Although they provide price information for policies, they offer little or no assistance in figuring how much life insurance you need or what type of policy you should buy. Such services offer computer-generated comparisons among the 20 to 80 companies they represent to help you select the least expensive life insurance policies and companies.

Life insurance premiums are usually quoted in dollars per $1000 of coverage. Generally, the higher the face amount of the policy, the lower the rate per $1000 will be. For example, a company might sell term life insurance for $1 per $1000 per year when purchased in face amounts of $100,000 or more and $1.25 per $1000 per year for policies under $100,000. In fact, policies with face amounts of $1 million can cost less than $0.50 per $1000 per year for people under age 35. It is easy to pay too much for term life insurance, however, especially if you do not comparison-shop. The rates shown in Table 12.4 represent good values for term insurance.

Table 12.4

Fair Prices for Term Life Insurance

Age	Nonsmokers		Smokers	
	Male	Female	Male	Female
18 to 30	$0.76	$0.68	$1.05	$1.01
35	0.80	0.74	1.36	1.26
40	1.03	0.95	2.06	1.65
45	1.45	1.20	2.95	2.30
50	2.60	1.76	4.16	3.30

Note: The CFA Insurance Group recommends multiplying the rate by each $1000 of coverage desired and then adding $60 to cover estimated administrative fees.

Source: Taking the Bite Out of Insurance, A Comprehensive Guide to Life Insurance, available for $14 [(202) 387-6121], which is periodically updated, including tables.

Reprinted by permission of the Consumer Federation of America Insurance Group, 1424 16th Street, Suite 604, Washington, D.C. 20036.

Comparing Cash-Value Policies The cost of insurance measured in dollars per $1000 is not an appropriate decision criteria when comparing term and cash-value insurance or when examining various types of cash-value insurance. Table 12.5 on the following page lists annual premiums that are near the average required for various types of insurance policies.

Table 12.5

Typical Premiums for Various Types of Life Insurance (Face Amount $100,000)

Policy Type	Policy Year 1	2	3	5	10	11	20	Age 65
Annual renewable term (guaranteed renewability to age 70)	$80	$81	$82	$83	$90	$92	$110	$2400
Decreasing term (over 20 years)	160	160	160	160	160	160	160	0
Convertible term (within 5 years)	170	170	170	170	940	940	940	940
Whole life	870	870	870	870	870	870	870	870
Universal life	590	590	590	590	680	730	760	790
Limited-pay life (paid at age 65)	920	920	920	920	920	920	920	0

Premiums quoted are for a 21-year-old male nonsmoker. Smokers pay 30 to 100 percent extra because they typically live seven years less than nonsmokers, according to data from the State Mutual Life Assurance Company of America.

• *The Net Cost Method.* The **net cost** of a life insurance policy equals the total of all premiums to be paid minus any accumulated cash value and accrued dividends. It is calculated for a specific point in time during the life of the policy—for example, at the end of the tenth or twentieth year. The net cost is often a negative figure, giving a false impression that the policy will pay for itself. You should ignore net cost calculations provided by a life insurance agent.

• *The Interest-Adjusted Cost Index Method.* A **cost index** is a numerical method to compare the costs of similar plans of life insurance. The **interest-adjusted cost index (IACI)** measures the cost of life insurance, taking into account the interest that would have been earned had the premiums been invested rather than used to buy insurance. The lower the IACI, the lower the cost of the policy. The IACI is calculated for a specific point in time—usually the twentieth year—during the life of the policy.

Reputable agents should have IACI information on hand. In fact, agents in most states are required to disclose the information (usually an IACI for the twentieth year) if asked. Ask for five-, ten-, and 30-year IACIs as well, because companies have been known to manipulate their dividend and cash value accumulations to look especially good at the 20-year point. You should insist on being told the index *before* you agree to buy a policy, and you should shop elsewhere if the agent refuses, resists, or tries to imply that the index has little value. Unfortunately, the IACI does not provide an accurate means of comparing types of policies that differ widely. It is totally inappropriate, for example, when comparing term insurance and cash-value insurance.

Plan Your Life Insurance Program

A life insurance and investment plan recommended for the income-producing years in an individual's life cycle is depicted in the figure given here. The plan is built on two cornerstones: (1) the purchase of term insurance for the bulk of life insurance needs, because term insurance is more flexible than cash-value insurance and provides more protection for each premium dollar, and (2) a systematic, regular investment program.

At the age of 20, as shown in the figure, the average person needs little or no life insurance. If desired, a small term or cash-value policy with guaranteed insurability is usually sufficient. Over time, however, an individual's responsibilities for the financial well-being of others may increase. These responsibilities will, in turn, increase the need for protection. As the early years of an investment program will not yield enough protection, life insurance likely should be purchased. The amount purchased will depend on the individual's needs (the amounts in the figure are intended only as examples). At about the age of 45, the probable losses from a premature death will begin to diminish because the investment program started at the age of 20 will have grown sufficiently to offer some protection from a premature death. Thus, life insurance needs will level off or decrease around the same time that term insurance pre-miums become more expensive. By the age of 65, life insurance needs will be greatly reduced or eliminated, and the investment program will have grown sufficiently to provide retirement income.

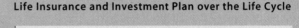

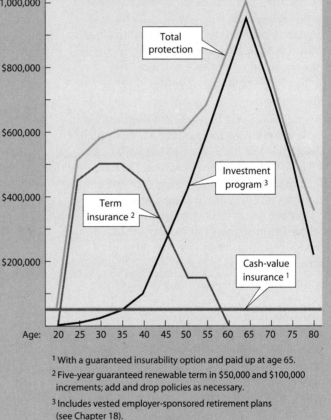

Life Insurance and Investment Plan over the Life Cycle

[1] With a guaranteed insurability option and paid up at age 65.

[2] Five-year guaranteed renewable term in $50,000 and $100,000 increments; add and drop policies as necessary.

[3] Includes vested employer-sponsored retirement plans (see Chapter 18).

• ***The Interest-Adjusted Net Payment Index Method.*** The IACI assumes that the policy will be cashed in and surrendered at the end of a certain period (usually 20 years) rather than remaining in force until the death of the insured. If the policy is to remain in force until death, however, you can use the **interest-adjusted net payment index (IANPI)** to more effectively measure the cost of cash-value insurance. Again, the lower the IANPI, the lower the cost of the policy.

Summary

1. Life insurance is designed to provide protection from the financial losses that result from death.

2. The reasons to purchase life insurance change over the life cycle. During childhood and singlehood, the need for life insurance is very small or even nonexistent. Factors affecting life insurance needs include the need to replace income, final-expense needs, readjustment-period needs, debt-repayment needs, college-expense needs, availability of government programs, and ownership of other life insurance and assets. Two methods to calculate life insurance needs are the multiple-of-earnings approach and the needs approach.

3. Basically only two types of life insurance exist: term life insurance and cash-value life insurance. Variations of term life insurance include decreasing term insurance, guaranteed renewable term insurance, convertible term insurance, and credit life insurance. Variations of cash-value insurance include whole life insurance, limited-pay life insurance, and universal and variable life insurance.

4. A life insurance policy is a written contract between the insurance purchaser and the insurance company spelling out in detail the terms of the agreement. When buying life insurance, special attention should be paid to the policy's general terms and conditions, special features of cash-value life insurance, and settlement options.

5. You should purchase life insurance only after you have determined the actual dollar amount and type of policy you need and analyzed comparative premiums. Term life insurance provides the most insurance protection for each premium dollar. The interest-adjusted cost index can provide a means of comparing similar policies, but its use is limited when comparing dissimilar policies.

Key Words & Concepts

beneficiary   *341*
cash surrender value   *354*
cash-value life insurance   *339*
conditions   *349*
decreasing term insurance   *340*
face amount   *339*
grace period   *351*
guaranteed insurability option   *356*
guaranteed renewable term insurance   *340*
insuring agreements   *349*
interest-adjusted cost index (IACI)   *360*
interest-sensitive life insurance   *345*
life insurance   *332*
needs approach   *336*
nonforfeiture values   *354*
owner   *341*
premium quote service   *359*
settlement options   *353*
Social Security survivor's benefits   *335*
term life insurance   *339*
variable–universal life insurance   *348*

Questions for Thought & Discussion

1. Briefly explain why the name "life insurance" may be considered a misnomer.

2. Identify the role that actuaries play in the life insurance business.

3. What is the major financial loss suffered upon the death of a family's primary income earner?

4. Describe five factors affecting the need for life insurance.

5. What is the multiple-of-earnings approach toward estimating lost income for a family or individual?

6. What is the difference between the multiple-of-earnings approach and the needs approach in estimating income losses?

7. How do term life insurance and cash-value life insurance differ?

8. Distinguish between the owner, the insured, the beneficiary, and the contingent beneficiary of a life insurance policy.

9. Describe level-premium term insurance.

10. Why might you want to buy a decreasing term policy?

11. What is guaranteed renewable term insurance?

12. Why might a convertibility option be a desirable part of a term life policy?

13. What is the major reason for not buying credit life insurance?

14. Give two reasons why you might want to buy group life insurance.

15. How does a limited-pay life insurance policy differ from a whole life policy?

16. What three pieces of information do interest-sensitive life insurance purchasers have about their policies that purchasers of more traditional cash-value policies lack?

17. How does variable–universal life insurance differ from variable life insurance?

18. Distinguish between the guaranteed minimum rate and the current rate paid on an interest-sensitive life insurance policy.

19. What is low-load life insurance?

20. Why is it misleading to say that a life insurance policy will "pay for itself"?

21. Describe the five sections of an insurance policy.

22. How does the IRS classify insurance dividends?

23. Distinguish between participating and nonparticipating insurance policies.

24. Distinguish between underwriting and investment profit of insurance companies.

25. Why does the death benefit usually differ from the face amount of a life insurance policy?

26. What advantage does a grace period offer to a life insurance policyholder?

27. What value does a guaranteed insurability option have for a life insurance policyholder?

28. What is meant by the term "settlement options," and what options are available to life insurance beneficiaries?

29. Name three factors that influence the cost of life insurance.

30. What might you gain by "buying term and investing the difference"?

31. What is the most important factor to consider when choosing a life insurance company?

32. What is a premium-quote service, and what benefit might consulting such a service offer?

33. What is the interest-adjusted cost index?

DECISION-MAKING CASES

Case 1 Life Insurance for a Newly Married Couple

Just-married couples sometimes overindulge in the type and amount of life insurance that they buy. Bryson and Jeanette Greenwood of Gunnison, Colorado, took a different approach. Both were working and had a small amount of life insurance provided through their respective employee benefit programs: Bryson, $35,000, and Jeanette, $15,000. During their discussion of life insurance needs and related costs, they decided that if Jeanette completed her master's degree in industrial psychology, she would have better employment opportunities. Consequently, they decided to use money they had available for additional life insurance to pay for Jeanette's education. They both feel, however, that they do not want to become "life insurance poor."

(a) In what way does Jeanette's return to school alter the Greenwoods' life insurance concerns?

(b) Would you agree that the amount of life insurance provided by the Greenwoods' respective employers is adequate while Jeanette is in school? Explain your response.

(c) How might the Greenwoods' life insurance needs change over the life cycle?

Case 2   Fraternity Members Contemplate Permanent Life Insurance

Lee Chen is a college student from Santa Ana, California. He is about to graduate, and was approached recently by a life insurance agent who set up a group meeting for several members of Lee's fraternity. During the meeting, the agent presented six life insurance plans and was very persuasive about the benefits of a plan that his company calls Affordable Life II. Under the plan, the soon-to-graduate student can buy $100,000 of permanent life insurance for a very low premium during the first five years and then pay a higher premium later when income presumably will have increased. Lee was confused after the meeting, as were his friends. Armed with your knowledge from this personal finance book, you have been asked to respond to some of their questions.

(a) Do you think the Affordable Life II plan is a good deal for these young people? Why or why not?

(b) How can the fraternity members decide how much life insurance they need?

(c) Is life insurance really as confusing as the agent made it seem? If not, what simpler explanation would you give?

(d) What type of life insurance program would you advise for the fraternity brothers?

(e) How would they know if a life insurance policy is offered at a fair price?

Financial Math Questions

1. Glenda Crahcrow of Portland, Maine, has a $100,000 participating cash-value policy written on her life. The policy has accumulated $4700 in cash value, of which Glenda has borrowed $3000. The policy also has accumulated unpaid dividends of $1666. Yesterday Glenda paid her premium of $1200 for the coming year. What is the current death benefit from this policy?

2. Wanda and Raymond Hensley of Savannah, Georgia, are a married couple in their mid-thirties. They have two children, aged 5 and 3, and Wanda is pregnant with their third child. Wanda is a book indexer who earned $15,000 after taxes last year. Because she performs much of her work at home, it is unlikely she will need to curtail her work after the baby is born. Raymond is a family therapist with a thriving practice; he earned $48,000 last year after taxes. Because both are self-employed, Wanda and Raymond do not have access to group life insurance. They are each covered by $50,000 universal life policies they purchased three years ago. In addition, Raymond is covered by a $50,000 five-year renewable term policy, which will expire next year. The Hensleys are currently reassessing their life insurance program. As a preliminary step in their analysis, they have determined that Wanda's account with Social Security would yield the family about $1094 per month, or an annual benefit of $13,128, if she were to die. For Raymond, the figure would be $2072 per month, or an annual benefit of $24,864. (See Appendix B for the determination of these benefits.) Both agree that they would like to support each of their children to age 22, but have been unable to start a college savings fund. They estimate that it would cost $30,000 to put each child through college as measured in today's dollars. They expect that burial expenses for each would total about $6000, and they would like to have a lump sum of life insurance clearly marked for paying off their $70,000 home mortgage. They also feel that each spouse would want to take a six-month leave from work if the other were to die.

(a) Calculate the amount of life insurance that Wanda needs using the information given. Use the Decision-Making Worksheet on page 337 or the *Garman/Forgue* Web site. Assume a 3 percent after-tax and after-inflation rate of return and an income need for 22 years, because the unborn child will need financial support for that many years.

(b) Calculate the amount of life insurance that Raymond needs using the information given. Use the Decision-Making Worksheet on page 337 or the *Garman/Forgue* Web site. Assume a 3 percent rate of return after taxes and inflation and an income need for 22 years, because the unborn child will need financial support for that many years.

(c) If Wanda and Raymond purchased term insurance to cover their additional needs, how much more would each need to spend?

MONEY MATTERS: LIFE-CYCLE CASES

Victor and Maria Hernandez Contemplate Switching Life Insurance Policies

Victor and Maria have a total of $200,000 in life insurance. Victor has a $50,000 cash-value policy purchased more than 20 years ago when they were first married and a $100,000 group term policy through his employer. Maria has a $50,000 group term insurance policy through her employer. The couple has been approached by a life insurance agent who thinks that they need to change their policy mix because they have inadequate insurance. Specifically, the agent has suggested that Victor cash in his cash-value policy and buy a new variable–universal life policy.

1. If Victor cashes in his policy, what options would he have when receiving the cash value?

2. As the Hernandez children are now grown and on their own, and both Victor and Maria are employed full-time, give general reasons why Victor may need more or less insurance.

3. Why would it be a bad idea for Victor to buy a variable–universal life policy?

4. Determine what the $8000 in cash value in Victor's life insurance policy would be worth in 20 years if that sum were invested somewhere else and earned an 8 percent annual return. (Hint: Use the *Garman/Forgue* Web site.)

The Johnsons Change Their Life Insurance Coverage

Harry and Belinda Johnson spend $9 per month on life insurance in the form of a premium on a $10,000 paid-at-65 cash-value policy on Harry. Belinda receives a group term insurance policy from her employer with a face amount of $38,700 (1.5 times her annual salary). By choosing a group life insurance plan from his "menu" of fringe benefits, Harry now has $20,400 (his annual salary) of group term life insurance. Harry and Belinda have decided that, since they have no children, they could reduce their life insurance needs by protecting one another's income for only four years, assuming the survivor would be able to fend for himself or herself after that time. They also realize that their savings fund is so low that it would have no bearing on their life insurance needs.

Harry and Belinda are basing their calculations on a projected 4 percent rate of return after taxes and inflation. They also estimate the following expenses: $8000 for final expenses, $4000 for readjustment expenses, and $5000 for repayment of short-term debts.

1. Should the $3000 interest earnings from Harry's trust fund be included in his annual income for the purposes of calculating the likely dollar loss if he were to die? (See the discussions about the Johnsons at the end of Chapter 2.) Explain your response.

2. Based on your response to the previous question, how much more life insurance does Harry need? Use the Decision-Making Worksheet on page 337 to arrive at your answer.

3. Repeat the calculations to arrive at the additional life insurance needed on Belinda's life.

4. How might the Johnsons most economically meet any additional life insurance needs you have determined they may have?

5. In addition to their life insurance planning, how might the Johnsons begin to prepare for their retirement years? See "How to: Plan Your Life Insurance Program," on page 361.

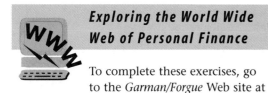

Exploring the World Wide Web of Personal Finance

To complete these exercises, go to the *Garman/Forgue* Web site at

www.hmco.com/college/business/

Select Personal Finance. Click on the exercise link for this chapter and answer the questions that appear on the Web page.

1. Use the Decision-Making Worksheet on page 337 of the text or on-line at the *Garman/Forgue* Web site to calculate your life insurance needs. Are you underinsured, overinsured, or appropriately insured? Also visit the Web site for FinanCenter, which provides a life insurance needs calculator. Follow the directions to calculate your life insurance needs. Why do you think the *Personal Finance* text worksheet and the FinanCenter calculator yield differing results? (Hint: Note how the two versions handle income replacement.)

2. Visit the Web site for QuoteSmith to obtain a quote for the annual premium on a $100,000 guaranteed renewable, ten-year term policy for you. Then call a life insurance agent in your community for a quote on the same term insurance policy. How do the term rates quoted by your local agent compare with the rates found over the Internet? Also, ask for the quote on a $100,000 universal life policy with guaranteed insurability and waiver-of-premium options. Ask the agent to explain why the quotes for the two types of policies differ. Analyze his or her response based on what you learned in this chapter.

3. Consult the Web site for the Insurance News Network, and click on Ratings to check the rating for the insurance company recommended by the agent in Exercise 2 and the lowest-cost company for term insurance that you found on the Web. What do those ratings tell you about the strength of those companies?

4. Call a local life insurance office and talk to one of the agents about the potential for someone interested in a career in life insurance. As part of the discussion, ask his or her advice about what professional certifications are most valuable. Also, visit the Web site for the American College to read up on the requirements for the professional designation of chartered life underwriter (CLU) mentioned in the text.

5. Visit the Web site for the National Association of Insurance Commissioners and find its map of the states to bring up the site of the insurance regulatory agency in your home state. Explore the information your state provides to assist consumers in the purchase of life insurance. Then visit the insurance regulatory agency for California, New York, or Florida. How does the information provided by your state compare with that provided by one of those states?

6. Visit the Web site for the Social Security Administration to obtain a copy of your Personal Earnings and Benefits Estimate statement. This statement will provide you with baseline information on your eligibility for Social Security benefits, including survivor benefits. The statement will be sent to you by U.S. mail although it is planned that this information will be available on-line in the future.

PART FOUR

Investment Planning

Investment Fundamentals and Portfolio Management

13

O B J E C T I V E S

After reading this chapter, you should be able to:

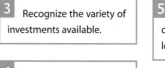

1 Summarize reasons why people invest, what is required before beginning, how returns are earned, and some ways to obtain funds to invest.

2 Determine your own investment philosophy.

3 Recognize the variety of investments available.

4 Identify the major factors that affect the return on investment.

5 Specify some strategies of portfolio management for long-term investors.

6 List three guidelines to use when deciding the best time to sell investments.

At many points in this book, we have encouraged you to set aside funds for the future, especially by accumulating funds through regular savings. This approach is a wise course of action, but building real wealth requires an additional consideration—earning a good return on your money. The difference in the return is a major distinction between mere savings and investing. Successful investors ultimately become able to live off the earnings on their accumulated wealth, often without spending the wealth itself. The most common ways that people invest involve putting money into assets like stocks, mutual funds, and real estate. Investments can increase your income and help maximize your enjoyment of life. Of course, to achieve this higher level of living in the future you cannot spend every dollar that you earn, but must instead set aside some of your income and invest it to help secure that future lifestyle. Moreover, you—and no one else—are responsible for your financial success.

This chapter begins by examining why and how people start to invest. Next, we provide tools to help you identify your personal investment philosophy. A variety of investments are then introduced. The following section describes major factors that affect the return on investment, including investment risk, diversification, leverage, taxes, buying and selling costs, and inflation. We then present reasons why people fail to succeed financially and give ideas on how to succeed. Next, strategies for long-term investors are discussed in detail. The chapter concludes by listing guidelines to use in deciding the best time to sell investments.

Preparations for Investing

1 Summarize reasons why people invest, what is required before beginning, how returns are earned, and some ways to obtain funds to invest.

Before undertaking an investment plan, you need to know why people invest, some prerequisites for investing, the sources of investment returns, and how to obtain money to invest. Fortunately, opening an investment account is just as easy as opening a checking account.

Why People Invest

People invest for one or more of four general reasons: (1) to achieve financial goals, such as purchase of a new car, a down payment on a home, payment of a child's education, and so on; (2) to increase current income; (3) to gain wealth and a feeling of financial security; and (4) to have funds available during retirement years. People who place funds in investments must accept occasional losses, setbacks, and unexpected occurrences; over the long term, however, they typically earn much higher returns than those obtained through savings.

Prerequisites to Investing

Before you embark on an investment program, make sure you have taken the following steps:

1. *Live within your means.* If you find yourself constantly running short of cash toward the end of the month, you may need to institute better budget controls and probably will not have any money available for investments. On the other hand, if you are not overly indebted and generally have money available for regular expenses, small gifts, and occasional self-indulgences, you should begin thinking about an investment program.

2. *Continue a savings program.* A good financial manager saves regularly to acquire goods and services or to build an emergency fund. Investors also save so that they can make periodic investments with accrued savings.

3. *Establish lines of credit.* A line of credit can help you meet personal financial emergencies and reduce the need to keep large amounts of savings readily available. For example, you might maintain a line of credit of $3000 at a local bank, $5000 at a brokerage firm, or $4000 on a bank credit card.

4. *Carry adequate insurance protection.* Liability insurance protects your assets and lifestyle in the event you are sued, and health insurance can defray your expenses if you or a member of your family falls ill. Life insurance is

Get Money to Invest

Unless you inherit money or win a lottery, you must save to build up funds to invest. Some suggestions follow:

- *Pay yourself first through forced savings plans.* You should "pay yourself" every time you receive income—that is, you should treat savings as a fixed expense in your budget. When asked, most employers will direct a portion of your salary to a savings account at a bank, credit union, or savings and loan association, or even a savings plan at work. You never "see" this money, because it is deposited automatically. An advantage of a forced savings plan is that you have to take action not to save, thus making it easier to continue saving.

- *Save—don't spend—extra funds.* When unexpected money arrives, you will be able to add substantially to your savings balance. Examples of extra money might include a year-end bonus from an employer, the after-tax amount of a raise above your previous salary, money gifts, and income tax refunds. In addition, when bud-

geted costs do not exceed income for a given time period, you should put the surplus (or part of it) in savings.

- *Make installment payments to yourself.* If you make installment repayments on a debt, you have an unusual opportunity to save after making the last repayment on the debt. Simply continue to make the payments—but to your savings account.

- *Break a habit.* Put aside the amount you would have spent.

- *Scrimp one month each year.* If you make a concerted effort to scrimp on all expenses one month each year, you can accumulate a sizable amount of money for savings and investment. To accomplish this goal, cut back on some planned expenditures and question every possible variable expense. Knowing that this level of frugality will end after 30 days will help motivate you toward success.

frequently purchased in conjunction with investments to protect the lifestyle of dependents in the event of an investor's death.

5. *Establish investment goals.* When you have specific reasons to invest, you will be more likely to consider "investments" as a high-priority category in your budget.

Investment Returns

Investment returns come from two sources: current income and capital gains. **Current income** is money received from an investment, usually on a regular basis, in the form of interest, dividends, rent, or other such payment. As noted earlier, interest is the amount you receive for allowing a financial institution or individual to use and invest the money you lent (the principal). **Dividends** are distributions of profits to owners of shares in a corporation. Corporations typically retain some profits to use for continued growth and distribute the remainder as dividends. **Rent** is payment received in return for allowing someone to use your real property, such as land or a building.

The Long-Term Rates of Return on Investments

According to Ibbotson Associates, for the past 60 years common stocks have recorded gains of 11.4 percent annually compared with 15.1 percent for small company stocks, 5.5 percent for long-term corporate bonds, 5.1 percent for long-term government bonds, and 3.9 percent for 30-day Treasury bills. The inflation rate during that time averaged 4.1 percent. The 11.4 percent return on common stocks typically consists of an 8.4 percent capital gain plus a 3.0 percent dividend yield.

A **capital gain** is income that results from an increase in the value of an investment. It is calculated by subtracting the total amount paid for the investment (including transaction costs) from the higher price at which it is sold (minus any transaction costs). Of course, a **capital loss** results if the selling price (minus transaction costs) is lower than the original amount invested (plus transaction costs). For example, the value of a small apartment building might increase from $200,000 to $275,000 over a few years. The value of a share of common stock might increase from $80 to $100 per share in six months. Note, however, that you realize a capital gain on an investment only when you sell it. For most investments, a trade-off exists between capital gains and current income: Investments with high capital gains potential often pay little current income, and investments that pay substantial current income generally have little or no potential for capital gains. Long-term investors are usually willing to forgo much current income in favor of possibly earning substantial future capital gains.

The **return** is the total income from an investment, including current income plus capital gains or minus capital losses. The **rate of return**, or **yield**, is the return on an investment expressed as a percentage of the current price; it is usually stated on an annualized basis. For example, Nina Torres, a married home builder from Gainesville, Florida, purchased shares of H&M stock for $1000, including the broker's commissions. She received $50 in cash dividends during the year. If Nina then sells the stock for $1100, minus the $60 in broker's commissions, she will have a capital gain of $40 ($1100 − $60 − $1000). Adding this $40 gain to the $50 in cash dividends provides a total return of $90, or a 9 percent annual yield on the investment ($90 ÷ $1000).

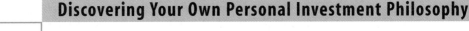

Discovering Your Own Personal Investment Philosophy

2 Determine your own investment philosophy.

Have you ever known someone who received a substantial inheritance and quickly lost it on poor investments? Such events have occurred often, but especially when people forget to match their financial decisions with their usual manner of thinking, feeling, and acting.

How Do You Handle Risk?

Risk—and your ability to handle it—greatly influences your personal investment philosophy. **Risk** represents the uncertainty that the yield on an investment will deviate from what is expected. Placing money in a federally insured savings account incurs virtually no risk because the government guarantees both the principal and the yield. Buying stock in a corporation is riskier because no one can guarantee the future success of a company. For most investments, the greater the risk, the greater the potential yield. This potential for gain is what motivates people to accept increasingly greater levels of risk.

As an investor trying to figure out your own investment philosophy, you first need to determine your ability to handle risk. Basically, you need to determine how much anxiety related to your investments you can handle. We sometimes call this ability your "stomach and sleep quotient" (SSQ). Ask yourself: What is my basic temperament or natural disposition? How well do I handle stress? How well do I sleep at night? Will my financial decisions cause loved ones to worry? Can I afford a 10, 20, or 30 percent market decline on my investments? Answering these questions honestly will help you match investments to your temperament and investment philosophy.

Ultraconservative "Investment" Strategies

There are many ways to save with no risk of losing your principal and still obtain respectable, although limited, returns: federally insured savings accounts, certificates of deposit, and EE and HH Savings Bonds. Ultraconservative investors, especially those who cannot sleep at night if they think their money is at risk, do not consider investments because they stick with the 100 percent safe options backed by the U.S. federal government. An ultraconservative investor of $1000 will not lose a penny and likely will gain $40 or more over the course of a year. In actuality, ultraconservative investors are not investors, but are, in fact, savers. They find it difficult to get ahead over the long term.

Your Investment Philosophy:
Conservative, Moderate, or Aggressive

True investors develop an **investment philosophy**—a personal investment strategy that anticipates specific returns and risks and contains tactics for accomplishing your investment goals. If you record your strategy and tactics in writing, you may avoid making inconsistent investment decisions. Successful investors match investment philosophy with investment goals.

Conservative The financial goal of obtaining a specific potential rate of return is accompanied by varied degrees of risk. If you have a **conservative investment philosophy**, you accept very little risk and are generally rewarded with relatively low rates of return for seeking the twin goals of a moderate current income and preservation of capital. You could be characterized as a "risk averter." Conservative investors often protect themselves by carefully avoiding losses and trying to stay with investments that have gains, often for long time periods (perhaps for five or ten years). Tactically, they might sell investments when the price rises or falls 15 percent. Most investors approaching retirement or who are planning to withdraw money from their investments in the near future adhere to a conservative investment philosophy.

Conservative investors typically consider investing in obligations issued by the government (such as Treasury bills, notes and bonds, and municipal bonds), high-quality (blue-chip) corporate bonds and stocks, balanced mutual funds (which own both stocks and bonds), certificates of deposit, and fixed annuities.

They also tend to spread their funds among a large number of investment alternatives. A conservative investor with $1000 might lose $50 over the course of a year or gain $60 during the same period.

Moderate People with a **moderate investment philosophy** seek capital gains through slow and steady growth in the value of their investments and some current income. They invite only a fair amount of risk of capital loss. Most have no immediate need for the funds and are instead laying the investment foundation for later years or building upon such a base. Moderate investors are fairly comfortable during rising and falling market conditions, remaining secure in the knowledge that they are investing for the long term. Their tactics might include selling investments when the price has risen 25 percent, selling if the price drops by 25 percent, and spreading investment funds among several choices.

People seeking moderate returns consider investing in dividend-paying common stocks, growth and income mutual funds, high-quality corporate bonds, government bonds, variable annuities, and real estate. A moderate investor with $1000 might lose $200 over the course of a year or gain $150.

Aggressive If you choose to strive for a very high return by accepting a high level of risk, you have an **aggressive investment philosophy** and could be characterized as a "risk seeker." Aggressive investors primarily seek capital gains. Many such investors take a short-term approach, confident that they can profit substantially during major upswings in market prices.

People seeking aggressive returns consider investing in common stocks of new or fast-growing companies, high-yielding junk bonds, aggressive-growth mutual funds, limited real estate partnerships, undeveloped land, precious metals, gems, commodity futures, stock-index futures, and collectibles of every stripe. Devotees of an aggressive investment philosophy sometimes do not spread their funds among many alternatives, and they may also adopt short-term tactics to increase capital gains. For example, an aggressive investor might place most of his or her investment funds in a single stock in the hope that it will rise 10 percent over 90 days, giving an annual yield of more than 40 percent. Those shares can then be sold and the money used to invest elsewhere. Investment tactics for aggressive investors are discussed in Chapter 17, "Real Estate and Advanced Portfolio Management." (A **portfolio** is a collection of stocks and bonds, collectively called **securities**, plus other investments such as mutual funds, real estate, and gold.)

Aggressive investors must be emotionally and financially able to weather substantial short-term losses—for example, a downward swing in price of 30 or 40 percent—with the expectation that an even stronger upswing in price might occur in the future. An aggressive investor with $1000 might lose $400 during a year or gain $400 over the same time frame.

Investment Selection

3 Recognize the variety of investments available.

You have two key decisions to make when choosing investments: (1) Do you want to lend your money or own an asset? (2) Do you want to invest for the short or long term?

Do You Want to Lend or Own?

You can invest money in two ways, by lending and by owning. When you lend your money, you receive some form of IOU and the promise of future income. You can lend by depositing money in banks, credit unions, and savings and loan associations (via savings accounts and certificates of deposit) or by lending money to governments (via Treasury notes and bonds as well as state and local bonds), businesses (corporate bonds), mortgage-backed bonds (such as Ginnie Maes), and life insurance companies (annuities). Such lending investments, or **debts**, generally offer both a fixed maturity and a fixed income. With a **fixed maturity**, the borrower agrees to repay the principal to the investor on a specific date. With a **fixed income**, the borrower agrees to pay the investor a specific rate of return for use of the principal. Such investments allow lenders to be fairly confident that they will receive a certain amount of interest income for a specified period of time and that the lent funds will eventually be returned. Thus, the return is somewhat assured. No matter how much profit the borrower makes with your funds, however, the investing lender receives only the fixed return promised at the time of the initial investment.

You may also invest money through ownership. When you buy an investment asset, you typically either own the asset outright or purchase it on credit. These investments are often called **equities.** You can buy common or preferred corporate stock (to obtain part-ownership in a corporation), purchase shares in a mutual fund company (which then invests the funds in corporate stocks and bonds), put money into your own business, purchase real estate, buy commodity futures (pork bellies or oranges), or buy investment-quality collectibles (such as rare antiques or stamps). Investment owners have the potential of a substantial return because they typically share the profits.

Do You Want to Make Short-Term or Long-Term Investments?

Most individual investors lack the expertise, time, and money to reap substantial short-term financial gains from investments (**short-term** means less than one year). Short-term gains often are offset by commissions and fees. For these reasons, most individual investors make **long-term investments**, keeping their funds in the same investment for two, five, or ten years or more. Regardless of the length of the investment period, you should periodically reexamine your investments with an eye toward maximizing return. An overview of the types of investments that match specific investment time frames is provided in Table 13.1.

Choosing an Investment Vehicle

This chapter provides the background information and tools of analysis that will permit you to decide on the types of investments that best suit your needs. We also provide specific guidelines for deciding when each investment should be sold. The following four chapters examine the details of such investments. Chapter 14 focuses on investing in individual stocks and bonds. Chapter 15 examines investing in mutual funds—the most popular of all investments owned by individuals and families. The focus of Chapter 16 is on the complexi-

Table 13.1

Match the Investment Alternatives to the Time Frame of Your Goals

Time	Investment Goals	Trade-Offs	Possible Investments
Less than 2 years	Easy access to funds Moderate yields Steady income Stable prices	Low returns Vulnerable to inflation	NOW checking account Savings account Money market account Certificates of deposit Treasury issues and corporate bonds maturing within 2 years

2 to 5 years	Moderately high yields
	Steady income
	Narrow price movements
		Less safety than for
		   shorter-term investments
		Lower returns than for
		   longer-term investments
		Some vulnerability to inflation
			Corporate bonds maturing
			   within 5 years
			Ginnie Mae bonds
			Stocks paying high dividends
			Balanced mutual funds

6 to 10 years	Moderately high yields
	Predictable price
	   movements
		Less safety than for
		   shorter-term investments
		Lower returns than for
		   longer-term investments
			Stocks paying high dividends
			Ginnie Mae bonds
			Short-term bonds
			Long-term bonds
			Long-term certificates of deposit (CDs)
			Growth and income mutual funds
			Real estate

More than 10 years	High long-term yields
	Potential for appreciation
	Returns that outpace
	   inflation
		Price volatility
		May have limited liquidity
		   and marketability
		Patience required
			Growth stocks
			Long-term bonds
			Precious metals
			Aggressive-growth mutual funds
			Real estate

ties of buying and selling all types of investments. Finally, Chapter 17 examines real estate (when viewed as an investment rather than as property for personal use) and speculative investments, such as commodities, options, and precious metals. After reading these chapters, you should have learned enough about investments to make wise decisions on your own.

Major Factors That Affect the Rate of Return on an Investment

4 Identify the major factors that affect the return on investment.

A number of factors affect the rate of return on an investment: various types of risk, investment risk, diversification, leverage, taxes, buying and selling costs, and inflation.

Investment Risk

"Pure risk," which concerns the uncertainty of events occurring with no potential for gain, was discussed in Chapter 10. Investments, however, are subject to

speculative risk, which involves the potential for either gain or loss. Common stock, for example, may rise or fall in value; which event will occur is an unknown. Because of the uncertainty that surrounds investments, many people choose conservatively to keep their risk low. Yet, to get high yields, they must accept greater unknowns and higher risk.

Figure 13.1 graphically presents the **risk pyramid,** which illustrates the trade-offs between risk and return for a number of investments. All four investments guaranteed by the U.S. government (savings bonds, certificates of deposit, insured bank accounts, and Treasury securities) offer a virtually "risk-free return" and, accordingly, offer a relatively low return.

Types of Investment Risk Investment risk can be categorized as follows:

- **Inflation risk.** Inflation risk is the risk that an investment's return may be diminished or reversed by the cumulative effects of inflation. To maintain the same buying power, returns must significantly exceed the inflation rate because investors typically must pay taxes on income earned. Otherwise, earnings from investments will lose purchasing power because the income received is paid in ever-cheaper dollars. Inflation risk is present for all types of investments.

- **Deflation risk.** Houses, real estate, and other ownership investments are subject to the deflation risk that the general price level in the economy might drop, thereby reducing the investment's value. Such events have occurred recently in certain regional real estate markets.

- **Interest-rate risk.** Interest-rate risk stems from the possibility that interest rates will rise and the value of certain investments will fall. Interest-rate risk affects fixed-interest-rate obligations such as bonds and preferred stocks,

Figure 13.1

The Risk Pyramid Reveals the Trade-Offs between Investment Risk and Return

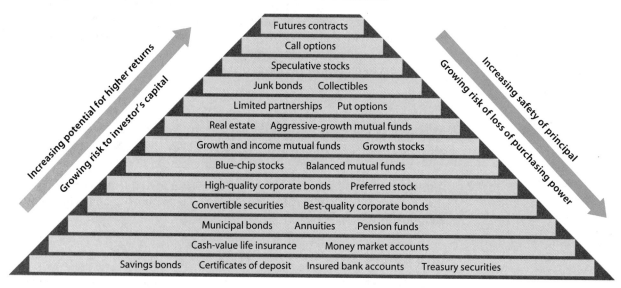

which have an almost guaranteed rate of return. For example, suppose that you buy a 20-year $1000 government bond at 6 percent. The government is obligated to pay you $60 per year ($1000 × 0.06) and to repay the $1000 principal 20 years from now. If interest rates in the economy rise substantially, perhaps to 8 percent, the market value of the 6 percent bond will decline. Because investors could buy a new bond for $1000 that pays 8 percent, they might offer to buy your 6 percent bond for $750, which would raise their effective yield to 8 percent ($60 ÷ $750). Note that your capital loss would be realized only if you actually sold your bond.

- **Financial risk.** Financial risk relates to the possibility that the investment will fail to pay a return to the investor. A corporation might temporarily experience difficult financial times and fail to pay dividends on its shares of stock. In addition, there is always a risk that the company could go bankrupt.

- **Market-volatility risk.** All investments are subject to occasional sharp changes in price due simply to changes in the overall market for such investments. This market-volatility risk must be considered. For example, the value of similar stocks being traded can change 2 to 4 percent in a single day, and the value of a single stock might change even more dramatically. The price of a typical stock fluctuates about 50 percent in an average year; thus, a stock selling for $30 per share in January might range in price from $15 to $45 before the end of the following December.

- **Marketability risk.** When you have to sell an illiquid asset quickly, you may face a marketability risk—the uncertainty of loss you might have to absorb if forced to sell an investment before its planned disposal. Selling real estate in a hurry, for example, often requires the seller to make price concessions because few potential buyers may emerge. An investment with marketability risk is illiquid because the asset cannot be quickly converted to cash.

- **Political risk.** The political environment can often dramatically influence the value of investments. Imposition of wage and price controls, government efforts to settle labor strikes, and election of officials who change defense spending, tariff policies, and income tax rates can all affect investments negatively or positively.

Table 13.2 on the following page summarizes the degrees of each kind of risk for each type of investment. You may want to return to this table, as well as to Table 13.1, as you encounter these types of investments in more depth in the following chapters.

Random and Market Risk **Random risk** (also called **unsystematic risk**) is the risk associated with owning only one investment (such as stock in one company) that, by chance, may do very poorly in the future due to uncontrollable or random factors, such as labor unrest, lawsuits, and product recall. If you invest in only one stock, its value might rise or fall; if you invest in two stocks, however, the odds are lessened that both will fall in price. Such **diversification**—the process of reducing risk by spreading investment money among several investment opportunities—provides one effective method of managing random risk. It results in a potential rate of return on all of the investments that is generally

Table 13.2

Types of Investments and Degrees of Risk

Type of Investment	Type of Risk							
	Inflation	Deflation	Interest Rate	Financial	Market Volatility	Market-ability	Liquidity	Political
Insurance (cash value)	Medium	Low	Low	Low	Low	Low	Low	Low
Insurance annuities	High	Low	Low	Low	Low	Low	Low	Low
Bonds (best quality)	High	Low	High	Low	Medium	Low	Low	Low
Bonds (high quality)	High	Low	High	Medium	Medium	Low	Low	Low
Common stocks	Medium	Medium	Medium	Medium	High	Low	Low	High
Mutual funds	Medium	Medium	Medium	Medium	High	Low	Low	High
Real estate	Low	Low	Medium	Low	Low	High	High	High
Precious metals, options, and commodities	Low	Low	Low	High	High	High	Low	High

lower than the potential return on a single alternative. This lower return on investment represents the opportunity cost of reducing the risk of loss.

At a minimum, an investor should diversify between stocks and bonds while maintaining some funds in cash equivalents awaiting investment opportunities, as illustrated in Figure 13.2. Note that the overall total return of the diversified portfolio (9.6 percent) shown in the figure is *less* than the portion earning the greatest return on equities (12 percent); observe also that the risk of loss is reduced.

As a practical matter, you will need to accept many types of investment risk to achieve your long-term financial goals. It is important to accept investment risks without being irrationally frightened, and then manage the risk.

Research suggests that you can eliminate random risk by holding 15 or more stocks and bonds, and that such risk can be cut in half by diversifying into as few as five stocks and bonds. If you were very confident that interest rates would decline in future years, for example, you might be wise to put $10,000 into high-yielding corporate bonds (perhaps paying 9 percent) before the interest rates slipped further. If you were wrong and interest rates increased, pulling bond rates upward as well, the value of your bonds would temporarily decline sharply. The third column in Table 13.2 shows that bonds carry a high risk related to interest rates and that real estate is associated with a low risk from inflation (real estate prices generally rise during inflationary times). By making several investments (perhaps including bonds and real estate), you can reduce your random risk. As rational investors diversify, they reduce random risk.

Figure 13.2

The Effect of Diversification Results in a Lower Total Return

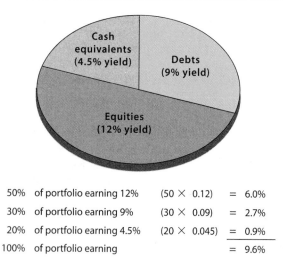

50%	of portfolio earning 12%	(50 × 0.12)	= 6.0%
30%	of portfolio earning 9%	(30 × 0.09)	= 2.7%
20%	of portfolio earning 4.5%	(20 × 0.045)	= 0.9%
100%	of portfolio earning		= 9.6%

Diversification cannot reduce all risks, however. Some risks would exist even if you owned all of the stocks in a market because prices will move up and down over time. This uncertainty of loss is called **market risk**, also known as **systematic risk**. Market risk tends to be caused by influences and events that operate independently of a particular investment, such as economic, social, or market conditions, fluctuations in investor preferences, or political factors. Examples include inflation and an aging population. Market risk has averaged about 8 percent through the years, meaning that any single securities investment, through no fault of its own, might vary up and down about 8 percent annually. The total risk in an investment consists of the sum of the random risk and market risk.

Leverage

Another factor that can affect return on investment is **leverage**. This process involves using borrowed funds ("OPM," meaning "other people's money") to make an investment with the goal of earning a rate of return in excess of the after-tax costs of borrowing. Investing in real estate for its rental income provides an illustration of leverage, as shown in Table 13.3. Assume that a person can buy a small office building either by making a $10,000 down payment and borrowing $90,000 or by paying $100,000 cash. If the rental income is $12,000 annually ($1000 per month) and the person pays income taxes at a 28 percent rate, it would be better to use credit to buy the building because the yield would be 18.14 percent versus an 8.64 percent yield when paying cash.

Leverage can prove particularly beneficial when substantial capital gains occur, as this strategy sharply boosts the return on the investment. Assume that at the end of one year, the value of the building described above has appreciated 7 percent and you could sell it for $107,000 (excluding commission costs). If you had purchased the property for $100,000 cash and then sold it for $107,000, the

Table 13.3

Illustration of Leverage: Buying Real Estate Using Credit

	Pay Cash	Use Credit
Purchase price of office building	$ 100,000	$ 100,000
Amount borrowed	0	– 90,000
Amount invested	100,000	10,000
Rental income ($1000 per month)	12,000	12,000
Minus tax-deductible interest (10.0 percent, 30-year loan on $90,000)	– 0	– 9,480
Net earnings before taxes	12,000	2,520
Minus income tax liability (28 percent bracket)	– 3,360	– 706
Rental earnings after taxes	$ 8,640	$ 1,814
	÷ 100,000	÷ 10,000
Percentage return on amount invested	8.64 percent	18.14 percent

Use Beta to Estimate Risk for Your Investment Portfolio

Beta is a ratio measure of an investment's price volatility—or risk—compared with a specific market index, usually for similar investments. In stocks, for example, beta is a statistically determined measure of the relative risk of a common stock compared with the market for all stocks. The average for all stocks in the market has arbitrarily been assigned a beta of +1.0. Betas for an individual stock can be either positive or negative.

Most individual stocks have positive betas between +0.5 and +2.0. A beta of zero suggests that the price of the stock is independent of the market, much like that of a risk-free U.S. Treasury security. A beta of less than 1.0 (0.0 to 0.9) means that the stock price is less sensitive to the market because it moves in the same direction as the general market, albeit not to the same degree. A beta of +1.1 to +2.0 (or higher) indicates that the price of the security is more sensitive to the market because its price moves in the same direction as the market but by a greater percentage. A stock with a negative beta is considered a countercyclical stock because it exhibits price changes that are contrary to downward movements in the business cycle (such as cigarette and utility company stocks); thus, prices of such stocks remain steady or go up during an economic recession.

As an illustration of how to use beta to estimate the amount of risk in your investment portfolio, assume that you are willing to accept more risk than the general investor and that you buy a stock with a beta of 1.5. If the average price of all stocks rises by 20 percent over time, the price of the stock you chose will probably rise by 30 percent, which is the beta of 1.5 multiplied by the increase in the market (1.5 × 20 percent). If the average market drops in value by 10 percent, the price of the stock you chose might drop by 15 percent (1.5 × 10 percent). Betas for individual stocks, mutual funds, and other investments are available from brokerage firms, reference books, advisory services, and investment magazines.*

---

* *Alpha* is a quantification of the difference between an investment's expected return, based upon its beta, and how it actually performs given its beta risk, or its expected performance (outperforming or underperforming it). A stock or mutual fund with a positive alpha means the company did better than expected for its level of risk; negative alphas indicate poor performance. Like betas, alphas are published by a variety of sources.

capital gain on the sale would be 7 percent (the $7000 return divided by $100,000 originally invested). If you had bought it using credit, however, the capital gain would be 70 percent (the $7000 return divided by the $10,000 originally invested, ignoring transaction costs, taxes, and inflation).

Leverage has a potentially negative side as well. In the preceding example, if you used credit to purchase the property, you would need a minimum rental income of $9480 to be able to make the mortgage loan payments. A few months of vacancy or expensive repairs to the building could result in a losing situation. Furthermore, a decline in value would be magnified using leverage. You can become financially overextended by using leverage for investments, a factor that you should not ignore.

Taxes

When comparing similar investments, your objective should be to earn the best **after-tax return**—that is, the net amount remaining after selling the investment and subtracting the initial cost, selling expenses, and all income taxes. You

The best kinds of investment returns often are those that are **tax-free** because the investor keeps the entire return. When an investment pays a higher taxable return than a tax-free investment, it may be a better choice. Smart investors do the math and find out (and the math is shown on page 81).

The next-best return is **tax-sheltered** because no taxes are due on the profits until one or more years in the future. Thus, the profits can grow free of taxes. When taxes must eventually be paid, the tax rates might be lower. Wise investors consider making tax-free and tax-sheltered investments before making investments that are subject to current income taxes.

should analyze investments carefully in terms of anticipated income, potential capital gains, and after-tax effects of total investment income. Increasing the after-tax return on your investments requires an understanding of your marginal tax rate and the concept of taxable versus tax-free income.

Marginal Tax Rate The **marginal tax rate** is the tax rate on your last dollar of earnings. It gives you two pieces of information: (1) the amount that the taxpayer keeps after paying income taxes, and (2) the tax savings benefit of a tax-deductible expense. Assume that the person considering the real estate investment in Table 13.3 has a taxable income of $50,000 and pays income taxes at a rate of 28 percent. If the annual rental income on the property was increased $1000, the investor would gain $720 after paying $280 in income taxes. Alternatively, if the investor had to spend $1400 recarpeting and painting after a tenant moved out, that amount would be tax-deductible and would, therefore, reduce the investor's tax liability by $392 ($1400 × 0.28). Thus, the government becomes a partner in sharing tax-deductible expenses. The concept of the marginal tax rate is discussed in more detail in Chapters 1 and 3.

Taxable versus Tax-Free Income Investors should consider the after-tax return of comparable taxable and tax-free alternatives. For example, Ibrahim Sallah, a member of a two-income family in Ames, Iowa, is comparing a $1000 corporate bond paying a 7.6 percent return with a municipal bond paying a 5.9 percent return. Because he is in the 28 percent marginal tax bracket, $21 of the $76 interest earned annually on the corporate bond would go to income taxes ($76 × 0.28). Ibrahim would be left with an after-tax return of 5.5 percent ($76 − $21 = $55 ÷ $1000). The municipal bond's annual interest of $59 would be exempt from federal income taxes. Ibrahim should choose the municipal bond because the after-tax return is 5.9 percent ($59 ÷ $1000), which is 0.4 percentage point higher than the corporate bond (5.9 percent − 5.5 percent). Your decision to invest in tax-free opportunities should depend on the yields available and your marginal tax rate. Equations 3.1 and 3.2 (on page 81) demonstrate how to determine tax-equivalent yields on any type of investment. In addition, Chapter 14, "Investing in Stocks and Bonds," provides details on tax-free investments.

Buying and Selling Costs, Including Commissions

Buying and selling investments may result in a number of transaction costs, such as "fix-up costs" when preparing a home for sale, appraisals for collectibles, and storage costs for precious metals. The largest transaction cost in investments, however, usually comprises **commissions**. These fees or percentages are paid to salespersons, agents, and companies for their services—that is, to buy or sell an investment. The commission charged to buy an investment (one commission) and then later sell it (a second commission) is partially based on the value of the transaction. Typical ranges for commissions are as follows: stocks, 1.5–2.5 percent; bonds, 0–2.0 percent; mutual funds, 0–8.5 percent; real estate, 6.0–7.0 percent; options and futures contracts, 4.0–6.0 percent; limited partnerships, 10.0–15.0 percent; and collectibles, 15.0–30.0 percent. You can increase your return by holding down commission expenses. (Additional details on commissions are provided in later chapters.)

Inflation

Inflation is an extremely important factor when considering an investment because it can significantly impact the "real" return on investments. Consider Shirley Robinson, a manufacturing worker from Ruston, Louisiana, who thought she had hedged against inflation by depositing $1000 in a bank account paying 3 percent interest. Her account earned $30 interest during the year; unfortunately, the inflation rate for the year was 4 percent. To beat inflation, Shirley must invest her money so that it earns a higher return than the inflation rate.

Most investors expect inflation to occur. The only question is how quickly prices will rise in the future; over the long term, increases have averaged approximately 3.0 percent per year. During periods of high inflation, the real value of most assets declines, although the value of some rises. Historically, common stocks and real estate rise with inflation over several years. On the other hand, bonds lose value during inflationary times because they are fixed-dollar investments that offer the return of a certain number of dollars—dollars that are losing their original purchasing power.

Investors who fail to earn a return that exceeds the rate of inflation lose money because of the effects of inflation and the income taxes that must be paid

Calculate the Real Rate of Return (After Taxes and Inflation) on Investments

Step 1. *Identify the anticipated before-tax rate of return.* Perhaps you think that a stock will pay a rate of return of 11 percent in one year, including current income and capital gain.

Step 2. *Subtract the impact of your marginal tax rate on the anticipated rate of return to obtain the net return after taxes.* This step reveals your **tax-equivalent yield.** Assume that you are in the 28 percent federal income tax bracket, so $(1 - 0.28) \times 0.11 = 0.0792$, or 7.9 percent.

Step 3. *Subtract an estimate of anticipated inflation from the anticipated net return after taxes to obtain the real rate of return on investment (after taxes and inflation).* You estimate annual inflation of 5 percent for the coming year; therefore, 7.9 percent − 5 percent = 2.9 percent. Thus, your anticipated rate of return of 11 percent provides a real return of 2.9 percent after taxes and inflation.*

* The simple subtraction method illustrated here is quite useful even though it slightly overestimates the return. For precision, the following formula provides a more accurate indicator of the real rate of return after taxes and inflation: "1 plus the tax-equivalent yield" divided by "1 plus the inflation rate" equals a quotient from which "1" is subtracted; the result is then multiplied by "100." This calculation results in a return of 2.78 percent.

on the gain. The challenge is to analyze the risks of making investments carefully so as to earn the highest possible **real return on investment** (the yield after subtracting the effects of taxes and inflation).

Portfolio Management Strategies for Long-Term Investors

5 Specify some strategies of portfolio management for long-term investors.

A **long-term investor** generally operates under a moderate or conservative investment philosophy and wants to hold an investment as long as it provides a return commensurate with its risk, usually for five years or more. Knowledgeable amateurs can obtain long-term investment results that are superior to those produced by most professionals, but it takes some discipline, time, and effort to achieve this outcome. If you like the idea of getting together with others in an investment club, contact the National Association of Investors Corporation [(800) 320-6242 or *www.naic.com*] to find a club located nearby.

In addition to understanding the overall economic picture (see Chapter 1), long-term investors need to know how well the **securities markets** (places where stocks and bonds are traded) are performing. A securities market in which prices have declined in value 20 percent or more from previous highs, often over several weeks or months, is called a **bear market**. Since 1926 there have been 22 bear markets. In contrast, a **bull market** results when securities prices have risen 20 percent or more over time. Historically, there have been 23 bull markets with an average gain of 110 percent. A **bull** in the market is a person who expects securities prices to go up; a **bear** expects the general market to decline. The origin of these terms is unknown, but some suggest that they refer to the ways that the animals attack: bears thrust their claws downward, and bulls move their horns upward. Bear markets last, on average, about nine months; bull markets average 29 months in length.

The person who understands the concepts of rising and falling markets can take advantage of appropriate investment opportunities. Four strategies of portfolio management for long-term investors are business-cycle timing, dollar-cost averaging, portfolio diversification, and asset allocation.

Strategy: Business-Cycle Timing

All long-term investors must be able to withstand some volatility (the likelihood of some large price swings), as well as recognize that occasions when market prices decline are, in fact, opportunities to invest in companies with promising futures as prices are depressed. This logic fits investors who follow the **business-cycle timing approach**. The investor seeks to be part of the market when long-term prices are rising and to conservatively reduce the likelihood of major losses by exiting the market when declines appear probable. The object is to not maximize profits in a bull market and eliminate all losses when the market declines— this is **market timing**, and it is impossible to predict short-term price changes. Research shows that the direction of long-term investments accounts for 50 to 70 percent of the gains in the average stock or mutual fund.

A typical business cycle—from boom to bust—lasts five years. Business-cycle timing requires investing in securities when the general economy is in a recession and prices have been declining over a number of months (a bear market). Although the perfect time to buy is at the "bottom" of the market, few people are lucky enough to guess this point correctly. Thus, business-cycle investors must begin buying as the market begins to rebound; the challenge is knowing when it is safe to return to the market. The investor should sell securities later, when the general economy is prospering and a bull market characterizes the investments scene. Figure 1.1 (on page 7) illustrates various phases of the business cycle.

The challenge confronting the investor is to have the courage to buy during times of economic recession when most other investors contemplate selling in case prices drop even further. In fact, six months into the next recession probably will be an excellent time to buy stocks and mutual funds. The prices of these securities typically rebound just before a recession ends in anticipation of better times ahead.

Many long-term investors give up the attempt to time their investments in bull and bear markets because it proves too difficult. To be successful, you must consistently outguess the market. Instead, many smart investors choose one or a combination of the other strategies of long-term investing (dollar-cost averaging, portfolio diversification, and asset allocation) and—very importantly—they remain invested. People wishing to earn the historic long-term average returns of the equities markets (11.4 percent) can do so only if they stay invested in the market.

Strategy: Dollar-Cost Averaging

Dollar-cost averaging is a systematic program of investing equal sums of money at regular intervals regardless of the price of the investment. In this approach, the same fixed dollar amount is invested in the same stock or mutual fund at regular intervals over a long time. As a result, you purchase more shares when the price is down and fewer shares when the price is high. This objective is one of the goals of business-cycle timing. Most of the shares are, therefore, accumulated at below-average costs. This strategy avoids the risks and responsibilities of investment timing because the stock purchases are made regularly (probably every month) regardless of the price. It also ignores all outside events and short-term gyrations of the market, providing the investor with a disciplined buying strategy. It is important to note that the dollar-cost averaging method assumes that the investor has done basic research on the quality of the investment and selected one with good future prospects. Chapters 14 through 17 are designed to improve your ability to identify quality investments.

Table 13.4 shows the results of systematic investments in a stock under varying market conditions. (Commissions are excluded.) As an example, assume that you invest $300 into a stock every three months. To illustrate dollar-cost averaging, assume that the funds were first invested during the "fluctuating market" shown in Table 13.4. Because the initial price is $15 per share, you receive 20 shares for your investment. Then the market drops—an extreme but easy-to-follow example—and the price falls to $10 per share. When you buy $300 worth of the stock now, you receive 30 shares. Three months later, the market price rebounds to $15 and you invest another $300, receiving 20 shares. It then drops and rises again.

Table 13.4

Dollar-Cost Averaging for a Stock or Mutual Fund Investment

Fluctuating Market			Declining Market			Rising Market		
Regular Investment	Share Price	Shares Acquired	Regular Investment	Share Price	Shares Acquired	Regular Investment	Share Price	Shares Acquired
$ 300	$15	20	$ 300	$15	20	$ 300	$ 6	50
300	10	30	300	10	30	300	10	30
300	15	20	300	10	30	300	12	25
300	10	30	300	6	50	300	15	20
300	15	20	300	5	60	300	20	15
Total $1500	$65	120	$1500	$46	190	$1500	$63	140

Average share price: $13.00 ($65 ÷ 5)*	Average share price: $9.20 ($46 ÷ 5)*	Average share price: $12.60 ($63 ÷ 5)*
Average share cost: $12.50 ($1500 ÷ 120)†	Average share cost: $7.89 ($1500 ÷ 190)†	Average share cost: $10.71 ($1500 ÷ 140)†

* Sum of share price total ÷ number of investment periods.
† Total amount invested ÷ total shares purchased.

You now own 120 shares, with a total investment of $1500. The **average share price** is a simple calculation of the amounts paid for the investment made by dividing the share price total by the number of investment periods. In this example, the average share price is $13.00 ($65 ÷ 5). The **average share cost,** a more meaningful figure, is the actual cost basis of the investment used for income tax purposes. It is calculated by dividing the total amount invested by the total shares purchased. In this example, it is $12.50 ($1500 ÷ 120). Based on the recent price of $15 per share, each of your 120 shares is worth on average $2.50 ($15 − $12.50) more than you paid for it. Thus, your gain is $300 (120 × $2.50; or $15 × 120 = $1800, $1800 − $1500 = $300).

Markets may also decline over a time period. The "declining market" portion of Table 13.4 (representing a prolonged bear market of 15 months) shows purchases of 190 shares for increasingly lower prices that eventually reach $5 per share at the bottom of the business cycle. In a declining market, if you keep investing using dollar-cost averaging, you will purchase a large volume of shares. If you sell when the market is down substantially, you will not profit. In this example, you have purchased 190 shares at an average cost of $7.89, and they now have a depressed price of $5. Selling at this point would result in a substantial loss of $550 [$1500 − (190 × $5)]. Dollar-cost averaging requires that you continue to invest if the longer-term prospects suggest an eventual increase in price.

During the "rising market" in Table 13.4, you continue to invest but buy fewer shares. The $1500 investment during the bull market bought only 140 shares for an average cost of $10.71. In this rising market, you profit because

About Direct-Investment Plans and DRIP Plans

You can buy shares directly from more than 130 well-known companies without a broker and then continue to invest without paying brokerage commissions. This tactic involves a **direct-investment plan.** Not only is the broker eliminated, which saves you money, but a direct-investment plan also allows you to purchase additional shares on a regular basis without paying brokerage commissions. Companies offering such a plan include Ameritech, AT&T, Exxon, Home Depot, McDonald's, Pepsico, Sears, Tenneco, and Walgreen. [For a list of companies offering direct purchases, see the Securities Transfer Association at *www.netstockdirect.com* or call the Direct Stock Purchase Plan Clearinghouse at (800) 774-4417.]

Buying shares using a direct-investment plan automatically enrolls you into a **dividend reinvestment plan (DRIP).** Under a DRIP plan, quarterly dividends are automatically reinvested in new shares purchased directly from the company for little or no cost. You can also buy additional new shares without a commission or for a small fee. Wal-Mart is illustrative. It requires a minimum investment of $250 and $50 thereafter. The enrollment fee is $20 plus $0.10 per share. Most companies will buy back shares for a transaction fee of $10. Buying shares regularly through a DRIP plan is an example of dollar-cost averaging.

your 140 shares have a recent market price of $20 per share, for a total value of $2800 (140 × $20).

Almost anyone can profit in a rising market. If you use dollar-cost averaging over the long term, you will continue to buy in rising, falling, and fluctuating markets. The overall result will be that you buy more shares when the cost is down, thereby lowering the average share cost to below-average prices. The totals in Table 13.4, for example, reveal an overall investment of $4500 ($1500 + $1500 + $1500) used to purchase 450 shares (120 + 190 + 140) for an average cost of $10 per share ($4500 ÷ 450). With the recent market price at $20, you will realize a long-term gain of $4500 ($20 current market price × 450 shares = $9000; $9000 − $4500 invested = $4500 gain). Note that the dollar-cost averaging method would remain valid if the time interval for investing were monthly, quarterly, or even semiannually; benefits are derived from the regularity of investing.

Dollar-cost averaging offers two advantages. First, it reduces the average cost of shares of stock purchased over a relatively long period. Profits occur when prices for an investment fluctuate and eventually go up. Although the possibility of loss is not eliminated, losses are limited during times of declining prices. The most important factor is that profits accelerate during rising prices. Second, dollar-cost averaging dictates investor discipline. This strategy of investing is not particularly glamorous, but it is the only approach that is *almost guaranteed* to make a profit for the investor. It takes neither brilliance nor luck, just discipline.*

* People who invest through an *individual retirement account (IRA),* employee stock ownership programs, and 401(k) retirement plans (discussed in Chapter 18) similarly enjoy the benefits of dollar-cost averaging when they invest regularly.

Employee Stock Ownership Programs

Another application of dollar-cost averaging is an **employee stock ownership program (ESOP).** Many corporations offer an ESOP as a fringe benefit for employees. This plan permits employees to buy shares of stock in the company and gives them an extra incentive to do a good job, with the anticipated result being growth of the corporation's profitability and a higher value for the stock. Generally, the purchase price of the stock is fixed in ESOPs and the amount that may be purchased is limited. In some cases, the employer will make a matching contribution of stock, which greatly accelerates the purchasing efforts of the individual investor-employee. For example, for every $100 of stock the employee purchases (perhaps up to a maximum of $2000 annually), the company might donate $50 of additional stock.

Strategy: Portfolio Diversification

Portfolio diversification is the practice of selecting a collection of investments (such as stocks, bonds, mutual funds, real estate, and gold) that have dissimilar risk–return characteristics. As noted earlier, the decreased risk provides a lower, but quite acceptable, overall potential return. Portfolio diversification represents an effective long-term investment strategy as it offsets the riskiness of individual investments and evens out the ups and downs of individual investment returns.

Investors in securities can diversify within an investment medium (such as different stocks in one industry) or across alternatives (such as in stocks, bonds, and mutual funds). Investors in bonds can diversify by type and quality of bond as well as by maturity. The extent of diversification you choose depends on your personal investment philosophy and the amount you have to invest. Figure 13.3 illustrates some portfolios for people with differing investment philosophies.

Figure 13.3

Illustrative Diversified Investment Portfolios

Conservative

Blue-chip stocks	Balanced mutual funds	Growth stocks	Long-term bonds	CDs and short-term bonds	Money market funds
15%	10%	10%	15%	30%	20%

Moderate

Aggressive-growth stocks	Mutual funds	Blue-chip stocks	Foreign mutual funds	Long-term bond funds	CDs and short-term bonds	Money market funds
10%	25%	10%	10%	25%	10%	10%

Aggressive

Aggressive-growth stocks or mutual funds	Growth mutual funds	Foreign growth mutual funds	Small-cap stocks	Long-term bonds	Money market funds
30%	10%	20%	15%	15%	10%

Strategy: Asset Allocation

Historical data suggest that 60 to 90 percent of the returns earned by long-term investors who do little trading is not obtained from specific investments; rather, it is derived from owning the right asset categories at the right time. The remaining 10 to 40 percent of returns comes from specific choices and market timing. **Asset allocation** is a method of deciding what portion of the investment portfolio to allocate to various categories of assets: stocks, bonds (generically called debts), and cash or cash equivalents. Asset allocation requires that you keep your equities, debts, and cash equivalents at a fixed ratio for long time periods. The objective is to increase the return on assets while decreasing risk. In effect, asset allocation represents a form of diversification.

The manner in which a portfolio is divided among equities, debts, and cash equivalents will vary according to how much an investor is willing to sacrifice in potential return in exchange for a gain in overall return. Investors willing to accept a total return lower than stocks alone might provide, in hopes of a better return than cash management instruments offer (a conservative investment philosophy), might divide their assets equally between cash management instruments, equities, and stocks. The apportionment also depends on the investor's time horizon. No two investors will develop the same allocations because age, income, family situation, overall financial goals, and personal tolerance for risk vary.

Figure 13.4 illustrates decisions about how much to allocate to each type of security. A young investor might decide to keep most of his or her funds in equities (an aggressive approach), because they perform better over the long term and younger investors have more time to make up any major losses. Middle-aged investors might decide on more balanced portfolios (a moderate approach), because equities can be volatile over any given five-year period and such investors may not want all of their money there. A retired investor might decide to keep only a small portion of the portfolio in equities (a conservative approach). Once you decide how much to invest in each allocation, stick with your plan; you need not change your proportions until your broad investment goals change—probably for at least another five or ten years.

Figure 13.4

Examples of Investment Portfolios Using Asset Allocation

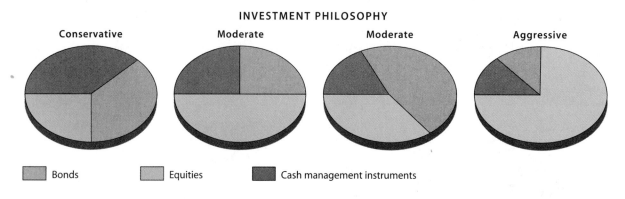

Individual investors usually find that they must move funds once each year to practice effective asset allocation, particularly if portions get out of line by 10 to 15 percent. This is because the value of groups of assets rises and falls and their proportion in the total portfolio also changes. Thus you must readjust your holdings to reestablish the allocation proportions to your original plan. When rebalancing you will be selling high and buying low—the goal of all investors. Maintaining the balance is the key, because you cannot predict the future, but you can control your exposure to risk.

The Best Time to Sell

6 List three guidelines to use when deciding the best time to sell investments.

Following the guidelines presented here will help you profit from your investments because they improve your understanding about the best time to sell investments.

Take Your Profits

The great financier Bernard Baruch was once asked how he made so much money in investments. He replied, "I always sold too soon!" Baruch's advice is that one should not be too greedy. Sell when you have reached your goal. Don't be paralyzed into missing modest and respectable profits in hopes of bigger gains. When you have earned a satisfactory profit—an amount that only you can determine—sell and take the real profit to avoid the risk of later drops in prices.

Cut Losses Quickly

When you have bought an investment as a result of an error in judgment, sell it. Temporary shifts in prices of 10 to 25 percent happen frequently, but when the momentum slows and it becomes clear that an earlier decision to buy was incorrect, don't wait for a 20 percent loss to develop into a 30 or 50 percent loss some weeks or months later. Don't hold on to a loser. Accept your error, sell, and make a better investment with the proceeds.

If You Wouldn't Buy It Now, Sell It

As you review your portfolio of investments, don't think about the price you originally paid and the possible income tax impact. Ask yourself, "If I had extra money to invest, would I put it into this investment?" Then carefully analyze that alternative. If your answer is no, sell the investment, and don't let a 2 or 5 percent commission stop you.

Summary

1. Investing requires an understanding of why people invest, what they should have accomplished before beginning to invest, how to figure investment returns, and how to obtain the initial funds for investing.

2. Your personal tolerance for risk is a critical factor in discovering your own investment philosophy, whether it is conservative, moderate, or aggressive.

3. When choosing investments, you must make two key decisions: (a) Do you want to lend your money or own an asset? (b) Do you want to invest for the short or long term? Once you have answered these questions, you can begin to compare and choose among investments.

4. The major factors affecting the rate of return on investment include types of investment risks, diversification, leverage, taxes, buying and selling costs, and inflation.

5. Four long-term investment strategies may be followed for portfolio management: business-cycle timing, dollar-cost averaging, portfolio diversification, and asset allocation. Ultimately, however, the degree of investor success depends upon the quality of investments selected.

6. Guidelines on when to sell an investment include "Take your profits," "Cut losses quickly," and "If you wouldn't buy it now, sell it."

Key Words & Concepts

capital gain   *371*
current income   *370*
diversification   *377*
dividends   *370*
dollar-cost averaging   *384*
equities   *374*
financial risk   *377*
fixed income   *374*

inflation risk   *376*
interest-rate risk   *376*
investment philosophy   *372*
leverage   *379*
marketability risk   *377*
market-volatility risk   *377*
moderate investment philosophy   *373*
random risk   *377*
real return on investment   *383*
return   *371*
risk   *371*
yield   *371*

Questions for Thought & Discussion

1. Identify the four reasons why most people are motivated to invest.

2. Name four prerequisites to investing.

3. Name five ways that you can obtain funds for investment.

4. Distinguish between current income and capital gain.

5. What is the difference between an ultraconservative investor and the other types of investors?

6. Compare and contrast the three primary types of investment philosophies.

7. Describe the difference between lending investments and owning investments, and give examples of each.

8. Why do more investors make long-term investments rather than short-term ones?

9. What is interest-rate risk?

10. What is marketability risk?

11. What is market risk?

12. Explain how diversification works, and give an example.

13. Identify the advantages of using leverage in the investment process.

14. Give an example of how your marginal tax rate affects return on investment.

15. Cite an investment that offers little protection against inflation and one that offers ample protection against inflation.

16. How is the real return on an investment calculated, and why is it important to know?

17. Give an example of how an intelligent investor might use a business-cycle timing approach for long-term investing.

18. List some of the benefits of a dividend reinvestment plan (DRIP).

19. What two goals does dollar-cost averaging accomplish, and how does it work?

20. Explain how portfolio diversification works, and give an example of how to use it.

21. Describe the logic behind the asset-allocation strategy for long-term investing.

22. Discuss one guideline that will help you know when to sell securities.

DECISION-MAKING CASES

Case 1   A Veteran Invests to Buy a Condominium

Ron Witherspoon, a paraplegic disabled veteran of the U.S. Navy and self-employed "computer nerd" from Omaha, Nebraska, hopes to continue his savings and investment program for three more years before making a down payment on a condominium. The home that he wants to purchase is currently priced at $90,000.

(a) If inflation is 4 percent for each of the next three years, how much will the condominium probably cost? See Appendix A.1 or use the *Garman/Forgue* Web site. (See the section on time value of money in Chapter 1 beginning on page 15.)

(b) If Ron wants to make a 20 percent down payment, how much money will he need in the future given the projected value of the condominium?

(c) Should Ron invest his money during the next three years by lending or owning? Why?

Case 2   Investing a Gift of Cash

Kay Zick, a recently married mental health counselor from Boulder, Colorado, is thinking about investing a $2000 gift that her uncle gave her. Perhaps you can help Kay with some questions about return.

(a) How much will Kay's real return be (after taxes and inflation) if she earns a 12 percent total return on a stock investment this year, assuming that inflation is 4 percent and she and her husband are in the 28 percent marginal tax bracket? Use the information on page 382 or the *Garman/Forgue* Web site.

(b) How much will Kay's real return be if she earns a 14 percent total return on the investment? Use the information on page 382 or the *Garman/Forgue* Web site.

(c) If Kay invests the money in a mutual fund that earns a 12 percent return for the next 20 years, how much will the account be worth at that time (assume that no income taxes must be paid and all dividends are reinvested)? Use Appendix A.1 or the *Garman/Forgue* Web site.

(d) How much will the account be worth in 30 years if it continues to compound at 12 percent? Use Appendix A.1 or the *Garman/Forgue* Web site.

Financial Math Questions

1. George and Carolyn Clemson have decided to establish a college fund for their newborn daughter. They estimate that they will need $100,000 in 18 years. Assuming that the Clemsons could get a return of 9 percent, how much would they need to invest annually to reach their goal? Use Appendix A.3 or the *Garman/Forgue* Web site.

2. George Clemson's mother wants to help pay for her grandchild's education. How many years will it take if she invests $1000 a year, earning 8 percent, to reach a goal of $30,000? Use Appendix A.3 or the *Garman/Forgue* Web site.

3. If one year of college currently costs $15,000, how much will it cost the Clemsons' daughter in 18 years, assuming a 5 percent annual rate of inflation? Use Appendix A.1 or the *Garman/Forgue* Web site.

4. Louis and Charles, who are twins, took different approaches to investing. Louis saved $2000 per year for ten years starting at age 22 and never added any more money to the account. Charles saved $2000 per year for 20 years starting at age 35. Assuming that the brothers earned a 10 percent return, who had accumulated the most by the time they were age 65? Use Appendix A.3, Appendix A.1, or the *Garman/Forgue* Web site.

5. Martha Robinson has a choice of two investments. She can buy a $1000 tax-free municipal bond that pays 4.3 percent interest or a $1000 taxable corporate bond that pays 6.3 percent interest. Both bonds will mature in five years. If Martha is in the 28 percent tax bracket, which bond should she choose?

MONEY MATTERS: LIFE-CYCLE CASES

Victor and Maria Hernandez Try to Catch Up on Their Investments

The expenses of sending two children through college prevented Victor and Maria Hernandez from adding substantially to their investment program. Now that their younger son John has completed school and is working full-time, however, they would like to build up their investments quickly. Victor is 47 years old and wants to retire early, perhaps by age 60. In addition to the retirement program at his place of employment, Victor believes that their present investment portfolio valued at $70,000 will need to triple to $210,000 by retirement time.

1. What rate of return is needed on the $70,000 portfolio to reach the goal of $210,000? Use the *Garman/Forgue* Web site.

2. Victor and Maria think they will need a total of $400,000 for a retirement nest egg. Therefore, they will need to create an additional sum of $190,000 through new investments.

Assuming an annual return of 10 percent, how much do the Hernandezes need to invest each year to reach the goal of $190,000? Use Appendix A.3 or Quicken.

3. If they assume only an 8 percent annual return, how much do the Hernandezes need to invest each year to reach the goal of $190,000? Use the *Garman/Forgue* Web site.

The Johnsons Start an Investment Program

Harry and Belinda's finances have improved in recent months, even though they have incurred new debts for an automobile loan and a condominium. The improvement has occurred because they cut back in their spending on discretionary items (clothing, food, and entertainment) and because Harry recently received a sizable raise after changing employers. His new job is that of assistant designer at Medical Facilities, Inc., and it pays $6000 more than his other job. The new job is also a mile closer to home, reducing Harry's commuting time.

The Johnsons have decided to concentrate on getting a solid investment program under way while they have two incomes available. They are willing to accept a moderate amount of risk and expect to invest between $200 and $400 per month over the next five years. Assuming that they have an adequate savings program, respond to the following questions:

1. In what types of investments (choose only two) might the Johnsons place the first $2000? (Review Tables 13.1 and 13.2 for ideas and available options, and consider the types of investment risks inherent in each choice.) Give reasons for your selections.

2. In what types of investments might they place the next $4000? Why?

3. What types of investments should they choose for the next $10,000? Why?

4. If inflation is 4 percent, what would their earnings for the year be if they earn 15 percent on a $400 monthly investment? Calculate the projected earnings using the *Garman/Forgue* Web site.

Exploring the World Wide Web of Personal Finance

To complete these exercises, go to the *Garman/Forgue* Web site at

www.hmco.com/college/business/

Select Personal Finance. Click on the exercise link for this chapter and answer the questions that appear on the Web page.

1. Visit the Web site for the National Association of Investors (click on Frequently Asked Questions) for an overview of the corporation's investment principles. Also, ask several people for their personal guidelines on how they would select investments. Compare the results from your discussions with the principles found on the Web and with what you have read in this chapter.

2. Visit the Web site for the Alliance for Investor Education and take its risk quiz. What do the results of the quiz tell you about your tolerance for risk? Also, survey a number of people to ascertain their investment philosophy—conservative, moderate, or aggressive. Probe further by asking them questions similar to those found on the risk quiz. Are their perceptions of their risk tolerance congruent with the results they might find from taking the risk quiz? Check the core investing principles cited by the Alliance for Investor Education. Compare them with what you found on the National Association of Investors Web site in Exercise 1.

3. Visit the Web site for the Vanguard family of mutual funds. Read the Plain Talk chapter on reasonable stock market expectations and answer the following questions:

(a) What likely rate of return should you expect as an investor with a moderate risk philosophy?

(b) What types of investments are recommended for persons with such a philosophy?

4. Visit the Web site for the Vanguard family of mutual funds. Read the Plain Talk chapter on dollar-cost averaging and answer the following questions:

(a) What are the principal benefits of using the dollar-cost averaging approach?

(b) What investment philosophy(s) are most congruent with dollar-cost averaging?

5. Visit the Web site for Bank of America for an overview of its recommendations for asset allocation mixes for specific investment goals. Compare three of the strategies and speculate on why the particular mix of stocks, bonds, and cash was recommended for each.

6. Visit the Web site for the *Wall Street Journal.* Determine today's closing stock price for one of the following companies for each of the past ten years [Coca-Cola (KO), IBM (IBM), General Electric (GE), or General Motors (GM)]. Assume that you had invested $10,000 at the end of each year using dollar-cost averaging to purchase shares of the particular company you chose. Calculate the following:

(a) how many shares you would have purchased

(b) the average share price

(c) the average share cost

(d) the total value of those shares today (you will also have to look up the stock's current market price)

Investing in Stocks and Bonds 14

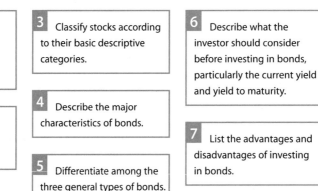

OBJECTIVES

After reading this chapter, you should be able to:

1 Describe stocks and bonds and how they are used by corporations and investors.

2 Define everyday terms in the language of stock investing.

3 Classify stocks according to their basic descriptive categories.

4 Describe the major characteristics of bonds.

5 Differentiate among the three general types of bonds.

6 Describe what the investor should consider before investing in bonds, particularly the current yield and yield to maturity.

7 List the advantages and disadvantages of investing in bonds.

If you keep all of your extra money in ultraconservative cash equivalents, such as certificates of deposit, you likely will be frustrated by the low returns, which will be barely adequate to cover inflation. To do better, you must begin to think about increasing risk to increase the potential yield. When you learn about investments and choose stock, bond, and mutual fund investments carefully, you can increase returns significantly while simultaneously increasing risk only slightly. These investments belong in almost everyone's investment portfolio because they provide opportunities for conservative, moderate, and aggressive investors alike. This chapter focuses on stocks and bonds, while Chapter 15 examines mutual funds.

We begin by describing stocks and bonds and how investors use them. We then illustrate how a corporation uses stocks and bonds to finance its objectives. This discussion is followed by a review of important investment terms. Next, we describe the basic classifications of stocks (such as growth stocks) as well as three approaches people use when investing. A section on the advantages and disadvantages of common stocks is provided to help you discover whether they are right for you, followed by some guidelines for selling stock. The chapter then turns to important terminology used in bond investing. After describing the three major types of bonds, we detail the advantages and disadvantages of owning bonds and discuss key factors that the investor should consider before investing in bonds.

Stocks and Bonds and How They Are Used

1 Describe stocks and bonds and how they are used by corporations and investors.

The corporate form of business ownership is popular in the United States partly because of its potential to raise large sums of money that can then be used to expand the business. A **corporation** is a state-chartered legal entity that can conduct business operations in its own name. The ability of a corporation to sell shares of ownership to investors offers a company the potential to develop into a firm of considerable size. A corporation may have a large number of investors and can continue to exist even as the shares change hands.

A corporation's financial needs may vary over time. To begin business, a new corporation needs money for **startup capital** (funds initially invested in a business enterprise). During its life, a corporation may need additional money to grow. To raise capital and finance its goals, a corporation may issue three different types of **securities** (negotiable instruments of ownership or debt): common stock, preferred stock, and bonds.

Common Stock

Stocks are shares of ownership in the assets and earnings of a business corporation. **Common stock** is the most basic form of ownership of a corporation. The owner of stock—called a **shareholder** or **stockholder**—has a claim on the assets and earnings of the firm. Common stockholders have a residual claim after any claims made by bondholders and preferred stockholders (discussed below). A corporation may have a single owner/shareholder or have millions of shares that are owned by numerous owners/shareholders. Each shareholder has a proportionate interest in the ownership and, therefore, in the assets and income of the corporation.

Each common stockholder may vote to elect the board of directors, which sets policy and names the principal officers of the company that run the day-to-day operations of the firm. The number of votes each shareholder has depends on the number of shares he or she owns. If the corporation becomes bankrupt, the common stockholder's equity consists of the amount left after the claims of all creditors are satisfied. This risk of loss is balanced by the potential to share in

> **Did You KNOW?**
>
> ### Some Common Stock Shareholders Receive Perks
>
> Many companies send new shareholders samples of their products or give all shareholders special prices on products and services. For example, Tandy Corporation give its shareholders a 10 percent discount on purchases at its Radio Shack stores. Wrigley, the chewing gum company, sends shareholders 20 packs of gum every year. Check with a stockbroker to research the perks offered by other companies.

substantial profits when the corporation performs well. A shareholder's liability for business losses is limited to the amount invested in the shares of stock owned.

Stocks represent potential income for investors because stockholders own a piece of the future profits of the company. People who own stocks typically have two expectations: (1) that the corporation will be profitable enough to pay **dividends** (a share of profits distributed in cash), and (2) that the **market price** of the stock, which is the current price that a buyer is willing to pay a willing seller, will increase.

Preferred Stock

Preferred stock is a type of fixed-income ownership security in a corporation. Owners of preferred stock receive a fixed dividend per share that the corporation must distribute before any dividends are paid out to common stockholders. Preferred stockholders typically have no voting privileges, and they usually do not share in any extraordinary profits made by a corporation.

The market price of shares of preferred stock is primarily based on prevailing interest rates. When interest rates rise, the market price of a preferred stock will drop so that the real yield remains competitive with similar-risk investments. For example, a preferred stock that costs $100 and pays an annual cash dividend of $6 would, therefore, provide a 6 percent return. If returns on other investments of similar risk later climbed to 8 percent, the market price that others would be willing to pay for your preferred stock would drop to reflect the differences in return. After all, who would pay $100 for a preferred stock with a dividend of $6 when they could put their money into a similar investment (such as a corporate bond) and receive $8? With a cash dividend of only $6, the market price of the preferred stock would have to drop to approximately $75 to increase the yield to approximately 8 percent ($6 ÷ 0.08 = $75).

Sometimes a corporation decides not to pay dividends to preferred stockholders because it lacks profits or simply wishes to retain and reinvest all of the earnings. With **cumulative preferred stock**, when the board of directors votes to skip **(pass)** making a cash dividend to preferred stockholders, the dividend must be paid to these stockholders before any future dividends are distributed to the common stockholders. For example, assume that a company passes on the first two quarterly dividends of $2.25 each to preferred stockholders, who expect to receive $9 each year ($2.25 × 4 quarters). If the company prospers and wants to give a cash dividend to its common stockholders in the third quarter, it must first pay the passed $4.50 to the cumulative preferred stockholders. Furthermore, the usual third-quarter cash dividend of $2.25 must be made to the preferred stockholders before the common stockholders can receive any dividends. In the case of **noncumulative preferred stock,** the preferred stockholders would have no claim to previously skipped dividends.

Bonds

Fixed-asset investments require a specific amount of money to be invested for a certain amount of time. Examples of fixed-asset investments include certificates of deposit (discussed in Chapter 5), government bonds, corporate bonds, and annuities (annuities are examined in Chapter 18). A **bond** is an interest-bearing negotiable certificate of long-term debt issued by a corporation, municipality (such as a city or state), or the U.S. federal government. When an investor buys a bond, he or she essentially lends money to the issuer. Bonds are basically IOUs. The initial purchaser of the bond lends the issuer a certain amount of money—the **principal**—and, in return, the issuer makes two promises: (1) to pay interest over the life of the bond, and (2) at some point in the future—the **maturity date**—to repay the investor's principal. The proceeds from bonds are often used by corporations and governments to finance expensive construction projects and to purchase costly equipment. Once bonds are initially issued, they can be bought and sold many times by investors.

Investment-grade fixed-asset investments offer a reasonable certainty of regularly receiving the **periodic income** (interest) and retrieving the amount originally invested. For taking this relatively small financial risk, one typically earns an appropriately low return, particularly when compared with the higher total returns earned on most investments in common stocks and mutual funds. You should consider investing in bonds if you have a conservative or moderate investment philosophy and desire a steady source of income from part of your investment portfolio. Good-quality bonds also represent attractive investments because those held to maturity carry little financial risk relative to investments in common stocks or real estate. The total annual after-tax return on bonds is historically about one-half that of stocks.

An Illustration: Running Paws Catfood Company

To better understand how a corporation finances its goals by issuing common and preferred stock while paying returns for stockholders, consider the example of Running Paws Catfood Company. This small family business was started in New Jersey by Linda Webtek, who developed a wonderful recipe for cat food and sold the product to the local grocery store. As sales increased, Linda decided to incorporate the business and expand its operations. Running Paws issued 10,000 shares of common stock at $10 per share. Three friends each bought 2500 shares, and Linda signed over the cat food formula and equipment to the corporation itself in exchange for the remaining 2500 shares. At that point, Running Paws had $75,000 in working capital (7500 shares sold at $10 each), some equipment, and a four-person board of directors. Each of the directors worked for the firm, although they paid themselves very low salaries.

The **revenues** of a corporation like Running Paws are used to pay (1) expenses, (2) interest to bondholders, (3) taxes, (4) cash dividends to preferred stockholders, and (5) cash dividends to common stockholders, in that order. If there is money left over after items 1 and 2 are paid, the corporation has earned a **profit**, and after item 3 is paid, a **net (after-tax) profit**. The average corporation pays out 40 to 60 percent of its after-tax profit in cash dividends to stockholders. The remainder, called **retained earnings**, is left to accumulate and finance the company's goals—often expansion and growth. In its early years, Running Paws retained all of its profits and declared no dividends.

Common stockholders, like the stockholders of Running Paws Catfood Company, are not guaranteed dividends, although most profitable companies pay common stockholders a small dividend on a quarterly basis until increased earnings justify paying out a higher amount. Given that Running Paws retained all its earnings, you may wonder why people invest in stocks. There are two reasons. First, as a company becomes more efficient and profitable, cash dividends to common stockholders may not only begin but also rise—sometimes sharply. Second, the market price of the stock may rise as more investors become interested in the future profitability of a growing company. Common stock comprises a share of ownership; as the company grows, the price of its common stock follows suit unless additional shares are sold even faster than the corporation grows. Remember, the retained earnings are owned by the common stockholders.

At Running Paws Catfood Company, capacity quickly expanded, with ensuing increases in sales. Soon more orders were coming in from New York City than the firm could handle. After three years, the owners of Running Paws decided to expand once again. They wanted to borrow an additional $100,000, but their business was so new and uncertain that lenders demanded an extremely high interest rate. They considered issuing bonds as debts of the corporation, but found that their new business was viewed as too risky for investors to consider lending money to it by purchasing bonds. The owners then decided to issue 5000 shares of preferred stock at $20 per share, paying a cash dividend of $1.20 per share annually. Cash dividends to preferred stockholders are a set amount per share and often remain the same each year, whether profits are good or bad. When the owners of Running Paws found that no one wanted to buy preferred shares with that yield ($1.20 ÷ $20 = 6 percent), they voted to increase the dividend to $1.80 annually, providing a 9 percent yield to investors. The preferred stock was then sold to outside investors; the original investors retained control of the company through their common stock because the preferred stockholders could not vote for the board of directors.

Following its pattern of expanding into new markets, Running Paws soon developed new lines of cat food, which sold well. With the proceeds from the sale of preferred stock, and after a new plant in Los Angeles opened, the income of the four-year-old business finally exceeded expenses, and it had a profit of $13,000. The board of directors declared a dividend of $9000 to preferred stockholders, but no dividend for common stockholders. In the following year, net profits after taxes amounted to $28,000. Again the board paid a $9000 dividend to the preferred stockholders but retained the remainder of the profits to finance continued expansion and improved efficiency.

One of the original partners wanted to exit the business and needed to sell her 2500 shares of stock, for which she had originally paid $25,000. Because Running Paws was beginning to show some profits, two other private investors recommended by a local stockbroker made offers to purchase her shares. The shares were sold at $16 per share, with 1500 shares going to one investor and 1000 shares to another investor. Thus, this original investor gained $15,000 in price appreciation ($16 × 2500 = $40,000; $40,000 − $25,000 = $15,000) when she sold out. (Note that the corporation did not profit from this transaction.) Now five owners of the common stock, including the two new ones, voted for the board of directors; each share has one vote.

During the sixth year, sales again increased and earnings totaled $39,000. This time the board voted $9000 for the preferred stockholders and $5000 ($0.50 per share) for the common stockholders and retained the remaining $25,000. Thus, the common stockholders finally began to receive cash dividends.

Even with its success, Running Paws faced another difficult decision. To distribute its products nationally would mean another $200,000 to $250,000 in expansion costs. After much discussion, the board voted to sell an additional 10,000 shares of common stock at $25 per share. This action diluted the owners' proportion of ownership by half (although they could buy some of the shares themselves to maintain their proportionate interest), but the potential for profit was considered to be much higher with the increased production capacity.

It took several months to sell all of the new common stock, because so few people knew that the company had stock available for sale. Various local stockbrokers also took selling commissions totaling $16,000, leaving $234,000 available for the company to use for expansion. If Running Paws continues to prosper, its board of directors might work toward having its stock listed on a regional stock exchange (see Chapter 16) to facilitate trading of shares and to further enhance the company's image.

The Language of Stock Investing

2 Define everyday terms in the language of stock investing.

Before you seriously consider stocks as an investment, you need to understand the everyday terms used in the language of stock investing.

Earnings per Share (EPS)

Earnings per share (EPS) indicates the income a company has available, on a per-share basis, to pay dividends and reinvest as retained earnings. The EPS value is a dollar figure determined by dividing the corporation's total after-tax annual earnings (before common stock cash dividends are distributed but after payment of dividends to preferred stockholders) by the total number of shares of common stock held by investors. It provides a measure of the firm's profitability on a common stock per-share basis, which investors can then use to compare financial conditions at several companies. The EPS is reported in the business section of many newspapers. In our example, assume that, next year after payment of dividends to preferred stockholders, Running Paws Catfood Company had a net profit of $43,000 and paid $11,000 in dividends to preferred stockholders. With 20,000 shares of stock, the EPS would be $2.15 ($43,000 ÷ 20,000).

Price/Earnings Ratio (P/E Ratio)

The **price/earnings ratio (P/E ratio** or **P/E multiple)** is the most widely used measure of a stock's relative price. A ratio of the current market price of a common stock to its earnings per share (EPS), it indicates how many times a stock's selling price is greater than its earnings per share. The P/E ratio shows how the market values the stock because it describes the amount that investors are willing to pay for each dollar of a company's earnings [either actual earnings for the previous 12 months, called **trailing earnings**, or earnings projected by analysts (**forward earnings**) for the coming 12 months]. Furthermore, the ratio measures investor confidence in a stock's future over the next five years or so. For example, if the market price of a share of Running Paws stock is currently $25 and its

EPS is $1.70, the P/E ratio will be 15 ($25 ÷ $1.70 = 14.7, which rounds to 15). This value also could be called a 15-to-1 ratio or a P/E multiple of 15. The price/earnings ratios of many corporations are widely reported as financial news (e.g., in newspapers). In general, low P/E stocks tend to have higher dividend yields, less risk, lower prices, and a slower earnings growth rate.

To use a P/E ratio to assess a company's financial status, compare it with other P/E ratios for firms in the same industry. The P/E ratios for most corporations typically range from 5 to 25. Financially successful companies that have been paying good dividends through the years might have a P/E ratio of 7 to 10. Rapidly growing companies would most likely have a much higher P/E ratio—15 to 25. Speculative companies might have P/E ratios of 40 or 50, because they have low earnings now but anticipate much higher earnings in the future. Firms that are expected to have strong earnings growth generally have a high stock price and P/E ratio. A relatively low P/E means that investors expect sluggish growth or perhaps an uncertain future.

Cash Dividends per Share

Cash dividends are distributions made in cash to holders of stock. The firm's board of directors usually declares a dividend on a quarterly basis according to the fiscal year, typically at the end of March, June, September, and December. Dividends are ordinarily paid out of current earnings, but, in the event of unprofitable times (i.e. a recession or low earnings), the money might come from previous earnings. Occasionally, a company will borrow to pay the dividend so as to maintain its reputation of consistently paying dividends. Of course, later profits must be used to repay any funds borrowed.

The **dividends per share** measure translates the total cash dividends paid out by a company to common stockholders into a per-share figure. For example, Running Paws Catfood Company might elect to declare a total cash dividend of $8000 for the year to common stockholders. In this case, cash dividends per share amount to $0.40 ($8000 ÷ 20,000 shares).

The **dividend yield**—the cash dividend return to an investor expressed as a percentage of the price of a security—also can be determined. For example, the $0.40 cash dividend of Running Paws Catfood Company divided by the current $25 market price reveals a dividend yield of 1.6 percent ($0.40 ÷ $25). Growth and speculative companies typically pay little or no cash dividend.

Dividend Payout Ratio

The **dividend payout ratio** measures the percentage of total earnings paid out to stockholders as cash dividends. For example, Running Paws Catfood Company earned $32,000 (after paying preferred stockholders), paid out a cash dividend of $8000 to company stockholders, and retained the remaining $24,000 to facilitate growth of the company. Thus, the dividend payout ratio equals 0.25 ($8000 ÷ $32,000). For that year, Running Paws paid a dividend equal to 25 percent of earnings. Newer companies usually retain most, if not all, of their profits to facilitate growth. An investor interested in growth would seek a company with a low payout ratio. The lower the payout ratio, the greater the odds that the company's earnings will sustain future dividend payments.

Market Price

The **market price** of an investment is the amount that a willing buyer would currently pay a willing seller for the asset. Sales commissions are not included in this value. In stock transactions, the market price represents the current price of a single share of stock. It may be estimated by looking at prices quoted in financial newspapers, as described in Chapter 16, "Buying and Selling Securities." True market price is the amount you receive when selling an investment or pay when buying an investment. For example, if Running Paws stock has recently been selling at $25 per share, this value represents its market price on paper. The true market price at the point that you actually sell or buy Running Paws stock might be higher or lower.

Price-to-Sales Ratio (PSR)

The **price-to-sales ratio (PSR)** is obtained by dividing the total current market value of a stock (the current market price multiplied by the number of shares outstanding) by the total corporate revenue (sales) for the past year. For example, if Running Paws Catfood Company's common stock currently sells for $25 per share and 20,000 shares are outstanding, its total current market value is $500,000. If company revenues (sales of cat food) were $750,000 over the past year, the stock's PSR would be 0.67 ($500,000 ÷ $750,000). The lower the PSR ratio, the better the marketability of the stock. Market analysts generally suggest that investors avoid companies with a PSR greater than 1.5 in favor of those having PSRs of less than 0.75. Research by James O'Shaughnessy, published in the book *What Works on Wall Street,* shows that PSR is a more reliable method of choosing winning stocks than the P/E ratio.

Book Value and Price-to-Book Ratio

The **book value** is the net worth of a company, which is determined by subtracting the company's total liabilities from its assets. Also known as **shareholder's equity**, it theoretically indicates a company's worth if its assets were sold, its debts paid off, and the net proceeds distributed to common shareholders.

Book value per share reflects the book value of a company divided by the number of shares of common stock outstanding. Running Paws has a net worth of $230,000, which, when divided by 20,000 shares, gives a book value per share of $11.50. Often little relationship exists between the book value of a company and its earnings or the market price of its stock. Note, however, that the market price for a company's common stock usually exceeds its book value per share because stockholders anticipate earnings and dividends in the future and expect the market price to rise. When the value of the assets per share exceeds the price per share, the stock may truly be underpriced.

The **price-to-book (P-B) ratio** compares the market price of a common stock to its book value per share. To obtain a P-B ratio, the company's book value per share is divided into the price per share. In the Running Paws example, the book value per share of $11.50 would be divided into the most recent price at which the stock was sold ($25 in this case); thus, the P-B ratio for Running Paws is 2.17. The current P-B ratio for most stocks lies between 2.1 and 1.0. The lower the ratio, the less highly a company's assets have been valued, indicating that the stock may be currently underpriced. If the ratio is less than 1, the assets may be utilized ineffectively. In such cases, an underperforming and undervalued company may become a target of a corporate takeover.*

Par Value

Historically, **par value** meant the dollar amount assigned to a share of stock by the company's charter when the corporation issued it. Many people have falsely assumed that this value was a minimum price. In fact, par value bears no relation to the current market price of common stock. In the case of preferred stocks, par value signifies the dollar value upon which dividends are based. After issuance, the market price of preferred stocks may rise or fall, but the dividends paid are still calculated on the original par value.

Total Return

Total return is the combination of the cash dividends paid and the capital gain. The **capital gain** or **price appreciation**—the net income received from the sale of capital assets beyond the expenses incurred in the purchase and sale of those assets—is realized when the stock is sold. Until then, such gains are only paper profits. A **paper profit** is an unrealized profit on an investment still held; in contrast, a **paper loss** is an unrealized loss on an investment. If you purchased Running Paws common stock at $25 per share and sold it at $30 per share, you would realize a gain of $5. Assuming that you bought 200 shares and paid a commission of $60, your cost was $5060 [($25 × 200) + $60]. If you sold at $30 per share and paid a sales commission of $70, the proceeds would be $5930 [($30 × 200) − $70]. Your capital gain is, therefore, $870 ($5930 − $5060). Based on the invested amount of $5060, the capital gain of $870 represents a 17.2 percent yield ($870 ÷ 5060). If you sold your Running Paws common stock after one year, the return would include $870 in capital gains plus $110 in cash dividends (200 shares × $0.55) for a total return of $980 ($870 + $110), or a 19.4 percent yield on $5060 invested ($980 ÷ $5060).

The alternative would have been to hold the shares in anticipation of a further increase in the stock's market price. For instance, the price of Running Paws stock could rise to $35 in the next several months. Of course, the price could also drop to $27 and reduce your gain, or it might drop even further to $20 and result in a capital loss if you sold the stock.

Preemptive Rights

When Running Paws Catfood Company issued additional shares of its stock to finance growth in its fifth year, current stockholders were concerned that they would lose their proportionate interest in the company. Common stockholders

---

* A new measure of the worth of a company is **economic value added** (EVA). Reported by some investment publications, EVA subtracts the cost of a company's capital from its after-tax operating profit in a given year. It is a reliable measure of return on invested capital. **Market value added** is a projection of future EVAs.

usually have a **preemptive right** to purchase additional shares, frequently at a discount from the market price before new shares are offered to the public. Exercising this right enables them to maintain their proportionate ownership.

Stock Dividends

A **stock dividend** is a dividend paid in the form of securities instead of cash. The dividend may comprise additional shares of the issuing company or shares of another company (usually a subsidiary) owned by the issuing company. Shares are distributed to existing stockholders on the basis of their current proportional ownership. For example, the board of directors of Running Paws could decide to declare a 10 percent stock dividend to stockholders who currently own the 20,000 outstanding shares. If you owned 2000 shares, the company would give you an additional 200 shares. If you owned 55 shares, the company would mail you documentation for five shares and ask how you would like to handle the value of the remaining half share. You might be given the option of either receiving the cash equivalent of the half share or paying for an additional half share so that you could receive six full shares.

Many people incorrectly assume that the value of their holdings increases when they receive a stock dividend. Although the price of the stock might rise for a day or so after declaration of a stock dividend, it then corrects for the additional shares of stock available and drops accordingly. This market correction occurs because the book value of the company is unchanged but the number of shares outstanding has gone up. Assume that the 20,000 shares of Running Paws stock were priced at $25 per share. If a stock dividend of 10 percent was declared, 22,000 shares of ownership would be available. If you had owned 2000 shares of the 20,000 total shares, you would have owned 10 percent of the company. After the stock dividend, you would own 2200 shares out of a total of 22,000—still exactly 10 percent.

What effect would a stock dividend have on cash dividends? Suppose that Running Paws continues to pay a $0.40 per share cash dividend the year after it declares a 10 percent stock dividend. The company will need greater earnings because it will be paying out $8800 rather than $8000—a cash dividend 10 percent greater than the previous year. Alternatively, the company could reduce the per-share cash dividend to reflect the greater number of shares. Declaration of a stock dividend slightly dilutes stock ownership and reduces the market price of the stock by a similar percentage while maintaining the actual value of each stockholder's investment.

Stock Splits

A **stock split** is a trade of a given number of existing shares of stock for a certain number of newly issued shares. A two-for-one stock split increases the number of shares outstanding by 100 percent and reduces cash dividends per share by 50 percent. For example, in a two-for-one stock split at Running Paws, the owners of the 22,000 shares (remember the 10 percent stock dividend) would be issued 44,000 new shares. If the market price of the old stock was $25 per share, the new stock will be worth approximately $12.50, or 50 percent of the previous price, because the number of shares was doubled.

The effects of a stock split are fourfold: (1) no change in the proportion of ownership held by the original stockholders; (2) no change in the proportion of cash dividends per share; (3) a proportional decrease in the market price of the stock; and (4) an indication that the stock will outperform the market over the next 12 months.

A company whose stock is selling at $90 per share might use a stock split to reduce the market price to $45 (two for one) or even $30 (three for one) to encourage more investors to buy and sell stock. Stock splits, therefore, can have the effect of opening up trading to a greater number of investors. For this reason, they ordinarily require the consent of the board of directors and a two-thirds approval by the current stockholders.

A company opts for a **reverse stock split** when it wishes to increase the market price of its stock. For example, a company with stock selling at $10 per share could have a one-for-three or one-for-four reverse split to increase the price per share to $30 or $40. Reverse splits are often viewed as an indication that the company is in trouble, particularly when the original price was less than $10.

Voting Rights

Owners of common stock normally have **voting rights**—the proportionate authority to express an opinion or choice in matters affecting the company. Each share of common stock gives the holder one vote. (Companies rarely issue nonvoting common stock.) At the annual meeting of the company, the board of directors is elected (or reelected), and stockholders vote on matters of special interest. Each stockholder may participate in these activities by either attending the meeting or voting by **proxy**. A proxy is written authorization given by a shareholder to someone else to represent him or her and to vote his or her shares at a stockholder's meeting. It is usually easier to vote by mail through a proxy than to attend the meeting in person.

In reality, most issues facing a corporation are foreseen by the board of directors, which then obtains control, by means of proxies, of a large voting bloc to ensure that its desires are met. On rare occasions, a **proxy battle** occurs, as two competing forces (often the existing board of directors and an outsider group that may be seeking a merger or buyout) actively campaign for stockholders' voting rights to gain control of the company. In such instances, the competing forces write letters to stockholders soliciting their proxies.

Three Basic Classifications of Common Stock

3 Classify stocks according to their basic descriptive categories.

Many investment brokers and individual investors group certain stocks according to specific characteristics. These classifications can then be used to match an investor's preferences with investment options. The three basic classifications of corporate stock are as follows: (1) income stocks, (2) growth stocks, and (3) speculative stocks. Other terms are used to characterize classifications as well.

Income Stocks

A company whose stock is classified as an **income stock** characteristically has paid a cash dividend higher than that offered by most companies year after year because the company has fairly high earnings and chooses to retain only a small portion of the earnings. To declare high cash dividends regularly, the company must have a steady stream of income—utility companies, for example, fit this profile. Stocks issued by telephone, electric, and gas companies are normally labeled income stocks. Investors in these companies usually are not very concerned with the P/E ratio or the growth potential of the price of the stock. Betas (see page 380) are often less than 1.0. Many retired persons are often attracted to income stocks, for example.

Growth Stocks

The term **growth stock** describes a company with a consistent record of relatively rapid growth in earnings in all economic conditions. The return to investors from growth stocks comes primarily from increases in share price. Such stocks typically pay low or no dividends because most of their earnings are retained to maintain company growth.

Stocks of companies that are leaders in their fields, that dominate their markets, and that have several consecutive years of above-industry-average earnings are considered **well-known growth stocks**. Investor awareness of such corporations is widespread, and expectations for continued growth are high. The P/E ratio is high, too. Many growth stocks have a glamorous reputation that improves or declines sharply in conjunction with the overall market and, therefore, have betas of 1.5 or more. Investors generally seem to prefer growth stocks of well-known companies, because they typically pay some dividends and offer a good opportunity for price appreciation. In the past, well-known growth stocks have included those offered by Coca-Cola, The Gap, Nike, and Wal-Mart stores.

How Most Investors Select Stocks

The premise of **fundamental analysis**—and most investors take this approach to investing—assumes that each stock has an intrinsic (or true) value based on its expected future earnings; therefore, some stocks can be identified that will outperform others. The fundamental approach presumes that current and future earnings trends, industry outlook, and management's expertise determine a stock's price movement. Furthermore, because knowledge about companies' futures is not perfect, some stocks are underpriced and others are over-priced. The investor studies certain fundamental factors, such as the company's sales, assets, earnings, products or services, markets, and management, to determine a company's basic value. He or she then estimates the value of one company by comparing its history and expected future profitability with those of competing firms. The aim is to seek out sound stocks—perhaps even unfashionable ones—that are priced well below the market's multiples of earnings, cash flow, and book value.

Because some lesser-known growth stocks are not as popular with investors, the P/E ratios for such firms are generally lower (although still high) than those of the more glamorous, well-known growth stocks. Often such firms represent regional businesses with strong earnings or may be the third- or fourth-leading firm in an industry. Some of these lesser-known growth stocks in recent years have been Gibson Greetings, Long's Drug Stores, and Healthdyne. Their betas are usually 1.5 or more.

Speculative Stocks

The term **speculative stock** describes a company that has an apparent potential for substantial earnings at some time in the future, even though such earnings may never be realized. Speculative stocks often have a spotty earnings record or are so new that no earnings pattern has emerged. Investors in these types of firms incur some risk because the recent history of earnings and dividends is likely to be poor or highly inconsistent. As a result, investors in speculative stocks rank the safety of their principal as a secondary factor. With meager dividends anticipated, the investor hopes that the company will make a new discovery, invent a new product, or generate valuable information that later may push up the price of the stock and create substantial capital gains.

Examples of speculative companies include computer-graphics and video-game companies, Internet applications, small oil businesses, genetic engineering firms, and some pharmaceutical manufacturers. For these firms, the P/E ratio fluctuates widely along with the company's fortunes, and a beta exceeding 2.0 is common. For every speculative company that succeeds, many others do poorly or fail altogether.

Other Characterizations for Common Stocks

A variety of other terms are used to describe particular stocks within the four basic classifications in greater detail. These terms include *blue-chip, value, cyclical,* and *countercyclical.*

Blue-Chip Stocks   The term **blue-chip stock** suggests a company that has a well-regarded reputation, that dominates its industry (often with annual revenues of $1 billion or more), that has a long history of both good earnings and consistent cash dividends, that grows at approximately the same rate as the overall economy, and whose shares are widely held by individual investors and institutions. The earnings of blue-chip companies (which are usually considered income stocks or well-known growth stocks) are expected to grow at a consistent but unspectacular rate because these highly stable firms are the leaders in their industries. Examples of such stocks include Dow Chemical, General Electric, Exxon, and H. J. Heinz. Investing in such companies is considered much less risky than investing in other types of firms.

Value Stocks   When the price of a company's common stock is low given its historical earnings record and the current value of its assets, it is described as a **value stock.** Such a stock is said to be underappreciated by most investors; thus,

The Advantages and Disadvantages of Investing in Common Stock

There are several advantages and disadvantages of investing in common stock.

Advantages

- **The likelihood of cash dividends and price appreciation.** Historically, the combined annual cash dividend and price appreciation of all stocks is about 11 percent.

- **A low minimum investment.** A share of stock could sell for as little as $5 or $10 (although it is rare to buy one share at a time).

- **Limited investors' liability.** If the corporation goes bankrupt, you lose only the price of the stock.

- **Excellent marketability.** Common stocks can generally be sold with ease.

Disadvantages

- **Risk.** A financial risk exists that the company will not be successful.

- **Investment of time.** Stocks require a significant amount of time for personal management. Because the prices of many common stocks vary with certain news events, world happenings, and economic and political variables, investors need to stay alert to current happenings to know when to buy or to sell quickly so as to reap profits or reduce losses.

- **Uncertain return.** Even a company with an excellent record of paying cash dividends might have to skip one or two quarterly dividends during times of low profitability.

- **Inflation risk.** During times of high inflation, many common stock prices are depressed. As inflation rises, interest rates rise as well, increasing the cost of doing business (and thus lowering profits). Inflation provides a high rate of return to savers because interest rates rise. As a result, many people move their money into safer alternatives such as bonds or savings, thereby further depressing stock prices.

- **Market-volatility risk.** The price of a stock might be depressed when you want to sell it. For example, assume that your child's college fund consists of common stock investments and prices of all stocks are depressed when the child turns 18. At that point, the value of the investments could be sharply lower, and it might not be wise to sell the stocks to pay tuition bills.

its current price makes it look like an investment bargain. Such companies often operate within industries that benefit from a growing economy. Although their stock prices have changed, some past examples of value stocks have included DuPont, Eastman, IBM, Lockheed, Time Warner, and Westinghouse Electric.

Cyclical Stocks The term **cyclical stock** describes a company whose profits are greatly influenced by changes in the economic business cycle. Typically, such companies operate in the major consumer-dependent industries, such as automobiles, housing, airlines, and publishing. The market prices of cyclical stocks mirror the general state of the economy and reflect the various phases of the business cycle. During times of prosperity and economic expansion, corporate earnings rise, profits grow, and stock prices climb; during a recession, these measures decline sharply. In addition to companies in the basic industries (such as retailing, steel, tires, and heavy machinery), many firms characterized as

Make a Decision about When to Sell Stocks

It is hard for an investor to know exactly when to sell owned stocks, although the following guidelines should assist in the decision-making process. You should consider selling when

1. The stock reaches your target price.

2. Favorable developments occur that temporarily push up the price.

3. Good profits are unlikely to continue.

4. The stock lags behind others in its industry group.

5. Company profits begin to fall short of analysts' projections.

6. Industry and company prospects are deteriorating.

7. Losses are moderate (before they become enormous).

8. The stock's price/earnings ratio appears too high.

9. You have found a better place for the money.

---

blue-chip, income, growth, value, or speculative stocks can also be described as cyclical stocks. Most cyclical stocks have a beta of about 1.0.

Countercyclical Stocks Even when economic activity suffers a general decline, some companies maintain substantial earnings because their products are always in demand. These firms are considered **countercyclical** (or **defensive**) **stocks** because they perform well even in an environment characterized by weak economic activity and sliding interest rates. Most cigarette smokers, for example, do not quit during a recession, and people usually continue to go to movies, consume soft drinks, purchase kitty litter, buy electric utility service, have their clothes dry-cleaned, visit hospitals, have their cars washed, and buy groceries. Similarly, utility companies generally continue to have good earnings during periods of economic decline. During rising markets, the prices of these recession-resistant stocks tend to rise less quickly than cyclical stocks, and they still may drop somewhat in a declining market. Countercyclical stocks, by definition, have a beta that is less than 1.0 or even negative. Investors interested in receiving cash dividends regularly sometimes choose these stocks.

The Language of Bond Investing

> 4   Describe the major characteristics of bonds.

A **bond** is a certificate that represents a debt obligation of the bond issuer (a corporation or government) to the bondholder/investor. The major characteristics of bonds are discussed below.

The Indenture

An **indenture** is a written legal agreement between a group of bondholders (representing each bondholder) and the debtor describing the terms of the debt by setting forth the maturity date, interest rate, and other factors. For corporate bonds, this lengthy document specifies many of the debtor's responsibilities regarding the use of the borrowed money, the date(s) on which the bond principal must be repaid, and the dates on which interest payments must be made. A trustee—a bank or trust company—is normally appointed to represent the bondholders and to ensure that the obligations of the indenture are met. State laws require issuers of corporate bonds to pay interest due to bondholders even if the company does not turn a profit. Government bonds usually do not include indentures, because the authorizing statute typically details the responsibilities of the public agency issuing the bond.

Face Value, Coupon Rate, and Maturity Date

Bonds are usually issued at a **face value** (also known as **par value**) of $1000; this amount is specified on the certificate. The term **coupon rate** (also known as **coupon, coupon yield,** and **stated interest rate**) refers to the stated interest rate printed on the certificate when the bond is issued. It reflects the total annual fixed rate of interest that will be paid at regular intervals (usually every six months). For example, Flora Johnson, a retired postal worker from West Lafayette, Indiana, bought a 20-year $1000 Running Paws Catfood Company bond last week with a coupon rate of 7 percent that promises to pay her $70 in interest annually (normally bonds pay two semiannual installments: $35 in this instance).

The coupon rate of a bond remains the same until the **maturity date**, when the face amount is due and the debt must be paid off (or retired). Most corporate bonds mature in 20 to 30 years. Government securities often mature in ten to 20 years, although the maturity time could be as short as five years or as long as 40 years. Occasionally, bonds are retired serially; that is, each bond is numbered consecutively and matures according to a prenumbered schedule at stated intervals. These investments are known as **serial bonds.**

Secured and Unsecured Bonds

Bonds are issued as either secured or unsecured. A corporation issuing a **secured bond** would pledge specific assets as collateral in the indenture or have the principal and interest guaranteed by another corporation or a government agency. In the event of default, the trustee could take legal action to seize and sell such assets. Three types of secured bonds are **mortgage bonds** (which use land and buildings as collateral), **collateral trust bonds** (stocks and perhaps other bonds as collateral), and **equipment bonds** (certain equipment, such as airplanes or railroad cars, as collateral). In the event of bankruptcy, the claims of secured creditors are paid first.

An **unsecured bond** does not name collateral as security for the debt and is backed only by the good faith and reputation of the issuing agency. Thus, an unsecured bond, which is called a **debenture**, is backed by the general credit of the issuer and is not secured by a mortgage or lien on any specific property. Although secured bonds might appear safer than unsecured bonds at first glance, often this assumption is not true. All government bonds are unsecured, for example, and U.S. government bonds are debentures that are backed by the "full faith, credit, and taxing power of the government." In addition, the strong financial reputations of many large corporations enable them to offer unsecured bonds that are safer than the secured bonds of some other companies.

Investors in bonds want to be as confident as possible that interest payments will be made on time and that the principal will be repaid as scheduled. For this reason, many bonds include a **sinking fund**, through which money is set aside each year for repayment of the principal portion of the debt. The trustee receives these funds and oversees this responsibility. The added assurance of a sinking fund reduces investor risk and, therefore, permits the agency to issue bonds at interest rates lower than those offered for similar bonds.

Senior and Subordinated Bonds

A corporation that issues unsecured bonds several times over the years must rank the bonds for repayment priority in the event of default. A **senior debenture** gives holders a first right to all assets not pledged to secured bondholders. A **subordinated debenture** gives holders a lesser claim to assets than that provided by a senior debenture. Of course, the greater the risk associated with a bond, the higher the interest rate should be.

Registered and Bearer Bonds

In the past, all corporations issued **bearer bonds** (also called **coupon bonds**). The owners of such bonds were unknown to the corporation; a series of post-dated coupons attached to the bond signified their ownership. When an interest payment was due, a bondholder detached the proper coupon and presented it to the corporation, a paying agent, or a bank to receive payment. The principal was claimed in the same manner. Some older issues of coupon bonds are still traded. By law, all bonds issued in recent years have been **registered bonds**, which provide for the recording of the bondholder's name so that checks or electronic funds transfers for interest and principal can be safely forwarded when due. The Internal Revenue Service is notified of the payments as well. A registered bond can be transferred only when it is endorsed by the registered owner.

Bonds today are issued in **book-entry form**, which means that certificates are not issued. Instead, an account is set up in the name of the issuing organization or the brokerage firm that sold the bond. Interest is paid into the account when due. The U.S. government uses the book-entry form for bonds that it issues.

Callable Bonds

Most bonds (and preferred stocks) are **callable**—that is, the issuer can buy back the security from the investor before the maturity date if the issuer so requests. The issuer repurchases the bond at par value or by paying a slight surcharge, perhaps 5 percent above par value, if the price reaches a certain level. Precise call dates must be stated in advance to investors.

A company might desire to exercise a call option when interest rates drop substantially. For example, assume that a company issues bonds paying a $90 annual dividend (9% coupon rate). When interest rates drop to 7 or perhaps 6 percent, the 9 percent bonds may represent a high cost for money for the corporation. Therefore, if the bonds have a callable feature, the company might seek to redeem the bonds early. Approximately 80 to 90 percent of long-term bonds and preferred stocks are classified as callable.

Warrants

A bond sold with a warrant attached bestows some of the benefits of stock ownership on bondholders. A **warrant** (also called a **purchase warrant**) is a type of security attached to a bond, a preferred stock, or some issues of common stock that gives the holder the right to purchase a specific number of shares at a stipulated price within a specified time limit or for the life of the bond. A warrant is offered with securities as an added inducement to buy.

To illustrate, assume that you own a Running Paws Catfood Company bond with a face value of $1000, an 8 percent interest rate, and a warrant attached. For the next five years, the warrant gives you the right to buy ten shares of common stock for $30 per share. If the price of the common stock rises above $30, the warrant will have substantial value. If the price climbs to $36, for example, you can purchase ten shares at $30, for a total of $300 (saving $60 on the market price of $360). In this case, the warrant has a value of $60, and the price of the bond will increase by the same amount. If you do not want to use the warrant, you may sell it, assuming it is "detachable" from the bond. If the common stock price never rises above $30 per share, the warrant has no value.

Convertibility

Some bonds and some preferred stocks have a **convertibility privilege** that allows them to be exchanged for a certain number of shares of the issuing company's common stock during a specified time period. This option gives the investor the chance for both income and equity participation if the stock price increases.

Convertible securities take priority over common shareholders in the event of bankruptcy. Investors receive a fixed cash return while they wait for the underlying common stock to appreciate; then, if conditions warrant, they can make the swap. Investors often prefer convertibles because they provide reduced volatility and greater safety than most stocks. Moreover, convertible securities offer a steady yield unless they are swapped for shares of common stock.

Let's say that you have a $1000 Running Paws Catfood Company convertible bond that was issued at 9 percent and permits conversion to 30 shares of Running Paws common stock at any time during the next 20 years. During this period, you will receive interest payments from the bond and hope that the stock price will rise. The conversion feature begins to affect the price of the bond when Running Paws stock rises above $33.33 per share ($1000 ÷ 30 shares). If the stock price climbs to $36, for example, the bond price will increase to $1080 (30 shares × $36), regardless of general interest rates, which also affect bond prices. If the price of the common stock continues to rise, the price of the bond follows suit. If the common stock price remains below $33.33, the conversion privilege makes no difference.

Types of Bonds Available to Investors

5   Differentiate among the three general types of bonds.

Three general types of bonds are available: (1) corporate bonds, (2) U.S. government securities, and (3) municipal bonds.

Corporate Bonds

Corporate bonds are interest-bearing certificates of long-term debt of a company. They represent an important source of funds for corporations—every dollar of newly issued common stock is countered by three dollars of newly issued corporate bonds. Because of tax regulations, corporations often finance major projects by issuing long-term bonds instead of selling stocks. Payments of dividends to common and preferred stockholders are not tax-deductible for corporations, unlike interest paid to bondholders.

State laws require corporations to make bond interest payments on time. Therefore, companies in financial difficulty must pay bondholders before paying any short-term creditors. Before buying corporate bonds, investors must assess the financial quality of the company, considering both its current profitability and the likelihood of long-term financial stability. Every year more than 100 corporations that issue bonds go bankrupt, with their bondholders suffering losses of principal and interest.

It is important for investors to compare the risks and potential rewards of bond investments. To help you in appraising such risks, independent advisory services grade bonds for credit risk: Moody's Investors Service, Inc. and Standard & Poor's Corporation. These firms publish unbiased ratings of the financial conditions of corporations and municipalities that issue bonds. A **bond rating** represents the opinion of an outsider on the quality—or creditworthiness—of the issuing organization. It reflects the likelihood that the issuing organization will be able to repay its debt. Thus, investors have access to measures of the **default risk** (or **credit risk**), which is the uncertainty associated with not receiving the promised periodic interest payments and the principal amount when it becomes due at maturity. Moody's and Standard & Poor's examine the financial strength of each bond issuer, the quality of its management, its prospects for the future, its strength compared with its competitors or other municipalities, future directions of the industry or region, and a variety of other factors. Such bond rating directories are available in most large libraries; they are also available on-line. Ratings for each bond issue are continually reevaluated, and they are frequently changed after the original security has been sold to the public.

After bonds have been purchased, most can easily be sold in a **secondary market** prior to maturity. This market is also called an **aftermarket**, because it is where existing securities that have already been sold to the public are bought and sold. A stock and bond exchange is an example of such an aftermarket.

Table 14.1 shows the rating scales used by Moody's and Standard & Poor's. The higher the rating, the greater the probable safety of the bond and the lower the default risk. In contrast, the lower the rating of the bond, the higher the stated interest rate or the effective interest rate when such bonds are reduced in price from their face amount, as more risk is involved. Higher ratings denote confidence that the issuer will not default and, if necessary, that the bond can readily be sold before maturity in a secondary market.

Table 14.1

Summary of Municipal and Corporate Bond Ratings

Rating		Interpretation of Rating
Moody's	**Standard & Poor's**	
Aaa Aa A	AAA AA A	High investment quality suggests ability to repay principal and interest on time. Aaa and AAA bonds are generally referred to as "gilt-edged" because they have demonstrated profitability over the years and have paid their bondholders their interest without interruption; thus, they carry the smallest risk.
Baa Ba	BBB BB B	Medium-quality investments that adequately provide security to principal and interest. They are neither highly protected nor poorly secured; thus, they may have some speculative characteristics.
B Caa Ca	CCC CC C	Lack characteristics of a desirable investment, and investors have decreasing assurance of repayment as the rating declines. Elements of danger may be present regarding repayment of principal and interest.
C	DDD DD D	In default with little prospect of regaining any investment standing.

Note: Bonds rated Baa and higher by Moody's and BBB and higher by S&P are investment-grade quality; Ba and BB and lower are junk bonds.

U.S. Government Securities

U.S. government securities are classified into two general groups: (1) Treasury bills, notes, and bonds, and (2) federal agency issue notes, bonds, and certificates.* The interest rates on federal government securities are usually lower than those on corporate bonds because they are virtually risk-free—the possibility of default is near zero. Conservative investors are often attracted to the certainty offered by U.S. government securities. They also know that U.S. Treasury securities cannot be called early if interest rates drop. Federal government securities provide an additional advantage in that the interest income remains exempt from state and local income taxes.

Unlike Series EE and HH savings bonds, most government bonds are transferable and can be sold by one investor to another. You may purchase a U.S. Treasury security directly from the government, through banks, or in the securities market through brokerage firms.

Treasury Bills, Notes, and Bonds Treasury bills, notes, and bonds—collectively known as **Treasury securities**—are debt instruments used by the federal government to finance the public national debt. Benefits of Treasury securities are that they represent a safe source of current income, have excellent liquidity, and are simple to acquire and sell. You may purchase all Treasury securities in units of $1000 each directly from any Federal Reserve Bank or its branch office.

---

* U.S. savings bonds (both Series EE and HH) represent another type of government security. They are discussed from a cash-management perspective in Chapter 5, "Managing Your Cash." See *www.ny.frb.org* for data useful to investors and government securities.

About Junk Bonds

So-called **junk bonds** are high-risk, high-interest-rate corporate or municipal bonds rated below BBB by Standard and Poor's or below Baa by Moody's bond-rating agency. These bonds carry ratings that are below traditional investment grade. The default rate on high-quality bonds is less than 1 percent; the default rate on junk bonds exceeds 3 percent. Fewer than 800 of the 23,000 large U.S. companies that issue bonds meet the highest credit-risk rating standards. Junk bonds are typically issued by young companies with short track records or those with questionable financial strength.

"Junk bond" is also a term used to describe high-interest bonds used to fund corporate takeovers. **Leveraged buy-outs (LBOs)** are takeovers of a company, usually by its officers and other private investors, that are financed with the assets of the corporation pledged as security for borrowing large amounts of money. They typically saddle a corporation with a huge amount of debt, increasing the chance that the company might default in the future. When growth in the economy slows, more overindebted companies may default on their bonds. More than 60 well-known corporations have defaulted on junk bonds in the past five years.

Because junk bonds pay 2 to 6 more interest points than high-quality bonds, large numbers of investors have purchased these bonds in recent years despite the higher risk to obtain the anticipated higher returns. Wise investors avoid buying individual junk bonds because of the risk involved. Instead, many people invest in a "high-yield income" bond mutual fund that owns junk bonds. Money invested in such a mutual fund is safer because the fund's diversification reduces risks. Mutual funds are discussed in Chapter 15.

Treasury bills, also called **T-bills**, are short-term U.S. government securities that mature in one year or less, such as in 13, 26, or 52 weeks. The 13- and 26-week bills are sold every week, and the 52-week bills are sold every four weeks. Treasury bills do not pay current interest income because they are sold at a **discount** from face value, where the difference between the selling price and the T-bill's value at maturity—the gain—represents the interest for federal income tax purposes. Stated as an interest rate, the return on such investments is called a **discount yield**. For example, if you purchase a new 52-week $1000 T-bill for $950, it will mature in one year. At that point, the U.S. Treasury Department will electronically forward $1000 to you. The discount yield would be 5.3 percent ($1000 − $950 = $50; $50 ÷ $950 = 0.0526) on your investment of $950.

Individuals buy new issues of T-bills on a noncompetitive bid basis. The price individuals pay for the bill will represent the average of all competitive offers made by large institutions that buy millions of dollars' worth of T-bills that week. To buy a T-bill, you simply submit a certified or cashier's check for the face amount along with the proper form. A few days later, you will receive notification that you own the T-bill and an electronically wired refund that represents the difference between the face value of the bill and the purchase price.

U.S. **Treasury notes** are intermediate-term U.S. government securities that are issued in two-, three-, five-, and ten-year maturities; they pay interest semiannually. These notes are registered and sold with a fixed interest rate, which is slightly higher than rates for Treasury bills because the lending period is longer.

Treasury bonds are long-term U.S. government securities that have a maturity period of 11 to 30 years or more. Interest is paid semiannually on these registered bonds. The fixed interest rates are higher than on notes because they are longer-term securities.

New Treasury securities can be purchased only by using the Treasury Direct Plan. To open a **Treasury Direct account,** obtain Form PD 5182 by calling the Bureau of Public Debt at (800) 943-6864, or download it from the Internet at *www.publicdebt.treas.gov.* You must provide the government with both your Social Security number and your bank account number. Purchases are recorded electronically, with all interest, principal, and other payments deposited with your local financial institution, and a written statement of the transactions is forwarded to the investor. No commissions, charges, or fees are due when buying and redeeming Treasury securities directly with the government. When a bank or stock brokerage firm handles such transactions, fees of $50 to $60 per transaction are charged.

Federal Agency Issues of Bonds, Notes, and Certificates   More than 100 different bonds, notes, and certificates are issued by various federal agencies, such as the Government National Mortgage Association (Ginnie Mae), the Federal National Mortgage Association (Fannie Mae), the Federal Home Loan Mortgage Corporation (Freddie Mac), and the Student Loan Marketing Association (Sallie Mae). These **agency issues** generally are backed by the assets and resources of the issuing agency *instead of* the full faith and credit of the U.S. government. For example, Ginnie Mae certificates are backed by the Government National Mortgage Association, and each security represents interest in a pool of mortgages that are sold to institutions and investors in units of $25,000 (they can also be purchased in smaller units through a mutual fund). When homeowners make their monthly mortgage payments to Ginnie Mae, a part of the principal and interest is passed to investors. Agency issues are not as widely recognized as Treasury securities, yet they often pay a yield that is 0.5 to 1.5 percentage points higher than the yield for comparable-term Treasury securities because of their somewhat higher degree of risk.

Municipal Bonds

Municipal bonds (also called **munies**) are long-term debts issued by local governments (cities, states, and various districts and political subdivisions) and their agencies that are used to finance public improvement projects, such as roads, bridges, and parks, or to pay ongoing expenses. Moody's *Bond Record* rates some 20,000 munies, and twice as many unrated securities exist. Bonds range in quality from AAA-rated state highway bonds to unrated securities issued by local governmental parking authorities.

Among the dozen or more types of specialized municipal bonds, two are most frequently issued: revenue bonds and general obligation bonds. **Revenue bonds** are sold to investors to raise money for specific projects, and they pay interest out of the revenues of those projects. They are backed only by the income from the user fees levied on projects built or maintained, such as dormitories, airports, sewers, power plants, hospitals, and toll roads—thus, they are not backed by a government's taxing power. The most popular type of state and local government security, revenue bonds typically have yields about a half percentage point higher than yields for general obligation bonds. **General obligation bonds** are issued by states, cities, and government agencies that have taxing authority. They are backed by the full faith and credit of the issuer. Because a government or government agency has the responsibility to repay these debts, such bonds are usually considered safer than revenue bonds. Some states offer general obligation bonds known as "minibonds" that are issued in denominations as small as $500 or $100.

The U.S. Constitution requires that municipal bond interest be exempt from federal income tax. Thus, municipal bonds are also known as **tax-free bonds** or **tax-exempt bonds** because the interest income is tax-free. In addition, interest income on munies is exempt from state and local income taxes if the investor lives in the state that issued the bond. Municipal bonds almost always offer a lower stated return than other bonds.

Capital gains on the sale of munies, on the other hand, are taxable. Such gains may be realized when bonds are bought at a discount and then sold at a higher price or redeemed for full value at maturity. In addition, bonds bought in the secondary market at a premium may appreciate to produce a gain.

Although defaults occur on more than 100 municipal bond securities every year, they are generally safer than corporate bonds, but, of course, not as safe as U.S. government securities. Both Moody's and Standard & Poor's rate municipal bonds. Approximately 40 percent of all new municipal bonds sold today carry insurance that guarantees the timely repayment of principal and interest in case

 Did You KNOW ?   *Zero-Coupon Bonds Pay No Annual Interest*

Zero-coupon bonds (also called **zeros** or **deep discount bonds**) are municipal, corporate, and Treasury bonds that pay no annual interest. They are sold to investors at sharp discounts from their face value, and then redeemed at full value upon maturity. For example, a 7 percent, $1000 zero-coupon bond to be redeemed in the year 2008 might sell today for $308. Zeros pay no current income to investors, so investors do not have to worry about reinvesting any interest payments. The interest, which is usually compounded semiannually, accumulates within the bond itself, and the return to the investor comes from redeeming the bond at its stated face value. In this manner, zeros operate much like Series EE savings bonds and T-bills. Zeros, therefore, pay "phantom" interest. Although no interest money is received, you must pay income taxes on the interest every year unless the securities are held in a qualified tax-sheltered retirement plan, such as an IRA or 401(k). In that case, income taxes are deferred until the funds are withdrawn.

The maturity date for a zero could range from a few months to as long as 30 years. Treasury zeros, unlike most other zeros, are noncallable. Such bonds are ideal for people planning for their retirement years because they know exactly how much will be received upon maturity. In addition, many parents invest in **zero-coupon college bonds** to help pay for their children's education. With these bonds, the income paid in the name of the child is generally so small that little if any income taxes are charged.

the issuer defaults. Because this insurance reduces the return by only about 0.16 percent, insured municipal bonds may represent a wiser choice.

What Should You Consider Before Investing in Bonds?

6 Describe what the investor should consider before investing in bonds, particularly the current yield and yield to maturity.

A number of factors should be considered before investing in bonds: certain risks, premiums and discounts, current yield, yield to maturity, and tax-equivalent yields.

The Susceptibility of Bonds to Certain Risks

Four types of risk particularly affect the bond investor: (1) credit risk, (2) callability risk, (3) inflation risk, and (4) interest-rate risk.

Credit Risk Puts the Investor's Original Investment in Jeopardy During the years until the bond matures, the investor's funds remain at risk because the issuer might possibly get into financial difficulty and be unable to make interest payments or repay the original principal invested. Should the issuing company or municipality experience financial difficulty, one of the major bond-rating services is likely to downgrade its bonds credit rating. In such an event, the market price of the bonds generally drops. If the issuer cannot honor its obligations, the bonds are in **default.** In this situation, a corporation usually seeks protection under Chapter 11 of the bankruptcy code so that it can reorganize its business under the supervision of a court-appointed trustee. If the creditors approve the reorganization plan, the business remains in operation, although it usually must sell substantial assets in the process. If a bond issuer becomes bankrupt, its assets are sold and the proceeds used to repay secured and unsecured debts.

Callability Risk May Reduce the Investor's Expected Return Investors who purchase callable bonds run the risk that the security will be bought back from the investor by the issuer before the maturity date. Issuers make such requests so that they can sell new bonds with a lower interest rate. If the investor owns a bond that has been called, he or she will have to reinvest the proceeds earlier than expected, most likely at a lower interest rate. If the bond was purchased at a premium, a bondholder could suffer a significant loss.

Inflation Risk May Lower the Investor's Return **Inflation risk** represents the possibility that the investor's money will lose purchasing power due to inflation. He or she will not be able to purchase as much after making the investment as before. Investors who lend for long time periods require higher interest rates because it is difficult to project the effect of inflation on the future values of money with great accuracy. Should interest rates rise, the long-term investor will be locked into a lower rate of return for more years than with a shorter-term security. As a result, bonds are priced to achieve current and future values and, therefore, include an **inflation premium**—that is, an extra amount of interest equal to a projection of rising prices in the economy. If the premium proves too low, the investor loses some or all of the profit, as well as perhaps some of the purchasing power of the initial investment. If inflation and interest rates fall, bond prices will increase to provide exceptional levels of return.

The U.S. Treasury sells **inflation-indexed savings bonds** that guarantee that the investor's return will outpace inflation. These bonds are also called **I-bonds** or **Treasury inflation protection securities (TIPS)**. The interest earned on the I-bond will equal the inflation rate plus a fixed rate of return. Once purchased, the fixed rate stays the same until the bond stops earning interest after ten, 20, or 30 years. The total interest rate, however, changes every May and November based on the current inflation rate. As a result, the principal value will increase over the life of the bond in line with increases in the consumer price index.

For example, if the inflation rate was 4 percent during the first six months of the year, then by midyear the principal of the bond would be valued at $1020 ($1000 × 0.04/2). Also at mid-year the investor receives the first semiannual interest payment of $17.85 ($1020 × 0.035/2). If inflation accelerated so that it reached 4.5 percent for the full year, then the principal of the bond would be valued at $1045 by the second semiannual interest payment. The second semiannual payment would be $18.29 ($1045 × 0.035/2).

As a result, both the investor's income and the principal keep pace with inflation. A guarantee that the investor's return will beat inflation for the next 30 years is a promise that other ultraconservative investments cannot match. To avoid having to pay current income taxes on an annual inflation adjustment (because the money is considered earned, even though it is not actually received), investors can either elect to defer the tax until the bond reaches maturity or keep I-bonds in tax-deferred retirement accounts (discussed in Chapter 18). As with traditional savings bonds, the interest is exempt from state and local taxes.

Interest-Rate Risk Results in Variable Value A bond's value (its price on any given day) is affected by its type, coupon rate, availability in the marketplace, demand for the bond, prices for similar bonds, the underlying credit quality of the issuer, the number of years that must elapse before its maturity, and fluctuations in current market interest rates in the general economy. The state of the economy and the supply and demand for credit affect **market interest rates**,

The Relative Market Interest Rates for Bond Investment

Market interest rates for various bond investments on any particular day might be: Treasury bills, 5.0 percent; U.S. Treasury notes, 5.4 percent; U.S. Treasury bonds, 6.8 percent; federal agency issues, 7.2 percent; high-quality corporate bonds, 7.9 percent; long-term certificates of deposit, 7.0 percent; junk bonds, 11.2 percent; and high-quality municipal bonds, 5.1 percent. These market interest rates usually change frequently. For a debt to represent an attractive investment, it must return the market interest rate or better for debts with similar risks. Historically, long-term Treasury bonds have paid a return of 2 percent beyond inflation.

which are the current long- and short-term interest rates paid on various types of corporate and government debts that carry similar levels of risk. Long-term rates are largely set by investors in the bond market, primarily based upon their expectations of future inflation. Short-term interest rates, on the other hand, are manipulated by the Federal Reserve Board, also known as the **Fed.** When the economy slumps, the Fed often lowers the interest rates on short-term Treasury issues in an attempt to stimulate economic activity. When inflation rises, the Fed raises interest rates. Changes in short-term interest rates generally affect rates paid on intermediate- and long-term bonds.

When market interest rates increase, interest rates paid on newly issued bonds will rise and the price of existing bonds will fall. This action occurs so that the existing bond and the new bond offer potential investors approximately the same yield. As a result, bonds generally have a **fixed yield** (the interest income payment remains the same) but a **variable value.**

To the investor, **interest-rate risk** reflects the uncertainty of the market price of an asset in the future that results from possible interest-rate changes. This uncertainty is also called **market risk.** For example, assume that you buy a 20-year, $1000 bond with a stated annual interest rate of 8 percent, or an annual return of $80 ($1000 $\times$ 0.08). If interest rates in the general economy jump to 10 percent after one year, no one will want to buy your bond for $1000 because it pays only $80 per year. Should you want to sell it at that time, the price of the bond will have to be lowered, probably to $800 [see Equation (14.2) on page 420 for the calculation involved].

On the other hand, if interest rates on newly issued bonds slip to 6 percent after one year, the price of your bond will increase sharply (probably to $1333), because investors will be willing to pay a **premium** (a sum of money paid in addition to a regular price) to own your bond paying 8 percent when other rates are only 6 percent. It is important to remember that bond yields and prices move in opposite directions—that is, as one goes up, the other goes down.

Because they offer the possibility of capital gains, bonds represent a unique investment opportunity for moderate, conservative, and aggressive investors alike. If the bond is held to maturity (19 more years in this example), no matter how much the market price fluctuates over the life of the bond, the issuer is obligated to repay the face value of $1000 (i.e., the stated price printed on the certificate). Therefore, investors who own bonds until maturity can ignore any interest-rate risk.

Bond prices are most volatile when: (1) bonds are sold at less than face value when first issued, (2) the stated rate is low, and (3) the bond maturity time is long. The investor who holds a bond to maturity might ignore such information, but the person considering selling before maturity might be shocked to see price swings of 20 percent or more. A speculator might regard such rapid price changes as opportunities.

Premiums and Discounts

When a bond is first issued, it is sold in one of three ways: (1) at its face value (the value of the bond as stated on the certificate), which is also the amount the investor will receive when the bond matures, (2) at a discount below its face value, or (3) at a premium above its face value. Later, because the stated interest

Estimate the Selling Price of a Bond After Interest Rates Have Changed

Bond prices are influenced partially by supply and demand, but mostly by the cost of money. If you paid $1000 for a 20-year, 7 percent bond and were forced to sell it after interest rates on comparable bonds had increased to 9 percent, you would lose more than $200. You can estimate the selling price of an existing bond (assuming it is more than a few years from maturity) after interest rates change by using the **bond-selling price formula**:

In Equation (14.1), the selling price equals $777.78 ($70 ÷ 0.09). If you bought the bond for $1000, you will lose $222.22 if you sell it for $777.78. Alternatively, if interest rates drop to 5½ percent, you could sell your 7 percent bond at a profit of $272.72 ($70 ÷ 0.055 = $1272.72 − $1000). Of course, if you keep the bond until maturity, the issuer is obligated to retire it for $1000. Exact calculations of selling prices can be performed by a brokerage firm. This formula is duplicated on the *Garman/Forgue* Web site.

$$\text{Bond selling price} = \frac{\text{annual interest income in dollars}}{\text{current market interest rate}} \quad (14.1)$$

rate on the bond remains fixed, the market price changes to provide a competitive effective rate of return.

As an example, assume that Running Paws Catfood Company decided to issue 20-year bonds at 8.8 percent. While the bonds were being printed and prepared for sale, the market interest rate on comparable bonds rose to 9 percent. In this instance, Running Paws will sell the bonds at a slight discount to provide a competitive return. Discounts and premiums on bonds reflect changing interest rates in the economy and the number of years to maturity.

Current Yield

The **current yield** equals the bond's fixed annual interest payment divided by its bond price. It is a measure of the current annual income (the total of both semiannual interest payments in dollars) expressed as a percentage when divided by the bond's current market price. When you buy a bond at par (for example, for $1000), its current yield equals its coupon yield. As bond prices fluctuate because of interest rate changes and other factors, the current yield also changes. For example, if Flora Johnson paid $940 for a $1000 bond paying $70 per year, the bond's current yield is 7.45 percent, as shown by the **current yield formula**:

$$\text{Current yield} = \frac{\text{current annual income}}{\text{current market price}} \quad (14.2)$$

$$= \frac{\$70}{\$940}$$

$$= 7.45\%$$

Financial sections of larger newspapers usually publish the current yields for a great number of bonds based on that day's market prices. While this information is useful, it does not tell an investor the current yield that a previously purchased bond earns because it was probably obtained at a price different from the current market price (at a premium or discount) rather than at precisely $1000 (as was the case for Flora). Realize, too, that a bond's current yield is based upon the purchase price, not on the prices at which it later trades.

The total return on a bond investment is made up of the same components as for any investment: current income *and* capital gains. In Flora's case, she will receive $1000 at the maturity date (20 years from now) even though she paid only $940 for the bond; therefore, her anticipated total return (or effective yield) will be higher than the 7.45 percent current yield. How much higher is accurately revealed by the yield to maturity (discussed below).

Yield to Maturity

Yield to maturity (YTM) is the total annual effective rate of return earned by a bondholder on a bond when it is held to maturity. It reflects *both* the current income *and* any difference if the bond was purchased at a price other than face value spread over the life of the bond. In reality, the market price of a bond equals the present value of its future interest payments and the present value of its face value when the bond matures. Three generalizations can be made about the yield to maturity: (1) if a bond is purchased for exactly its face value, the YTM is the same as the coupon rate printed on the certificate; (2) if a bond is purchased at a premium, the YTM will be lower than the coupon rate; and (3) if a bond is purchased at a discount, the YTM will be higher than the coupon rate.

For example, because Flora Johnson bought her 20-year bond with a coupon rate of 7 percent at a discount for $940, her yield to maturity must be greater than the coupon rate because she will receive $60 more than she paid for the bond when she receives the $1000 at maturity. Exactly how much higher can be determined by calculating an approximate yield to maturity when contemplating a bond purchase, because bonds that seem comparable may have different YTMs. The **yield to maturity (YTM) formula**, which is duplicated on the *Garman/Forgue* Web site, factors in the approximate appreciation when a bond is bought at a discount or at a premium:

$$YTM = \frac{I + [(FV - CV) / N]}{(FV + CV) / 2} \qquad (14.3)$$

where

$$
\begin{aligned}
I &= \textbf{interest} \text{ paid annually in dollars} \\
FV &= \textbf{face value} \\
CV &= \textbf{current value (price)} \\
N &= \textbf{number} \text{ of years until maturity}
\end{aligned}
$$

For example, if Flora Johnson paid $940 for a 20-year bond with a 7 percent coupon rate, the YTM is calculated as follows:

$$
\begin{aligned}
YTM &= \frac{\$70 + [(\$1000 - \$940) / 20]}{(\$1000 + \$940) / 2} \\
&= \frac{\$73}{\$970} \\
&= 7.53\%
\end{aligned}
$$

How Far Bond Prices Will Move When Interest Rates Change

On any given day, the major determinant of bond prices is the prevailing level of interest rates in the economy. The following figure illustrates the price changes for bonds when interest rates rise or fall. In general, rising interest rates reduce bond prices, and falling rates increase bond prices. In addition, the longer the time until maturity of a bond, the more sensitive the price to changes in interest rates. Thus, prices for long-term bonds fluctuate much more than those for short-term securities.

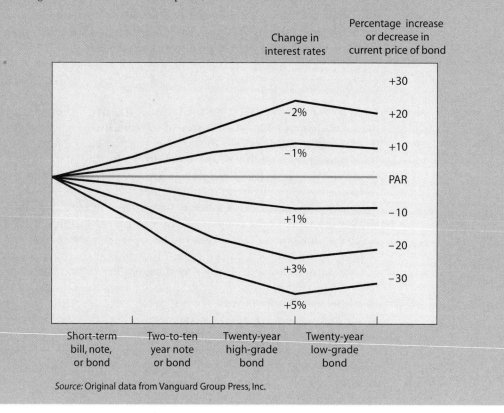

Source: Original data from Vanguard Group Press, Inc.

If you plan to buy and hold a bond until maturity, you should compare YTMs instead of current yields when considering a purchase because YTMs fairly represent all factors. The current yield on a bond is not an effective measure of the total annual return to the investor; in fact, the fewer years until maturity, the worse an indicator it becomes. As calculated above, Flora Johnson's 20-year bond with a coupon rate of 7 percent and a current yield of 7.45 percent has a YTM of 7.53 percent. If it had been purchased with only ten years until maturity, the YTM would be 7.84 percent; with five years until maturity, the YTM would be 8.45 percent; and with two years until maturity, the YTM would be 10.3 percent. Exact YTMs are listed in detailed bond tables available at large libraries or a broker's office.

| TAX | **Considerations & Consequences** | *Capital Gains and Losses* |

People generally invest in stocks and bonds with the intention of receiving current income and capital gains. Current income is taxed at one's regular tax rate. Short-term capital gains (sales of assets held for one year or less) and long-term capital gains (on assets held more than one year) can also occur. Net short-term gains are taxed at one's marginal tax rate. Net long-term gains are taxed at 20 percent (10 percent for those in the 15 percent tax bracket). Beginning in 2001, the 20 percent and 10 percent tax rate for gains on assets held more than 5 years drop to 18 percent and 8 percent.

Capital losses are deductible from capital gains and as much as $3000 of ordinary income; any excess over $3000 may be carried over to future years.

Tax-Equivalent Yields

Because municipal bonds receive special tax treatment, many investors consider buying them. In general, the higher your federal tax bracket, the more favorable municipal bonds become as an investment (as compared with taxable bonds).

The task of the investor is to determine the tax-equivalent yield so as to choose between a municipal bond (a tax-exempt investment) and a corporate bond (a taxable investment). The **tax-equivalent yield** compares the after-tax return on a taxable investment with the return on a tax-free investment. An investor who knows the tax-equivalent yield should choose the investment with the best "after-tax return." For example, a taxpayer in the 28 percent bracket will find that a 10.0 percent yield on a corporate bond pays the same after-tax return as a tax-free muni earning 7.2 percent [7.2 percent = $0.10 \times (1.00 - 0.28)$]. Thus, the investor would have to earn more than 10 percent on a taxable investment to equal the yield on this particular tax-exempt bond. The two formulas for tax-equivalent yields are discussed in detail on page 81.

When to Sell Bonds

In a few distinct instances, a bondholder should consider selling before a bond matures:

- *When interest rates have dropped and you can profit.* When interest rates drop, the price of a bond necessarily increases. If, for example, you own an 8 percent bond and interest rates decline to 6 percent, the price of your bond could rise to $1333, as determined by Equation (14.1). You may wish to take your profits by selling.

- *When the bond rating has seriously slipped.* Despite your efforts to choose a quality bond, unexpected events can cause a bond's rating to change. Perhaps the corporation suffered some economic setbacks, or the municipality had a loss in taxing authority. Be alert to any changes in bond ratings. A decreased bond rating can mean greater financial risk and a lower market price.

Select a Bond in Which to Invest

The process of selecting a bond involves the following four decisions:

1. *Decide on risk level.* The level of financial risk is related to the likely rate of return; the safest bonds offer the lowest yields. Securities of the U.S. government offer virtually no risk. For slightly more risk, consider the highest-rated corporate and municipal bonds. Lower-rated bonds, such as Baa or B, offer higher yields but carry substantial risk.

2. *Decide on maturity.* Consider the time schedule of your financial needs. Bonds with a short maturity generally have a lower current yield but greater price stability.

3. *Decide on tax equivalents.* Carefully consider the impact of the return from bonds on the total income taxes to be paid. As shown in Equations (3.1) and (3.2), tax-exempt securities sometimes offer a higher after-tax return than taxable alternatives.

4. *Select the highest yield to maturity (YTM).* Given similar bond securities with comparable risks, maturity, and tax equivalency, investors should choose the one that offers the highest yield to maturity (YTM), as calculated by Equation (14.3).

- ***When you definitely expect shifts in interest rates.*** Interest rates change continually, but some events clearly suggest that substantial changes in interest rates are forthcoming. Perhaps a conservative (or liberal) government is elected; perhaps federal budget deficits are growing larger (or smaller) with corresponding forecasts of greater deficits (or surpluses) in the future. Your reaction to a likely interest-rate shift depends on the types of bonds you own and the direction of the shift. If you expect interest rates to rise, you could sell short-term bonds and reinvest the proceeds when the rates have increased. In a market of falling interest rates, you can realize capital gains by selling bonds with higher coupon rates.

Advantages and Disadvantages of Investing in Bonds

7 List the advantages and disadvantages of investing in bonds.

The advantages and disadvantages of investing in bonds are as follows:

Advantages

- Bonds pay higher interest rates than savings accounts.
- Bonds generally offer a safe return of principal.
- Bonds usually have less volatility than stocks.
- Bonds offer regular income.
- It costs only $1000 to invest in bonds.

- Management of bonds is fairly easy because they require less careful attention than most alternative investments.

- Income from municipal bonds is exempt from federal income taxes and possibly from state and local taxes.

Disadvantages

- Bonds offer no hedge against inflation because inflation causes market interest rates to rise. In turn, bond interest rates rise, spurring declines in bond prices.

- Bond prices can be quite volatile because market interest rates vary after a bond has been issued.

- **Compounding** (earning interest on principal and interest) is almost impossible because most bondholders cannot reinvest dividends to receive the benefits of compounding.

- Except for tax-exempt bonds, the interest and capital gains on bonds are subject to an investor's (perhaps high) marginal tax rate.

- Poor marketability may exist if the security does not trade frequently.

- Diversification within bonds may be difficult to achieve (at $1000 each) because proper spreading of risk requires investing in several different securities.

Summary

1. Stocks are shares of ownership in the assets and earnings of a business corporation. They are initially sold to investors to finance corporate goals. Stocks represent potential income for investors because stockholders own a stake in the future direction of the company. Bonds are interest-bearing negotiable certificates of long-term debt issued by a corporation, a municipality (such as a city or state), or the federal government. Bond investors expect to receive periodic income every six months in the form of interest; in addition, they anticipate receiving the amount originally invested when the bond matures.

2. In the study of stock investments, several important terms need to be understood, such as earnings per share, price/earnings ratio, market price, and preemptive rights.

3. Stocks can be classified as income stocks (which pay higher-than-average dividends), growth stocks (which emphasize growth over income), and speculative stocks. Speculative stocks may have a spotty earnings record or be so new that no earnings pattern has emerged, but they may have an apparent potential for substantial earnings at some time in the future.

4. The likelihood of dividends and the potential for sharp price appreciation are perceived as major advantages of common stock investments. Disadvantages include financial risk, market-volatility risk, and the time required to personally manage the stock portfolio.

5. As evidence of debt, bonds include a number of major characteristics, such as legal indenture, denominations of value, coupon rate, maturity time, secured or unsecured, senior or subordinated, registered or bearer,

sinking fund, callability, warrants, and convertibility.

6. Three general types of bonds are available: corporate bonds (issued by private companies), U.S. government securities (virtually risk-free, with interest income that is exempt from state and local income taxes), and municipal bonds (whose interest income is exempt from federal income taxes).

7. Before investing in bonds, the investor should consider both the price and yield of a bond. These measures are functions of current market interest rates, prices for similar bonds, the current yield, and the yield to maturity.

8. Advantages of investing in bonds include higher interest rates than on savings accounts, safe return of principal, regular income, and ease of management. Disadvantages include the ability of interest-rate movements to affect the market price of a bond before it reaches maturity, the lack of appreciation of the principal, and the lack of compounded interest.

Key Words & Concepts

blue-chip stock   *406*

bond-selling price formula   *420*

callable   *410*

common stock   *395*

countercyclical stocks   *408*

current yield   *420*

default risk   *412*

earnings per share (EPS)   *399*

fundamental analysis   *405*

interest-rate risk   *419*

junk bonds   *414*

P/E ratio   *399*

registered bonds   *410*

retained earnings   *397*

secondary market   *412*

shareholder   *395*

tax-equivalent yield   *423*

Treasury bills   *414*

yield to maturity (YTM)   *421*

zero-coupon bonds   *416*

Questions for Thought & Discussion

1. Explain how common stocks represent ownership to the investor.

2. Summarize the differences between common and preferred stock.

3. Explain the general characteristics of a fixed-asset investment, and give examples of such investments.

4. Summarize the kinds of capitalization it takes to start up and operate a new corporation.

5. What does the price/earnings ratio mean, and how would you interpret a P/E ratio of 8 to 1?

6. Explain why one company might have a dividend payout ratio of 0.65 and another a ratio of 0.30.

7. Explain the likely relationship of the market price of a stock with its par value and its book value per share.

8. What effect do stock dividends have on the individual investor who already owns shares of stock in a company?

9. Identify a reason why some companies undertake stock splits.

10. Discuss the value of voting rights for a stockholder.

11. Differentiate between growth stocks and speculative stocks.

12. Explain why a particular growth stock could also be called a cyclical stock.

13. Identify two advantages and two disadvantages of investing in common stock.

14. List three guidelines on when to sell stocks.

15. Explain how indentures work and why government bonds do not include them.

16. Explain the difference between a senior debenture and a subordinated debenture.

17. Describe a situation in which a bond issuer would exercise a bond's callable feature.

18. Explain why some bonds include warrants.

19. What is the value of having a convertible bond?

20. Compare and contrast the three general types of bonds.

21. What are junk bonds, and why do people invest in them?

22. Summarize the differences among Treasury bills, notes, and bonds.

23. Distinguish between the two most popular types of municipal bonds.

24. What tax characteristic is unique to municipal bonds?

25. Explain how zero-coupon bonds work and which types of investors might be attracted to them.

26. Why might an investor in bonds be concerned about interest-rate risk?

27. Explain how changes in market interest rates cause bonds to be sold at a premium or at a discount.

28. Explain how bonds have a variable value and a fixed yield.

29. Summarize how the principal on an inflation-indexed savings bond can increase over the life of the bond, and explain why it is important to the investor.

30. What is the difference between current yield and yield to maturity?

31. Give a mathematical example (different from the text illustration) of how to estimate the selling price of a bond after interest rates have changed.

32. List some advantages and disadvantages of investing in bonds.

33. Describe three situations in which it may be wise to sell bonds.

DECISION-MAKING CASES

Case 1 Two Sisters' Attitudes Toward Investments

Ellen Daniel, an English instructor in Searcy, Arkansas, has purchased several types of bonds over the years, and her total bond investment now exceeds $40,000. She prefers a variable-value and fixed-yield investment. Her sister Mary, a physician, has more than $50,000 invested in various blue-chip income common stocks in a variety of industries.

(a) Justify Ellen's attitude toward bond investments.

(b) Justify Mary's attitude toward stock investments.

Case 2 A College Student Ponders Investing in the Stock Market

Richard Ford of Athens, Georgia, has $5000 that he wants to invest in the stock market. Richard is in college on a scholarship and does not plan on needing the $5000 or any dividend income for another five years, when he plans to buy a new automobile. Richard is currently considering a stock selling for $25 with an EPS of $1.25. Last year, the company earned $900,000, of which $250,000 was paid out in dividends.

(a) What classification of common stock would you recommend to Richard? Why?

(b) Calculate the price/earnings ratio and the dividend payout ratio for this stock. Given this information and your recommendation, would this stock be an appropriate purchase for Richard? Why?

(c) Identify the components of the total return Richard might expect, and estimate how much he might expect annually from each component.

Case 3 An Aggressive Investor Seeks Rewards in the Bond Market

Karen Varcoe, who is single, works as a drug manufacturer's representative based in Riverside, California. She is an aggressive investor who believes that interest rates will drop over the next year or two because of an economic slowdown. Karen wants to profit in the bond market by buying and selling during the next several months. She has asked your advice on how to invest her $15,000.

(a) If Karen buys corporate or municipal bonds, what rating should her selections have? Why?

(b) Karen has a choice between two comparable $1000 corporate bonds: one with a coupon rate of 8.4 percent, and a convertible bond with a coupon rate of 8 percent. The convertible right allows the owner to purchase 30 shares of Running Paws common stock with a current market price of $30 over the next five years. Which bond is the better choice for Karen? What assumptions about the market price of the stock did you make?

(c) If Karen buys 15 30-year, $1000 corporate bonds with an 8.5 percent coupon rate for $960 each, what is her current yield? [Hint: Use Equation (14.2).]

(d) If market interest rates for comparable bonds drop 2 percent over the next 12 months (from 8.5 percent to 6.5 percent), what will be the approximate market price of each of Karen's bonds in (c)? [Hint: Use Equation (14.1).]

(e) Assuming rates drop 2 percent in 12 months, how much is Karen's capital gain on the $15,000 investment if she sells? How much was her current return for the two semiannual interest payments? How much was her total return, both in dollars and as an annual yield? (Ignore transaction costs.)

(f) If Karen is wrong in her projections and interest rates go up 1 percent over the year, what would be the probable market price of each of her bonds? [Hint: Use Equation (14.1).] Explain why you would advise her to sell or not to sell.

Financial Math Questions

1. A stock sells at $15 per share.

   (a) What is the EPS for the company if it has a P/E ratio of 20?

   (b) If the company's dividend yield is 5 percent, what is its dividend per share?

   (c) What is the book value of the company if the price-to-book ratio is 1.5 and it has 100,000 shares of stock outstanding?

2. What is the market price of a $1000, 20-year, 8.8 percent bond if comparable market interest rates drop to 7.0 percent?

3. What is the market price of a $1000, 20-year, 8.3 percent bond if comparable market interest rates drop to 7.0 percent?

4. What is the market price of a $1000, 20-year, 8.8 percent bond if comparable market interest rates rise to 9.6 percent?

5. What is the market price of a $1000, 20-year, 8.3 percent bond if comparable market interest rates rise to 9.6 percent?

6. What is the tax-equivalent yield of a municipal bond paying 5.4 percent for a taxpayer in the 28 percent tax bracket?

7. What is the tax-equivalent yield of a municipal bond paying 5.7 percent for a taxpayer in the 31 percent tax bracket?

8. What is the tax-equivalent yield of a corporate bond paying 8.7 percent for a taxpayer in the 28 percent tax bracket?

9. A corporate bond maturing in 20 years with a coupon rate of 8.9 percent was purchased for $980.

   (a) What is its current yield?

   (b) What will its selling price be if comparable market interest rates drop 2 percent in two years?

   (c) Calculate the bond's YTM using Equation (14.3) or the *Garman/Forgue* Web site.

10. A corporate bond maturing in 18 years with a coupon rate of 8.2 percent was purchased for $1100.

    (a) What is its current yield?

(b) Calculate the bond's YTM using Equation (14.3) or the *Garman/Forgue* Web site.

(c) What will the bond's selling price be if comparable market interest rates rise 1.5 percent in two years?

MONEY MATTERS: LIFE-CYCLE CASES

Victor and Maria Hernandez Wonder about Investing

Victor and Maria are considering making investments in stocks and bonds. They plan to invest between $8000 and $9000 every year for the next 13 years.

1. Why should Victor and Maria consider buying common stock as an investment?

2. Advise Victor and Maria on major cautions they should observe when investing in common stocks.

3. If Victor and Maria bought a stock with a market price of $50 and a beta value of 1.8, what would be the likely price of an $8000 investment after one year if the general market for stocks rose 20 percent?

4. What would the same investment be worth if the general market for stocks dropped 20 percent?

5. Advise Victor and Maria on major cautions they should observe when investing in bonds.

6. Assume that Victor and Maria bought $8000 in 13-year bonds with a coupon rate of 8 percent and that interest rates dropped to 7 percent after one year. What is the approximate current price of their bonds if they were to sell? [Hint: Use Equation (14.1) or visit the *Garman/Forgue* Web site.]

7. If inflation averages 5 percent for the next 13 years and their $8000 bond is redeemed by the issuer, how much buying power will the Hernandez family have with their $8000?

The Johnsons Want Greater Yields on Investments

Harry and Belinda Johnson have saved $6000 toward a down payment on a very expensive luxury automobile they hope to purchase in the next three to five years. Because they are not receiving a very high return on their money market account, they are seeking greater yields with bond investments. Examine the table below, which identifies eight investment alternatives, and then respond to the questions that follow.

1. What is the current yield of each investment alternative? Use Equation (14.2) or visit the *Garman/Forgue* Web site. (Write your responses in the proper column in the table.)

2. What is the yield to maturity for each investment alternative? (Write your responses in the proper column in the table.) You may calculate the YTMs using Equation (14.3) or visiting the *Garman/Forgue* Web site.

Name of Issue	Bond Denomination	Coupon Rate %	Years Until Maturity	Moody's Rating	Market Price	Current Yield	YTM
Corporate ABC	$1000	9.0	4	Aa	$ 980		
Corporate DEF	1000	9.5	20	Aa	1020		
Corporate GHI	1000	8.4	12	Baa	735		
Corporate JKL	1000	8.8	5	Aaa	990		
Corporate MNO	1000	10.1	15	B	820		
Corporate PQR	1000	6.0	11	B	450		
Treasury Note	1000	8.1	3	—	995		
Municipal Bond	1000	6.6	20	Aa	960		

3. Knowing that the Johnsons follow a moderate investment philosophy, which one of the six corporate bonds would you recommend? Why?

4. Given that the Johnsons are in the 28 percent federal marginal tax bracket, what is the tax-equivalent yield for the municipal bond choice? Should they invest in your recommendation in question 3 or in the municipal bond? Why? You may calculate tax-equivalent yields using the formulas on page 423.

5. Which three of the eight alternatives would you recommend as a group so that the Johnsons would have some protection for their $6000 because of diversification? Why do you suggest that combination?

6. Assume that the Johnsons bought all three of your recommendations in question 5. If market interest rates drop by 2 percent in two years (for example, from 9.4 percent to 7.4 percent), what are your recommendations for buying or selling each alternative? Why? Support your answer by calculating the selling price for each bond using Equation (14.1) or visiting the *Garman/Forgue* Web site.

Exploring the World Wide Web of Personal Finance

To complete these exercises, go to the *Garman/Forgue* Web site at

www.hmco.com/college/business/

Select Personal Finance. Click on the exercise link for this chapter and answer the questions that appear on the Web page.

1. Visit Quicken's Stock Search Web page. Search for stocks with a five-year price/earnings ratio growth rate exceeding 50 percent, $5 billion or more capitalization, and a P/E ratio from 0 to 10. How many companies meet these criteria? Select again using a P/E ratio from 0 to 20. How many companies meet this new criteria? Why is this list longer? Do you recognize any of the companies on either list?

2. Visit the Stock Evaluator Web site for Quicken. Type in the symbols for the following companies: Coca-Cola (KO), General Motors (GM), Microsoft (MSFT), and Disney (DIS). Evaluate the four on the basis of earnings per share, dividend yield, price/earnings ratio, and five-year earnings per share growth. What do these data suggest to you about the relative attractiveness of these companies for investors?

3. Visit the Web site for Checkfree Investment Services. Click on "quotes" to obtain current price quotes on the companies from question 2. At the right of the price quotes is a box from which you can select "price history." Which of the four has seen the best stock price appreciation over the past year?

4. Visit the Web site for the Bureau of Public Debt of the Federal Treasury Department, where you will find the results of recent auctions for Treasury notes and bonds. What do the results of auctions over the past year tell you about market expectation for movement of interest rates in the future? (Hint: Compare auction rates for bonds and notes with similar maturity periods.)

5. Visit CNN's Financial News Web site. Click on "industry watch" and select one industry sector to review. Browse through the financial news articles on that sector for information about its recent and prospective results for investors.

6. Visit the Web site for The Motley Fool. Compare the information provided in the "13 Steps to Foolish Investing" with information in this text chapter. Develop a list of five key points every beginning investor in stocks and bonds should know.

15

Investing Through Mutual Funds

O B J E C T I V E S

After reading this chapter, you should be able to:

1 Identify why people invest in mutual funds.

2 Distinguish among the four major objectives of mutual funds.

3 Classify mutual funds by portfolio.

4 List the unique benefits of mutual funds.

5 Describe the various charges and fees associated with investing in mutual funds.

6 Explain how to select a mutual fund in which to invest.

7 Recognize valid reasons for selling a mutual fund investment.

Mutual funds are the most common form of investment company in the United States. An **investment company** is a corporation, trust, or partnership in which investors with similar financial goals pool their funds to utilize professional management and to diversify their investments in securities and other investments. Spreading the risk enables an occasional loss in one investment to be offset by profits from many other investments. A **mutual fund** is an investment company that combines the funds of investors who have purchased shares of ownership in the investment company and then invests that money in a diversified portfolio of securities issued by other corporations or governments. Figure 15.1 on the following page graphically illustrates the concept of mutual funds.

This chapter examines the appeal and logic of mutual funds as an investment. We first explain why people might want to invest in a mutual fund. We then distinguish among the major objectives of mutual funds and classify them

Figure 15.1

How a Mutual Fund Works

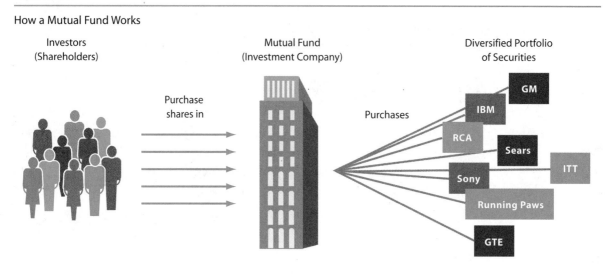

according to their portfolio holdings. Next, we discuss unique benefits of mutual funds. After describing the various fees and charges that add to the cost of investing, we summarize advantages and disadvantages of mutual funds. A number of key questions on how to go about selecting a mutual fund are addressed as well. The last section discusses when to sell shares in a mutual fund.

Reasons for Investing Through Mutual Funds

1 Identify why people invest in mutual funds.

About half of all working adults currently invest through mutual funds—the highest proportion in history. Growth in this type of investment has been spurred by several factors: newer and more attractive types of funds have been created; many funds carry few or no sales charges; some have performed much better than the average common stock; and widespread marketing efforts have been used to promote mutual funds. In addition, selecting a mutual fund through which to invest is much easier than selecting specific stocks or bonds (topics discussed in Chapter 14). In fact, it is a relatively simple task to identify a mutual fund that has investment objectives similar to your own. Experts agree that mutual funds represent appropriate investment choices for both beginning and sophisticated investors. The intelligent investor in mutual funds, using common sense and a little knowledge of the world of investments, can "perform with the pros."

The kind of mutual fund in which most people invest is called an **open-end investment company** because it is always ready to sell new shares of ownership in the investment company and to buy back previously sold shares at the fund's current market value. Today more mutual funds exist (more than 11,000) than companies listed on the New York Stock Exchange (approximately 1450), although the funds hold only about 10 percent of the nation's corporate stocks.

About 90 percent of all mutual funds are open-end funds, which are the focus of this chapter.* Shares can be purchased from the mutual fund itself, from a financial planner, from a bank, or through a brokerage firm; shares can always be sold back to the fund. Thus, no trading occurs among individual investors.

Mutual Funds Dispense Profits to Investors

All investment companies operate in a similar manner. They pool funds obtained by selling shares to investors and then make investments in particular stocks and bonds to achieve the financial goal of income or growth (or sometimes both). **Stocks** are shares of ownership in the assets and earnings of a business corporation, such as General Motors, IBM, Sears, or Running Paws Catfood Company. **Bonds** are interest-bearing negotiable certificates of long-term debt (often ten to 30 years) issued by a corporation, municipality (such as a city or state), or the federal government. For example, General Motors might sell bonds to finance the development of a new line of automobiles, and the U.S. government might sell bonds to refinance the national debt.

The challenges of security selection and portfolio management are taken on by the professional mutual fund managers. A **portfolio** comprises a collection of securities (such as stocks and bonds) and other investment alternatives chosen to achieve a particular investment goal. Management typically retains the voting rights to elect a mutual fund's board of directors, and investors pay a fee for the management service. Mutual funds, which operate as regulated investment companies, distribute virtually all of their income annually to avoid paying income tax on the earnings.

Investors Expect Dividend Income

The first type of return expected by the investor in mutual funds is **mutual fund dividends**—that is, income paid to investors out of profits earned by the mutual fund. An investor in a profitable mutual fund receives a mutual fund dividend check that represents both ordinary income dividend distributions and capital gains distributions. **Ordinary income dividend distributions** occur when the fund distributes dividend income that has been received from securities owned and interest from any net operating revenues. These distributions to the fund shareholders may be made on a monthly, quarterly, or annual basis. A **capital gains distribution** represents the net gains (capital gains minus capital losses) that a fund realizes on its sale of securities from its portfolio during the year. Capital gains distributions are usually made on an annual basis.

Because both types of distributions represent investment income to the shareholders, mutual fund investors must pay personal income taxes on such short- and/or long-term gains. Taxes on these earnings can be deferred while those amounts are kept in an IRS-qualified tax-sheltered retirement account (as

---

* A second type of mutual fund is a **closed-end investment company**, which issues a limited and fixed number of shares and does not buy them back. Thus, after the original issue is sold, the price of a share depends upon the performance of the investment trust company in particular and market conditions in general. Closed-end shares are traded much like the common stock or bonds of a corporation.

discussed in Chapter 18), and avoided when the earnings represent interest from municipal bonds (which is tax-exempt from federal income tax and sometimes from state income tax).

Investors Expect Price Appreciation

The investor in mutual funds also expects a return in the form of price appreciation. The investor hopes that the market value of the mutual fund—known as the NAV—will increase. **Net asset value (NAV)** is the current market value of one share in a mutual fund. It is calculated by adding the value of all securities in a fund's portfolio, subtracting expenses, and then dividing the total by the number of shares outstanding. A fund's accountants calculate the NAV at the end of each business day by totaling the market value of the stocks, bonds, and cash, adding in the day's worth of interest and dividends, and subtracting that day's worth of management expenses. The NAV is similar to the market price of a stock in that it rises or falls with the success of the investments of the mutual fund company. A mutual fund always sells and buys back its shares at the NAV, plus or minus any sales charges or fees. The business section of most newspapers publishes mutual funds NAVs every day.

For example, if your mutual fund owns IBM and General Electric common stocks and the market values of those two companies increase, the rising prices will push up the worth of the mutual fund. The increased value of the underlying securities is directly reflected in the net asset value of fund shares. Technically, such increases in the NAV represent **unrealized capital gains** because at this point they are only "paper profits" on the accounts of the mutual fund.* Logically, the mutual fund company desires to remain invested in a number of quality stocks and bonds whose values are still growing. These unrealized capital gains, when not distributed, will continue to increase the mutual fund's NAV. The individual mutual funds investor profits from the gains in the NAV by selling shares after the NAV has risen. When realized, such gains are considered taxable income to individual investors (again unless the money is kept in an IRS-qualified tax-sheltered retirement account, discussed in Chapter 18).†

The Different Objectives of Mutual Funds

> **2** Distinguish among the four major objectives of mutual funds.

A mutual fund's objectives must be stated in its **prospectus.** This legally prescribed written disclosure to the Securities and Exchange Commission (SEC) and prospective investors details pertinent operational and financial facts about a corporation, including the experience of its management, its financial status, any anticipated legal matters that could affect the company, and potential risks

---

*   When such gains are "realized" by the mutual fund company, they are paid to fund investors as capital gains distributions. Note also that when a fund pays a capital gain distribution, the fund's NAV is reduced accordingly. If no distribution occurs, the NAV is not reduced, and shareholders do not have a tax liability.

†   The capital gain, if any, will consist of the difference between the **basis** on the shares redeemed and the amount of the redemption. The basis is the price paid for the shares, plus all reinvested dividends and capital gains distributions.

TAX Considerations & Consequences — *Mutual Funds*

Mutual funds investors should think about two possible tax consequences before purchasing or selling.

First, unlike stocks that incur a taxable event only when shares are sold or a dividend is paid, mutual fund investors have tax liabilities every year, regardless of whether they sold shares. This occurs because mutual funds are required to distribute the bulk of the capital gains, along with dividend or interest income. Thus, when considering investing in a mutual fund, especially toward the end of the calendar year, you should check with the mutual fund company about any planned year-end capital gains distributions. If the fund expects to make a significant payout, consider waiting until just after the distribution, known as the record date, before making your investment. On the **record date**, investors who own shares receive the capital gains distribution. If you invest before this date, two things may occur: (1) you will owe income taxes on the capital gains distribution even though it is just a paper gain, and (2) the fund's share price typically will drop by an amount equal to the payout.

Second, when selling mutual funds shares, take the time to review which shares might be the best ones to sell. Assuming good recordkeeping, you might specifically sell those shares that result in the lowest tax liability. For example, you might want to sell losers and take those capital losses against other funds sold for a profit. If you do not know the prices paid for various shares, you will have to use the **average cost basis method** to determine capital gain or loss, where an investor uses the average price paid for all of his or her shares. Mutual fund companies can provide that figure.

You do *not* have to be concerned about these mutual fund income tax liability possibilities if your transactions are made within a tax-qualified retirement plan, pertain to tax-sheltered mutual fund purchases, or involve a relatively small number of shares that will result in minimal taxes.

of investing in the corporation. Such a prospectus also identifies one of four major objectives for the fund: (1) income, (2) long-term growth, (3) growth and income, and (4) balanced. A fund's objectives should reflect the individual investor's investment objectives, time horizon, and tolerance for risk.

Funds with a Current Income Objective

A mutual fund that has income as its primary focus aims almost exclusively to earn a high level of current interest and dividends from the investments in its portfolio. Long-term capital gains represent a secondary consideration. Such a mutual fund would purchase investment-quality corporate bonds, preferred stocks, and blue-chip income stocks. It typically provides the investor with a high income dividend and very little likelihood of long-term price appreciation in its NAV.

Funds with a Long-Term Growth Objective

A mutual fund with a growth objective focuses on long-term growth in the value of the securities (price appreciation) held in its portfolio rather than a flow of dividends. Such a fund buys and holds the common stocks of growing companies whose earnings are expected to increase at a better-than-average rate under all economic conditions. These firms (such as Wal-Mart, Microsoft, and Coca-Cola) tend not to declare cash dividends but instead reinvest most of their earnings to facilitate future growth. Stocks of such companies generally increase in price over long periods of time, which consequently pushes up the mutual fund's NAV. Funds with a growth objective strive to provide a very good total return for the investor who is willing to accept some risk. The return should take the form of small income dividends and long-term appreciation in NAV.

Funds with a Growth and Income Objective

A mutual fund whose objective is a combination of growth and income aims for an above-average return—that is, one not as low as that offered by funds with an income objective nor as high as that offered by funds with a growth objective. The portfolio of such a fund would include a variety of securities, with an emphasis on common stocks. The return should take the form of some income dividends and long-term price appreciation in the fund's NAV.

Funds with a Balanced Objective

Mutual funds with a balanced objective typically emphasize preservation of the invested capital along with moderate growth and income. The objectives of growth and income vary according to economic times, but stability remains a paramount concern in a portfolio of stocks and bonds (typically held in a 60:40 ratio). The portfolio might include many blue-chip growth stocks and high-quality bonds to ensure a flow of income. The return should take the form of some income dividends and long-term price appreciation in its NAV.

Classification of Mutual Funds According to Their Portfolios

3 Classify mutual funds by portfolio.

The thousands of different mutual funds available mean that some fund will fit almost every investor's needs. Each mutual fund tries to achieve its investment objectives by selecting securities from a wide range of investment opportunities. Sometimes funds are classified according to the four objectives described earlier, but they may also be categorized on the basis of their portfolio holdings.

Common Stock Funds

Many diversified mutual funds include only common stocks in their portfolios. The primary objective of a **common stock fund** is to increase its net asset value over the long term through price appreciation of the securities in its portfolio. Several types of common stock funds pursue this goal.

Aggressive Growth Funds An **aggressive growth fund**, also widely known as a **maximum capital gains fund**, seeks the greatest long-term capital appreciation and incurs the greatest fluctuation in the price of its shares. It does not emphasize income dividends, but relies primarily on NAV appreciation to produce a return. Holdings could involve small companies whose share prices are more volatile than the norm, such as rapidly growing companies, firms developing new technologies, and other emerging businesses with good long-term profit potential, located both in the United States and abroad. Such funds often employ high-risk investment techniques, such as borrowing money for leverage, short selling, hedging, and options (see Chapter 17). Popular maximum capital gains funds include Kaufmann, Enterprise Capital Appreciation, Thomson Opportunity B, and AIM Constellation.

Growth Funds **Growth funds** seek long-term capital appreciation without undue risk, although they also experience substantial price fluctuation. They take a more conventional approach to investing than aggressive growth funds, buying stock in both small and large, longer-established and perhaps better-known companies that pay few or no dividends. Popular growth funds include Janus Twenty, Berger 100, Twentieth Century Growth, and Fidelity Magellan.

Value Funds A **value fund** specializes in stocks whose prices appear to be low (those with low price-to-book or price-to-earnings ratios), based on the logic that such stocks are currently out of favor and underpriced. The underappreciated common stocks in a value fund are expected to benefit from a growing economy, especially during the early stages of an economic recovery. Some experts say that the term "value fund," rather than describing a type of fund, actually refers to a manager's style of investing because he or she purposefully seeks out underpriced stocks. Mutual funds that are currently described as value funds include Quest for Value Small Capitalization Fund, Royce Premier Fund, Founders Discovery Fund, and Legg Mason Special Investment Trust.

Growth and Income Funds A **growth and income fund** invests in common stocks that pay reasonable dividends, as well as stocks from lesser-known firms with strong growth potential, thereby combining expected growth with a strong income foundation. Growth and income funds should entail less risk than aggressive growth and growth funds; not surprisingly, such funds are quite popular among investors. Examples of growth and income funds include AIM Charter, Cigna Value, SteinRoe Prime Equities, and Vanguard Quantitative.

Small Company Funds A **small company fund** (also called a **small cap** fund) specializes in investing in lesser-known common stocks that pay little, if any, dividends but offer strong growth potential. Examples of popular small company funds include Twentieth Century Ultra Investors, Alger Small Capitalization, Hartwell Emerging Growth, and Robertson Stephens Emerging Growth.

Sector Funds A **sector fund** heavily invests in common stocks from one industry or one portion of the economy. Of course, investing in only one sector increases risks as well as potential returns—even in a diversified portfolio. Popular sector funds include Vanguard Special Health Portfolio, Fidelity Select Biotechnology, and Fidelity Technology.

Global and International Funds A **global fund** invests in stocks and/or bonds of companies listed on U.S. and foreign exchanges. Popular global funds include Harbor International, Vanguard World-International Growth, and GT Japan

Growth. **International funds** hold only foreign stocks; in addition, some such funds focus on a single country or geographic region. Examples of diversified international funds include Van Eck Work Income, MFS Worldwide Governments, and Merrill Lynch Global B. **Emerging market funds** seek out stocks listed on the relatively illiquid and inefficient stock exchanges of newly industrialized countries and those evolving away from socialistic economies.

Index Funds   An **index fund** is composed of a large number of securities carefully structured to match, as closely as possible, the total return performance of a standard group of securities, or "target index." The S&P 500 is an example of a target index. The return in an index fund is expected to equal that of all stocks listed in the index, which offers a benefit as the market rises. Market growth is, of course, the long-term trend; historically, stocks have provided an average annual return of about 11.2 percent. Popular index funds include the Wilshire 5000 Index and Vanguard 500 Portfolio. More than one-fourth of all equity funds are index funds.

Balanced Funds

Balanced funds seek to preserve **principal** (the money initially invested), provide current income, and provide moderate long-term growth of NAV. The funds invest in a mixtue of bonds, preferred stocks, and common stocks. Their investment policy calls for the fund to maintain a balance of such holdings and vary them according to economic conditions. Balanced funds include Twentieth Century Balanced, Pasadena Balanced Return, Equitable Balance B, and Kemper Investment Portfolio Total Return.

Bond Funds

Bond funds aim to earn current income without undue risk and pay ordinary income dividend distributions. The term "bond fund" is actually a misnomer because these funds usually hold a portfolio of bonds and other investments,

The Total Return for Various Types of Stock Mutual Funds Is about the Same

New data from the Investment Company Institute reveal that it makes very little difference which type of stock mutual fund in which you invest over the long term. Over time (e.g., ten years), the average annual returns for different types of diversified stock funds (growth, domestic equity, growth and income, equity income, and balanced) converge at around 11 percent (11.2 percent according to Ibbot- son Associates). The only secret to such a good return is to remain patient and keep investing. Returns over one, three, and five years vary widely, but over the long term the returns of major categories of diversified mutual funds are roughly the same. The moral: put your cash into several highly rated stock mutual funds and relax. Ten years later your money will have doubled or tripled.

such as preferred stocks and common stocks that pay high dividends. Short-term bond funds feature little fluctuation in price and a moderate return; intermediate- to long-term bond funds provide more income accompanied by moderate fluctuations in price. In addition, some bond funds specialize in investing in riskier, high-yielding bonds that are popularly known as **junk bonds.** Selected bond funds include Pacific Horizon Capital Income, Concord Income Convertible, Vanguard Convertible Securities, and American Capital Harbor A.

Municipal bond (tax-exempt) funds attempt to earn current tax-exempt income by investing solely in municipal bonds issued by cities, states, and various districts and political subdivisions. The interest income earned on these bonds is exempt from federal personal income taxes. Popular municipal bond funds include General Municipal Bond and Financial Tax-Free Inc. Shares.

Specialty Funds

Specialty funds have been created to serve almost every investment need that requires both concentration and diversification in a field. Popular specialty funds include Franklin Utilities, National Aviation and Technology, and Dean Witter Natural Resources Development. **Mutual fund funds,** such as Vanguard Star, Rightime Fund, and FundTrust Aggressive Growth, earn a return by investing in other mutual funds, thereby providing extensive diversification. **Precious metals and gold funds** seek long-term capital appreciation by investing in securities associated with gold, silver, and other precious metals. Popular precious metal funds include Enterprise Precious Metals, Vanguard Specialized Gold, and Keystone Precious Metals. **Mortgage funds** invest in mortgage-backed securities, such as Ginnie Mae issues. Examples of mortgage funds include Alliance Mortgage Securities Income and American Capital Federal Mortgage.

Money Market Funds

A **money market fund,** also called a **money market mutual fund (MMMF),** invests exclusively in cash and cash equivalents (debt securities). Such funds specialize in securities that have very short-term maturities, always less than one year. The average maturity for the portfolio of investments cannot, by law, exceed 90 days for an MMMF. Government regulations further require that MMMFs place 99 percent of their investments in securities that receive the highest ratings from outside ranking services.

This strategy reduces price swings in the value of the MMMF investments; as a result, the fund maintains a virtually constant share value ($1 per share) and only the yield varies. Fund assets include Treasury bills and notes, certificates of deposit, commercial paper, and repurchase agreements. Thus, the investor's principal incurs almost no risk. By staggering the maturities of the securities held in the portfolio, the MMMF can earn the current cost of money on its investments. Some such funds invest in only tax-exempt securities, so the investor avoids federal income taxes on any dividends. Most large mutual fund families offer MMMFs, including Dreyfus, Lexington, and American Century. Money market funds represent an important part of most investors' cash management plans, as discussed in Chapter 5, because they provide a convenient place to keep money while awaiting other investment opportunities.

About Check Writing on Money Market Fund Accounts

Most money market mutual funds permit you to withdraw money by writing special checks drawn on your account, thereby acting as high-yielding cash management accounts. Usually, checks must be written in amounts no smaller than $100 or $200, and only a limited number of checks may be written per month. Writing a check on a money market fund account essentially redeems the number of shares necessary to honor the check. For example, if Conglomerate Cat and Dog Food Mutual Fund shares had a net asset value of $10 and you wrote a check for $500, the fund would redeem 50 shares ($10 × 50 = $500).

Unique Benefits of Mutual Funds

4   List the unique benefits of mutual funds.

Mutual funds have distinct features that make this form of investing both unique and investor-friendly.

Automatic Reinvestment

Unlike most other investment alternatives, mutual funds permit **automatic income reinvestment.** This provision allows for the automatic reinvestment of ordinary income dividend distributions and capital gains distributions to buy additional shares of the fund. Fractional shares are purchased as needed. More than three-fourths of mutual fund shareholders have their income reinvested, which greatly compounds share ownership. Figure 15.2 illustrates the tremendously positive results that can be obtained by reinvesting all dividends and capital gains distributions.

Most funds permit you to reinvest dividend income without paying any commission, and those companies that assess sales charges on reinvested dividends should be avoided. Fund policies related to this process will be described in the prospectus.

IRS-Qualified Tax-Sheltered Retirement Accounts

Most mutual funds provide programs that "qualify" as tax-deferred ways to invest money for retirement and, accordingly, are registered with the IRS. Depending on eligibility qualifications, you can put thousands of dollars into a mutual fund each year, deduct the amount from your taxable income, watch the fund grow, and pay no income taxes on any of the profits until funds are withdrawn during retirement. Such programs include individual retirement accounts (IRAs), 403(b), 401(k), 457, Salary Reduction Simplified Employee Pension Plans,

Figure 15.2

The Value of Automatic Reinvestment of Income (Dividends and Capital Gains)

An initial investment of $10,000 grew to almost $29,000 in ten years (because the value of the underlying securities pushed up the net asset value).

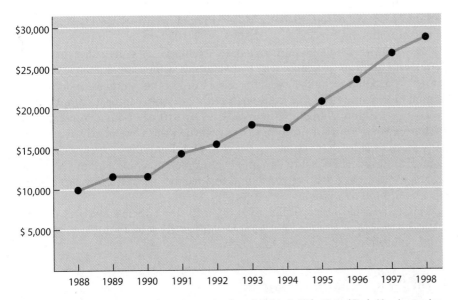

Source: Used with the permission of Morningstar, Inc. from *Principia Pro™ for Mutual Finds.* Morningstar, Inc., 2/28/99. *www.morningstar.net,* (312) 696-6000. Data based on more than 1000 stock and bond mutual funds in operation over the past ten years.

and Keogh retirement programs. (Chapter 18 discusses these mechanisms in retirement planning.*)

Easy Purchase and Sale

Shares in an open-end mutual fund can be liquidated almost immediately simply by communicating with the company via telephone, wire, or facsimile, or in writing. Each share is redeemed at the closing price—that is, the NAV—at the end of the trading day.

After you have opened an account with a mutual fund company, you can easily buy and sell shares by telephone. To open an account, you fill out a brief application form and forward the initial investment, which generally must be a minimum amount of $250 to $2000. You can then call a toll-free number—where operators record your verbal instructions—to order the mutual fund company to electronically transfer funds from one account to another or to and from your local financial institution.

*   Another unique benefit is that mutual funds purchased within an IRS-qualified tax-sheltered retirement account contain a **beneficiary designation clause.** The shareholder can name a beneficiary so that in the event of death, the proceeds go to the beneficiary without going through probate. (The delays and expenses of probate are discussed in Chapter 19.)

Electronic funds transfers (EFT) allow shareholders to purchase and redeem shares of a fund via the telephone. In addition, mutual fund investors may have periodic investment payments automatically forwarded from checking or savings accounts to the mutual fund company using EFT. Wire transfers also can be made to and from a mutual fund company. Both the mutual fund and the financial institution send written notification of each transaction, and automatic withdrawals may be stopped at any time. EFT transactions eliminate delays associated with mailing checks.

A **switching privilege** (also called an **exchange** or **conversion privilege**) permits mutual fund shareholders, if their needs or objectives change, to swap shares on a dollar-for-dollar basis for shares in another mutual fund within a mutual fund family. Transfer from one fund to another can be accomplished at no cost or for only a small fee, typically $5 or $10 per transaction, called an **exchange fee.** A **mutual fund family** exists when the same management company (such as Fidelity Investments, Dreyfus, or T. Rowe Price) operates a variety of mutual funds. The Fidelity Group, for example, offers more than 180 funds, ranging from an aggressive-growth fund to a technology sector fund to a municipal bond fund to a money market fund.

Payroll transfer plans permit investors to instruct their employers to automatically forward a specified portion of each paycheck to a mutual fund. Some funds permit transfers directly from Social Security checks.

Recordkeeping and Reporting

In addition to a prospectus, mutual fund companies must send shareholders periodic reports and annual tax statements. This information helps keep the investor apprised of fund performance. **Confirmation statements** (which indicate the number of shares owned and the value of the holdings) must also be forwarded to the mutual fund shareholder every time a transaction occurs in the account. These confirmation statements provide evidence of ownership as well. Investors in a mutual fund family receive **consolidated statements** that report all of their holdings and transactions in the mutual fund family. Recordkeeping is a vital part of mutual fund investments because taxable gains and losses must be carefully calculated for income tax purposes (unless such investments are made within an IRS-qualified tax-sheltered retirement account, discussed in Chapter 18).

Collateral for Loans

Mutual fund shares may be used as collateral for loans from banks and other lenders. Money invested in mutual fund shares that are kept within some IRS-qualified tax-sheltered retirement accounts (discussed in Chapter 18) may be borrowed directly from the trustee (often the investor's employer) of the account.

Withdrawal Plans

All mutual funds make various types of **withdrawal plans** (also called **systematic withdrawal plans**) available to shareholders who want a periodic income

Children Can Invest Through a Mutual Fund

Many parents and grandparents find that mutual funds are a perfect gift for savvy students who want to learn more about saving and investing. Most mutual funds reduce the minimum investment to $1000, $500, or even $250 for a **custodial account,** where assets are held in the name of an adult on behalf of a child. These accounts are permitted under the federal Uniform Gifts to Minors Act. Many mutual funds also lower their minimums for

investors who agree to invest small amounts regularly, to perhaps as little as $20 per month. Even mutual fund gift certificates are available. As investment objectives change, young investors can switch among investment alternatives within a mutual fund family. The child is responsible for the payment of income taxes on mutual fund dividend income in excess of $700 (see Chapter 3).

from their mutual fund investments. To be eligible for such a plan, your investment usually must have a total net asset value of at least $5000. In addition, each withdrawal must be at least $50. The firm forwards the amounts to you (or to anyone you designate) at regular intervals (monthly or quarterly). You can take your funds out of a mutual fund using one of four methods: (1) by taking a set dollar amount each month, (2) by cashing in a set number of shares each month, (3) by taking the current income as cash, or (4) by taking a portion of the asset growth.

The Costs of Investing Through Mutual Funds

5 Describe the various charges and fees associated with investing in mutual funds.

The costs of investing in mutual funds become more complicated every year. Mutual funds charge investors a variety of fees, some of which can be avoided.

Management Fees

All mutual funds charge a **management fee,** which is an annual assessment for operating the mutual fund. The professional managers who operate mutual funds are compensated for their investment expertise and managerial abilities with a percentage of the investment company's assets as specified in the articles of incorporation. Because the management fee is always figured as an annual percentage of the assets in the mutual fund, it is part of what is called an **expense ratio,** although other marketing costs are contained in this figure. Depending on the size and type of fund, management fees typically range from 0.4 to 1.9 percent of the fund's assets and are assessed annually; management fees for diversified stock funds average less than 1.4 percent and fees for index funds are usually less than 0.7 percent. Avoid funds with high management fees, especially since research consistently shows that low-expense funds outperform those with high administrative costs by at least 1.5 percentage points annually. Low expenses stack the odds of future fund performance in the investor's favor.

Load Funds

Mutual funds can be classified as to whether they have a **sales charge** or **commission**, also called a **load.** This sales commission is charged whenever a person invests in a particular mutual fund. Mutual funds that assess such sales charges are called **load funds**, and they are generally sold by brokerage firms, banks, and financial planners.

Load funds sold to the public by a broker, banker, or financial planner require payment of a sales commission on the amount invested at the time of purchase. The commission—typically 5.5 to 8.5 percent—is called a **front-end load** because it is paid at the time of each purchase. For example, assume that you have discussed the investment potential of the Conglomerate Cat and Dog Food Mutual Fund with a salesperson. After examining the prospectus, you decide to invest $10,000. Because this load fund charges a commission of 8.5 percent (the maximum permitted by the Securities and Exchange Commission), the salesperson receives $850 ($10,000 × 0.085). As a result, only $9150 is actually available to earn dividends and capital gains. This commission is much higher than stock transaction costs, which are usually about 2 percent.

The sales charge may be shown either as the stated commission or as a percentage of the amount invested. The stated commission (8.5 percent in our example) is always somewhat misleading. In contrast, the percentage of the amount invested is a more accurate figure because it is based on the actual money invested and working. A stated commission of 8.5 percent actually amounts to 9.3 percent of the amount invested: $10,000 − $9150 = $850; $850 ÷ $9150 = 9.3%. If you want to invest a full $10,000, you will need to pay out $10,930 [$10,930 − ($10,930 × 8.5 percent) = $10,000].

Investments of $10,000 or more often receive a discount on the load. So-called **low-load funds** may have only a 1 to 3 percent sales charge. These funds may also be sold by brokers, but are sometimes sold via mail and through retailers in shopping centers. About half of all mutual funds levy a load.

No-Load Funds

A mutual fund that does not assess a sales charge at the time of the investment purchase is called a **no-load fund.** These mutual fund companies let people invest directly, without the services of a broker, banker, or financial planner. In general, no charge is assessed when you sell a mutual fund. No-load mutual funds sell their shares at net asset value without the addition of sales charges, but the SEC allows such funds to be called "no-load" even if they assess a "service fee" of 0.25 percent or less. The fee is supposedly used for ongoing personal service and/or account maintenance, although no-load funds traditionally do not employ sales personnel or charge fees. Interested investors simply seek out advertisements for these funds in financial newspapers and magazines and buy shares directly from the company. Many no-load funds are described and analyzed in publications such as *Business Week, Consumer Reports, Forbes, Fortune, Kiplinger's Personal Finance Magazine,* and *Money.*

Hidden Fees

About 60 percent of all no-load mutual funds and many load funds charge **hidden fees.*** These charges, commissions, and other costs often are not apparent to the mutual fund investor, but reduce the fund's anticipated total return. The negative impact of such fees is illustrated in Table 15.1.

Deferred Load Fees The most common alternative to a front-end load is a **contingent deferred sales charge**, also known as a **back-end load.** This sales commission is imposed if an investor redeems shares within a specified number of years after purchase (often five or six years). Typically the fee declines 1 percentage point for each year the investor owns the fund. For example, a fund might charge a 6 percent fee if an investor redeems the shares within one year of purchase, and then steadily decline on an annual basis, until it reaches zero after six years or less.

Redemption Fees A **redemption fee** (or **exit fee**) is a charge the investor pays on any shares sold back to the fund; the fee typically disappears after the investment has been held for six months or a year. This increasingly common fee is designed to discourage frequent trading in and out of particular mutual funds. The fee usually represents 1 percent of the value of the shares redeemed. Long-term investors should not shy away from funds with redemption fees that disappear after a year.

12b-1 Fees The most common charge assessed to shareholders is a **12b-1 fee** (named for the Securities and Exchange Commission rule that permits the charge), which is an annual charge that pays for advertising, marketing, distribution, and promotional costs of the fund. The 12b-1 fees are also known as a **distribution fees.** Such charges pay for items like advertising and sales brochures,

Table 15.1

The Effect of Loads and Fees on Mutual Fund Returns
(Estimated figures based on a $10,000 investment assuming a 10 percent gain each year)

Years	No-Load*	3% Front-End Load	8.5% Front-End Load	5.5% Front-End Load with 0.25% 12b-1	5% Back-End Load with 1% 12b-1†
1	$10,890	$10,560	$9,960	$10,260	$10,280
3	12,900	12,500	11,800	12,150	12,230
5	15,320	14,860	14,020	14,380	14,460
7	18,170	17,620	16,620	18,000	16,930
10	23,470	22,770	21,480	22,800	21,200

* 1 percent annual management fee.
† A declining redemption fee of 5 percent the first year that goes to zero after the fifth year.

* Technically, the existence and amount of any and all fees assessed by a mutual fund are not hidden, as they must be disclosed in the fund prospectus.

as well as **trailing commissions**, which are compensation fees paid to salespersons for months or years in the future. Although the funds do not call 12b-1 fees "loads" because they are not charged up front, they act just like loads.

A 12b-1 fee is actually a "perpetual sales load" because it is assessed on the investment, as well as on reinvested dividends, every year, forever. If you pay 1 percent per year in 12b-1 fees for a mutual fund in which you invest for ten years, you will be giving up nearly 10 percent of your initial investment amount in trailing commissions. Such commissions can prove quite costly for the shareholder over a period of years. In general, you would be well-advised to invest in a load fund rather than pay 12b-1 assessments if you plan to own the fund for more than five years. The SEC caps 12b-1 fees at 0.75 percent, although it permits a 0.25 percent "service fee," which brings the total cap to 1 percent. Some funds stop assessing 12b-1 fees after four to eight years.

Disclosure of Fees

To assist the investing public, the SEC requires that a mutual fund's prospectus include a **standardized expense table** in its first three pages that describes and illustrates its fees projected over five years. It estimates hypothetical total costs that a mutual fund investor would pay on a $1000 investment that earns 5 percent annually and is withdrawn after ten years. Funds are required to report projected returns for periods of one, three, five, and ten years. The data in a table do not offer an exact representation of past charges; rather, they illustrate the effect of all sales costs (front- and back-end), management fees, and other expenses that an investor would have to pay. Such tables make it easier to compare fees and expenses across various mutual funds.

 About Flexible Pricing of Mutual Funds

A growing number of mutual fund companies now offer different classes of shares in the same portfolio. Mutual fund investors, therefore, face a choice of fee structures—the only difference among the classes. Of course, each class has a different NAV because each charges different fees. The distinct classes give investors a clear choice about the type of commission they will pay.

Class A shares have a front-end load (typically 2.5 to 5.5 percent, most of which goes to the salesperson who sold the fund) and possibly a low 12b-1 distribution fee (in the 0.25 to 0.35 percent range). **Class B shares** have no up-front sales load, but do assess a contingent deferred sales fee if the shares are sold within a certain number of years, plus a 12b-1 distribution fee (typically around 0.75 percent). After a certain amount of time, typically six to eight years, many funds automatically convert B shares to A shares, which carry the lower 12b-1 fees. **Class C shares**, also called **level-load shares** or **pay-as-you-go shares**, have only a permanent 12b-1 distribution fee (typically 1 percent).

Such classifications are bound to cause confusion because none of these is truly a "no load" fund. In addition, with three possible classes for each existing mutual fund, the total number of choices is over 11,000. Of course, if you want to have all of your money working for you, invest in no-load mutual fund shares.

Regulations compel stock and bond mutual fund operators to present standardized performance calculations when reporting returns. In advertisements, fund performance may be quoted in terms of yield or total return. Such data on performance are based on historical results and, of course, do not indicate future results. According to SEC regulations, the **yield of a mutual fund** must be expressed as the rate of income the fund earns on its investments as a percentage of the fund's share price. A fund that has been in operation less than one year must disclose its total return since inception. All figures must be adjusted to reflect the impact of loads and fees.

Which Is Better, a Load or No-Load Fund?

The sales commissions charged by load funds indisputably reduce total returns. When investment results are adjusted for the impact of sales charges, no-load mutual funds have an initial advantage because the investor has more money at work. In general, the shorter the time period, the greater the negative impact of loads on the total return for the mutual fund investor. About half of the highest-performing growth-oriented funds are no- or low-load funds.

The Advantages and Disadvantages of Open-End Mutual Funds

As you consider investing in open-end mutual funds, you should review their advantages and disadvantages, as listed below:

Advantages

- The variety of families of funds and specific funds available makes it fairly easy to choose a fund that matches your investment objectives.

- The switching privilege within a mutual fund family permits easy exchange if your investment objectives change.

- No-load funds put all of your money to work.

- Mutual funds can be used to invest through various tax-deferred retirement plans.

- You carry less financial risk because the fund diversifies investments.

Disadvantages

- Contingent deferred sales charges make it difficult to determine the better-performing companies.

- Hidden fees often reduce the annual return to investors. In addition, management fees may exceed 1 percent of the assets of the funds annually.

- Most no-load funds must be sought out and researched by the investor because they usually are not heavily advertised.

- Income taxes generally must be paid on dividends as well as capital gains distributions (unless the money is kept in an IRS-qualified tax-sheltered retirement account, discussed in Chapter 18).

- The return on the average mutual fund is 1 to 2 percent less than the total yield possible on the average performance of common stocks.

The hidden loads associated with gradually declining redemption fees, 12b-1 fees, and excessive management fees do not necessarily buy better management. Over time, steep costs can dampen the total return. Overall, up-front load charges are more costly to the investor in the short run (less than five years), and annual 12b-1 charges are more costly over the long run. People who decide to investigate mutual funds on their own usually invest in no-load funds.

Research shows that people who buy funds with the aid of a commission-charging broker, banker, or planner are less likely to bail out and sell when markets become unstable. More patient investors generally realize a better return than those who try to time the market by buying and selling frequently. Load mutual funds are typically kept by investors twice as long as by no-load investors (four or more years versus two or more years). Moreover, long-term investors earn better returns than those who trade often.

Strategies for Selecting a Mutual Fund

| 6 | Explain how to select a mutual fund in which to invest. |

Selecting a mutual fund involves gathering information and comparing the performance of various funds. Fortunately, a tremendous amount of objective information is available to help in your decision making.

Match Your Goals

Your first task is to match your interpretation of a mutual fund's objectives with your own investment philosophy (conservative, moderate, or aggressive) and investment goals. Figure 15.3 illustrates the general risk–return trade-off for various types of funds that have different objectives. To realize one specific objective (such as preservation of capital), you must usually sacrifice another objective (such as appreciation of capital). **Preservation of capital** is similar to freedom from financial risk; it also can be defined in terms of relative performance when the value of your shares in a declining market does not fall as much as the values of other shares.

Locate Sources of Comparative Performance Data

Current information about mutual funds is available from a great number of useful services. When comparing the track records of mutual funds, investors should focus on three factors: expenses, volatility, and past performance. To compare funds on a consistent basis, you might want to use the figures of only one of the investment publications mentioned below.

The Financial Press   The most useful news publications are the *Wall Street Journal (www.wsj.com)* (the Friday edition provides mutual fund performance measures), *Barron's, Investor's Business Daily,* and the business section of newspapers, such as *The New York Times* and *USA Today.* In addition, a number of on-line news and quote services are priced for the small investor, including Compu-Serve, Dow Jones News/Retrieval—Private Investor Edition, Farcast, Personal Journal, Quotecom, and Reuters Money Network.

Figure 15.3

The Risk–Return Trade-Offs of Mutual Funds

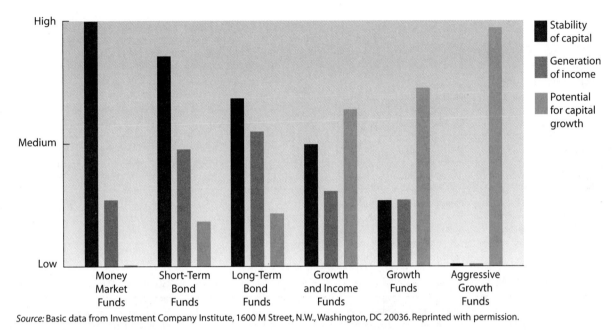

Source: Basic data from Investment Company Institute, 1600 M Street, N.W., Washington, DC 20036. Reprinted with permission.

Magazines that Rate Mutual Funds Magazines that are extremely helpful in comparing performance over time include *Business Week, Consumer Reports, Forbes, Fortune, Kiplinger's Personal Finance Magazine, Money,* and *Worth.* The late August issue of *Forbes,* the October issue of *Money,* the late February issue of *Business Week,* and the September issue of *Kiplinger's Personal Finance Magazine* feature comprehensive examinations of the performance of numerous mutual funds.

Specialized Mutual Fund Investment Publications A number of specialized publications examine mutual funds in considerable detail; these resources are often available in large libraries. Among the best for ranking funds by total return over long periods of time are *Morningstar Mutual Funds, Morningstar No-Load Funds, Mutual Funds Update, Investment Companies Yearbook, Johnson's Investment Company Charts, IBC/Donoghue's Mutual Funds Almanac, Standard & Poor's/ Lipper Mutual Fund Profiles,* and *The Value Line Mutual Fund Survey.* Moody's Investment Service now rates mutual funds.

Data from specialized mutual fund investment publications are very informative for the potential investor. Dozens of newsletters that specialize in mutual funds are available as well.

Interpret Comparative Performance Information over Time

Publications that offer comparative performance information about mutual funds generally rank each fund according to one-, three-, five-, and ten-year

Table 15.2

Mutual Fund Performance

	Load	OPI	Trading Style	Volatility Grade			Returns			
				Down-side	Overall	1998 Down-Market	10-year (%)	5-year (%)	3-year (%)	1998 (%)
Firstar Growth and Income Institutional	no load	86.5	LV/MV	B+	B+	B+	—	176.8	105.0	22.76
Forum Investors Bond	low load	77.5	—	B+	A	B	—	39.7	25.7	6.13
Investment Company of America	load	82.0	LV/LG	B+	B+	B+	390.6%	149.2	90.5	22.94
T. Rowe Price Dividend Growth	no load	80.6	LV/MV	A	A	B+	—	153.8	88.6	15.04
Transamerica Premier Balanced	no load	77.4	LG/MG	—	C+	A	—	—	101.8	29.30
UAM FMA Small Company	no load	53.6	MV/SV	C	B	B	—	108.9	73.6	−2.03
Vanguard 500 Index	no load	88.3	LG/LV	C+	C+	C+	471.5%	192.7	110.5	28.62
Vanguard Bond Index Total Bond	no load	85.7	—	C+	C+	C+	136.8%	41.6	23.1	8.59

Trading Style abbreviations: LG=Large-cap growth, LV=large-cap value, MG=mid-cap growth, MV=mid-cap value, SV=small-cap value.
Source: Copyright, February 1, 1999, *U.S. News & World Report.* Visit us at our Web site *www.usnews.com* for additional information.

performance. For example, *U.S. News & World Report* uses **OPI** (**overall performance index**) as a measure of investment returns and volatility compared to similar funds. *Kiplinger's Personal Finance Magazine* provides a **volatility ranking** for mutual funds. Its system measures the volatility of a fund's results on a scale of 1 (least volatile) to 10 (most volatile), indicating how much it could decline in a falling market or increase in a rising market relative to other mutual funds. High volatility suggests greater long-term rewards and a greater-than-normal risk of short-term losses during economic downturns. Conservative investors can avoid the most volatile stock funds, while aggressive investors might seek them out.

Consider a Fund's Long- and Short-Term Performance A complication in comparing performance arises when distinctions are drawn between long- and short-term performance. Some funds have operated for less than a decade, whereas some older funds may have changed managers, grown substantially, and modified their investment styles. Long-term investors usually focus on a fund's long-term performance.

Consider the Size of the Fund The size of the mutual fund is important because smaller funds (those that have less than $100 million in assets to invest) have greater flexibility than more stable, larger funds. For example, Fidelity Investment's enormous $80 billion Magellan Fund owns one million or more shares in dozens of major corporations; consequently, its buying and selling decisions can

In 3 years, $1000 grew to...	Expense Ratio	Assets (billions)	Telephone
$2050	0.87	$0.506	800 982-8909
$1210	0.70	$0.083	800 953-6786
$1795	0.56	$46.840	800 421-9900
$1886	0.80	$1.260	800 225-5132
$2018	1.45	$0.054	800 892-7587
$1736	1.03	$0.218	877 828-5465
$2105	0.19	$69.550	800 635-1511
$1231	0.20	$7.550	800 635-1511

seriously affect overall trading in those stocks and may inhibit Magellan from making decisive moves.

Consider Fund Performance in Up and Down Markets
While long-term investors may seek out funds that have performed well over the past several years, it is also useful to compare the performance of mutual funds in up (rising) and down (declining) markets. A **down market** or an **up market** (when prices of securities are generally falling or rising) usually lasts six months to a year—sometimes even longer. *Money* magazine uses its "risk-adjusted grade" to rate each fund's return in light of the risks it took over the previous five years. Table 15.2 contains recent performance data for a number of growth and maximum growth mutual funds from *Money* magazine.

Read Prospectuses and Annual Reports

An **annual report** is a published summary of the financial activities of a mutual fund company (or any other corporation) for the year. Both annual reports and prospectuses detail a mutual fund's operations and finances. The SEC requires mutual fund prospectuses to be updated annually and to present yields, expenses, and returns in a standardized format. In addition, funds must compare their short- and long-term performance, after expenses, with the performance of a standard market index, such as Standard & Poor's 500-stock index. The SEC prohibits the dissemination of false and misleading investment literature. The ultimate authority on a fund's track record is its current prospectus.

When to Sell a Mutual Fund

7 Recognize valid reasons for selling a mutual fund investment.

Because people invest in mutual funds for different reasons, and because the objectives of the funds vary widely, it is difficult to generalize about the best time to sell a particular mutual fund. In general, a fund probably should not be sold if a portfolio manager has a single bad year when the fund's long-term performance record has been good. Nonetheless, you might consider selling in the following circumstances:

- Your fund performs poorly compared with similar funds during two successive down markets or two successive up markets.

- Your perception of general economic trends indicates that peaks and valleys in the business cycle are being rounded or will soon smooth out.

- Your fund is growing too rapidly or has become too large, which may make it difficult for the manager (and the newly hired assistants) to follow the same investment principles that initially led to success.

The SEC Is Educating Investors about Mutual Fund Risk

Risk in the minds of investors consists of the chance of loss; it is the possibility that an investment will not perform as expected. The Securities and Exchange Commission (SEC), which regulates mutual funds, wants the investing public to become more informed about mutual fund risk.

The currently used statistical measures of risk are as follows:

1. **Standard deviation,** a historical measure of volatility that gauges the likelihood that a fund's return will skip up and down from month to month, varying from its average rate of return for a particular period of time. During a recent three-year time period, the S&P 500 Equity Index had a standard deviation of 11.8, a balanced fund of 6.9, and a money market fund of 3.1.

2. **Beta,** a measure that shows a fund's price volatility as compared with a specific market index of other mutual funds.

3. **Alpha,** which measures the difference between an investment's expected return, based upon its beta, and how it actually performs given its beta risk or expected performance (outperforming or underperforming it).

4. **Duration,** which measures a bond fund's sensitivity to changes in interest rates.

- Your fund manager radically changes investment style or strategy, as shown by the investments made and described in a recent prospectus.

- Your fund is taken over by a new manager who does not possess a strong track record of success in running another fund or in managing private accounts.

- Your investment goals become more conservative, such as when you near retirement age.

- You need cash for a child's education, a down payment on a home, an emergency, or for any other worthwhile purpose.

Summary

1. More people are investing through mutual funds than ever before because newer and more attractive funds have been recently created, because many funds carry low or no sales charges, and because some funds have performed much better than the average common stock.

2. Mutual funds have one of four broad objectives, which a company must report in the prospectus: current income, long-term growth, long-term growth and income, and balanced.

3. Mutual funds can be classified according to their portfolio of investments, such as common stock funds, bond and preferred stock (income) funds, balanced funds, municipal bond (tax-exempt) funds, specialty funds, and money market mutual funds.

4. As a specialized form of securities investment, mutual funds offer several unique features, such as automatic dividend reinvestment and easy purchase and sale.

5. Investors in mutual funds may be confronted with sales charges (on load funds), contingent deferred sales charges (on load and no-load funds), management fees, and hidden fees that reduce income from the

funds. All such fees must be disclosed to investors.

6. Mutual funds offer numerous advantages (such as switching privileges), as well as some disadvantages (such as management fees that reduce returns).

7. Selection of a mutual fund involves matching your goals to those of the fund, reading the prospectus and annual reports, locating sources of comparative performance data, and interpreting comparative performance data over time.

8. Investors in mutual funds should think about selling when a fund shows mediocre performance compared with similar funds, when general economic trends indicate that peaks and valleys in the business cycle are being rounded, and when the fund manager changes.

Key Words & Concepts

automatic income reinvestment   *440*

back-end load   *445*

bond funds   *438*

common stock fund   *436*

contingent deferred sales charge   *445*

expense ratio   *443*

front-end load   *444*

investment company   *431*

management fee   *443*

money market mutual fund   *439*

mutual fund   *431*

mutual fund dividends   *433*

mutual fund family   *442*

net asset value (NAV)   *434*

no-load fund   *444*

open-end investment company   *432*

prospectus   *434*

standardized expense table   *446*

switching privilege   *442*

12b-1 fee   *445*

Questions for Thought & Discussion

1. Explain in one sentence how a mutual fund works.

2. Distinguish between income from an ordinary income dividend distribution and income from a capital gains distribution.

3. Summarize how the net asset value (NAV) of a mutual fund can increase.

4. Compare and contrast a mutual fund with a balanced objective to one with a growth and income objective.

5. Describe two types of common stock funds.

6. Explain the value of a mutual fund that offers automatic reinvestment of dividends and capital gains distributions.

7. List three examples of the easy purchase and sale of a mutual fund company.

8. Explain the value of automatically reinvesting dividends and capital gains in mutual funds.

9. Why do mutual funds charge management fees, and what is the typical fee amount?

10. Distinguish between a load mutual fund and a no-load mutual fund.

11. How can an 8.5 percent stated sales charge on a mutual fund be misleading?

12. List and briefly describe some hidden fees attached to some no-load mutual funds.

13. Under what circumstances is it better to buy a load fund? A no-load fund? Summarize your reasons.

14. Name and briefly explain two advantages of investing in open-end mutual funds.

15. Name and briefly explain two disadvantages of investing in open-end mutual funds.

16. What is a volatility rating, and how can it be used by a mutual fund investor?

17. List three key factors to consider when interpreting comparative performance information about mutual funds over time.

19. Describe two situations that might cause you to consider selling your mutual fund shares.

DECISION-MAKING CASES

Case 1   Matching Mutual Fund Investments to Economic Projections

Glenn Sandler, a veterinarian for the past ten years in Green Bay, Wisconsin, is married and has one child. He is interested in investing in mutual funds. Glenn wants to put half of his $20,000 of accumulated savings into a stock mutual fund and then continue to invest $200 monthly for the foreseeable future, perhaps using the money for retirement starting in about 25 years. Glenn has limited his choices to the mutual funds listed in Table 15.2.

(a) Glenn wants to invest the full $10,000 now and diversify his holdings into two mutual funds. His personal economic projections for the next few years include low interest rates, moderate inflation, and medium-to-high economic growth. Given those assumptions, which two funds listed in Table 15.2 do you recommend for his $10,000? Why? (You may want to review the section on making economic projections in Chapter 1 before responding.)

(b) If Glenn's short-term economic forecast had projected high interest rates, moderate-to-high inflation, and sluggish economic growth (perhaps even with a recession), would you recommend that he put the $10,000 into mutual funds right now? If yes, explain why and suggest a fund from Table 15.2. If no, explain why not and suggest an alternative investment option for the $10,000.

(c) Glenn also wants to invest $200 per month into one mutual fund over the next 25 years. Assuming favorable long-term economic projections, which of the funds listed in Table 15.2 would you recommend? Why?

Case 2   Selection of a Mutual Fund as Part of a Retirement Plan

Etta Mae Westbrook, a single mother of a six-year-old child, works in a marketing firm in Knoxville, Tennessee, and is willing to invest $2000 to $3000 per year in a mutual fund. She wants the invest-

ment income to supplement her retirement pension starting in approximately 20 years. Her investment philosophy is moderate. Advise Etta Mae by responding to the following questions:

(a) Would you recommend that Etta Mae invest in a mutual fund with growth as its objective or growth and income? Why?

(b) Etta Mae wants to invest in a mutual fund that focuses on common stocks. Which two stock funds in Table 15.2 would you recommend that she avoid? Why?

(c) Explain your reasons for having Etta Mae invest in a load fund or a no-load fund.

(d) Assume that after 20 years Etta Mae's investments have done very well. In fact, she's considering a plan for periodically withdrawing income. Advise her on the advantages and disadvantages of this plan given her long-term investment objective.

Financial Math Questions

1. Last January Mike invested $1000 for 100 shares in the "Can't Lose Mutual Fund," an aggressive growth no-load mutual fund. After reinvesting dividends all year, the NAV for Mike's investment has risen from $10 per share to $13.25.

   (a) What is the percentage increase in the value of Mike's mutual fund?

   (b) If Mike redeemed his mutual fund investment for $13.25 per share, how much profit would he realize?

   (c) Assuming Mike pays income taxes at the 28 percent rate, what is the amount of income tax he will have to pay if he sells his shares?

   (d) Assuming Mike pays income taxes at the 28 percent rate, what is the amount of income tax he will have to pay if he chooses not to sell his shares but to remain invested?

2. Two years ago Jane invested $1000 for 125 shares ($8 per share NAV) in the "Can't Lose Mutual Fund," an aggressive growth no-load

mutual fund. Last year she made two additional investments of $500 each (50 shares at $10 and 40 shares at $12.50). After reinvesting all dividends, the NAV for her investment has risen from $8 per share to $13.25. Late in the year, she sold 60 shares at $13.25.

(a) What were the proceeds on Jane's sale of the 60 shares?

(b) To use the Internal Revenue Service's *average cost basis method** of determining the average price paid for one share, begin by calculating the average price paid for the shares. In this instance, the $2000 is divided by 215 shares (125 shares + 50 shares + 40 shares). What was the average price paid by Jane?

(c) To finally determine the average cost basis of shares sold, one multiplies the average price per share times the number of shares sold—in this case, 60. What is the total cost basis for Jane's 60 shares?

(d) Assuming that Jane must pay income taxes on the difference between the sales price for the 60 shares and their cost, how much is the difference?

(e) If Jane's mutual fund transactions were conducted within an IRS-qualified tax-sheltered retirement account, what would her income tax liability be if she were paying income taxes at the 28 percent rate?

MONEY MATTERS: LIFE-CYCLE CASES

Victor and Maria Invest for Retirement

Victor and Maria Hernandez plan to retire in less than 15 years. Their current investment portfolio is distributed accordingly: 40 percent in growth mutual funds, 40 percent in corporate bonds and bond mutual funds, and 20 percent in cash equivalents. They have decided to increase the amount

of risk in their portfolio by taking 10 percent from cash equivalent investments and investing in some mutual funds with strong growth possibilities.

1. Of the mutual funds listed in Table 15.2, which two would you recommend to meet the Hernandezes' goals? Why?

2. If those two investments perform over the next decade as well as they did in the past, would you recommend that the Hernandezes remain invested in those two funds during their retirement years? Why or why not?

The Johnsons Decide to Invest Through Mutual Funds

After learning about mutual funds, the Johnsons are convinced that they are a good investment, especially because of the diversification and professional management such funds offer. The couple has a nest egg of $9500 to invest through mutual funds. In addition, they want to invest another $300 per month on a regular basis.

Although not yet completely firm, Harry and Belinda's goals at this point are as follows:

(1) they want to continue to build for retirement income;

(2) they will need about $10,000 in six to eight years to use as supplemental income if Belinda has a baby and does not work for six months; and

(3) they might buy a super-expensive luxury automobile requiring a $10,000 down payment if they decide not to have a child.

Knowing that the Johnsons have a moderate investment philosophy, that they live on a reasonable budget, and that they have a well-established cash-management plan, advise them on their mutual fund investments by responding to the following questions:

1. Using Figure 15.3, which two separate types of funds would you recommend to meet the Johnsons' goals? Why?

2. How would you divide the $9500 between the two types of funds? Why?

---

* The IRS permits other methods to calculate share costs, including "first in, first out" and "designated shares." For more information, call the IRS at (800) TAX-FORM and ask for Publication 564.

3. How much of the $300 monthly investment amount would you allocate to each type of fund? Why?

4. Some comparable mutual fund performance data on stock funds are shown in Table 15.2. Using only that information and assuming that you are recommending some funds for the Johnsons' retirement needs, which three funds would you recommend? Why?

5. Assume that all three funds perform above average for the next ten years. A bear market then occurs, causing the NAVs to drop 25 percent from the previous year. What conditions must exist before you would recommend that the Johnsons sell their accumulated shares in the funds?

6. Determine the value of their $9500 investment in ten years, assuming that the three funds increase 13 percent annually for the next ten years. (Use the *Garman/Forgue* Web site.)

Exploring the World Wide Web of Personal Finance

To complete these exercises, go to the *Garman/Forgue* Web site at

www.hmco.com/college/business/

Select Personal Finance. Click on the exercise link for this chapter and answer the questions that appear on the Web page.

1. Visit the Web site for T. Rowe Price. Access its "Insights Library." Compare the information provided in the "Investing with Mutual Funds" article with information in this text chapter. Develop a list of five key points every beginning investor in mutual funds should know. Also list four advantages that investing in stock mutual funds provide as opposed to direct purchase of stock.

2. Visit Morningstar's Mutual Funds OnDemand Web site. Complete the requested information on fund return, objective, and so on to search for mutual funds that meet your criteria. From the search results, select one fund to research further. Type in the ticker symbol for that fund in the "advice" box at the top of the page to obtain research information on that fund. How would the information provided be of assistance to the mutual fund investor? (Hint: You may need to use trial and error to obtain a list of funds and find one that has been researched.) Telephone some mutual fund companies and request that they send you (1) an application to open an account and (2) recent performance information.

3. Visit the Web sites for three of the more prominent mutual fund families: Value Line, Fidelity, and American Century. What types of information do these sites provide to entice investors to buy fund shares through these families of funds? What types of information of a general nature do these sites provide investors regardless of where they decide to invest? For one or two of the funds, request that they send you (1) an application to open an account and (2) recent performance information.

4. Visit the Web site of the Motley Fool. In the search site dialog box, type "index funds." Read one or more of the articles found to ascertain the Motley Fool's views of index mutual funds. What five strengths do you see in this approach to mutual fund investing?

5. Visit the Web site of Mutual Fund Interactive. Click on "profile," and read three or four of the profiles of mutual fund managers provided. What common themes do you see in their professional training and background?

6. Visit the Web site for *Kiplinger's Personal Finance Magazine* to see its ratings of the recent performance of mutual funds. Browse through the ratings for the top large funds and stock funds over the past one, three, and five years. What mutual fund families seem to consistently rank highly?

Buying and Selling Securities 16

OBJECTIVES

After reading this chapter, you should be able to:

1 Explain the operation and regulation of securities markets.

2 Discuss types of brokerage firms.

3 Interpret newspaper quotations for listed securities.

4 Describe the process of buying and selling securities.

5 List the major sources of investment information about securities.

6 Estimate and calculate potential returns on investments.

7 Explain the 12-step investment process.

The actual process of buying and selling securities is rather simple. It takes only a telephone call to a brokerage firm or a mutual fund company; most transactions can even be carried out via a home computer. A **brokerage firm** specializes in buying and selling negotiable securities, such as stocks, bonds, and mutual funds.

This chapter provides specific information about how to buy and sell securities, with the sequence of topics following the steps in the investment process. First, you must understand how securities markets are operated and regulated. You then need to choose a brokerage firm to perform many of your buying and selling transactions. Next, you need to know how the securities markets operate, including how to read newspaper quotations for stocks, bonds, and mutual funds. In our discussion, we also provide details about the actual process of buying and selling securities. With that knowledge, you can begin to explore key sources of investment information, such as data on general economic conditions, securities market indexes, various industries, and specific companies. You should also be able to estimate and calculate potential rates of return on investments. Finally, we present a 12-step process for investing.

Securities Markets

Securities markets exist to raise capital and arrange the buying and selling of stocks and bonds. Individual securities are bought and sold in primary and secondary markets. A **primary market** is anywhere issuers and buyers of new offerings of stocks and bonds are brought together. For example, when Linda Webtek sold the original shares in Running Paws Catfood Company to her three friends, the primary market was her living room. A **secondary market** (also called the **aftermarket**) is where the trading of previously purchased securities takes place. Aftermarkets include organized stock exchanges and over-the-counter markets. The activities of securities markets are regulated by various government agencies and self-regulated by the securities industry itself.

Primary Markets

In the primary markets, companies that need capital to begin their operations sell new issues of stocks, bonds, or both to the investing public. New issues of stock are referred to as **initial public offerings (IPOs)**. Later capital needs, perhaps for expansion of the business, may be financed through corporate profits or by selling additional new issues. **Investment banking firms** serve as intermediaries between the issuing company and the investing public in the primary markets.

Figure 16.1

Flow of Stocks and Bonds in Primary Markets

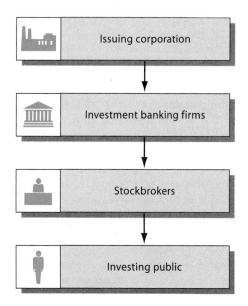

For example, assume that Running Paws, now a successful small corporation, wants to sell its products nationally. The owners have calculated that they will need about $5 million for this expansion. After careful analysis, they estimate that the per-share market value of their new 100,000 shares of stock will likely be about $25. (The remainder of the needed funds will be raised by issuing long-term bonds and taken out of profits.) The investment banker negotiates a purchase price—perhaps $24—after assessing the likely marketability of the stock and the expenses anticipated in selling it. The $1 difference between the purchase price and the expected resale price represents the potential profit for both the investment banker and the brokerage firm that eventually sells the stock to the investing public. When negotiations are complete, the investment banker publicly announces the availability of the stock as of a certain date. The investment banker sells blocks of shares to brokerage firms, which in this example will pay $24.50 per share, thus earning $0.50 per share for the investment banker. When the shares are sold to the investing public for $25, the other $0.50 represents the brokerage firms' per-share profit. Brokerage firms charge no sales commissions on the sale of new securities. When firms are too small to use the services of an investment banker, they use **venture capitalists** (private lenders) or stockbrokers instead. Figure 16.1 illustrates this flow of stocks and bonds in the primary markets.

Secondary Markets

After securities have been sold in the primary markets, they are resold in the secondary markets, which are composed of organized stock exchanges and the over-the-counter market. These secondary markets are commonly known as **securities markets**.

You can buy or sell securities in the organized exchanges through a **stockbroker** who works for a brokerage firm. A stockbroker is licensed to buy and sell securities on behalf of clients, provides them with investment advice and information, and generally collects a commission on each purchase or sale of such securities. A stockbroker may also be called an **account executive, registered representative**, or **sales representative.** He or she may either buy securities for the firm's own account that are then sold to investors or arrange the transactions between buyers and sellers. Stockbrokers must disclose when they are selling securities owned by the firm for which they work. Figure 16.2 shows the flow of stocks, bonds, and other securities in secondary markets. Note that the issuing corporations are no longer involved in any of the transactions.

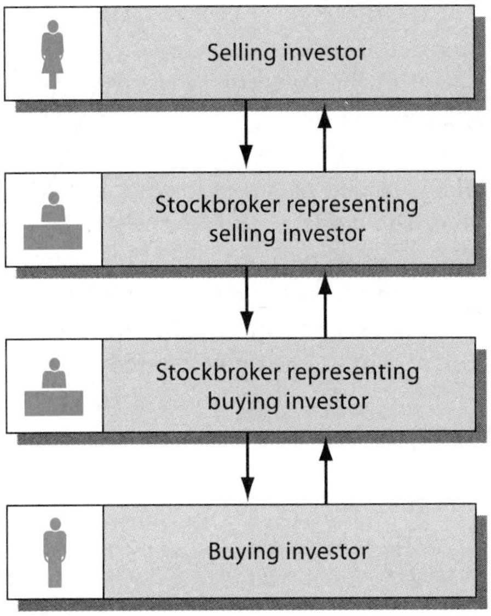

Organized Stock Exchanges

An **organized stock exchange** (or **stock market**) is a market where agents of buyers and sellers meet and trade a specified list of securities, usually the stocks and bonds of the larger, more well-known companies. More than three-fourths of all securities bought and sold are traded on one of the organized exchanges, which include the New York Stock Exchange, the American Stock Exchange, and regional stock exchanges (such as the Pacific Stock Exchange).

Only members of each stock exchange can trade securities on the floor of the exchange. A **member firm** is an organization that has purchased a seat on the exchange, which gives the firm the legal right to buy and sell securities on the exchange. The New York Stock Exchange contains 1366 seats, a fixed number, and large brokerage firms have multiple seats.

Each exchange trades only **listed securities.** Securities with this designation have been approved by the exchange for sale on its floor and the issuing companies have met various criteria regarding number of stockholders, numbers of shares owned by the public (outstanding shares), market value of each share, and corporate earnings and assets. These minimum requirements provide some assurance to investors

Figure 16.2

Flow of Securities in Secondary Markets

that the stocks traded are issued by reputable companies. Companies may be delisted if they fail to meet the minimum requirements at a later date.

New York Stock Exchange Founded in 1792, the New York Stock Exchange (NYSE) is by far the largest exchange in the world and has the most stringent requirements for listing. Corporations must have minimum earnings of $2.5 million before taxes, net assets of at least $16 million, a minimum of 1.2 million shares publicly held, a market value of outstanding stocks of no less than $18 million, and a minimum of 2000 shareholders owning at least 100 shares each to be listed on the "Big Board." More than 3250 stocks offered by the approximately 2750 companies on the NYSE account for about 97 percent of the market value of all listed stocks on the various exchanges. The average price per share on the NYSE is $33. The same stocks can be sold on more than one exchange, and the NYSE exchange accounts for about 80 percent of all stock trades.

American Stock Exchange The American Stock Exchange (ASE or AMEX), also located in New York City, is the second-largest exchange in the United States. The AMEX was started in 1849 when people traded securities on a corner of Wall Street, which has since become the financial nerve center of the United States. Today the American Stock Exchange lists more than 940 stocks and 260 bonds. Its listing requirements are less stringent than those of the NYSE. Consequently, the AMEX lists primarily smaller and younger companies than does the NYSE; the average per share price on the AMEX is $24. The American Stock Exchange may be merging with NASDAQ (see below).

Regional Stock Exchanges Regional stock exchanges trade securities mainly of interest to investors living in certain areas (as well as other securities). Many stocks listed on the NYSE and the AMEX are also listed on some regional exchanges to encourage more trading; smaller firms are also listed. The Pacific Stock Exchange (PSE), for example, requires net assets of only $1 million for listing, in addition to other criteria. Owing to the difference in time zones, the PSE stays open for trading for a few hours later than the New York-based exchanges. Other regional stock exchanges include the Boston, Cincinnati, Intermountain, Midwest, Philadelphia, and Spokane exchanges.

NASDAQ Over-the-Counter Market Publicly traded securities not sold on an organized exchange are traded on the **over-the-counter (OTC) market.** In the OTC market, buyers and sellers negotiate transaction prices, often using a sophisticated telecommunications network connecting brokerage firms throughout the United States that is run by the National Association of Securities Dealers (NASD). Its NASDAQ system provides prices on securities offered by more than 4900 small domestic and foreign companies. These securities often include the stocks and bonds of small firms that do not have many shares outstanding and do not have much trading interest; a few large companies are also listed, however. No central exchange floor for transactions exists, and trades are accomplished via computer screens. The OTC market has few listing requirements, and the price per share for a typical OTC stock is $11. The NASDAQ may be merging with the AMEX.

In an OTC sale, a stockbroker at a brokerage firm representing a buyer communicates with another brokerage firm that has the desired securities. The second brokerage firm is more accurately known as a **broker/dealer** because, in addition to offering the usual brokerage services, it can "make a market" for one or more securities. Thus, broker/dealers both buy and sell securities. **Market making** occurs when a broker/dealer attempts to provide a continuous market by maintaining an inventory of specific securities to sell to other brokerage firms and stands ready to buy reasonable quantities of the same securities at market prices. To avoid potential conflicts of interest with a client, when a stockbroker sells securities in which the brokerage firm has made a market, the buying investor must be informed of that fact.

The transaction price is negotiated because two prices are involved. The **bid price** is the highest price anyone has declared he or she wants *to pay* for a security. Thus, it also represents the amount a brokerage firm is willing to pay for a particular security. The **asked price** is the lowest anyone *will accept* at that time for a particular security. Thus, it also represents the amount for which a brokerage firm is willing *to sell* a particular security. The **spread** comprises the difference between the bid price, at which a broker will buy shares, and the higher asked price, at which the broker will sell shares. The spread can be as little as $12\frac{1}{2}$ cents per share, but typically ranges from 25 to 50 cents for most over-the-counter stocks. In addition to paying the asked price, the investor typically pays the broker a nominal sales commission.

Electronic Communications Networks The traditional organized stock markets are being challenged by **electronic communications networks (ECNs)** where all middlemen are excluded from transactions. ECN computers look for matching buy and sell orders and execute the trades. Popular ECNs are Island and Instinet.

Regulation of Securities Markets

Self-regulation is important in the securities industry because the public must trust the market before it will invest. Accordingly, organized exchanges dictate rules and regulations for listing and for trading. Similarly, the over-the-counter market is regulated by its **self-regulatory organization (SRO)**, the National Association of Securities Dealers. An SRO is a private organization designated by Congress to operate and oversee an aspect of the securities business. SROs aim to provide investors with accurate and reliable information about securities, maintain ethical standards, and prevent fraud against investors. All states now require registration of securities to be sold within the state.

Federal regulation of securities began with the Securities Act of 1933 and the formation of the Securities and Exchange Commission (SEC) in 1934. The SEC has focused on requiring disclosure of information about securities to the investing public and on approving the rules and regulations employed by the larger organized securities exchanges. It requires registration of listed securities with appropriate and updated information. In addition, it regulates all exchange members and prohibits manipulative practices, such as using insider information for illegal personal gain or falsely causing the price of a security to rise or fall. As part of its duties, this agency regulates the advertising of securities and requires that proxies and proxy statements be mailed in a timely manner to all stockholders. The SEC, which possesses investigative police powers, has been characterized as a government agency that "strictly regulates the honesty and practices of the securities industry" and depends upon effective self-regulation. The SEC's toll-free number for inquiries and complaints is (800) 732-0330.

Investor's insurance further protects the investing public. The Security Investors Protection Corporation (SIPC) is a government agency that safeguards the funds entrusted by investors to a brokerage firm in case the firm fails, provided that the firm is registered with the SEC as required. Each of an investor's accounts at a brokerage firm is protected against financial loss as a result of unreturned securities and cash up to a total of $500,000, but no more than $100,000 cash. Investment losses are not covered; instead, the SIPC protects investors only when brokerage firms go bankrupt.

All brokerage firms have a number of legal fiduciary obligations to their investors. Although abuses in the securities industry are rare, a small minority of unethical stockbrokers practice **churning** of investors' accounts—that is, they encourage investors to buy and sell securities frequently in an effort to earn more commissions for themselves. Other abuses occur when brokers forecast unrealistic investment returns and when clients are encouraged to select inappropriate types of investments for their portfolios. Brokers have the duty to protect customers from pursuing investment strategies that are destined to fail as well as the duty to supervise the client's suitability as an investor on an ongoing basis.

As a matter of convenience, more than 60 percent of investors prefer to leave securities certificates in the name of their brokerage firm rather than to take physical possession themselves. Securities certificates kept in the brokerage firm's name instead of the name of the individual investor are known as the security's **street name**. This is done to facilitate resale. Securities held in the street name are also afforded SIPC protection.

Operation of a Brokerage Firm

2 Discuss types of brokerage firms.

The great majority of securities transactions in the primary and secondary markets are executed with the assistance of a brokerage firm that owns seats on the various organized exchanges. You can use either a general brokerage firm or a discount brokerage firm; both charge commissions for any trading they conduct on your behalf. You should make clear to the brokerage firm, in writing, your investment objectives and your desired level of risk.

General Brokerage Firms

A traditional **general brokerage firm** typically offers full services to customers, including a company investment newsletter that discusses general economic trends and offers investment recommendations, periodic reports that cover particular market trends and industries, capsule-written research analyses that assess

Investigate Brokerage Sales Representatives

You can check the background of a stockbroker or a brokerage firm by filling out an information request form obtained from the National Association of Securities Dealers (P.O. Box 9401, Gaithersburg, MD 20898). Upon request, the NASD will inform you whether a securities firm or any of its employees have been subject to disciplinary proceedings. The NASD's toll-free number is (800) 289-9999. Visit its Web site at *www.nasdr.com/2000.htm.*

hundreds of individual companies (available to customers just for the asking), and the personal advice and attention of one of the thousands of stockbrokers working in the United States. The philosophy of general brokerage firms, such as Merrill Lynch or Smith Barney, is geared toward the value-added benefit of having someone personally advise you about investments. These firms maintain up-to-the-minute contact with the investment world through electronic equipment (usually including a **quotation board,** which is an electronic display that reports all security transactions on the major exchanges as they occur) and subscribe to expensive but valuable news wire services that can keep customers apprised of world news affecting particular investments. The interested investor may obtain price quotations on securities over the telephone. Brokerage firms also maintain a reference library and provide custodial services to safely hold securities for customers. Investors receive monthly statements summarizing all of their transactions and commissions, dividends, and interest.

Commissions and Fees

Brokerage firms receive a commission on each securities transaction to cover the direct expenses of executing the transaction and other overhead expenses. Most brokerage firms have an established fee schedule that they use when dealing with any but the largest investors. These fees reflect a commission rate that declines as the total value of the transaction increases. For example, in lieu of a minimum commission charge of $25, a brokerage firm might charge 2.8 percent on a transaction amounting to less than $800, 1.8 percent on transactions between $800 and $2500, 1.6 percent on amounts between $2500 and $5000, and 1.2 percent on amounts exceeding $5000.

Transaction costs are based on sales of **round lots,** which are blocks of stock in units of 100 shares, or one $1000 bond. **Odd lots** comprise transactions in units of more or other than units in multiples of 100 shares. When brokerage firms buy or sell shares in odd lots, they may charge a fee of 12.5 cents (called an **eighth**) per share on the odd-lot portion of the transaction. For example, an order for 140 shares at $25 each (total value $3500) could carry a round-lot commission fee of $40 (100 shares × $25 = $2500; $2500 × 0.016 = $40) plus an odd-lot fee of $5 (40 shares × $0.125), for a total fee of $45.

The payment of commissions can quickly reduce the return on any investment. A purchase commission of 2 percent added to a sales commission of another 2 percent means that the investor must earn a 4 percent yield just to pay the transaction costs. Broker's commissions typically range from 1 to 20 percent, depending on the investment bought or sold. The easiest way to hold down investing costs is to find a brokerage firm that charges low commissions.

Discount Brokerage Firms

In recent years, many investors have chosen to use **discount brokerage firms,** which can execute trades for about 50 to 70 percent less than full-service brokers. They feature especially low commission charges because they provide limited services to customers. They focus on a single function: efficiently executing orders to buy and sell securities. Discount brokerage firms do not normally conduct research or provide specific investment advice to customers. To initiate a transaction, an investor calls the discount brokerage firm at a toll-free telephone number to get price quotes, check accounts, and buy and sell securities without talking to a human. Examples include Accutrade [(800) 882-4887], Brown [(800) 822-2021], and Charles Schwab [(800) 435-4000].

Some discount brokers allow investors to purchase no-load mutual funds as well as stocks and bonds, although those funds charge 12b-1 fees every year. In addition, more than 30 brokerage firms offer **on-line trading** at deeply discounted brokerage fees. Examples include: Datek [*www.datek.com,* (888) 463-2835], E*trade [*www.etrade.com,* (800) 387-2331], and Scottsdale, [*www.scottrade.com,* (800) 906-7268]. Typically, if you have an account balance of $10,000, you can trade as many as 5000 shares for about $10.

Opening an Account

If you decide not to buy and sell securities through a discount brokerage firm, you must select a suitable general brokerage firm and a specific stockbroker at that firm to represent your interests. Make your decisions with care. The brokerage firm should be exchange-registered, meaning that it agrees to comply with the rules and regulations mandated by the exchange. Avoid brokerage firms with even a slightly suspect reputation.

You can open three kinds of accounts with a brokerage firm: (1) a cash account, (2) a margin account, and (3) a discretionary account.* A **cash account** requires an initial deposit (perhaps as little as $50) and specifies that full settlement is due the brokerage firm within three business days after a buy or sell order has been given. After a transaction, your account is debited or credited and written confirmation immediately forwarded to you. Uninvested money may be placed in the brokerage firm's money market account, with interest being credited to you.

About Ownership of Securities Investments

Like other assets, securities may be owned in joint tenancy with right of survivorship, tenancy in common, or tenancy by the entirety (as discussed in Chapters 4 and 17). In contrast, assets in employee-benefit retirement plans, such as 401(k) accounts, are always owned by the employee. Rules generally permit only the worker to name the person to receive the proceeds upon death. For investments held outside of such accounts, splitting the form of ownership using joint tenancy with right of survivorship may help avoid estate taxes because separately titled assets can be transferred to a bypass trust (a topic examined in Chapter 19).

---

* Many brokerage firms also offer a separate **wrap account** where the company offers advice and then both selects and manages a client's portfolio of mutual funds for a fee of 1 to 2 percent of assets per year. This charge comes in addition to the funds' annual expenses and any sales charges (loads) associated with the funds. Many mutual fund companies also offer wrap accounts.

In a **margin account**, the brokerage firm agrees to lend the customer part of the funds for the purchase of securities. Such an account requires a deposit of substantial cash or securities ($2000 or more) but permits you to buy additional securities on credit using funds borrowed from the firm. Both the Federal Reserve Board and the brokerage firm establish rules on the maximum amount of credit that can be used to purchase other securities. (Buying on margin is discussed in Chapter 17, "Real Estate and Advanced Portfolio Management.") A **discretionary account** gives the brokerage firm discretion to buy and sell securities on your account. Both margin and discretionary accounts require that the investor and the brokerage firm agree to operate under a specific set of guidelines.

Interpretation of Stock, Bond, and Mutual Fund Quotations

3 Interpret newspaper quotations for listed securities.

The daily buying and selling transactions of stocks and bonds on secondary markets are summarized in the *Wall Street Journal,* the most widely read financial newspaper in the United States (*http://update.wsj.com*). Additional information can be found in the weekly newspaper *Barron's.* Most daily newspapers also publish abbreviated information.

To keep abreast of market information, you should know how to read newspaper quotations for listed stocks, over-the-counter stocks, bonds, and mutual funds. Figure 16.3 on the following page gives quotations for listed stocks on the New York Stock Exchange on one particular day. The companies listed have an abbreviated trading symbol. We will examine the common stock listing for Mobil Corporation, indicated by the MOB symbol, following the quotations column by column.

Columns 1 and 2: **52 Weeks, High and Low** The first two columns show that Mobil traded stock at a high price of 102 and a low of 76 5/8 during the past 52 weeks plus the current week, not including the previous trading day. Stock transactions are reported in eighths, with each eighth representing 12.5 percent of the base price (dollars in this case). Thus, during the past 12 months, Mobil stock ranged in price from $102 to $76.25.*

Column 3: **Stock** This column gives the name of the stock—in this example, Mobil.

Column 4: **Sym** This column provides the abbreviated symbol used to identify the name of the stock—in this example, MOB for Mobil.

Column 5: **Div** The dividend amount is based on the last quarterly declaration by the company. For example, Mobil last paid a dividend (perhaps quarterly or semiannually) that, when converted to an annual basis, amounts to an estimated $3.70 annual dividend.

Column 6: **Yld%** The figure in this column represents the yield of dividend income calculated by dividing the current price of the stock into the most

---

* The stock markets are expected to soon convert to quoting prices in decimals, like the dollars and cents of everyday currency, rather than fractions. Until then, markets will switch to sixteenths instead of eighths, with each sixteenth representing 6.25 cents.

Figure 16.3

How Stocks Are Quoted

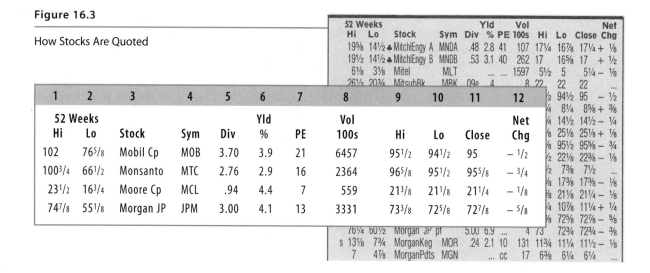

	1	2	3	4	5	6	7	8	9	10	11	12
	52 Weeks					Yld		Vol				Net
	Hi	Lo	Stock	Sym	Div	%	PE	100s	Hi	Lo	Close	Chg
	102	76⁵⁄₈	Mobil Cp	MOB	3.70	3.9	21	6457	95¹⁄₂	94¹⁄₂	95	− ¹⁄₂
	100³⁄₄	66¹⁄₂	Monsanto	MTC	2.76	2.9	16	2364	96⁵⁄₈	95¹⁄₂	95⁵⁄₈	− ³⁄₄
	23¹⁄₂	16³⁄₄	Moore Cp	MCL	.94	4.4	7	559	21³⁄₈	21¹⁄₈	21¹⁄₄	− ¹⁄₈
	74⁷⁄₈	55¹⁄₈	Morgan JP	JPM	3.00	4.1	13	3331	73³⁄₈	72⁵⁄₈	72⁷⁄₈	− ⁵⁄₈

recent estimated annual dividend. The price of the Mobil stock ($95) is found in column 11; thus $3.70 ÷ $95 = 3.9 percent.

Column 7: **P/E** This figure provides the price/earnings ratio based on the current price. The earnings figure used to calculate the P/E ratio is not published in the daily newspaper but is the latest available 12-month earnings amount published by the company. Because the P/E ratio is based on actual performance, it is known as a **trailing P/E.** When Mobil's closing price of $95 is divided by the earnings, it gives a P/E ratio of 21. From this figure, we can deduce that Mobil's previous 12 month's earnings were $4.52 ($95 ÷ 21).

Column 8: **Vol 100s** This figure indicates the total volume of trading activity for the stock measured in hundreds. Thus, 645,700 shares of Mobil were traded on this day.

Columns 9, 10, and 11: **High, Low, and Close** These three figures indicate the range of prices at which the stock traded on this day. *High* is the highest price at which it traded, *Low* is the lowest price, and *Close* is the last trade of the day before the market closed.

Column 12: **Net Chg** The net change represents the difference between the closing price on this day and the closing price on the previous trading day. The Mobil closing price of $95 was down ¹⁄₂ from the previous closing price, which must have been $95.50.

Figure 16.4 shows recent over-the-counter stock quotations, known as NASDAQ. New Jersey Steel common stock (NJST symbol), for example, ranged in price over the past year from 17¹⁄₂ to 9¹⁄₂. NJST has not paid a dividend during the past 12 months. On this day, 1400 shares were traded at prices between 11 and 10³⁄₄, and the price of the closing sale (11) was down ¹⁄₂ from the last sale of the previous day.

Figure 16.5 shows corporate bond quotations for the Lilly Corporation for one particular day. The line for Lilly shows that 5000 bonds (volume of 5 × 1000), due in the year 2001, with a coupon yield of 8¹⁄₈ ($8.125), were traded. In bond quotations, typically only the closing price of the day is reported—108³⁄₈ ($108.375) in this instance. The last sale of the day of the Lilly bonds was priced

Figure 16.4

How Over-the-Counter Stocks Are Quoted

1	2	3	4	5	6	7	8	9	10	11	12
52 Weeks Hi	Lo	Stock	Sym	Div	Yld %	PE	Vol 100s	Hi	Lo	Close	Net Chg
17 1/2	9 1/2	NJSteel	NJST		...	...	14	11	10 3/4	11	− 1/2
11 7/8	8	Noblns	NOBLF	.20	1.7	5	15	11 5/8	11 5/8	11 5/8	− 1/4
61	52	Nordsn	NDSN	.64	1.1	21	361	57 3/4	57	57 3/8	− 1/4
11 3/4	5 13/16	NoAmBiol	NBIO		...	16	7719	10 1/8	8 3/4	9	−1 3/8

at \$108.375 (108 3/8), which represented a 1 7/8 (\$1.875) increase from the last sale of the previous day. The current yield (Cur Yld) is rounded to 7.5 percent (\$8.125 ÷ \$108.375 = 7.49 percent).

Financial tables in newspapers list mutual fund prices and sales activity, as illustrated in Figure 16.6 on the following page. The name of the fund is followed by its investment objective as stated in the company's prospectus. For example, within the group listing for Fidelity mutual funds, the Magellan Fund (abbreviated as Magln) has an objective listed as GRO (growth).

Fidelity's Magellan Fund (Magln) has a net asset value (NAV) of \$89.62. An NL in the Offer Price column stands for no-load, meaning that no front-end sales charge is assessed; in Fidelity Magellan's case, however, the column lists a price of \$92.39. Thus, this load fund has an Offer Price (offering price) of \$92.39, and

Figure 16.5

How Bonds Are Quoted

Bonds	Cur Yld	Vol	Close	Net Chg
Lilly 8 1/8 01	7.5	5	108 3/8	+ 1 7/8
LoneStr 10s03	10.0	149	100 1/2	− 1/8
LglsLt 8.9s19	9.3	43	96 1/8	− 1 1/8
LglsLt 9s22	9.2	60	98	− 3/8
McDnlDg 8 1/400	7.9	10	104 3/4	− 1/4

Figure 16.6

How Mutual Funds Are Quoted

	Inv. Obj.	NAV	Offer Price	NAV Chg	YTD	13 wks	3 yrs	R
Fidelity Invest								
HiYld	HYM	11.89	NL	...	+ 9.8	+ 0.2	+ 5.6	E
MagIn p	GRO	89.62	92.39	− 0.05	+ 34.7	+ 14.9	+ 20.7	A
NewMkt r	WBD	9.05	NL	− 0.01	− 5.8	+ 3.5	NS	..
Puritn	EQI	16.69	NL	+ 0.01	+ 14.3	+ 5.3	+ 14.3	A

(column header: — Total Return —)

Background quotation excerpt:

	Inv. Obj.	NAV	Offer Price	Chg	YTD	13 wks	3 yrs	R
EmrMkt r	ITL	15.98	16.47	−0.02	− 0.9	+ 3.2	+14.3	B
Eq Inc	EQI	36.11	NL	+0.05	+20.6	+ 7.1	+16.5	A
EQII	EQI	20.70	NL	+0.03	+18.1	+ 6.6	+16.3	A
Eqldx	G&I	20.69	NL	+0.03	+23.8	+ 7.5	+13.4	B
Europ	ITL	22.55	23.25	−0.25	+12.8	+ 3.3	+12.3	C
ErCapAp	ITL	12.08	12.45	−0.09	+12.7	+ 1.0	NS	..

	Inv. Obj.	NAV	Offer Price	Chg	YTD	13 wks	3 yrs	R
IntEq	ITL	9.76	10.22	+0.03	+ 3.9	+ 2.2	NS	..
MidCap	MID	12.70	13.30	−0.03	+23.1	+10.9	NS	..
OhioTF	IDM	10.01	10.48	...	+10.3	+ 1.6	NS	..
QualBd	BIN	9.75	10.21	−0.02	+10.7	+ 1.0	NS	..
QualGr	GRO	11.76	12.31	+0.01	+21.7	+ 7.1	NS	..

Franklin Group:

			Offer Price	Chg	YTD	13 wks	3 yrs	R
p	BHI	2.78	2.90	...	+14.1	+ 3.2	+10.4	B
	BST	9.35	9.57	...	+ 6.9	+ 1.3	+2.3	E
	BST	9.78	9.78	−0.01	+ 5.8	+ 1.7	NA	..
I p	SSM	11.47	11.98	...	+ 9.6	+ 0.7	+6.4	B
I p	SSM	11.27	11.77	...	+ 9.2	+ 0.7	+6.4	B
p	CAP	26.55	26.95	−0.04	+23.5	+ 6.7	NA	..
	GRO	16.57	17.35	+0.01	+38.9	+17.3	NA	..
d p	MCA	9.77	10.20	...	+11.6	+ 0.1	NS	..
p	ISM	11.95	12.48	...	+ 9.7	− 0.2	+6.2	B
	IDM	10.53	10.77	+0.01	+10.4	+ 1.4	NS	..
p	MCA	7.14	7.46	...	+ 9.3	+ 0.6	+6.3	B
I p	SSM	11.57	12.08	...	+ 9.6	+ 1.0	+6.6	A
I p	SSM	10.77	11.25	...	+ 9.0	+ 0.8	+6.0	C
	SEC	12.33	12.91	+0.06	+24.4	+ 8.5	+14.7	C
p	GRO	7.52	7.87	−0.02	+25.2	+ 9.3	+12.6	D
	EQI	14.88	15.58	...	+13.8	+ 3.7	+11.5	C
p	IDM	10.73	10.98	...	+ 9.3	+ 1.4	NS	..
	GLM	11.87	12.40	...	+ 9.8	+ 1.2	+6.5	A
RS p	BST	9.79	10.02	−0.01	+ 5.5	+ 1.6	NA	..
I p	MFL	11.50	12.01	−0.01	+ 9.5	+ 0.8	+6.6	B
p	MFL	9.68	10.11	...	+12.9	− 0.2	NS	..
I p	SSM	11.69	12.21	...	+ 9.1	+ 0.8	+6.4	B

MagIn	GRO	89.62	92.39	−0.05	+34.7	+14.9	+20.7	A
MktIn r	G&I	41.64	NL	+0.08	+23.7	+ 7.5	+13.3	B
MA TF	DMA	11.18	NL	−0.01	+11.0	0.0	+6.5	A
MidCap	MID	13.47	NL	−0.06	+27.9	+12.2	NS	..

GIGvini p	WBD	8.09	8.45	−0.01	+ 9.3	+ 0.6	+5.0	B
GIHlth p	SEC	13.76	14.41	−0.18	+26.1	+17.5	NA	..
GIUtili p	SEC	12.58	13.17	−0.04	+12.9	+ 1.3	NA	..
Goldl p	SEC	15.29	16.01	−0.12	+ 3.2	+ 4.0	+13.9	C

the NAV Chg (net asset value changed) dropped $0.05 from the closing quotation of the previous day. The next three columns refer to Total Return. The YTD column (year to date) total return figure assumes that all dividends were reinvested and sales charges are omitted; for Fidelity, the year to date return is 34.7 percent. Calculations for the total return over the previous 13 weeks (13 wks) and past three years (3 yrs) are also provided; in this example, Fidelity Magellan returned 14.9 percent over the previous 13 weeks and 20.7 percent over the past three years. The final column labeled R reveals the ranking (by quintiles on an A through E scale) for the fund compared with others grouped by the same investment objective. Fidelity Magellan received an A ranking, placing it in the upper 20 percent of funds with a similar investment objective over the past year.

In mutual funds, the NAV is also known as the **mutual fund bid price**. Shareholders receive this amount per share when they cash in (**redeem**) their shares—that is, the company is willing to pay this amount to buy the shares back. On this day, Fidelity Magellan Fund is bidding $89.62 to repurchase any shares outstanding. For mutual funds, the **mutual fund asked price** (or **offer price**) is the price at which a mutual fund's share can be purchased by investors; it equals the current net asset value per share *plus* sales charges, if any. Thus, if you wanted to buy Fidelity's Magellan Fund, the company would offer to sell it to you for $92.39. The sales commission (load) may be calculated as a factor of the difference between the two prices ($92.39 − $89.62 = $2.77; $2.77 ÷ $92.39 = 3.0 percent). By law, this load must be the same whether you purchase shares from a fund or through a brokerage firm.

The SEC requires that listings show a **footnote p** to mark those that assess an annual 12b-1 fee for marketing expenses; no-load mutual funds may be listed as NL even if they assess this fee, however. Funds that have authorized 12b-1 fees but are not currently using them do not have to put a *p* next to their names. In addition, the SEC requires that **footnote r** be placed after the names of mutual funds to identify those that assess redemption charges or exit fees. A redemption charge may be small and either permanent or temporary; alternatively, it may be large—perhaps starting at 6 percent—and decline gradually until it disappears. A mutual fund may assess a redemption charge and still be called no-load. A listing with both a *p* and an *r* means that the fund levies both 12b-1 fees and redemption charges; such funds may not be listed as a no-load. Some newspapers use the **footnote t** to indicate mutual funds that charge both 12b-1 and redemption fees. Fidelity Magellan has no footnotes.

The newspapers' quotations for no-load mutual funds are easier to comprehend. In Figure 16.6, the Fidelity New Markets Fund (NewMkt) has a net asset value (NAV) of $9.05, is a no-load fund (NL), and had a change in the net asset value (NAV Chg) of down $0.01 from the closing price of the previous trading day. Thus, if you wanted to buy or sell shares of this Fidelity fund on this day, the price would be $9.05 per share. Note that the Fidelity New Markets Fund assesses a redemption fee (it has a footnote *r*).

Securities Transactions and the Investor

4 Describe the process of buying and selling securities.

As many as 50 million shares of stocks may be traded daily on the over-the-counter market in the United States and another 400 million shares traded on the New York Stock Exchange. Between 75 and 80 percent of the trading is conducted by large investment banks and mutual funds. Every trade brings together a buyer and a seller to conclude the transaction at a given price.

The Trading Process

To illustrate the process of trading securities, assume you instruct brokerage firm A to purchase a certain number of shares at a specific price. The firm relays the buy order to representative A, who coordinates brokerage firm A's trading. Because brokerage firm A has a seat on the exchange, the buy order is then given to floor broker A, the brokerage firm's contact person at the exchange. This broker contacts a **specialist,** who is a person on the floor of the exchange who handles trades of the particular stock in an effort to maintain a fair and orderly market. The buy order is filled, either by taking shares from the specialist's own inventory or by matching another investor's sell order.

Matching or Negotiating Prices

On the organized exchanges, a match must occur between the buyer's price and the seller's price for a sale to take place. Therefore, a specialist could hold a specific order for a few minutes, a few hours, or even a week before a match is made. With actively traded issues, a transaction normally is completed in just a few minutes. A slower-selling security can be traded more quickly if an investor is willing to accept the current market price (as discussed below).

On the over-the-counter market, the bid and asked prices represent negotiation of a final price. If a buyer does not want to pay the asking price, he or she instructs the stockbroker to offer a lower bid price, which may or may not be accepted. If it is refused, the buyer might cancel the first order and raise the bid slightly in a second order in the hope that the owner will sell the shares at that price. Otherwise, the buyer may have to pay the full asked price to complete the picture. Generally, OTC trades occur at prices between the bid and asked figures.

Types of Orders

Only two types of orders exist—buy and sell. A stockbroker buys or sells securities according to prescribed instructions in a process called executing an order. The constraints that can be placed on the prices of those orders are called market, limit, and stop orders.

Market Order   A **market order** instructs the stockbroker to execute an order at the prevailing market price—that is, the current selling price of a security. A stockbroker can generally secure a transaction within a few minutes. In reality, the floor broker tries to match the instructions from many investors with the narrow range of prices available from the specialist. Traders on the floor of the stock market typically shout and signal back and forth as part of this effort to match buyers and sellers. Most trades are market orders.

Limit Order   A **limit order** instructs the stockbroker to buy or sell at a specific price. A limit order may involve instructions to buy at the best possible price but not above a specified limit, or to sell at the best possible price but not below a specified limit. It provides some protection against buying a security at a price higher than desired or selling at too low a price. The stockbroker transmits the limit order to the specialist. The order is executed if and when the specified price or better is reached and all other previously received orders on the specialist's book have been considered.

A disadvantage for a buyer who places a limit order is that the investor might miss an excellent opportunity. For example, assume that you place a limit order with your stockbroker to buy 100 shares of Running Paws common stock at $60^{1}/_{2}$ or lower. You have read in the newspaper that the stock has recently been selling at 61 and $61^{1}/_{4}$, and you hope to save $0.50 to $1.00 on each share. That same day the company announces publicly that it plans to expand into the dog food area for the first time. Investor confidence in the new sales effort pushes the price up to 70. If you had given your stockbroker a market order instead, you would have purchased 100 shares of Running Paws at perhaps $61^{1}/_{4}$ or $61^{1}/_{2}$, which would have given you an immediate profit of $850 ($70 - 61^{1}/_{2} = 8^{1}/_{2}$; $8^{1}/_{2} \times 100$ shares = $850) on an initial investment of $6150 ($61^{1}/_{2} \times 100$).

A disadvantage for a seller placing a limit order is that it could result in no sale if the price drops because of negative news. Assume that you bought stock at 50 that is currently selling at 58 and that you have placed a limit order to sell at a price of no less than 60 in order to take your profit. The price could creep up to 59 and then fall back to 48, however. In this event, you did not sell the securities because the limit order was priced too high, and they are now worth less than what you originally paid for them. A limit order is best used when you expect great fluctuations in the price of a stock and when you buy or sell infrequently traded securities on the over-the-counter market. Limit orders account for 35 percent of all trades.

Stop Order A **stop order** instructs a stockbroker to sell your shares at the market price if a stock declines to or goes below a specified price. It is often called a **stop-loss order** because the investor uses it to protect against a sharp drop in price and thus to stop a loss. The specialist executes the order as soon as the stop-order price is reached and a buyer is matched at the next market price.

As an example of how to stop a loss, assume that you bought 100 shares of Running Paws stock at 70. You are nervous about its entry into the competitive dog food business and fear that the company might lose money. Therefore, you place a stop order to sell your shares if the price drops to 56, thus limiting your potential loss to 20 percent ($70 − $56 = $14; $14 ÷ $70 = 0.20). Some months later, you read in the financial section of your newspaper that even after six months Running Paws still has less than 1 percent of the dog food market. You call your stockbroker, who informs you that the price of Running Paws stock dropped drastically in response to the article, which was published the previous day in the *Wall Street Journal*. He reports that all of your shares were sold at 55, that the current price is 49, and that the sales transaction notice is already in the mail to your home. The stop order cut your losses to slightly more than 20 percent ($70 − $55 = $15; $15 ÷ $70 = 21.4 percent) and saved an additional loss of $6 ($55 − $49) per share. Thus, the stop order reduced your loss to $1500 [(100 × $70 = $7000) − (100 × $55 = $5500)] instead of $2100 [(100 × $70 = $7000) − (100 × $49 = $4900)].

You can use a stop order to protect profits, too. Assume that you bought 100 shares of Alpo Dog Food Company at $60 per share, which now has a current selling price of $75. Your paper profit is $1500 ($75 − $60 = $15; $15 × 100 shares = $1500), less commissions. To protect part of that profit, you place a stop order with your stockbroker to sell at $65 if the price drops that low. If your stock is sold, you realize a real profit of $500 ($65 − $60 = $5; $5 × 100 shares = $500). If Alpo Dog Food stock climbs in price instead, perhaps in response to the bad news about Running Paws, the stop order would have cost you nothing. If the price does climb, you might replace the stop order with one having a higher price to lock in an even greater amount of profit.

Use Computer Software to Manage Your Investment Portfolio

Computers can help manage your investment portfolio. Keeping track of several stock, bond, and mutual fund investments, as well as buying and selling transactions, requires careful recordkeeping, especially for income tax purposes. These tasks can be performed easily using a computer software program. In addition, an investment portfolio manager program permits you to monitor your investments by maintaining current values of the items in your portfolio. Some programs even allow you to trade securities through a brokerage firm by placing orders on your computer.

Popular investment programs (and the publishers) include StreetSmart (Charles Schwab), Principia (Morningstar), WealthBuilder (Reality), Compustock (A. S. Gibson), Market Analyzer Plus (Dow Jones and Company), and Your Personal Investment Manager (Timeworks).

Time Limits

Investors have several ways to place time limits on their orders. A **fill-or-kill order** instructs the stockbroker to buy or sell at the market price immediately or else cancel the order. A **day order** is valid only for the remainder of the trading day during which it was given to the brokerage firm. Unless otherwise indicated, any order received by a stockbroker is assumed to be a day order. A **week order** remains valid until the close of trading on Friday of the current week. A **month order** is effective until the close of trading on the last business day of the current month. An **open order**, also called a **good-till-canceled (GTC) order**, remains valid until executed by the stockbroker or canceled by the investor. If you give an order longer than a week in duration, you must carefully monitor events and then alter the order if the situation changes substantially.

Purchasing Mutual Funds

Shares in mutual funds may be purchased through a brokerage firm or from an investment company itself. Investors use one of two ways to buy mutual funds: direct purchase and contractual accumulation.

Direct Purchase   A **direct purchase** involves the acquisition of shares in a mutual fund by simply ordering and paying for the shares, plus any commissions; each transaction is considered a one-time purchase. A direct purchase can be made by mail or through a sales representative of the investment company, or through a financial planner or a brokerage firm. The investor's account is credited with ownership of fractional shares measured to three decimal places. The firm mails out a written confirmation for each transaction, and after receipt of an invested amount; after the confirming statement is issued, you may make additional purchases or redemptions at any time.

People generally invest in no-load shares directly with an investment company, and in load shares through a brokerage firm or financial planner.* Any commissions and fees are deducted from each investment amount. If you invest in a load fund, the commission reduces the number of shares purchased. For example, if you buy shares of Conglomerate Cat and Dog Food Mutual Fund, which has a net asset value of $16.50 per share, a commission of 8 percent might be charged on the load fund. The purchase of 25 shares might cost $445.50: $412.50 for the shares (25 × $16.50) plus $33 in commission (0.08 × $412.50).

Contractual Accumulation Plan   A **contractual accumulation plan** is a formalized, long-term program to purchase shares in a load mutual fund. Investors sign an agreement to invest a specific dollar amount periodically over a certain number of years (usually ten). Commissions are paid as shares are purchased, although they are often accelerated and deducted during the first two years. This plan can be used to meet a financial goal to invest a specific amount.

The Investment Companies Amendments Act of 1970 protects mutual fund investors using contractual accumulation plans who change their minds and

---

*   A number of discount brokers now sell no-load funds without a commission or transaction fee. As their compensation, they collect a charge equal to 0.25 percent of sales directly from the fund sponsors. The funds also assess 12b-1 fees.

decide to liquidate. Under the law, any investor is entitled to a full refund within 45 days. A partial refund, up to 85 percent in some instances, depending on the net asset value of the mutual fund, is available within 16¹/₂ months. Primarily because the front-end load commission structure generates a negative effect, only a handful of plans are still being sold.

Information about Securities

5 List the major sources of investment information about securities.

To reduce investment risks and increase returns, the wise investor seeks out and utilizes investment information. By following up your own hunches with research, you can build a portfolio of common stocks, bonds, mutual funds, and other investments that is superior to a portfolio created by simply relying on suggestions and tips from stockbrokers. Individual investors often enjoy an edge over the more than 20,000 professional analysts working for large institutions, such as mutual funds and pension funds, because they can change the mix in their portfolios more quickly and have more choices than those trading big blocks of securities.

This section takes a "how-to" approach to gathering investment information about general economic conditions, securities market indexes, industry data, and company news. By spending a few hours with reference materials available in most public libraries and with documents from the companies themselves, you should be able to identify investments with profit potential and avoid those that suggest trouble.

General Economic Conditions

Knowing when to buy or sell securities requires an assessment of general economic conditions. You need to know the stage of the business cycle (recession or prosperity) and the current interest and inflation rates. In addition, you should project economic conditions over the next 12 to 18 months. (These topics were examined in Chapters 1 and 13.)

By reading a local daily newspaper and a weekly newsmagazine, you can gain insights into the economic conditions, especially if you select big-city newspapers like the *Los Angeles Times, Miami Herald, New York Times,* or *Washington Post.* Many big-city newspapers are available in libraries or by mail subscription. You can also obtain specific economic news from the *Wall Street Journal* and *Barron's,* the two most popular financial newspapers in the country. These publications are usually available at public and college libraries as well as at brokerage firm offices. *Business Week, Fortune, U.S. News & World Report, Money,* and *Kiplinger's Personal Finance Magazine* provide excellent information on economic conditions as well. Select a few publications to read regularly to keep abreast of general economic conditions.

Securities Market Indexes

Securities market indexes measure the average value of a number of securities chosen as a sample to reflect the behavior of a more general market. Investors use such indexes to determine trends that might guide them in investment decisions because short-run price movements may or may not be important compared with longer-term situations. Ideally, for example, an investor would buy low and sell high. That is, you try to buy securities at low prices during the depth of a **bear market**, which is defined as a protracted period when stock shares fall in value, perhaps with a 20 percent drop from the peak or a 50 percent drawback of bull market gains. Bear markets, on average, last about 14 months. You should seek, in turn, to sell at high prices during the height of a **bull market**, a protracted period when stock shares rise in value. The most popular indexes are described in the following paragraphs.

Dow Jones Industrial Average (DJIA)   The DJIA is the most widely reported of all indexes, having been used continuously since 1884. In determining the DJIA, the prices of only 30 actively traded blue-chip stocks are followed. The 30 stocks include well-known companies like American Express, Caterpillar, DuPont, Exxon, General Motors, Hewlett-Packard, IBM, Sears, Wal-Mart, and Walt Disney. When an evening newscaster reports that "the Dow rose 200 points today in heavy trading," realize that these "points" are changes in the index, not actual dollar changes in the value of the stocks. The average is calculated by adding the closing prices of the 30 stocks and dividing by a number adjusted for splits, spin-offs, and dividends. The index has served as a popular barometer of daily activity of securities traded on the New York Stock Exchange for many years, because the stocks chosen broadly represent the interests of the investing public.

Standard & Poor's 500   S&P's 500 index reports price movements of 500 stocks of large, established, publicly traded firms. It includes stocks of 400 industrial firms, 40 financial institutions, 40 public utilities, and 20 transportation companies. Although not as popularly reported as the DJIA, S&P's 500 more accurately reflects daily transactions of the investing public. Companies with the greatest market value influence the index the most.

New York Stock Exchange Composite   This index includes all stocks traded on the NYSE (approximately 3250). Consequently, it provides a comprehensive measure of the price movements and value changes of those stocks.

American Stock Exchange (AMEX)   This index is based on the market value of the more than 1300 stocks and bonds traded on the AMEX. It provides a measure of companies not as popular as those traded on the NYSE.

NASDAQ Composite   This index represents about 4700 over-the-counter stocks in the automated quotations system of the National Association of Securities Dealers. Most of these companies are young and more risky enterprises.

Nikkei Dow   Japan's best-known barometer of stock prices represents the activity of 300 stocks. Because this market is open at night in the United States, U.S. investors often check the Nikkei Dow in the morning as an indicator of what might happen that day.

Information about Industries

The current prices of individual companies' securities are often affected by the performance of the industry as a whole. Economic events can have considerable impact on entire industries, such as aerospace, apparel, automobiles, beverages, chemicals, construction, pharmaceuticals, electronics, finance, foods, machinery, and metals; they may even depress the stock of a very profitable company. For example, JCPenney could be having a highly profitable year, but if investors anticipate a recession and expect retail sales to drop, the value of its stock might be held down even if the company is enjoying a good year. Figure 16.7 on the following page illustrates profitability data for selected industries from Johnson's Charts.

Studying industries of interest to you will help you make intelligent buying and selling decisions. Excellent reference sources often found in large libraries include *Value Line Investment Survey* (Volume 1), Standard & Poor's *Industry Surveys*, and Moody's *Industry Review*. Specific information about industries is also available from trade associations and investment publications.

Trade Associations A **trade association** is an organization representing the interests of companies in the same industry. For example, the American Council of Life Insurance is composed of representatives of life insurance companies, and the American Bankers Association represents the interests of the banking industry. In addition to lobbying elected officials to present the views of their members, trade associations gather a tremendous amount of detailed information on the history, current activities, and future prospects of the industry. Although their projections for the future often appear overly optimistic, it is useful to know how an industry views its own prospects.

To contact the trade associations of interest to you, look up their names and addresses in the *Encyclopedia of Associations*, published by Gale Research Company, and *National Trade and Professional Associations*, published by the U.S. Department of Commerce. Both references are available in larger libraries.

Industry-Oriented Investment Publications Industry information is reported in such publications as *Business Week* and *Forbes* (one issue of *Forbes* analyzes the performance of all major industries each year). You can also spend a great deal of money subscribing to investment publications and advisory services, including *Industry Surveys* and *The Outlook* (published by Standard & Poor's), *Value Line Investment Survey* (Value Line Publishing, Inc.), the *Monthly Economic Letter* (Citibank), and *Industrial Manual* (Moody's). Fortunately, many of these publications can be found in large libraries (especially at colleges) and in brokerage firm offices.

Information about Specific Companies and Funds

Investment guru Peter Lynch wisely says that investors should buy only when they have a clear, simple understanding of why the value of their investment is likely to rise. Therefore, before buying any securities, you should learn about the company that offers them. You can obtain this information from a number of sources, including the key ones described below. In your analysis, focus on the

Figure 16.7

Percentage Increase of Stocks of 71 Industries over Ten Years, 1989–1998

The wide range of investment results for the past ten years of 71 different industries, as shown by Standard & Poor's, reveals the difficulty of selecting common stocks.

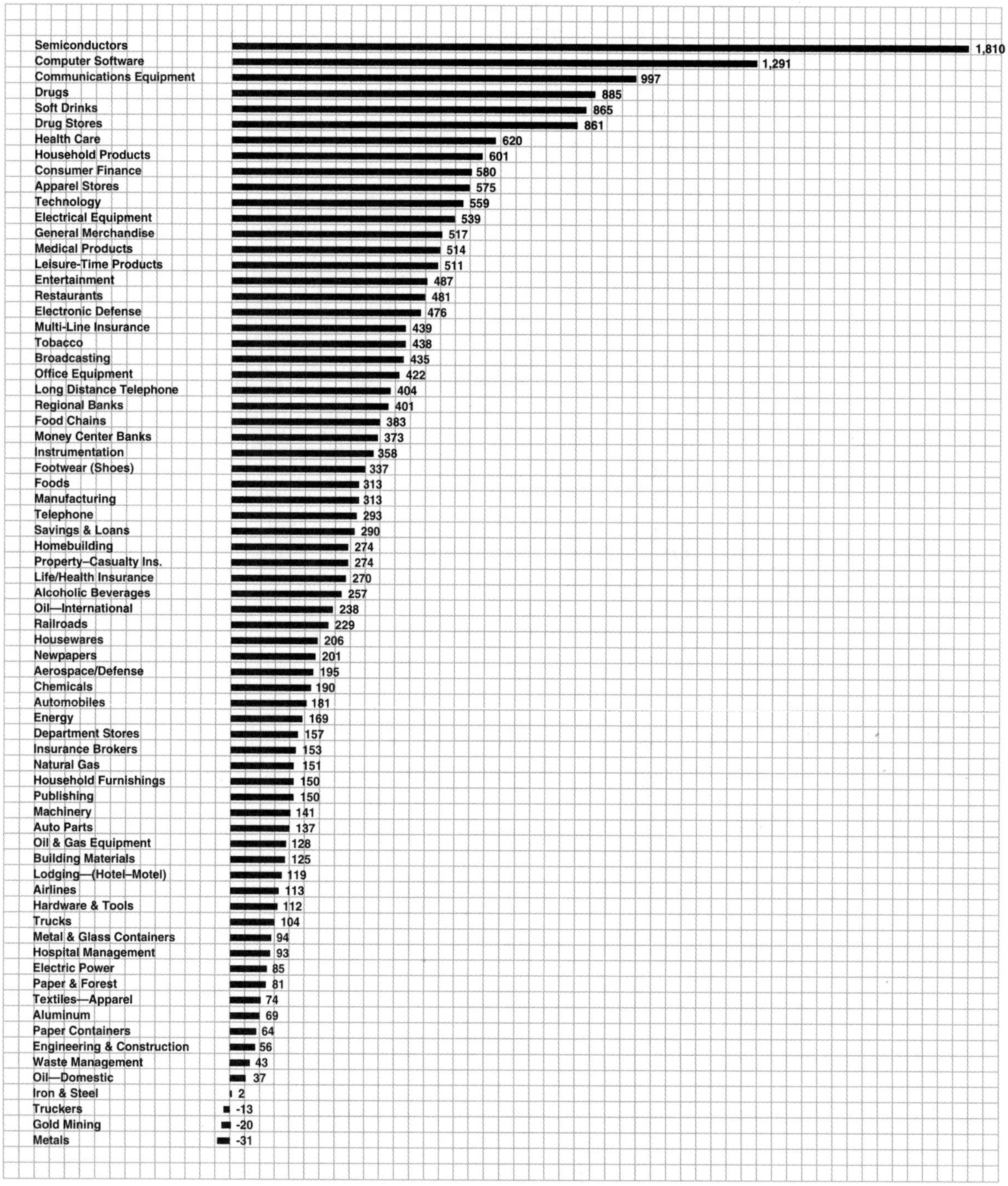

Industry	Percentage Increase
Semiconductors	1,810
Computer Software	1,291
Communications Equipment	997
Drugs	885
Soft Drinks	865
Drug Stores	861
Health Care	620
Household Products	601
Consumer Finance	580
Apparel Stores	575
Technology	559
Electrical Equipment	539
General Merchandise	517
Medical Products	514
Leisure-Time Products	511
Entertainment	487
Restaurants	481
Electronic Defense	476
Multi-Line Insurance	439
Tobacco	438
Broadcasting	435
Office Equipment	422
Long Distance Telephone	404
Regional Banks	401
Food Chains	383
Money Center Banks	373
Instrumentation	358
Footwear (Shoes)	337
Foods	313
Manufacturing	313
Telephone	293
Savings & Loans	290
Homebuilding	274
Property–Casualty Ins.	274
Life/Health Insurance	270
Alcoholic Beverages	257
Oil—International	238
Railroads	229
Housewares	206
Newpapers	201
Aerospace/Defense	195
Chemicals	190
Automobiles	181
Energy	169
Department Stores	157
Insurance Brokers	153
Natural Gas	151
Household Furnishings	150
Publishing	150
Machinery	141
Auto Parts	137
Oil & Gas Equipment	128
Building Materials	125
Lodging—(Hotel–Motel)	119
Airlines	113
Hardware & Tools	112
Trucks	104
Metal & Glass Containers	94
Hospital Management	93
Electric Power	85
Paper & Forest	81
Textiles—Apparel	74
Aluminum	69
Paper Containers	64
Engineering & Construction	56
Waste Management	43
Oil—Domestic	37
Iron & Steel	2
Truckers	-13
Gold Mining	-20
Metals	-31

Source: From *Johnson's Charts, 51st Annual Edition.* Copyright © 1999. Used by permission of Johnson's Charts, Inc.

quality of management, the firm's financial stability, the company's earnings stream, and its competitive position. A large number of sources provide on-line price quotes and background reports on stocks and mutual funds, including *Money* magazine's Personal Finance Center (*http://pathfinder.com/money*).

Annual Reports Every public corporation publishes an **annual report** that summarizes its financial activities for the year. Investors use these reports to compare results from recent years and to find out about management's views of the immediate future. These reports often speak with an optimistic voice, because the company wants investors to think highly of its prospects. Interesting information—sometimes negative—is often found in the footnotes. To receive an annual report, ask a brokerage firm or write directly to the corporation.

Prospectuses When a company issues any new security, it must file a **prospectus** with the Securities and Exchange Commission. This disclosure about a corporation describes the experience of its management, its financial status, any anticipated legal matters that could affect the company, and potential risks of investing in the corporation. The language is legalistic and full of technical jargon, but the interested investor can sift through the details. Many firms update their prospectuses regularly, and they are available on-line from the SEC (*www.sec.gov*).

Profile Prospectuses A **profile prospectus** supplements the lengthier prospectuses required by the Securities and Exchange Commission that are provided to mutual fund investors. It offers a two- to four-page summary presentation of information contained in a legal prospectus that specifically answers 11 key investor questions (including details about the fund's ten-year performance record) and is written in lay language.

Search for Investments on the Internet

Corporate and mutual fund filings that are required by the Securities and Exchange Commission are available on the Internet from the Electronic Data Gathering and Retrieval (Edgar) project. On-line browsers can perform a company search using (*http://town.hall.org/edgar/edgar.html*). A list of World Wide Web pages maintained by public corporations can be accessed using (*http://networth.galt.com/www/home/insider/publicco.html*). A directory service like Yahoo lets you electronically search thousands of Web sites (*http://yahoo.com*).

10-K Reports Every company registered with the Securities and Exchange Commission must report many financial particulars to the SEC by filing a **10-K report** once each year to ensure public availability of accurate, current information about the firm. This comprehensive official document contains much of the same type of information as a prospectus or annual report and additional updated financial details on corporate activities. You can obtain 10-K reports from the SEC (also available on-line from the SEC at *www.sec.gov*) or find them in many college libraries.

Investment Ratings Publications You can read about specific public corporations in the United States in a number of investment ratings publications, including the highly popular *Standard & Poor's Stock Reports*. These publications rank and rate the projected future

Use a Computer to Search Investment Alternatives

A variety of software is available to help you analyze and evaluate stocks, bonds, and other investments. In addition, software programs are available to help manage your investment portfolio.

The difficult task of reviewing all of the stocks and bonds in various industries can be made much easier with the aid of a computer. Database systems enable you to quickly sift through and screen hundreds of companies to find those that best suit your investment objectives. A financial database system provides on-line access to information on 1500 or more stock and bond investments that can be screened on a personal computer. Some systems work using disks, while others offer on-line access via a modem and telephone. Historical information, current financial statements, current prices, and up-to-date news are available around the clock.

A stock-screening program allows you to identify stocks that meet your specific investment criteria. You can rate companies according to a number of factors, such as price, earnings, sales, dividend, P/E ratio, current assets, and profits. Subscribers pay a modest fee to hook up to one or more financial database systems.

Popular financial diskette database systems include Value/Screen (Value Line, 711 Third Avenue, New York, NY 10017) and Stockpak II (Standard & Poor's Corporation, 25 Broadway, New York, NY 10004). On-line systems include CompuServe (5000 Arlington Centre Boulevard, Columbus, OH 43220), Dow Jones News/Retrieval (P.O. Box 300, Princeton, NJ 08540), The Source (1616 Andern Road, McLean, VA 22102), and Trade Plus (82 Devonshire Street, Boston, MA 02109).

earnings and profitability of corporations in a concise **stock report.** A stock report for a corporation typically contains a brief summary description and current outlook, important developments, comparisons with competitors, and tables with financial data going back ten years. You can find such publications in larger libraries, college libraries, and in the offices of brokerage firms.

Research Reports Basic investment research tries to separate companies that are on the way up financially from those on the way down. Hundreds of analysts produce research reports each day at major brokerage firms (such as PaineWebber and Merrill Lynch) and investment banks (such as Kidder Peabody, Donaldson, Lufkin & Jenrette), and most of these reports are available through a general brokerage firm. Although the research reports usually recommend that investors buy certain stocks, they rarely recommend selling. Hence, it is prudent to interpret their "hold" recommendations as a clear signal to sell. Although the quality of advice is uneven, ranging from brilliant to pedestrian (analysts have a tendency to run with the herd and make similar recommendations), collectively this research is the best conducted on securities investments. Simply ask your stockbroker which reports can be made available to you.

Estimating and Calculating Potential Returns on Investments

6   Estimate and calculate potential returns on investments.

To be a successful investor, your rate of return on investments should be in excess of inflation and income taxes. The return on short-term U.S. Treasury bills, which are virtually risk-free and exempt from federal income taxes, has historically exceeded the rate of inflation by a slight degree. Thus, when T-bills pay 5 percent interest, the inflation rate might hover around 4.0 percent. This circumstance provides almost no gain for the investor. For this reason, investors often use the yield on Treasury bills as a base number that provides a zero **real rate of return**—that is, the return on an investment after inflation and income taxes. The objective of conservative, moderate, and aggressive investors then becomes to earn a higher return than that offered on T-bills—but how much higher?

Estimating and calculating returns on potential investments involve three steps: (1) Use beta* to calculate an estimated required yield on an investment given its risk; (2) calculate the potential rate of return on the investment; and (3) compare the required rate of return with the projected rate of return on the investment. Armed with these data, you will be better able to make a good decision.

Use Beta to Calculate an Estimated Required Rate of Return on an Investment Given Its Risk

Beta provides a useful measure of risk when calculating your estimated required rate of return on an investment, whether it involves stock, bonds, or mutual funds. You can obtain the betas for specific stocks from a brokerage firm, mutual fund company, realtor, library reference book, or magazines that write about investments. Some recent betas for groups of mutual funds are as follows: growth and income, 1.50; global, 1.88; aggressive growth, 2.3; and precious metals, 3.0. Given a beta for a particular investment, you can begin to calculate your total estimated required rate of return on an investment.

To complete the calculation, you will need estimates of both the current Treasury-bill rate and the market risk—information that is readily available. For example, the T-bill rate is published in the business section of most newspapers. **Market risk**, also known as **systematic risk**, is the risk associated with the impact of the overall economy on securities markets. It often causes the market price of a particular stock or bond to change, even though nothing has changed in the underlying fundamental values of the security. Historical records indicate that 8 percent represents a realistic estimate of market risk.

---

*   Recall that the concept of **beta** (discussed in Chapter 13) statistically estimates the relative risk of a particular investment compared with the market risk for all investments by using historical data. A beta figure shows how responsive the price of an individual investment has been to overall market fluctuations. For example, if Running Paws Catfood Company stock has a historical performance beta of 1.5, if the stock market as a whole goes up 10 percent, Running Paws stock will probably go up 15 percent. Should the market fall 10 percent, Running Paws will likely decline 15 percent. Higher betas mean greater risk relative to the market.

To calculate the total estimated required rate of return on an investment, multiply the beta value of an investment times the estimated market risk return and then add the risk-free T-bill rate, as illustrated in Equation (16.1).

$$\text{Total Estimated Rate of Return Required on an Investment} = \text{T-bill rate} + (\text{beta} \times \text{market risk}) \quad (16.1)$$

For example, assume that you are considering investing in Running Paws Catfood Company, which has a beta of 1.5. If you assume a market risk of 8 percent (the historical average) and the current T-bill rate is 5.0 percent, the total estimated required rate of return on this investment is 17.0 percent [5.0 + (1.5 × 8.0)].

Calculate the Potential Rate of Return on a Particular Investment

The **potential return** for any investment over a period of years can be determined by adding anticipated income (from dividends, interest, rents, or other sources) to the future value of the investment minus its original cost. Table 16.1 illustrates how to sum up the projected income and price appreciation. You can then convert these figures into a **potential rate of return** by calculating the approximate compound yield, as shown in Equation (16.2), and this figure can be compared with returns on other investments.

Example: Running Paws Catfood Company Based on a recommendation from his stockbroker, Tony Schiano is considering Running Paws Catfood Company as a potential investment that might provide a better return than inflation and income taxes for about five years. Tony has determined the following information about this stock investment: It is currently priced at $30 per share, its most recent 12-month earnings amounted to $2.40 per share, and the cash dividend for the same period was $0.66 per share.

Tony began the task of projecting the future value of one share of the stock by using the earnings per share information. He first calculated the price/earnings ratio to be 12.5 ($30 ÷ $2.40). Next, as illustrated in Table 16.1, Tony applied a 15 percent rate of growth estimate (the same rate that occurred in previous years, according to Running Paws' annual report) for the earnings per share for each year ($2.40 × 1.15 = $2.76; $2.76 × 1.15 = $3.17; and so forth). Using a P/E ratio of 12.5 (the same as the current ratio), Tony estimated the market price at the end of the fifth year to be $60.38 (12.5 × $4.83). This calculation gives a projected net appreciation in stock price over five years of $30.38 ($60.38 minus the current price of $30).

To project the future income of the investment in Running Paws—the anticipated cash dividends—Table 16.1 shows that Tony estimated a 15 percent growth rate in the cash dividend ($0.66 × 1.15 = $0.76; $0.76 × 1.15 = $0.87; and so forth). Adding the projected cash dividends over five years gives a total of $5.11. Tony obtained the potential

Table 16.1

One Investor's Projections of the Earnings and Dividends for Running Paws Catfood Company

End of Year	Earnings	Dividend Income
1	$2.76	$0.76
2	3.17	0.87
3	3.65	1.00
4	4.20	1.15
5	4.83	1.33
Total dividends		$5.11

return for one share of Running Paws over five years by adding anticipated dividend income ($5.11) to the future value of the investment ($60.38) less its original cost ($30.00), for a result of $35.49 ($5.11 + $30.38). Thus, Tony has projected that $30 invested in one share of Running Paws will earn a potential total return of $35.49 in five years.

The question now becomes, what is the percentage yield for this dollar return? The **approximate compound yield (ACY)** formula provides a measure of the annualized compound growth of any long-term investment. You can determine this value by using Equation (16.2) and, if needed, varying the components slightly for different investments.* Note that the calculation requires use of an *annual average dividend* rather than the specific projected dividends. In this example, the annual average dividend computes to $1.02 by dividing the $5.11 in dividend income by five years. Substituting the data from Table 16.1 into Equation (16.1) and using the average annual dividend figure results in an approximate compound yield of 15.7 percent on the potential investment in one share of Running Paws stock for five years. This formula can be found on the *Garman/Forgue* Web site.

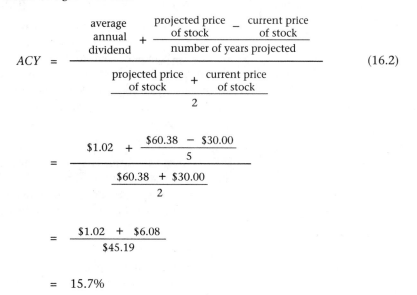

$$ACY = \frac{\begin{array}{l}\text{average} \\ \text{annual} \\ \text{dividend}\end{array} + \dfrac{\begin{array}{c}\text{projected price} \\ \text{of stock}\end{array} - \begin{array}{c}\text{current price} \\ \text{of stock}\end{array}}{\text{number of years projected}}}{\dfrac{\begin{array}{c}\text{projected price} \\ \text{of stock}\end{array} + \begin{array}{c}\text{current price} \\ \text{of stock}\end{array}}{2}} \qquad (16.2)$$

$$= \frac{\$1.02 + \dfrac{\$60.38 - \$30.00}{5}}{\dfrac{\$60.38 + \$30.00}{2}}$$

$$= \frac{\$1.02 + \$6.08}{\$45.19}$$

$$= 15.7\%$$

Compare the Estimated Required Rate of Return with the Projected Rate of Return on an Investment

Now the moment is at hand for decision making. You must compare the estimated required rate of return on an investment given its risk to the investment's potential projected rate of return. In our example involving Running Paws Catfood Company, the risk suggested a required rate of return of 17.0 percent. Its

---

* For example, for a mutual fund investment, change the numerator in the ACY formula to include the dividends and capital gains distributions, plus a one-year time period divided into the result of subtracting the beginning price from the ending price; change the denominator to include the ending price plus the beginning price divided by 2.

potential rate of return was projected to be only 15.7 percent, however, which suggests that Running Paws Catfood Company may not be a good buy for this investor at the current stock selling price of $30—that is, the stock is "overpriced." If the market value of Running Paws declines somewhat, perhaps to $29 per share, the investor might consider buying because the mathematics would reveal a projected rate of return more comparable to the required rate of return. Moreover, once armed with projected rate of return information for an investment, you may compare it with other investments.

How to Invest: A Twelve-Step Process

7 Explain the 12-step investment process.

Follow this 12-step process to attain your long-term investment goals:

1. *Identify your personal investment philosophy.* Before you make any investment, you must ascertain whether you follow a conservative, moderate, or aggressive philosophy (examined in Chapter 13).

2. *Identify your desired total rate of return.* It is imperative to take reasonable risks in the search for higher long-term rates of return. You must, therefore, identify the range of total return you desire, given the amount of risk you will accept. For example, a conservative investor might be satisfied with safe investments yielding 7 to 8 percent annually, a moderate investor might prefer a return of 9 to 12 percent, and an aggressive investor could aim for a total annual return of 13 to 30 percent.

3. *Keep an eye on local situations.* Peter Lynch, the former manager of the Fidelity Magellan Fund, says that amateur investors have an advantage over the large investors because three to five years before analysts really start to follow such developments, local people can be among the first to see the industry in which they work start to turn around. They may also see nearby businesses with bright futures.

4. *Set a time horizon for investing objectives.* Are you building up an amount for a down payment on a home, creating a college fund for a child, or putting money away for retirement? Keep in mind why you are investing and proceed accordingly.

5. *Choose your preferred investment medium.* Study carefully and decide which type of investment you prefer to earn the desired total return. Some people love stocks and hate bonds, and others prefer real estate to either type of security. Still others seek to earn good yields using mutual funds.

6. *Study available investment alternatives.* Take your time because you do not have to make a particular investment today, this week, or even this year. Carefully research the industry, the firm, and the competition. If you cannot find attractive investments, do not invest.

7. *Choose an investment for its components of total return.* Your task is to select an investment that will provide the necessary potential total return through income and price appreciation in the proportions that you desire. One stock might provide an anticipated cash dividend of 1.5 percent and an

TAX Considerations & Consequences — *Investment Profits and Losses*

From an income tax perspective, it is wise to consider balancing any investment losses against investment profits. Otherwise, too much money may be spent on income taxes.

For example, Barney Smith pays federal and state income taxes at a 30 percent rate. His investment portfolio has included two mutual funds and two stocks for some years. Both mutual funds have risen in value, but the stocks have declined. If all four investments were sold today, Barney would see the following net profit and loss figures: mutual fund A (+$5000); mutual fund B (+$10,000), stock C (−$7000), and stock D (−$9000).

If Barney sold his winning mutual funds, his profit would be $15,000 ($5000 + $10,000),

although $4500 of that amount would go to pay income taxes ($15,000 × 0.30). Therefore, Barney's proceeds would be reduced to $10,500 ($15,000 − $4500).

Barney could reduce his tax liability by selling one or both of his losing stocks. If he sold all of his stocks, his tax loss would be $16,000 ($7000 + $9000), and those losses would offset any income tax liability because they exceeded the profits of the mutual fund sales ($16,000 − $15,000). Thus, Barney's proceeds remain at $15,000 after taxes. IRS regulations permit Barney to carry forward the $1000 net loss ($16,000 in losses against $15,000 in profits) to place against next year's securities profits or ordinary income.

expected annual price appreciation of 10 percent for a total anticipated return of 11.5 percent. Another choice offering the same projected total return might be a stock with expected annual cash dividends of 4.5 percent and capital gains of 7 percent.

8. ***Invest in companies that will outearn competitors.*** If you are a long-term investor, you should consider only the companies that will likely be industry leaders—not necessarily the largest firms, but the pacesetters in terms of profitability. You should invest because you have good reasons related to profitability, such as a new division that is turning around, certain competitors that are losing ground, or product research that looks promising.

9. ***Develop a plan for investing and stick with it.*** Investors often do best by setting target prices and making a list of probable strategies and actions. For example, you might decide to buy a certain stock currently selling at $37 when its price slips to $35 and then hold it for five years or a little longer. In addition, you may decide that if the price appreciates more than 20 percent during any given year after you have held the stock for two years, you will sell to take your profits. Alternatively, if the issue loses more than 20 percent of its value over any 12-month time period, you will seriously consider selling and investing the proceeds elsewhere. If the economy seems to be peaking out, with a probable recession forecast, you may follow a path of immediately selling out and putting the proceeds in bonds or a money market account.

10. ***Diversify your portfolio.*** It is critical that you not put all of your investment eggs in one basket. For example, you might eventually buy a number of

mutual funds, perhaps including a balanced fund, an asset-allocation fund, a life-cycle fund, and a growth fund. Similarly, you could invest in three or four stocks within an industry group instead of just one. Do not diversify into unknown investments just for the sake of diversification, however.

11. ***Invest regularly.*** Successful investing requires making investments over a long time period, preferably a lifetime.

12. ***Reinvest your earnings.*** This approach allows invested sums to grow, which will almost certainly boost your investment profits.

Summary

1. After securities have been sold in the primary market, organized stock exchanges (such as the New York Stock Exchange) offer a secondary market.

2. To buy and sell securities, you must open an account at a general brokerage firm or discount brokerage firm and pay specific fees on each transaction.

3. Stock, bond, and mutual fund quotations from secondary market transactions are published in the business section of most newspapers.

4. The actual transaction to buy or sell securities involves brokers matching or negotiating the final price. Use of stop orders can help you reduce losses as well as protect gains in securities transactions.

5. Watching information on general economic conditions and the securities markets indexes, along with industry data and news about corporations, can help reduce investment risks and increase returns.

6. When considering an investment, you need to calculate an investment's potential rate of return.

7. The 12-step investment process includes identifying your desired return as well as making a list of probable actions you can take during certain investment conditions.

Key Words & Concepts

approximate compound yield (ACY)   *481*

bid price   *461*

cash account   *464*

churning   *462*

contractual accumulation plan   *472*

day order   *472*

discount brokerage firm   *464*

footnote t   *469*

limit order   *470*

market making   *461*

mutual fund bid price   *468*

odd lots   *463*

organized stock exchange   *459*

over-the-counter (OTC) market   *460*

securities market indexes   *473*

self-regulatory organization (SRO)   *461*

specialist   *469*

stockbroker   *459*

stop order   *471*

10-K report   *477*

Questions for Thought & Discussion

1. Explain why securities markets exist and describe the difference between primary and secondary markets.

2. Explain the role of an investment banking firm in the securities business.

3. Summarize the role of a brokerage firm in the process of trading securities in the secondary market.

4. Briefly describe how the organized stock exchanges differ.

5. Explain the over-the-counter concepts of market making, bid price, and asked price.

6. Summarize the benefits that an investor realizes by using a general brokerage firm.

7. What might be the commissions at a full-service general brokerage firm and a discount brokerage firm on a purchase of 350 shares of a stock priced at $10 per share?

8. Distinguish between a cash account and a margin account, and identify advantages of using each from an investor's point of view.

9. What is meant by the following stock transaction terms: stock, div, yld%, sales 100s, P/E ratio, high/low, close, net chg?

10. Summarize the meaning of newspaper quotations for mutual funds.

11. When are prices matched or negotiated?

12. Give reasons why investors would want to use a market order, a limit order, and a stop order.

13. Distinguish between the two ways of buying mutual funds: direct purchase and contractual accumulation.

14. Why is it important to obtain information about an industry in which you are considering investing?

15. What are the major factors considered in regulating in the securities market?

16. Summarize the insurance coverage provided investors by the Securities Investors Protection Corporation (SIPC).

17. Identify two popular stock indexes used by investors and briefly distinguish between them.

18. Summarize the logic in identifying a good return on a stock investment, including the concept of beta.

19. Summarize the essence of how to figure the potential rate of return on an investment.

20. Summarize how to use beta in estimating rate of return on an investment.

21. Choose three of the 12 steps in investing and summarize what they mean.

DECISION-MAKING CASES

Case 1 An Accountant Buys Computer Company Stock

Ronald Wall, an accountant from Honolulu, Hawaii, is interested in investing in Greenfield Computer Company. He notices that the market price for its common stock has hovered around $80 in recent months, and he wants to buy 100 shares. Give Ronald advice as he ponders the following questions:

(a) Should he use a general or discount brokerage firm for this purchase? Why?

(b) Should he give the stockbroker a market order or a limit order? Why?

(c) Should it be a day order or a good-till-canceled order? Why?

(d) What would the discount brokerage firm's commission probably be if Ronald bought Greenfield Computer for $79^{1}/_{2}$?

(e) As Ronald is an investor interested in cutting his losses and taking his gains, explain why he might put in stop orders at 67 and 92.

Financial Math Questions

1. Michael Margolis is a single parent and a motivational training consultant from Kansas City, Missouri. He is wondering about potential returns on investments given certain amounts of risk. Michael recently invested a total of $6000 in three stocks ($2000 in each) with different betas (stock A with a beta of 0.8, stock B with a beta of 1.7, and stock C with a beta of 2.5).

(a) If the stock market rises 12 percent over the next year, what is the likely value of each investment?

(b) If the stock market rises 19 percent over the next year, what is the likely value of each investment?

(c) If the stock market declines 8 percent over the next year, what is the likely value of each investment?

(d) Compare the value of the total portfolio in parts (a) and (c). Would Michael have had better results if he owned any one stock (i.e., would a $6000 investment in one stock leave him better off if the market went up or down the next year?).

2. Mary Porterfield, a married mother of three and part-time Mary Kay Cosmetics sales representative from DeKalb, Illinois, is trying to explain to her friend Elizabeth Shrader how to read the newspaper financial data on mutual funds. Mary turned to the financial section of the newspaper and located the part on mutual funds. Using Figure 16.6, help Mary explain by responding to the following questions about the Fidelity Investments group of mutual funds:

(a) How much would it cost to buy 100 shares of Fidelity Puritan (Puritn)?

(b) What would the commission charge be in terms of dollars and as a percentage of the amount invested?

(c) If Elizabeth already owned 100 shares of Puritan, how much would she receive per share if she redeemed them?

(d) Calculate the commission rates to buy shares in Fidelity Magellan (Magln) and New Market (NewMkt).

(e) How much would it cost to buy 100 shares of Fidelity HiYield (HiYld)?

(f) How much would it cost to sell 100 shares of Fidelity Magellan (Magln)? Explain why.

3. Xiao and Shiao Jing-jian, newlyweds from Kingston, Rhode Island, have decided to begin investing for the future. Xiao is a 7-Eleven store manager, and Shiao is a high school math teacher. They intend to take $3000 out of savings for investment and then continue to invest an additional $200 to $400 per month. Both have a moderate investment philosophy and seek some cash dividends as well as price appreciation.

(a) Calculate the five-year return on the investment choices in the table below. Put your calculations in tabular form like that shown in Table 16.1. (Hint: At the end of the first year, the EPS for Running Paws will be $2.40 with a dividend of $0.66, while the EPS for Eagle Packaging will be $2.76 with a projected dividend of $0.86.)

(b) Using the appropriate P/E ratios, what are the estimated market prices of Running Paws and Eagle after five years?

(c) Show your calculations in determining the projected price appreciations for the two stocks over the five years.

(d) Add the projected price appreciation of each stock to its projected cash dividends, and show the total five-year percentage returns for the two stocks.

	Running Paws	Eagle Packaging
Current price	$30.00	$8.00
Current earnings per share (EPS)	$2.00	$2.30
Current quarterly cash dividend	$0.15	$0.18
Current P/E ratio	15	21
Projected earnings annual growth rate	20%	20%
Projected cash divided growth rate	10%	10%

(e) Determine the average annual dividend for each stock, and use these figures in calculating the approximate compound yields for each.

(f) Check your responses by entering the data on the *Garman/Forgue* Web site. Which stock offers the largest potential rate of return?

(g) Assume that inflation is approximately 5 percent and the return on high-quality long-term corporate bonds is 9 percent. Given the Jing-jians' investment philosophy, explain why you would recommend
(1) Running Paws,
(2) Eagle, or
(3) a high-quality, long-term corporate bond as a growth investment. Support your answer by calculating the projected real return using the information on page 382 or by using the *Garman/Forgue* Web site. The Jing-jians are in the 28 percent marginal tax bracket.

MONEY MATTERS: LIFE-CYCLE CASES

The Hernandez Family Has Some Investment Questions

In recent years, the Hernandez family has been saving toward retirement, which Victor and Maria plan to begin in eight years. Through payroll deductions, Victor now has $25,000 saved at his credit union. Maria has put away $10,000 from her part-time employment. These amounts are in addition to Victor's investments through the retirement plan offered by his employer. Thinking that the past performance of various industries might be a fairly good predictor of earnings in the future, they seek your advice on where to invest the funds. They expect to sell some of the investments immediately after their retirement begins to have money for living expenses.

1. Suggest to the Hernandez family three industries that have had successful earnings in recent years (see Figure 16.7).

2. Give your personal opinion on why those industries might be successful in the future decade.

3. Briefly tell the Hernandezes how and when to obtain information about those industries and particular companies.

4. If their $35,000 investment earns an annual return of 9 percent, what will be the future value of the investment after eight years? (Hint: Use Appendix A.1 or the *Garman/Forgue* Web site.)

5. Assume that the $35,000 grows to $70,000 by the time that Victor and Maria retire and that it will continue to earn a return of 9 percent annually. If they plan on living an additional 20 years, how much can they withdraw each year so that the fund will be liquidated only after 20 years? (Hint: Use Appendix A.4 or the *Garman/Forgue* Web site.)

The Johnsons Want to Invest in Stock

After reviewing several types of investments, Harry and Belinda have decided to invest $1200 now and then $200 to $400 per month for the next two years. All income from their investments will be automatically reinvested, but they expect some price appreciation as well. Harry and Belinda are busy learning about different investments and generally "following the market."

1. Harry has been watching Mobil stock, and Belinda is interested in Monsanto. Which stock had the greatest volume of trading? Which stock reported the greatest net change in price? (See Figure 16.3.)

2. Based on only the P/E ratios for the two stocks, which is the better value?

3. If the Johnsons had a "windfall" and purchased 100 shares of Monsanto stock, how much commission would they pay? How much commission would they pay on 100 shares of Mobil stock? Assume the purchases were made at the highest price of the day.

4. Briefly discuss the factors the Johnsons should consider in choosing a stock brokerage firm, particularly given that they plan to invest regularly.

Exploring the World Wide Web of Personal Finance

To complete these exercises, go to the *Garman/Forgue* Web site at

www.hmco.com/college/business/

Select Personal Finance. Click on the exercise link for this chapter and answer the questions that appear on the Web page.

1. Visit the Web site for the General Motors Corporation annual report. Then visit the Securities and Exchange Commission Web site for a recent report for General Motors (type General Motors Corporation in the keyword box). How do the tone and feel of the two reports differ?

2. Visit the Web site for the New York Stock Exchange. Click on Market Regulation and then Protecting the Consumer. Describe the mechanism available to consumers who have disputes within the securities industry.

3. Visit the Web site of the National Association of Securities Dealers, where you will find a description of the Office of Ombudsman. What is the role of this office and how might investors use it to their advantage?

4. Visit the Web site for E*Trade and read up on the services provided by clicking on About E*Trade. How do the services provided compare and contrast with those provided by traditional full-service brokers? What effect might the advent of web trading services have on traditional investment houses?

5. Visit the Web site for Equity Analytics, Ltd., where you will find information on using various stop and limit orders to protect your stock investments from market swings. What are the advantages of these techniques?

Real Estate and Advanced Portfolio Management

17

OBJECTIVES

After reading this chapter, you should be able to:

1 Identify the advantages and disadvantages of investing in real estate and in using advanced portfolio management techniques.

2 Explain an effective way to determine the proper price to pay for real estate.

3 Distinguish between the types of direct and indirect ownership investments in real estate.

4 Detail ways of speculating in the securities markets.

5 Describe the speculative aspects of tangible investments.

M ost homeowners intuitively realize that the money used to buy their homes accomplishes more than just putting a roof over their heads. Homes also have an investment aspect, because they typically increase in value over the long term. Homes and other forms of real estate investment sometimes create quite substantial profits. This potential for profit encourages homeowners and other investors to consider real estate as an alternative investment to stocks, bonds, or mutual funds. Similarly, many people turn to more speculative investments in an attempt to increase the overall return on their investment portfolio.

This chapter begins with a discussion of the advantages and disadvantages of real estate and speculative investments. We then consider how to determine the value—that is, the price that might be paid—for a particular piece of property. Next comes a review of the types of direct and indirect ownership of real estate investments. It is followed by sections on techniques of advanced portfolio management involving speculative investing in the securities markets and tangible investments. The chapter concludes with a description of how to determine when to sell speculative investments.

Advantages and Disadvantages of Real Estate and Techniques of Advanced Portfolio Management

1 Identify the advantages and disadvantages of investing in real estate and in using advanced portfolio management techniques.

Real estate is property consisting of land and all permanently attached structures and accompanying rights and privileges, such as crops and mineral rights. People invest in real estate for both economic and noneconomic reasons. One noneconomic reason is that most investors like the feeling of being closely involved with their investments and the pride and satisfaction associated with owning property. The ultimate goal of investing in real estate is economic—the maximization of after-tax returns. (Real estate carries special income tax provisions that often increase after-tax income.) Residential real estate today offers an investor a yield roughly equal to the rate of inflation in the economy, although the return may be higher in some communities. The best returns from investing in real estate often come from commercial properties. In return for owning real estate, the investor must sacrifice substantial liquidity. Most real estate investments are not speculative, of course. Rather, they represent an alternative form of investment made by many investors who prefer low to moderate risk.

Speculative (or high-risk) investments are investment alternatives that carry considerable risk of loss along with the chance of large gains. In addition to the high potential profits, such investments carry a clear danger of losing some or all of the funds that have been invested. This potential high return can be enhanced further by using **leverage**, in which borrowed funds are used to make investments. Most speculative investments offer little or no potential for return from current income, such as cash dividends. Instead, most of the returns take the form of capital gains.

We refer to investing in speculative investments as advanced portfolio management because these alternative investments are not wise choices for the casual investor. **Advanced portfolio management** employs speculative mechanisms that round out the portfolios of some investors. Speculative investments should represent a relatively small portion of one's overall investment mix—perhaps 5 to 25 percent depending on investment philosophy, net worth, and stage in the life cycle. In any event, investors should be aware that they are dealing in very sophisticated markets when investing in such items as rights, options, precious metals, and collectibles.

Many of the speculative investing techniques described in this chapter are a **zero-sum game** in which the wealth of all investors remains the same, as the trading simply redistributes the wealth among the traders. Each profit must be offset by an equivalent loss. Thus, the average rate of return for all investors is zero, and the return actually becomes negative if transaction costs are included. Accordingly, investment funds used for speculative purposes should be only those that you can afford to lose.

Advantages of Real Estate Investments

Real estate investments provide four advantages: (1) the possibility of a positive cash flow, (2) the potential for price appreciation, (3) the availability of leverage, and (4) a number of special tax treatments.

Positive Cash Flow For an income-producing real estate investment, you pay operating expenses out of rental income. If the property has a mortgage (a common occurrence), payments toward the mortgage principal and interest also must be made out of rental income. The amount of rental income you have left after paying all operating expenses, including repairs and mortgage expenses, is called **cash flow**. The amount of cash flow—obtained by simply subtracting cash outlays from cash inflow—depends on the amount of rent received, the amount of expenses paid, and the amount necessary to repay the mortgage debt. Positive cash flow is a form of current income and is analogous to cash dividends received by owners of common stock and mutual funds. Those investors can obtain a return from two sources: current income (dividends) and capital gains. Likewise, real estate investors can realize a profit from current income (positive cash flow) and capital gains. Capital gains on real estate are taxed as long- or short-term rates (see Chapter 3). Investors usually prefer a positive cash flow to a negative cash flow because any shortages represent out-of-pocket expenses for the investor. Many investors, however, can manage a negative cash flow for a few years while waiting for capital gains to materialize through an increase in the market value of the property.

Price Appreciation **Price appreciation** comprises the amount above ownership costs for which an investment is sold; it is similar to the capital gains on a stock investment. In real estate, ownership costs include the original purchase price as well as expenditures for any capital improvements made to a property prior to sale. **Capital improvements** are costs incurred in making changes in real property that add to its value. Paneling a living room, adding a new roof, and putting up a fence represent capital improvements. In contrast, **repairs** are expenses (usually tax-deductible against an investor's cash-flow income) necessary to maintain the value of the property. Repainting, mending roof leaks, and fixing plumbing are examples of repairs. For instance, assume that Keith Carson, an unmarried schoolteacher from Detroit, Michigan, bought a small rental house as an investment five years ago for $80,000. He fixed some roof leaks (repairs) for $1000 and then added a new shed and some kitchen cabinets (capital improvements) at a cost of $5000 before selling the property this year for $105,000. As a result, Keith happily realized a price appreciation of $20,000 ($105,000 − $80,000 purchase price − $5000 capital improvements).

Leverage Lenders normally permit real estate investors to borrow from 75 to 95 percent of the price of an investment property. This leverage can increase the yield on an investment. Suppose that Keith Carson, instead of paying cash for the house, had made a down payment of $25,000 and borrowed the remainder. What effect would this borrowing have on his yield? In the first instance, Keith paid $80,000 cash for the property and thus earned a 25 percent yield on his investment ($20,000 ÷ $80,000) over the five years. In the second situation, using leverage, he would have an apparent yield of 80 percent ($20,000 ÷

$25,000). The true yield would be lower because of mortgage payments, interest expenses, property taxes, and repairs, but would still be a substantial double-digit return. Details of how to calculate the yield associated with real estate are provided later in this chapter.

The **loan-to-value ratio** measures the amount of leverage in a real estate investment project. It is calculated by dividing the amount of debt by the value of the total original investment. For example, Keith had a loan-to-value ratio of 68.75 percent, or 68.75 percent leverage, because his down payment was only $25,000 on the $80,000 property ($55,000 ÷ $80,000 = 0.6875).

Beneficial Tax Treatments   The U.S. Congress, through provisions in the Internal Revenue Code, encourages real estate investments by permitting investors a variety of special tax treatments. These provisions include depreciation, interest deductions, tax-free exchanges, and rental income tax regulations.

Depreciation Deduction   Investors in real estate become successful by understanding the "numbers" of real estate investing. For example, assume that Marilyn Furry, a lawyer from University Park, Pennsylvania, invested $115,000 in a residential building ($100,000) and land ($15,000). She rents the property to a tenant for $10,000 per year. The tenant pays all variable costs, such as real estate taxes ($600), insurance ($380), and maintenance ($240). You may think that, because the tenant pays all expenses, Marilyn must pay income taxes on the entire $10,000 in rental income; the IRS, however, allows her to deduct depreciation from this income. **Depreciation** represents the decline in value of an asset over time due to normal wear and tear and obsolescence. A proportionate amount of a capital asset representing depreciation may be deducted against income each year over the asset's estimated life. (Land cannot be depreciated.)

According to the straight-line method of depreciation, Marilyn can deduct an equal part of the building's cost over the estimated life of the property. According to the IRS guideline, residential properties may be depreciated over 27.5 years and commercial real estate for 39 years. Thus, Marilyn calculates the amount she can annually deduct from income to be $3636 ($100,000 ÷ 27.5). Table 17.1 shows the effects of depreciation on her income taxes, assuming Mar-

Table 17.1

Effect of Depreciation on Income Taxes and Yield

			Without Depreciation	With Depreciation
Total amount invested	$115,000	Gross rental income	$10,000	$10,000
Cost of land	− 15,000	Less annual depreciation expense	0	$ 3,636
Cost of rental building	$100,000	Taxable income	$10,000	$ 6,364
Depreciation permitted for 27.5 years	$ 3,636	Income taxes (33 percent marginal tax rate)	$ 3,300	$ 2,100
		Return after taxes	$ 6,700	$ 7,900
		Yield after taxes (divide return by $115,000)	5.8 %	6.9 %

Table 17.2

Additional Effect of Interest Paid on Income Taxes and Yield

Gross rental income	$ 10,000
Less annual depreciation deduction	– 3,636
Subtotal	$ 6,364
Less interest expense ($64,000, 9 percent mortgage loan)	– 6,179
Taxable income	$ 185
Return after interest expense ($10,000 – $6,179)	$ 3,821
Minus income taxes (0.33 × $185)	– 61
Return after taxes	$ 3,760
Yield after taxes [$3760 ÷ ($115,000 – $64,000)]	7.4%

ilyn is in the 33 percent effective marginal tax bracket (federal and state combined). In this example, the depreciation deduction lowers taxable income from $10,000 to $6364 ($10,000 − $3636) and raises the yield on the investment from 5.8 percent to 6.9 percent, a 19 percent increase [(6.9 − 5.8) ÷ 5.8]. This yield is based on the total investment of $115,000.

Interest Deduction Real estate investors incur several general business expenses in attempting to earn a profit: interest on a mortgage, real estate taxes, insurance, utilities, capital improvements, and repairs.* The largest of these costs often comprises the interest expense, as most properties are purchased with a mortgage loan. Table 17.2 illustrates the effect of interest expenses on income taxes. Assume Marilyn Furry borrowed $64,000 to purchase her $115,000 property. After she deducts interest expenses, her income flow is reduced to $3821; after she deducts depreciation, her *taxable* income is reduced to a mere $185. Because the income tax liability is only $61 ($185 × 0.33), the after-tax return on her leveraged investment increases to 7.4 percent. This yield is based on an investment of $51,000 ($115,000 − $64,000).

Because the tax laws permit investors to deduct interest expenses, part of the real cost of financing investment property is shifted to the government. The amount transferred depends on the investor's marginal tax bracket. Marilyn's interest deduction gives her an after-tax cash return of $3760. In essence, the $6179 in interest is paid with $2039 (33 percent tax bracket) of the money that was not sent to the federal and state governments and $4140 ($6179 − $2039) of Marilyn's money. Essentially, a major aspect of using borrowed money to invest is that the government "pays" part of the interest costs for the investor.

Tax-Free Exchanges Another special tax treatment results when a real estate investor trades equity in one property for equity in a similar property. If none of the people involved in the trade receives any other form of property or money, the transaction is considered a **tax-free exchange.** If one person receives some money or other property, only that person must report the extra proceeds as a taxable gain. For example, assume that you bought a duplex five years ago for $80,000 and now trade it with your friend, giving $5000 in cash for your friend's $135,000 commercial building. Your friend needs to report only the $5000 as income this year. In contrast, you must report your long-term gains ($135,000 − $5000 − $80,000 = $50,000) only when you actually sell the new property.

* Some commercial leases require that taxes, insurance, and utilities be paid by the lessee, which increases the investor's return.

Rental Income Tax Regulations If the real estate is "business property," expenses associated with the rental use of the property may be deductible—even if they produce a net loss that may be used to shelter other income from taxes. All real estate income and losses are classified for income tax purposes as **passive income** and **passive losses** (in contrast to other forms of income, such as that from a job or dividends from stock and mutual fund investments). Generally, passive losses cannot be used to offset income produced by a taxpayer's active (nonrental real estate) income.

Taxpayers who use a real estate investment residence (such as a vacation home) for 14 or fewer days and **materially participate*** in "actively managing" the property may take passive losses to reduce income taxes. When adjusted gross income (AGI) is less than $100,000, as much as $25,000 in passive losses may be used to shelter income from any source, such as salary or other investment income. The limit is gradually phased out as the AGI moves between $100,000 and $150,000. Thus, this ability to shelter income from taxes represents a terrific benefit for most people who invest in real estate on a small scale.

When personal use of a real estate investment residence (usually a vacation property) exceeds 14 days, income tax deductions (such as for interest, property taxes, and advertising) are limited to the amount of rental income from the property. Excess losses can be carried forward to future years to offset future income generated by the real estate investment residence.

Disadvantages of Real Estate Investments

The potential for a high total return from real estate investment carries with it a high degree of risk and uncertainty. Over the past decade, the average annual return on real estate investments in the United States has ranged from 3 to 15 percent. In some areas, however, property values have actually declined. The following list describes this and other disadvantages of real estate investments.

- *Financial Risk*   It is quite possible to lose money in real estate investments.

- *Complexity*   Real estate investments require more study and careful investigation than do most other investments.

- *Large Initial Investment*   Investment in real estate generally requires many thousands of dollars, often with an initial outlay of $15,000 to $30,000 or more.

- *Time-Consuming Management Demands*   Managing a real estate investment requires time.

- *Low Current Income*   Sometimes expenses may reduce cash-flow return to less than 2 percent or even generate a loss.

- *Unpredictable Costs*   Estimating costs presents many difficulties.

---

*   The Internal Revenue Service requires that to "materially participate" the investor must meet one of seven IRS tests. One test is if the taxpayer participates in the activity for more than 500 hours per year. If the participation is less than 500 hours, one qualifies if the participation constitutes substantially all of the participation of all individuals (including nonowners) during the year.

- *Difficulty in Selling* Because real estate is expensive, the market for investment property is much smaller than the securities market.

- *Liquidity* Because of liquidity problems, it may take months or even years to find a buyer, arrange the financing, and close the sale of a real estate investment.

- *High Transfer Costs* Substantial transfer costs, often 6 to 7 percent of the property's sale price, are incurred when real estate is bought or sold.

What Should You Pay for a Real Estate Investment?

2 Explain an effective way to determine the proper price to pay for real estate.

The **discounted cash-flow method** is an effective way to estimate the value or asking price of a real estate investment. It emphasizes after-tax cash flow and the return on the invested dollars discounted over time to reflect a discounted yield. Computer software programs are available to help calculate discounted cash flows. You also can use Appendix A.2, as shown in Table 17.3. To illustrate how this method works, assume that you require a rate of return of 10 percent on a piece of real estate property advertised for sale at $80,000. You estimate that rents can be increased each year for five years. After all expenses are paid, you expect to have an after-tax cash flow of $4000, $4200, $4400, $4600, and $4800 for the five years. Assuming some price appreciation, you anticipate selling the property for $100,000 after all expenses are incurred. How much should you pay now to buy the property?

Table 17.3 explains how to answer this question. Multiply the estimated after-tax cash flows and the expected proceeds of $100,000 to be realized on the sale of the property by the present value of a dollar at 10 percent (the required rate of return). Add the present values together to obtain the total present value of the property—in this case, $78,632. Thus, the asking price of $80,000 is too high for you to earn an after-tax return of 10 percent. Your choices are to negotiate the price down, accept a return of less than 10 percent, or consider another

Table 17.3

Discounted Cash-Flow Method Illustration

	After-Tax Cash Flow	Present Value of $1 at 10 Percent*	Present Value of After-Tax Cash Flow
1 year	$ 4,000	0.909	$ 3,636
2 years	4,200	0.826	3,469
3 years	4,400	0.751	3,304
4 years	4,600	0.683	3,142
5 years	4,800	0.621	2,981
Sell property	$100,000	0.621	62,100
Present value of property			$78,632

* From Appendix A.2.

investment. The discounted cash-flow method provides an effective way to estimate real estate values because it takes into account the selling price of the property, the effect of income taxes, and the time value of money.

Direct and Indirect Ownership Investments in Real Estate

3   Distinguish between the types of direct and indirect ownership investments in real estate.

A real estate investment is known as **direct ownership** when an investor holds actual legal title to the property. You can invest directly as an individual—buying an apartment building, for example—or jointly with other investors.

Direct Ownership Investments in Real Estate

There are three general types of direct ownership investments in real estate: (1) residential property units and commercial properties, (2) second or vacation homes, and (3) raw land and residential lots.

Residential Units and Commercial Properties   **Residential units** are properties designed for residential living, such as houses, duplexes, apartments, mobile homes, and condominiums, that offer a potential to produce investment profits. **Commercial properties** are properties designed for business uses, such as office buildings, medical centers, gasoline stations, and motels, that also carry a potential to produce a profit. Realizing a good investment income from these properties normally requires that you take an active interest in their management.

Residential units are probably the least complex real estate investments with which to begin, the easiest to sell, and the least profitable. One popular way to start in real estate investment is to purchase **sweat equity property.** In this approach, you would seek a property that needs repairs but has good underlying value. You buy it at a favorable price and "sweat" by spending many hours cleaning, painting, and repairing it to sell at a profit or to rent to tenants.

Commercial properties carry more risk of remaining unrented than residential units. In addition, business tenants usually expect more extensive and costly services, and the buildings have a greater likelihood of obsolescence. Accordingly, you can charge higher rents on commercial properties to offset the higher risk involved.

When choosing income-producing rental property, you need to consider several criteria: good location, dependability of income, current value of the property, condition of the property, likely impact of future competition of similar real estate, availability of reasonable financing, moderately priced utilities, stable real estate property taxes, and, of course, return on investment after taxes.

Second or Vacation Homes   Many people own a second or vacation home, usually a house, condominium, or mobile home located near a lake or a beach, in the mountains, or at some resort area. The IRS generally considers a second or vacation home to be just another piece of property. Thus, owners can deduct amounts spent for mortgage interest and real estate property taxes. For example, Leslie Cain, a librarian from Lynchburg, Virginia, has bought vacation property on the west coast of Florida for which she makes a $600 monthly payment. Monthly interest and taxes amount to $500. Because Leslie is in the 28 percent tax bracket, she realizes tax savings of $140 monthly ($500 × 0.28). Thus, her property's net cost is $460 ($600 − $140) per month, or $5520 annually.

If she rents out her property, Leslie can qualify for additional tax savings if her adjusted gross income is less than $150,000. IRS regulations allow investors to take all or a portion of passive losses on a vacation home used as rental property as long as the investor: (1) materially participates in rental operations; (2) rents the property for 15 days or more; (3) attempts to rent the property, either by listing it with a rental agent or advertising it; and (4) the owner's personal use does not exceed 14 days or 10 percent (whichever is greater) of the total number of days the home is rented at a "fair rental value." Rental losses for depreciation, repair costs, utility bills, and other expenses may be taken as tax deductions. For example, income for Leslie could amount to $2000 for 20 days of rentals. In Leslie's case, rental losses might total $3500 and result in a tax loss of $1500, but only if she did not personally use the property more than 14 days herself. Remember, too, that Leslie stands to gain from long-term price appreciation.

When to Sell a Real Estate Investment

Generally, you should sell a real estate investment in the following situations:

- **Your investments are unwise.** No matter how careful the real estate investor is, some investments just do not work out. Perhaps the apartment building is located in the wrong neighborhood or the vacation property is deteriorating and actually declining in value. When troubles and expenses mount, it is time to consider selling.

- **You are tired of ownership.** At some point, you may no longer enjoy collecting rents, arranging maintenance, and making capital improvements, or your vacation spot may lose its attractiveness. Consider selling the property and finding another investment that you like better.

- **Alternative investments pay more.** Some people buy a piece of real estate and feel they must keep it forever. You may have owned a vacation property for many years and paid off the mortgage in

full, or a rental building you bought years ago may still be bringing in a stream of income. Could you make more money by selling or refinancing and then investing the proceeds elsewhere? For example, a vacation home valued at $90,000 with no mortgage debt represents a $90,000 asset earning no current income for the owner. An alternative would be to refinance it, perhaps obtaining $70,000, and to invest that amount elsewhere.

- **You need money.** Many owners of real estate go through crisis times when they simply need money. In these instances, you do not necessarily need to sell your property. When you refinance property instead of selling, you may receive a substantial amount of cash in addition to a new mortgage.

- **You want to invest "upward."** You can use leverage to enhance profits in real estate. You may want to sell your home and invest those proceeds (including price appreciation) into a more expensive property.

A special provision in the tax law pertains to vacation properties that are rented out for fewer than 15 days during the year. Under the law, you cannot take any deductions, except for mortgage interest and property taxes, but the rental income you collect is not taxable; instead, it is considered tax-free income.

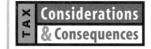

An Income-Producing Real Estate Investment

When you are considering a real estate investment, you use your investment amount (purchase price or down payment) to estimate the likely rate of return. This estimate may be compared with other investment alternatives. The following table shows five-year estimates for a hypothetical residential property with a purchase price of $100,000. The building will be purchased with a $75,000 mortgage loan, so the buyer has to make a $25,000 down payment and also pay $4000 in closing costs. The gross income is projected to rise at an annual rate of 5 percent, vacancies and unpaid rent at 10 percent, real estate taxes at 7 percent, insurance at 8 percent, and mainte-

nance at 10 percent. Virtually the entire payment for the 30-year, $75,000, 12 percent fixed-rate mortgage loan is assumed to be interest during these early years. For income tax purposes, the land is valued at $10,000, and the building is depreciated over 27.5 years. Thus, the amount of annual straight-line depreciation is calculated to be $3272 ($100,000 − $10,000 = $90,000; $90,000 ÷ 27.5 = $3272). The buyer is in the 28 percent marginal tax bracket.

Note how difficult it is to earn current income from rental properties when financing costs are relatively high. During the first year, the total cash flow loss is projected to be $2261. Furthermore, because

Estimates for a Successful Real Estate Investment

		Year				
		1	2	3	4	5
A.	Gross possible income	$10,000	$10,500	$11,025	$11,576	$12,155
	Less vacancies and unpaid rent	− 500	− 550	− 605	− 666	− 733
B.	Projected gross income	$ 9,500	$ 9,950	$10,420	$10,910	$11,422
C.	Less operating expenses					
	Interest and principal (P + I)	$ 9,261	$ 9,261	$ 9,261	$ 9,261	$ 9,261
	Real estate taxes (T)	900	963	1,030	1,103	1,180
	Insurance (I)	400	432	467	504	544
	Maintenance	1,200	1,320	1,452	1,597	1,757
	Total operating expenses	$11,761	$11,976	$12,210	$12,465	$12,742
D.	Total cash flow (negative)	$(2,261)	$(2,026)	$(1,790)	$(1,555)	$(1,320)
E.	Less depreciation expense	− 3,272	− 3,272	− 3,272	− 3,272	− 3,272
F.	Taxable income (or loss) (D − E)	$(5,533)	$(5,298)	$(5,062)	$(4,827)	$(4,592)
G.	Annual tax savings (28 percent marginal rate)	1,549	1,483	1,417	1,352	1,286
H.	Net cash flow income (or loss) after taxes (G − D)	$ (712)	$ (543)	$ (373)	$ (203)	$ (34)

Raw Land and Residential Lots Investing in raw land or residential lots on which you do not intend to build is a speculative affair. **Raw land** is undeveloped acreage, typically far from established communities, with no utilities and no improvements except perhaps a substandard access road. A **residential lot** is subdivided acreage with utilities—typically water, electricity, and sewerage—

the income tax laws permit depreciation to be recorded as a real estate investment expense, even though it is not an out-of-pocket cost, the total taxable loss is projected to be $5533. This loss is deductible on the investor's income tax. Because the investor is in the 28 percent tax bracket, the loss of $5533 results in a first-year annual tax savings of $1549 ($5533 × 0.28). Instead of sending the $1549 to the government in taxes, the investor can use it to pay the operating expenses of the investment. Therefore, the cash-flow loss of $2261 is reduced by $1549 for a net cash-flow loss after taxes of $712 ($2261 − $1549). During the first year of ownership, the investor will have to come up with the additional $712 (about $60 monthly) to make ends meet.

Assume that the property appreciates in value at an annual rate of 6 percent and will be worth $133,823 in five years ($100,000 × 1.06 × 1.06 × 1.06 × 1.06 × 1.06). If it sold at this price, a 6 percent real estate sales commission would reduce the proceeds by $8029 to $125,794.

Now we can calculate the crude annual rate of return on the property, as the following table shows. A **crude rate of return** is a rough measure of the yield on amounts invested that assumes that equal portions of the gain are earned each year. The total return in this example was substantial. There were out-of-pocket cash investments of $25,000 for the down payment, $4000 in closing costs, and $1865 in net cash-flow losses ($712 + $543 + $373 + $203 + $34), for a total investment of $30,865. The investor has a capital gain of $38,154, or a crude annual rate of return (before taxes) of 124 percent over five years, roughly 25 percent annually (124 percent ÷ 5 years).

Crude Rate of Return on a Successful Real Estate Investment

Taxable cost (adjusted basis)

Purchase price ($25,000 down payment, $75,000 loan)	$ 100,000
Closing costs	− 4,000
Subtotal	104,000
Less accumulated depreciation	− 16,360
Taxable cost (adjusted basis)	$ 87,640

Proceeds (after paying off mortgage)

Sale price	$ 133,823
Less sales commission	− 8,029
Net proceeds	$ 125,794
Less taxable cost	− 87,640
Taxable proceeds (capital gain)	$ 38,154

Amount invested

Down payment	$ 25,000
Closing costs	4,000
Accumulated net cash flow losses	+ 1,865
Total invested	$ 30,865

Crude annual rate of return

Total invested	$ 30,865
Taxable proceeds (capital gain)	$ 38,154
Before-tax total return ($38,154 ÷ $30,865)	124%
Crude before-tax annual rate of return (124 percent ÷ 5 years)	25%

Note: Using a financial calculator yields an internal rate of return for this investment of 23.3 percent. Thus, the crude rate of return calculations given here provide a reasonably close estimate in this instance.

located within or adjacent to established communities. Land speculators buy raw land and residential lots to sell to people who "think" they will build in the future. You should not buy any acreage unless you firmly believe that: (1) the price paid today is substantially less than what it might be in the future, (2) comparable acreage will not be available in the future when needed by buyers, or (3) you will later build on the property yourself.

Although they are not sufficient by themselves, "location, location, and location" are regarded as the first three rules of successful real estate investing. Beware of speculating in unknown land in some distant new city, retirement village, or resort. A potential investor should always see the land, hire an attorney to review the deal, read the **property report** (a document legally required under the federal Interstate Land Sales Act for properties offered for sale across state lines), and obtain a private property appraisal.

You Are Asked to Invest in Time Sharing

Time sharing is often promoted as a way to simultaneously invest and obtain vacation housing. For between $5000 and $20,000, buyers can purchase one or more week's use of luxury vacation housing furnished right down to the salt and pepper shakers. Vacationers also pay an annual maintenance fee for each week of ownership, perhaps amounting to $100 per week.

Legally, the terms "time sharing" and "interval ownership" are not interchangeable. A **right-to-use purchase** of a limited, preplanned, time-sharing period of use of a vacation property actually represents only a vacation license. It does not grant legal real estate ownership interest to the purchaser, but instead provides a long-term lease permitting use of a hotel suite, condominium, or other accommodation. This practice is also known as **nondeeded time sharing.** As in some other situations that involve leasing, if the true owner of the property—the developer—becomes bankrupt, the time share purchasers (actually tenants) can be locked out of the premises by the creditors.

In contrast, an **interval ownership purchase** provides time-sharing buyers with actual titles and deeds to limited time periods of use of real estate.

Purchasers thus become secured creditors who are guaranteed continued use of the property throughout any bankruptcy proceedings. This practice is also known as **deeded time sharing.**

Time sharing and interval ownership should be viewed as a prepaid vacation expense—not as a real estate investment. (It is an investment for the developer, however, as a $100,000 apartment unit that is time-shared for 52 weeks at $5000 per week brings the developer $260,000.) In fact, time sharing is not a wise investment for most people. It is very difficult to sell a time-share investment, and people rarely receive more than 50 percent of their original investment in the sale. A survey from the Resort Property Owners Association estimates that the average time-share unit languishes on the market for 4.4 years before being sold. At any point in time, 60 percent of all time shares are up for sale. If you are interested in such property for vacation purposes, you should be leery of gifts and awards offered to promote time-sharing units, avoid right-to-use time sharing, demand a 15-day cancellation clause in the contract, and require that your money be placed in escrow until the construction of any yet-to-be-built time-sharing project is completed.

Indirect Ownership Investments in Real Estate

In an **indirect investment in real estate**, the investors do not hold actual legal title to the property. Examples include real estate syndicates, real estate investment trusts, and ownership of mortgages. Investors can obtain information on these alternatives from brokerage firms.

A **real estate syndicate** is an indirect form of real property investment, often organized as a limited partnership, in which a required minimum number of shares (often five) are sold to investors for as little as $500 per share to raise capital for real estate projects. Syndicates finance the building of many office buildings, shopping centers, factories, apartment houses, supermarkets, and motels. The **limited partnership** form of real estate syndicate involves two classes of partners: the general partner and the limited partners. The **general partner** (usually the organizer and initial investor) operates the syndicate and has unlimited financial liability. The **limited partners** (the outside investors) receive part of the profits and the tax-shelter benefits but remain inactive in the management of the business and have no personal liability for the operations of the partnership beyond their initial investment.

A **real estate investment trust (REIT)** is an unincorporated business that raises money by selling shares to the public, much in the same way as a closed-end mutual fund, and owns property or provides mortgage lending to developers. Offering the potential of high profits, REITs typically specialize in a segment of the real estate market, such as apartment buildings or medical facilities.

Speculation in the Securities Markets

4 Detail ways of speculating in the securities markets.

Several techniques of speculating in securities markets are used in advanced portfolio management. Speculation in securities markets occurs when investors make use of margin buying or selling securities "short," as well as when they invest in specialized securities such as rights, options, and futures contracts.

Margin Buying

One technique to increase the return on an investment is margin buying. A **margin account** requires a deposit of substantial cash or securities ($2000 or more) and permits the purchase of other securities using credit granted by the brokerage firm. Using a margin account to purchase securities, or **margin buying**, allows the investor to apply leverage that magnifies returns by borrowing money from a brokerage firm to buy securities. As a result, the investor can buy more stocks and bonds than would be possible with available cash. Both brokerage firms and the Federal Reserve Board regulate use of credit to buy securities. The **margin rate** is the percentage of the value (or equity) in an investment that is not borrowed. In recent years, it has ranged from 30 to 80 percent. Thus, if the margin rate is 40 percent, you can buy securities by putting up only 40 percent of the total price and borrowing the remainder from the brokerage firm. The securities purchased, as well as other securities in the margin account, are used as collateral. Margin lending is financed at competitive rates.

Buying on margin is commonly used to increase return on investment. For example, assume that Running Paws common stock is selling for $80 per share and you wish to buy 100 shares for a total of $8000. Using your margin account, you will make a cash payment of $3200 (0.40 × $8000), with the brokerage firm lending you the difference of $4800 ($8000 − $3200). For the sake of simplicity, we will omit commissions and assume the brokerage firm lends the funds at 10 percent interest. Thus, your equity (market value minus amount borrowed) in the investment is $3200. If, as illustrated in Table 17.4, the price of Running Paws stock increases from $80 to $92 at the end of a year, you can sell your

Table 17.4

How Buying on Margin Affects the Return on Investment

	Cash Transaction	40% Margin Transaction
Price of stock rises (from $80 to $92 a share)		
Buy 100 shares @ $80 (amount invested)	−$8000	−$3200
Sell 100 shares @ $92 (proceeds)	9200	9200
Net proceeds	$1200	$6000
Minus amount borrowed	—	− 4800
Net	$1200	$1200
Minus cost of borrowing	—	− 480
Return	$1200	$ 720
Yield (return ÷ amount invested)	+ 15.0%	+22.5%
Price of stock declines (from $80 to $70 a share)		
Buy 100 shares @ $80 (amount invested)	−$8000	−$3200
Sell 100 shares @ $70 (proceeds)	7000	7000
Net proceeds	−$1000	$3800
Minus amount borrowed	—	− 4800
Net	−$1000	$1000
Minus cost of borrowing	—	− 480
Return	−$1000	−$1480
Yield (return ÷ amount invested)	−12.5%	−46.25%
Price of stock declines (from $80 to $60 a share)		
Buy 100 shares @ $80 (amount invested)	−$8000	−$3200
Sell 100 shares @ $60 (proceeds)	6000	6000
Net proceeds	−$2000	$2800
Minus amount borrowed	—	−4800
Net	−$2000	−$2000
Minus cost of borrowing	—	−480
Return	−$2000	−$2480
Yield (return ÷ amount invested)	−25.0%	−77.5%

investment for a proceed of $9200, minus the amount invested ($3200), the amount borrowed ($4800), and the cost of borrowing ($4800 × 0.10 = $480), for a yield of $720. Because you invested an equity of only $3200 for a profit of $720, you have earned a return of 22.5 percent ($720 ÷ $3200). If you had instead put up the entire $8000 and not bought on margin, your return on investment would have been only 15 percent ($9200 − $8000 = $1200; $1200 ÷ $8000 = 0.15). In this way, "other people's money" can be used to increase the rate of return on your investment.

Aggressive investors also like to buy on margin because leverage potentially allows them to make significant gains over short time periods. For example, assume that the margin rate is 50 percent and you want to purchase 1000 shares of a $10 stock. Buying on margin, you need put up only $5000 (0.50 × $10,000). If the price of the stock rises to only $11 over the course of a month, you make a handsome profit. The $1000 in proceeds ($11 × 1000 = $11,000; $11,000 − $10,000 = $1000) might be reduced by a brokerage firm's interest charges of $100, for a return of $900. Thus, you achieve a yield of 18 percent on the amount invested ($900 ÷ $5000) in only one month, or more than 200 percent annually. By not buying on margin, the short-term investor just described would have been forced to wait until the price reached 11⁷/₈ (almost a full point higher than the margin investor) to realize a similar return ($11,875 − $10,000 = $1875; $1875 ÷ $10,000 = 18.75 percent).

Buying on margin can be dangerous as well. If the price of a security bought on margin declines, leverage can work against you, as Table 17.4 illustrates. For example, if the Running Paws stock bought at $80 dropped to $70 after a year, you would lose $10 per share on the 100 shares, for a total loss of $1000. Proceeds would be only $7000. If you bought the stock on 40 percent margin, this amount is offset by the cost of the investment ($3200), the margin loan from the broker ($4800), and interest on the loan ($480), for a total deduction of $8480 and a net loss of $1480 ($7000 − $8480). Thus, a loss of $1480 on an investment of $3200 is a negative return of 46.25 percent (−$1480 ÷ $3200). The same $10 loss per share (from $80 to $70 per share) would have been a negative loss of only 12.5 percent if the stocks were not bought on margin ($7000 − $8000 = −1000; −$1000 ÷ $8000 = −0.125). In this manner, leverage obtained when buying stocks on margin can enhance both profits and losses dramatically.

Determine a Margin Call Price

To determine at what price a margin call will occur, use the **margin call formula** given in Equation (17.1). Substituting the figures from the preceding illustration, the investor will not receive a margin call unless the stock price drops below $64, as equity at this point remains 25 percent. This formula also appears on the *Garman/Forgue* Web site.

$$\text{Margin call price} = \frac{\text{amount owed broker} ÷ (1 - \text{margin call requirement})}{\text{number of shares bought}} \quad (17.1)$$

Similarly, the example cited in Table 17.4 illustrates the magnitude of the loss due to a $20 decline in value as a negative return of 77.5 percent, compared with a loss of only 25 percent if the investor had not bought on margin.

In addition, a **margin call** could hurt the financial position of the margin buyer. With this approach, the margin investor is required to contribute more funds if the value of the security declines to the point where the investor's equity is less than a required percentage (such as 25 percent) of the current market value. If the investor fails to put up the additional cash or securities, the broker can legally sell the securities. The margin call concept protects the broker who has loaned money on securities. In Table 17.4, the 100 shares of Running Paws priced at $80 were originally valued at $8000, with investor's equity of $3200, or 40 percent ($3200 ÷ $8000), and $4800 borrowed from the brokerage firm. Assume that the stock price drops to $60 per share, which makes the current market value $6000. Because the investor still owes $4800, the equity has dropped to $1200 ($6000 − $4800), which is only 20 percent of the value of the securities ($1200 ÷ $6000). The broker will immediately make a margin call, demanding that funds be added to the account (perhaps within 72 hours) to bring the equity up to a minimum of 25 percent. In this example, an additional $300 ($6000 × 0.25 = $1500; $1500 − $1200 = $300) would be required.

If the investor cannot meet the margin call, the broker will sell the securities as soon as possible (at whatever price is obtainable), and a sharp financial loss will result. The investor must repay the broker for any losses.

Selling Short

Buying a security in the hope that it will go up in value—the goal of most investors—is called **buying long**. You might suspect, however, that the price of a security will drop. You can earn profits when the price of a security declines by first selling short, although it is a tricky business. **Selling short** is a trading technique by which investors sell a security they do not own (borrowing it from a broker) and later buy the same number of shares of the security at a lower price (and return it to the broker), thus earning a profit on the transaction. It's "buy low, sell high," but reversed to "sell high, buy low." Brokerage firms require an investor to maintain a margin account when selling short because it provides some assurance that the investor can repay the value of the stock if necessary. As a result, some or all of an investor's funds deposited in a margin account are effectively tied up during a short sale. Many brokers hold the proceeds of a short sale, without paying interest, until the customer "covers the position" by buying it back for delivery to the broker.

For example, you believe that the price of Running Paws stock will drop substantially over the next several months. You have heard that some top managers of the company may resign and that competitors are expected to introduce newer products. Accordingly, you instruct your broker to sell 100 shares of Running Paws at $80 per share ($80 × 100 = $8000). In this illustration, assume that you have a 40 percent margin requirement, which means you have committed $3200 (0.40 × $8000). The shares are actually borrowed by the broker from another investor or another broker. Several months later, Running Paws announces lower profits because of strong competition, and the share price drops to $70. Now you instruct your broker to buy 100 shares at the new price.

You gain a profit of $1000 ($8000 − $7000), ignoring commissions, providing a yield of 31.3 percent ($1000 ÷ $3200).

A very small price drop can provide big profits for the short-term investor who sells short and uses margin buying techniques. For example, imagine that you sell 100 shares of a $10 stock with a 40 percent margin requirement. The committed funds amount to $400 (0.40 × $1000). Even if the price of the stock declines by only $1, you still earn a significant profit: 100 shares sold at $10 equals $1000, minus 100 shares bought at $9 equals $900, for a profit of $100 and a yield of 25 percent ($100 ÷ $400).

On the other hand, almost unlimited losses can occur if the price rises rather than falls. If the $10 stock soars to $22, the loss will exceed the original investment: 100 shares sold at $10 equals $1000, minus 100 shares bought at $22 equals $2200, for a loss of $1200 and a negative yield of 550 percent ($2200 ÷ $400). In addition, when the price of a security rises, short sellers are subject to margin calls. Clearly, selling short and buying on margin are techniques to be used only by sophisticated investors.*

Trading in Rights

When corporations raise additional capital by selling new shares of stock, current stockholders may experience dilution of their ownership position. For example, assume that Road Runners Shoe Company has 100,000 shares of stock outstanding and wants to sell an additional 100,000 shares. A stockholder who owns 10,000 shares would see his or her ownership in the company go from 10 percent (10,000 divided by 100,000) to 5 percent (10,000 divided by 200,000). The bylaws of many corporations and the statutes of most states give a **preemptive right** to existing stockholders, which is the legal right that the stockholder be given the opportunity to purchase a proportionate share of any new stock issue so that he or she can maintain a proportionate ownership share. Each current stockholder is issued a **right**, which is a legal instrument to purchase a number of shares of corporate stock at a specific price during a limited time period. Most rights lapse after 16 days, although some have a one-month limit. The rights can be used to buy shares of the new stock offering, or the holders of rights can sell them to other investors.

Rights normally allow purchase of the new shares at a price somewhat lower than the current market value of the stock. Consequently, a market exists for the buying and selling of rights, in which speculators may choose to participate. A typical speculative investment is to use margin to buy rights with the hope that the value of the stock—and hence the rights—will rise.

For example, the right to buy one share of the new Road Runners stock at $18 is worth approximately $2 if the current selling price is $20 ($20 − $18 = $2). If other investors perceive this new stock offering as an indication that Road Runners will be more profitable in the future, the price of the stock might rise to

---

* The short seller also must pay the brokerage firm any dividends paid by the company until the position is covered. These dividends are passed on to the person whose stock was borrowed. The investor whose stock was borrowed usually does not know that his or her securities were used because the brokerage firm uses certificates held in the name of the firm—the **street name**—and posts dividends as if they were paid by the company.

perhaps $21 or $22 and the price of the right will follow suit. Imagine that you purchase 1000 rights at $2 each and put up only $500 in cash, using margin for the remaining $1500. (Special margin rules exist for rights transactions.) If the price of the stock rises to $22, you will realize a tremendous profit. The value of each right will have risen to about $4 ($22 − $18), and it may be even higher if investor interest remains particularly strong. Selling the right or exercising it to purchase the shares at the specified price will bring you proceeds of $2000 ($4000 − $1500 − $500) on an investment of only $500. Your yield of 400 percent ($2000 ÷ $500) will be realized in just a few days or weeks. You should realize, however, that the price of the stock could have dropped below $18, forcing down the value of the right and possibly resulting in a total loss of $2000 ($500 invested plus the $1500 borrowed) for the investor.

Using Options to Profit

An **option** is a contract that gives the holder the right to buy or sell a specific asset at a predetermined price within a specified time period. Markets exist for options related to common stocks, debt instruments, foreign currencies, stock indexes, and even unleaded gasoline. The most common are **stock options**, which are contracts giving the holder the right to buy or sell a specific number of shares (normally 100) of a certain stock at a specified price (the **striking price**) before a specified date (the **expiration date**, typically three months).* Buying and selling options are techniques used by both conservative and aggressive investors. Options are examples of a **derivative**, a financial instrument that is based on the values of other financial indicators (such as interest rates, foreign exchange rates, commodity prices, or stock market indexes).

Writing Options   Options are created by an **option writer**. Through a stock brokerage firm, an option writer issues an option contract promising either to buy or to sell a specified asset for a fixed striking price; in return, the option writer receives an **option premium** (the price of the option itself) for standing ready to buy or sell the asset at the wishes of the option purchaser. Once written and sold, an option may change hands many times before its expiration. The **option holder** is the person who actually owns the option contract. The original option writer always remains responsible for buying or selling the asset if requested by the holder of the option contract.

Two types of options exist: puts and calls. A **call option** is an option contract that gives the option holder the right to *buy* the optioned asset from the option writer at the striking price. A **put option** is an option contract that gives the option holder the right to *sell* the optioned asset to the option writer at the striking price. The feature "How to Make Sense of Options" illustrates the relationships between option writers and option holders for both puts and calls.

Most options expire without being exercised by the option holder, and the option writer is the only person to earn a profit. The profit results from the premium charged when the option was originally sold. An option writer can approach the market from the position of either a conservative investor or a speculative investor.

---

*   A new, longer-term option called **Long-term Equity AnticiPation Securities (LEAPS)** is available for more than 150 stocks. These options have lives as long as two and one-half years.

Conservative Writers Profit by Selling Covered Calls Conservative option writers own the underlying asset (the stock), and when they sell a call, for example, it is described as a **covered option** because the writer has an ownership position. (If the writer does not own the asset, it is a **naked option**, a speculative position.) When used effectively by conservative option writers, calls can potentially pick up an extra return of perhaps 1 to 2 percent every three months.

As a conservative investor, you can profit by selling a call on stock already owned, giving the buyer the right to purchase your shares at a fixed strike price for a time period. Assume that you have 1000 shares of ABC stock originally bought for $56 (total investment of $56,000) and you write a call to sell the shares at a strike price of $60. The option price is $2, so you gain an instant premium of $2000 (omitting commissions). Three scenarios are possible:

1. If the stock price does not change in three months, the call expires and, as the covered call writer, you profit from the $2000 premium.

2. If the stock price rises to $65, the holder exercises the call and buys the stock at $60. Your profit is $6000 ($4000 from appreciation in the stock price from $56 to $60, plus the $2000 premium. You missed out on potentially greater profits, however, because you sold the stocks at the striking price of $60. Without the option, you could have sold the stock at $65 per share.

3. If the stock price drops to $50, the buyer of the call will not exercise it because the market price is less than the strike price. You keep the $2000 premium, which cuts your loss from $6000 ($56 − $50 = 6 × 1000) to $4000.

Conservative Investors Reduce Risks by Purchasing Covered Puts Conservative investors who own the asset also use puts to set up a **collar** to safeguard their profits, similar to the way one buys collision insurance on an automobile. Puts

---

Make Sense of Options

An option is a contract that gives its holder the right to buy or sell an asset at a specified price. The two principal players in the options game are the option writer and the option holder. Their relationship may be summarized as follows:

	Call	Put
Option Writer (gets a premium for taking this position)	If requested by the option holder, the option writer must sell the asset to the option holder at the striking price.	If requested by the option holder, the option writer must buy the asset from the option holder at the striking price.
Option Holder (owns the contract)	Can force the option writer to sell him or her the asset at the striking price, or may sell the option through an options market, or may let the option expire.	Can force the option writer to buy the asset from him or her at the striking price, or may sell the option through an options market, or may let the option expire.

allow the holder of the contract to sell an asset at a specific striking price for a certain time period, commonly three months. For example, if you own 1000 shares of ABC stock originally purchased at $56 per share (total investment of $56,000), you hope that the market price of the stock will go up. If it goes down instead, you may suffer a loss. To reduce this risk, you could buy a put for 1000 shares at a striking price close to the purchase price of the stock—for example, $52. The total price of the option contract might be $2000 ($2 per share). Three scenarios are possible:

1. If the stock price does not change in three months, the put expires, and you are out only the $2000.

2. If the stock price rises to $65, you allow the put to expire because it is greater than the striking price, and again you are out only the $2000. Alternatively, you could sell your shares at $65 and realize a profit of $7000 ($65 × 1000 = $65,000 − $56,000 − $2000).

3. If the stock price drops to $50, you would exercise the put and sell your stock at the striking price of $52, thereby hedging your loss from $6000 ($56 − $50 = $6 × 1000) to $4000 ($56 − $52 = $4 × 1000).

Thus, conservative investors might buy put options for protection against severe price declines.

Speculative Investors Try to Profit with Options Aggressive investors speculating in the options markets attempt to profit in two ways: (1) Because a market typically exists for each security for a period of three months, the investor can hope for an increase in the value of the option. For example, if the price of a stock is rising, a holder of a call option might sell it to another investor for a higher price than that originally paid. (2) The investor can exercise the option at the striking price, take ownership of the underlying securities, and sell them at a profit.

Aggressive investors take a particularly speculative position when they do not own the underlying asset, as when they buy naked options or sell naked puts. Option traders can suffer considerable losses, however. For example, the holder of a call may be forced to take a loss when the market price of the optioned asset rises above the striking price instead of declining. The investor would then be forced to buy the asset at its current price and then sell it at the lower striking price. Conversely, the writer of a put may take a loss when the market price of an optioned asset drops below the striking price. The writer would be forced to buy the asset from the option holder at a price higher than the market price. Clearly, writing naked options is a highly speculative activity.

Options Markets The actual buying and selling of stock options and other forms of options take place in five major options markets: the Chicago Board Options Exchange (CBOE), which is the largest of these markets; the American Stock Exchange (AMEX); the New York Stock Exchange (NYSE); the Philadelphia Exchange; and the Pacific Exchange. Even though these markets are dominated by professionals, data from the Securities and Exchange Commission reveal that four out of every five option traders lose money.

In reality, option holders rarely buy or sell the underlying assets. Instead, they simply buy and sell the options. The market price of calls goes down when the market price of the underlying asset declines; it rises, in turn, when the market price of the underlying asset goes up. The market price of puts goes down when the market price of the underlying asset climbs; it goes up when the market price of the underlying asset declines. As the option nears expiration, its value tends to fall. In fact, more than 90 percent of all options are worthless when they expire. This fact should not be of grave concern, however, because speculator-trader profits are based on rises and declines in the market prices of the options rather than the expiration value of the options. The various classes of options (stock options, stock-index options, and so forth) each have specified expiration dates—usually at the close of the market on the third Friday of specified months.

Buying Calls Why would someone want to buy calls from a writer or holder? Remember that calls simply allow the holder of the contract to buy an asset at a specified price. The lure of a call is that the option holder can control a relatively large asset with a small amount of capital for a specified period of time. If the market price of the asset rises to exceed the striking price plus the premium, the holder could make a substantial profit. For example, Connie Kratzer, a bank examiner from Kalamazoo, Michigan, bought a stock option call on Xerox in March, when the stock was selling for $55 per share. The striking price is $60,

Calculate Break-Even Prices for Option Contracts

Investors need to know the **break-even price** for options contracts. At this price, the cost of a contract is negated by a profit (or the cost is reduced by hedging a loss). The break-even price for options contracts are calculated according to Equations (17.2) and (17.3). If the striking price on a put option contract were $52 and the option contract cost $2000 and provided for the control of 1000 shares of stock, the break-even price of a share of the stock would be $50, as the calculation below shows.

If the striking price on a call were $60 and the option contract cost $200 and provided for the control of 100 shares of stock, the break-even price of a share of the stock would be $62. Both formulas appear on the *Garman/Forgue* Web site.

$$\text{Break-even price on puts} = \text{striking price} - \frac{\text{contract cost}}{\text{number of shares under control}} \quad (17.2)$$

$$= \$52 - \frac{\$2000}{\$1000}$$

$$= \$50$$

$$\text{Break-even price on calls} = \text{striking price} + \frac{\text{contract cost}}{\text{number of shares under control}} \quad (17.3)$$

$$= \$60 - \frac{\$200}{\$100}$$

$$= \$62$$

the expiration date is the third Friday in March, and the price (premium) of the call is $2 per share. Thus, the option contract cost $200 ($2 × 100 shares under her control). Connie hopes that the per-share price for Xerox will rise. She prefers not to buy the stock outright because 100 shares of Xerox would cost her a great deal more—$5500 ($55 × 100).

For Connie to break even on the call option deal, the price of Xerox shares must rise to $62 before the call expires, as shown in Equation (17.3). If Connie exercises the call option, she can buy the stock at $60 from the option writer and sell it on the market for the current market price of $62 (ignoring commissions). In this instance, she earns $2 per share ($62 − $60), which offsets the $2 per share purchase price of the option. If the price of Xerox stock rises to $65, Connie would make a $3 profit per share on the stock, for a total profit of $300. Based on her $200 investment, this gain amounts to a 150 percent yield ($300 ÷ $200) earned over a short period. On the other hand, if the Xerox stock price fails to reach $60 by late March, Connie's $200 in calls will expire with no value at all and she will lose her entire investment.

Selling Options   You would want to sell a put or a call when its market price has risen sufficiently due to changes in the market price of the underlying asset to ensure a profit. Alternatively, you might sell an option if its market price is dropping to prevent further losses.

Did You KNOW?

The Advantages and Disadvantages of Speculative Investments

You can begin speculative investing with a relatively small amount of capital, perhaps only $300 to $500. Sellers of speculative investment opportunities rarely screen customers to be sure that they can afford to take the risk. While you make the decision as to whether you should become involved in speculative investments, the prudent investor limits speculative investments to less than 10 percent of his or her total investment portfolio.

People who pursue speculative investments need even temperaments and strong stomachs. The high rewards from many speculative investments frequently represent the profits garnered during short-term market fluctuations. The speculator must typically act in a matter of hours, days, or weeks (rather than years) and must have a consider-able amount of investment knowledge. To succeed in any area of investing, you must perform careful research and make intelligent decisions. To succeed in speculative investing, however, you need to stay constantly alert to any developments, become thoroughly familiar with the intricacies of each type of investment, utilize expert resources (such as a brokerage firm) that provides specialized information in your desired type of investment, and act decisively to ensure profits and cut losses.

In most areas of speculative investment, losers outnumber winners by three or four to one. Depending on your own investment philosophy, you may want to rule out high-risk investments entirely, consider speculative risks on an occasional basis, or seek out such opportunities regularly.

Trading in Futures Contracts

Investors can profit from increases or decreases in the prices of various commodities and commercial products by buying and selling **futures contracts**. A **future** is a type of forward contract that is standardized (usually in terms of size of contract, quality of product to be delivered, and delivery date) and traded on an organized exchange. Futures contracts usually focus on certain agricultural and mining products. Organized securities markets include the Chicago Mercantile Exchange (trading commodities such as pigs, pork bellies, eggs, potatoes, and cattle); the Chicago Board of Trade (corn, wheat, soybeans, soybean oil, oats, silver, and plywood); the New York Coffee and Sugar Exchange; the New York Cocoa Exchange; the International Monetary Market, which is part of the Chicago Mercantile Exchange (foreign currencies and U.S. Treasury bills); the New York Commodity Exchange (gold and silver); and the New York Mercantile Exchange (platinum). Stock futures are also traded on the New York Futures Exchange; in this case, the "commodity" is S&P's 500 or the index of another exchange. Futures are an example of investing in a derivitive.

An economic need creates futures markets. For example, a farmer planting a 10,000-bushel soybean crop might want to sell part of it now to ensure a certain price is received when the crop is actually harvested. Similarly, a food-processing company might want to purchase corn or wheat now to protect itself against sharp price increases in the future. An orange juice manufacturer might want to lock in a certain supply of oranges at a definite price now rather than run the risk that a winter freeze might push up prices. The speculator who buys (or sells) a commodity contract is hoping that the market price of the commodity will rise (or fall) before the contract matures, usually three to 18 months after it is written.

Aggressive investors seek out futures because of the potential for extremely high profits. Depending on the commodity, the volatility of the market, and the brokerage house requirements, the investor can put up as little as 5 to 15 percent of the total value of the contract. Some contracts require a deposit of only $300. Commissions average about $20 for each purchase and sale. To illustrate the use of leverage in buying futures contracts, assume that Sharon Laux, a scuba-diving instructor from the U.S. Virgin Islands, purchases a wheat contract for 5000 bushels at $3.80 per bushel in July. The contract value is $19,000 ($3.80 × 5000), but Sharon puts up only $2500. Each $0.01 increase in the price of wheat represents a total of $50 to her ($0.01 × 5000). If the price rises $0.50, to reach $4.30, by late July, Sharon will make $2500 ($0.50 × 5000 bushels) and double her investment. In essence, she could buy the wheat for $3.80 per bushel (as stipulated in the contract) rather than the market price of $4.30 in late July. Of course, as a speculator, Sharon does not actually want the wheat. On the other hand, she certainly could find a flour mill to buy her futures contract.

The potential for loss exists, too. If the price drops $0.50 to reach $3.30, Sharon would lose $2500. If the price declines, the broker will make a margin call and ask Sharon to provide more money to back up the contract. If Sharon does not have these additional funds, the broker can legally sell Sharon's contract and "close out" the position, which results in a true cash loss for Sharon. Because of the risks involved, most brokerage houses require their futures customers to have a minimum net worth of $50,000 to $75,000, exclusive of home and life insurance.

Approximate Rates of Return on Alternative Investments

Yields on investments vary from year to year. Listed at right are the approximate returns for several investments over the past decade.

Type of Asset	Annual Rate of Return (%)
S&P 500	12.9
Small capitalization stocks	14.5
U.S. Treasury long-term bonds	5.0
U.S. Treasury intermediate bonds	5.7
Corporate long-term bonds	5.8
Corporate junk bonds	6.8
Residential housing	6.0
Commercial real estate	7.0
Gold	5.0
Silver	4.8
Art	8.6
Consumer price index	3.7

Sources: Authors' estimates based on original data from Art Market Research, Ibbotson Associates, Lehman Brothers, Morgan Stanley Research, National Association of Realtors, T. Rowe Price, Salomon Brothers, and the *Wall Street Journal.*

In each commodity transaction, a winner and a loser will emerge. A buyer of a futures contract benefits if the price of the commodity increases, but the seller suffers. When prices decline, the reverse is true. Thus, futures trading is a zero-sum game. An estimated 90 percent of investors in the futures market lose money; 5 percent (mostly the professionals) make good profits from the losers; and the remaining 5 percent break even.

Speculation with Tangible Investments

5 Describe the speculative aspects of tangible investments.

Tangible investments are physical items that are owned primarily for their investment value. They are often speculative in nature. Two tangible investments are discussed in the following sections: (1) precious metals and (2) collectibles.

Precious Metals

Gold, silver, and platinum are precious metals much in demand worldwide. Silver and platinum, unlike gold, have numerous industrial uses. Many people around the world invest in precious metals to preserve capital in difficult economic times, reasoning that if their national economies experience difficulty, they will still be able to trade gold even if the paper money is devalued. Using a similar rationale, some people in the United States invest 5 or 10 percent of their investment portfolio in precious metals as a hedge against political, military, and economic uncertainty.

The prices of precious metals tend to increase in times of economic and political turmoil, especially when inflation is high. Fluctuating demand for precious metals also affects the market values. For example, in a recent three-month period, the price of gold rose from $375 to $430 per ounce, before settling around $400. Speculators can earn high profits on such sharp price swings that occur over a period of months or weeks.

Precious metals pay no dividends. Furthermore, only the wealthy can afford to buy the actual product, which is referred to as bullion. Because gold bullion must be purchased in minimum amounts of 100 troy ounces (slightly more than 8 pounds), an investor may need $40,000 or more for an initial outlay. Investors interested in smaller quantities turn to other ways of owning precious metal investments: coins, certificates, companies that mine metals, and metals futures. Bags of silver coins are sold on the New York Mercantile Exchange. Gold coins are generally available in minimum lots of five, although some banks will sell smaller amounts and, naturally, charge higher commissions. Gold coins that are easy to trade include the American "Eagle," the Canadian "Maple Leaf," and the South African "Krugerrand"; silver coins include the American "Eagle" silver dollar. Some banks sell gold certificates, which provide evidence of ownership of small amounts of gold kept by the institution for safety; of course, these banks charge commissions and storage fees.

Stocks of gold-, silver-, and platinum-mining companies have offered mixed returns in recent years. Such stocks are risky, but most pay small dividends, unlike the actual metals. The stocks also have a daily liquidity by wire or mail. Gold and silver futures contracts are available as well.

Numerous scams exist in the area of precious metals. These frauds inevitably start with salespersons calling future victims to urge them to invest in precious metals and telling tales about skyrocketing prices and high profit potentials.

Collectibles

Collectibles are cultural artifacts that have value because of their beauty, age, scarcity, or simply popularity. Buying collectibles as investments can also become a relaxing hobby. Many collectibles are not particularly liquid, such as stamps, art, rare coins, antique cars, baseball cards, matchbooks, and other items thought to have value. Yet, stamps, art, and rare coins are collectibles with a sizable resale market. Like all tangible investments, the only return on collectibles is through price appreciation, and you must sell to realize a profit.

Stamps More than 30 million people in the United States engage in **philately**—the collection and study of stamps, envelopes, and similar material. You may have heard of the rare and valuable 24¢ 1918 "inverted Jenny" U.S. airmail stamp that was printed upside down or the $1.60 brown Graf Zeppelin issue, which soared to a value of $10,000 for a very fine mint set of three. Recently, the 1918 stamp was valued at more than $30,000, but the price of the Graf Zeppelin had slipped to $3000, reflecting changes in collector demand for each.

Any hobbyist needs to attain a high level of expertise before seriously considering stamps as an investment. Forgeries abound among unscrupulous traders. The wise buyer should deal with only the most reputable sellers, diversify stamp holdings, and purchase rare stamps of only the highest quality.

Rare Coins   A **numismatist** collects coins, medallions, and selected commemoratives. As with other collectibles, values of some of these assets do increase. An uncirculated, high-quality 1829 Indian cent with large letters bought in 1948 for $11, for example, has increased in value by more than 2500 percent, because its price has risen to $300. The values of many other coins have risen by more than 10 or 15 percent per year in the past decade.

In all cases, the rarer the coin and the higher the quality, the better the price and the greater the likelihood of appreciation. A "type" collection includes one coin for each year of a specific coin design made over a period of years. A type-coin collection could focus on such issues as Morgan dollars minted between 1878 and 1921, Liberty walking half-dollars minted between 1907 and 1964, and Buffalo nickels minted between 1923 and 1956. The value of a complete type set is always higher than that of the same coins on an individual basis. Investors in rare coins should deal only with reputable sellers, obtain a written guarantee of genuineness from the dealer or auctioneer, and seek another professional opinion to corroborate the grade and value of rare coins.

When to Sell Speculative Investments

The following suggestions relate to when to sell speculative investments.

Act when investment targets are reached.
You should set investment targets for gains and losses, and always take actions to stick with these goals. For example, a purchaser of warrants might decide to sell when profits reach 30 percent or when losses reach 20 percent.

Cut losses short.
You should cut losses short by graciously and faithfully accepting losses when they occur. For example, an option you purchased at 3 that has now declined to 2 has caused you to lose $33^1/3$ percent. If you had earlier decided to sell when losses reached 20 percent, the time to sell is now (or an hour ago).

Be patient.
You need to be patient before selling tangible assets such as rare coins, stamps, art, and diamonds. The high sales commission costs on these assets can offset most of the paper gain achieved in a year or two. Such assets usually should be held at least five years for maximum appreciation.

Use contrarianism.
Consider practicing **contrarianism**. This investment approach suggests that once the general public has seized on an idea, its usefulness is over and the wise investor should take the opposite action.

Baseball Cards About 20 million people collect and trade baseball cards. A Mickey Mantle card that once was enclosed in a bubble gum package 40 years ago, for example, may now be worth hundreds of dollars. As with the stamp and coin markets, amateurs often do not get their money's worth when making purchases, however.

Summary

1. Speculative investments involve considerable risk in exchange for the chance of large gains. Thus, funds used for speculative purposes should be only those that one can afford to lose.

2. People invest in real estate to maximize after-tax returns and to experience the four advantages of real estate investing: the possibility of a positive cash flow, the potential for price appreciation, the availability of leverage, and special tax treatments that can enhance profits. Disadvantages of real estate investing include the effort and cost of buying a real estate investment, the frequent need to actively manage the investment, and difficulties and costs associated with selling the property.

3. You can determine the value of, or the price to pay for, a selected piece of real estate property using the discounted cash flow method.

4. Types of direct ownership investment in real estate include raw land and residential lots, income-producing properties, second or vacation homes, time sharing, and interval ownership. Examples of indirect ownership include real estate investment trusts (REITs) and limited partnerships.

5. Investors should consider selling investments when they have achieved their target for gains or to cut losses short.

6. Buying on margin and short selling are speculative ways of investing in securities markets. Rights have an intrinsic financial value and, if bought on margin, can represent a highly speculative investment. The speculative investor can profit in both buying and selling stock options, although buying puts can be a conservative move. Profit can be made in the volatile area of futures contracts based on increases or decreases in the prices of various commodities.

7. Tangible investments are usually speculative investments. The prices of precious metals—such as gold, silver, and platinum—tend to increase in times of economic, military, and political turmoil, especially if inflation rises quickly. Buying collectibles—such as stamps, rare coins, and baseball cards—can provide a hobby as well as investment benefits.

Key Words & Concepts

advanced portfolio management *490*

call option *506*

capital improvements *491*

contrarianism *514*

depreciation *492*

discounted cash-flow method *495*

futures contracts *511*

leverage *490*

limited partnership *501*

loan-to-value ratio *492*

margin call *504*

option *506*

option writer *506*

price appreciation *491*

put option *506*

right *505*

selling short *504*

speculative investments *490*

tax-free exchange *493*

zero-sum game *490*

1. Briefly explain three advantages to investing in real estate.

2. Explain the difference between capital improvements and repairs, and give examples of each.

3. Explain how leverage can help a real estate investor.

4. Describe how a negative cash flow can occur in a real estate investment. Explain why a real estate investment can be successful while simultaneously having a negative cash flow.

5. Summarize how depreciation and interest costs can help the real estate investor.

6. Describe a circumstance in which a real estate investor might undertake a tax-free exchange with another real estate investor.

7. Cite five disadvantages to investing in real estate.

8. What distinguishes speculative from other investments?

9. Describe the elements that make the discounted cash-flow method of estimating the value of a real estate property effective.

10. Distinguish between a right-to-use purchase and an interval-ownership purchase of vacation property.

11. Explain the difference between limited and general partners in a limited partnership.

12. Describe two situations in which the conservative real estate investor might seriously consider selling a real estate investment.

13. What are the benefits of using a margin account when investing?

14. What are the potential negative impacts of a margin call?

15. Describe how money can be made by the trading technique called selling short.

16. Which two options are available to the holder of a right?

17. Identify the risks of writing a naked option.

18. Distinguish between a put and a call.

19. How are put options used as a conservative investment strategy?

20. What is a futures contract? Give examples of the types of commodities that are traded with such a contract.

21. Why is investing in futures contracts a speculative investment?

22. Distinguish between intangible and tangible investments.

23. How is money made from an investment in precious metals?

24. What are the major forms of investment in collectibles?

25. List two criteria to use as guidelines when considering selling speculative investments.

Case 1   A Florist Takes Up Speculation

Ruth Hayden, a florist from St. Paul, Minnesota, has a house with a small mortgage, a good life insurance plan for herself and her two children, and several thousand dollars in secure savings accounts. She recently inherited more than $90,000 in cash from a relative. In addition, Ruth inherited stocks and bonds worth more than $100,000 that bring her about $1000 per month in extra earnings. An annuity guarantees her a monthly income of $1800 until her death. Ruth has talked to an investment counselor about making some speculative investments. Because she has a steady income, she feels she can absorb any losses without detriment to herself or her children.

(a) Considering the information given, do you feel that Ruth is in a position to make speculative investments?

(b) What precautions should Ruth take before making speculative investments?

(c) Assuming that Ruth knows little about speculative investments, advise her as to the most important positive and negative features of the major speculative investments available today.

(d) Ruth can't understand why she should pay $250 to borrow money for investments, when she clearly has adequate funds available. Explain why buying 100 shares of stock for $50 per share and selling it at $65 per share offers less return than the same deal purchased at a 40 percent margin. Ignore commissions, and show your calculations in tabular form like that of Table 17.4.

(e) Ruth was also puzzled because a friend was elated that the price of a stock had fallen in a short-selling deal. Ruth thought a good deal required that the stock price rise. Help Ruth understand how short selling works.

Financial Math Questions

1. Gerald Fitzpatrick, an electrician from Scranton, Pennsylvania, is interested in the numbers of real estate investments. He has reviewed the figures in Table 17.2 and is impressed with the potential 7.4 percent yield after taxes. Gerald is in the 15 percent marginal tax bracket. Answer the following questions to help guide his investment decisions:

(a) Substitute Gerald's 15 percent marginal tax bracket in Table 17.2 and calculate the taxable income, return after taxes, and yield after taxes.

(b) Why does real estate appear to be a favorable investment for Gerald?

(c) As the IRS allows only so much for depreciation expense, what other two factors might be changed in Table 17.2 to increase Gerald's yield?

(d) Calculate the yield after taxes for Gerald, assuming that he bought the property and financed it with a $64,000, 8 percent mortgage with annual interest costs of $5500.

2. Donna Ramirez, a caterer from Winslow, Arizona, is considering buying a vacation condominium apartment for $165,000 in Park City, Utah. Donna hopes to rent the condo

to others to keep her costs down. Respond to the following questions to help Donna with her decisions:

(a) If Donna's monthly payments are $1090—of which $890 goes for interest, $90 for principal, $70 for property taxes, and $40 for homeowner's insurance—plus another $40 for the monthly homeowner's association fee, which of these costs will be tax-deductible? List the costs and total on an annualized basis.

(b) If Donna is in the 28 percent marginal tax bracket, how much less in taxes will she pay if she buys this condo?

(c) Given that she would like to personally use the condo for vacations amounting to ten to 12 days per year, how many days will Donna have to rent it out before she would become eligible to deduct rental losses from her taxes?

(d) Because Park City is mostly a winter ski resort and few condo renters can be found in the off season, Donna is concerned about qualifying to deduct rental losses. Assuming she could rent the condo for $120 per day, describe the IRS-approved rental alternative she could use to generate income. Calculate the maximum amount of money Donna could obtain using that plan.

(e) Figure Donna's annual net out-of-pocket cost to buy the condominium and rent it out minimally for tax-free income. Start with her $10,680 annual cost for monthly payments of $890 and homeowner's association fees of $40 per month. Next, deduct the savings on income taxes as well as the presumed rental for 14 days.

(f) Using the figure derived in part (e), what would Donna's out-of-pocket cost per day be to use the condo herself if she stayed there ten days each year? Fifteen days each year?

3. John Lewis, a health manager from Toledo, Ohio, wants to buy 100 shares of DEF Company stock on margin. Assume that the margin requirement is 50 percent, DEF stock sells

for $40 per share, and commissions are ignored.

(a) How much can John borrow?

(b) If the interest rate is 10 percent per year compounded annually, how much interest will John pay if he keeps the position open for one year?

(c) If John sells the stock at the end of the year for $30 per share, how much money will he lose, expressed both in dollars and as a percentage of the amount he invested?

(d) If John sells the stock for $50 per share at the end of one year, what is the amount of his gain, expressed both in dollars and as a percentage of the amount he invested?

4. Cecilia Alvarez, a physical therapist from Miami, Florida, wants to sell 100 shares of XYZ Company stock short because she feels the price will decline during the next month. The XYZ stock currently sells at $30 per share. Assume that the margin rate is 50 percent and ignore commissions.

(a) How much will the brokerage firm hold in the short sale account?

(b) If Cecilia closes the position in one month with the stock priced at $40 per share, how much will she lose, expressed both in dollars and as a percentage of the amount she invested?

(c) If Cecilia's forecast is right and the price drops to $25 per share, how much will she gain, expressed both in dollars and as a percentage of the amount she invested?

MONEY MATTERS: LIFE-CYCLE CASES

Victor and Maria Consider Hedging an Investment with Puts

Victor and Maria Hernandez recently invested in 200 shares of Pharmacia & Upjohn Pharmaceuticals common stock at $93 per share. They purchased the stock because the company is testing a new drug that may represent a significant medical breakthrough. The stock's value has already risen $8 in three months, in anticipation of the U.S. Food and Drug Administration's approval of the new drug. Many observers believe that the price of the stock could reach $100 if the drug is successful. If it is not the breakthrough anticipated, however, the price of the stock could drop back to the $85 range. The Hernandezes are optimistic but feel that they should hedge their position a bit. As a result, they have decided to purchase two nine-month Pharmacia & Upjohn 100-share puts for $3 per share at a striking price of $93 per share. Ignore commissions when answering the following questions:

1. What price would the Pharmacia & Upjohn stock need to reach for the Hernandezes to break even on the investment?

2. How much would the Hernandezes gain if they sold the stock for $102 six months from now?

3. How much would the return be as a percentage on an annualized basis?

4. If the price of the stock dropped to $85 in six months, how much would the Hernandezes lose?

The Johnsons Consider a Real Estate Investment

Harry and Belinda Johnson are considering purchasing a residential income property as an investment. The Johnsons desire an after-tax total return of 10 percent. They are considering a property with an asking price of $190,000 that produces $27,000 in gross rental income and $15,000 in net operating income. Calculate the present value of after-tax cash flow for the property, assuming that the after-tax cash-flow numbers are $8000 for the first year, $8400 for the second year, $8800 for the third year, $9200 for the fourth year, and $9600 for the fifth year, and that the selling price of the property will be $220,000 in five years. Prepare your information in a format similar to Table 17.3, using Appendix A.2, or the *Garman/Forgue* Web site, to discount the future after-tax cash flows to their present values.

Give the Johnsons your advice on whether they should invest in the property at its current price of $190,000.

Exploring the World Wide Web of Personal Finance

To complete these exercises, go to the *Garman/Forgue* Web site at

www.hmco.com/college/business/

Select Personal Finance. Click on the exercise link for this chapter and answer the questions that appear on the Web page.

1. Visit the Web site for the Chicago Board of Trade (CBOT). Select the "Answers to Frequently Asked Questions" section to answer the following questions:

    (a) What is a futures contract?

    (b) What is the difference between a stock exchange and a futures exchange?

    (c) Where are the actual commodities that are traded on the CBOT?

    (d) Browse the site further to determine what commodities are traded on the CBOT.

2. Visit the Web site of the National Association of Real Estate Investment Trusts (NAREIT). Select the "Answers to Frequently Asked Questions" section to answer the following questions:

    (a) Why were REITs created?

    (b) How are REITs managed?

    (c) What makes a REIT attractive to investors?

    (d) How are the REITs of today different from the REITs of 25 years ago?

    (e) How many REITs are currently available in the United States?

3. Visit the Web site for Equity Analytics, Ltd., where you will find information on the basics of option investing, buying a put, and buying a call. When might an investor want to use options in his or her investment portfolio? Identify several exchanges on which options are traded.

4. Visit the Web site for Vanguard Securities, where you will find information on using a margin account. What are the current margin rates for the following types of investments: equities (stocks), municipal bonds, corporate bonds, and short sales?

PART FIVE

Retirement and Estate Planning

Retirement Planning

18

OBJECTIVES

After reading this chapter, you should be able to:

1 Summarize some of the radical changes in retirement planning that affect today's workers and retirees.

2 Estimate retirement expenses and the sources of income during retirement.

3 Calculate the relative advantages of tax-sheltered versus non–tax-sheltered retirement plans.

4 Describe the types and characteristics of employer-sponsored retirement plans.

5 Explain the purposes and benefits of personal retirement plans.

6 Describe how to qualify for the Social Security retirement program and the role that Social Security plays in retirement planning.

7 Estimate the dollar amount you should be saving for retirement.

Today's workers are healthier, are better educated, will live longer, and have higher expectations than those of earlier generations. When they retire, these workers will want a comfortable and happy life with less stress and more leisure. Having financial security during retirement years is not a matter of luck; it takes planning. As this chapter amply illustrates, one of the skills that workers must clearly possess today is financial planning, both for their pre-retirement money management opportunities and for their retirement years. People who start investing for retirement in their twenties should aim to reserve 12 to 15 percent of pretax income every year, including employer contributions. Those who have delayed planning for retirement until their thirties or forties should begin investing 20 to 25 percent annually in an effort to catch up; they will also have to be more aggressive in their investments. In addition, late savers must be flexible on the age at which they retire.

This chapter first discusses retirement expenses and the sources of income during retirement years. Next, we turn to the benefits of using tax sheltering in retirement planning. Employer-sponsored retirement plans are examined as an essential consideration in most people's retirement planning. We then move on to the important topic of personal retirement plans. Social Security is also discussed, because it represents a key source of retirement funds. We cover Social Security last because it is important that you take charge of your own retirement planning, rather than assuming that government programs, which are subject to change, will take care of you. To aid in your planning, we provide an illustration for determining the dollar amount you should be saving each year for retirement.

Radical Changes for Workers and Retirees

1 Summarize some of the radical changes in retirement planning that affect today's workers and retirees.

Times have changed dramatically for today's workers and retirees. Most important has been the shift from the employer to the employee of both the obligation to invest and the risk of making poor investments. Clearly, retirement planning is not the same process that it once was. Today's workers and retirees can expect that:

- The "safety net" of Social Security will not represent the most significant source of funding for your retirement.

- A "guaranteed" pension plan funded solely by your employer is unlikely to form the cornerstone of your retirement program.

- Most workers must manage their own retirement plan and make the savings and investment decisions themselves.

- Inflation will increase the cost of living during your retirement years and affect the value of your investments.

- Retiree medical benefits will be trimmed or canceled altogether, so that you will need to allocate sufficient funds in retirement to pay for this expense.

- You probably will live a very long time after retirement (actuarial tables indicate that women who reach age 65 will live another 18.3 years while men age 65 are expected to live an additional 13.9 years).

- You will probably have to pay income taxes on the pension benefits you receive, reducing the after-tax value of your investments.

- Your income tax situation and management of personal finances will become more complicated after retirement, not simpler.

Retirement Expenses and Income Sources

2 Estimate retirement expenses and the sources of income during retirement.

Estimation of retirement needs is a three-step process: (1) estimate your retirement expenses, (2) estimate your sources of retirement income, and (3) estimate the additional retirement savings to meet your goals. These questions may not have precise answers. The further away your retirement, the fuzzier the picture may be because you are attempting to predict the future.

Experts estimate that retirees need 75 to 90 percent of their working income level to enjoy a comfortable retirement lifestyle. The lower your preretirement income, the greater the proportion of that income you will probably need after retirement. Because women are less likely to get retirement benefits from their employers (32 percent compared with 55 percent for men) and they get less from Social Security (about $650 per month compared with $825 for men), women need to save more money for retirement than men.

Assume that a couple retiring today with estimated retirement expenses of $30,000 will live for 20 years past retirement and that they could earn an after-tax and after-inflation rate of return of 3 percent on their investments. What amount of **nest egg** (total accumulated savings and investments) should they have built up over the years and have available at retirement? Calculations (using Appendix A.4) for 20 years at 3 percent reveal an amount of $446,340 ($30,000 × 14.878) needed at retirement.

The situation is even more dramatic for younger workers contemplating retirement. Again assume $30,000 in retirement expenses in today's dollars. For someone aged 25 with 40 years to go before retirement, inflation (assuming 3%) will raise that expense figure to $97,860 ($30,000 × 3.262 from Appendix A.1). Using the same inflation and rate of return assumptions as in the paragraph above, the 25-year-old would need a nest egg of $1,455,961 ($97,860 × 14.878) at age 65.

On the income side of the retirement equation, smart personal finance managers expect to depend less on Social Security and Medicare and to rely more on their own investments for financial security during retirement. According to a report prepared by the Social Security Administration, the average retired couple with income in excess of $20,000 now receives income from several sources, as illustrated in Figure 18.1. Today Social Security represents about 22 percent of a couple's income, although the proportion is lower for higher-income people. In the next century, most retirees are expected to receive Social Security retirement benefits that are higher (even after adjusting for inflation) than those received by today's retirees, but it will represent a lower percentage of their income. A retirement plan should therefore include a combination of employer-sponsored retirement plans, personal retirement planning mechanisms, and additional investments.

Figure 18.1

Sources of Retirement Income

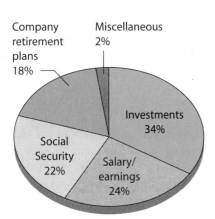

Another source of income for many retirees is the equity in their homes. By selling a home at retirement and then moving into a smaller home or an apartment, a couple might be able to use this equity to fund expenditures for many years. Alternatively, it might be advantageous to consider a reverse mortgage (see Chapter 9, page 248) in which the lender sends monthly checks to the homeowner.

One of the roadblocks to an early start on retirement planning is motivation. Don't let the mathematics and long-term estimating stop you from taking positive actions to save and invest for retirement.* The longer you have until retirement, the more

---

*   Top-rated retirement planning computer software programs (ranging in price from $15 to $100) include Vanguard's Retirement Planner [(800) 876-1840], Retire ASAP [(800) 225-8246], Fidelity's Retirement Planning Software [(800) 554-8888], Dow Jones' Plan Ahead [(800) 522-3567], Intuit's Quicken Financial Planner [(800) 624-8742], Price Waterhouse's Retire Secure [(800) 752-6234], and T. Rowe Price Retirement Planning Kit [(800) 541-1472].

aggressive an approach to investing you can pursue. If you save regularly, you will make progress toward your goal. The remainder of this chapter shows you how to build your retirement nest egg and culminates with an illustration of how one investor can save enough to retire comfortably.

Tax-Sheltered Retirement Plans

3 Calculate the relative advantages of tax-sheltered versus non–tax-sheltered retirement plans.

Employers usually offer employees retirement plans because the promise of a secure retirement represents an effective way to recruit and keep valuable employees. Many pension plans are classified as **tax-sheltered retirement plans** (also called **qualified retirement plans**). These retirement plans, which have been approved by the Internal Revenue Service as vehicles to deposit tax-sheltered contributions and/or earn tax-sheltered returns, offer advantages that can increase eventual retirement benefits. Plans you set up for yourself may also carry these tax advantages.

Recall from Chapter 1 that tax sheltering can occur in several ways. First, some plans allow for a reduction in current income subject to tax each time a deposit is made into the plan. Referred to as **pretax dollars**, these deposits are not taxed until they are withdrawn. This approach allows people to put more money away for retirement, as the government subsidizes deposits through lower tax bills. Second, all qualified plans allow the earnings on the deposited funds (interest, dividends, and so on) to be sheltered from taxation while the plan is growing. By not paying taxes, depositors can see all of their plan earnings stay on deposit to greatly enhance the power of compounding over time. Plan earnings will be taxed only when they are withdrawn. Third, in a unique type of plan, the Roth IRA (discussed later in this chapter), the earnings will not even be taxed when withdrawn, provided certain conditions are met.

Withdrawals from a Tax-Sheltered Plan

The tax sheltering resulting from allocation of money to a qualified retirement plan generally represents a deferment of taxes rather than a permanent avoidance of taxes. As noted earlier, income tax must be paid when the funds are withdrawn.* If money is withdrawn prior to a certain age—usually 59^1/$_2$—a 10 percent penalty may be assessed in addition to the usual income tax. People who do a good job of saving and investing for retirement may find themselves in the same tax bracket after retirement as before. Nonetheless, it is generally better to pay taxes later rather than sooner, because you have tax-deferred buildup over time.

Distributions from tax-sheltered retirement plans may be fully or partially taxable, depending upon whether your account includes nondeductible contributions. If the account comprises only deductible contributions, any distributions are fully taxable when received. If you also made nondeductible contributions, logically those distributions should not be taxed at withdrawal as they have already been taxed earlier. The IRS assumes that withdrawals from any account

---

* A major exception is the Roth IRA, discussed later in this chapter, which is not taxable at withdrawal.

will consist of both previously taxed and previously untaxed funds. IRS regulations require you to apply a complex formula that assumes that any withdrawal consists of pre- and post-tax money in the same proportion as the deposits were made up of pre- and post-tax money. Because this assumption may result in over-taxation, you should maintain adequate records of all contributions—even for 40 years or more.

Employer-Sponsored Qualified Retirement Plans

4 Describe the types and characteristics of employer-sponsored retirement plans.

Approximately one-third of all workers at small firms participate in an employer-sponsored qualified retirement plan, compared with more than 75 percent of workers in medium to large firms. If you participate in such a plan,* it can serve as the cornerstone of your retirement planning. If you do not have access to an employer-sponsored qualified plan, you should make alternative preparations for retirement.

Because employer-sponsored qualified retirement plans play such an important role, the U.S. Congress passed the Pension Reform Act of 1974, also called the Employee Retirement Income Security Act (ERISA). While not requiring companies to offer retirement plans, ERISA does regulate existing plans. The following sections describe several important aspects of employer-sponsored qualified retirement plans.

Participation and Vesting

To be eligible for any benefits, employees must participate in their employer-sponsored retirement plan. Under ERISA, employers must choose one of two approaches in allowing full-time workers to participate in the retirement plan: (1) admitting every employee who has worked for the firm for one year or who is at least age 21, whichever is later, or (2) admitting every employee who has worked for the company for at least two years if immediately vested at 100 percent.

ERISA places stringent requirements on **vesting,** a process by which employees during their working years obtain permanent rights to retirement benefits provided by employers that cannot be taken away in case of dismissal or resignation. While you always have a right to the money you personally put into a retirement plan at work, vesting gives you the legal right to benefits based on money your employer contributes to your retirement plan. Retirement plans must offer one of two government-approved vesting alternatives. With **five-year vesting** (also known as **cliff vesting**), an employee is not vested during the first five years but becomes fully vested at the end of the fifth year. **Seven-year vesting,** also known as **graduated vesting,** requires employees to be 20 percent vested after three years, 40 percent after four years, 60 percent after five years, 80 percent after six years, and 100 percent at the end of seven years of employment. All previous time worked for the employer since the worker was aged 18 must count toward vesting. Employers are free to offer more generous (earlier) vesting rules.

Defined-Benefit Plans—Yesterday's Standard

A **defined-benefit plan** is defined by the level of "benefits" received by an employee who has retired. Often referred to as a "pension," those benefits are determined by a specified formula linked to the number of years of employment and the worker's income. For example, an employee might have a defined annual retirement benefit of 2 percent multiplied by the number of years of service and multiplied by the average annual income during the last five years of employment. In this example, a worker with 30 years' service and an average income of $48,000 over the last five years of work would have an annual benefit of $28,800 (30 × 0.02 × $48,000), or $2400 a month. Defined-benefit plans were the "standard" pensions a generation ago, but are used by an ever-decreasing percentage of employers today.

Funded or Unfunded Plans Defined-benefit plans are either funded or unfunded. In a **funded pension plan**, the employer makes full payments annually to a trustee, who places the funds in conservative and relatively safe investments so that promised benefits will be available to all employees when they retire. In an **unfunded pension plan**, retirement expenses are paid out of current earnings rather than from funds previously set aside to cover current and future liabilities. These "owe-as-you-go" plans are more risky, especially if the employer should go bankrupt. A new law requires that employers notify employees if the company's pension plan is less than "90 percent funded"—that is, if the firm went bankrupt today, it would have less than 90 percent of the assets required to meet its pension responsibilities.

Most state and local government defined-benefit plans are unfunded, as is Social Security. Thus, benefits are partially paid out of current revenues. The "guarantee" of government programs comes primarily from the political pressure of retirees and current workers who expect similar benefits.

ERISA established the Pension Benefit Guarantee Corporation (PBGC) *www.pbgc.gov*, which provides an insurance program that guarantees certain benefits to eligible workers whose employers' defined-benefit plans are not financially sound enough to pay their obligations. The PBGC covers only defined-benefit plans, not the more widely utilized defined-contribution plans (discussed below), and the coverage is limited to a maximum of $31,704 per year. Another major exemption from PBGC coverage occurs when an employer transfers a pension plan to an insurance company. In this case, the insurer becomes responsible for making the payments; the retirees, therefore, face a dilemma if the insurer gets into financial difficulty, unless a state guaranty corporation steps in.

Integration of Benefits with Social Security Benefits from defined-benefit plans are sometimes integrated with benefits from Social Security. This practice can have detrimental effects because increases in the amount of Social Security benefits received by the retiree may reduce company-paid benefits. For example, assume that you retire with a company pension of $900 per month and Social Security benefits of $600 per month. If your Social Security payments increase $100 to $700, the company pension may drop by $100 to $800, offsetting the increase in Social Security benefits. The net effect is that you lose ground to inflation despite increases in Social Security benefits.

Normal or Early Retirement? The earlier you retire, the smaller your monthly retirement benefit from a defined-benefit plan will be because you are expected to receive income for more years as a retired person. On average, a man retiring at age 62 has 17.3 years of life remaining to collect retirement benefits; a man retiring at age 65, in contrast, is likely to collect benefits for only 15.2 years. Monthly benefits for the early retiree in a defined-benefit plan are smaller so that he or she receives, in theory, the same total dollar amount of benefits as the person who retires later. The U.S. Supreme Court has ruled that men and women who contribute equal amounts must receive the same company retirement benefits, even though their average life expectancies differ. (In the United States, women live approximately six years longer than men.)

The financial benefits of early retirement will depend on the retiree's life expectancy and the rate at which benefits are reduced, as illustrated in Table 18.1. Workers expecting to live less than the average expectancy may achieve a better financial position by retiring early. The opposite is true if family history or health status indicates the probability of an extremely long life. Most employees are allowed to work for as long as they choose, but companies generally do not increase benefits for employees who postpone retirement beyond age 65.

Defined-Contribution Plans—Today's Standard

A **defined-contribution plan** is defined by its "contributions"—that is, the amount of money deposited in each person's individual account. The balance amassed in such a plan consists of the contributions plus any investment income and gains, minus expenses and losses.

In these plans, the employer, the employee, or both set aside money during the working years to establish a fund that pays retirement benefits to the covered worker. The money contributions devoted to the plan are clearly specified, but the amount of the benefit remains unknown until the benefits are withdrawn. This variation arises because the sum available depends greatly on the success of the investments made with the deposited funds. In a defined-contribution plan, the worker—not the employer—bears the risk of investment losses and the success of investment profits.

Table 18.1

Impact of Early Retirement on Pension Benefits

Age at Retirement	Monthly Benefit	Life Expectancy in Months*	Present Value (at Age 55) of Projected Benefits†
65	$1,000	208	$100,520
62	880	236	108,860
60	800	255	112,430
55	500	304	95,460

* Female retiree.
† Assumes a 4 percent after-inflation rate of return.

Defined-contribution plans are replacing many traditional defined-benefit pensions as the main source of retirement income for millions of workers; indeed, they represent the only retirement plans now available at many companies. Employers use this strategy because unfunded pension liability is eliminated, but workers must bear greater uncertainty about the amount of benefits that will ultimately be received. On the plus side, defined-contribution plans generally permit earlier vesting and allow more flexible investment choices and easier portability than old-style pensions. In addition, each employee's funds are placed in a separate account, which remains out of reach of corporate creditors should the company go bankrupt.

Contributory versus Noncontributory Plans In a **noncontributory retirement plan**, the employer deposits *all* of the funds in the plan. In a **contributory retirement plan**, the employee, and possibly the employer, place funds in the plan. Often, employee and employer shares are equal. For example, each might contribute 5 percent of the employee's salary up to a certain dollar amount.

Portability If the option is available, an employee also might benefit from **portability**, which is a contract clause that permits workers to maintain and transfer accumulated funds to another employer's plan. Workers who change jobs usually have the choice of keeping their retirement money invested in the former employer's retirement plan until retirement, transferring it to their new employer's plan, or rolling it over to an individual retirement account (discussed later in this chapter).

Salary-Reduction Plans **Salary-reduction plans** comprise a group of defined-contribution plans available to people who work for various types of organizations. Salary-reduction plans include the 401(k), 403(b), and 457 plans, which are named after sections of the IRS tax code. Each type of plan is restricted to a specific group of workers. When the employing organization has 100 or fewer employees, it may set up a **Savings Incentive Match Plan for Employees (or SIMPLE)** that is inexpensive for employers to operate.

The funds contributed each year by the employee, in effect, reduce the amount of income subject to tax and, along with any employer contributions, accumulate tax-free until they are withdrawn at retirement. The funds are then invested by the employee in mutual funds, annuities, or individual securities from a list of options established by the employer. Often the employee has from three to twenty or more investment options from which to choose; government regulations encourage employers to educate their employees without giving direct investment advice. Because each individual employee makes his or her own investment decisions, a salary-reduction plan could be described as a **self-directed retirement plan.** You should place only funds that you will not need until retirement in a salary-reduction plan.

The **401(k) salary-reduction plan**, or **401(k) plan**, is the best known of the salary-reduction plans. It is designed for employees of private corporations who may contribute as much as .15 percent of their gross earnings each year, up to a maximum amount set by law ($10,000 in 1999). Eligible employees of nonprofit organizations (colleges, hospitals, religious organizations, and some other not-for-profit institutions) may contribute to similar **403(b) salary-reduction plans** that have the same contribution limits. State and local government employees may contribute to **457 plans.**

Many employers limit to about 10 percent the proportion of the annual salary that an employee may contribute to a salary-reduction plan, which prevents many workers from reaching the $10,000 limit. In addition, many employers will not contribute to an employee's retirement plan unless the employee contributes as well. Workers participating in SIMPLE salary-reduction plan may contribute up to $6000 a year. Employers may match the contribution up to 3 percent of salary.

A tremendous bonus for employees who participate in salary-reduction plans is that many employers will partially or fully **match** (put funds into the retirement account) the contributions of employees. For example, an employer might contribute $0.50 for each $1 contributed by the employee, up to 6 percent of the worker's salary. Thus, a person who puts $3000 into a retirement plan that is 50 percent matched by his or her employer ($1500) receives an immediate "return on investment" of a fantastic 50 percent ($1500 ÷ $3000). Almost 90 percent of employers match some proportion of the retirement money saved by their employees. Workers can accumulate substantial retirement funds by using a salary-reduction plan with matching contributions. For example, if contributions of $1200 per year into such a fund were matched 100 percent by the employer for 25 years at an interest rate of 8 percent, the fund would accumulate to $175,464 (from Appendix A.3, the calculation is $2400 × 73.11). Without

HOW to . . .

Invest Your 401(k) Funds

Federal guidelines encourage employers to give their employees at least three investment choices (beyond the employer's own stock) with differing risk and return characteristics for defined-contribution plans. Employers also must provide the employee with sufficient information to make intelligent decisions about these options. The actual choices are the responsibility of the employee, who can put all of the funds into a single option or allocate the funds across the options. A typical plan has seven or eight choices, perhaps including the employer's own stock, a growth stock mutual fund (often an index fund), a bond fund, a fixed annuity, and a variable annuity. Following these guidelines reduces an employer's liability against lawsuits if investments in a tax-deferred retirement plan do poorly or disappear because of poor investment choices.

Many employers offer an annuity called a **guaranteed investment contract (GIC).** A GIC is an annuity contract purchased through an insurance company as part of a qualified retirement plan. GICs promise to pay a certain level of interest for a given period of time, much like a certificate of deposit. Although GICs have a guaranteed return for at least the first year, they generally provide a low return because the insurance company places the funds in low-risk investments. Over the long term, they usually do not perform as well as more risk-oriented options such as stock mutual funds.

Because retirement plans are designed for long-term investing, it is appropriate to accept higher levels of risk. Depending on their age, employees might be best served by putting the bulk of their funds into higher-risk choices.

a match, the retirement fund would amount to only $87,732 ($1200 × 73.11). Amazingly, nearly half of employees eligible to participate in salary-reduction plans still do not take full advantage of this free money.

Other Types of Employer-Sponsored Retirement Plans

In addition to providing employees with a defined-contribution or defined-benefit plan, many employers offer other retirement plans to employees. Six such plans are described below.

Cash-Balance Pension Plans An increasing number of employers have established or amended existing retirement plans as hybrid forms of the traditional pension plans. The most popular of these hybrids, the **cash-balance pension plan**, is a defined-benefit plan with features of a defined-contribution plan. Under this plan, benefits are still "defined" based on years of service and income levels as they are under defined-benefit plans. However, each employee has an "account" into which the employer makes "deposits" to fund the defined benefit. The dollar value of the account can be determined at any time. The investment earnings

---

The Questions to Ask about Your Employer-Sponsored Retirement Plan

As you plan for retirement, find out as much as you can about your company's retirement plan by asking the following questions:

1. When is an employee eligible to participate in the plan? Is the plan optional or required?

2. Is it a defined-benefit or defined-contribution plan?

3. If it is a defined-benefit pension, how are benefits calculated?

4. Is the plan insured by the Pension Benefit Guaranty Corporation (PBGC)?

5. If it is a defined-contribution plan, what shares are contributed by the employer and employee? What investment options are available? Under what rules may the employee switch among investment options?

6. How do employees become vested?

7. Can the plan be discontinued by the company? Can it be changed? How?

8. Are benefits integrated with Social Security benefits? How?

9. What is the earliest retirement age, and what reductions for early retirement or increases for late retirement apply?

10. Are defined-benefit retirement benefits guaranteed for life once you retire?

11. What are the survivor's and disability benefits?

12. What are the procedures for applying for benefits?

13. Will health care benefits (if any) continue after retirement?

14. Are financial planning services offered to assist workers in making retirement and other financial decisions?

of the account are specified; e.g., at 8 percent (annual adjustments can be made to reflect economic conditions). If the pension plan fund earns a rate of return that exceeds the specified rate, the employer owns the additional earnings. Vesting requirements are the same as for the traditional plans.

At separation from employment or retirement, the employee has the right to the vested lump-sum amount rather than to a monthly pension. This may absolve the employer of any further obligations to the employee. The employee can purchase an annuity with the funds (thereby funding his or her own pension) or deposit the lump-sum into a rollover IRA (see below) or to a new employer's retirement plan.

After-Tax Salary-Reduction Plans   An **after-tax salary-reduction plan** (sometimes called a **corporate thrift program**) is a fringe benefit offered by employers as an additional inducement to retain the loyalty of employees. Under this program, employees can make excess salary-reduction contributions to a plan, up to a ceiling of 15 percent of annual income, that accumulate tax-free. Although the employees pay current-year income taxes on their contributions, the investment earnings are tax-deferred. Many employers will match or partially match the money contributed by an employee. This mechanism offers substantial benefits for two groups of people: (1) those approaching retirement who realize that they have too little set aside and need to catch up, and (2) those who want to contribute more to a salary-reduction program but have already reached the maximum in a qualified plan. The total contribution to all salary-reduction plans, including pretax and after-tax money, is limited to 25 percent of gross earnings or $30,000, whichever is less.

Participating employees do not pay income taxes when they receive a distribution of principal, as this amount will have already been taxed when it was contributed. Earnings distributed from an after-tax plan, of course, become subject to income taxes. Participants in after-tax pension money should keep these accounts separate from pretax pension accounts. If the accounts are combined, the IRS will assume that all contributions were made with after-tax money. As a result, the money put into any after-tax retirement plans would be unfairly penalized (that is, taxed twice).

Nonqualified Deferred-Compensation Plans   A **nonqualified deferred-compensation plan** permits an employee and employer to agree to defer large payments for services rendered to a later date, perhaps when the employee enters a lower marginal tax bracket. Highly paid athletes and executives, for example, often prefer such arrangements and frequently request that some of their compensation be paid during their retirement years. **Deferred income** is not income until it is paid and, thus, is not taxed until received by the employee.

ESOPs   An **employee stock-ownership plan (ESOP)** is a qualified retirement plan whose funds must be invested primarily in the stock of the employing corporation. In effect, the retirement fund consists of stock in the company. If the stock does well, the retirement nest egg will grow significantly. Of course, the opposite can occur as well. Employees who have been in an ESOP plan for ten years may diversify into other investments by transferring up to 25 percent of their account at age 55 and 50 percent at age 60.

Profit-Sharing Plans **Profit-sharing plans** are defined-contribution plans to which the employer makes "substantial and recurring" contributions. The level of contributions put into the plan reflects the employee's income and the level of profits achieved by the employer. Profits are not necessary in most profit-sharing plans, however. Contributions might be fixed (perhaps at 10 percent of profits) or be discretionary, although a definite formula must be established to determine the contributions of participants. Some profit-sharing plans use both age and compensation as a basis for calculating employer contributions. A **stock bonus plan** is similar to a profit-sharing plan except that benefit payments must be made with company stock. While distributions may be made in cash, the participants receive a guaranteed right to purchase stock.

Methods of Payout

You generally have three choices with employer-sponsored retirement plans when you retire or change employers:

- Some plans allow you to keep your account invested. You can then defer income taxes until you begin receiving payouts, usually in the form of monthly payments.

- Some plans allow you to take the money in a **lump sum** and pay the income taxes due. Depending upon your age, the lump-sum distribution might be eligible for special IRS rules that allow for averaging the distrinution over a period of ten years, thereby reducing the tax liability in the first year and spreading it out over several subsequent years. In this way, averaging reduces the overall tax liability.

- Your plan may permit you to transfer the entire lump sum, via a rollover, to an individual retirement account (see below), where it continues to grow tax-deferred. This strategy also delays income taxes until you begin receiving payouts. If you later get the opportunity to participate in a 401(k) plan—for example, by going to work for a new employer—you can transfer funds from an IRA rollover account to the new 401(k) plan, as long as the rollover IRA money was not mixed with a regular IRA.

Internal Revenue Service regulations require that you begin taking distributions from a qualified retirement plan at age $70^1/2$. Otherwise, severe IRS penalties apply for making withdrawals too late (an exception is the Roth IRA).

Disability and Survivor's Benefits

The prospect of financial security during retirement is heartening, but disability and survivor's benefits also represent a concern for workers who have spouses or children. One's full retirement benefits form the basis for any disability or survivor's benefits. People receiving disability or survivor's benefits are generally entitled to an amount that is substantially less than the full retirement amount. For example, if you were entitled to a retirement benefit of $2000 per month, your disability benefit might be only $1500 per month. If a survivor is entitled

How Long Your Money Will Last

Part of your retirement income will likely derive from some accumulated savings and investments built up over the years. The key question is, "How long will the money last during your retirement years?" The answer depends upon three factors: (1) the amount of money in the nest egg; (2) the rate of return earned on the funds; and (3) the amount of money that is withdrawn from the account each month.

By spending at a rate that will not deplete the fund too rapidly, retirees can ensure that the funds will last the desired number of years. The table

below provides factors that can be multiplied by the amount in the retirement fund to determine the amount available for spending each month. Consider the example of a Jimmy Stewart, a 58-year-old early retiree from Potterville, Missouri, who wants his $250,000 nest egg to last 15 years, assuming that it will earn a 6 percent annual return in the future. The value in the table in the "15 years" column and the "6 percent" row is 0.00844. Multiplying 0.00844 times $250,000 reveals that Jimmy could withdraw $2110 every month for 15 years before the fund was depleted.

	Number of Years				
Rate of Return	5	10	15	20	25
3%	0.01797	0.00966	0.00691	0.00555	0.00474
4%	0.01842	0.01012	0.00740	0.00606	0.00527
5%	0.01887	0.01061	0.00791	0.00660	0.00585
6%	0.01933	0.01110	0.00844	0.00716	0.00644
7%	0.01980	0.01161	0.00899	0.00775	0.00707
8%	0.02028	0.01213	0.00956	0.00836	0.00772

to benefits, that pension amount must be paid over two people's lives instead of a single person's life; consequently, the monthly payment is lower. If your surviving spouse is five years older than you, he or she might be entitled to $1300 per month; in contrast, if your spouse is five years younger, he or she might be entitled to only $1000 per month.

A retirement plan with **survivor's benefits** is legally required to provide benefits to a surviving spouse in the event of the death of the entitled worker. This requirement can be waived if desired, but only after marriage (not in a prenuptial agreement). Federal law dictates that a spouse or ex-spouse who qualifies for benefits under a plan must agree in writing to a waiver of the spousal benefit. This stipulation protects the interests of surviving spouses. If the spouse does waive his or her survivor's benefits, the worker's retirement benefit is higher. Of course, upon the worker's death, the spouse will not receive any survivor's benefits when a waiver exists. Unless a spouse has his or her own retirement benefits, it is usually wise to keep the spousal benefit.

Collect Pension Money from a Divorced Spouse

The Retirement Equity Act of 1984 allows states to split pensions between husbands and wives at divorce. To receive a share of a defined-benefit or defined-contribution pension plan, a former spouse needs a **qualified domestic-relations order (QDRO).** This specialized court order legally authorizes the pension plan administrator to take specific action not outlined in the pension plan regulations. The order must be approved by the pension plan administrator to ensure that it fits within the plan's rules to be effective. ERISA requires that pension plan administrators respond within 30 days of a written request to inquiries from former spouses who cite their rights as plan beneficiaries.

With a QDRO, the payout from a pension plan may be divided upon divorce or as soon as the employee leaves a job or reaches retirement age. Annuities and individual retirement accounts may also be divided as part of a divorce agreement.

Because divorce and splitting retirement money have income tax ramifications, it is wise to obtain appropriate legal counsel and tax advice.

To qualify for Social Security retirement benefits based on your former spouse's earnings, the marriage must have lasted at least ten years and both you and your ex-spouse must be at least 62 years old. Your checks cannot begin until two years after the divorce. Your Social Security benefits are not affected if the ex-spouse remarries. If you remarry, however, you lose the right to benefits based upon your former spouse's earnings, unless your second marriage also ended in divorce. If both marriages lasted at least ten years, you could elect benefits based upon which former spouse's earnings generate the higher benefit. Your benefit amount consists of 50 percent of a divorced spouse's benefit; if the ex-spouse dies, the benefit increases to 100 percent of the ex-spouse's benefit.

Personal Retirement Plans

5 Explain the purposes and benefits of personal retirement plans.

Not all workers are offered employer-sponsored qualified retirement plans. Even if you can take advantage of an employer-sponsored qualified retirement plan, its benefits may fall short of providing adequate preparation for your retirement. Fortunately, IRS regulations also allow you to take advantage of other personally established qualified retirement planning mechanisms, all of which provide some tax-shelter opportunities. These mechanisms include individual retirement accounts (IRAs), Keogh plans (pronounced "key-oh"), simplified employee pension–individual retirement account plans (SEP-IRAs), and annuities.

Individual Retirement Accounts

An **individual retirement account (IRA)** is a tax-deferred retirement plan established by people who have wage, salary, or net self-employment earnings. IRAs are typically opened with banks, mutual funds, insurance companies, and stock brokerage firms. You can set up an IRA in one of two ways: (1) by making annual contributions, and (2) by rolling over a distribution received from a qualified employer plan or from another IRA, creating a **rollover IRA.**

You can invest IRA money almost any way you desire, and change your investments whenever you please, without paying taxes on any gains. IRAs are self-directed, meaning that you decide how to invest the money; you also assume responsibility for following the rules.

Deposits into an IRA may be tax-deductible even if the taxpayer does not itemize deductions on his or her income tax return. In this way, such contributions reduce taxable income. Investment earnings on IRA funds are not taxable until they are withdrawn, so your investments grow faster.

You may contribute as much of your earnings as you desire, up to a maximum of $2000 per year. In general, you may not contribute more than you earn. An exception is made for spouses who do not earn money income. In a **spousal account** for one-income couples, the maximum contribution is $4000. The amounts deposited may be allocated between spouses in any way as long as neither spouse makes a contribution exceeding $2000.

If you deposit more into an IRA account than the amount legally permitted, you will owe a penalty to the IRS. You may also choose to contribute to an IRA account once and then never add any other funds.

Withdrawals of IRA funds prior to age 59$\frac{1}{2}$ are taxed as ordinary income, and a 10 percent tax penalty must be paid unless used for qualifying education expenses. Withdrawals from an IRA must begin by April 1 of the year after the account owner turns 70$\frac{1}{2}$ and be withdrawn at a rate that will deplete the funds during one's remaining life expectancy. This rule was instituted to prevent people from using an IRA to pass funds tax-free to heirs. Although you may not borrow from an IRA account, you may pull IRA money out of an account providing that you redeposit the full amount within 60 days.

Fully Deductible IRA Accounts Three-fourths of all U.S. workers qualify for tax-deductible individual retirement accounts, including all who are *not* "active participants" in an employer-sponsored qualified retirement plan. Thus, the question becomes, "Are you an active participant in an employer retirement plan?" Members of defined-benefit plans are active participants. Those who participate in a defined-contribution plan—meaning that they actually contribute and are not simply eligible—are active participants as well. Married workers are not considered active participants simply because their spouse is participating in a retirement plan.

You must make deductible IRA contributions by April 15 for the previous tax year. The maximum tax-deductible contribution is $2000 per year or the amount of compensation earned, whichever is less. A married couple may contribute as much as $4000 annually; up to $2000 each.

Partially Deductible IRA Accounts Even if you are a participant in an employer-sponsored plan, you may be allowed to put tax-deductible money into an IRA account. The level of allowable tax-sheltered contributions depends on the amount of the adjusted gross income (AGI) for federal income tax purposes. Single workers with an AGI less than $30,000 and married workers with a joint AGI less than $50,000 may shelter IRA contributions up to $2000. For those with AGIs exceeding these amounts, the allowable tax-deductible contribution is reduced $1 for each $5 increase in income until the allowable contribution is entirely phased out ($40,000 for single workers and $60,000 for married workers). For example, a single worker with an adjusted gross income of $35,000 would be able to shelter $1000 in IRA contributions: $2000 − [($35,000 − $30,000) ÷ 5 × 1].

Non-Deductible IRAs May Still Offer Benefits **Non-deductible IRAs** are established by people who cannot deduct the contribution from their income taxes. Even though contributed funds are not tax-deductible, the amounts that accumulate remain sheltered from income taxes. Because a non-deductible IRA is funded with after-tax money, it is better to contribute the maximum to any salary-reduction pension plan that offers the opportunity of a deductible contribution before funding a non-deductible IRA. Separate IRA accounts should be created for tax-deductible contributions and non–tax-deductible contributions to simplify the calculation of income taxes when withdrawals are eventually made. IRS form 8606 must be filed each year with your federal income tax return once you have made a non-deductible IRA contribution. You should keep copies of all 8606 forms so you do not overpay income taxes when money is finally withdrawn.

The Roth IRA Tax law revisions in 1997 created the **Roth IRA.** The contributions into a Roth IRA are not tax-deductible, but they are tax-free when withdrawn. As with other IRAs, the earnings on the funds in the account grow tax-free over the years. Even more importantly, if the Roth IRA has been in place for more than five years and you have reached age 59$\frac{1}{2}$ (or the earnings have been used for qualified education expenses or up to $10,000 to purchase a first home), these earnings are

About Retirement Rollover Penalties

If money in a qualified pension plan is withdrawn by an employee departing from an employer, the IRS may consider it taxable income because such amounts were sheltered from taxes earlier. The result might be a substantial tax bill.

A **rollover** is a transfer of retirement money from one retirement plan to another. The IRS's **20 percent withholding rule** applies to lump-sum distributions from pension plans and other qualified retirement plans. It requires that an employer withhold a 20 percent tax from a lump-sum distribution paid directly to a former employee. To avoid income tax withholding, a direct **trustee-to-trustee rollover** must occur in which the funds go directly from the previous employer's pension fund to the trustee of the new pension account, with no payment to the employee.

For example, a $300,000 lump-sum distribution made directly to an employee would result in that person receiving $240,000 and the employer withholding $60,000 for the IRS. Government regulations further require that the employee put the entire $300,000 into a new account or a rollover IRA within 60 days—even though only $240,000 was received. The investor must supply the difference ($60,000 in this instance) on his or her own. Substantial penalties are incurred for noncompliance. The 20 percent amount that was withheld may be retrieved the following tax year by filing an income tax return to claim a refund. The IRS wants taxpayers to transfer retirement funds in such a way that the previously untaxed money remains accountable and, eventually, taxable.

not taxed or penalized at withdrawal. This feature of the Roth IRA represents an enormous tax break. A $2000 deposit at age 25, for example, might be worth $64,000 at age 65—and completely tax-free. The total contribution into all IRAs is limited to $2000 per year. All of this amount can go into a Roth IRA as long as adjusted gross income is less than $95,000 for single taxpayers and less than $150,000 for joint filers. Smaller Roth IRA contributions are allowed for those with AGIs up to $110,000 and $160,000, respectively. Individuals can contribute to Roth IRAs even if they are not allowed to contribute to tax-deductible IRAs because they participate in an employer-sponsored retirement plan.

Simplified Employee Pension Plan– Individual Retirement Accounts

A **simplified employee pension plan–individual retirement plan** (also called a **SEP-IRA** or **SEP,** or SIMPLE plan if set up after 1996) is a retirement plan that allows employers to contribute a discretionary amount into employees' IRAs each year. Used by people who are self-employed and small business owners, a SEP-IRA is simple to set up and easy to maintain. With a SEP-IRA, each participant can make tax-sheltered contributions representing 0 to 15 percent of net self-employment income, or $22,500, whichever is less. Participants may vary the percentage of earned income contributed each year, or even skip a year if desired. The investment alternatives for a SEP-IRA are quite flexible.

Keogh Plans

If you are self-employed either full- or part-time, you may want to consider a **Keogh plan** for yourself and any employees. Although a Keogh plan is more expensive to set up and requires more administrative time to operate than other retirement plans, it enables you to contribute a percentage of self-employment income each year. Depending upon the type of Keogh plan established (profit sharing, money purchase, or paired plan), you can save as much as 25 percent of self-employment income, with most plans capped at $30,000 per participant. While withdrawals before age 59$1/2$ are penalized, contributions can still be made after age 70$1/2$ (unlike other retirement plans). Keogh investors are also allowed to invest in real estate. The same worker may have a salary-reduction plan, an IRA, a SEP-IRA, and a Keogh.

Annuities

An **annuity** is a contract made with an insurance company that provides for a series of payments to be received at stated intervals (usually monthly) for a fixed or variable time period. All annuities represent hybrids of investment and insurance, with earnings growing tax-free until payouts begin. As a result, they are sometimes called **tax-sheltered annuities (TSAs).** Although these contracts are sold by life insurance companies, annuities are often described as being the opposite of life insurance because they generally provide funds during life, not after death. Annuities may be classified as either immediate or deferred.

Get at Your Qualified Retirement Funds Early

If you take money out of a qualified tax-sheltered retirement account prior to age 59½, you will usually incur a 10 percent penalty on what you take as well as owe regular income taxes on the amount withdrawn. In some instances, such as disability, it is possible to gain access to the funds and avoid the 10 percent penalty (but not the taxes). Three other mechanisms also are available under IRS rules, although your employer may have rules that restrict withdrawals.

Hardship conditions.

You can withdraw money for hardships such as a funeral, medical expenses, tuition, and a down payment on a home. You must prove that you have exhausted all other sources and have been turned down for loans to meet the expense. Such withdrawals represent taxable income if taxes had not yet been paid on the funds. Hardship withdrawals are not allowed from an IRA.

Early retirement.

If you retire between ages 55 and 59½, you may withdraw funds from an IRS-qualified plan or may be allowed to take the money out of the plan and use the lump sum to establish a rollover IRA (see page 535). Consequently, you might qualify for a special early withdrawal opportunity for owners of IRAs. You could then withdraw funds from the rollover IRA account without penalty if you take the money in substantially equal periodic payments designed to last the rest of your life expectancy. You must continue to receive the equal payments for a minimum of five years or until age 59½, whichever is longer, at which point you can change the payment amount to fit your income needs.

Loans from the retirement fund.

Most employers allow workers to borrow money from their qualified retirement plans without paying a penalty. Borrowing limits are $10,000 for accounts that contain $10,000 or less or 50 percent of the balance if the account contains more than $10,000, with an overall maximum loan of $50,000. Except for loans to purchase primary residences, the money must be repaid in five years, usually through payroll deduction. About 60 percent of workers with such plans have an outstanding loan. You cannot borrow from an IRA or use an IRA account as collateral for a loan. Borrowing money from your plan may appear to be an easy, low-cost way of getting a loan, but borrowed funds do not continue to grow and thus borrowing puts retirement security at risk.

For people still working, the most familiar annuity is the **deferred annuity**, which builds up funds prior to retirement. In this plan, you regularly give money (typically every payday) to an insurance company, which invests it. At a date specified in the contract (such as a sixtieth birthday or retirement), the annuity begins providing a stream of payments while the **annuitant** (the person receiving the annuity) remains alive, often for the remainder of the recipient's life.

Other Annuity Variations As illustrated in Figure 18.2 on the following page, the purchaser of annuity may choose among other factors to tailor the annuity plan to fit his or her goals. An annuity can be purchased in installments over time (**installment premium annuity**) or as a **single-premium annuity**. This latter type is often used to roll over funds from a retirement plan or receive

Figure 18.2

Classifying Annuities

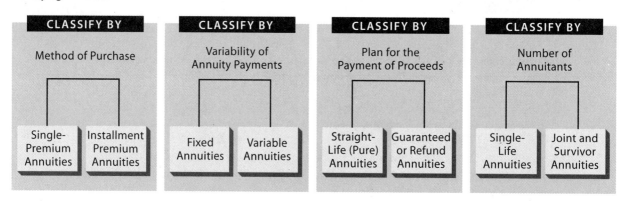

the death benefit from a life insurance policy. Some annuities are **fixed annuities**, for which both the rate of return and the income received are fixed. Others are **variable annuities**, which allow the purchaser to choose among alternatives for investing the funds, thereby allowing for variable rates of return and hence income. A **straight-life (pure) annuity** provides an income for the life of the annuitant; payments cease when that person dies. Alternatively, guaranteed annuities can be set up to pay a minimum number of installments (**installments-certain annuity**), payments for a specified time period regardless of how long the beneficiary lives (**period-certain annuity**), or a lump sum to a beneficiary should the annuitant die prior to some agreed-upon date (**cash-refund annuity**). Some annuities will cover the lives of more than one person (**joint and survivor annuities**) and are most often used by married couples.

How to Use Annuities in Retirement Planning   Although the earnings from the funds invested in an annuity accumulate tax-free, you should not buy annuities simply to shelter earnings until all other avenues for sheltering contributions—that is, tax-sheltered retirement plans—have been exhausted. For example, if Johanna Jensen, a high-income worker, was trying to save $15,000 per year toward retirement, first she should put $10,000 into her 401(k) retirement plan at work. In this manner, she reduces her taxable income by $10,000. The remaining $5000 ($15,000 − $10,000) could be invested in an after-tax salary-reduction plan, tax-free municipal bonds, a cash-value life insurance policy, annuities, or Roth IRA. If an annuity is not part of a qualified retirement program, the portion of monthly payouts that is a return of principal would be excluded from taxable income.

Because annuities carry high administrative expenses and sales commissions (loads), people often choose at retirement to roll their lump-sum pension payouts into IRA-rollover accounts. Retirees who prefer not to take responsibility for investment decisions and money management often choose annuities. Investors who purchase annuities when interest rates are low may find that their pay-

Tax Considerations & Consequences — *Retirement*

Wise managers of their personal finances take full advantage of tax sheltering for funds intended for retirement. The following examples assume that a person who pays income taxes at the 28 percent rate invests $1000 at the end of each year for 20 years and the funds earn 8 percent annually.

Example 1. *Make investments that tax-shelter both contributions and growth—in a qualified retirement plan, such as a salary-reduction plan—and invest both the planned sum and the tax money saved.* A $1000 contribution into a qualified plan results in a $280 reduction in income taxes owed for someone in the 28 percent marginal tax bracket. If you invest the planned sum ($1000 in this example) plus the amount of income taxes saved each year ($280), the resulting accumulation can be quite significant. With an 8 percent annual return over 20 years, the $1280 ($1000 + $280) investment will grow to $58,575 and you will pay taxes only as funds are withdrawn.

Example 2. *Make investments that tax-shelter both contributions and growth—in a qualified retirement plan, such as a salary-reduction plan—but invest only the planned sum.* If you invest the planned sum of $1000 each year into a qualified plan, but choose not to invest the income tax savings of $280, the account will accumulate to $45,760 over 20 years and you will pay taxes as growth accumulated is withdrawn.

Example 3. *Make investments that tax-shelter growth but not contributions—in an after-tax salary-reduction plan, a nonqualified IRA account, or a deferred variable annuity.* In this case, only $1000 is available to invest each year because no income tax savings are generated by the contribution. With an 8 percent annual return over 20 years, the $1000 investment will grow to $45,760 and you will pay taxes as growth accumulated is withdrawn.

Example 4. *Use a Roth IRA.* Once again, only $1000 is available to invest because no income tax savings are generated on the contribution. With an 8 percent annual return over 20 years, the $1000 annual investment will grow to $45,760 with no taxes owed as it is withdrawn. Hence, you will earn $25,760 [$45,760 − (20 × $1000)] in tax-free money.

Example 5. *Make non–tax-sheltered investments for retirement, such as mutual funds and high-quality stocks and bonds.* Once again, only $1000 is available to invest because no income tax savings are generated by the contribution. The 8 percent return is subject to income taxes, however, which reduces the annual tax-equivalent yield to 5.76 percent [8 percent × (1 − 0.28)]. With a 5.76 annual return over 20 years, $1000 will grow to $35,850.

If you have both tax-sheltered investments (example 1 above) and those that shelter growth but not contributions (examples 2 and 3 above), you must keep meticulous records of which investments were made with deductible and non-deductible money. Otherwise, you risk having to pay income taxes on your *non*-deductible contributions, thus paying taxes twice. Many people find it helpful to use separate financial institutions for the deductible and non-deductible contributions.

ments do not keep pace with inflation. Buying tax-sheltered annuities in installments is likely to become less popular due to the recent reductions in capital gains tax rates and the advent of the Roth IRA.

Social Security Retirement Benefits

6   Describe how to qualify for the Social Security retirement program and the role that Social Security plays in retirement planning.

The Social Security program comprises an amalgam of 55 government programs for the elderly and others who qualify for benefits. Almost 50 million pension, survivor, and disability checks are mailed each month. Social Security focuses on providing Americans with minimum—but not necessarily adequate—protection against the loss of income from retirement, disability, or death of a family wage earner. Last year (1999), the average monthly Social Security retirement check amounted to $780.

Funding for Social Security benefits comes from a compulsory payroll tax split equally between employee and employer. The Social Security taxes withheld from wages are called **FICA taxes** (for Federal Insurance Contributions Act). Amounts withheld are deposited in the Social Security trust fund accounts, although more than three-fourths of those funds have been lent back to the U.S. Treasury to finance budget deficits. Social Security is considered an unfunded pension plan run by the federal government because taxes collected from current workers pay the benefits for current retirees. As a result, the ability of the Social Security system to meet Americans' retirement needs continues to be challenged. Nevertheless, Social Security benefits constitute one of the most important assets in the life of a wage earner.

Contributions to Social Security

Wage earners pay Social Security FICA taxes on wage income up to the **maximum taxable yearly earnings**, which comprise the maximum amount to which the full Social Security tax rate is applied. The maximum taxable yearly earnings figure—$72,600 last year—is adjusted annually for inflation. In recent years, the total Social Security tax rate has been 7.65 percent, consisting of a 6.2 percent FICA tax and a 1.45 percent Medicare tax. Higher-income taxpayers pay the 1.45 percent Medicare tax on all of their earned income. For example, a person earning $25,000 pays a Social Security tax of $1912.50 ($25,000 × 0.0765) and a person earning $75,000 pays $5588.70 {($72,600 × 0.0765) + [($75,000 − $72,600) × 0.0145]}. The employer pays taxes that match each of these amounts. Self-employed workers pay a Social Security tax rate twice that of wage earners because their contributions are not matched by an employer.

Eligibility for Social Security Retirement Benefits

When a worker retires, various members of his or her family can receive benefits: the retiree; unmarried children under age 18, or age 19 if still in high school; unmarried children 18 or older who were severely disabled before age 22 and who are still disabled; the retiree's spouse if aged 62 or older; and the retiree's spouse younger than age 62 if caring for a child under 16 (or over 16 and disabled) who receives benefits. Electing to delay receipt of Social Security benefits beyond age 65 produces a higher monthly benefit later, with an adjustment of plus 3 percent for each year (0.25 percent for each month). Since 1990, the adjustment has been gradually increased and will continue to do so until it reaches a total of 8 percent per year in 2008.

Social Security retirement benefits can be received as early as age 62, but starting benefits before age 65 permanently reduces the benefits to account for the longer period of likely benefits. The size of the reduction is 0.556 percent for each month prior to age 65 that benefits begin. A reduction of 20 percent occurs at age 62, $13^1/3$ percent at age 63, and $6^2/3$ percent at age 64. Thus, someone who would be entitled to a monthly benefit of $800 at age 65 would receive only $640 [$800 − (0.20 × $800)] per month if he or she chose to start receiving benefits at age 62.

For persons attaining age 65 in 2003, the full-benefit age will be gradually increased until it reaches 67 years in 2022. Reduced benefits will still be available at age 62, but the reduction for early benefits will increase (ultimately as high as 30 percent of the full benefit) as the full-benefit retirement age increases. This change affects people born after 1937.

Qualifying for Social Security Benefits

The Social Security program covers nine out of every ten U.S. employees. Some federal, state, and local government employees are exempt because their employers have instituted other plans. To qualify for benefits, a worker accumulates credits for employment in any work covered by Social Security, including part-time and temporary employment. To qualify, the employment need not be consecutive. Military service also provides credits. **Credits** (formerly called **quarters of coverage**) are calendar units credited by the Social Security Administration (SSA) based on earnings in a calendar year. Last year, for example, workers received one credit if they earned $740 and the annual maximum of four credits if they earned $2960 (4 × $740). The dollar figure required for each credit earned is raised annually to keep pace with inflation.

The number of credits determines eligibility for benefits. The Social Security Administration recognizes four statuses of eligibility (described below), and Table 18.2 on the following page shows the length-of-work requirements for benefits.

- **Fully insured.** Fully insured status requires 40 credits and provides the worker and family with benefits under the retirement, survivor's, and disability programs. Once obtained, this status cannot be lost even if the person never works again. It is required to receive retirement benefits. "Fully insured" does not imply that the worker will receive the maximum benefits allowable, because the actual dollar amount of benefits is based on the average of the highest 35 years of earnings during the working years.

- **Currently insured.** To achieve currently insured status, six credits must be earned in the most recent three years. This status provides for some survivor's or disability benefits but no retirement benefits. To remain eligible for these benefits, a worker must continue to earn at least six credits every three years or meet a minimum number of covered years of work established by the Social Security Administration.

- **Transitionally insured.** Transitionally insured status applies only to retired workers who reach the age of 72 without accumulating 40 credits (ten years). These people are eligible for limited retirement benefits.

- **Not insured.** Workers younger than age 72 who have fewer than six credits of work experience are not insured.

Table 18.2

Length-of-Work Requirements for Social Security Benefits

Types of Benefits	Payable to	Minimum Years of Work under Social Security
Retirement	You, your spouse, child, dependent spouse 62 or over	10 years (fully insured status) (If age 62 prior to 1991, you may need only $7^3/_4$ to $9^1/_4$ years.)
Survivors*		
Full	Widow(er) 60 or over, disabled widow(er) 50–59, widow(er) if caring for child 18 years or younger, dependent children, dependent widow(er) 62 or over, disabled dependent widow(er) 50–61, dependent parent at 62	10 years (fully insured status)
Current	Widow(er) caring for child 18 years or younger, dependent children	$1^1/_2$ years of last 3 years before death (currently insured status)
Disability	You and your dependents	If under age 24, you need $1^1/_2$ years of work in the 3 years prior to disablement; if between ages 24 and 31, you need to work half the time between when you turned 21 and your date of disablement; if age 31 or older, you must have 5 years of credit during the 10 years prior to disablement.
Medicare		
Hospitalization (Part A: automatic benefits)	Anyone 65 or over plus some others, such as the disabled	Anyone qualified for the Social Security retirement program is qualified for Medicare Part A at age 65; others may qualify by paying a monthly premium for Part A.
Medical expense (Part B: voluntary benefits)	Anyone eligible for Part A and anyone else 65 or over (payment of monthly premiums required)	No prior work under Social Security is required.

Source: U.S. Department of Health and Human Services.

* A lump-sum death benefit no greater than $255 is also granted to dependents of those either fully or currently insured.

Calculation of Retirement Benefits

An **indexing method** is used for calculating Social Security benefits. This method revalues previous wage earnings to adjust for inflation. Because of indexing, retirement benefits can only be "guesstimated" as the indexing formula for future years is unknown. Appendix B, "Estimating Social Security Benefits," explains how to make a fair estimate of your benefits.

You also may obtain an official estimate of your benefits from the Social Security Administration.* A **personal earnings and benefit estimate statement**

---

* Telephone the Social Security Administration at (800) 772-1213 or write the SSA at Box 56, Baltimore, MD 21203. You can estimate your benefits using the SSA's program called "ANYPIA" on the Internet at *www.ssa.gov*.

(PEBES) is available for each worker in the United States. This free statement shows the SSA's record of your lifetime taxable earnings covered under Social Security regulations, the estimated taxes paid on those earnings, and estimates of your monthly Social Security benefits if you retire at age 62, 65, or 70. It also shows the monthly amount that your survivors would receive if you died in the current year and the monthly disability benefit you and your family would receive if you became unable to work. All workers aged 25 and older will automatically receive an annual PEBES statement beginning in 2000. Having this information will help you calculate an estimate of benefits and compare this estimate with your personal records for any discrepancies. Earnings records held by the Social Security Administration (SSA) should be kept up-to-date and accurate. Workers have only three years to correct errors.

For workers who have substantial total earnings in retirement, a portion of the amount of Social Security benefit represents taxable income. The marginal tax rate applied is the individual's normal rate—usually 15 or 28 percent. In addition, limits are placed on how much income a person may earn while collecting Social Security retirement benefits. If earned income exceeds these limits, the Social Security retirement benefit will be reduced.

Supplemental Security Income

For people who are 65 or older, blind, or disabled, the federal **supplemental security income (SSI)** program might provide limited monetary benefits. To qualify, you must have no more than $2000 in assets ($3000 for a couple) excluding a home or car, and your income must fall below a certain level. The basic monthly check amounts to approximately $450 for a single person and $670 for a couple. Some states also pay a supplemental benefit beyond SSI payments.

A Retirement Planning Illustration

7 Estimate the dollar amount you should be saving for retirement.

Knowing your annual retirement expenditures in current dollars and being knowledgeable about the sources of income that might support these expenditures leads logically to the question of how much money must be set aside to provide that support. The Decision-Making Worksheet "Estimating Retirement Needs in Today's Dollars" can be used to calculate this amount. In the following example, a worker uses this worksheet to arrive at the amount that would need to be saved each year. Couples could use the same worksheet by simply combining their dollar amounts where appropriate. Consider the case of William Handy, aged 35 and single, who is a medical lab technician for a small firm in Taos, New Mexico. Bill currently earns $30,000 per year and has worked for his employer since age 24. He plans to retire at age 62.

1. Bill has chosen not to develop a retirement budget at this time. Instead, he multiplied his current salary by 80 percent to arrive at an annual income (in current dollars) needed in retirement of $24,000 ($30,000 × 0.80). This amount was entered on line 1 of the worksheet.

Estimating Retirement Needs in Today's Dollars

This worksheet will help you calculate the annual amount you need to set aside in today's dollars so that you will have adequate funds during your retirement. The example below assumes that a married person is now 35 years old, will retire at age 62, has a current income of $30,000, currently saves and invests about $2000 per year, gives zero to the company's new 401(k) savings and investment program, anticipates needing a retirement income of $24,000 per year assuming a spending lifestyle at 80

percent of current income ($30,000 × 0.80), and will live an additional 20 years beyond retirement. Investment returns are assumed to be 3 percent after inflation—a fair estimate for a typical portfolio. The financial needs would differ if the growth rate of the investments is greater than 3 percent. This approach simplifies the calculations and puts the numbers to estimate retirement needs into today's dollars. The amount saved must be higher if substantial inflation occurs.

	Example	Your Numbers
1. Annual income needed at retirement in today's dollars (Use carefully estimated numbers or a certain percentage, such as 70% or 80%.)	$24,000	_____
2. Estimated Social Security retirement benefit in today's dollars [Use Appendix B or telephone the Social Security Administration at (800) 772-1213 for a projection of your benefits.]	$ 7,248	_____
3. Estimated employer pension benefit in today's dollars (Ask your retirement benefit advisor to make an estimate of your future pension, assuming that you remain in the same job at the same salary, or make your own conservative estimate.)	$ 5,800	_____
4. Total estimated retirement income from Social Security and employer pension in today's dollars (line 2 + line 3)	$13,048	_____
5. Additional income needed at retirement in today's dollars (line 1 – line 4)	$10,952	_____
6. Amount you must have at retirement in today's dollars to receive additional annual income in retirement (line 5) for 20 years (from Appendix A.4, assuming a 3% return over 20 years, or 14.878 × $10,952)	$162,944	_____
7. Amount already available as savings and investments in today's dollars (add lines 7-A through 7-D, and record total on line 7-E)		
A Employer savings plans, such as a 401(k), SEP, or profit-sharing plan	0	
B IRAs and Keoghs	$4,000	
C Other investments, such as mutual funds, stocks, bonds, real estate, and other assets available for retirement	$8,000	
D If you wish to include a portion of the equity in your home as savings, enter its present value minus the cost of another home in retirement	0	
E Total retirement savings (add lines A through D)	$12,000	_____
8. Future value of current savings/investments at time of retirement (Using Appendix A.1 and a growth rate of 3% over 27 years, the factor is 2.221; thus, 2.221 × $12,000)	$26,652	_____
9. Additional retirement savings and investments needed at time of retirement (line 6 – line 8)	$136,292	_____
10. Annual savings needed (to reach amount in line 9) before retirement (Using Appendix A.3 and a growth rate of 3% over 27 years, the factor is 40.71; thus, $136,292 ÷ 40.71)	$ 3,348	_____
11. Current annual contribution to savings and investment plans	$ 2,000	_____
12. Additional amount of annual savings that you need to set aside in today's dollars to achieve retirement goal (in line 1) (line 10 – line 11)	$ 1,348	_____

2. Bill called the Social Security Administration to obtain his personal earnings and benefit estimate statement. According to the statement, at age 62 he could expect a monthly benefit of $604 (in current dollars). Multiplying by 12 gave an expected annual Social Security benefit of $7248 (in current dollars), which he entered on line 2 of the worksheet.

3. Line 3 of the worksheet, which calls for Bill's expected pension benefit, is appropriate for defined-benefit plans. After discussing his expected employer pension with the benefits counselor at work, Bill found that the company retirement plan had recently changed from a defined-benefit plan to a defined-contribution plan. His anticipated benefit under the old plan would amount to approximately $5800 annually, assuming that he remained with the company until his retirement, so he entered that figure on line 3.

4. Bill adds lines 2 and 3 to determine his total estimated retirement income from Social Security and employer pension. The amount on line 4 would be $13,048 ($7248 + $5800).

5. Subtracting line 4 from line 1 reveals that Bill would need an additional income of $10,952 ($24,000 − $13,048) in today's dollars from savings and investments to meet his annual retirement income needs.

6. At this point, Bill has considered only his annual needs and benefits. Because he plans to retire at age 62, Bill will need income for 20 years based on his life expectancy. (It is possible that Bill could live well into his eighties, so that he would need the inflation-adjusted equivalent of his annual retirement expenditures for more than 20 years.) Using Appendix A.4 and assuming a return 3 percent above the inflation rate, Bill finds the multiplier 14.878 where 3 percent and 20 years intersect and calculates that he needs an additional amount of $162,944 (14.878 × $10,952) at retirement.

7. Bill's current savings and investments can be used to offset the $162,944 he will need for retirement. Bill has zero savings through his employer's new 401(k) plan, but he does have some money invested in an IRA, plus some other investments. These amounts are totaled ($12,000) and recorded on line 7.

8. If left untouched, the $12,000 that Bill has built up will continue to earn interest and dividends until he retires. Because he has 27 more years until retirement, Bill can use Appendix A.1 and, assuming a growth rate of 3 percent over 27 years, find the factor 2.221 and multiply it by the total amount in line 7. Bill's $12,000 should have a future value of $26,652 at his retirement, so he puts this amount on line 8.

9. Subtracting line 8 from line 6 reveals that Bill will need a nest egg of $136,292 at the time of retirement.

10. Using Appendix A.3 and a growth rate of 3 percent over 27 years, Bill finds a factor of 40.71. When divided into $136,292, it reveals that he needs savings and investments of $3348 per year until retirement.

11. Bill records his current savings and investments of $2000 per year on line 11.

12. Bill subtracts line 11 from line 10 to determine the additional amount of annual savings that he should set aside in today's dollars to achieve his retirement goal. His shortfall totals $1348 per year. By saving about $112 each

month ($1348 ÷ 12), he can reach his retirement goal established in step 1. Bill would be wise to discuss with his benefits counselor how much he can save and invest via the company's new 401(k) program.

Bill could take steps to catch up by contributing an additional $1348 per year into the company 401(k) plan—that is, almost 4¹/₂ percent of his salary. For a margin of safety, and if the rules of his employer's pension plan permit, he could save an additional 1 to 1¹/₂ percent of his salary. His employer may also possibly match some or all of Bill's 401(k) contributions.

Note that Bill needs to set aside an additional $1348 in *current* dollars. That amount assumes that the growth of his investments will be 3 percent greater than the inflation rate, a reasonable assumption. But, as his income goes up, Bill should increase this amount.

Reframe Your Thinking about Retirement Savings

The large dollar amount required for a retirement nest egg can be very scary. A novel approach to thinking about retirement saving has been developed by Dennis R. Ackley of Watson Wyatt Worldwide. He suggests looking at your retirement as something you "buy." The "retail price" is the nest egg itself. From that amount you can subtract "discounts" for employer-based retirement plans, Social Security, and any funds you have already accumulated. Then you identify the difference—the shortfall indicted on line 9 of the Decision-Making Worksheet—and buy it on the "layaway plan." The additional amounts you periodically save and invest are therefore the "layaway payments" with which you "buy" your retirement.

Summary

1. Times have radically changed for workers and retirees, particularly with the shift from the employer to the employee of both the obligation to invest and the risk of making poor investments.

2. Experts estimate that retirees need 75 to 90 percent of their income to maintain a comfortable lifestyle, and higher-income people must rely upon employer-provided and supplemental retirement plans as well as savings and investments to support an appropriate level of living.

3. The two advantages of qualified retirement plans are that tax-deductible contributions create larger returns and tax-deferred growth enhances earnings.

4. Analyzing any employer-sponsored retirement plan is vital in retirement planning. The Employee Retirement Income Security Act (ERISA) regulates such plans, including employee participation and vesting. The once-traditional defined-benefit plan is being replaced today by defined-contribution plans. A number of other types of employer-sponsored retirement plans also exist.

5. Personal retirement plans include individual retirement accounts (IRAs), simplified

employee pension plan–individual retirement accounts (SEP-IRAs), Keogh plans, and annuities.

6. Social Security retirement benefits are funded by worker- and employer-paid taxes and may provide an important—but insufficient—portion of income needed during retirement years.

7. An illustration of planning for retirement reveals that it is possible to avoid having to accumulate the money needed for retirement in a hurry. The process begins with estimating retirement expenses and sources of income and ends with estimating the additional dollar amount to be set aside for retirement each year.

Key Words & Concepts

after-tax salary-reduction plan   *532*

defined-benefit plan   *527*

defined-contribution plan   *528*

401(k) salary-reduction plan   *529*

guaranteed investment contract (GIC)   *530*

individual retirement account (IRA)   *535*

Keogh plan   *538*

maximum taxable yearly earnings   *542*

personal earnings and benefit estimate statement (PEBES)   *544*

portability   *529*

qualified domestic-relations order (QDRO)   *535*

qualified retirement plans   *525*

rollover   *537*

salary-reduction plans   *529*

self-directed retirement plan   *529*

tax-sheltered retirement plans   *525*

unfunded pension plan   *527*

variable annuities   *540*

vesting   *526*

Questions for Thought & Discussion

1. List three examples of the radical changes for workers and retirees that have occurred in recent years.

2. What are the three steps to estimating retirement needs?

3. What are the likely sources and amounts of income for the average person considering retirement?

4. What is a tax-sheltered (qualified) retirement plan? In what two ways can such a plan help decrease your income tax liability?

5. Using an example, explain how putting money into a tax-sheltered retirement plan can create larger returns than putting the same money into a bank.

6. Using an example, explain how putting money into a tax-sheltered retirement plan enhances earnings.

7. Summarize why it is best to begin a tax-sheltered retirement plan at an early age.

8. What penalties are levied if you take money out of a tax-sheltered retirement plan prior to age 59 1/2?

9. Why is vesting important to a person covered by an employer-sponsored retirement plan?

10. Distinguish between cliff vesting and graduated vesting.

11. Distinguish between a defined-contribution plan and a defined-benefit plan.

12. Distinguish between funded and unfunded plans.

13. What disadvantage arises when retirement benefits are integrated with Social Security benefits?

14. What effect does early retirement have on a worker's benefit? Why does it occur?

15. Why are defined-contribution plans gradually replacing defined-benefit plans?

16. Distinguish between contributory and noncontributory retirement plans.

17. Define "portability" as a feature of pension plans.

18. Explain the 20 percent withholding rule for early withdrawals from retirement plans.

19. What bonus situation do many employers provide with salary-reduction plans? Explain how this approach is useful to the employee.

20. What is the benefit to the employee of taking an early retirement payout using ten-year averaging?

21. What dangers exist if a married worker is considering changing his or her survivor's retirement benefit from a joint and survivor annuity to a single-life annuity?

22. What is an after-tax salary-reduction plan, and what advantage does it offer the financial manager?

23. Differentiate between an employee stock-ownership plan (ESOP) and a profit-sharing plan.

24. List two questions that might be asked about an employer-sponsored retirement plan.

25. What is an IRA, and how can it be used as a tax-sheltered retirement plan?

26. Distinguish between a deductible IRA account and a Roth IRA.

27. Who should consider establishing a Keogh plan?

28. What three reasons can a person use to receive his or her qualified retirement funds early?

29. Distinguish between a fixed annuity and a variable annuity.

30. What impact does early retirement have on Social Security retirement benefits?

31. Distinguish between "fully insured" and "currently insured" for Social Security benefits.

DECISION-MAKING CASES

Case 1   Estimating Early and Normal Retirement Benefits

Ben Dietrick of St. Louis, Missouri, age 35, is single and does not expect to marry. He is busily making plans for his retirement. He is anxious to maintain his current lifestyle without "scrimping," but still wants to actively start saving for his retirement to take advantage of compounding. Currently, Ben earns $40,000 per year, with an adjusted gross income of $39,135 and an after-tax income of $28,750. He anticipates receiving $10,265 from Social Security annually, and $12,865 per year in pension benefits upon his retirement at age 65. If he retires at age 55, his pension benefits will be approximately $9500. To date, Ben has about $10,000 of investments.

(a) Using the Decision-Making Worksheet on page 546, calculate the additional amount of annual savings that Ben needs to set aside to reach his goal of retiring at age 55 with 70 percent of his current income.

(b) What amount of savings for retirement would Ben need if he decided to work to age 65? Use the same worksheet to solve for the answer.

(c) Would you recommend Ben invest in an IRA or a Roth IRA? Why or why not?

Case 2   Calculation of Annual Savings Needed to Meet a Retirement Goal

Melinda Smith, age 40, single and from San Diego, California, is trying to estimate the amount she needs to save annually to meet her retirement needs. Melinda currently earns $40,000 per year. She expects to need 80 percent of her current salary to live on at retirement. She expects $825 per month in Social Security benefits. Using the Decision-Making Worksheet on page 546, calculate answers to the following questions:

(a) What annual income would Melinda need for retirement?

(b) What would her annual expected Social Security benefit be?

(c) Melinda expects to receive $500 per month from her pension at work. What is her annual benefit?

(d) How much annual retirement income will she need from savings?

(e) How much will Melinda need to save by retirement in today's dollars if she plans to retire at age 65?

(f) Melinda currently has $5000 in an IRA account. Assuming a growth rate of 8 percent, what will the value of her IRA savings be when she retires?

(g) How much will she still need to save?

(h) What is the annual amount she needs to save to reach this goal?

Financial Math Questions

1. Mike Shanahan is considering the tax consequences of investing $2000 at the end of each year for 20 years, assuming that the investment earns 6 percent annually.

   (a) How much will the account total if both contributions and growth of the investment remain sheltered from taxes?

   (b) How much will the account total if growth remains tax-sheltered but not contributions?

   (c) How much will the account total if the investments are not sheltered at all from taxes? See the examples in the "Tax Considerations and Consequences" on page 541 for guidance. [Hint: Use Appendix A.3 or the *Garman/Forgue* Web site.]

2. Over the years, Joe and Marie Paget have accumulated $200,000 and $220,000, respectively, in their qualified retirement plans. If the amounts in the two plans earn a 6 percent rate of return over Joe and Marie's anticipated 20 years of retirement, how large an amount could be withdrawn from the two funds each month? Use the table in the boxed feature on page 534 to make your calculations or the *Garman/Forgue* Web site or Appendix A.4.

3. As Joe Paget is an aggressive investor and he is lucky, assume that his $200,000 nest egg will earn 8 percent while his wife Marie's investments earn 6 percent. How large an amount could be withdrawn from the two funds each month over the next 20 years? Use the table in the boxed feature on page 534 to make your calculations or the *Garman/Forgue* Web site or Appendix A.4.

4. Madeline and Grover Murray desire an annual retirement income of $40,000 and they expect to live for 20 years past retirement. Assuming that they could earn a 3 percent after-tax and after-inflation rate of return on their investments, what amount of accumulated savings and investments would they need? Use Appendix A.4 or the *Garman/Forgue* Web site to solve for the answer.

5. Raul and Juanita Selenas hope to sell their large home for $280,000 and retire to a smaller residence valued at $150,000. After they sell, they plan to invest the $130,000 in equity ($280,000 − $150,000 omitting selling expenses) and earn a 6 percent after-tax return. Approximately how much annual income will that money earn? Use Appendix A.4 or the *Garman/Forgue* Web site to solve for the answer.

6. Laura Graves plans to invest $3000 in a mutual fund for the next 25 years to accumulate a retirement fund. Her twin sister Linda plans to invest the same amount for the same length of time in the same mutual fund but, instead of investing with after-tax money, she will invest through a tax-sheltered salary-reduction retirement plan. If both mutual fund accounts provide a 9 percent rate of return, how much more will Linda have in her retirement account after 25 years if she also invests the taxes she saves each year? Assume both women pay income taxes at a 28 percent rate. Use Appendix A.3 or the *Garman/Forgue* Web site to solve for the answer.

7. Rita Jones is currently putting $9500 per year into her tax-sheltered salary-reduction program at work. Rita's employer offers to match $0.50 for each $1 contributed to the retirement plan up to 6 percent of salary— $4200 in Rita's case, as her annual salary is $70,000. How much will Rita accumulate after 18 years if her annual $9500 investments plus the employer's $2100 contributions grow at a 2 percent rate of return after taxes and inflation? (Rita assumes that her increases in salary will equal the value of inflation and income taxes, and thus her real income will not change.) Use Appendix A.3

or the *Garman/Forgue* Web site to solve for the answer.

8. Roy Wells wants to invest $4000 annually for his retirement 30 years from now. He has a conservative investment philosophy and expects to earn a return of 4 percent in a tax-sheltered account. If he took a more aggressive investment approach and earned a return of 6 percent, how much more would Roy accumulate? Use Appendix A.3 or the *Garman/Forgue* Web site to solve for the answer.

MONEY MATTERS: LIFE-CYCLE CASES

Victor and Maria's Retirement Plans

Victor, now aged 61, and Maria, aged 59, are retiring at the end of the year. Since his retail management employer changed from a defined-benefit to a defined-contribution retirement plan ten years ago, Victor has been contributing the maximum amount of his salary to several different mutual funds offered through the plan, although his employer never matched any of his contributions. Victor's tax-sheltered plan, which now has a balance of $144,000, has been growing at a rate of 9 percent through the years. Under the previous defined-benefit plan, Victor is entitled to a single-life pension of $360 per month or a joint and survivor option paying $240 monthly. The value of Victor's investment of $20,000 in Pharmacia & Upjohn eight years ago has now grown to $56,000.

Maria's earlier career as a dental hygienist provided no retirement program, although she did save $10,000 via her credit union, which was later used to purchase zero-coupon bonds now worth $28,000. Maria's second career as a pharmaceutical representative for Pharmacia & Upjohn allowed her to contribute about $27,000 to her pension plan over the past nine years. Pharmacia & Upjohn matched a portion of her contributions, and that account is now worth $112,000; its growth rate has been about 8 to 10 percent annually. When Maria's mother died last year, she inherited her mother's home, which is rented for

$900 per month; the house has a market value of $120,000. The Hernandezes' personal residence is worth $180,000. They pay income taxes at a 28 percent rate.

1. Sum up the present values of the Hernandezes' assets, excluding their personal residence, and identify which assets derive from tax-sheltered plans.

2. Assume that the Hernandezes sold their stocks, bonds, and the rental property and realized $188,000 after income taxes and commissions. If that amount earned a 7 percent rate of return over the Hernandezes' anticipated 20 years of retirement, how large an amount could be withdrawn each month? How large a monthly amount could be withdrawn if the proceeds earned 6 percent? Use the table in the boxed feature on page 534 to make your calculations, or use Appendix A.4.

3. Victor's $144,000 and Maria's $112,000 pensions have been sheltered from income taxes for many years. Explain the advantages the couple received by leaving the money in the tax-sheltered accounts. Offer them a reason not to keep the money in the accounts.

The Johnsons Consider Retirement Planning

Harry Johnson's father, William, was recently forced into early retirement at age 63 because of poor health. In addition to the psychological impact of the unanticipated retirement, William's financial situation is poor because he had not planned adequately for retirement. The situation has inspired Harry and Belinda to take a look at their own retirement planning. Together they now make about $57,000 per year and would like to have a similar level of income when they retire. Harry and Belinda are both 28 years old and, although retirement is a long way off, they know that the sooner they start a retirement plan, the larger their nest egg will be.

1. Belinda believes that the couple could maintain their current level of living if their retirement income represented 75 percent of their current annual income after adjusting for inflation. Assuming a 4 percent

inflation rate, what would Harry and Belinda's annual income need to be when they retire at age 65? (Hint: Use Appendix A.1 or visit the *Garman/Forgue* Web site.)

2. Both Harry and Belinda are covered by a defined-contribution pension plan at work. Harry's employer contributes $1000 per year and Belinda's employer contributes $2000 per year. Assuming a 7 percent rate of return, what would their nest egg total at retirement 40 years from now? (Hint: Use Appendix A.3 or visit the *Garman/Forgue* Web site.)

3. For how many years would the nest egg provide the amount of income indicated in question 1? Assume a 4 percent return after taxes and inflation. (Hint: Use Appendix A.4 or visit the *Garman/Forgue* Web site.)

4. One of Harry's dreams is to retire at age 55. What would the answers to questions 1, 2, and 3 be if he and Belinda were to retire at that age?

5. How would early retirement at age 55 affect their Social Security benefits?

6. What would you advise Harry and Belinda to do to meet their income needs for retirement?

Exploring the World Wide Web of Personal Finance

To complete these exercises, go to the *Garman/Forgue* Web site at

www.hmco.com/college/business/

Select Personal Finance. Click on the exercise link for this chapter and answer the questions that appear on the Web page.

1. Use the Retirement Planning Worksheet on page 546 of the text or on the *Garman/Forgue* Web site to estimate the additional amount you would need to save to reach your retirement goal. Then visit the T. Rowe Price Web site, where you will find a similar worksheet. Use it to estimate your retirement savings needs using similar assumptions. What explanation can you give to account for the differences in the two estimates?

2. Download the electronic version of the Social Security Administration's Social Security Benefits Estimate software. Use the program to estimate your Social Security benefits or order your personal earnings and benefits estimate statement on-line.

3. Visit the Web site of the American Association of Retired Persons (AARP). Investigate AARP's answers to the following questions: Is the Social Security system broke? Will Social Security be there for you when you retire? Would you do better investing your money on your own?

4. Visit the Web site for the Evergreen Funds. Use its IRA calculator to determine whether you would be better off using a traditional IRA or a Roth IRA account.

5. Visit the Web site for Valic. Click on "sponsoring a plan" and then "setting up a plan." There you will find a compilation of the relative attributes of traditional defined-benefit plans and traditional defined-contribution plans from the perspective of an employer. Describe three benefits of each from the perspective of a worker based on what you have read.

6. Visit the Web site for CNNFN, where you will find an article on 401(k) fees and the effect they can have on retirement savings. Develop a list of four or five questions that employees with a 401(k) plan might ask their employer about the fees charged under their plan. Then visit the Web site for the U.S. Department of Labor, where you can download a copy of its brochure on understanding 401(k) fees.

Estate Planning

19

OBJECTIVES

After reading this chapter, you should be able to:

1 Describe how an estate is distributed by a probate court when one dies with or without a will.

3 Explain how to use trusts to transfer assets and reduce taxes.

2 Summarize two ways that assets may be distributed using prearranged actions outside of probate court.

4 Understand techniques used to protect the value of an estate from gift, estate, and inheritance taxes.

You will likely work hard over the course of your lifetime to build an **estate** (the wealth accumulated over a lifetime) that could total as much as $1 or $2 million. It would be unfortunate to have this wealth decimated upon your death because of incorrect transfers of pension and life insurance benefits and excessive expenditures on lawyers, estate administration, and taxes.

Estate planning encompasses managing, conserving, and distributing an estate in the manner that most efficiently and effectively accomplishes your personal objectives. It involves establishing, implementing, and revising plans to protect wealth from taxes and other costs that can erode wealth. Managing the proper ownership of assets both during one's life and after one's death can ensure the proper distribution of assets and income to heirs. Thus, estate planning offers benefits both before and after death. Estate planning no longer applies only to the "rich" because rising values of real estate and pension plans have pushed many people's wealth toward higher levels. This chapter examines the basic steps in estate planning. It is arranged to first consider distributions by probate court and then distributions by prearrangement (including trusts). The final section discusses ways to protect the value of an estate from transfer taxes. We recommend that you read further on the subject and consult with a competent attorney before taking specific actions.

Distributions by Probate Court

1 Describe how an estate is distributed by a probate court when one dies with or without a will.

Probate is a court-supervised transfer of a decedent's assets to the rightful beneficiaries. The probate process ensures that the assets are distributed according to a properly executed and valid will, or, when no will exists, to the persons, agencies, or organizations required by state law. The probate court also attempts to see that the debts, taxes, and expenses of the deceased are paid.

State laws usually require the probate period to last a minimum of six months to give sufficient time for persons to file claims against the estate. Probate costs can claim as much as 4 to 10 percent of the assets in the estate. Thus, an estate loses value when going through probate because it is eroded by the costs of executing the transfers. Most states permit small estates (usually less than $60,000 in assets subject to probate) to be distributed with minimal probate court involvement.

Avoiding probate means that the court does not oversee the process of publicly administering an estate. It also ensures faster settlement and lower administrative costs.

Not all property goes through this court-supervised process. Thus, a distinction must be made between probate and nonprobate property. **Nonprobate property,** which does not go through probate, includes assets transferred to survivors by contract or by operation of law rather than via a will. Examples include insurance proceeds not payable to the estate, retirement plan benefits, personal pension plans, annuities, and assets jointly owned with right of survivorship. Essentially, nonprobate property transfers are prearranged. Nonprobate assets do not become subject to claims for the decedent's debts and expenses against the estate. If the entire estate consists of nonprobate assets, probate procedures generally are unnecessary and the assets are simply distributed as required. Techniques for this type of estate planning are examined later in the chapter.

Probate property, which goes through the probate process, includes property transferred by a will, the value of assets owned solely in the name of the deceased, that person's proportionate share of any tenancies in common (but not that jointly owned with right of survivorship), the proceeds of life insurance payable to the estate of the deceased, and, in some states, the decedent's half of community property owned with a spouse. These assets are known as the **probate estate.** Generally, a decedent's probate estate consists of property that the decedent owned individually. Ownership is discussed on pages 138–140.

Distributions Dictated by a Will

If you die with a will, the probate court will distribute your assets according to its provisions. A **will** is a written document that directs the disposition of your assets at death; it generally serves as the basis for estate planning. The major functions of a will are: (1) to transfer assets to particular people and organizations; (2) to choose the executor, trustees, and others who will administer the estate; and (3) to reduce the tax liability on the estate of the deceased.

Legal Terms Used in a Will   The person who makes a will is called a **testator** and upon death is legally referred to as the **decedent**. A person who dies with a valid will has died **testate**, rather than intestate. Anyone who has reached the age of majority in a particular state (usually 18 years of age) and is of sound mind may "have the capacity" to make a legally valid will. A person receiving property identified in a will is called a **beneficiary**.

The will names an **executor** or **executrix** (female executor), also known as a **personal representative**, to carry out the directions and requests contained in the will. The executor must petition the probate court to be officially designated as the personal representative. Once the petition is approved, the executor is then provided a certain amount of legal power by the state to carry out appropriate functions for the deceased. This person has a large number of duties, as noted in the boxed feature, "Did You Know? The Responsibilities of an Executor of an Estate." A person with basic accounting skills who can handle standardized forms is probably well suited to be an executor. In addition, your executor needs to understand the personal aspects of your estate. Because that combination may be difficult to find, many wills name co-executors. These executors also may sometimes need guidance from an attorney.

Types of Wills   Some people write their own informal wills—most of which are later deemed invalid. Many are thrown out by the courts because state laws typically do not recognize such wills; others are voided because of some seemingly minor error in drafting. When the court rejects a will, the deceased is assumed to have died intestate.

A **holographic will** is handwritten entirely by the person signing it and often is, as some states require, dated and signed with the same handwriting. Approximately 35 states will not recognize the authority of a holographic will, and, in general, even witnessed holographic wills are often not honored by courts. Typed or preprinted wills that are signed but lack witnesses are typically rejected as well. All states declare invalid a videotape of a person reciting his or her bequests because tapes can be easily altered. Another frequently discredited informal will is a **nuncupative will**—an oral will spoken by a dying individual to another person or persons. Clearly, making a will is not a casual undertaking.

For a will to be valid in a decedent's state of residence, the signatures of two or three witnesses are usually needed. A proper witness is a person who will not profit from the will. When properly drafted, signed, and witnessed, the form is usually termed a **formal will**. A will drafted by an attorney is an example of a formal will. It is least likely to be successfully challenged. A simple formal will prepared by an attorney can cost $100 to $200, and a complex one costs more.

Some people choose to complete a fill-in-the-blank document as a will. To complete such a will, the individual answers a series of written or computer-generated questions from commercially available sources.* Such wills have drawbacks, however, in that they usually do not effectively provide for tax planning

---

*   Examples include WillMaker (Nolo Press), Home Lawyer (MECA Software), Personal Lawyer (Imsi Software), and Quicken Family Lawyer (Intuit).

The Responsibilities of an Executor of an Estate

Because of the many duties and obligations required of the person who is named the executor of an estate, many people direct in their will that an attorney be appointed to perform the tasks. This provision spares a friend or relative from the challenging and time-consuming efforts required. The following list outlines the basic tasks required of someone who has taken on this important duty:

- Make the funeral and burial arrangements in accordance with the wishes of the deceased.

- Submit a copy of the will to probate court.

- Make provisions for adequate living arrangements for dependent survivors of the deceased until the estate has been settled.

- Hire outside professionals, such as an attorney, accountant, and appraiser.

- Take steps to examine and maintain the deceased's assets, including opening an estate checking account.

- Find, catalog, and valuate all assets of the estate, including securities, real estate, personal property, and any trusts established by the deceased.

- Notify concerned parties of the death, including creditors, debtors, others with a business relationship, and newspapers.

- Collect all amounts owed to the estate, including salary, pension, and insurance proceeds, as well as Social Security and other government benefits.

- Pay all debts of the estate, including any last-illness health care expenses.

- Oversee the management of the estate's assets and any business interests of the deceased until the distribution is complete.

- Oversee the preparation of tax forms for income and estate taxes.

- Pay income and estate taxes for the deceased as well as all estate expenses.

- Distribute the estate to heirs in accordance with the provisions of the will.

- Submit a final accounting and file the necessary reports with the court on the executor's activities.

considerations, the circumstances of those who were previously married and had children, or complex estates.

The original will should be kept in a safe place, such as a safe deposit box; copies may be kept at home, at work, or with relatives. For many years, most people kept their original wills in a lockbox at their attorneys' offices; court decisions that increased the liability of attorneys who held wills for safekeeping have, however, discouraged lawyers from providing this service. Today, bank executives typically allow appropriate survivors to inspect the contents of a decedent's safe-deposit box (even if sealed) to search for a will or a life insurance policy, allowing such documents to be removed. Obviously, you must let your family or other heirs know the location of your will.

Codicils Circumstances that should cause people to consider changing their wills include moving to another state, marrying or divorcing, having children, undergoing a substantial change in assets, or experiencing the death of heirs, executors, or guardians named in the will. You can update a will either by writing a new will or, more simply, by adding a **codicil**. This legal amendment to a

 **The Major Provisions of a Will**

1. Identification of the testator and places of residence.

2. Introductory clause to provide validity of the will, such as, "This is my will and testament . . ."

3. Revocation-of-prior-wills clause if prior wills have been written.

4. Final instructions for the payment of taxes, debts, funeral, burial, and administrative costs of the estate.

5. Specific bequests for particular items, such as stamp collections or jewelry.

6. General bequests related to the assets of the estate that usually provide for money to be given to individuals.

7. Charitable gifts to various organizations.

8. Allocation of residual estate statement explaining where the remaining portion of the estate goes after the preceding bequests are satisfied.

9. Survivorship clause indicating the guardian(s) for children if both husband and wife die.

10. Trust provisions to create and give directions to trusts.

11. Appointment clauses to designate the executor of the estate and guardians that represent the interests of children (if any).

12. Executive clauses that add to the validity of the will, such as dating, witnessing, and signing.

will adds or deletes a bequest or other provision. A codicil should be drawn up by an attorney, properly witnessed, and signed by the testator.

Letter of Last Instructions   Many people prepare a personally signed **letter of last instructions** (also called a **letter precatory**), given to the executor of an estate prior to death. It provides a detailed inventory of assets and liabilities, describes personal preferences about transfers of many pieces of personal property (both valuable and sentimental), and contains funeral and burial instructions. Although the letter offers guidance to heirs and beneficiaries, the instructions are not legally binding unless they are specifically incorporated into a will. Nevertheless, such bequeaths are generally honored.

The letter should include information about the location of all assets, including various checking and savings accounts, life insurance policies, and accounts at brokerage firms; a list identifying the location of important legal and financial documents; organ donation instructions; the location of the original will; and a list of names, addresses, and telephone numbers of people to notify upon your death. Because it is generally not presented in probate court, a letter of last instructions remains somewhat private. It provides a way to bequeath art, antiques, jewelry, and collectibles to specific heirs, assuming that they agree to abide by the instructions.

Distributions in the Absence of a Will

State laws require that everyone's estate be disposed of at death by transferring it to legal heirs or, if none exists, to the state government itself. If you die with-

Use Advance Directives

Many illnesses such as Alzheimer's disease, strokes, and cancer can result in a period of mental incompetence before death. An **advance directive** is any document that establishes in advance who will make medical and other decisions for you should you become mentally incompetent and that specifies your desires related to those decisions. Three such advance directives are described below.

A **durable power of attorney** provides an inexpensive legal process to assign the power to control your affairs and execute contracts on your behalf should you ever become mentally incapacitated. (A regular power of attorney is ineffective for this purpose.) A durable power of attorney remains valid and operative as long as you live, unless you explicitly revoke it. It should detail the specific aspects of your affairs that it covers and should even mention specific institutions (banks or brokerage firms, for example) and account numbers. A durable power of attorney gives virtually absolute power to manage your affairs, so choose a trusted individual who knows your wishes. In many states, a durable power of attorney becomes effective immediately after being drawn up. Thus, you may choose instead to establish a **springing durable power of attorney** that does not take effect until incapacitation occurs.

A **living will** is a written statement indicating that its signer does not wish extraordinary medical measures to be taken if he or she has no reasonable expectation of recovery from a desperate medical problem. This document relieves family members of making a difficult, painful decision. To be effective and to avoid varying interpretation, living wills must speak to specific circumstances. For example, if death is imminent, a living will could direct that life-support measures, such as a respirator, be removed. A federal law requires hospitals to inform patients of their rights to make such decisions about medical care. Living wills need to conform precisely to the statutes in the state where the person lives.

A number of states have adopted a **health care proxy** (also called a **health care power of attorney**) that permits the signer to authorize named individuals to make health care decisions on his or her behalf if the signer becomes unable to make such decisions. This document differs from a durable power of attorney in two ways. First, only the specified individuals are given the legal right to make the life-support decision. Second, a health care proxy cannot address financial affairs. Give copies of all of these documents to members of your family and other responsible persons in your life.

out leaving a valid will, you have died **intestate.** The state where you lived prior to death then assumes the complete right to determine how your estate will be divided. This legal determination usually forces your heirs to share money in ways you did not intend. A will represents your opportunity to ensure that the distribution is fair and in accordance with your wishes.

About 70 percent of the U.S. adult population do not have a will. In most states, if you die without a will, a **public administrator** or **public conservator**—usually a spouse or close relative—is appointed by the probate court to distribute your estate in accordance with the laws of that state. A commission of perhaps 3 to 5 percent of the estate's value is charged to cover the administrator's fee. If you have minor children and no surviving parent, a state court must appoint someone to act as a guardian to manage each child's affairs, which will represent additional costs to the estate.

The powers given to an administrator by the court are limited. As a result, the administrator must frequently seek the court's permission for specific legal actions, all of which generate expenses in the form of court fees. For example, a court order is required to sell securities and real estate in most states. If the heirs are of legal age, they must all agree on the sale of real estate or the method of maintaining the property; when agreement proves difficult to obtain, the court makes the decisions. The net estate ultimately distributed to heirs is reduced by the costs of these administrative actions.

If you have children, you should appoint a legal guardian in your will. Both single parents and married couples should take this step. The guardian should be someone who shares your values and views on child-rearing. Consider naming an alternate candidate in case your first choice cannot take this responsibility. If none is legally named, the court will appoint a guardian.

When a person dies without a will, the manner in which the assets are divided varies enormously from state to state. For example, one state might make the following distributions of a $120,000 estate: If a person with no surviving kin except a spouse dies without a will, the spouse receives the entire estate of $120,000. If the deceased had children with that spouse, the spouse takes $60,000 and the balance is divided equally by the spouse and the children. If the surviving spouse had children from another marriage, one-half of the estate goes to the spouse and the balance is divided among the children. If the decedent is survived by a spouse and a parent, the spouse receives $60,000 and one-half of the balance, with the remainder passing to the parent. If the deceased is survived by a spouse, no children, and other relatives, the situation becomes even more complicated. If no will has been prepared and no surviving relatives exist (extremely rare), the share goes to the state by right of **escheat**. In escheat, property is turned over to the state when no one is legally qualified to inherit or make claim on a deceased's property.

As you can see, state law contains a bewildering number of complexities that govern who constitutes a legal heir and to how much (if any) of an estate an heir may be entitled. What may appear least fair in the intestate distributions just described is that, if the decedent has no children, your spouse may be required to share the assets with a distant relative.

The Partnership Theory of Marriage Rights

The **partnership theory of marriage rights** is the basis for the presumed intent of wedded couples to share their fortunes equally. Thus, property acquired during the marriage and titled in the name of only one partner (other than property acquired by gift or inheritance) becomes the property of both spouses. A decedent who disinherits a surviving spouse or who leaves that person with less than a fair share of the estate is judged to have reneged on the partnership theory of marriage. Thus, a disinherited surviving spouse has some claim to a portion of the decedent's estate, if he or she chooses to elect that option. The amount usually represents one-third to one-half of the decedent's estate. Moreover, you are not allowed to disinherit a spouse unless this right is voluntarily given up by the spouse in a signed agreement, and even that type of document may be challenged. Some states limit the right to challenge a will by providing that survivors have six months to challenge it and claim a legal share.

In certain states,* when a marriage ends by the death of one partner, **community property laws** provide for similar spousal rights. **Community property** consists of property acquired during marriage, except for separable property. **Separable property** is a property wholly owned by one spouse. Such property belonged to the spouse before marriage or was received as a gift or an inheritance during the marriage.

When one spouse dies, community property laws assume that this property was jointly owned and equally shared by the spouses, no matter how much was actually contributed by either and even if only one spouse held legal title. Thus, upon the death of one spouse, one-half of the community property is retained by the surviving spouse, and the remaining half may pass to other heirs.

Distributions by Prearranged Actions Outside Probate Court

2 Summarize two ways that assets may be distributed using prearranged actions outside of probate court.

Two major types of prearranged actions may be taken to distribute assets outside the control of a probate court: (1) transfers by operation of law, and (2) transfers by contract. Such transfers occur outside the provisions of a will and lie beyond the control of the probate court. While an asset may transfer out of the reach of probate court, it may still be subject to estate taxes (discussed later in this chapter).

Transfers by Operation of Law

State laws stipulate how property owned in specified ways will transfer at the death of one of the owners beyond the supervision of a probate court. In ownership by **joint tenancy with right of survivorship**, each person owns the whole of an asset and can dispose of it without the approval of the other owner or owners. Upon the death of one owner, the surviving owners receive the property by operation of law rather than through the provisions of a will. Many married couples maintain their checking and savings accounts in joint tenancy with right of survivorship so that the surviving spouse will not lose access to that money. In about 30 states, the courts recognize **tenancy by the entirety** between spouses where the asset cannot be disposed of without the permission of the other. Again, such property transfers at death to the survivor without going through probate.

Transfers by Contract

Several types of nonprobate assets can be directly assigned to beneficiaries by contract, including life insurance proceeds, annuities, employer-provided pensions, profit-sharing plans, individual retirement accounts (IRAs), Keogh

* These states include Arizona, California, Idaho, Louisiana, Nevada, New Mexico, Texas, Washington, and Wisconsin. In some instances, community property rules are disregarded for tax purposes.

accounts, government bonds, bank accounts with a payable-on-death beneficiary named, and certain trusts established before death. These assets generally will pass out of the reach of a probate court according to beneficiary designation forms that were completed and signed during the person's life. Because trusts represent a widely used method of transferring assets and reducing taxes, this topic is examined in depth in the next section.

Use of Trusts to Transfer Assets and Reduce Taxes

3 Explain how to use trusts to transfer assets and reduce taxes.

An estate can be protected by creating one or more contractual **trusts** to which property is transferred. A trust is a contract between the creator and the trustee that permits the latter to manage wealth and direct income for a specific purpose for the benefit of the creator and others. A **trustee** is a person or agent (such as an attorney or bank trust department) that holds legal title to property and promises to faithfully and wisely administer it for the creator and others.

Trusts can be established during the creator's life as well as upon his or her death. People who should consider setting up a trust are those who have complex estates, hold relatively few liquid assets, own property in more than one state, have heirs who will need the assets immediately, desire privacy for their heirs, fear a battle over the provisions of a will, or live in a state with high probate costs or cumbersome probate procedures. Trusts may be created to safeguard the inheritances of survivors, reduce estate taxes, provide financial assistance for minor children, manage property for young children or disabled elders, and provide income for future generations.[*]

Some of the important terms associated with trusts follow:

Grantor	The person who makes a grant of assets to establish a trust. Also called the **settlor, donor,** or **trustor.**
Trustee	The person or corporation to whom the property is entrusted to manage for the use and benefit of the beneficiary or beneficiaries.
Corpus	The assets put into a trust. Also called the **trust estate** or **fund.**
Beneficiary	The person for whose benefit a trust is created. Also called the **donee.**
Remainder beneficiaries	The parties named in the trust who are to receive the corpus upon termination of the trust agreement.

---

[*] A **generation-skipping trust** can be utilized at the time of death. A federal **generation-skipping transfer tax** will be applied in addition to relevant estate and gift taxes, although a $1 million exemption (indexed for inflation) on transfers is made. A **bypass trust** (also known as a **credit-shelter trust, exemption trust,** or **family trust**) can transfer separately titled assets (including stocks and mutual funds held outside a retirement plan) to children or grandchildren.

Living Trusts

Trusts fall into two broad categories: (1) **living trusts** (established while the creator is alive), and (2) **testamentary trusts** (established upon death). For estate planning purposes, the greatest distinction between living trusts is their permanency. This section examines the two forms of living trusts—revocable and irrevocable—and the following section examines testamentary trusts. Transfers to a trust made within three years of death may, however, be brought back into the decedent's estate for tax purposes.

Irrevocable Living Trust   An **irrevocable living trust** is used to give away assets to reduce estate taxes. An irrevocable living trust is not subject to any modification by the grantor during his or her lifetime, thus permanently bypassing probate and estate taxes applied to the person who instituted the trust. The grantor gives up three key rights under an irrevocable living trust: (1) control of the property, (2) change of the beneficiaries, and (3) change of the trustees. Because irrevocable trusts are generally considered separate tax entities, the trust pays any income taxes due. To set up such a trust, a one-time fee ranging from $750 to $2500—at least twice as much as a typical will—is required.

Revocable Living Trust   A **revocable living trust** is used to protect and manage a person's assets. The person creating the trust maintains the right to change its terms or cancel the trust at any time, for any reason, during his or her lifetime. Thus, the grantor retains control over the assets for as long as he or she lives, and any taxable events must be reported by the person who established the trust. Most revocable living trusts also establish the grantor as the trustee.

TAX Considerations & Consequences

Use of a Charitable Remainder Trust to Boost Current Income

Effective use of an irrevocable **charitable remainder trust (CRT)** can boost your income. A CRT is a split-interest gift with a charitable organization designated as the remainder beneficiary. You set up the CRT trust and irrevocably give it assets. The trust pays you income for a set period, usually for life, and possibly your spouse's life as well; the charity then receives the corpus. For example, Frankie Solowiej, a widow from Hyattsville, Maryland, increased the after-tax income on her $60,000 investment portfolio from $1000 to $4800 per year by earmarking the assets for the National Wildlife Federation. According to her attorney, Tony Shostak, the charitable trust that Frankie created to hold the gift until her death first sold the assets without capital gains taxes and then reinvested the proceeds to obtain a higher return.

A bonus associated with a CRT is that the projected future value of the gift can be discounted to a present value, which can be written off as a charitable contribution on Frankie's current income tax return, saving her even more money. It is wise to give appreciated assets (i.e., stocks, art, collectibles) to a charitable remainder trust because the donor can avoid capital gains taxes while still realizing the full benefit of the asset's current value. Thus, a CRT works well for people who show wealth on paper because of appreciated assets.

A revocable living trust can provide for the orderly management and distribution of assets should the grantor become incapacitated or incompetent, as a new trustee can easily be named. Revocable trusts are commonly used to establish newly created trusts upon the death of the grantor (called testamentary trusts, and discussed below) that are governed by the terms established in the revocable living trust. A revocable living trust operates much like a will and can prove more difficult to contest. Revocable living trusts do not reduce gift and estate taxes. If a trust is revocable, its assets stay in the taxable estate of the grantor.

Testamentary Trusts

The second broad category of trusts used in connection with estate planning comprises **testamentary trusts.** A testamentary trust is created under the terms of a will and becomes effective upon the death of the grantor according to the terms of the grantor's will or revocable living trust. Testamentary trusts can be designed to provide money or asset management after the grantor's death, to provide income for a surviving spouse and children, to give assets to grandchildren or great-grandchildren while providing income from the assets to the surviving spouse and children, and for most of the purposes cited previously.

In summary, properly drawn trusts can save you and your family time, trouble, and money. These laudable objectives can be achieved only with the assistance of an experienced attorney who specializes in carefully drafting, planning, and executing strategies and techniques in estate planning.

Protection of an Estate from Taxes

4 Understand techniques used to protect the value of an estate from gift, estate, and inheritance taxes.

Under federal law, a person must pay gift taxes on excess portions of gifts made during his or her lifetime as well as estate taxes on assets that transfer at death. The **federal gift and estate tax** is assessed on property owned and/or controlled by a deceased before its transfer to heirs. (This definition immediately suggests a fundamental loophole in estate taxes—if property is not controlled, it will not be taxed; as discussed above, this can be accomplished using irrevocable trusts.) When combined, transfer taxes on gifts and estates are sometimes called **death taxes.** Note that the federal gift and estate tax is levied against the person who created the estate. Many states also levy an **inheritance tax** on heirs who have the right to receive a decedent's property. Such inheritance taxes are based upon the value of the property received and the relationship of the beneficiary to the deceased. This topic is examined later in the chapter.

The federal gift and estate tax is a combined and cumulative tax. The **federal gift tax** is imposed on the transfer of income and gifts made by an individual during his or her lifetime. A transfer is a gift when no payment or consideration is received in return. The **federal estate tax** is applied to the transfer of assets at death. It applies to net taxable estates worth more than $675,000,* after allowing for certain deductions, such as for charitable bequests and property passing

---

* In 2000–2001; $650,000 in 1999 to rise to $1 million by 2006.

to a surviving spouse. Thus, the combined federal gift and estate tax affects certain gifts made during one's lifetime as well as transfers made at death. Table 19.1 shows the **unified federal gift and estate tax rate schedule** that is used for *both* gift and estate tax purposes. It is applied to the sum of your taxable estate at death and any taxable lifetime gifts made.

Ways to Reduce the Federal Gift and Estate Tax

Federal laws encourage gift giving. To be defined as a **gift** by the IRS, the donor must relinquish control over the asset and, as a result, the recipient must have a present or a future interest in the money or property given, meaning that the recipient has a legal right to the gift. Thus, according to IRS regulations, gifts may not be loans or payments for services rendered; the latter are classified as taxable income by the IRS and the recipient must pay income taxes. Gifts and bequests—in any amount and at any time—made to certain recognized charitable and educational organizations always escape the federal gift and estate tax. Gifts allow the donor to reduce the size of his or her taxable estate, which results in a lower gift and estate liability.

Table 19.1

Unified Federal Gift and Estate Tax Rates, 2000–2001

(1) Taxable Estate plus Taxable Gifts	(2) Tax	(3) Rate of Tax on Excess over Amount in Column 1	(4) Unified Gift and Estate Tax Credit	(5) Federal Gift and Estate Tax Liability
Under $10,000	18% of amount	—	$220,550	—
$ 10,000	$ 1,800	20%	220,550	—
20,000	3,800	22	220,550	—
40,000	8,200	24	220,550	—
60,000	13,000	26	220,550	—
80,000	18,200	28	220,550	—
100,000	23,800	30	220,550	—
150,000	38,800	32	220,550	—
250,000	70,800	34	220,550	—
500,000	155,800	37	220,550	—
750,000	248,300	39	220,550	$27,750
1,000,000	345,800	41	220,550	125,250
1,250,000	448,300	43	220,550	245,750
1,500,000	555,800	45	220,550	353,250
2,000,000	780,800	49	220,550	578,250
2,500,000	1,025,800	53	220,550	823,250
3,000,000	1,290,800	55	220,550	1,088,250

Source: Internal Revenue Service.

In addition to making charitable and educational gifts, the gift and estate tax may be eliminated or reduced in four ways: (1) annual gift exclusion, (2) split gifts, (3) unlimited gift tax marital deduction, and (4) unified gift and estate tax credit.

The Annual Gift Tax Exclusion   The federal gift and estate law allows an initial portion of taxable gifts (in cash or property) made during one's lifetime to be excluded from any gift and estate tax. You are permitted to give away as much as $10,000* in cash or other assets tax-free to each of any number of donees per year under a provision known as the **annual gift tax exclusion.** Such gifts may be given to individuals or other entities, including charitable organizations. For the recipient, gifts are tax-free. Gifts of $10,000 or less in cash or other assets reduce the size of the donor's taxable estate because the donated assets reduce the owner's gross estate. In addition, voluntary payments in any amount made directly to an educational institution or to a medical care provider to pay for another's educational tuition or medical expenses are exempt from being classified as taxable gifts to the donor. The recipient does not have to be a dependent or even a relative.

A **taxable gift**—one that is subject to the federal gift and estate tax—represents that portion of any gift to one donee in excess of $10,000 in one year. Taxable gifts must be added back and included in the donor's taxable estate as part of the gift and estate tax calculation after death. Donors must report such gifts annually by filing IRS Form 709. This filing requirement notifies the IRS of those taxable gifts that later must be added to the donor's gross taxable estate at death. Those who report taxable gifts in effect defer gift and estate taxes that may be assessed at a later date when the donor's taxable estate is totaled at death.

From a tax perspective, wealthy people can give gifts to reduce estate tax liability. For example, a gift of a $25,000 painting in 1999 is valued in 1999 dollars, not at its inflated value if the donor dies perhaps eight years later. As a gift given to a relative, the painting would add only $15,000 ($25,000 − $10,000) to the donor's taxable estate at death. Alternatively, if the painting increased in value 10 percent per year and was transferred as part of the estate eight years later, the painting would have a value of $53,600 ($25,000 × 2.144, from Appendix A.1) in 2007, assuming 10 percent annual inflation. At that time, transfer of the painting would require payment of more taxes by the decedent's estate than an earlier gift. Although gifts provide a valuable way to reduce estate taxes, logical limitations exist on how much should be given away before death.

Once assets have been transferred, any appreciation in value, as well as any income earned from the asset, becomes the responsibility of the recipient—not the donor. For example, the recipient of shares of stock valued at $50,000 at the time of the transfer (the price the donor paid does not matter) must pay income taxes on any future dividends as well as any capital gains made between the date that the asset was received and when it is sold.

Split Gifts   Gifts made by married couples to a third party may be **split.** When spouses consent, the gift can be treated as if half were made by each spouse, even

---

* The $10,000 annual gift tax exclusion is potentially subject to an inflation adjustment for gifts made after 1998. Given the adjustment formula, however, it is unlikely that the $10,000 exclusion will be raised for several years.

if only one contributed the whole amount. Gift splitting, therefore, doubles the annual gift tax exclusion to $20,000 per donee. Making two smaller gifts results in a lower tax than one large gift.

Consider the example of Bobby Joe and Betty Turner from Moscow, Idaho, who several years ago consented to give a split gift of $50,000 to their son Jeffrey to use as a down payment on a home. The first $20,000 of that gift remains exempt from the gift and estate tax. The $30,000 exceeding the two annual exclusion amounts is attributed to Bobby and Betty on a 50:50 basis. Thus, each person will have been deemed to have made a $15,000 taxable gift, which will consume $15,000 of each unified credit or trigger a gift tax to both Bobby and Betty.

The Unlimited Gift Tax Marital Deduction The **unlimited gift tax marital deduction** eliminates the tax on gifts between spouses because a married person

---

  Give Money to Children for College

From a personal finance perspective, when giving money to a child to attend college, it is smart to reduce taxes on that money so that more will be devoted to the intended purpose. The following suggestions are aimed at reducing both income and gift and estate taxes:

• *Open a no-fee custodial account* at a bank, brokerage, or mutual fund under the Uniform Transfers to Minors Act (or the Uniform Gifts to Minors Act). Contributions of less than $10,000 (or $20,000 from a married couple) qualify as exclusions from the annual gift tax. With this strategy, you appoint someone you trust to manage the assets given to a child. This **custodian** controls the assets until the child reaches a designated age, such as 18 or 21. The child then gains full control of the account's contents.

• *Recognize that the custodian can spend the money* for the benefit of the child (perhaps for music lessons or foreign travel); any money spent on "parental support items," however, cause the income from the account to be considered taxable income for the parents if they act as custodians.

• *Consider limiting the amount in the custodial account* while the child is under age 14 so that it

generates no more than $1400 per year in earnings. The first $700 will be free of income taxes to the child, while the next $700 will be taxed at the child's rate (typically 15 percent). (Figures are adjusted annually by the IRS for inflation.)

• *Realize that income and capital gains will be taxed at the child's low rate* (typically 15 percent) after the child turns age 14. For example, the next $24,350 above $1400 in income is taxed at a rate of 15 percent.

• *When the child reaches age 14, ask a college financial aid office* to calculate whether the amount in the custodial account will significantly lower the child's eligibility for college aid. If necessary, restrict future contributions to the account and save additional amounts outside the account. Under most financial aid formulas, students must spend 35 percent of their assets on education.

• *Establish a Section 529 College Savings Plan* if one is offered by your state. These plans allow gifts to children under 15. The taxes on the earnings are generally exempt from state income taxes, and federal taxes are deferred until earnings are withdrawn.

may give his or her spouse an unlimited amount free of any gift tax. Thus, gifts between spouses (over and above the $10,000 amount of the annual exclusion) may be transferred tax-free. (Federal tax laws place limits on such transfers when a spouse is not a U.S. citizen.*) Keep in mind, however, that when the surviving spouse dies, all or part of the estate could be taxed, including assets that the first spouse might otherwise have passed tax-free to other heirs. The estate may ultimately be taxed more heavily after the surviving spouse dies. To reduce the federal estate taxes, alternatives such as trusts should be explored.

The Unified Federal Gift and Estate Tax Credit   Little or no tax may be owed on the taxable portion of a gift because of the **unified gift and estate tax credit.** This dollar-for-dollar reduction in the gift and estate tax represents the amount that one may give away or bequeath free of federal estate taxes. This credit of $220,550 in 2000–2001 is equivalent to the tax on an estate valued at $675,000, as can be seen in Table 19.1. The first $675,000 of an estate remains free of federal gift and estate taxes. Gifts can become immediately taxable when they exceed the combination of the annual exclusion and the unified credit—that is, $685,000 per year to one person. The value of taxable gifts made during your lifetime is subtracted from your $675,000 exemption upon your death. The credit will increase to $345,800 in 2006.

Calculation of the Federal Gift Tax: An Example

Over the past five years, Randy McNelis, a widower, has made a number of taxable gifts totaling $150,000, which were reported to the IRS. This year he gave $100,000 to his son. The tax on this year's gift is calculated as follows: previous taxable gifts ($150,000) plus this year's taxable gift to his son ($100,000) less this year's annual gift exclusion ($10,000) equals total taxable gifts ($240,000). Using Table 19.1 reveals a tentative tax of $67,600 [$38,800 + 0.32 × ($240,000 − $150,000)]. After applying a portion of the $220,550 unified gift and estate tax credit ($67,600 in this instance), Randy has a zero tax liability for this year's gift to his son, as well as an unused unified gift and estate tax credit of $152,950 ($220,550 − $67,600). Randy does not have to pay any gift and estate tax until his taxable gifts exceed the threshold ($675,000 plus $10,000 given over one or more years).

Calculation of the Federal Estate Tax: An Example

A **gross estate** includes the fair market value of everything owned at the time of death, such as bank deposits, securities, business interests, real estate, personal property, life insurance, personal pension plans, and employer-provided pensions, as well as the decedent's ownership share of everything owned jointly with others (i.e., homes, automobiles) subject to federal estate taxes. It is also known as the **gross estate for federal estate tax purposes.** Any gift and estate taxes due will be paid on the **taxable estate.** It consists of the gross estate *minus* liabilities (current bills, credit card balances, mortgages, loans, and taxes owed),

---

*   If your spouse is not a U.S. citizen, no marital deduction for estate taxes is available unless you create a special trust called a **qualified domestic trust (QDOT).** Further, a $100,000 annual limit applies to tax-exempt gifts that a noncitizen may receive from his or her spouse.

Arrange Your Life Insurance to Avoid Estate Taxes

Although beneficiaries owe no income tax on the proceeds from a life insurance policy, the proceeds of a policy often *are* considered part of the policy-holder's estate. When life insurance proceeds become part of the estate and therefore subject to the decedent's estate tax, the beneficiary receives a reduced amount. For example, a person who has substantial life insurance coverage and a home valued in the six figures may very well have an estate worth more than $675,000. Recall that estates whose values exceed $675,000 are subject to federal estate taxes, which begin at a rate of 37 percent and quickly move up to a voracious 55 percent.

Life insurance proceeds are included in an estate when the benefits are payable to or will benefit one's estate, when the insured possessed any rights of ownership associated with the policy (i.e., can change the beneficiary, can borrow against it, or has surrender rights), or when the policy ownership has been transferred within three years of the insured's death.

Two appropriate estate planning techniques exist to remove the value of life insurance policies from one's estate. First, the ownership of a life insurance policy can be legally transferred to someone else, such as a spouse. To take this step, simply obtain and complete an *assignment form* from an insurance agent. Note, however, that you must permanently give up all rights and powers over the policy and its benefits, such as changing beneficiaries or borrowing against any cash value. Second, giving a life insurance policy to an irrevocable trust for the benefit of children or a spouse keeps the death benefit out of one's estate. Such transfers do not avoid estate taxes unless you give the policy away more than three years before your death.

To keep a future life insurance policy out of your estate, another technique may be used. Someone other than yourself—such as your children or the trustee of an irrevocable trust—must negotiate for the policy and initially own it. It does not matter who pays the premiums because the IRS has ruled that life insurance policies owned by others remain out of the decedent's estate.

expenses for settling the estate (including funeral expenses), and charitable transfers (to religious, benevolent, scientific, literary, and educational organizations) *plus* any taxable gifts.

Thanks to the unified gift and estate tax credit, about 95 percent of Americans are not expected to owe federal gift and estate taxes based on the current value of their estate. The rise in home prices, accumulations of savings in retirement accounts, life insurance, and increasing values of investment securities has propelled many average-income people into this category, however. The tax rates are also extremely high—after the unified gift and estate tax credit is applied, the rates *begin* at 37 percent. Therefore, owners of estates worth more than $675,000 would be wise to think about property transfers that may reduce or avoid the estate tax.

The information in the Decision-Making Worksheet "Calculation of Federal Gift and Estate Tax Liability" shows the forecasted tax liability for the estate of Bobby Joe Turner. If he dies, he will be survived by his spouse Betty. His gross estate of $1,125,000 includes the following items:

- $635,000 of assets held in only his name [a vacation home inherited from his parents before he married, $110,000; securities, $90,000; part-ownership of a business, $250,000; an art collection, $100,000; cash, $25,000; miscellaneous personal assets (such as jewelry and clothing), $60,000].

- $140,000 in a Keogh retirement plan.

- $350,000 in jointly owned property with right of survivorship (one-half of the values of the Turners' primary residence after subtracting the mortgage balance, $230,000; checking and savings, $30,000; securities, $90,000).

In addition, Bobby Joe's will bequeaths $25,000 to the National Wildlife Federation, and his miscellaneous personal assets are designated for his wife. The will directs that the remainder of his assets be divided between his wife and son. A $150,000 life insurance policy that Betty purchased on Bobby Joe's life will be excluded from his estate, as will $20,000 in an irrevocable life insurance trust set up some years ago. In addition, Bobby Joe's half of the value of the $30,000 tax-

Calculation of Federal Gift and Estate Tax Liability

In the blank spaces below, insert the estimated values pertaining to your estate to calculate (using Table 19.1) the amount of your federal gift and estate tax liability, if any. The figures in the left column below represent the case of Bobby Joe Turner, which is discussed in the text.

	Example of Bobby Joe Turner	Worksheet
1. Gross estate	$1,125,000	_____
2. Less funeral and administrative expenses and debts		
Funeral	– 8,000	_____
Estate administrative costs	– 22,000	_____
Debts	– 5,000	_____
3. Less marital deduction of jointly owned property with right of survivorship (1/2 value)	– 175,000	_____
4. Less unlimited marital deduction	– 0	_____
5. Less charitable bequests	– 25,000	_____
6. Less transfers by trust	– 0	_____
7. Tentative taxable estate	890,000	_____
8. Add taxable gifts (his portion of excess gifts)	+ 15,000	_____
9. Total taxable estate	905,000	_____
10. Tentative federal gift and estate tax*	308,750	_____
11. Less unified tax credit	– 220,550	_____
12. Net federal gift and estate tax	$ 88,200	_____

* Using Table 19.1, the calculations are $248,300 + 0.39 × ($905,000 – $750,000).

able gift to his son for a home down payment must be added back to his estate upon his death.

Better estate planning by making some gifts under the taxable threshold limitations (including joint gifts) and creating some trusts could have eliminated this tax liability and permitted most, if not all, of the $88,200 to transfer to heirs instead of going to the government. Alternatively, Betty, acting as Bobby Joe's personal representative, could elect the unlimited gift tax marital deduction to eliminate the entire estate tax liability. Upon her death, a substantial estate tax may be due. As you can see, without proper planning, a substantial portion of your estate may be eroded by gift and estate taxes, especially if your taxable estate totals more than $675,000.

State Death Taxes: Estate and Inheritance

Two kinds of state death taxes may be required: estate and inheritance.

Estate taxes are levied by four states (Mississippi, New York, Ohio, and Oklahoma) in a manner similar to the federal estate tax. Some of these states tax estates valued at less than $600,000. Tax rates range from 1 percent or less on property passing to children to 32 percent on property going to unrelated parties. The decedent's estate must pay these taxes.

Roughly half of the states use a **pickup tax**, which is applied only to estates that pay federal estate taxes. This tax is designed to obtain for the state some of the money that otherwise would go to the federal government. It represents the amount of the credit that the Internal Revenue Service allows for state death taxes (i.e., the IRS assumes a certain level of state taxes). The revenue comes from the federal government's share of the estate taxes, not from the estate of the deceased. States using the pickup tax merely set their tax at the level assumed by the IRS. The estate pays the tax directly to the state.

Heirs must pay state inheritance taxes in 16 states* based on the value of the assets they receive. Even though the heirs and beneficiaries pay the inheritance taxes, as a practical matter they are often paid out of the cash remaining in an estate. After all bequests have been distributed, then the beneficiaries and heirs divide what remains and use the funds for the taxes. If insufficient cash assets exist in the estate, however, the heirs themselves must pay the inheritance taxes in proportion to their share of the total bequests. When the heirs do not have the cash available to pay the taxes, inherited items must be sold, usually at an auction.

Consider the case of Reggie Harmon of Hartford, Connecticut, who had an estate of

Did You KNOW?

Estate Planning for Single People

Single people and those living with a cohabitant do not receive the benefit of the unlimited gift tax marital deduction to reduce estate taxes. If they have substantive assets, single people should give gifts and put money into irrevocable living trusts (with one cohabitant as trustee and the other as beneficiary) to transfer assets to their desired heirs and to reduce estate taxes. Unmarried people with large estates generally need a substantial amount of life insurance because it is more difficult to reduce estate taxes. Such insurance should be owned in such a way that the proceeds avoid estate taxes; for details, see the feature on how to arrange your life insurance to avoid estate taxes (page 569).

---

* Connecticut, Delaware, Indiana, Iowa, Kansas, Kentucky, Louisiana, Maryland, Montana, Nebraska, New Hampshire, New Jersey, North Carolina, Pennsylvania, South Dakota, and Tennessee.

$300,000 and who left one-half of his estate to his wife, $125,000 to his children, and $25,000 to his sister. Under Connecticut law, the $150,000 left to his wife was exempt from taxes. As required by Connecticut law, the $125,000 left to his children was taxed at 4.29 percent on the amount exceeding $50,000 ($75,000 × 0.0429 = $3217.50). The $25,000 left to his sister was taxed at 5.72 percent on the amount over $6000 ($19,000 × 0.0572 = $1086.80). Thus, an inheritance tax totaling $4304.30 ($3217.50 + $1086.80) was levied.

Tax rates and exemptions vary among the states and can be complicated. Contacting a tax attorney familiar with state taxes can be most helpful because exemptions and deductions are much smaller than the federal allowances. As a result, substantial state taxes may be levied on a relatively small estate. In addition, many surviving children have been forced to "sell the family farm" just to pay inheritance taxes. Heirs of lottery winners sometimes face the same dilemma.

One solution to legally avoid paying estate and inheritance taxes is to establish an **irrevocable life insurance trust** where the trust becomes the life insurance beneficiary. At the death of the grantor/insured, the trust receives the funds needed to pay the taxes. Another solution is to have the donor's children buy a **last-to-die insurance policy** (also called a **survivorship insurance policy**) on the donor, which is life insurance coverage purchased to pay estate taxes. Under the IRS's **three-year rule**, however, the proceeds of a life insurance policy are returned to the estate for tax purposes when the decedent's money was used to pay for a policy within three years of death. This rule also applies to gifts.

Summary

1. A probate court generally oversees the distribution of assets in an estate. If you die with a valid will, the court will distribute your assets according to the provisions of that will. If you die without a will, state laws will determine how your assets will be distributed, often utilizing the partnership theory of marriage rights (if you are married).

2. Two major types of prearranged actions may be taken to distribute assets outside the provisions of a will and outside the control of a probate court: transfers by operation of law and transfers by contract. These actions also assure privacy.

3. As contracts, trusts can be used to manage wealth and direct income for a specific purpose for the benefit of the creator and others. They are classified as either living trusts (established while the creator is alive) or testamentary trusts (established upon death).

4. It is vital to protect the value of your estate through avoidance of both federal gift and estate taxes and inheritance taxes. Four methods are available to eliminate or reduce these taxes: (1) annual gift exclusion, (2) split gifts, (3) unlimited gift tax marital deduction, and (4) unified gift and estate tax credit.

Key Words & Concepts

beneficiary   *556*
codicil   *557*
durable power of attorney   *559*
estate planning   *554*
federal gift and estate tax   *564*
formal will   *556*
inheritance tax   *564*
intestate   *559*

Questions for Thought & Discussion

1. Define "estate planning" and explain its purposes.
2. Why should probate be avoided if possible?
3. Distinguish between probate property and nonprobate property.
4. What are the main reasons for having a will?
5. Identify the parties who would be named in a will.
6. Cite some key responsibilities for an executor of a will.
7. Distinguish between a holographic will and a nuncupative will.
8. Identify some of the key provisions that should be noted in a will.
9. How is a letter of last instructions used?
10. Distinguish between a durable power of attorney and a health care proxy.
11. Distinguish between a living will and a health care proxy.
12. Distinguish between a public administrator and a guardian.
13. How might a state law handle an estate in the event of the death of a single person without a will? A married person with one child without a will?
14. Describe the partnership theory of marriage rights.
15. Distinguish between community property and separable property.
16. List some assets that can be transferred by operation of law and by contract.
17. List five reasons why people create trusts.
18. Distinguish between a living trust and a testamentary trust.
19. How does a revocable living trust differ from an irrevocable trust?
20. Give an example of how people use charitable remainder trusts to boost current income.
21. What is the purpose of the unified gift and estate tax credit?
22. Distinguish between the federal gift and estate tax and an inheritance tax.
23. Describe the use of the gift tax exclusion.
24. List three key ways to give money to children for college.
25. Why is the cost basis an important consideration when making a gift?
26. Summarize how gifts might reduce your estate taxes.
27. Cite an advantage and a disadvantage of passing assets from one spouse to another utilizing the unlimited gift tax marital deduction.
28. What subtractions are taken from a gross estate for federal estate tax purposes to calculate the taxable estate?
29. List the ways to arrange your life insurance to avoid estate taxes.
30. Distinguish between state estate taxes and state inheritance taxes.

DECISION-MAKING CASES

Case 1 A Couple Considers the Ramifications of Dying Intestate

Louise Parker of Seattle, Washington, is a 34-year-old police detective earning $45,000 per year. She and her husband, Chris, have two children in elementary school. They jointly own (with survivorship rights) a modestly furnished home and two late-model cars; along with a snowmobile, these items are their principal physical assets. Each spouse is covered by a $50,000 term life insurance policy. They have $5000 in a joint savings account (without survivorship rights). Neither Louise nor Chris has a will.

(a) List four possible negative things that could happen if either Louise or Chris were to die without a will.

(b) What would be the most important negative consequence of not having a will if both Louise and Chris were to die in some type of accident?

(c) Louise often mentions the cost of an attorney as a reason for not having a will. How might the problem of not having a will be solved at a lower cost?

Case 2   A Lottery Winner Practices Estate Planning

Your good friend and next-door neighbor, Robert, has just announced that he has the single winning ticket in the $7,000,000 lottery drawing of last week. Robert is 60 years old and divorced and has two adult children (Mary and Kitty) and four grandchildren. Recognizing that you are not an attorney, but knowing that your friend needs personal financial advice, offer some estate planning suggestions regarding the following points:

(a) Assume that Robert's taxable estate now amounts to $7,200,000 and, after using Table 19.1 to calculate Robert's estate tax liability total (if he died tomorrow), give him that figure while offering him a single piece of general advice.

(b) What advice can you offer about the amount of each gift that Robert might give that would be excluded from his estate?

(c) Name three specific types of trusts that Robert might consider to reduce his eventual estate taxes.

(d) Offer some suggestions on how Robert might arrange his life insurance to avoid estate taxes.

(e) Offer Robert some suggestions on how to pay for the college educations of his grandchildren.

Financial Math Questions

1. Christie and Darryl DeGuzman regularly saved and invested to the point where they are now in a financial position to be able to afford many of their dreams. They have decided to help pay for the college education of Christie's divorced sister's child, Christopher, who is five years of age. The DeGuzmans put $8000 into a custodial mutual fund account for Christopher. Answer the following questions.

(a) If Christopher's account grows at an annual rate of 8 percent and all dividends are reinvested, how many years will it take for the account to grow to the point where the child must pay income taxes?

(b) If the custodial account eventually earns annual dividends of $1500, how much will the child owe in income taxes, assuming Christopher must pay at a tax rate of 15 percent? (Hint: See the feature "How to Give Money to Children for College.")

(c) If the custodial account eventually earns annual dividends of $2000, how much will the child owe in income taxes, assuming a tax rate of 28 percent?

(d) If Christopher's account of $8000 grows at an after-tax annual rate of 5 percent with all dividends reinvested, how much will the account contain 13 years later when the child is ready to begin college? [Hint: Use Appendix A.1 or the *Garman/Forgue* Web site to solve for the answer.]

(e) If college expenses for one year will amount to $40,000 in 13 years, how much should the DeGuzmans put into a custodial account growing at an after-tax rate of 5 percent to have enough to pay the first year of schooling? [Hint: Use

Appendix A.1 or the *Garman/Forgue* Web site to solve for the answer.]

2. Mel Stafford of Boston, Massachusetts, has been named executor of the estate of his aunt, who recently died. As executor, he wishes to determine the estate taxes that must be paid. The following data apply to the estate: gross estate, $1,430,000; deductible expenses for settlement of the estate, $75,000; debts of the estate, $30,000; charitable contributions, $75,000; and irrevocable trusts of $100,000 to each of the five nieces and nephews. Not long before her death, the aunt gave Mel an additional $10,000. Develop a table similar to that contained in the Decision-Making Worksheet on page 570 using Mel's information, and then answer the following questions:

   (a) What is the gross estate?

   (b) What is the taxable estate?

   (c) What is the unified estate tax credit for this estate?

   (d) What amount of estate taxes will be owed?

   (e) Will taxes be assessed on the $10,000 gift to Mel?

3. Randy Carter died recently without a valid will. His gross estate for federal estate tax purposes was $2.2 million. Randy's wife, Imelda, and three children were his only survivors. Answer the following questions, assuming that Randy's state of residence followed the typical guidelines of division (one-half for the spouse with the children splitting the remainder):

   (a) What will be the proportional division of assets for the wife and the children?

   (b) What dollar amount will be inherited by Imelda?

   (c) If Imelda now dies without a will, what will be the proportional division of assets, assuming that she has no other living relatives other than her children?

   (d) If Imelda has personal assets (beyond her inheritance from Randy) that have a fair market value of $400,000, when she dies, how much will her gross estate total?

   (e) Assuming Imelda's estate paid $6000 for her funeral expenses and $180,000 to pay off the remaining debts, use Table 19.1 to calculate the amount of federal gift and estate tax on Imelda's estate.

4. Jennifer and John Martin have three children. She is a teacher and he is a pharmacist. Jennifer's sole and separate property and their fair market values are an automobile ($5000), paintings ($10,000), personal property ($25,000), an individual retirement account ($25,000, for which John is the beneficiary), and a state teacher's retirement plan ($50,000, for which John is the beneficiary). John's sole and separate property are a condominium ($90,000), an automobile ($13,000), a boat ($5000), personal property ($20,000), a mutual fund ($60,000), and an employer pension plan ($100,000, for which Jennifer is the beneficiary). Their jointly owned property includes a checking account ($6000), a money market fund ($25,000), a certificate of deposit ($50,000), a mutual fund ($60,000), home furnishings ($20,000), and personal property ($10,000). The details of their life insurance follow:

	Owner	Insured	Beneficiary	Amount	Cash Value
Policy 1	Jennifer	Jennifer	John	$100,000	$15,000
Policy 2	John	Jennifer	John	$ 50,000	$ 8,000
Policy 3	John	John	Jennifer	$100,000	0
Policy 4	Jennifer	John	Jennifer	$250,000	$ 1,500

   (a) Calculate Jennifer's probate estate.

   (b) Calculate Jennifer's gross estate.

   (c) Calculate John's probate estate.

   (d) Calculate John's gross estate.

MONEY MATTERS: LIFE-CYCLE CASES

Victor and Maria Update Their Estate Plans

Since retiring earlier this year, Victor and Maria have found that their assets amount to approximately $800,000, made up of the following: Victor's half-interest in their home ($90,000), his tax-sheltered pension plan ($144,000), his stock ($56,000), and personal property ($50,000); Maria's half-interest in their home ($90,000), the inherited home from her mother ($120,000), her tax-sheltered pension plan ($112,000), the present value (obtained from Victor's employer) of the survivor's benefits under her husband's defined-benefit pension plan ($60,000), personal property ($50,000), and her zero-coupon bonds ($28,000).

1. Offer the Hernandezes advice about how each might establish a durable power of attorney.

2. Should both Victor and Maria have living wills and health care proxies? Why or why not?

3. Victor purchased his $100,000 term life insurance policy through his employer, and he has been paying on his privately purchased $50,000 whole life policy for many years (which now has a cash value of $30,000). Maria is listed as the beneficiary on both policies. Assuming that Victor owns both policies, what advice can you offer regarding ownership of the two policies?

4. If Victor were to die tomorrow (before ownership of the insurance policies could be changed), what would Victor's gross estate be for tax purposes?

5. If Maria were to die one day after Victor's death, what would Maria's gross estate be for tax purposes? (Hint: Add in the life insurance death benefits.)

6. Offer Victor and Maria some suggestions on how to ease the transfer of assets to their adult children and grandchildren.

7. Calculate the estimated value of Victor and Maria's tax-sheltered pension plans, now

$256,000 ($144,000 + $112,000), if those assets increase at a rate of 10 percent annually for the next ten years.

Belinda Johnson Helps Her Uncle Plan His Estate

Belinda Johnson has been approached by her uncle, David Lawrence, who seeks advice about planning his estate. She has been handling some of David's investments, and he trusts her judgment on financial matters. David has a net worth of $2,340,000. At age 54, he is concerned about preparing his finances so that as much as possible of his estate will go to his heirs according to his wishes. David has no will but has written down some of his ideas. He has no wife or children but wants to provide for his mother, four nephews, Belinda, and a disabled sister.

1. What is the first action David should take in planning his estate? Why?

2. How might David use gifts to help reduce his estate taxes?

3. Why might a revocable living trust be a good idea for David in providing for his mother and sister?

4. What other types of trusts might David use in his estate planning?

Exploring the World Wide Web of Personal Finance

To complete these exercises, go to the *Garman/Forgue* Web site at *www.hmco.com/college/business/*

Select Personal Finance. Click on the exercise link for this chapter and answer the questions that appear on the Web page.

1. Visit the Web site for State Farm Insurance. Take the estate planning quiz provided and list two actions you would take as a result of what you learned from your right and wrong answers to the quiz.

2. Visit the Web site of Diane Reis, Attorney at Law, where you will find an estate tax calculator. Assume a person has a $100,000 (do not use commas when entering data) life insurance policy, a paid-for home valued at $135,000, $435,000 in a retirement plan, and $44,000 in other assets. Assume $17,000 in debts and a desire to give $20,000 to a university scholarship fund at death. What would be the estimated estate tax on such an estate, and how much could be saved using a bypass trust? Assuming a home valued at $350,000 and other assets of $444,000, answer these same questions. Explore the site further to determine two groups of people who might benefit from bypass trusts.

3. Visit the Web site of Recer Estate Services to determine if your state has an inheritance tax. If so how, how does your state's top tax rate compare with the rates of the other states? Use the Yahoo search feature to search for additional information on your state's inheritance tax by typing the words "yourstatename+inheritance+tax" in the appropriate box.

4. Upon death, one's will may become a public document through the probate process. Visit the Court TV Web site, where the wills of a number of famous people have been posted. Select a person whose will interests you. Identify three estate planning techniques outlined in this chapter that were used by that person.

5. Visit the Web site for Choices in Dying, where you will find an explanation of advance directives and can download forms and information on the laws in all states and the District of Columbia. Read and/or download the information and forms for your state. Is an advance directive something you would consider based on your understanding of your state's laws?

APPENDIXES

Present and Future Value Tables

A

Many problems of personal finance involve decisions about money values at varying points in time. These values can be directly and fairly compared only when they are adjusted to a common point in time. Chapter 1 introduced the basic time value concepts. This appendix offers more details about the time value of money; it also provides tables listing the future and present value of $1 with which to make calculations.

Four assumptions must be made to eliminate unnecessary complications:

1. Each planning period is one year long.

2. Only annual interest rates are considered.

3. Interest rates are the same during each of the annual periods.

4. Interest is compounded and continues earning a return in subsequent periods.

Tables of present and future values can be constructed to make these adjustments. Future values are derived from the principles of compounding the dollar values ahead in time. Present values are derived by discounting (which is the inverse of compounding) the dollar values and transferring them to an earlier point in time.

It is usually unnecessary to precisely identify whether the interest is paid/received at the *beginning* of a period or at the *end* of a period, to know whether interest compounds daily or quarterly instead of annually. (These calculations require even more tables.) The following present and future value tables assume that money is accumulated, received, paid, compounded, or whatever at the *end* of a period. The tables can be used to compute the mathematics of personal finance with high certainty and to confirm (or reject as inaccurate) what people tell you about financial matters.

The most significant task is to determine the correct table. Accordingly, each table is clearly described, and illustrations of its use appear on the facing page where possible. In addition, the appropriate mathematical equation is shown and can be easily solved using a calculator.

Illustrations Using Appendix A.1: Future Value of $1

To use the table on page A-5, locate the future value factor for the time period and the interest rate.

1. You invest $500 at a 15 percent rate of return for 12 years. How much will you have at the end of that 12-year period?

   The future value factor is 5.350; hence, the solution is $500 × 5.350, or $2675.

2. Property values in your neighborhood are increasing at a rate of 5 percent per year. If your home is presently worth $90,000, what will its worth be in 7 years?

   The future value factor is 1.407; hence, the solution is $90,000 × 1.407, or $126,630.

3. You need to amass $40,000 in the next 10 years to meet a balloon payment on your home mortgage. You have $17,000 available to invest. What annual interest rate must be earned to realize the $40,000?

   $40,000 ÷ $17,000 = 2.353. Read down the periods *(n)* column to 10 years and across to 2.367 (close enough), which is found under the 9 percent column. Hence, the $17,000 invested at 9 percent for 10 years will grow to a future value of slightly more than $40,000.

4. An apartment building is currently valued at $160,000, and it has been appreciating at 8 percent per year. If this rate continues, in how many years will it be worth $300,000?

   $300,000 ÷ $160,000 = 1.875. Read down the 8 percent column until you reach 1.851 (close enough to 1.875). This number corresponds to a period of 8 years. Hence, the $160,000 property appreciating at 8 percent annually will grow to a future value of $300,000 in slightly more than 8 years.

5. You have the choice of receiving a down payment from someone who wants to purchase your rental property as $15,000 today or as a personal note for $25,000 payable in 6 years. If you could expect to earn 8 percent on such funds, which is the better choice?

   The future value factor is 1.587; hence, the future value of $15,000 at 8 percent is $15,000 × 1.587, or $23,805. Thus, it would be better to take the note for $25,000.

6. How much will an automobile now priced at $20,000 cost in 4 years, assuming an annual inflation rate of 5 percent? Read down the 5 percent column and across the row for 4 years to locate the future value factor of 1.216. Hence, the solution is $20,000 × 1.216, or $24,320.

7. How large a lump-sum investment do you need now to have $20,000 available in 5 years, assuming a 10 percent annual rate of return?

   The $20,000 future value is divided by 1.611 (10 percent at 5 years), resulting in a current lump-sum investment of $12,415.

8. You have $5000 now and need $10,000 in 9 years. What rate of return is needed to reach that goal?

   Divide the future value of $10,000 by the present value of the lump sum of $5000 to obtain a future value factor of 2.0. In the row for 9 years, locate the future value factor of 1.999 (very close to 2.0). Read up the column to find that an 8 percent return on investment is needed.

9. How many years will it take your lump-sum investment of $10,000 to grow to $16,000, given an annual rate of return of 7 percent?

   Divide the future value of $16,000 by the present value of the $10,000 lump sum to compute a future value factor of 1.6; look down the 7 percent column to find 1.606 (close enough). Read across the row to find that an investment period of 7 years is needed.

   An alternative approach is to use a calculator to determine the future value, *FV*, of a sum of money invested today, assuming that the amount remains in the investment for a specified number of time periods (usually years) and that it earns a certain rate of return each period. The equation is

   $$FV = PV (1.0 + i)n \qquad\qquad (A.1)$$

   where

   FV = the future value
   PV = the present value of the investment
   i = the interest rate per period
   n = the number or periods the *PV* is invested

Appendix A.1

Future Value of $1 at the End of n Periods

(Used to Compute the Compounded Future Value of a Given Present Value Lump-Sum Investment)

n	1%	2%	3%	4%	5%	6%	7%	8%	9%	10%	11%	12%	13%	14%	15%	16%	17%	18%	19%	20%
1	1.0100	1.0200	1.0300	1.0400	1.0500	1.0600	1.0700	1.0800	1.0900	1.1000	1.1100	1.1200	1.1300	1.1400	1.1500	1.1600	1.1700	1.1800	1.1900	1.2000
2	1.0201	1.0404	1.0609	1.0816	1.1025	1.1236	1.1449	1.1664	1.1881	1.2100	1.2321	1.2544	1.2769	1.2996	1.3225	1.3456	1.3689	1.3924	1.4161	1.4400
3	1.0303	1.0612	1.0927	1.1249	1.1576	1.1910	1.2250	1.2597	1.2950	1.3310	1.3676	1.4049	1.4429	1.4815	1.5209	1.5609	1.6016	1.6430	1.6852	1.7280
4	1.0406	1.0824	1.1255	1.1699	1.2155	1.2625	1.3108	1.3605	1.4116	1.4641	1.5181	1.5735	1.6305	1.6890	1.7490	1.8106	1.8739	1.9388	2.0053	2.0736
5	1.0510	1.1041	1.1593	1.2167	1.2763	1.3382	1.4026	1.4693	1.5386	1.6105	1.6851	1.7623	1.8424	1.9254	2.0114	2.1003	2.1924	2.2878	2.3864	2.4883
6	1.0615	1.1262	1.1941	1.2653	1.3401	1.4185	1.5007	1.5869	1.6771	1.7716	1.8704	1.9738	2.0820	2.1950	2.3131	2.4364	2.5652	2.6996	2.8398	2.9860
7	1.0721	1.1487	1.2299	1.3159	1.4071	1.5036	1.6058	1.7138	1.8280	1.9487	2.0762	2.2107	2.3526	2.5023	2.6600	2.8262	3.0012	3.1855	3.3793	3.5832
8	1.0829	1.1717	1.2668	1.3686	1.4775	1.5938	1.7182	1.8509	1.9926	2.1436	2.3045	2.4760	2.6584	2.8526	3.0590	3.2784	3.5115	3.7589	4.0214	4.2998
9	1.0937	1.1951	1.3048	1.4233	1.5513	1.6895	1.8385	1.9990	2.1719	2.3579	2.5580	2.7731	3.0040	3.2519	3.5179	3.8030	4.1084	4.4355	4.7854	5.1598
10	1.1046	1.2190	1.3439	1.4802	1.6289	1.7908	1.9672	2.1589	2.3674	2.5937	2.8394	3.1058	3.3946	3.7072	4.0456	4.4114	4.8068	5.2338	5.6947	6.1917
11	1.1157	1.2434	1.3842	1.5395	1.7103	1.8983	2.1049	2.3316	2.5804	2.8531	3.1518	3.4785	3.8359	4.2262	4.6524	5.1173	5.6240	6.1759	6.7767	7.4301
12	1.1268	1.2682	1.4258	1.6010	1.7959	2.0122	2.2522	2.5182	2.8127	3.1384	3.4985	3.8960	4.3345	4.8179	5.3503	5.9360	6.5801	7.2876	8.0642	8.9161
13	1.1381	1.2936	1.4685	1.6651	1.8856	2.1329	2.4098	2.7196	3.0658	3.4523	3.8833	4.3635	4.8980	5.4924	6.1528	6.8858	7.6987	8.5994	9.5964	10.6993
14	1.1495	1.3195	1.5126	1.7317	1.9799	2.2609	2.5785	2.9372	3.3417	3.7975	4.3104	4.8871	5.5348	6.2613	7.0757	7.9875	9.0075	10.1472	11.4198	12.8392
15	1.1610	1.3459	1.5580	1.8009	2.0789	2.3966	2.7590	3.1722	3.6425	4.1772	4.7846	5.4736	6.2543	7.1379	8.1371	9.2655	10.5387	11.9737	13.5895	15.4070
16	1.1726	1.3728	1.6047	1.8730	2.1829	2.5404	2.9522	3.4259	3.9703	4.5950	5.3109	6.1304	7.0673	8.1372	9.3576	10.7480	12.3303	14.1290	16.1715	18.4884
17	1.1843	1.4002	1.6528	1.9479	2.2920	2.6928	3.1588	3.7000	4.3276	5.0545	5.8951	6.8660	7.9861	9.2765	10.7613	12.4677	14.4265	16.6722	19.2441	22.1861
18	1.1961	1.4282	1.7024	2.0258	2.4066	2.8543	3.3799	3.9960	4.7171	5.5599	6.5436	7.6900	9.0243	10.5752	12.3755	14.4625	16.8790	19.6733	22.9005	26.6233
19	1.2081	1.4568	1.7535	2.1068	2.5270	3.0256	3.6165	4.3157	5.1417	6.1159	7.2633	8.6128	10.1974	12.0557	14.2318	16.7765	19.7484	23.2144	27.2516	31.9480
20	1.2202	1.4859	1.8061	2.1911	2.6533	3.2071	3.8697	4.6610	5.6044	6.7275	8.0623	9.6463	11.5231	13.7435	16.3665	19.4608	23.1056	27.3930	32.4294	38.3376
21	1.2324	1.5157	1.8603	2.2788	2.7860	3.3996	4.1406	5.0338	6.1088	7.4002	8.9492	10.8038	13.0211	15.6676	18.8215	22.5745	27.0336	32.3238	38.5910	46.0051
22	1.2447	1.5460	1.9161	2.3699	2.9253	3.6035	4.4304	5.4365	6.6586	8.1403	9.9336	12.1003	14.7138	17.8610	21.6447	26.1864	31.6293	38.1421	45.9233	55.2061
23	1.2572	1.5769	1.9736	2.4647	3.0715	3.8197	4.7405	5.8715	7.2579	8.9543	11.0263	13.5523	16.6266	20.3616	24.8915	30.3762	37.0062	45.0076	54.6487	66.2474
24	1.2697	1.6084	2.0328	2.5633	3.2251	4.0489	5.0724	6.3412	7.9111	9.8497	12.2392	15.1786	18.7881	23.2122	28.6252	35.2364	43.2973	53.1090	65.0320	79.4968
25	1.2824	1.6406	2.0938	2.6658	3.3864	4.2919	5.4274	6.8485	8.6231	10.8347	13.5855	17.0001	21.2305	26.4619	32.9190	40.8742	50.6578	62.6686	77.3881	95.3962
26	1.2953	1.6734	2.1566	2.7725	3.5557	4.5494	5.8074	7.3964	9.3992	11.9182	15.0799	19.0401	23.9905	30.1666	37.8568	47.4141	59.2697	73.9490	92.0918	114.4755
27	1.3082	1.7069	2.2213	2.8834	3.7335	4.8223	6.2139	7.9881	10.2451	13.1100	16.7386	21.3249	27.1093	34.3899	43.5353	55.0004	69.3455	87.2598	109.5893	137.3706
28	1.3213	1.7410	2.2879	2.9987	3.9201	5.1117	6.6488	8.6271	11.1671	14.4210	18.5799	23.8839	30.6335	39.2045	50.0656	63.8004	81.1342	102.9666	130.4112	164.8447
29	1.3345	1.7758	2.3566	3.1187	4.1161	5.4184	7.1143	9.3173	12.1722	15.8631	20.6237	26.7499	34.6158	44.6931	57.5755	74.0085	94.9271	121.5005	155.1893	197.8136
30	1.3478	1.8114	2.4273	3.2434	4.3219	5.7435	7.6123	10.0627	13.2677	17.4494	22.8923	29.9599	39.1159	50.9502	66.2118	85.8499	111.0647	143.3706	184.6753	237.3763
40	1.4889	2.2080	3.2620	4.8010	7.0400	10.2857	14.9745	21.7245	31.4094	45.2593	65.0009	93.0510	132.7816	188.8835	267.8635	378.7212	533.8687	750.3783	1051.668	1469.772
50	1.6446	2.6916	4.3839	7.1067	11.4674	18.4202	29.4570	46.9016	74.3575	117.3909	184.5648	289.0022	450.7359	700.2330	1083.657	1670.704	2566.215	3927.357	5988.914	9100.438

Illustrations Using Appendix A.2: Present Value of $1

To use this table, locate the present value factor for the time period and the interest rate.

1. You want to begin a college fund for your newborn child; you hope to accumulate $30,000 by 18 years from now. If a current investment opportunity yields 7 percent, how much must you invest in a lump sum to realize the $30,000 when needed?

    The present value factor is 0.296; hence, the solution is $30,000 × 0.296, or $8880.

2. You hope to retire in 25 years and want to deposit a single lump sum that will grow to $250,000 at that time. If you can now invest at 8 percent, how much must you invest to realize the $250,000 when needed?

    The present value factor is 0.146; hence, the solution is $250,000 × 0.146, or $36,500. The present value of $250,000 received 25 years from now is $36,500 if the interest rate is 8 percent.

3. You have the choice of receiving a down payment from someone who wants to purchase your rental property as $15,000 today or as a personal note for $25,000 payable in 6 years. If you could expect to earn 8 percent on such funds, which is the better choice?

    The present value factor is 0.630; hence, the solution is $25,000 × 0.630, or $15,750. Thus, the present value of $25,000 received in 6 years is greater than $15,000 received now, and the personal note is the better choice.

4. You own a $1000 bond paying 8 percent annually until its maturity in 5 years. You need to sell the bond now even though the market rate of interest on similar bonds has increased to 10 percent. What discounted market price for the bond will allow the new buyer to earn a yield of 10 percent?

    First, compute the present value of the future interest payments of $80 per year for 5 years at 10 percent (using Appendix A.4): $80 × 3.791, or $303.28. Second, compute the present value of the future principal repayment of $1000 after 5 years at 10 percent: $1000 × 0.621, or $621.00. Hence, the market price is the sum of the two present values ($303.28 + $621.00), or $924.28.

An alternative approach is to use a calculator to determine the present value, *PV*, of a single payment received some time in the future. The equation, which is a rearrangement of the future value equation (A.1), is

$$PV = \frac{FV}{(1.0 + i)^n} \qquad (A.2)$$

where

$$
\begin{aligned}
PV &= \text{the present value of the investment} \\
FV &= \text{the future value} \\
i &= \text{the interest rate per period} \\
n &= \text{the number or periods the } PV \text{ is invested}
\end{aligned}
$$

Appendix A.2

Present Value of $1

(Used to Compute the Present Value of Some Known Future Single Payment Amount)

n	1%	2%	3%	4%	5%	6%	7%	8%	9%	10%	11%	12%	13%	14%	15%	16%	17%	18%	19%	20%
1	0.9901	0.9804	0.9709	0.9615	0.9524	0.9434	0.9346	0.9259	0.9174	0.9091	0.9009	0.8929	0.8850	0.8772	0.8696	0.8621	0.8547	0.8475	0.8403	0.8333
2	0.9803	0.9612	0.9426	0.9246	0.9070	0.8900	0.8734	0.8573	0.8417	0.8264	0.8116	0.7972	0.7831	0.7695	0.7561	0.7432	0.7305	0.7182	0.7062	0.6944
3	0.9706	0.9423	0.9151	0.8890	0.8638	0.8396	0.8163	0.7938	0.7722	0.7513	0.7312	0.7118	0.6931	0.6750	0.6575	0.6407	0.6244	0.6086	0.5934	0.5787
4	0.9610	0.9238	0.8885	0.8548	0.8227	0.7921	0.7629	0.7350	0.7084	0.6830	0.6587	0.6355	0.6133	0.5921	0.5718	0.5523	0.5337	0.5158	0.4987	0.4823
5	0.9515	0.9057	0.8626	0.8219	0.7835	0.7473	0.7130	0.6806	0.6499	0.6209	0.5935	0.5674	0.5428	0.5194	0.4972	0.4761	0.4561	0.4371	0.4190	0.4019
6	0.9420	0.8880	0.8375	0.7903	0.7462	0.7050	0.6663	0.6302	0.5963	0.5645	0.5346	0.5066	0.4803	0.4556	0.4323	0.4104	0.3898	0.3704	0.3521	0.3349
7	0.9327	0.8706	0.8131	0.7599	0.7107	0.6651	0.6227	0.5835	0.5470	0.5132	0.4817	0.4523	0.4251	0.3996	0.3759	0.3538	0.3332	0.3139	0.2959	0.2791
8	0.9235	0.8535	0.7894	0.7307	0.6768	0.6274	0.5820	0.5403	0.5019	0.4665	0.4339	0.4039	0.3762	0.3506	0.3269	0.3050	0.2848	0.2660	0.2487	0.2326
9	0.9143	0.8368	0.7664	0.7026	0.6446	0.5919	0.5439	0.5002	0.4604	0.4241	0.3909	0.3606	0.3329	0.3075	0.2843	0.2630	0.2434	0.2255	0.2090	0.1938
10	0.9053	0.8203	0.7441	0.6756	0.6139	0.5584	0.5083	0.4632	0.4224	0.3855	0.3522	0.3220	0.2946	0.2697	0.2472	0.2267	0.2080	0.1911	0.1756	0.1615
11	0.8963	0.8043	0.7224	0.6496	0.5847	0.5268	0.4751	0.4289	0.3875	0.3505	0.3173	0.2875	0.2607	0.2366	0.2149	0.1954	0.1778	0.1619	0.1476	0.1346
12	0.8874	0.7885	0.7014	0.6246	0.5568	0.4970	0.4440	0.3971	0.3555	0.3186	0.2858	0.2567	0.2307	0.2076	0.1869	0.1685	0.1520	0.1372	0.1240	0.1122
13	0.8787	0.7730	0.6810	0.6006	0.5303	0.4688	0.4150	0.3677	0.3262	0.2897	0.2575	0.2292	0.2042	0.1821	0.1625	0.1452	0.1299	0.1163	0.1042	0.0935
14	0.8700	0.7579	0.6611	0.5775	0.5051	0.4423	0.3878	0.3405	0.2992	0.2633	0.2320	0.2046	0.1807	0.1597	0.1413	0.1252	0.1110	0.0985	0.0876	0.0779
15	0.8613	0.7430	0.6419	0.5553	0.4810	0.4173	0.3624	0.3152	0.2745	0.2394	0.2090	0.1827	0.1599	0.1401	0.1229	0.1079	0.0949	0.0835	0.0736	0.0649
16	0.8528	0.7284	0.6232	0.5339	0.4581	0.3936	0.3387	0.2919	0.2519	0.2176	0.1883	0.1631	0.1415	0.1229	0.1069	0.0930	0.0811	0.0708	0.0618	0.0541
17	0.8444	0.7142	0.6050	0.5134	0.4363	0.3714	0.3166	0.2703	0.2311	0.1978	0.1696	0.1456	0.1252	0.1078	0.0929	0.0802	0.0693	0.0600	0.0520	0.0451
18	0.8360	0.7002	0.5874	0.4936	0.4155	0.3503	0.2959	0.2502	0.2120	0.1799	0.1528	0.1300	0.1108	0.0946	0.0808	0.0691	0.0592	0.0508	0.0437	0.0376
19	0.8277	0.6864	0.5703	0.4746	0.3957	0.3305	0.2765	0.2317	0.1945	0.1635	0.1377	0.1161	0.0981	0.0829	0.0703	0.0596	0.0506	0.0431	0.0367	0.0313
20	0.8195	0.6730	0.5537	0.4564	0.3769	0.3118	0.2584	0.2145	0.1784	0.1486	0.1240	0.1037	0.0868	0.0728	0.0611	0.0514	0.0433	0.0365	0.0308	0.0261
21	0.8114	0.6598	0.5375	0.4388	0.3589	0.2942	0.2415	0.1987	0.1637	0.1351	0.1117	0.0926	0.0768	0.0638	0.0531	0.0443	0.0370	0.0309	0.0259	0.0217
22	0.8034	0.6468	0.5219	0.4220	0.3418	0.2775	0.2257	0.1839	0.1502	0.1228	0.1007	0.0826	0.0680	0.0560	0.0462	0.0382	0.0316	0.0262	0.0218	0.0181
23	0.7954	0.6342	0.5067	0.4057	0.3256	0.2618	0.2109	0.1703	0.1378	0.1117	0.0907	0.0738	0.0601	0.0491	0.0402	0.0329	0.0270	0.0222	0.0183	0.0151
24	0.7876	0.6217	0.4919	0.3901	0.3101	0.2470	0.1971	0.1577	0.1264	0.1015	0.0817	0.0659	0.0532	0.0431	0.0349	0.0284	0.0231	0.0188	0.0154	0.0126
25	0.7798	0.6095	0.4776	0.3751	0.2953	0.2330	0.1842	0.1460	0.1160	0.0923	0.0736	0.0588	0.0471	0.0378	0.0304	0.0245	0.0197	0.0160	0.0129	0.0105
26	0.7720	0.5976	0.4637	0.3607	0.2812	0.2198	0.1722	0.1352	0.1064	0.0839	0.0663	0.0525	0.0417	0.0331	0.0264	0.0211	0.0169	0.0135	0.0109	0.0087
27	0.7644	0.5859	0.4502	0.3468	0.2678	0.2074	0.1609	0.1252	0.0976	0.0763	0.0597	0.0469	0.0369	0.0291	0.0230	0.0182	0.0144	0.0115	0.0091	0.0073
28	0.7568	0.5744	0.4371	0.3335	0.2551	0.1956	0.1504	0.1159	0.0895	0.0693	0.0538	0.0419	0.0326	0.0255	0.0200	0.0157	0.0123	0.0097	0.0077	0.0061
29	0.7493	0.5631	0.4243	0.3207	0.2429	0.1846	0.1406	0.1073	0.0822	0.0630	0.0485	0.0374	0.0289	0.0224	0.0174	0.0135	0.0105	0.0082	0.0064	0.0051
30	0.7419	0.5521	0.4120	0.3083	0.2314	0.1741	0.1314	0.0994	0.0754	0.0573	0.0437	0.0334	0.0256	0.0196	0.0151	0.0116	0.0090	0.0070	0.0054	0.0042
40	0.6717	0.4529	0.3066	0.2083	0.1420	0.0972	0.0668	0.0460	0.0318	0.0221	0.0154	0.0107	0.0075	0.0053	0.0037	0.0026	0.0019	0.0013	0.0010	0.0007
50	0.6080	0.3715	0.2281	0.1407	0.0872	0.0543	0.0339	0.0213	0.0134	0.0085	0.0054	0.0035	0.0022	0.0014	0.0009	0.0006	0.0004	0.0003	0.0002	0.0001

Illustrations Using Appendix A.3: Future Value of an Annuity of $1 per Period

To use this table, locate the future value factor for the time period and the interest rate.

1. You plan to retire after 16 years. To provide for that retirement, you initiate a savings program of $7000 per year in an investment yielding 8 percent. What will the value of the retirement fund be at the beginning of the seventeenth year?

   Your last payment into the fund will occur at the end of the sixteenth year, so scan down the periods *(n)* column for period 16, and then move across until you reach the column for 8 percent. The future value factor is 30.32. Hence, the solution is $7000 × 30.32, or $212,240.

2. What will be the value of an investment if you put $2000 into a retirement plan yielding 7 percent annually for 25 years?

   The future value factor is 63.250. Hence, the solution is $2000 × 63.250, or $126,500.

3. You are trying to decide between putting $3000 or $4000 annually for the next 20 years into an investment yielding 7 percent for retirement purposes. What is the difference in the value of investing the extra $1000 for 20 years?

   The future value factor is 41.0. Hence, the solution is $1000 × 41.0, or $41,000.

4. You will receive an annuity payment of $1200 at the end of each year for 6 years. What will be the total value of this stream of income invested at 7 percent by the time you receive the last payment?

   The appropriate future value factor for 6 years at 7 percent is 7.153. Hence, the solution is $1200 × 7.153, or $8584.

5. How many years of investing $1200 annually at 9 percent will it take to reach a goal of $11,000?

   Divide the future value of $11,000 by the lump sum of $1200 to find a future value factor of 9.17. Look down the 9 percent column to find 9.200 (close enough). Read across the row to find that an investment period of 7 years is needed.

6. If you plan to invest $1200 annually for 9 years, what rate of return is needed to reach a goal of $15,000?

   Divide the future value goal of $15,000 by $1200 to derive the future value factor 12.5. Look across the row for 9 years to locate the future value factor of 12.49 (close enough). Read up the column to find that you need an 8 percent return.

   An alternative approach is to use a calculator to determine the total future value, *FV*, of a stream of equal payments (an annuity). The equation is

$$FV = \frac{[(1.0 + i)n - 1.0] \times A}{i} \tag{A.3}$$

where

$$
\begin{aligned}
FV &= \text{the future value} \\
i &= \text{the interest rate per period} \\
n &= \text{the number or periods the } PV \text{ is invested} \\
A &= \text{the amount of the annuity}
\end{aligned}
$$

Appendix A.3

Future Value of a Stream of Equal Payments (an Annuity) of $1 per Period

(Used to Compute the Future Value of a Stream of Income Payments)

n	1%	2%	3%	4%	5%	6%	7%	8%	9%	10%	11%	12%	13%	14%	15%	16%	17%	18%	19%	20%
1	1.0000	1.0000	1.0000	1.0000	1.0000	1.0000	1.0000	1.0000	1.0000	1.0000	1.0000	1.0000	1.0000	1.0000	1.0000	1.0000	1.0000	1.0000	1.0000	1.0000
2	2.0100	2.0200	2.0300	2.0400	2.0500	2.0600	2.0700	2.0800	2.0900	2.1000	2.1100	2.1200	2.1300	2.1400	2.1500	2.1600	2.1700	2.1800	2.1900	2.2000
3	3.0301	3.0604	3.0909	3.1216	3.1525	3.1836	3.2149	3.2464	3.2781	3.3100	3.3421	3.3744	3.4069	3.4396	3.4725	3.5056	3.5389	3.5724	3.6061	3.6400
4	4.0604	4.1216	4.1836	4.2465	4.3101	4.3746	4.4399	4.5061	4.5731	4.6410	4.7097	4.7793	4.8498	4.9211	4.9934	5.0665	5.1405	5.2154	5.2913	5.3680
5	5.1010	5.2040	5.3091	5.4163	5.5256	5.6371	5.7507	5.8666	5.9847	6.1051	6.2278	6.3528	6.4803	6.6101	6.7424	6.8771	7.0144	7.1542	7.2966	7.4416
6	6.1520	6.3081	6.4684	6.6330	6.8019	6.9753	7.1533	7.3359	7.5233	7.7156	7.9129	8.1152	8.3227	8.5355	8.7537	8.9775	9.2068	9.4420	9.6830	9.9299
7	7.2135	7.4343	7.6625	7.8983	8.1420	8.3938	8.6540	8.9228	9.2004	9.4872	9.7833	10.0890	10.4047	10.7305	11.0668	11.4139	11.7720	12.1415	12.5227	12.9159
8	8.2857	8.5830	8.8923	9.2142	9.5491	9.8975	10.2598	10.6366	11.0285	11.4359	11.8594	12.2997	12.7573	13.2328	13.7268	14.2401	14.7733	15.3270	15.9020	16.4991
9	9.3685	9.7546	10.1591	10.5828	11.0266	11.4913	11.9780	12.4876	13.0210	13.5795	14.1640	14.7757	15.4157	16.0853	16.7858	17.5185	18.2847	19.0859	19.9234	20.7989
10	10.4622	10.9497	11.4639	12.0061	12.5779	13.1808	13.8164	14.4866	15.1929	15.9374	16.7220	17.5487	18.4197	19.3373	20.3037	21.3215	22.3931	23.5213	24.7089	25.9587
11	11.5668	12.1687	12.8078	13.4864	14.2068	14.9716	15.7836	16.6455	17.5603	18.5312	19.5614	20.6546	21.8143	23.0445	24.3493	25.7329	27.1999	28.7551	30.4035	32.1504
12	12.6825	13.4121	14.1920	15.0258	15.9171	16.8699	17.8885	18.9771	20.1407	21.3843	22.7132	24.1331	25.6502	27.2707	29.0017	30.8502	32.8239	34.9311	37.1802	39.5805
13	13.8093	14.6803	15.6178	16.6268	17.7130	18.8821	20.1406	21.4953	22.9534	24.5227	26.2116	28.0291	29.9847	32.0887	34.3519	36.7862	39.4040	42.2187	45.2445	48.4966
14	14.9474	15.9739	17.0863	18.2919	19.5986	21.0151	22.5505	24.2149	26.0192	27.9750	30.0949	32.3926	34.8827	37.5811	40.5047	43.6720	47.1027	50.8180	54.8409	59.1959
15	16.0969	17.2934	18.5989	20.0236	21.5786	23.2760	25.1290	27.1521	29.3609	31.7725	34.4054	37.2797	40.4175	43.8424	47.5804	51.6595	56.1101	60.9653	66.2607	72.0351
16	17.2579	18.6393	20.1569	21.8245	23.6575	25.6725	27.8881	30.3243	33.0034	35.9497	39.1899	42.7533	46.6717	50.9804	55.7175	60.9250	66.6488	72.9390	79.8502	87.4421
17	18.4304	20.0121	21.7616	23.6975	25.8404	28.2129	30.8402	33.7502	36.9737	40.5447	44.5008	48.8837	53.7391	59.1176	65.0751	71.6730	78.9791	87.0680	96.0217	105.9306
18	19.6147	21.4123	23.4144	25.6454	28.1324	30.9057	33.9990	37.4502	41.3013	45.5992	50.3959	55.7497	61.7251	68.3941	75.8364	84.1407	93.4056	103.7403	115.2659	128.1167
19	20.8109	22.8406	25.1169	27.6712	30.5390	33.7600	37.3790	41.4463	46.0185	51.1591	56.9395	63.4397	70.7494	78.9692	88.2118	98.6032	110.2846	123.4135	138.1664	154.7400
20	22.0190	24.2974	26.8704	29.7781	33.0660	36.7856	40.9955	45.7620	51.1601	57.2750	64.2028	72.0524	80.9468	91.0249	102.4436	115.3797	130.0329	146.6280	165.4180	186.6880
21	23.2392	25.7833	28.6765	31.9692	35.7193	39.9927	44.8652	50.4229	56.7645	64.0025	72.2651	81.6987	92.4699	104.7684	118.8101	134.8405	153.1385	174.0210	197.8474	225.0256
22	24.4716	27.2990	30.5368	34.2480	38.5052	43.3923	49.0057	55.4568	62.8733	71.4027	81.2143	92.5026	105.4910	120.4360	137.6316	157.4150	180.1721	206.3448	236.4384	271.0307
23	25.7163	28.8450	32.4529	36.6179	41.4305	46.9958	53.4361	60.8933	69.5319	79.5430	91.1479	104.6029	120.2048	138.2970	159.2764	183.6014	211.8013	244.4868	282.3618	326.2368
24	26.9735	30.4219	34.4265	39.0826	44.5020	50.8156	58.1767	66.7648	76.7898	88.4973	102.1741	118.1552	136.8315	158.6586	184.1678	213.9776	248.8075	289.4945	337.0105	392.4842
25	28.2432	32.0303	36.4593	41.6459	47.7271	54.8645	63.2490	73.1059	84.7009	98.3471	114.4133	133.3339	155.6196	181.8708	212.7930	249.2140	292.1048	342.6035	402.0424	471.9811
26	29.5256	33.6709	38.5530	44.3117	51.1135	59.1564	68.6765	79.9544	93.3240	109.1818	127.9988	150.3339	176.8501	208.3327	245.7120	290.0883	342.7626	405.2721	479.4305	567.3773
27	30.8209	35.3443	40.7096	47.0842	54.6691	63.7058	74.4838	87.3508	102.7231	121.0999	143.0786	169.3740	200.8406	238.4993	283.5688	337.5024	402.0323	479.2211	571.5223	681.8527
28	32.1291	37.0512	42.9309	49.9676	58.4026	68.5281	80.6977	95.3388	112.9682	134.2099	159.8173	190.6989	227.9499	272.8892	327.1041	392.5027	471.3778	566.4808	681.1116	819.2233
29	33.4504	38.7922	45.2188	52.9663	62.3227	73.6398	87.3465	103.9659	124.1354	148.6309	178.3972	214.5827	258.5834	312.0937	377.1697	456.3032	552.5120	669.4474	811.5228	984.0679
30	34.7849	40.5681	47.5754	56.0849	66.4389	79.0582	94.4608	113.2832	136.3075	164.4940	199.0209	241.3327	293.1992	356.7868	434.7451	530.3117	647.4390	790.9479	966.7121	1181.882
40	48.8864	60.4020	75.4013	95.0255	120.7998	154.7620	199.6351	259.0565	337.8824	442.5925	581.8260	767.0914	1013.704	1342.025	1779.090	2360.757	3134.522	4163.212	5529.829	7343.856
50	64.4632	84.5794	112.7969	152.6671	209.3480	290.3359	406.5289	573.7701	815.0834	1163.908	1668.771	2400.018	3459.507	4994.522	7217.714	10435.65	15089.50	21813.09	31515.33	45497.17

Illustrations Using Appendix A.4:
Present Value of an Annuity of $1 per Period

To use this table, locate the present value factor for the time period and the interest rate.

1. You are entering a contract that will provide you with an income of $1000 at the end of the year for the next 10 years. If the annual interest rate is 7 percent, what is the present value of that stream of payments?

    The present value factor is 7.024; hence, the solution is $1000 × 7.024, or $7024.

2. You expect to have $250,000 available in a retirement plan when you retire. If the amount invested yields 8 percent and you hope to live an additional 20 years, how much can you withdraw each year so that the fund will just be liquidated after 20 years?

    The present value factor for 20 years at 8 percent is 9.818. Hence, the solution is $250,000 ÷ 9.818, or $25,463.

3. You have received an inheritance of $60,000 that you invested so that it earns 9 percent. If you withdraw $8000 annually to supplement your income, in how many years will the fund run out?

    Solving for *n*, $60,000 ÷ $8000 = 7.5. Scan down the 9 percent column until you find a present value factor close to 7.5, which is 7.487. The row indicates 13 years; thus, the fund will be depleted in approximately 13 years with $8000 annual withdrawals.

4. A seller offers to finance the sale of a building to you as an investment. The mortgage loan of $280,000 will be for 20 years and requires an annual mortgage payment of $24,000. Should you finance the purchase through the seller or borrow the funds from a financial institution at a current rate of 10 percent?

    $280,000 ÷ $24,000 = 11.667. Scan down the periods *(n)* column to 20 years and then read across to locate the figure closest to 11.667, which is 11.470. The column indicates 6 percent; thus, seller financing offers a lower interest rate.

5. You have the opportunity to purchase an office building for $750,000 with an expected life of 20 years. Looking over the financial details, you see that the before-tax net rental income is $90,000. If you want a return of at least 15 percent, how much should you pay for the building?

    The present value factor for 20 years at 15 percent is 6.259, and $90,000 × 6.259 = $563,310. Thus, the price is too high for you to earn a return of 15 percent.

    An alternative approach is to use a calculator to determine the present value, *PV,* of a stream of payments. The equation is

$$PV = \frac{[1.0 - 1.0/(1.0 + i)n] \times A}{i} \qquad \text{(A.4)}$$

where

$$
\begin{aligned}
PV &= \text{the present value of the investment} \\
i &= \text{the interest rate per period} \\
n &= \text{the number or periods the } PV \text{ is invested} \\
A &= \text{the amount of the annuity}
\end{aligned}
$$

Appendix A.4

Present Value of a Stream of Equal Payments (an Annuity) of $1 per Period

(Used to Compute the Future Value of a Stream of Income Payments)

n	1%	2%	3%	4%	5%	6%	7%	8%	9%	10%	11%	12%	13%	14%	15%	16%	17%	18%	19%	20%
1	0.9901	0.9804	0.9709	0.9615	0.9524	0.9434	0.9346	0.9259	0.9174	0.9091	0.9009	0.8929	0.8850	0.8772	0.8696	0.8621	0.8547	0.8475	0.8403	0.8333
2	1.9704	1.9416	1.9135	1.8861	1.8594	1.8334	1.8080	1.7833	1.7591	1.7355	1.7125	1.6901	1.6681	1.6467	1.6257	1.6052	1.5852	1.5656	1.5465	1.5278
3	2.9410	2.8839	2.8286	2.7751	2.7232	2.6730	2.6243	2.5771	2.5313	2.4869	2.4437	2.4018	2.3612	2.3216	2.2832	2.2459	2.2096	2.1743	2.1399	2.1065
4	3.9020	3.8077	3.7171	3.6299	3.5460	3.4651	3.3872	3.3121	3.2397	3.1699	3.1024	3.0373	2.9745	2.9137	2.8550	2.7982	2.7432	2.6901	2.6386	2.5887
5	4.8534	4.7135	4.5797	4.4518	4.3295	4.2124	4.1002	3.9927	3.8897	3.7908	3.6959	3.6048	3.5172	3.4331	3.3522	3.2743	3.1993	3.1272	3.0576	2.9906
6	5.7955	5.6014	5.4172	5.2421	5.0757	4.9173	4.7665	4.6229	4.4859	4.3553	4.2305	4.1114	3.9975	3.8887	3.7845	3.6847	3.5892	3.4976	3.4098	3.3255
7	6.7282	6.4720	6.2303	6.0021	5.7864	5.5824	5.3893	5.2064	5.0330	4.8684	4.7122	4.5638	4.4226	4.2883	4.1604	4.0386	3.9224	3.8115	3.7057	3.6046
8	7.6517	7.3255	7.0197	6.7327	6.4632	6.2098	5.9713	5.7466	5.5348	5.3349	5.1461	4.9676	4.7988	4.6389	4.4873	4.3436	4.2072	4.0776	3.9544	3.8372
9	8.5660	8.1622	7.7861	7.4353	7.1078	6.8017	6.5152	6.2469	5.9952	5.7590	5.5370	5.3282	5.1317	4.9464	4.7716	4.6065	4.4506	4.3030	4.1633	4.0310
10	9.4713	8.9826	8.5302	8.1109	7.7217	7.3601	7.0236	6.7101	6.4177	6.1446	5.8892	5.6502	5.4262	5.2161	5.0188	4.8332	4.6586	4.4941	4.3389	4.1925
11	10.3676	9.7868	9.2526	8.7605	8.3064	7.8869	7.4987	7.1390	6.8052	6.4951	6.2065	5.9377	5.6869	5.4527	5.2337	5.0286	4.8364	4.6560	4.4865	4.3271
12	11.2551	10.5753	9.9540	9.3851	8.8633	8.3838	7.9427	7.5361	7.1607	6.8137	6.4924	6.1944	5.9176	5.6603	5.4206	5.1971	4.9884	4.7932	4.6105	4.4392
13	12.1337	11.3484	10.6350	9.9856	9.3936	8.8527	8.3577	7.9038	7.4869	7.1034	6.7499	6.4235	6.1218	5.8424	5.5831	5.3423	5.1183	4.9095	4.7147	4.5327
14	13.0037	12.1062	11.2961	10.5631	9.8986	9.2950	8.7455	8.2442	7.7862	7.3667	6.9819	6.6282	6.3025	6.0021	5.7245	5.4675	5.2293	5.0081	4.8023	4.6106
15	13.8651	12.8493	11.9379	11.1184	10.3797	9.7122	9.1079	8.5595	8.0607	7.6061	7.1909	6.8109	6.4624	6.1422	5.8474	5.5755	5.3242	5.0916	4.8759	4.6755
16	14.7179	13.5777	12.5611	11.6523	10.8378	10.1059	9.4466	8.8514	8.3126	7.8237	7.3792	6.9740	6.6039	6.2651	5.9542	5.6685	5.4053	5.1624	4.9377	4.7296
17	15.5623	14.2919	13.1661	12.1657	11.2741	10.4773	9.7632	9.1216	8.5436	8.0216	7.5488	7.1196	6.7291	6.3729	6.0472	5.7487	5.4746	5.2223	4.9897	4.7746
18	16.3983	14.9920	13.7535	12.6593	11.6896	10.8276	10.0591	9.3719	8.7556	8.2014	7.7016	7.2497	6.8399	6.4674	6.1280	5.8178	5.5339	5.2732	5.0333	4.8122
19	17.2260	15.6785	14.3238	13.1339	12.0853	11.1581	10.3356	9.6036	8.9501	8.3649	7.8393	7.3658	6.9380	6.5504	6.1982	5.8775	5.5845	5.3162	5.0700	4.8435
20	18.0456	16.3514	14.8775	13.5903	12.4622	11.4699	10.5940	9.8181	9.1285	8.5136	7.9633	7.4694	7.0248	6.6231	6.2593	5.9288	5.6278	5.3527	5.1009	4.8696
21	18.8570	17.0112	15.4150	14.0292	12.8212	11.7641	10.8355	10.0168	9.2922	8.6487	8.0751	7.5620	7.1016	6.6870	6.3125	5.9731	5.6648	5.3837	5.1268	4.8913
22	19.6604	17.6580	15.9369	14.4511	13.1630	12.0416	11.0612	10.2007	9.4424	8.7715	8.1757	7.6446	7.1695	6.7429	6.3587	6.0113	5.6964	5.4099	5.1486	4.9094
23	20.4558	18.2922	16.4436	14.8568	13.4886	12.3034	11.2722	10.3711	9.5802	8.8832	8.2664	7.7184	7.2297	6.7921	6.3988	6.0442	5.7234	5.4321	5.1668	4.9245
24	21.2434	18.9139	16.9355	15.2470	13.7986	12.5504	11.4693	10.5288	9.7066	8.9847	8.3481	7.7843	7.2829	6.8351	6.4338	6.0726	5.7465	5.4509	5.1822	4.9371
25	22.0232	19.5235	17.4131	15.6221	14.0939	12.7834	11.6536	10.6748	9.8226	9.0770	8.4217	7.8431	7.3300	6.8729	6.4641	6.0971	5.7662	5.4669	5.1951	4.9476
26	22.7952	20.1210	17.8768	15.9828	14.3752	13.0032	11.8258	10.8100	9.9290	9.1609	8.4881	7.8957	7.3717	6.9061	6.4906	6.1182	5.7831	5.4804	5.2060	4.9563
27	23.5596	20.7069	18.3270	16.3296	14.6430	13.2105	11.9867	10.9352	10.0266	9.2372	8.5478	7.9426	7.4086	6.9352	6.5135	6.1364	5.7975	5.4919	5.2151	4.9636
28	24.3164	21.2813	18.7641	16.6631	14.8981	13.4062	12.1371	11.0511	10.1161	9.3066	8.6016	7.9844	7.4412	6.9607	6.5335	6.1520	5.8099	5.5016	5.2228	4.9697
29	25.0658	21.8444	19.1885	16.9837	15.1411	13.5907	12.2777	11.1584	10.1983	9.3696	8.6501	8.0218	7.4701	6.9830	6.5509	6.1656	5.8204	5.5098	5.2292	4.9747
30	25.8077	22.3965	19.6004	17.2920	15.3725	13.7648	12.4090	11.2578	10.2737	9.4269	8.6938	8.0552	7.4957	7.0027	6.5660	6.1772	5.8294	5.5168	5.2347	4.9789
40	32.8347	27.3555	23.1148	19.7928	17.1591	15.0463	13.3317	11.9246	10.7574	9.7791	8.9511	8.2438	7.6344	7.1050	6.6418	6.2335	5.8713	5.5482	5.2582	4.9966
50	39.1961	31.4236	25.7298	21.4822	18.2559	15.7619	13.8007	12.2335	10.9617	9.9148	9.0417	8.3045	7.6752	7.1327	6.6605	6.2463	5.8801	5.5541	5.2623	4.9995

Estimating Social Security Benefits

B

The Social Security Administration (SSA) has a basic benefit credited to you right now earned for your retirement, for a period of disability, or for your survivors, provided that you qualify based on the number of credits of coverage you have earned. The level of benefits received from Social Security depends on your income in past years that was subject to the Federal Insurance Contributions Act (FICA) taxes, commonly known as Social Security taxes. The tables that follow provide the authors' estimates of Social Security benefits for various income levels. They are based on 1999 Social Security benefit levels and allow you to estimate your own benefits by using your personal income data.

Social Security Retirement Benefits

To be eligible for Social Security retirement benefits, any worker born after 1928 must have earned 40 credits of coverage. As noted in the text, it is possible to receive four credits per year. In 1999, a worker would earn one quarter credit for each $740 of income subject to Social Security taxes. Dependent children, spouses caring for dependent children, and retired spouses at age 62 (including former spouses if the marriage lasted at least ten years) may also collect benefits based on the eligibility of the retired worker. To obtain figures more specific than those given in Table B.1, contact the Social Security Administration for a personal earnings and benefits estimate statement as described in Chapter 18.

You can use Table B.1 to estimate a person's Social Security retirement benefits in today's dollars, assuming the retiree worked steadily and received average pay raises and retired at the full benefit retirement age. Note that if more than one person would receive a benefit under the retiree's account (a retiree and spouse, for example), the amount of the second person's benefit would be one-half of the retiree's benefit, giving a total family benefit 50 percent higher than the figure in Table B.1.

Social Security Disability Benefits

Social Security will pay disability benefits to an insured worker, dependent children up to age 18 (or 19, if the child is still in high school), a spouse caring for a dependent child who is younger than age 16 or disabled, and a spouse (even if

Table B.1

Monthly Retirement Benefits at age 65 in Today's Dollars

	Present Annual Earnings				
	$15,000	$24,000	$36,000	$48,000	$72,600 and Higher
Per month	$675	$918	$1,203	$1,299	$1,379
Per year	$8,100	$11,016	$14,436	$15,588	$16,548
As a percentage of income	54.0%	45.9%	40.1%	32.5%	22.8%

divorced, but not remarried, provided the marriage lasted ten years) aged 62 or older. The benefit amount will depend on two factors. The first factor is the eligibility of the disabled worker. To be eligible for disability benefits, workers need at least 40 credits of coverage under Social Security, with at least 20 of the credits attained in the previous ten years (depending on year of birth). A worker younger than age 31 must have attained at least six credits, or one more than one-half of the total credits possible after age 21, whichever is greater. (For example, a 26-year-old worker would have five years, or 20 credits, possible and would need ten credits of coverage.) The second factor affecting benefit levels is the pre-disability income of the covered individual that was subject to the FICA tax.

You can use Table B.2 to estimate an individual's Social Security disability benefits in today's dollars, assuming the disabled person worked steadily and received average pay raises. The estimated family benefit is 150 percent of the benefit for the covered worker.

Table B.2

Monthly Disability Benefits

	Present Annual Earnings				
	$15,000	$24,000	$36,000	$48,000	$72,600 and Higher
Individual benefit per month	$687	$932	$1,215	$1,301	$1,377
Individual benefit per year	$8,244	$11,184	$14,850	$15,612	$16,524
As a percentage of income	55.0%	46.6%	40.5%	32.5%	22.8%
Maximum family benefit per month	$1,030	$1,398	$1,822	$1,951	$2,065
Maximum family benefit per year	$12,360	$16,776	$21,864	$23,412	$24,780
As a percentage of income	82.4%	69.9%	60.7%	48.8%	34.1%

Social Security Survivor's Benefits

Social Security will pay benefits to surviving children younger than age 18 (or 19, if the child is still in high school), to a surviving spouse (even if divorced from the deceased, but not remarried) caring for surviving children under age 16, and to a surviving spouse (even if divorced, if the marriage lasted at least ten years) aged 60 or older. Two factors are important. The first factor is the eligibility of the covered worker. The deceased worker must have accrued as many as 40 credits of coverage to be "fully insured," depending on his or her year of birth. Workers who have earned at least as many credits of coverage as years since turning age 21 will be fully insured as well. Other individuals may be considered "currently insured" if they have six credits of coverage in the previous 13 calendar credits. The survivors of currently insured workers receive limited types of benefits compared to those of fully insured workers. The second factor is the covered worker's level of earnings, as indicated in Table B.3.

You can use Table B.3 to estimate monthly survivor's benefits from Social Security in today's dollars for eligible surviving family members. The table assumes that the deceased worker worked steadily and received average pay raises.

Table B.3

Monthly Survivor's Benefits if You Died in 1999

	Present Annual Earnings				
	$15,000	**$24,000**	**$36,000**	**$48,000**	**$72,600 and Higher**
Individual benefit per month*	$504	$685	$891	$955	$1,011
Individual benefit per year	$6,048	$8220	$10,692	$11,460	$12,132
As a percentage of income	40.3%	34.2%	29.7%	32.5%	16.7%
Maximum family benefit per month	$1,094	$1,487	$1,933	$2,072	$2,194
Maximum family benefit per year	$13,128	$17,844	$23,196	$24,864	$26,328
As a percentage of income	87.5%	74.3%	64.4%	51.8%	36.3%

* A surviving spouse aged 65 or older would receive a benefit approximately one-third higher than these figures.

Careers in Personal Financial Planning and Counseling

Personal financial planning and counseling is a professional field that addresses the financial concerns of individuals and families. The need for sound advice in personal finance is becoming increasingly apparent to the public, inspiring ever more well-qualified people to enter this growing service profession.

Academic study in this field provides education and training for professionals who hope to offer counseling, education, or advice on individual and family financial matters, such as debt management, budgeting, financial management strategies, and fundamental financial planning opportunities. Financial services providers focus on the evolving role of personal finances in the lives of U.S. families, considering how people should spend, save, manage, protect, and invest their resources. Careers in the financial services industry—in business, government, and the nonprofit sectors—have been identified as terrific employment opportunities for at least the next two decades.

Factors That Have Led to Growth in the Field of Personal Financial Planning and Counseling

Just 35 years ago, the average U.S. consumer did not have any credit cards, seldom owned stocks, bonds, or life insurance, and either opened a non–interest-bearing checking account at a local bank or did not have a checking account at all. Many people planned on working for the same employer until they retired, with their jobs typically providing some health care benefits and perhaps a small pension.

Today, consumer choices among financial products and services have never been greater. The problems, challenges, and opportunities in personal financial matters facing individuals and families can seem overwhelming. People must select and pay for their health care plans and take responsibility for investing thousands of dollars every year into their personal pension plans. Although mistakes in either area can prove very costly, the public remains poorly informed about these complicated areas of financial decision making.

Individuals and families today face an increasingly deregulated personal financial marketplace, the constant introduction of new financial products, a wider availability of choices in products and services, loss of real spendable income due to inflation, higher costs for vital necessities (i.e., housing, transportation, and education), substantial housing mobility, employment dislocations because of regional economic instability with the resulting need for job retraining, and a growing dependence on two incomes to make financial ends meet and live a chosen lifestyle. At the same time, marketplace transactions have become much more impersonal because of the use of automated teller machines, bill paying by computer, mail-order catalogs, mega-shopping malls, home shopping via television, and financial transactions on the Internet.

These changes increase the likelihood of making errors in personal finances. These mistakes occur, in part, because everyone is not equally adept or successful at handling personal finances. Mismanagement in the areas of credit, planned spending, risk management, and investing can have serious negative results.

While the personal financial practices of the U.S. family undergo this transformation, most people still rely upon themselves or other family members as their primary source of advice about financial matters. Many consumers know few sources of financial help available in their communities—let alone any unbiased sources. Because so few people are educated in personal financial management, most individuals and families are ill-prepared to deal with today's financial problems, challenges, and opportunities. Despite a general lack of educational preparation in personal financial management, however, the responsibility for a person's financial well-being today rests squarely upon the individual and family.

The Role of a Professional in Personal Financial Planning and Counseling

In response to these needs and opportunities, a sharp increase has been noted in the demand for qualified professionals who are willing to enter the rapidly growing field of personal financial planning and counseling to become financial services providers.

Career opportunities for professionals in financial planning and counseling historically have been divided into two areas: (1) financial planning and (2) budget/credit counseling. Individuals in financial planning occupations usually sell financial products (such as life insurance, stocks, or mutual funds) and offer planning advice (in the areas of cash-flow management, risk management, and capital appreciation for retirement) to middle- and high-income clients. Members of the budget/credit counseling occupations generally advise clients of all income levels who are experiencing some type of financial difficulty (such as credit abuse) or facing a basic challenge (such as the need to accumulate funds for a child's education).

The *financial services provider,* or *financial counselor,* works with clients in a proactive manner to aid in financial decision making and to help implement those decisions. The definition of a financial counselor has evolved through the years, but now describes a professional capable of offering advice to those who need assistance with budgeting and credit problems as well as to those who need guidance in financial planning and decision making. Thus, this role encompasses the duties of both financial planners and budget/credit counselors. The prototype of this newer type of financial services provider is often employed in a company's employee assistance program (EAP), where he or she handles inquiries on all types of financial concerns of employees. The well-educated financial services provider of today and tomorrow can provide remedial and preventive advice to individuals and families regarding debt management, financial budgeting, and fundamental financial planning opportunities. Their clients may or may not already be managing their personal finances effectively. Keep in mind, however, that most job opportunities today remain divided into the traditional financial planning or the budget/credit counseling occupations, where the financial planner offers suggestions on productive financial opportunities while the budget/credit counselor helps people resolve problems with overspending and poor budgeting techniques.

Graduates from academic programs who enter professional careers in personal financial planning and counseling should take a holistic perspective to financial concerns in helping clients resolve specific financial problems, take advantage of unique planning opportunities, and integrate all aspects of a client's finances into a comprehensive financial plan. This comprehensive approach to resource management distinguishes personal financial counselors from credit counselors, insurance agents, and stockbrokers, each of whom might focus on a single area of a client's finances rather than the client's total financial needs.

Today's professionally educated financial services provider should be able to provide counseling, education, and advice to families on financial matters, such as utilizing human and community assets, obtaining entitlements, resolving credit and budgeting problems, managing cash, and dealing with risk management, retirement planning, and capital accumulation. The financial services provider can present issues, alternatives, and possible courses of action for clients to consider, with the overall goal of empowering individuals and families to function in their own self-interest. Importantly, the financial services provider also tries to educate and empower clients so that they can achieve their goals themselves.

In addition, the financial services provider can help individuals and families determine whether and how they can meet their life goals through proper management of financial and human resources. The immediate task is to help clients articulate goals and identify problems that may impede progress toward achievement of those goals. The financial services provider then helps the client determine whether the goals are achievable and how to accomplish them. Next, the financial services provider coordinates the implementation of a financial plan to improve the likelihood that the client will attain his or her immediate goals. In most cases, the financial services provider periodically reviews the progress of clients and, if needed, assists them in making any revisions necessary.

In advising clients, the financial services provider tries to point out how decisions and actions undertaken at one stage of life affect economic security at other stages of life and ultimately affect their long-term quality of life. If necessary, both remedial and preventive advice is offered, as well as productive planning suggestions. The advice provided by a financial services provider is intended to help clients position their assets, debts, and income so that they can efficiently and effectively meet their personal and family financial objectives.

In counseling people about their finances, a number of sensitive issues may arise with clients, occasionally including unresolved conflicts, which may result in the financial services provider making appropriate referrals to other specialized professionals as well as social services agencies. Thus, in addition to clients, financial services providers often interact with professionals employed in social service and government agencies, educational institutions, legal firms, and a variety of businesses.

Major activities of financial service providers include responding to client inquiries; offering credit and budgeting advice; proposing a budgeting format; contacting creditors and public assistance organizations (if necessary); explaining the provisions of an employee benefits package; preparing reports for and about clients; making productive financial planning suggestions (perhaps on how to provide for a child's education, reduce income taxes, or invest funds for retirement); developing promotional and informational programs; writing news releases, informational brochures, and newsletters; attending seminars and workshops to update the provider's personal knowledge of financial issues; and speaking to various consumer, employee, educational, government, business, and professional groups.

Professional Certifications

Professional certifications are obtained by many successful financial service providers who have voluntarily undergone training and met various qualifications. For those in financial planning occupations, these certifications include Certified Financial Planner (CFP), Chartered Financial Consultant (ChFC), Certified Financial Analyst (CFA), Registry of Financial Planning Practitioners, Registered Investment Advisor (RIA), Certified Employee Benefits Specialist (CEBS), Certified Professional Insurance Woman (CPIW), and master of science (MS) degree in personal financial management. More than 90 academic programs across the United States are registered with the International Board of Standards and Practices for Certified Financial Planners, Inc. Graduates of IBCFP-registered curricula are automatically entitled to take the Certified Financial Planner (CFP) examination. For members of the budget/credit counseling occupations, two popular certifications are CCCS and AFC. The Certified Consumer Credit Counselor (CCCS) is available to counselors working in nonprofit consumer credit counseling agencies. The Chartered Mutual Fund Counselor (CMFC) serves that industry. The Accredited Financial Counselor (AFC) certification, offered through the Association for Financial Counseling and Planning Education,* is available to all financial service providers.

Career Opportunities

The financial services industry, of which careers in budget/credit counseling and financial planning constitute but one part, has been identified as one of the brighter career prospects in the new century. This expanding field offers career opportunities for well-educated financial service providers with social service agencies, military bases, government agencies, financial institutions, stock and insurance brokerage businesses, financial planning firms, and private practice.

The financial services provider is sometimes the only member of a team with special expertise in financial matters, and colleagues may rely on him or her

---

* Association for Financial Counseling and Planning Education, 6099 Riverside Drive, Suite 100, Dublin, OH 43017; telephone: (614) 798-4107; fax (614) 798-6560; e-mail: request@afcpe.org; Internet: *www.afcpe.org*.

accordingly. A growing number of large organizations employ such a financial services provider who informs, updates, and educates the firm's other workers. In other employment situations, three or four (or more) financial service providers with similar backgrounds and job responsibilities may work in the same office.

Appropriate entry-level employment positions for financial counseling graduates include credit counselor, budget counselor, consumer credit counseling service operations manager, employee assistance counselor, pre-retirement counselor, financial counselor, military financial educator, consumer relations coordinator, housing counselor, loan coordinator, loan officer, new accounts representative, debt collections coordinator, credit investigator, claims representative, bankruptcy court service worker, extension agent, coordinator of financial counseling volunteers, stockbroker, insurance broker, and financial planner.

Suitable entry-level positions for financial counseling graduates can be found within a number of nonprofit and service-oriented employers: consumer credit counseling services, credit unions, family service agencies, armed forces family/community service agencies, corporate and government employee assistance programs, employee benefits counseling firms, college financial aid offices, social welfare agencies, hospitals, consumer finance companies, mortgage lenders, corporate credit departments, credit bureaus, credit collection agencies, juvenile and domestic relations courts, marriage counseling firms, mental health associations, community programs for the elderly/low-income workers, ministerial organizations, divorce mediation firms, cooperative extension services, labor unions, as bankruptcy attorneys, U.S. bankruptcy courts, the Federal Home Administration, the Farmers Home Administration, Housing and Urban Development offices, banks, savings and loan associations, insurance companies, and financial planning companies.

In addition, many potential entry-level positions and employers exist in the financial services industry, such as account representative at a brokerage firm, customer service agent at a mutual fund company, accounts officer at a bank or savings and loan association, sales representative for a real estate agency or an insurance company, and junior associate at a financial planning firm. Positions in the financial services field are likely to be found in both small and large organizations. Potential employers are located throughout the country, in both small and large communities.

Professionals in the financial services industry may enjoy lifelong career development opportunities. Advanced positions in middle management require several years of successful financial service provider experience. Such managers direct and train other financial service providers, represent the organization at meetings, work with advisory committees, monitor legislative and regulatory issues, address legislative hearings, and reasonably advocate the interests of personal financial planning and counseling clients.

According to many job-satisfaction studies, financial service providers are challenged and satisfied by their work. Salaries for entry-level employment positions vary. Entry-level positions for those employed in nonprofit credit/budget counseling positions usually pay less than $20,000 annually; comparable positions in government or business may begin around $25,000 but can quickly rise to $50,000 or more. In general, financial service providers believe that they are making a significant contribution to their clients' economic well-being.

How to Use a Financial Calculator* D

M ost personal finance decisions involve calculations of the time value of money. Three methods are used to compute this value: time value of money tables (such as those found in Appendix A), computer software programs, and financial calculators.

Compared with time value of money tables and computer software programs, financial calculators offer some relative advantages. Using calculators provides more accurate answers than time value tables. In addition, a person using a calculator can find the answers more rapidly and with more flexibility than someone using tables for calculating the time value of money. While computer software programs may handle more sophisticated calculations, the calculators are easier to access, carry around, and learn how to use, and they are considerably less expensive. Using financial calculators may be the most practical way to compute the time value of money for personal finance decisions and obtain satisfactory results.

Financial calculators—also called business calculators—can not only calculate the time value of money, but also perform statistical, business, and basic arithmetic calculations. In this appendix, we focus on the calculation of the time value of money for personal finance decisions.

A variety of brands of financial calculators are available. The most commonly used and least expensive ones (less than $35) are Sharp's EL-733A, Hewlett-Packard's HP-10B, and Texas Instruments' BA-II PLUS. This appendix will illustrate how to perform financial calculations with these three brands of calculators.

This appendix is divided into four sections. The first section discusses the preparations necessary before financial calculations can be made. Because all financial calculations will fall into one of two categories [the time value of a single amount (lump sum) or a series of equal amounts (annuity)], the second and third sections, respectively, illustrate how to perform these calculations. The last section demonstrates how to deal with more complicated calculations that require multistep procedures. For more comprehensive information on other functions of financial calculators, refer to the user's manuals provided by the financial calculator manufacturers.

Preparations for Personal Finance Calculations

The preparations required before performing personal finance calculations include clearing the register and setting the decimal places, compounding

---

* Prepared by Jing J. Xiao, Associate Professor, University of Rhode Island.

methods, and financial calculation mode. Other related issues include changing signs and clearing error messages.

Clearing the Register

Make sure to clear all memory registers before making a calculation. Otherwise, the results could be wrong. To clear the memory registers, use the following key strokes:

Purpose	EL-773A	HP-10B	BA-II PLUS
Clear memory registers	0 $\boxed{\text{X}\rightarrow\text{M}}$	■ $\boxed{\text{Clear All}}$	$\boxed{\text{2nd}}$ $\boxed{\text{MEM}}$ $\boxed{\text{ENTER}}$ $\boxed{\text{2nd}}$ $\boxed{\text{QUIT}}$ $\boxed{\text{2nd}}$ $\boxed{\text{CLR Work}}$
Clear TVM registers	$\boxed{\text{2ndF}}$ $\boxed{\text{CA}}$	■ $\boxed{\text{Clear All}}$	$\boxed{\text{2nd}}$ $\boxed{\text{QUIT}}$ $\boxed{\text{2nd}}$ $\boxed{\text{CLR TVM}}$

Note: The ■ key for HP-10B refers to the square orange key on the calculator.

Setting Decimal Places

A fixed or floating decimal place may be set before performing a calculation. The following two examples demonstrate how to accomplish this action.

Purpose	EL-773A	HP-10B	BA-II PLUS
Set 4 decimal places	$\boxed{\text{2ndF}}$ $\boxed{\text{TAB}}$ 4	■ $\boxed{\text{DISP}}$ 4	$\boxed{\text{2nd}}$ $\boxed{\text{FORMAT}}$ 4 $\boxed{\text{ENTER}}$ $\boxed{\text{2nd}}$ $\boxed{\text{QUIT}}$
Set a floating decimal point	$\boxed{\text{2ndF}}$ $\boxed{\text{TAB}}$.	■ $\boxed{\text{DISP}}$.	$\boxed{\text{2nd}}$ $\boxed{\text{FORMAT}}$ 9 $\boxed{\text{ENTER}}$ $\boxed{\text{2nd}}$ $\boxed{\text{QUIT}}$

Setting Compounding Methods

HP-10B and BA-II PLUS require you to preset the compounding methods before personal finance calculations, unlike EL-773A. The following examples illustrate how to preset compounding methods annually or monthly (daily and other compounding periods are also possible). Failure to preset the correct compounding method will result in erroneous answers.

Purpose	EL-773A	HP-10B	BA-II PLUS
Compounding annually	not required	1 ■ $\boxed{\text{P/YR}}$	$\boxed{\text{2nd}}$ $\boxed{\text{P/Y}}$ 1 $\boxed{\text{ENTER}}$ $\boxed{\text{2nd}}$ $\boxed{\text{QUIT}}$
Compounding monthly	not required	12 ■ $\boxed{\text{P/YR}}$	$\boxed{\text{2nd}}$ $\boxed{\text{P/Y}}$ 12 $\boxed{\text{ENTER}}$ $\boxed{\text{2nd}}$ $\boxed{\text{QUIT}}$

Setting Financial Calculation Mode

HP-10B and BA-II PLUS can access financial calculations any time. To access financial calculations for EL-773A, use the key sequence: 2ndF MODE.

Changing Signs

Conventionally, all cash outflows or payments carry a negative sign, and all cash inflows or receipts carry a positive sign. To input a negative number, hit the +/– key after entering the number. Entering a number with a wrong sign will result in an incorrect answer or error message.

Clearing Error Messages

The following messages indicate that an error has occurred and explain how to clear the error messages:

	EL-773A	HP-10B	BA-II PLUS
Error message on screen	E	no Solution	Error 5
Clear error message	C · CE	C	CE/C

The Time Value of a Single Amount

Calculating the time value of a single amount always involves four factors: present value, future value, interest rate, and time periods. The personal finance question usually asks for one factor, given the other three factors. On HP-10B and BA-II PLUS, make sure to use the correct compounding method (annually, monthly, or other). For EL-773A, remember to convert the annual interest rate into a monthly (or other) rate when monthly (or other) compounding frequencies methods are used.

Example 1: Future Value of an Investment

If you invest $500 at an annual interest rate of 15 percent, how much will you have at the end of a 12-year period?

Input/Result	EL-773A	HP-10B	BA-II PLUS
Present value	500 +/– PV	500 +/– PV	500 +/– PV
Time period: year	12 n	12 N	12 N
Interest rate	15 i	15 I/YR	15 I/Y
Result: future value	COMP FV 2675.13	FV 2675.13	CPT FV 2675.13

Thus, at the end of a 12-year period, you will receive $2675.13.

Example 1 can be rephrased in three other ways: (1) If you invest $500 at an annual interest rate of 15 percent, in how many years will you receive $2675.13?; (2) If you invest $500, what should be the interest rate if you receive $2675.13 at the end of a 12-year period?; and (3) If you want to receive $2675.13 given an annual interest rate of 15 percent at the end of a 12-year period, how much should you invest now?

Based on Example 1, can you figure out answers for the three questions with the calculator? Finding the answers may give you a better understanding of how to use a financial calculator.

Following are more examples dealing with the time value of a single amount.

Example 2: Present Value of an Investment Goal

If you want $30,000 for a newborn child's college education 18 years from now, and if a current investment opportunity yields 7 percent, how much should you invest now?

Input/Result	EL-773A	HP-10B	BA-II PLUS
Future value	30000 FV	30000 FV	30000 FV
Time period: year	18 n	18 N	18 N
Interest rate	7 i	7 I/YR	7 I/Y
Result: present value	COMP PV −8875.92	PV −8875.92	CPT PV −8875.92

To achieve the investment goal, the initial amount to be invested should be $8876.

Example 3: Retirement Needs

If you need $250,000 for retirement purposes, and you would like to invest $36,000 now and let it grow for 25 years, what is the required annual interest rate?

Input/Result	EL-773A	HP-10B	BA-II PLUS
Present value	36000 +/− PV	36000 +/− PV	36000 +/− PV
Future value	250000 FV	250000 FV	250000 FV
Time period: year	25 n	25 N	25 N
Result: interest rate	COMP i 8.06	I/YR 8.06	CPT I/Y 8.06

To meet the retirement needs, the interest rate should be at least 8.06%.

Example 4: Impact of Inflation on the Value of an Asset

If a car is now priced at $20,000, how many years will it take for its price to reach $24,000 at a 5 percent annual inflation rate?

Input/Result	EL-773A	HP-10B	BA-II PLUS
Present value	20000 [PV]	20000 [PV]	20000 [PV]
Future value	24000 [+/-] [FV]	24000 [+/-] [FV]	24000 [+/-] [FV]
Interest rate	5 [i]	5 [I/YR]	5 [I/Y]
Result: time period	[COMP] [n] 3.74	[N] 3.74	[CPT] [N] 3.74

The car price will reach $24,000 in 3.74 years.

The Time Value of an Annuity (a Series of Equal Amounts)

Two general types of personal finance questions involve annuities. The first type of question focuses on an outflow of money in equal payments, such as an auto loan, home mortgage payment, or contributions to a retirement plan. The second type of question concerns an inflow of money in equal amounts, such as receiving monthly benefit checks from a retirement plan or government agency.

Calculating the time value of an annuity involves four factors: a series of equal payments (annuity), present value or future value of total amount, interest rate, and time periods. Many personal finance questions will ask for one factor given the other three factors. Thus, if you can identify the factors presented in a problem, understand the given factors, and know what factor you are calculating, you will comprehend the problem and solve it accurately.

But beware! Before calculating personal finance problems, be sure to clear the memory registers and to use the correct compounding methods.

Example 5: Future Value of Retirement Savings

If you are 49 years old and put $7000 per year from current income in a savings program yielding 8 percent, how much will you accumulate when you retire 16 years later? In this problem, you are given the annuity (a series of equal payments), interest rate, and time periods. You are asked to calculate the future value of the total retirement contributions and interest income.

Input/Result	EL-773A	HP-10B	BA-II PLUS
Each payment	7000 [+/-] [PMT]	7000 [+/-] [PMT]	7000 [+/-] [PMT]
Time period: year	16 [n]	16 [N]	16 [N]
Interest rate	8 [i]	8 [I/YR]	8 [I/Y]
Result: FV of total amount	[COMP] [FV] 212269.98	[FV] 212269.98	[CPT] [FV] 212269.98

You will accumulate about $212,270 after 16 years.

Example 6: Present Value of Loan Payments

If you acquire a car loan of $20,000 at an interest rate of 8 percent for four years, what is the amount of your monthly payment?

Input/Result	EL-773A	HP-10B	BA-II PLUS
PV of loan amount	20000 PV	20000 PV	20000 PV
Time period: month	48 n	48 N	48 N
Interest rate	8 ÷ 12 = i	8 I/YR	8 I/Y
Result: each payment	COMP PMT −488.26	PMT −488.26	CPT PMT −488.26

The monthly payment would be $488.26.

Example 7: The Annual Percentage Rate of a Loan

If you have a car loan of $20,000 with a monthly payment of $400 for five years, what is the annual percentage rate (APR)?

Input/Result	EL-773A	HP-10B	BA-II PLUS
PV of loan amount	20000 PV	20000 PV	20000 PV
Time period: month	60 n	60 N	60 N
Each payment	400 +/− PMT	400 +/− PMT	400 +/− PMT
Result: interest rate	COMP i .618	I/YR 7.42	CPT I/Y 7.42

The APR would be 7.42 percent. The EL-773A shows the monthly rate of 0.618 percent, which must be multiplied by 12 (months) to obtain the annual rate of 7.42 percent.

Example 8: Monthly Payment of a Fixed-Rate Mortgage Loan

If you take out a mortgage loan of $120,000 at a fixed rate of 8 percent for 30 years, what is the monthly payment?

Input/Result	EL-773A	HP-10B	BA-II PLUS
PV of loan amount	120000 PV	120000 PV	120000 PV
Time period: month	360 n	360 N	360 N
Interest rate	8 ÷ 12 = i	8 I/YR	8 I/Y
Result: each payment	COMP PMT −880.52	PMT −880.52	CPT PMT −880.52

The monthly payment would be $880.52.

You may want to obtain more information about the mortgage loan payment before clearing the data from your financial calculator. For example, to find out the loan amortization amount at the fiftieth payment, hit the following keys:

Input/Result	EL-773A		HP-10B		BA-II PLUS	
50th payment	50		50 INPUT ■ AMORT		2nd Amort 50 ENTER	
					↓ 50 ENTER	
Results:	(Principal)		(Interest)		(Balance)	
	AMRT −111.50		= −769.01		↓ 115240.58	
	(Interest)		(Principal)		(Principal)	
	AMRT −769.01		= −111.50		↓ −111.50	
	(Balance)		(Balance)		(Interest)	
	AMRT 115240.58		= 115240.58		↓ −769.01	

The principal and interest would be $111.50 and $769.01, respectively, and the unpaid balance would be $115,240.58 when payment 50 is made.

To review the fraction of your first 50 payments that went for interest and the portion used for the repayment of principal, you may use the following key sequences:

Input/Result	EL-773A		HP-10B		BA-II PLUS	
Payment 1–50	1 P_1/P_2 50 P_1/P_2		1 INPUT 50 ■ AMORT		2nd Amort 1 ENTER	
					↓ 50 ENTER	
Results:	(Principal)		(Interest)		(Balance)	
	ACC −4759.42		= −39266.45		↓ 115240.58	
	(Interest)		(Principal)		(Principal)	
	ACC −39266.45		= −4759.42		↓ −4759.42	
	(Balance)		(Balance)		(Interest)	
	Not available		= 115240.58		↓ −39266.45	

The first 50 payments for principal and interest would be $4759.42 and $39,266.45, respectively, and the unpaid balance would be $115,240.58.

Example 9: Yield to Maturity for Bonds

Calculating the yield to maturity (YTM) for bonds is similar to the calculation of annual percentage rates (APRs) for annuities. If you paid $740 for a 20-year bond with a face value of $1000 and a promised interest payment of 7 percent ($70 annually), the YTM can be calculated as follows:

Input/Result	EL-773A	HP-10B	BA-II PLUS
PV of market price	740 +/− PV	740 +/− PV	740 +/− PV
Time period: years to maturity	20 n	20 N	20 N
Interest payment	70 PMT	70 PMT	70 PMT
FV of face value	1000 FV	1000 FV	1000 FV
Result: yield to maturity	COMP i 10.07	I/YR 10.07	CPT I/Y 10.07

The yield to maturity would be 10.07 percent.

More Complicated Calculations

The following examples demonstrate how to use multiple-step procedures to solve more complicated problems.

Example 10: Home Equity Loan with Variable Interest Rates

Assume you take a home equity loan of $12,000 for four years with a variable interest rate. If the interest rate is 11 percent for the first two years and 12 percent for the last two years, what is the monthly payment? To solve this problem: calculate the monthly payment in the first two years, calculate the unpaid balance at the twenty-fourth payment, and figure the monthly payment during the last two years.

1. Monthly payment in the first two years.

Input/Result	EL-773A	HP-10B	BA-II PLUS
PV of loan amount	12000 PV	12000 PV	12000 PV
Time period: month	48 n	48 N	48 N
Interest rate	11 ÷ 12 = i	11 I/YR	11 I/Y
Result: each payment	COMP PMT −310.15	PMT −310.15	CPT PMT −310.15

The monthly payment for the first two years would be $310.15. Do not clear the data; hit the following keys:

2. The unpaid balance at payment 24.

Input/Result	EL-773A	HP-10B	BA-II PLUS
24th payment 24		24 INPUT ■ AMORT	2nd Amort 24 ENTER ↓ 24 ENTER
Results:	(Principal) AMRT −246.89 (Interest) AMRT −63.26 (Balance) AMRT 6654.38	(Interest) = −63.26 (Principal) = −246.89 (Balance) = 6654.38	(Balance) ↓ 6654.38 (Principal) ↓ −246.89 (Interest) ↓ −63.26

After payment 24 (at the end of the first two years), the unpaid balance would be $6654.38. Clear the memory register, then perform the following calculation:

3. Monthly payment in the last two years.

Input/Result	EL-773A	HP-10B	BA-II PLUS
PV of loan amount	6654.38 PV	6654.38 PV	6654.38 PV
Time period: month	24 n	24 N	24 N
Interest rate	12 ÷ 12 = i	12 I/YR	12 I/Y
Result: each payment	COMP PMT −313.24	PMT −313.24	CPT PMT −313.24

The monthly payment for the last two years would be $313.24.

Example 11: Life Insurance Needs

If your income-replacement needs are $27,000 per year for 30 years, your other needs total $114,000, and your surviving spouse can receive monthly Social Security benefits of $1800 for 15 years, what is your life insurance need, assuming the inflation rate is 4 percent? To solve this problem, you need to calculate four items: total income-replacement needs, total needs, total government benefits, and life insurance needs.

1. Total income-replacement needs.

Input/Result	EL-773A	HP-10B	BA-II PLUS
Income replacement payment	27000 `PMT`	27000 `PMT`	27000 `PMT`
Time period: year	30 `n`	30 `N`	30 `N`
Inflation rate	4 `i`	4 `I/YR`	4 `I/Y`
Result: PV of total replacement needs	`COMP` `PV` −466885	`PV` −466885	`CPT` `PV` −466885

The total income-replacement needs would be $466,885.

2. Total needs.

The total needs include the total income-replacement needs ($466,885) plus other needs ($114,000), which equals $580,885.

3. Total government benefits.

Input/Result	EL-773A	HP-10B	BA-II PLUS
Annual benefit payment	1800 `x` 12 `=` `PMT`	1800 `x` 12 `=` `PMT`	1800 `x` 12 `=` `PMT`
Time period: year	15 `n`	15 `N`	15 `N`
Inflation rate	4 `i`	4 `I/YR`	4 `I/Y`
Result: PV of total benefits	`COMP` `PV` −240157	`PV` −240157	`CPT` `PV` −240157

The total government benefits would be $240,157.

4. Life insurance needed.

The life insurance needed would be the total needs ($580,885) minus total government benefits ($240,157), which equals $340,728.

Glossary

Acceleration clause A clause that says that after one loan payment is late, the loan is in default and all remaining installments are due and payable at once or on the demand of the lender.

Account exception fees Charges and penalties assessed for what the financial institution considers unusual transactions.

Actual cash value The purchase price of property less depreciation.

Add-on method A traditional and widely used technique for computing interest on installment loans in which the finance charge is added to the principal to calculate the total amount to be repaid.

Adjustable-rate mortgage (ARM) A mortgage in which the interest rate can fluctuate according to an index of interest rates prevalent in the economy as a whole. Also called a *variable-rate mortgage*.

Adjustments to income A select group of legal subtractions from gross income, used when determining income taxes.

Advanced portfolio management Investing in real estate and speculative investments to round out the investment portfolio.

After-tax salary-reduction plan A fringe benefit program that allows employees to make excess salary-reduction contributions to a retirement plan up to a ceiling of 15 percent of annual income that accumulates tax-free. Also called a *corporate thrift program*.

Aggregate limits Limits that place an overall maximum on the total amount of reimursement available under a policy.

Amortization The process of gradually paying off a loan through a series of periodic payments to a lender.

Annual percentage rate (APR) The relative cost of credit on a yearly basis expressed as a percentage rate.

Approximate compound yield (ACY) A formula that provides a measure of the annualized compound growth of any long-term investment.

Arbitration A method of having a dispute between two or more parties resolved by the legally binding decision of an impartial person or persons knowledgeable in the area of controversy.

Automatic income reinvestment A provision of most mutual funds that allows for the automatic reinvestment of ordinary income dividend distributions and capital gains distributions to buy more shares of the fund.

Automobile insurance Insurance that combines liability and property insurance coverage needed by automobile owners and drivers into a single-package policy.

Average-balance account A bank account that assesses a service fee only if the average daily balance of funds in the account drops below a certain level during the time period.

Average daily balance The sum of the outstanding balances owed each day during the billing period divided by the number of days in the period.

Average tax rate A calculated figure showing a person's tax liability as a percentage of total income.

Back-end load A general term describing various deferred charges paid when a shareholder redeems mutual fund shares. Also called *contingent deferred sales charge*.

Balance sheet A statement describing an individual's or family's financial condition at a particular time, showing assets, liabilities, and net worth. Also called *net worth statement*.

Balloon clause A clause in a credit contract that permits the last payment of a loan to be abnormally large in comparison with the other installment payments.

Bankruptcy A constitutionally guaranteed right that permits people (and businesses) to ask a court to find them unable to meet their debts; when such a petition is granted, that party's assets and liabilities are then administered for the benefit of the creditors.

Beneficiary (insurance) The person or organization named in the policy that will receive the life insurance or other benefit payment in the event of the insured's death.

Beneficiary (will) A person receiving property identified in a will.

Benefit period In a disability income insurance policy, the maximum period of time for which benefits will be paid.

Best buy A product or service that, in one's opinion, represents acceptable quality at a fair or low price for that level of quality.

Bid price The amount a brokerage firm is willing to pay for a particular security.

Blue-chip stock Stock of a company that has a good reputation, that is dominant in its industry, that has a long history of both good earnings and consistent cash dividends, that grows at about the same rate as the economy, and whose shares are widely held by individual investors and institutions.

Bond funds Mutual funds whose primary aim is to earn current income without undue risk and pay ordinary income dividend distributions.

Bond-selling price formula A way of estimating the selling price of a bond after interest rates have changed; the annual interest income in dollars divided by the current market interest rate.

Budget A document or set of documents used to record both projected and actual income and expenditures over a period of time.

Budget controls Methods and techniques intended to keep income and expenditures within the planned budget totals.

Budget estimates The recorded amounts in a budget that are planned and expected to be received or spent during a certain period of time.

Budgeting A process of projecting, organizing, monitoring, and controlling future income and expenditures.

Business cycle A wavelike pattern of economic activity that includes temporary phases that undulate from boom to bust: expansion, recession (or depression), and recovery. Also called *economic cycle.*

Callable A feature of most bonds and preferred stocks that permits the issuer to buy the security back from the investor before the maturity date if the issuer so requests. The issuer sometimes repurchases the security by paying a slight surcharge if the price reaches a certain level.

Call option An option contract that gives the option holder the right to buy the optioned asset from the option writer at the striking price.

Capital gain Income received from the sale of a capital asset above the costs incurred to purchase and sell the asset.

Capital improvements Costs incurred in making changes in real property that add to its value.

Cash account An account at a brokerage firm that requires an initial deposit (perhaps as little as $50) and specifies that full settlement is due the brokerage firm within three business days after a buy or sell order has been given.

Cash advance A cash loan from a bank credit card account.

Cash-basis budgeting Financial recordkeeping that recognizes earnings and expenditures when money is actually received or paid out.

Cash-flow calendar A budgeting device on which annual estimated income and expenses are recorded for each budgeting time period in an effort to identify surplus or deficit situations.

Cash management The task of maximizing interest earnings and minimizing fees on all one's funds kept readily available for living expenses, recurring household expenses, emergencies, and saving and investment opportunities.

Cash surrender value The amount received when a cash-value life insurance policy is canceled or surrendered; it represents the cash value minus any back-end load surrender charges.

Cash-value life insurance A policy that not only pays benefits at death but also has a savings element while the insured is alive. Also called *permanent insurance.*

Certificate of deposit (CD) An interest-earning savings instrument offered by an institution that accepts deposits for a fixed amount of time.

Certified check A personal check drawn on an account, on which the financial institution imprints the word *certified,* signifying that the account has sufficient funds to cover its payment.

Certified financial planner (CFP) A person who has been approved by the International Board of Standards and Practices for Certified Financial Planners (IBCFP).

Chapter 7 A type of bankruptcy in which the petitioner is discharged from remaining debts once the bankruptcy trustee has approved the petition and listed the debts and sold assets to pay each creditor a pro-rata share of the debt owed. Also called *straight bankruptcy.*

Chargeback Occurs when a credit card transaction is charged back against the business where the transaction occurred.

Churning A stockbroker's unethical encouragement of an investor to buy and sell securities frequently in an effort to earn large commissions for the broker.

Civil court A state court in which numerous civil matters are resolved and a written record is made of the testimony; the proceedings are completed with the assistance of attorneys, witnesses, a judge, and sometimes a jury.

Claims adjuster A person designated by an insurance company to assess whether a loss is covered and to determine the dollar amount the company will pay.

Claims ratio The percentage of premiums collected by an insurance company that is subsequently paid out to reimburse the losses of insureds.

Closed-end lease A lease in which there is no charge if the end of lease market value of the asset is lower than its originally projected value. Also called a *walkaway lease.*

Closing The process of financially and legally transferring a home to a new buyer, which usually takes place in the office of the lender or an attorney.

Codicil A legal amendment to a will that adds or deletes a bequest or other provision.

Coinsurance cap A stipulation in a health insurance plan that limits the annual out-of-pocket payments of the insured when meeting the coinsurance requirement.

Coinsurance clause A clause in an insurance policy that requires the insured to pay a proportion of any loss suffered.

Collision insurance Automobile insurance that is designed to reimburse the insured for losses to his or her vehicle resulting from a collision with another car or object or from a rollover.

Common stock The most basic form of ownership of a corporation. Common stockholders have a residual claim to dividends after any claims made by bondholders and preferred stockholders.

Common stock fund A mutual fund consisting only of common stock. Its objective is to increase net asset value over the long term through price appreciation of the securities in its portfolio.

Comparison shopping The process of comparing products or services to determine the best buy.

Compound interest The process of earning interest on reinvested interest as well as on the original amount invested.

Comprehensive health insurance A health insurance plan that combines the protection provided by hospital insurance, surgical insurance, medical expense insurance, and major medical expense insurance into a single policy.

Conditional sales contract A credit contract under which the title to the property being financed does not pass to the buyer until the last installment payment has been paid. Also called a *financing lease.*

Conditions Provisions in insurance policies that impose obligations on both the insured and the insurer.

Consumer Credit Counseling organization (nonprofit) Nonprofit service that offers free or low-cost debt-counseling services for those with serious debt problems.

Consumer price index (CPI) A broad measure of prices, or the cost of living for consumers, published monthly by the U.S. Bureau of Labor Statistics. It tracks, records, weights, and totals the prices of a market basket of 400 consumer goods.

Contingent deferred sales charge See **Back-end load.**

Contractual accumulation plan A formalized, long-term program to purchase shares in a load mutual fund.

Contrarianism An investment approach suggesting that once the general public has seized on an idea, its usefulness is over and the wise investor should take the opposite action.

Conventional mortgage The traditional fixed-rate, fixed-term, fixed-payment mortgage loan.

Cosigner A person who agrees to repay a loan if the borrower should fail to do so.

Countercyclical stocks Stocks of companies with products always in demand, which perform well even in an environment characterized by weak economic activity. Also called *defensive stocks.*

Credit bureau An agency that provides lenders with financial information on potential borrowers, compiling data primarily from various merchants, utility companies, banks, court records, and creditors.

Credit card liability A liability for unauthorized use of a credit card that occurs only if the cardholder received notification of potential liability and accepted the card when it was first mailed, the company provided a self-addressed form to be used to notify it if the card disappeared, and the card was illegally used before the cardholder notified the company of its loss.

Credit controlsheet A form used to monitor credit use, amounts owed, and parties to whom debts are owed.

Credit history A continuing record of a borrower's debt commitments and how well they have been honored.

Credit limit The maximum outstanding debt allowed on a revolving credit account.

Credit union (CU) A not-for-profit cooperative venture developed to pool the deposits of members so as to invest or lend to member-owners. Members usually have some common bond, such as the same employer, church, union, or fraternal association.

Current income Money received from an investment, usually on a regular basis, in the form of interest, dividends, rent, or other such payment.

Current yield A measure of the current annual income of a bond expressed as a percentage when divided by the bond's current market price.

Day order Instructions to a stockbroker that are valid only for the remainder of the trading day during which they were given to the broker.

Debit card A plastic card that provides access to EFT systems via ATMs or the EFT point-of-sale system. Also called *ATM card* or *EFT card*.

Debt consolidation The borrower exchanges several smaller debts with varying due dates and interest rates for a single large loan and one monthly payment.

Debt limit The maximum people feel they should owe based on their ability to meet the repayment obligations.

Debt service-to-income ratio A comparison of the dollars spent on gross annual debt repayments (including mortgages) with gross annual income.

Decreasing term insurance Term life insurance whose face amount declines annually while premiums remain constant.

Deductibles Requirements in an insurance policy that an insured pay an initial portion of any loss before receiving insurance benefits.

Deed A written document used to convey real estate ownership.

Default The failure of a borrower to make a payment of principal or interest when due or to meet another key term of a legal credit agreement.

Default risk The likelihood that a bondholder will not receive the promised periodic interest payments and the principal amount when due at maturity. Also called *credit risk*.

Deficiency balance The sum of money that is owed after the collateral (if any) on a defaulted loan is sold and the proceeds of the sale (if any) are applied to the balance of the loan and the expenses involved in the repossession.

Defined-benefit plan A retirement plan that bases the level of retirement, survivor's, or disability benefits on the worker's income and years of employment.

Defined-contribution plan A retirement plan in which the employer, the employee, or both set aside money at a predetermined rate regularly during the working years to establish a fund that pays retirement benefits to the covered worker.

Depository institution A financial institution recognized and regulated by the federal government to offer loans and banking services to businesses and individuals.

Depreciation The decline in value of an asset over time due to normal wear and tear and obsolescence.

Disability income insurance Insurance that provides the income if the insured cannot work due to prolonged illness or injury.

Discount brokerage firm A brokerage firm that features especially low commission charges because it provides limited services to customers.

Discounted cash-flow method A technique for estimating the value or asking price of a real estate investment that emphasizes after-tax cash flow and the return on the invested dollars discounted over time to reflect a discounted yield.

Discretionary income The money people have left over when they have paid for the necessities of living.

Disposable income The income received after taxes and all other employer withholdings; the money available for spending, saving, and investing.

Diversification The process of reducing risk by spreading investment assets among several investments.

Dollar-cost averaging An investment approach that requires investing the same fixed dollar amount in the same stock or mutual fund at regular intervals over a long time with the result that more shares are purchased when the price is down and fewer shares when the price is high.

Dunning letters Notices from creditors that insistently demand repayment of debts.

Durable power of attorney A legal process to appoint a specific individual to control another person's affairs should that person become mentally incapacitated.

Earned income credit (EIC) A special income tax subsidy that the government pays to low-income working people with or without children.

Earnest money A deposit offered by a home buyer to ensure that the seller will not sell the house to someone else during the negotiations.

Earnings per share (EPS) A measure of the profitability of a firm on a per-share basis; it is a dollar figure determined by dividing the corporation's total after-tax annual earnings (before common stock cash dividends) by the total number of shares of common stock held by investors.

Electronic funds transfer (EFT) The use of electronic means to transfer funds directly from one account to another.

Elimination period In a disability income insurance policy, the time period between the onset of the disability and the date that disability benefits begin. Also called a *waiting period*.

Employer-sponsored retirement plan A retirement plan approved by the IRS as a vehicle in which to deposit tax-sheltered contributions.

Equities An investment asset that provides ownership (equity) interest in the asset.

Equity The dollar value of an asset in excess of the amount owed on it.

Escrow account A special reserve account used to pay third parties and often used in conjunction with real estate loans.

Estate planning The process of establishing, managing, implementing, and revising plans to protect wealth from taxes and other costs, and ensuring the proper distribution of assets and income after death.

Exemption A legally permitted deduction of a taxpayer's income for each person supported by that income. Also called a *personal exemption*.

Expenditure An amount of money that has been spent.

Expense ratio See **Management fee.**

Expenses Total expenditures made.

Express warranties Written and oral warranties that accompany many products and are offered by manufacturers on a voluntary basis to induce customers to buy.

Face amount In life insurance, the dollar value stated in the policy that will be paid on the death of the insured party.

Fair market value What a willing buyer would pay a willing seller for a good (not the amount originally paid).

Federal Deposit Insurance Corporation (FDIC) An agency of the federal government that insures bank accounts.

Federal funds rate An interbank lending rate that banks charge other banks for short-term loans.

Federal gift and estate tax A tax assessed on property owned and/or controlled by a deceased before its transfer to heirs.

Federal Housing Administration (FHA) A subdivision of the U.S. Department of Housing and Urban Development that insures mortgage loans that meet its standards.

Fee-only financial planner One who earns no commissions and works only on a fee-for-service basis.

Finance charge The total dollar amount paid to use credit, including interest costs, service charges, and related mandatory insurance premiums.

Financial goals The long- and short-term objectives that one's financial planning and management efforts are intended to attain.

Financial ratios Objective numerical yardsticks designed to simplify making judgmental assessments of financial strength over time.

Financial risk The risk that an investment will fail to pay a return to the investor.

Financial statements Compilations of personal financial data designed to communicate information on money matters.

Financial strategies Preestablished plans of action to be implemented in specific situations.

Financial success The achievement of financial aspirations that are desired, planned, or attempted.

Fixed expenses Expenditures that are usually paid in the same amount during each time period.

Fixed income A characteristic of lending investments in which the borrower agrees to pay the investor a specific rate of return for use of the principal.

Fixed-time deposits Deposits that must be left on deposit for a specific period of time.

Flexible spending account (FSA) A program that allows employee-paid fringe benefits to be paid with pretax dollars in order to reduce the employee's taxable income.

Footnote t In some newspapers' financial tables, the device used to indicate that a mutual fund charges both 12b-1 and redemption fees.

Foreclosure A legal proceeding by which the lender seizes a home for nonpayment of the mortgage.

Formal will A will that has been properly drafted, signed, and witnessed.

Form 1040-X Amended U.S. Individual Tax Return, which can be used to amend returns filed in error for the previous three years.

401(k) salary-reduction plan A salary-reduction plan in which employees of private corporations may contribute up to a maximum amount set by law ($10,000 in 1999) per year. Employers may also contribute a full or partially matching amount. Employers may limit the proportion of the annual salary contributed to such a plan (usually to 15 percent of salary). Also called a *401(k) plan.*

Front-end load A sales commission paid on the amount invested in a load fund at the time of initial purchase.

Full warranty As defined in the Magnuson–Moss Warranty Act, an express warranty that includes free repair or replacement of covered components.

Fundamental analysis The premise that each particular stock has an intrinsic, or true, value based on its expected future earnings; therefore, some stocks can be identified that will outperform others.

Futures contracts Marketable contracts that require the delivery of a specific amount of a commodity at a certain future date.

Future value The valuation of an asset projected to the end of a particular time period in the future.

Garnishment A court-sanctioned procedure by which a portion of the debtor's wages are set aside to pay debts.

Grace period (credit) The time period beyond the due date during which any new credit card purchases will avoid finance charges should the previous current balance be paid in full.

Grace period (insurance) A period after each insurance premium due date, usually 31 days, during which an overdue payment may be paid without a lapse of the policy.

Gross domestic product (GDP) The value of all goods and services produced by workers and capital in the United States, regardless of ownership.

Gross income All income received in the form of money, goods, services, and property that you must report; it excludes nontaxable income.

Guaranteed insurability option An option that permits a cash-value life insurance policyholder to buy additional stated amounts of life insurance coverage without evidence of insurability.

Guaranteed investment contract (GIC) An annuity contract purchased through an insurance company as part of a qualified retirement plan, which promises to pay a certain level of interest for a given period of time.

Guaranteed renewable policy A health insurance policy that must be continued in force as long as the participant pays the required premium.

Guaranteed renewable term insurance Term life insurance that eliminates the need to prove insurability when the policy is to be renewed.

Health care plan A general term used to describe health insurance or another plan that pays for or provides reimbursement for health care expenditures.

Health insurance Insurance that protects against financial losses resulting from illness, injury, and disability.

Health maintenance organization (HMO) A health plan that provides a broad range of health care services to members on a prepaid basis.

Homeowner's insurance Insurance that combines liability and property insurance coverage needed by homeowners and renters into a single-package policy.

Implied warranty A legal right based on state law that provides that products sold are warranted to be suitable for sale and will work effectively whether there is an express warranty or not.

Income and expense statement A listing and summary of a person's or family's income and expense transactions that have taken place over a specific period. Also called a *cash-flow statement.*

Index of leading economic indicators (LEI) A composite index of 11 components of economic growth that is reported monthly by the U.S. Commerce Department.

Individual retirement account (IRA) A retirement investment account with a bank, mutual fund, insurance company, or other trustee set up by workers who earn salary, wage, or net self-employment earnings. Deposits may be tax-deductible, and investment earnings on IRA funds are not taxable until withdrawn.

Inflation A steady rise in the general level of the prices of goods and services.

Inflation risk The risk that the general price level will rise faster than the yield from an investment.

Inheritance tax A state tax levied on inherited property when it is received by heirs.

Insolvent Owing more than you own.

Installment credit Requires that the consumer must repay the amount owed in a specific number of equal payments, usually monthly. Also called *closed-end credit.*

Insurable interest A situation that exists when a person or organization stands to suffer a financial loss resulting directly from a peril.

Insurance A mechanism for transferring and reducing risk through which a large number of individuals share in the financial losses suffered by members of the group.

Insurance agents People who sell insurance.

Insurance claim A formal request to an insurance company for reimbursement for a covered loss.

Insuring agreements Insurance policy provisions that broadly define coverages provided under a policy.

Interest-adjusted cost index (IACI) A measure of the cost of life insurance that takes into account the interest that would have been earned had the premiums been invested rather than used to buy insurance.

Interest-rate risk The uncertainty of the market value of an asset in the future that results from possible interest-rate changes.

Interest-sensitive life insurance Cash-value life insurance that employs rates of return that vary according to changing interest rates and investment returns.

Intestate The situation of dying without leaving a valid will.

Introductory rate A temporarily low rate used to entice a borrower to sign up for a new credit card. Also called a *teaser rate.*

Investment company A corporation, trust, or partnership in which investors with similar financial goals pool their funds to utilize professional management and diversify their investments.

Investment philosophy A personal investment strategy that anticipates specific returns and risks and contains tactics for accomplishing one's investment goals.

Invoice price The price of a car, which reflects the price the dealer paid for the vehicle. Also called *seller's cost.*

Joint tenancy with right of survivorship A joint account in which each person owns the whole of an asset and can dispose of it without the approval of the other(s). When an owner dies, his or her share is divided equally among the other owners. Also called *joint tenancy.*

Junk bonds High-risk, high-interest-rate bonds rated low by a bond-rating company.

Keogh plan A pension plan that allows self-employed persons to make tax-deductible payments for themselves and their eligible employees to a fund held by a trustee who, in certain circumstances, could be the self-employed person.

Kiddie tax rate A provision of the Internal Revenue Code whereby children under age 14 pay their parents' marginal tax rate on unearned income in amounts that exceed $1400.

Last-to-die insurance policy Life insurance coverage purchased to pay estate taxes. Also called a *survivorship insurance policy.*

Lease A legal contract specifying the responsibilities of both the tenant and the landlord.

Letter of last instructions A signed letter (often handwritten) that provides a detailed inventory of assets and liabilities, describes personal preferences about transfers of many odd pieces of personal property, and contains funeral and burial instructions. Also called a *letter precatory.*

Leverage The use of borrowed funds to make an investment with the goal of earning a rate of return in excess of the after-tax costs of borrowing.

Liabilities The dollar value of items owed; debts owed.

Liability insurance Insurance that provides protection against financial losses suffered by others for which the insured party is responsible.

Lien A legal right to take and hold property or to sell it for payment of a claim.

Life insurance Insurance that protects against financial losses resulting from death.

Limited partnership A form of real estate syndicate involving two classes of partners, the general partner (usually the organizer and initial investor), who operates the syndicate and has unlimited financial liability, and the limited partners (the outside investors), who receive part of the profits and the tax-shelter benefits but remain inactive in the management of the business and have no personal liability for the operations of the partnership beyond their initial investment.

Limited warranty A warranty that offers less than a full warranty as defined in the Magnuson–Moss Warranty Act.

Limit order An instruction to a stockbroker to buy at the best possible price but not above a specified limit or to sell at the best possible price but not below a specified limit.

Liquidity The speed and ease with which an asset can be converted to cash.

Listing agreement A contract permitting a real estate broker to list a property exclusively or with a multiple-listing service.

Living will A written statement that can be used to direct that "extraordinary life support," "heroic measures," and "life prolonging procedures" be withheld or discontinued should one become "terminally ill" with "no reasonable expectation of recovery" and mentally unable to make this decision for oneself.

Loan-to-value ratio A ratio that measures the amount of leverage in a real estate investment project, calculated by dividing the amount of debt by the value of the total original investment.

Long-term goals Targets or ends that an individual or family desires to achieve using financial resources one or more years in the future.

Lowballing An attempt by a seller to raise an orally agreed-upon price.

Major medical expense insurance A health insurance plan that provides reimbursement for a broad range of medical expenses (including hospital, surgical, and medical expenses) with policy limits as high as $1 million and annual deductibles as high as $1000.

Managed care plan A health plan that pays or reimburses for health care expenditures but also has significant control over the conditions under which health care can be obtained.

Management fee The assessment for the investment expertise and managerial abilities of the professional managers who operate mutual funds. Also called *expense ratio*.

Marginal cost The additional (marginal) cost of one more incremental unit of some item.

Marginal tax rate The tax rate at which the last dollar earned is taxed.

Margin call A requirement imposed by the broker that the margin investor contribute more funds if the value of a security declines to the point where the investor's equity is less than a required percentage of the current market value; if this is not done, the broker can legally sell the security.

Marketability risk The uncertainty of loss one might have to absorb if forced to sell an investment earlier than planned.

Market making When a broker/dealer attempts to provide a continuous market by maintaining an inventory of specific securities to sell to other brokerage firms and stands ready to buy reasonable quantities of the same securities at market prices.

Market-volatility risk The risk that arises from changes in the value of an investment.

Maximum taxable yearly earnings The maximum amount of wage income to which the full Social Security tax rate is applied.

Medicaid A jointly financed program of the federal government and the states that pays some medical expenses of the poor.

Medical expense insurance A health insurance plan that provides reimbursement for physician and medical services other than those directly connected with surgery.

Medicare A program administered by the Social Security Administration that provides payment for hospital and medical expenses of persons aged 65 and over and some others.

Moderate investment philosophy An investment philosophy by which one seeks capital gains through slow and steady growth in the value of investments and some current income, and invites only a fair amount of risk of capital loss.

Money market mutual fund (MMMF) A mutual fund that specializes in earning a relatively safe and high return by debt securities that have very short-term maturities (always less than one year). Also called a *money market fund.*

Monitoring unexpended balances A method for controlling overspending by keeping track of the total of each budget classification.

Mortgage loan A loan to purchase real estate, in which the real estate itself serves as collateral.

Mutual fund An open-end investment company that combines the funds of investors who have purchased shares of ownership in the investment company and then invests that money in a diversified portfolio of securities issued by other corporations or governments.

Mutual fund dividends Income paid to investors in mutual funds out of profits earned by the funds.

Mutual fund family A variety of mutual funds managed by one company.

Needs approach A means of estimating life insurance needs by considering all of the factors that might affect the level of need.

Negotiable order of withdrawal (NOW) account A checking account that earns interest or dividends as long as minimum-balance requirements are satisfied.

Negotiating The step in the buying process when the buyer discusses the actual terms of an agreement with the seller. Also called *haggling*.

Net asset value (NAV) The current market value of one share in a mutual fund.

Net gain (loss) Total income minus total expenses where income exceeds (falls short of) expenses.

Net surplus The amount of money remaining after all budget classification deficits are subtracted from those with surpluses.

New vehicle buying service A service that provides people with aid ranging from retail and wholesale price lists to third-party negotiation of a purchase price from one or more automobile dealers.

No-load fund A mutual fund that does not assess a sales charge at the time of investment purchase.

Nonforfeiture values Clauses in a life insurance contract that protect the cash value, if any, in the event that the policyholder chooses not to pay or fails to pay the required premiums.

Nonprobate property Assets not controlled by a will but transferred to survivors by contract or law.

Odd lots Blocks of stock other than whole number multiples of 100 shares.

Open-ended credit Credit extended in advance of any transaction, so that the borrower does not need to reapply each time credit is desired. Amounts owed are repaid in one payment or in a series of equal or unequal payments, usually monthly.

Open-end investment company A mutual fund that is always ready to sell new shares of ownership and to buy back previously sold shares at the fund's current market value.

Opportunity cost The most valuable alternative that must be sacrificed to satisfy a want. Also called *alternative cost*.

Option A contract that gives the holder the right to buy or sell a specific asset—e.g., real estate or common stock—at a specified price within a specified time period.

Option writer A person who issues an option contract promising either to buy or to sell a specified asset for a fixed striking price and receives an option premium for standing ready to buy or sell.

Organized stock exchange A market where agents of buyers and sellers meet and trade a specified list of securities, which are usually the stocks and bonds of larger, well-known companies. Also called a *stock market*.

Original source records Formal documents that record personal financial activities.

Over-the-counter (OTC) market Publicly traded securities that are not sold on an organized exchange but where buyers and sellers negotiate transaction prices.

Owner The person who retains all rights and privileges granted by an insurance policy, including the right to amend the policy and the right to designate who receives the proceeds. Also called the *policyholder*.

Partnership theory of marriage rights The presumption in law that the intention of wedded couples is to share their fortunes equally because marriage constitutes an economic alliance.

Passive activities Rental operations and all other businesses in which a taxpayer does not materially participate. Losses on passive activities generally may not be used to offset ordinary income.

Peril Any event that causes a financial loss.

Periodic rate The annual percentage rate for a charge account divided by the number of billing periods per year (usually 12).

Personal earnings and benefit estimate statement (PEBES) The Social Security Administration's record of lifetime taxable earnings covered under SSA's regulations, taxes paid, and estimates of retirement benefits.

Personal finance The study of personal and family resources considered important in achieving financial success.

Personal financial planning The process of developing and implementing long-range plans to achieve financial success.

Personal inflation rate The rate of increase in prices of items purchased by a person or household.

Personal spending style An individual's way of spending or dealing with money, which is influenced by the person's values, attitudes, emotions, and other factors shaped through the experiences of life.

PITI Abbreviation for "principal, interest, (real estate) taxes, and insurance," the components of many monthly mortgage loan payments.

Plaintiff A person who has filed a small claims or civil court case and is suing the defendant.

Point A fee equal to 1 percent of the total mortgage loan, which must be paid in full when a home is bought.

Policy limits The maximum dollar amounts that will be paid under an insurance policy.

Portability A retirement plan contract clause that permits workers to maintain and transfer accumulated pension benefits to another pension plan if they change jobs.

Preexisting condition A medical condition or symptoms that were known to the participant or diagnosed within a specified time period before the effective date of a health plan.

Preferred provider organization (PPO) A group of medical care providers (doctors, hospitals, and so on) who contract with a health insurance company to provide services at a discount to policyholders if the policyholders choose to be served by PPO members.

Premium quote service An independent life insurance agent or group of agents who concentrate on low rates.

Prenuptial agreement A contract specifying what (if any) share of each person's assets the other will be entitled to during marriage or in case of divorce.

Prepayment penalty A special charge to the borrower for paying off a loan earlier than the final due date.

Present value The current value of an asset that will be received in the future. Also called *discounting*.

Preshopping research The process of gathering information about products or services before actually shopping for them.

Price appreciation The amount above ownership costs for which an investment is sold for; it is similar to capital gains on a stock investment.

Price/earnings ratio (P/E ratio, P/E multiple) A ratio of the current market value (price) of a common stock to its earnings per share (EPS), which shows how the market is valuing the stock.

Principle of indemnity The concept that insurance will pay no more than the actual financial loss suffered.

Private mortgage insurance (PMI) Insurance sold by a company that typically insures the first 20 percent of a mortgage loan in case of default.

Probate A court-supervised transfer of a decedent's assets to the rightful beneficiaries. The probate court also attempts to see that the debts, taxes, and expenses of the deceased will be paid.

Professional liability insurance Insurance that protects individuals and organizations that provide professional services when they are held liable for the losses of their clients. Also called *malpractice insurance*.

Progressive tax A tax rate that increases as a taxpayer's income increases.

Property insurance Insurance that protects against financial losses resulting from damage to or destruction of property or possessions.

Prospectus A written disclosure to the Securities and Exchange Commission and prospective investors that details pertinent operational and financial facts about a mutual fund, or new stock offering.

Public administrator Someone appointed by the probate court to distribute an estate according to state laws when a person dies intestate.

Put option An option contract that gives the option holder the right to sell an optioned asset to the option writer at the striking price.

Qualified domestic-relations order (QDRO) A specialized court order legally authorizing the pension plan administrator to take specific action not outlined in the pension plan regulations. The order must be approved by the pension plan administrator.

Qualified retirement plans Retirement plans approved by the IRS for special tax advantages that can reduce taxes and increase retirement benefits. Also called a *tax-sheltered retirement plan*.

Random risk The risk associated with owning only one investment that, by chance, may do very poorly in the future due to uncontrollable or random factors. Also called *systematic risk*.

Real estate broker A person licensed by a state to provide advice and assistance, usually for a fee, to buyers and sellers of real estate. Also called a *real estate agent*.

Real estate property taxes Local (town, city, county, township, parish) taxes based on the determined value of buildings and land.

Real income Income measured in constant prices relative to some base time period.

Real return on investment The yield after subtracting the effects of inflation and taxes.

Reasonableness tests Computer-based test based on average amounts for each category of deductions; IRS subjects every tax return to these tests.

Reconciling budget estimates Reconciling conflicting needs and wants as one revises one's budget until total projected expenses do not exceed projected income.

Recordkeeping The process of recording the sources and amounts of dollars earned and spent.

Redress To right a wrong.

Registered bonds Bonds that provide for the recording of the bondholder's name so that checks or electronic funds transfers for interest and principal can be safely forwarded when due.

Restrictive endorsement A means of authorizing a financial institution to accept a check only as a deposit to an account by writing "For deposit only" on the back along with one's signature.

Retained earnings Past and current earnings not paid to shareholders but instead left to accumulate and finance the goals of a company.

Return The total income from an investment, including current income plus capital gains or minus capital losses.

Revocable living trust A trust subject to change, amendment, modification, or cancellation by the grantor.

Revolving charge account A credit account for which the user has the option to pay the bill in full or to spread repayment over several months. Also called an *option account.*

Revolving savings fund A variable expense classification in budgeting into which funds are allocated in an effort to create savings that can be used to balance the budget later so as to avoid running out of money.

Right A legal instrument to purchase a number of shares of corporate stock at a specific price during a limited time period.

Risk In insurance, the uncertainty about whether a financial loss will occur and how large it will be; in an investment, the uncertainty that the yield will deviate from what is expected.

Risk management The process of identifying and evaluating situations involving pure risk to determine and implement the appropriate means for its management.

Rollover A transfer of retirement money from one retirement plan to another.

Salary-reduction plans A group of defined-contribution retirement plans in which employees divert a portion of their salary to a tax-sheltered investment account, where it accumulates tax-free until it is withdrawn at retirement.

Secondary market A place where existing securities, which have already been sold to the public, are bought and sold. Also called an *aftermarket.*

Second mortgage Any loan above the amount owed on a first mortgage with the mortgaged property serving as collateral.

Secured credit card A relatively high-interest bank credit card offered to people with a poor or nonexistent credit rating who must put an amount on deposit to serve as collateral for a credit limit equal to that amount. Also called a *collateralized credit card.*

Secured loan A loan that requires that certain assets (collateral) be pledged to secure the debt or the assurance of another person (cosigner), who agrees to pay the loan should the borrower fail to do so.

Securities market indexes Indexes that measure the value of a number of securities chosen as a sample to reflect the behavior of a more general market.

Self-directed retirement plan A term describing salary-reduction retirement plans because each employee makes his or her own investment decisions.

Self-regulatory organization (SRO) A private organization designated by Congress to operate and oversee an aspect of the securities business (for example, the National Association of Securities Dealers).

Selling short A trading technique by which investors sell a security they do not own (by borrowing it from a broker) and later buy the same number of shares of the security at, hopefully, a lower price (and return it to the broker), thus earning a profit on the transaction.

Separable property Property wholly owned by one spouse, and that belonged to the spouse before marriage or was received as a gift or an inheritance during the marriage.

Series EE savings bond A U.S. government bond purchased for 50 percent of its face value.

Service contract An agreement between the contract seller and the buyer of a product to provide free (or nearly free) repair services to covered components of the product for a specified time period.

Settlement options The choices a life insurance beneficiary or policyholder has concerning the payment of the death benefit from a life insurance policy.

Share draft account The credit-union version of a NOW checking account in which members' accounts earn dividends that, for all intents and purposes, are "interest income."

Shareholder The owner of a stock who has a claim on the assets and earnings of the firm issuing the stock. Also called *stockholder.*

Short-term liability An obligation to be paid off within one year.

Simple-interest method Interest is calculated by applying an interest rate to the unpaid balance of the debt.

Small claims court A state court with no written record of testimony, where civil matters are often resolved without the assistance of attorneys, providing that the legal amount claimed is less than a generally low maximum set in each state. Also called *court not of record*.

Smart card A plastic payment device that uses a powerful built-in computer chip to store data and handle several different payment functions. Also called *stored value cards* or *electronic purses*.

Social Security disability income insurance Social Security Administration insurance that provides benefits that will help replace the lost income of eligible disabled workers during a period of disability expected to last 12 full months or until death.

Social Security survivor's benefits Payments by the Social Security Administration to a surviving spouse and children; the level of benefits depends on the amount of Social Security taxes paid by the deceased during his or her life.

Specialist A person on the floor of a stock exchange who handles trades of a particular stock ordered in an effort to maintain a fair and orderly market.

Speculative investments Investment alternatives that carry considerable risk of loss for the chance of large gains. Also called *high-risk investments*.

Standard deduction The amount all taxpayers, except some dependents, who do not itemize deductions may subtract from adjusted gross income when filing an income tax return; the government's legally permissible estimate of a person's tax-deductible expenses.

Standardized expense table An estimate of the hypothetical total costs a mutual fund investor would pay on a $1000 investment that earns 5 percent annually and is withdrawn after five years.

Sticker price The manufacturer's suggested retail price for a new car and its options as listed on the window sticker.

Stockbroker Someone who works for a brokerage firm and is licensed to buy and sell securities on behalf of clients, provides them with investment advice and information, and generally collects a commission on each purchase or sale of such securities. Also called an *account executive, registered representative,* or *sales representative*.

Stop order An instruction telling a stockbroker to sell one's shares at the market price as a stock declines to or goes below a specified price. Also called a *stop-loss order*.

Subordinate budget A detailed listing of planned expenses within a single budgeting classification.

Switching privilege A privilege for mutual fund shareholders that permits them, if their needs or objectives change, to swap shares on a dollar-for-dollar basis for shares in another mutual fund managed by the same corporation. Also called *exchange privilege* or *conversion privilege*.

Tangible assets Physical items that have fairly long lifespans and could be sold to raise cash but whose primary purpose is to provide maintenance of a lifestyle.

Taxable income Amount one pays in taxes, determined by subtracting one's allowable exclusions, adjustments, exemptions, and deductions from one's total income.

Tax audit A formal examination of a taxpayer's tax forms by the IRS for accuracy and completeness.

Tax avoidance An attempt to avoid paying taxes by reducing tax liability through legal techniques.

Tax credit A credit that directly reduces tax liability on a dollar-for-dollar basis.

Tax-exempt equivalent yield Compares the after-tax return on a taxable investment to the return on a tax-free investment.

Tax-exempt income Income not considered legally as income for federal tax purposes.

Tax-free exchange A transaction in which a real estate investor trades equity in one property for equity in a similar property and none of the people involved in the trade receives any other form of property or money.

Tax shelter A tax planning tool that provides a reduction or postponement of income tax liability.

Tax-sheltered Income or benefits exempt from current income taxes.

Tax-sheltered retirement plans See **Qualified retirement plans**.

10-K report A comprehensive official document filed with the SEC by a company that contains much of the same type of information as a prospectus or annual report and provides additional updated financial details on corporate activities.

Term life insurance A life insurance policy that contains no savings plan and that pays benefits only if the insured party dies within the time period of the contract.

Tiered interest rate A combination of a base rate and a higher rate, where the higher rate is applied to larger account balances.

Tiered pricing The practice whereby lenders segment their credit customer base so as to offer lower interest rates to their best customers while charging higher rates to others.

Time value of money The concept applied in the comparison and prediction of the present and future values of an asset.

Title The legal right of ownership interest in real property.

Title insurance Insurance often required of home buyers by lenders to protect against the possibility that a title later will be found faulty.

Treasury bills Short-term U.S. government securities that mature in one year or less. They do not pay interest because they are sold at a discount to face value. Also called *T-bills*.

12b-1 fee An annual charge assessed to shareholders that pays for advertising, marketing, distribution, and promotional costs of a mutual fund.

Two-cycle average daily balance including new purchases The least favorable method for consumers of determining a credit card balance, which eliminates the grace period on new purchases made during the current billing cycle and retroactively eliminates the grace period for the previous month each time the account carries a balance.

Umbrella liability insurance A personal catastrophe liability policy that covers both general and automobile liability protection.

Underwriting The insurer's procedure of deciding which insurance applicants to accept.

Unearned income Income from rents, dividends, interest, royalties, and capital gains.

Unfair discrimination Making distinctions among individuals based on unfair criteria.

Unfunded pension plan A pension plan in which retirement benefits are paid out of current earnings rather than from funds previously set aside to cover current and future liabilities.

Unlimited gift tax marital deduction A provision of federal tax laws that allows everything left to a surviving spouse to transfer tax-free.

Usury laws Legal interest-rate maximums that govern the charges assessed by lenders.

Values Principles, standards, or qualities considered important, worthwhile, or desirable that provide criteria for goals, thereby giving continuity to decisions.

Variable annuity An annuity that allows the purchaser to choose how the money is invested, usually in mutual funds. As a result, the payments to the purchaser vary according to the success of the investments.

Variable expenses Expenditures over which an individual has considerable control.

Variable-rate loan A loan that includes a periodic rate that fluctuates according to some measure of interest rates in the economy. Also called an *adjustable-rate loan*.

Variable-universal life insurance A form of life insurance that provides both the pure protection of term insurance and the cash-value buildup of whole life insurance and that gives the policyholder some choice in the investments made with the cash value accumulated by the policy.

Vesting A process by which employees during their working years obtain nonforfeitable rights to retirement benefits provided by employers that cannot be taken away if they resign or are dismissed.

Warranties Assurances by sellers to buyers that goods are as promised and that certain steps will be taken to rectify problems.

Will A written document that directs the disposition of an individual's assets at death.

Yield The return on an investment expressed as a percentage of the cost of the investment. Also called *rate of return*.

Yield to maturity (YTM) The total annual effective rate of return earned by a bondholder on a bond when it is held to maturity; it reflects both the current income and any difference if the bond was purchased at a price other than face value.

Zero-coupon bonds Municipal, corporate, or Treasury issues that pay no annual interest, are offered to investors at prices far lower than their face value, and are redeemed at full value upon maturity. The interest accumulates within the bond itself, and the return to the investor comes from redeeming the bond at its stated face value. Also called *zeros* or *deep discount bonds*.

Zero-sum game A type of investment technique in which the wealth of all investors remains the same, as the trading simply redistributes the wealth among the traders.

Index

Boldface italic type indicates terms that are boldface in the text.